# BMW 3-Series Automotive Repair Manual

## by Jay Storer
## and John H Haynes

Member of the Guild of Motoring Writers

### Models covered:

BMW 3-Series, E90, E91, E92, E93, F30, F31 and F34 chassis
2006 through 2014
320i, 320xi (2012 through 2014)
325i, 325xi, 330i, 330xi (2006)
328i, 328xi (2007 through 2014)

*Does not include information specific to M3 models, 335i models, Hybrid models, diesel models, 3.0L turbocharged models, or 2006 325Ci/330Ci Coupe and Convertible models based on the E46 chassis. Also does not include information on the convertible top or rollover protection system.*

(18023 - 7X5)

ABCDE
FGHIJ
KL

**Haynes Publishing Group**

Sparkford Nr Yeovil
Somerset BA22 7JJ England

**Haynes North America, Inc**

859 Lawrence Drive
Newbury Park
California 91320 USA
www.haynes.com

**A book in the Haynes Automotive Repair Manual Series**

**Printed in Malaysia**

**ISBN-13: 978-1-62092-216-3**
**ISBN-10: 1-62092-216-9**

**Library of Congress Control Number: 2015954219**

While every attempt is made to ensure that the information in this manual is correct, no liability can be accepted by the authors or publishers for loss, damage or injury caused by any errors in, or omissions from, the information given.

# Contents

**Haynes mechanic and photographer with a BMW 3-Series**

# About this manual

## Its purpose

The purpose of this manual is to help you get the best value from your vehicle. It can do so in several ways. It can help you decide what work must be done, even if you choose to have it done by a dealer service department or a repair shop; it provides information and procedures for routine maintenance and servicing; and it offers diagnostic and repair procedures to follow when trouble occurs.

We hope you use the manual to tackle the work yourself. For many simpler jobs, doing it yourself may be quicker than arranging an appointment to get the vehicle into a shop and making the trips to leave it and pick it up. More importantly, a lot of money can be saved by avoiding the expense the shop must pass on to you to cover its labor and overhead

costs. An added benefit is the sense of satisfaction and accomplishment that you feel after doing the job yourself.

## Using the manual

The manual is divided into Chapters. Each Chapter is divided into numbered Sections, which are headed in bold type between horizontal lines. Each Section consists of consecutively numbered paragraphs.

At the beginning of each numbered Section you will be referred to any illustrations which apply to the procedures in that Section. The reference numbers used in illustration captions pinpoint the pertinent Section and the Step within that Section. That is, illustration 3.2 means the illustration

refers to Section 3 and Step (or paragraph) 2 within that Section.

Procedures, once described in the text, are not normally repeated. When it's necessary to refer to another Chapter, the reference will be given as Chapter and Section number. Cross references given without use of the word "Chapter" apply to Sections and/or paragraphs in the same Chapter. For example, "see Section 8" means in the same Chapter.

References to the left or right side of the vehicle assume you are sitting in the driver's seat, facing forward.

Even though we have prepared this manual with extreme care, neither the publisher nor the author can accept responsibility for any errors in, or omissions from, the information given.

### NOTE

A **Note** provides information necessary to properly complete a procedure or information which will make the procedure easier to understand.

### CAUTION

A **Caution** provides a special procedure or special steps which must be taken while completing the procedure where the Caution is found. Not heeding a Caution can result in damage to the assembly being worked on.

### WARNING

A **Warning** provides a special procedure or special steps which must be taken while completing the procedure where the Warning is found. Not heeding a Warning can result in personal injury.

# Introduction

These BMW 3-Series vehicles are available in Sedan, Sports Wagon, coupe and convertible models.

This manual covers models with 2.0L turbocharged four-cylinder and the non-turbocharged 3.0L inline, DOHC six-cylinder engine.

The engines are mounted longitudinally and drive through the transmission to the rear

wheels. Optional AWD is available and utilizes a transfer case that drives a front differential with a driveshaft and driveaxles. Transmissions include a 6-speed manual transmission, a 6-speed automatic transmission or an 8-speed automatic transmission.

Suspension is independent at all four wheels; coil spring/shock absorber strut assemblies are used at the front end, with

a double-pivot hub control using many aluminum components. The rear suspension utilizes a five-link design, with separate coil springs and shock absorbers. The rack-and-pinion steering is attached to the front subframe.

Disc brakes are used at all four wheels, with power assist as standard. An Anti-lock Brake system is standard on all models.

# Vehicle identification numbers

Modifications are a continuing and unpublicized process in vehicle manufacturing. Since spare parts manuals and lists are compiled on a numerical basis, the individual vehicle numbers are essential to correctly identify the component required.

## Vehicle Identification Number (VIN)

This very important identification number is stamped on a plate attached to the dashboard inside the windshield on the driver's side of the vehicle (see illustration). The VIN also appears on the Vehicle Certificate of Title and Registration. It contains information such as where and when the vehicle was manufactured, the model year and the body style.

## Manufacturer's Certification Regulation label

The Manufacturer's Certification Regulation label is attached to the driver's side door opening (see illustration). The label contains the name of the manufacturer, the month and year of production, the Gross Vehicle Weight Rating (GVWR), the Gross Axle Weight Rating (GAWR) and the certification statement.

## VIN model year code

Counting from the left, the model year code letter designation is the 10th character. On all models covered by this manual the model year codes are:

| | |
|---|---|
| 6 | 2006 |
| 7 | 2007 |
| 8 | 2008 |
| 9 | 2009 |
| A | 2010 |
| B | 2011 |
| C | 2012 |
| D | 2013 |
| E | 2014 |

## Engine number

On all models, the engine identification number is stamped on a machined pad on the block, which is visible looking from the left side of the engine and looking between the second and third intake runners, just above the oil pan.

## Transmission identification

The transmission identification tag is at the left-rear of the automatic transmission and on a plate at the left side of the case on manual transmissions. Refer to Chapter 7A or 7B for the transmission code numbers.

The Vehicle Identification Number (VIN) is visible through the driver's side of the windshield

The Manufacturer's Certification Regulation label is located on the driver's door opening

# Recall information

Vehicle recalls are carried out by the manufacturer in the rare event of a possible safety-related defect. The vehicle's registered owner is contacted at the address on file at the Department of Motor Vehicles and given the details of the recall. Remedial work is carried out free of charge at a dealer service department.

If you are the new owner of a used vehicle which was subject to a recall and you want to be sure that the work has been carried out, it's best to contact a dealer service department and ask about your individual vehicle - you'll need to furnish them your Vehicle Identification Number (VIN).

The table below is based on information provided by the National Highway Traffic Safety Administration (NHTSA), the body which oversees vehicle recalls in the United States. The recall database is updated constantly. **Note:** *This a partial list containing only the BMW dealer recalls. There are additional aftermarket recalls available.* For the latest information on vehicle recalls, check the NHTSA website at www.nhtsa.gov, www.safercar.gov or call the NHTSA hotline at 1-888-327-4236.

| Recall date | Recall campaign number | Model(s) affected | Concern |
|---|---|---|---|
| October 9, 2006 | **06V400000** | 2006 3-Series | On certain vehicles, one of the suspension control arm and swivel bearing connection bolts was not tightened correctly. The bolted connection could loosen. The bolted connection could break, which could impair vehicle handling and control, increasing the risk of a crash. |
| July 18, 2008 | **08V384000** | 2006 3-Series | On some models with sport seats, depending on the manner and frequency of the front passenger's entry and exit, small cracks have developed in the mat. If this occurs, the front passenger airbags, with the exception of the head protection system, will be deactivated and the airbag warning lamp as well as the passenger airbag "ON-OFF" lamp will be illuminated. In this situation, the front passenger airbags will not deploy even in a sufficiently severe accident and occupant protection provided by the system would not be possible. |
| July 01, 2009 | **09V257000** | 2008 3-Series | On some models, incorrect crimp connectors may have been used on the side airbag and belt tensioner wiring. As a result, sufficient contact between the crimp connectors and the corresponding plug may not occur, which could lead to an increase in the electrical resistance of that connection. If that happened, it would be possible for the side airbag and/or the safety belt tensioner not to deploy, not properly protecting an occupant, increasing the risk of injuries. |

| Recall date | Recall campaign number | Model(s) affected | Concern |
|---|---|---|---|
| April 20, 2012 | 12V176000 | 2012 3-Series | On some models, the front seat head restraints may exceed the downward movement limit of 25mm in the highest position. Which fails to comply with the requirements of Federal Motor Vehicle Safety Standard No. 202A. In the event of a vehicle crash, the head restraint may unexpectedly move down slightly if it was adjusted to the fully extended position, increasing the risk of personal injury. |
| February 07, 2013 | 13V044000 | 2007, 2008, 2009, 2010, 2011 328i | On some models, the connector for the positive battery cable connector and the corresponding terminal on the fuse box may degrade over time. Over time, the high current flow and heat from electrical resistance may lead to a breakage of the connection, and a loss of electrical power to the vehicle. If there is a loss of electrical power to the vehicle, the vehicle may unexpectedly stall, increasing the risk of a crash. |
| September 26, 2013 | 13V454000 | 2012, 2013, 2014 328i | On some models, due to insufficient lubrication, the vacuum pump that supplies brake power assistance may fail. A failure of the brake vacuum pump results in a reduction in braking power that could increase the risk of a crash. |
| November 12, 2013 | 13V546000 | 2007 328i | On some models, the front passenger seat occupant detection mat that determines if and how the passenger frontal air bag should deploy in a crash may fatigue and develop cracks which could lead to a system failure. Should the system fail, in the event of a crash, the front passenger air bag would be deactivated, increasing the risk of personal injury. |
| April 10, 2014 | 14V176000 | 2010, 2011 328i | On some models, the bolts that secure the housing for the variable camshaft timing adjustment (VANOS) unit can loosen over time and may possibly break. If the bolts loosen or break the engine may have reduced power or stall. An engine stall increases the risk of a crash. |
| October 07, 2014 | 14V627000 | 2012, 2013, 2014 328i 2014 328xi | On some models, due to insufficient lubrication, the vacuum pump that supplies brake power assistance may fail. A failure of the brake vacuum pump results in a reduction in braking power that could increase the risk of a crash. |
| March 31, 2015 | 15V189000 | 2014 328i 2014 328xi | On some models, improper nickel plating of components within the fuel pump may result in the fuel pump failing. If the fuel pump fails, the vehicle may stall without warning, increasing the risk of a crash. |

# Notes

# Buying parts

Replacement parts are available from many sources, which generally fall into one of two categories - authorized dealer parts departments and independent retail auto parts stores. Our advice concerning these parts is as follows:

*Retail auto parts stores:* Good auto parts stores will stock frequently needed components which wear out relatively fast, such as clutch components, exhaust systems, brake parts, tune-up parts, etc. These stores often supply new or reconditioned parts on an exchange basis, which can save a considerable amount of money. Discount auto parts stores are often very good places to buy materials and parts needed for general vehicle maintenance such as oil, grease, filters, spark plugs, belts, touch-up paint, bulbs, etc. They also usually sell tools and general accessories, have convenient hours, charge lower prices and can often be found not far from home.

*Authorized dealer parts department:* This is the best source for parts which are unique to the vehicle and not generally available elsewhere (such as major engine parts, transmission parts, trim pieces, etc.).

*Warranty information:* If the vehicle is still covered under warranty, be sure that any replacement parts purchased - regardless of the source - do not invalidate the warranty!

To be sure of obtaining the correct parts, have engine and chassis numbers available and, if possible, take the old parts along for positive identification.

# Maintenance techniques, tools and working facilities

## Maintenance techniques

There are a number of techniques involved in maintenance and repair that will be referred to throughout this manual. Application of these techniques will enable the home mechanic to be more efficient, better organized and capable of performing the various tasks properly, which will ensure that the repair job is thorough and complete.

## Fasteners

Fasteners are nuts, bolts, studs and screws used to hold two or more parts together. There are a few things to keep in mind when working with fasteners. Almost all of them use a locking device of some type, either a lockwasher, locknut, locking tab or thread adhesive. All threaded fasteners should be clean and straight, with undamaged threads and undamaged corners on the hex head where the wrench fits. Develop the habit of replacing all damaged nuts and bolts with new ones. Special locknuts with nylon or fiber inserts can only be used once. If they are removed, they lose their locking ability and must be replaced with new ones.

Rusted nuts and bolts should be treated with a penetrating fluid to ease removal and prevent breakage. Some mechanics use turpentine in a spout-type oil can, which works quite well. After applying the rust penetrant, let it work for a few minutes before trying to loosen the nut or bolt. Badly rusted fasteners may have to be chiseled or sawed off or removed with a special nut breaker, available at tool stores.

If a bolt or stud breaks off in an assembly, it can be drilled and removed with a special tool commonly available for this purpose. Most automotive machine shops can perform this task, as well as other repair procedures, such as the repair of threaded holes that have been stripped out.

Flat washers and lockwashers, when removed from an assembly, should always be replaced exactly as removed. Replace any damaged washers with new ones. Never use a lockwasher on any soft metal surface (such as aluminum), thin sheet metal or plastic.

## Fastener sizes

For a number of reasons, automobile manufacturers are making wider and wider use of metric fasteners. Therefore, it is important to be able to tell the difference between standard (sometimes called U.S. or SAE) and metric hardware, since they cannot be interchanged.

All bolts, whether standard or metric, are sized according to diameter, thread pitch and length. For example, a standard 1/2 - 13 x 1 bolt is 1/2 inch in diameter, has 13 threads per inch and is 1 inch long. An M12 - 1.75 x 25 metric bolt is 12 mm in diameter, has a thread pitch of 1.75 mm (the distance between threads) and is 25 mm long. The two bolts are nearly identical, and easily confused, but they are not interchangeable.

In addition to the differences in diameter, thread pitch and length, metric and standard bolts can also be distinguished by examining the bolt heads. To begin with, the distance across the flats on a standard bolt head is measured in inches, while the same dimension on a metric bolt is sized in millimeters (the same is true for nuts). As a result, a standard wrench should not be used on a metric bolt and a metric wrench should not be used on a standard bolt. Also, most standard bolts have slashes radiating out from the center of the head to denote the grade or strength of the bolt, which is an indication of the amount of torque that can be applied to it. The greater the number of slashes, the greater the strength of the bolt. Grades 0 through 5 are commonly used on automobiles. Metric bolts have a property class (grade) number, rather than a slash, molded into their heads to indicate bolt strength. In this case, the higher the number, the stronger the bolt. Property class numbers 8.8, 9.8 and 10.9 are commonly used on automobiles.

Strength markings can also be used to distinguish standard hex nuts from metric hex nuts. Many standard nuts have dots stamped into one side, while metric nuts are marked with a number. The greater the number of dots, or the higher the number, the greater the strength of the nut.

Metric studs are also marked on their ends according to property class (grade). Larger studs are numbered (the same as metric bolts), while smaller studs carry a geometric code to denote grade.

It should be noted that many fasteners, especially Grades 0 through 2, have no distinguishing marks on them. When such is the case, the only way to determine whether it is standard or metric is to measure the thread pitch or compare it to a known fastener of the same size.

Standard fasteners are often referred to as SAE, as opposed to metric. However, it should be noted that SAE technically refers to a non-metric fine thread fastener only. Coarse thread non-metric fasteners are referred to as USS sizes.

Since fasteners of the same size (both standard and metric) may have different strength ratings, be sure to reinstall any bolts, studs or nuts removed from your vehicle in their original locations. Also, when replacing a fastener with a new one, make sure that the new one has a strength rating equal to or greater than the original.

## Tightening sequences and procedures

Most threaded fasteners should be tightened to a specific torque value (torque is the twisting force applied to a threaded component such as a nut or bolt). Overtightening the fastener can weaken it and cause it to break, while undertightening can cause it to eventually come loose. Bolts, screws and studs, depending on the material they are made of and their thread diameters, have specific torque values, many of which are noted in the Specifications at the beginning of each Chapter. Be sure to follow the torque recommendations closely. For fasteners not assigned a

Grade 1 or 2          Grade 5          Grade 8

Bolt strength marking (standard/SAE/USS; bottom - metric)

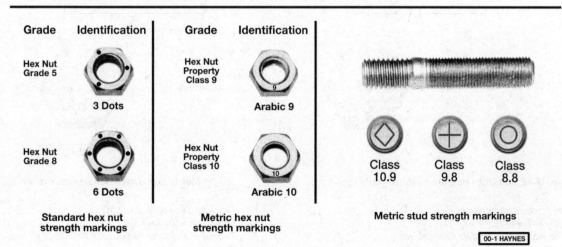

| Grade | Identification |
|---|---|
| Hex Nut Grade 5 | 3 Dots |
| Hex Nut Grade 8 | 6 Dots |

**Standard hex nut strength markings**

| Grade | Identification |
|---|---|
| Hex Nut Property Class 9 | Arabic 9 |
| Hex Nut Property Class 10 | Arabic 10 |

**Metric hex nut strength markings**

Class 10.9          Class 9.8          Class 8.8

**Metric stud strength markings**

specific torque, a general torque value chart is presented here as a guide. These torque values are for dry (unlubricated) fasteners threaded into steel or cast iron (not aluminum). As was previously mentioned, the size and grade of a fastener determine the amount of torque that can safely be applied to it. The figures listed here are approximate for Grade 2 and Grade 3 fasteners. Higher grades can tolerate higher torque values.

Fasteners laid out in a pattern, such as cylinder head bolts, oil pan bolts, differential cover bolts, etc., must be loosened or tightened in sequence to avoid warping the component. This sequence will normally be shown in the appropriate Chapter. If a specific pattern is not given, the following procedures can be used to prevent warping.

Initially, the bolts or nuts should be assembled finger-tight only. Next, they should be tightened one full turn each, in a criss-cross or diagonal pattern. After each one has been tightened one full turn, return to the first one and tighten them all one-half turn, following the same pattern. Finally, tighten each of them one-quarter turn at a time until each fastener has been tightened to the proper torque. To loosen and remove the fasteners, the procedure would be reversed.

### Component disassembly

Component disassembly should be done with care and purpose to help ensure that

| Metric thread sizes | Ft-lbs | Nm |
|---|---|---|
| M-6 | 6 to 9 | 9 to 12 |
| M-8 | 14 to 21 | 19 to 28 |
| M-10 | 28 to 40 | 38 to 54 |
| M-12 | 50 to 71 | 68 to 96 |
| M-14 | 80 to 140 | 109 to 154 |
| **Pipe thread sizes** | | |
| 1/8 | 5 to 8 | 7 to 10 |
| 1/4 | 12 to 18 | 17 to 24 |
| 3/8 | 22 to 33 | 30 to 44 |
| 1/2 | 25 to 35 | 34 to 47 |
| **U.S. thread sizes** | | |
| 1/4 - 20 | 6 to 9 | 9 to 12 |
| 5/16 - 18 | 12 to 18 | 17 to 24 |
| 5/16 - 24 | 14 to 20 | 19 to 27 |
| 3/8 - 16 | 22 to 32 | 30 to 43 |
| 3/8 - 24 | 27 to 38 | 37 to 51 |
| 7/16 - 14 | 40 to 55 | 55 to 74 |
| 7/16 - 20 | 40 to 60 | 55 to 81 |
| 1/2 - 13 | 55 to 80 | 75 to 108 |

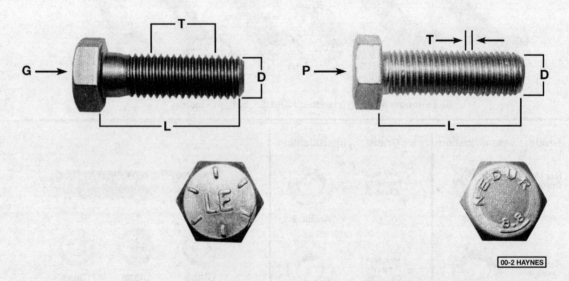

**Standard (SAE and USS) bolt dimensions/grade marks**          **Metric bolt dimensions/grade marks**

| G | Grade marks (bolt strength) | P | Property class (bolt strength) |
|---|---|---|---|
| L | Length (in inches) | L | Length (in millimeters) |
| T | Thread pitch (number of threads per inch) | T | Thread pitch (distance between threads in millimeters) |
| D | Nominal diameter (in inches) | D | Diameter |

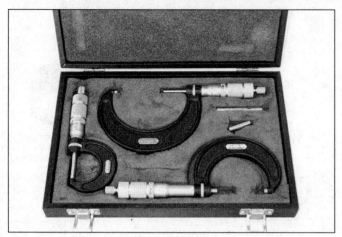

**Micrometer set**

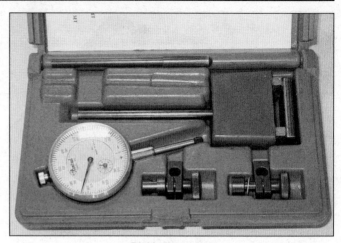

**Dial indicator set**

the parts go back together properly. Always keep track of the sequence in which parts are removed. Make note of special characteristics or marks on parts that can be installed more than one way, such as a grooved thrust washer on a shaft. It is a good idea to lay the disassembled parts out on a clean surface in the order that they were removed. It may also be helpful to make sketches or take instant photos of components before removal.

When removing fasteners from a component, keep track of their locations. Sometimes threading a bolt back in a part, or putting the washers and nut back on a stud, can prevent mix-ups later. If nuts and bolts cannot be returned to their original locations, they should be kept in a compartmented box or a series of small boxes. A cupcake or muffin tin is ideal for this purpose, since each cavity can hold the bolts and nuts from a particular area (i.e. oil pan bolts, valve cover bolts, engine mount bolts, etc.). A pan of this type is especially helpful when working on assemblies with very small parts, such as the carburetor, alternator, valve train or interior dash and trim pieces. The cavities can be marked with paint or tape to identify the contents.

Whenever wiring looms, harnesses or connectors are separated, it is a good idea to identify the two halves with numbered pieces of masking tape so they can be easily reconnected.

## Gasket sealing surfaces

Throughout any vehicle, gaskets are used to seal the mating surfaces between two parts and keep lubricants, fluids, vacuum or pressure contained in an assembly.

Many times these gaskets are coated with a liquid or paste-type gasket sealing compound before assembly. Age, heat and pressure can sometimes cause the two parts to stick together so tightly that they are very difficult to separate. Often, the assembly can be loosened by striking it with a soft-face hammer near the mating surfaces. A regular hammer can be used if a block of wood is placed between the hammer and the part. Do

not hammer on cast parts or parts that could be easily damaged. With any particularly stubborn part, always recheck to make sure that every fastener has been removed.

Avoid using a screwdriver or bar to pry apart an assembly, as they can easily mar the gasket sealing surfaces of the parts, which must remain smooth. If prying is absolutely necessary, use an old broom handle, but keep in mind that extra clean up will be necessary if the wood splinters.

After the parts are separated, the old gasket must be carefully scraped off and the gasket surfaces cleaned. Stubborn gasket material can be soaked with rust penetrant or treated with a special chemical to soften it so it can be easily scraped off. **Caution:** *Never use gasket removal solutions or caustic chemicals on plastic or other composite components.* A scraper can be fashioned from a piece of copper tubing by flattening and sharpening one end. Copper is recommended because it is usually softer than the surfaces to be scraped, which reduces the chance of gouging the part. Some gaskets can be removed with a wire brush, but regardless of the method used, the mating surfaces must be left clean and smooth. If for some reason the gasket surface is gouged, then a gasket sealer thick enough to fill scratches will have to be used during reassembly of the components. For most applications, a non-drying (or semi-drying) gasket sealer should be used.

## Hose removal tips

**Warning:** *If the vehicle is equipped with air conditioning, do not disconnect any of the A/C hoses without first having the system depressurized by a dealer service department or a service station.*

Hose removal precautions closely parallel gasket removal precautions. Avoid scratching or gouging the surface that the hose mates against or the connection may leak. This is especially true for radiator hoses. Because of various chemical reactions, the rubber in hoses can bond itself to the metal spigot that the hose fits over. To remove

a hose, first loosen the hose clamps that secure it to the spigot. Then, with slip-joint pliers, grab the hose at the clamp and rotate it around the spigot. Work it back and forth until it is completely free, then pull it off. Silicone or other lubricants will ease removal if they can be applied between the hose and the outside of the spigot. Apply the same lubricant to the inside of the hose and the outside of the spigot to simplify installation.

As a last resort (and if the hose is to be replaced with a new one anyway), the rubber can be slit with a knife and the hose peeled from the spigot. If this must be done, be careful that the metal connection is not damaged.

If a hose clamp is broken or damaged, do not reuse it. Wire-type clamps usually weaken with age, so it is a good idea to replace them with screw-type clamps whenever a hose is removed.

## Tools

A selection of good tools is a basic requirement for anyone who plans to maintain and repair his or her own vehicle. For the owner who has few tools, the initial investment might seem high, but when compared to the spiraling costs of professional auto maintenance and repair, it is a wise one.

To help the owner decide which tools are needed to perform the tasks detailed in this manual, the following tool lists are offered: *Maintenance and minor repair, Repair/overhaul* and *Special.*

The newcomer to practical mechanics should start off with the *maintenance and minor repair* tool kit, which is adequate for the simpler jobs performed on a vehicle. Then, as confidence and experience grow, the owner can tackle more difficult tasks, buying additional tools as they are needed. Eventually the basic kit will be expanded into the *repair and overhaul* tool set. Over a period of time, the experienced do-it-yourselfer will assemble a tool set complete enough for most repair and overhaul procedures and will add tools from the special category when it is felt that the expense is justified by the frequency of use.

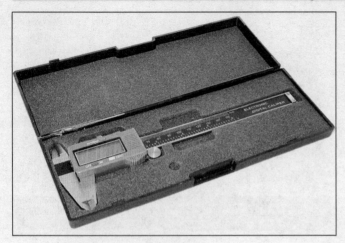

Dial caliper

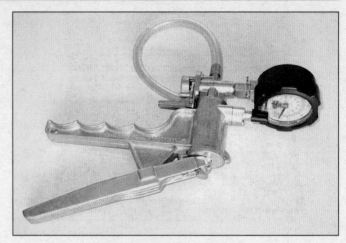

Hand-operated vacuum pump

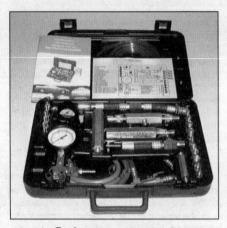

Fuel pressure gauge set

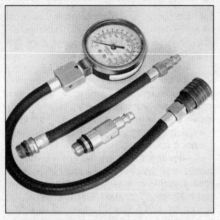

Compression gauge with spark plug
hole adapter

Damper/steering wheel puller

## Maintenance and minor repair tool kit

The tools in this list should be considered the minimum required for performance of routine maintenance, servicing and minor repair work. We recommend the purchase of combination wrenches (box-end and open-end combined in one wrench). While more expensive than open end wrenches, they offer the advantages of both types of wrench.

> *Combination wrench set (1/4-inch to*
>   *1 inch or 6 mm to 19 mm)*
> *Adjustable wrench, 8 inch*
> *Spark plug wrench with rubber insert*
> *Spark plug gap adjusting tool*
> *Feeler gauge set*
> *Brake bleeder wrench*
> *Standard screwdriver (5/16-inch x*
>   *6 inch)*
> *Phillips screwdriver (No. 2 x 6 inch)*
> *Combination pliers - 6 inch*
> *Hacksaw and assortment of blades*
> *Tire pressure gauge*
> *Grease gun*
> *Oil can*
> *Fine emery cloth*
> *Wire brush*

> *Battery post and cable cleaning tool*
> *Oil filter wrench*
> *Funnel (medium size)*
> *Safety goggles*
> *Jackstands (2)*
> *Drain pan*

**Note:** *If basic tune-ups are going to be part of routine maintenance, it will be necessary to purchase a good quality stroboscopic timing light and combination tachometer/dwell meter. Although they are included in the list of special tools, it is mentioned here because they are absolutely necessary for tuning most vehicles properly.*

## Repair and overhaul tool set

These tools are essential for anyone who plans to perform major repairs and are in addition to those in the maintenance and minor repair tool kit. Included is a comprehensive set of sockets which, though expensive, are invaluable because of their versatility, especially when various extensions and drives are available. We recommend the 1/2-inch drive over the 3/8-inch drive. Although the larger drive is bulky and more expensive, it has the capacity of accepting a very wide range of

large sockets. Ideally, however, the mechanic should have a 3/8-inch drive set and a 1/2-inch drive set.

> *Socket set(s)*
> *Reversible ratchet*
> *Extension - 10 inch*
> *Universal joint*
> *Torque wrench (same size drive as*
>   *sockets)*
> *Ball peen hammer - 8 ounce*
> *Soft-face hammer (plastic/rubber)*
> *Standard screwdriver (1/4-inch x 6 inch)*
> *Standard screwdriver (stubby -*
>   *5/16-inch)*
> *Phillips screwdriver (No. 3 x 8 inch)*
> *Phillips screwdriver (stubby - No. 2)*
> *Pliers - vise grip*
> *Pliers - lineman's*
> *Pliers - needle nose*
> *Pliers - snap-ring (internal and external)*
> *Cold chisel - 1/2-inch*
> *Scribe*
> *Scraper (made from flattened copper*
>   *tubing)*
> *Centerpunch*
> *Pin punches (1/16, 1/8, 3/16-inch)*
> *Steel rule/straightedge - 12 inch*

**General purpose puller**

**Hydraulic lifter removal tool**

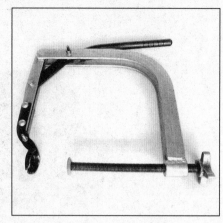

**Valve spring compressor**

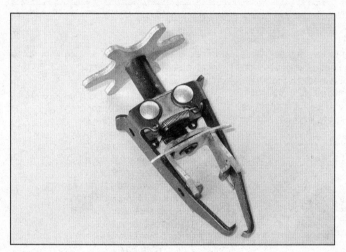

**Valve spring compressor**

**Ridge reamer**

*Allen wrench set (1/8 to 3/8-inch or
   4 mm to 10 mm)*
*A selection of files*
*Wire brush (large)*
*Jackstands (second set)*
*Jack (scissor or hydraulic type)*
**Note:** *Another tool which is often useful is an* electric drill with a chuck capacity of 3/8-inch and a set of good quality drill bits.

## Special tools

The tools in this list include those which are not used regularly, are expensive to buy, or which need to be used in accordance with their manufacturer's instructions. Unless these tools will be used frequently, it is not very economical to purchase many of them. A consideration would be to split the cost and use between yourself and a friend or friends. In addition, most of these tools can be obtained from a tool rental shop on a temporary basis.

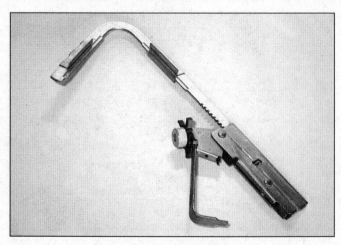

**Piston ring groove cleaning tool**

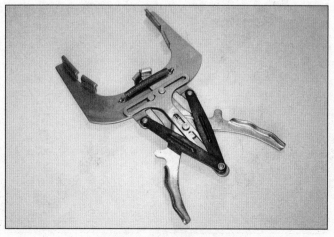

**Ring removal/installation tool**

**Ring compressor**

**Cylinder hone**

This list primarily contains only those tools and instruments widely available to the public, and not those special tools produced by the vehicle manufacturer for distribution to dealer service departments. Occasionally, references to the manufacturer's special tools are included in the text of this manual. Generally, an alternative method of doing the job without the special tool is offered. However, sometimes there is no alternative to their use. Where this is the case, and the tool cannot be purchased or borrowed, the work should be turned over to the dealer service department or an automotive repair shop.

Valve spring compressor
Piston ring groove cleaning tool
Piston ring compressor
Piston ring installation tool
Cylinder compression gauge
Cylinder ridge reamer
Cylinder surfacing hone
Cylinder bore gauge
Micrometers and/or dial calipers
Hydraulic lifter removal tool
Balljoint separator
Universal-type puller
Impact screwdriver
Dial indicator set
Stroboscopic timing light (inductive
    pick-up)
Hand operated vacuum/pressure pump
Tachometer/dwell meter
Universal electrical multimeter
Cable hoist
Brake spring removal and installation
    tools
Floor jack

**Brake hold-down spring tool**

**Torque angle gauge**

**Clutch plate alignment tool**

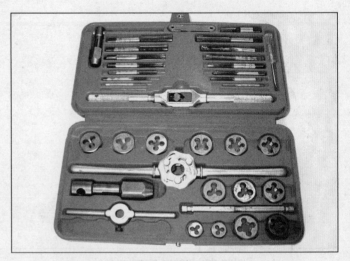

**Tap and die set**

## Buying tools

For the do-it-yourselfer who is just starting to get involved in vehicle maintenance and repair, there are a number of options available when purchasing tools. If maintenance and minor repair is the extent of the work to be done, the purchase of individual tools is satisfactory. If, on the other hand, extensive work is planned, it would be a good idea to purchase a modest tool set from one of the large retail chain stores. A set can usually be bought at a substantial savings over the individual tool prices, and they often come with a tool box. As additional tools are needed, add-on sets, individual tools and a larger tool box can be purchased to expand the tool selection. Building a tool set gradually allows the cost of the tools to be spread over a longer period of time and gives the mechanic the freedom to choose only those tools that will actually be used.

Tool stores will often be the only source of some of the special tools that are needed, but regardless of where tools are bought, try to avoid cheap ones, especially when buying screwdrivers and sockets, because they won't last very long. The expense involved in replacing cheap tools will eventually be greater than the initial cost of quality tools.

## Care and maintenance of tools

Good tools are expensive, so it makes sense to treat them with respect. Keep them clean and in usable condition and store them properly when not in use. Always wipe off any dirt, grease or metal chips before putting them away. Never leave tools lying around in the work area. Upon completion of a job, always check closely under the hood for tools that may have been left there so they won't get lost during a test drive.

Some tools, such as screwdrivers, pliers, wrenches and sockets, can be hung on a panel mounted on the garage or workshop wall, while others should be kept in a tool box or tray. Measuring instruments, gauges, meters, etc. must be carefully stored where they cannot be damaged by weather or impact from other tools.

When tools are used with care and stored properly, they will last a very long time. Even with the best of care, though, tools will wear out if used frequently. When a tool is damaged or worn out, replace it. Subsequent jobs will be safer and more enjoyable if you do.

## How to repair damaged threads

Sometimes, the internal threads of a nut or bolt hole can become stripped, usually from overtightening. Stripping threads is an all-too-common occurrence, especially when working with aluminum parts, because aluminum is so soft that it easily strips out.

Usually, external or internal threads are only partially stripped. After they've been cleaned up with a tap or die, they'll still work. Sometimes, however, threads are badly damaged. When this happens, you've got three choices:

1) Drill and tap the hole to the next suitable oversize and install a larger diameter bolt, screw or stud.
2) Drill and tap the hole to accept a threaded plug, then drill and tap the plug to the original screw size. You can also buy a plug already threaded to the original size. Then you simply drill a hole to the specified size, then run the threaded plug into the hole with a bolt and jam nut. Once the plug is fully seated, remove the jam nut and bolt.
3) The third method uses a patented thread repair kit like Heli-Coil or Slimsert. These easy-to-use kits are designed to repair damaged threads in straight-through holes and blind holes. Both are available as kits which can handle a variety of sizes and thread patterns. Drill the hole, then tap it with the special included tap. Install the Heli-Coil and the hole is back to its original diameter and thread pitch.

Regardless of which method you use, be sure to proceed calmly and carefully. A little impatience or carelessness during one of these relatively simple procedures can ruin your whole day's work and cost you a bundle if you wreck an expensive part.

## Working facilities

Not to be overlooked when discussing tools is the workshop. If anything more than routine maintenance is to be carried out, some sort of suitable work area is essential.

It is understood, and appreciated, that many home mechanics do not have a good workshop or garage available, and end up removing an engine or doing major repairs outside. It is recommended, however, that the overhaul or repair be completed under the cover of a roof.

A clean, flat workbench or table of comfortable working height is an absolute necessity. The workbench should be equipped with a vise that has a jaw opening of at least four inches.

As mentioned previously, some clean, dry storage space is also required for tools, as well as the lubricants, fluids, cleaning solvents, etc. which soon become necessary.

Sometimes waste oil and fluids, drained from the engine or cooling system during normal maintenance or repairs, present a disposal problem. To avoid pouring them on the ground or into a sewage system, pour the used fluids into large containers, seal them with caps and take them to an authorized disposal site or recycling center. Plastic jugs, such as old antifreeze containers, are ideal for this purpose.

Always keep a supply of old newspapers and clean rags available. Old towels are excellent for mopping up spills. Many mechanics use rolls of paper towels for most work because they are readily available and disposable. To help keep the area under the vehicle clean, a large cardboard box can be cut open and flattened to protect the garage or shop floor.

Whenever working over a painted surface, such as when leaning over a fender to service something under the hood, always cover it with an old blanket or bedspread to protect the finish. Vinyl covered pads, made especially for this purpose, are available at auto parts stores.

# Run-flat tires

All models covered by this manual are equipped with Run-flat tires. In the event of a puncture, the structure and construction of the tire allows the vehicle to be driven deflated at a maximum speed of 50 mph.

The maximum distance to be covered with a deflated tire is:
Low load (1 to 2 people without luggage) - 150 miles
Moderate load (2 people with luggage, 4 people without luggage) - 90 miles

Full load (4 or more people with luggage) - 30 miles

Because Run-flat tires are standard equipment, no spare wheel or vehicle jack is provided.

# Jump starting

When jump-starting a car using a booster battery, observe the following precautions:

a)  Before connecting the booster battery, make sure that the ignition is switched off.

b)  Ensure that all electrical equipment (lights, heater, wipers, etc) is switched off.

c)  Take note of any special precautions printed on the battery case.

d)  Make sure that the booster battery is the same voltage as the discharged one in the vehicle.

e)  If the battery is being jump-started from

the battery in another vehicle, the two vehicles MUST NOT TOUCH each other.

f)  Make sure that the transmission is in neutral (or PARK, in the case of automatic transmission).

**1** Unclip the plastic cover from the jump- start terminal (+) in the right-rear corner of the engine compartment, and connect the red jump lead to the terminal

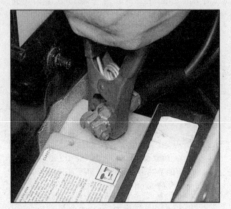

**2** Connect the other end of the red lead to the positive (+) terminal of the booster battery

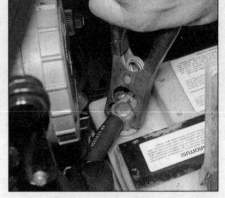

**3** Connect one end of the black jump lead to the negative (-) terminal of the booster battery

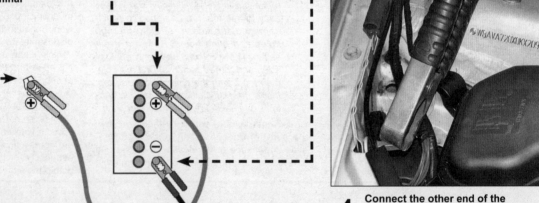

**4** Connect the other end of the black jump lead to the jump start negative terminal located on the right-hand inner fender panel in the engine compartment

**5** Make sure that the jump leads will not come into contact with the drivebelts or other moving parts on the engine

**6** Start the engine, then with the engine running at fast idle speed, disconnect the jump leads in the reverse order of connection; negative (black) lead first. Securely refit the plastic cover to the jump start positive terminal.

# Automotive chemicals and lubricants

A number of automotive chemicals and lubricants are available for use during vehicle maintenance and repair. They include a wide variety of products ranging from cleaning solvents and degreasers to lubricants and protective sprays for rubber, plastic and vinyl.

## Cleaners

**Carburetor cleaner and choke cleaner** is a strong solvent for gum, varnish and carbon. Most carburetor cleaners leave a dry-type lubricant film which will not harden or gum up. Because of this film it is not recommended for use on electrical components.

**Brake system cleaner** is used to remove brake dust, grease and brake fluid from the brake system, where clean surfaces are absolutely necessary. It leaves no residue and often eliminates brake squeal caused by contaminants.

**Electrical cleaner** removes oxidation, corrosion and carbon deposits from electrical contacts, restoring full current flow. It can also be used to clean spark plugs, carburetor jets, voltage regulators and other parts where an oil-free surface is desired.

**Demoisturants** remove water and moisture from electrical components such as alternators, voltage regulators, electrical connectors and fuse blocks. They are non-conductive and non-corrosive.

**Degreasers** are heavy-duty solvents used to remove grease from the outside of the engine and from chassis components. They can be sprayed or brushed on and, depending on the type, are rinsed off either with water or solvent.

## Lubricants

**Motor oil** is the lubricant formulated for use in engines. It normally contains a wide variety of additives to prevent corrosion and reduce foaming and wear. Motor oil comes in various weights (viscosity ratings) from 0 to 50. The recommended weight of the oil depends on the season, temperature and the demands on the engine. Light oil is used in cold climates and under light load conditions. Heavy oil is used in hot climates and where high loads are encountered. Multi-viscosity oils are designed to have characteristics of both light and heavy oils and are available in a number of weights from 0W-20 to 20W-50.

**Gear oil** is designed to be used in differentials, manual transmissions and other areas where high-temperature lubrication is required.

**Chassis and wheel bearing grease** is a heavy grease used where increased loads and friction are encountered, such as for wheel bearings, balljoints, tie-rod ends and universal joints.

**High-temperature wheel bearing grease** is designed to withstand the extreme temperatures encountered by wheel bearings in disc brake equipped vehicles. It usually contains molybdenum disulfide (moly), which is a dry-type lubricant.

**White grease** is a heavy grease for metal-to-metal applications where water is a problem. White grease stays soft under both low and high temperatures (usually from -100 to +190-degrees F), and will not wash off or dilute in the presence of water.

**Assembly lube** is a special extreme pressure lubricant, usually containing moly, used to lubricate high-load parts (such as main and rod bearings and cam lobes) for initial start-up of a new engine. The assembly lube lubricates the parts without being squeezed out or washed away until the engine oiling system begins to function.

**Silicone lubricants** are used to protect rubber, plastic, vinyl and nylon parts.

**Graphite lubricants** are used where oils cannot be used due to contamination problems, such as in locks. The dry graphite will lubricate metal parts while remaining uncontaminated by dirt, water, oil or acids. It is electrically conductive and will not foul electrical contacts in locks such as the ignition switch.

**Moly penetrants** loosen and lubricate frozen, rusted and corroded fasteners and prevent future rusting or freezing.

**Heat-sink grease** is a special electrically non-conductive grease that is used for mounting electronic ignition modules where it is essential that heat is transferred away from the module.

## Sealants

**RTV sealant** is one of the most widely used gasket compounds. Made from silicone, RTV is air curing, it seals, bonds, waterproofs, fills surface irregularities, remains flexible, doesn't shrink, is relatively easy to remove, and is used as a supplementary sealer with almost all low and medium temperature gaskets.

**Anaerobic sealant** is much like RTV in that it can be used either to seal gaskets or to form gaskets by itself. It remains flexible, is solvent resistant and fills surface imperfections. The difference between an anaerobic sealant and an RTV-type sealant is in the curing. RTV cures when exposed to air, while an anaerobic sealant cures only in the absence of air. This means that an anaerobic sealant cures only after the assembly of parts, sealing them together.

**Thread and pipe sealant** is used for sealing hydraulic and pneumatic fittings and vacuum lines. It is usually made from a Teflon compound, and comes in a spray, a paint-on liquid and as a wrap-around tape.

## Chemicals

**Anti-seize compound** prevents seizing, galling, cold welding, rust and corrosion in fasteners. High-temperature anti-seize, usually made with copper and graphite lubricants, is used for exhaust system and exhaust manifold bolts.

**Anaerobic locking compounds** are used to keep fasteners from vibrating or working loose and cure only after installation, in the absence of air. Medium strength locking compound is used for small nuts, bolts and screws that may be removed later. High-strength locking compound is for large nuts, bolts and studs which aren't removed on a regular basis.

**Oil additives** range from viscosity index improvers to chemical treatments that claim to reduce internal engine friction. It should be noted that most oil manufacturers caution against using additives with their oils.

**Gas additives** perform several functions, depending on their chemical makeup. They usually contain solvents that help dissolve gum and varnish that build up on carburetor, fuel injection and intake parts. They also serve to break down carbon deposits that form on the inside surfaces of the combustion chambers. Some additives contain upper cylinder lubricants for valves and piston rings, and others contain chemicals to remove condensation from the gas tank.

## Miscellaneous

**Brake fluid** is specially formulated hydraulic fluid that can withstand the heat and pressure encountered in brake systems. Care must be taken so this fluid does not come in contact with painted surfaces or plastics. An opened container should always be resealed to prevent contamination by water or dirt.

**Weatherstrip adhesive** is used to bond weatherstripping around doors, windows and trunk lids. It is sometimes used to attach trim pieces.

**Undercoating** is a petroleum-based, tar-like substance that is designed to protect metal surfaces on the underside of the vehicle from corrosion. It also acts as a sound-deadening agent by insulating the bottom of the vehicle.

**Waxes and polishes** are used to help protect painted and plated surfaces from the weather. Different types of paint may require the use of different types of wax and polish. Some polishes utilize a chemical or abrasive cleaner to help remove the top layer of oxidized (dull) paint on older vehicles. In recent years many non-wax polishes that contain a wide variety of chemicals such as polymers and silicones have been introduced. These non-wax polishes are usually easier to apply and last longer than conventional waxes and polishes.

# Conversion factors

### Length (distance)

| | | | | | |
|---|---|---|---|---|---|
| Inches (in) | X | 25.4 | = Millimeters (mm) | X 0.0394 | = Inches (in) |
| Feet (ft) | X | 0.305 | = Meters (m) | X 3.281 | = Feet (ft) |
| Miles | X | 1.609 | = Kilometers (km) | X 0.621 | = Miles |

### Volume (capacity)

| | | | | | |
|---|---|---|---|---|---|
| Cubic inches (cu in; in$^3$) | X | 16.387 | = Cubic centimeters (cc; cm$^3$) | X 0.061 | = Cubic inches (cu in; in$^3$) |
| Imperial pints (Imp pt) | X | 0.568 | = Liters (l) | X 1.76 | = Imperial pints (Imp pt) |
| Imperial quarts (Imp qt) | X | 1.137 | = Liters (l) | X 0.88 | = Imperial quarts (Imp qt) |
| Imperial quarts (Imp qt) | X | 1.201 | = US quarts (US qt) | X 0.833 | = Imperial quarts (Imp qt) |
| US quarts (US qt) | X | 0.946 | = Liters (l) | X 1.057 | = US quarts (US qt) |
| Imperial gallons (Imp gal) | X | 4.546 | = Liters (l) | X 0.22 | = Imperial gallons (Imp gal) |
| Imperial gallons (Imp gal) | X | 1.201 | = US gallons (US gal) | X 0.833 | = Imperial gallons (Imp gal) |
| US gallons (US gal) | X | 3.785 | = Liters (l) | X 0.264 | = US gallons (US gal) |

### Mass (weight)

| | | | | | |
|---|---|---|---|---|---|
| Ounces (oz) | X | 28.35 | = Grams (g) | X 0.035 | = Ounces (oz) |
| Pounds (lb) | X | 0.454 | = Kilograms (kg) | X 2.205 | = Pounds (lb) |

### Force

| | | | | | |
|---|---|---|---|---|---|
| Ounces-force (ozf; oz) | X | 0.278 | = Newtons (N) | X 3.6 | = Ounces-force (ozf; oz) |
| Pounds-force (lbf; lb) | X | 4.448 | = Newtons (N) | X 0.225 | = Pounds-force (lbf; lb) |
| Newtons (N) | X | 0.1 | = Kilograms-force (kgf; kg) | X 9.81 | = Newtons (N) |

### Pressure

| | | | | | |
|---|---|---|---|---|---|
| Pounds-force per square inch (psi; lbf/in$^2$; lb/in$^2$) | X | 0.070 | = Kilograms-force per square centimeter (kgf/cm$^2$; kg/cm$^2$) | X 14.223 | = Pounds-force per square inch (psi; lbf/in$^2$; lb/in$^2$) |
| Pounds-force per square inch (psi; lbf/in$^2$; lb/in$^2$) | X | 0.068 | = Atmospheres (atm) | X 14.696 | = Pounds-force per square inch (psi; lbf/in$^2$; lb/in$^2$) |
| Pounds-force per square inch (psi; lbf/in$^2$; lb/in$^2$) | X | 0.069 | = Bars | X 14.5 | = Pounds-force per square inch (psi; lbf/in$^2$; lb/in$^2$) |
| Pounds-force per square inch (psi; lbf/in$^2$; lb/in$^2$) | X | 6.895 | = Kilopascals (kPa) | X 0.145 | = Pounds-force per square inch (psi; lbf/in$^2$; lb/in$^2$) |
| Kilopascals (kPa) | X | 0.01 | = Kilograms-force per square centimeter (kgf/cm$^2$; kg/cm$^2$) | X 98.1 | = Kilopascals (kPa) |

### Torque (moment of force)

| | | | | | |
|---|---|---|---|---|---|
| Pounds-force inches (lbf in; lb in) | X | 1.152 | = Kilograms-force centimeter (kgf cm; kg cm) | X 0.868 | = Pounds-force inches (lbf in; lb in) |
| Pounds-force inches (lbf in; lb in) | X | 0.113 | = Newton meters (Nm) | X 8.85 | = Pounds-force inches (lbf in; lb in) |
| Pounds-force inches (lbf in; lb in) | X | 0.083 | = Pounds-force feet (lbf ft; lb ft) | X 12 | = Pounds-force inches (lbf in; lb in) |
| Pounds-force feet (lbf ft; lb ft) | X | 0.138 | = Kilograms-force meters (kgf m; kg m) | X 7.233 | = Pounds-force feet (lbf ft; lb ft) |
| Pounds-force feet (lbf ft; lb ft) | X | 1.356 | = Newton meters (Nm) | X 0.738 | = Pounds-force feet (lbf ft; lb ft) |
| Newton meters (Nm) | X | 0.102 | = Kilograms-force meters (kgf m; kg m) | X 9.804 | = Newton meters (Nm) |

### Vacuum

| | | | | | |
|---|---|---|---|---|---|
| Inches mercury (in. Hg) | X | 3.377 | = Kilopascals (kPa) | X 0.2961 | = Inches mercury |
| Inches mercury (in. Hg) | X | 25.4 | = Millimeters mercury (mm Hg) | X 0.0394 | = Inches mercury |

### Power

| | | | | | |
|---|---|---|---|---|---|
| Horsepower (hp) | X | 745.7 | = Watts (W) | X 0.0013 | = Horsepower (hp) |

### Velocity (speed)

| | | | | | |
|---|---|---|---|---|---|
| Miles per hour (miles/hr; mph) | X | 1.609 | = Kilometers per hour (km/hr; kph) | X 0.621 | = Miles per hour (miles/hr; mph) |

### Fuel consumption*

| | | | | | |
|---|---|---|---|---|---|
| Miles per gallon, Imperial (mpg) | X | 0.354 | = Kilometers per liter (km/l) | X 2.825 | = Miles per gallon, Imperial (mpg) |
| Miles per gallon, US (mpg) | X | 0.425 | = Kilometers per liter (km/l) | X 2.352 | = Miles per gallon, US (mpg) |

### Temperature

Degrees Fahrenheit = (°C x 1.8) + 32          Degrees Celsius (Degrees Centigrade; °C) = (°F - 32) x 0.56

*It is common practice to convert from miles per gallon (mpg) to liters/100 kilometers (l/100km), where mpg (Imperial) x l/100 km = 282 and mpg (US) x l/100 km = 235

## DECIMALS to MILLIMETERS

| Decimal | mm | Decimal | mm |
|---|---|---|---|
| 0.001 | 0.0254 | 0.500 | 12.7000 |
| 0.002 | 0.0508 | 0.510 | 12.9540 |
| 0.003 | 0.0762 | 0.520 | 13.2080 |
| 0.004 | 0.1016 | 0.530 | 13.4620 |
| 0.005 | 0.1270 | 0.540 | 13.7160 |
| 0.006 | 0.1524 | 0.550 | 13.9700 |
| 0.007 | 0.1778 | 0.560 | 14.2240 |
| 0.008 | 0.2032 | 0.570 | 14.4780 |
| 0.009 | 0.2286 | 0.580 | 14.7320 |
| | | 0.590 | 14.9860 |
| 0.010 | 0.2540 | | |
| 0.020 | 0.5080 | | |
| 0.030 | 0.7620 | | |
| 0.040 | 1.0160 | 0.600 | 15.2400 |
| 0.050 | 1.2700 | 0.610 | 15.4940 |
| 0.060 | 1.5240 | 0.620 | 15.7480 |
| 0.070 | 1.7780 | 0.630 | 16.0020 |
| 0.080 | 2.0320 | 0.640 | 16.2560 |
| 0.090 | 2.2860 | 0.650 | 16.5100 |
| | | 0.660 | 16.7640 |
| 0.100 | 2.5400 | 0.670 | 17.0180 |
| 0.110 | 2.7940 | 0.680 | 17.2720 |
| 0.120 | 3.0480 | 0.690 | 17.5260 |
| 0.130 | 3.3020 | | |
| 0.140 | 3.5560 | | |
| 0.150 | 3.8100 | | |
| 0.160 | 4.0640 | 0.700 | 17.7800 |
| 0.170 | 4.3180 | 0.710 | 18.0340 |
| 0.180 | 4.5720 | 0.720 | 18.2880 |
| 0.190 | 4.8260 | 0.730 | 18.5420 |
| | | 0.740 | 18.7960 |
| 0.200 | 5.0800 | 0.750 | 19.0500 |
| 0.210 | 5.3340 | 0.760 | 19.3040 |
| 0.220 | 5.5880 | 0.770 | 19.5580 |
| 0.230 | 5.8420 | 0.780 | 19.8120 |
| 0.240 | 6.0960 | 0.790 | 20.0660 |
| 0.250 | 6.3500 | | |
| 0.260 | 6.6040 | | |
| 0.270 | 6.8580 | 0.800 | 20.3200 |
| 0.280 | 7.1120 | 0.810 | 20.5740 |
| 0.290 | 7.3660 | 0.820 | 21.8280 |
| | | 0.830 | 21.0820 |
| 0.300 | 7.6200 | 0.840 | 21.3360 |
| 0.310 | 7.8740 | 0.850 | 21.5900 |
| 0.320 | 8.1280 | 0.860 | 21.8440 |
| 0.330 | 8.3820 | 0.870 | 22.0980 |
| 0.340 | 8.6360 | 0.880 | 22.3520 |
| 0.350 | 8.8900 | 0.890 | 22.6060 |
| 0.360 | 9.1440 | | |
| 0.370 | 9.3980 | | |
| 0.380 | 9.6520 | | |
| 0.390 | 9.9060 | 0.900 | 22.8600 |
| 0.400 | 10.1600 | 0.910 | 23.1140 |
| 0.410 | 10.4140 | 0.920 | 23.3680 |
| 0.420 | 10.6680 | 0.930 | 23.6220 |
| 0.430 | 10.9220 | 0.940 | 23.8760 |
| 0.440 | 11.1760 | 0.950 | 24.1300 |
| 0.450 | 11.4300 | 0.960 | 24.3840 |
| 0.460 | 11.6840 | 0.970 | 24.6380 |
| 0.470 | 11.9380 | 0.980 | 24.8920 |
| 0.480 | 12.1920 | 0.990 | 25.1460 |
| 0.490 | 12.4460 | 1.000 | 25.4000 |

## FRACTIONS to DECIMALS to MILLIMETERS

| Fraction | Decimal | mm | Fraction | Decimal | mm |
|---|---|---|---|---|---|
| 1/64 | 0.0156 | 0.3969 | 33/64 | 0.5156 | 13.0969 |
| 1/32 | 0.0312 | 0.7938 | 17/32 | 0.5312 | 13.4938 |
| 3/64 | 0.0469 | 1.1906 | 35/64 | 0.5469 | 13.8906 |
| 1/16 | 0.0625 | 1.5875 | 9/16 | 0.5625 | 14.2875 |
| 5/64 | 0.0781 | 1.9844 | 37/64 | 0.5781 | 14.6844 |
| 3/32 | 0.0938 | 2.3812 | 19/32 | 0.5938 | 15.0812 |
| 7/64 | 0.1094 | 2.7781 | 39/64 | 0.6094 | 15.4781 |
| 1/8 | 0.1250 | 3.1750 | 5/8 | 0.6250 | 15.8750 |
| 9/64 | 0.1406 | 3.5719 | 41/64 | 0.6406 | 16.2719 |
| 5/32 | 0.1562 | 3.9688 | 21/32 | 0.6562 | 16.6688 |
| 11/64 | 0.1719 | 4.3656 | 43/64 | 0.6719 | 17.0656 |
| 3/16 | 0.1875 | 4.7625 | 11/16 | 0.6875 | 17.4625 |
| 13/64 | 0.2031 | 5.1594 | 45/64 | 0.7031 | 17.8594 |
| 7/32 | 0.2188 | 5.5562 | 23/32 | 0.7188 | 18.2562 |
| 15/64 | 0.2344 | 5.9531 | 47/64 | 0.7344 | 18.6531 |
| 1/4 | 0.2500 | 6.3500 | 3/4 | 0.7500 | 19.0500 |
| 17/64 | 0.2656 | 6.7469 | 49/64 | 0.7656 | 19.4469 |
| 9/32 | 0.2812 | 7.1438 | 25/32 | 0.7812 | 19.8438 |
| 19/64 | 0.2969 | 7.5406 | 51/64 | 0.7969 | 20.2406 |
| 5/16 | 0.3125 | 7.9375 | 13/16 | 0.8125 | 20.6375 |
| 21/64 | 0.3281 | 8.3344 | 53/64 | 0.8281 | 21.0344 |
| 11/32 | 0.3438 | 8.7312 | 27/32 | 0.8438 | 21.4312 |
| 23/64 | 0.3594 | 9.1281 | 55/64 | 0.8594 | 21.8281 |
| 3/8 | 0.3750 | 9.5250 | 7/8 | 0.8750 | 22.2250 |
| 25/64 | 0.3906 | 9.9219 | 57/64 | 0.8906 | 22.6219 |
| 13/32 | 0.4062 | 10.3188 | 29/32 | 0.9062 | 23.0188 |
| 27/64 | 0.4219 | 10.7156 | 59/64 | 0.9219 | 23.4156 |
| 7/16 | 0.4375 | 11.1125 | 15/16 | 0.9375 | 23.8125 |
| 29/64 | 0.4531 | 11.5094 | 61/64 | 0.9531 | 24.2094 |
| 15/32 | 0.4688 | 11.9062 | 31/32 | 0.9688 | 24.6062 |
| 31/64 | 0.4844 | 12.3031 | 63/64 | 0.9844 | 25.0031 |
| 1/2 | 0.5000 | 12.7000 | 1 | 1.0000 | 25.4000 |

# Safety first!

Regardless of how enthusiastic you may be about getting on with the job at hand, take the time to ensure that your safety is not jeopardized. A moment's lack of attention can result in an accident, as can failure to observe certain simple safety precautions. The possibility of an accident will always exist, and the following points should not be considered a comprehensive list of all dangers. Rather, they are intended to make you aware of the risks and to encourage a safety conscious approach to all work you carry out on your vehicle.

## Essential DOs and DON'Ts

**DON'T** rely on a jack when working under the vehicle. Always use approved jackstands to support the weight of the vehicle and place them under the recommended lift or support points.

**DON'T** attempt to loosen extremely tight fasteners (i.e. wheel lug nuts) while the vehicle is on a jack - it may fall.

**DON'T** start the engine without first making sure that the transmission is in Neutral (or Park where applicable) and the parking brake is set.

**DON'T** remove the radiator cap from a hot cooling system - let it cool or cover it with a cloth and release the pressure gradually.

**DON'T** attempt to drain the engine oil until you are sure it has cooled to the point that it will not burn you.

**DON'T** touch any part of the engine or exhaust system until it has cooled sufficiently to avoid burns.

**DON'T** siphon toxic liquids such as gasoline, antifreeze and brake fluid by mouth, or allow them to remain on your skin.

**DON'T** inhale brake lining dust - it is potentially hazardous (see *Asbestos* below).

**DON'T** allow spilled oil or grease to remain on the floor - wipe it up before someone slips on it.

**DON'T** use loose fitting wrenches or other tools which may slip and cause injury.

**DON'T** push on wrenches when loosening or tightening nuts or bolts. Always try to pull the wrench toward you. If the situation calls for pushing the wrench away, push with an open hand to avoid scraped knuckles if the wrench should slip.

**DON'T** attempt to lift a heavy component alone - get someone to help you.

**DON'T** *rush or take unsafe shortcuts to finish a job.*

**DON'T** allow children or animals in or around the vehicle while you are working on it.

**DO** wear eye protection when using power tools such as a drill, sander, bench grinder, etc. and when working under a vehicle.

**DO** keep loose clothing and long hair well out of the way of moving parts.

**DO** make sure that any hoist used has a safe working load rating adequate for the job.

**DO** get someone to check on you periodically when working alone on a vehicle.

**DO** carry out work in a logical sequence and make sure that everything is correctly assembled and tightened.

**DO** keep chemicals and fluids tightly capped and out of the reach of children and pets.

**DO** remember that your vehicle's safety affects that of yourself and others. If in doubt on any point, get professional advice.

## Steering, suspension and brakes

These systems are essential to driving safety, so make sure you have a qualified shop or individual check your work. Also, compressed suspension springs can cause injury if released suddenly - be sure to use a spring compressor.

## Airbags

Airbags are explosive devices that can **CAUSE** injury if they deploy while you're working on the vehicle. Follow the manufacturer's instructions to disable the airbag whenever you're working in the vicinity of airbag components.

## Asbestos

Certain friction, insulating, sealing, and other products - such as brake linings, brake bands, clutch linings, torque converters, gaskets, etc. - may contain asbestos or other hazardous friction material. Extreme care must be taken to avoid inhalation of dust from such products, since it is hazardous to health. If in doubt, assume that they do contain asbestos.

## Fire

Remember at all times that gasoline is highly flammable. Never smoke or have any kind of open flame around when working on a vehicle. But the risk does not end there. A spark caused by an electrical short circuit, by two metal surfaces contacting each other, or even by static electricity built up in your body under certain conditions, can ignite gasoline vapors, which in a confined space are highly explosive. Do not, under any circumstances, use gasoline for cleaning parts. Use an approved safety solvent.

Always disconnect the battery ground (-) cable at the battery before working on any part of the fuel system or electrical system. Never risk spilling fuel on a hot engine or exhaust component. It is strongly recommended that a fire extinguisher suitable for use on fuel and electrical fires be kept handy in the garage or workshop at all times. Never try to extinguish a fuel or electrical fire with water.

## Fumes

Certain fumes are highly toxic and can quickly cause unconsciousness and even death if inhaled to any extent. Gasoline vapor falls into this category, as do the vapors from some cleaning solvents. Any draining or pouring of such volatile fluids should be done in a well ventilated area.

When using cleaning fluids and solvents, read the instructions on the container carefully. Never use materials from unmarked containers.

Never run the engine in an enclosed space, such as a garage. Exhaust fumes contain carbon monoxide, which is extremely poisonous. If you need to run the engine, always do so in the open air, or at least have the rear of the vehicle outside the work area.

## The battery

Never create a spark or allow a bare light bulb near a battery. They normally give off a certain amount of hydrogen gas, which is highly explosive.

Always disconnect the battery ground (-) cable at the battery before working on the fuel or electrical systems.

If possible, loosen the filler caps or cover when charging the battery from an external source (this does not apply to sealed or maintenance-free batteries). Do not charge at an excessive rate or the battery may burst.

Take care when adding water to a non maintenance-free battery and when carrying a battery. The electrolyte, even when diluted, is very corrosive and should not be allowed to contact clothing or skin.

Always wear eye protection when cleaning the battery to prevent the caustic deposits from entering your eyes.

## Household current

When using an electric power tool, inspection light, etc., which operates on household current, always make sure that the tool is correctly connected to its plug and that, where necessary, it is properly grounded. Do not use such items in damp conditions and, again, do not create a spark or apply excessive heat in the vicinity of fuel or fuel vapor.

## Secondary ignition system voltage

A severe electric shock can result from touching certain parts of the ignition system (such as the spark plug wires) when the engine is running or being cranked, particularly if components are damp or the insulation is defective. In the case of an electronic ignition system, the secondary system voltage is much higher and could prove fatal.

## Hydrofluoric acid

This extremely corrosive acid is formed when certain types of synthetic rubber, found in some O-rings, oil seals, fuel hoses, etc. are exposed to temperatures above 750-degrees F (400-degrees C). The rubber changes into a charred or sticky substance containing the acid. *Once formed, the acid remains dangerous for years. If it gets onto the skin, it may be necessary to amputate the limb concerned.*

When dealing with a vehicle which has suffered a fire, or with components salvaged from such a vehicle, wear protective gloves and discard them after use.

# Troubleshooting

**Contents**

This section provides an easy reference guide to the more common problems which may occur during the operation of your vehicle. These problems and their possible causes are grouped under headings denoting various components or systems, such as Engine, Cooling system, etc. They also refer you to the chapter and/or section which deals with the problem.

Remember that successful troubleshooting is not a mysterious black art practiced only by professional mechanics. It is simply the result of the right knowledge combined with an intelligent, systematic approach to the problem. Always work by a process of elimination, starting with the simplest solution and working through to the most complex - and never overlook the obvious. Anyone can run the gas tank dry or leave the lights on overnight, so don't assume that you are exempt from such oversights.

Finally, always establish a clear idea of why a problem has occurred and take steps to ensure that it doesn't happen again. If the electrical system fails because of a poor connection, check the other connections in the system to make sure that they don't fail as well. If a particular fuse continues to blow, find out why - don't just replace one fuse after another. Remember, failure of a small component can often be indicative of potential failure or incorrect functioning of a more important component or system.

Engine and transmission problems can often be diagnosed through a scan tool to check for trouble codes.

## Engine

### 1 Engine will not rotate when attempting to start

1 Battery terminal connections loose or corroded (Chapter 1).
2 Battery discharged or faulty (Chapters 1 and 5).
3 Automatic transmission not completely engaged in Park (Chapter 7) or clutch pedal not completely depressed (Chapter 6).
4 Broken, loose or disconnected wiring in the starting circuit (Chapters 5 and 12).
5 Starter motor pinion jammed in flywheel ring gear (Chapter 5).
6 Starter solenoid faulty (Chapter 5).
7 Starter motor faulty (Chapter 5).
8 Ignition switch faulty (Chapter 12).
9 Starter pinion or flywheel teeth worn or broken (Chapter 5).

### 2 Engine rotates but will not start

1 Fuel tank empty.
2 Battery discharged (engine rotates slowly) (Chapter 5).
3 Battery terminal connections loose or corroded (Chapter 1).
4 Leaking fuel injector(s), faulty fuel pump, pressure regulator, etc. (Chapter 4).
5 Broken timing chain (Chapter 2A).
6 Ignition components damp or damaged (Chapter 5).
7 Worn, faulty or incorrectly-gapped spark plugs (Chapter 1).
8 Broken, loose or disconnected wires at the ignition coil or faulty coil (Chapter 5).
9 Defective crankshaft or camshaft sensor (Chapter 6).

### 3 Engine hard to start when cold

1 Battery discharged or low (Chapter 1).
2 Malfunctioning fuel system (Chapter 4).
3 Faulty coolant temperature sensor or intake air temperature sensor (Chapter 6).
4 Faulty ignition system (Chapter 5).

### 4 Engine hard to start when hot

1 Air filter clogged (Chapter 1).
2 Fuel not reaching the fuel injection system (Chapter 4).
3 Corroded battery connections (Chapter 1).
4 Faulty coolant temperature sensor or intake air temperature sensor (Chapter 6).

### 5 Starter motor noisy or excessively rough in engagement

1 Pinion or flywheel gear teeth worn or broken (Chapter 5).
2 Starter motor mounting bolts loose or missing (Chapter 5).

### 6 Engine starts but stops immediately

1 Insufficient fuel reaching the fuel injector(s) (Chapters 1 and 4).
2 Vacuum leak at the gasket between the intake manifold/plenum and throttle body (Chapter 4).

### 7 Oil puddle under engine

1 Oil pan gasket and/or oil pan drain bolt washer leaking (Chapter 2).
2 Oil pressure sending unit leaking (Chapter 2).
3 Valve cover leaking (Chapter 2).
4 Engine oil seals leaking (Chapter 2).

### 8 Engine lopes while idling or idles erratically

1 Vacuum leakage (Chapters 2 and 4).
2 Air filter clogged (Chapter 1).
3 Malfunction in the fuel injection or engine control system (Chapters 4 and 6).
4 Leaking head gasket (Chapter 2).
5 Timing chain and/or sprockets worn (Chapter 2).
6 Camshaft lobes worn (Chapter 2).

### 9 Engine misses at idle speed

1 Spark plugs worn or not gapped properly (Chapter 1).
2 Faulty coil(s) (Chapter 1).
3 Vacuum leaks (Chapter 1).
4 Uneven or low compression (Chapter 2).
5 Problem with the fuel injection system (Chapter 4).

### 10 Engine misses throughout driving speed range

1 Fuel filter clogged and/or impurities in the fuel system (Chapters 1 and 4).
2 Low fuel pressure (Chapter 4).
3 Faulty or incorrectly gapped spark plugs (Chapter 1).
4 Faulty emission system components (Chapter 6).
5 Low or uneven cylinder compression pressures (Chapter 2).
6 Faulty ignition system (Chapter 5).
7 Vacuum leak in fuel injection system, intake manifold, air control valve or vacuum hoses (Chapters 4 and 6).

### 11 Engine stumbles on acceleration

1 Spark plugs fouled (Chapter 1).
2 Problem with fuel injection or engine control system (Chapters 4 and 6).
3 Fuel filter clogged (Chapters 1 and 4).
4 Intake manifold air leak (Chapters 2 and 4).
5 Problem with the emissions control system (Chapter 6).

### 12 Engine surges while holding accelerator steady

1 Intake air leak (Chapter 4).
2 Fuel pump or fuel pressure regulator faulty (Chapter 4).
3 Problem with the fuel injection system (Chapter 4).
4 Problem with the emissions control system (Chapter 6).

### 13 Engine stalls

1 Idle speed incorrect (Chapter 1).

2    Fuel filter clogged and/or water and impurities in the fuel system (Chapters 1 and 4).
3    Faulty emissions system components (Chapter 6).
4    Faulty or incorrectly-gapped spark plugs (Chapter 1).
5    Vacuum leak in the fuel injection system, intake manifold or vacuum hoses (Chapters 2 and 4).

## 14    Engine lacks power

1    Obstructed exhaust system (Chapter 4).
2    Faulty or incorrectly-gapped spark plugs (Chapter 1).
3    Problem with the fuel injection system (Chapter 4).
4    Dirty air filter (Chapter 1).
5    Brakes binding (Chapter 9).
6    Automatic transmission fluid level incorrect (Chapter 1).
7    Clutch slipping (Chapter 8).
8    Fuel filter clogged and/or impurities in the fuel system (Chapters 1 and 4).
9    Emission control system not functioning properly (Chapter 6).
10   Low or uneven cylinder compression pressures (Chapter 2).

## 15    Engine backfires

1    Emission control system not functioning properly (Chapter 6).
2    Problem with the fuel injection system (Chapter 4).
3    Vacuum leak at fuel injector(s), intake manifold or vacuum hoses (Chapters 2 and 4).

## 16    Pinging or knocking engine sounds during acceleration or uphill

1    Incorrect grade of fuel.
2    Fuel injection system faulty (Chapter 4).
3    Improper or damaged spark plugs or wires (Chapter 1).
4    Knock sensor defective (Chapter 6).
5    Vacuum leak (Chapters 2 and 4).

## 17    Engine runs with oil pressure light on

1    Low oil level (Chapter 1).
2    Idle rpm below specification (Chapter 1).
3    Short in wiring circuit (Chapter 12).
4    Faulty oil pressure sender (Chapter 2).
5    Worn engine bearings and/or oil pump (Chapter 2).

## 18    Engine continues to run after switching off

Defective start/stop button (Chapter 12) or car access system.

## Engine electrical systems

## 19    Battery will not hold a charge

1    Drivebelt or tensioner defective (Chapter 1).
2    Battery electrolyte level low (Chapter 1).
3    Battery terminals loose or corroded (Chapter 1).
4    Alternator not charging properly (Chapter 5).
5    Loose, broken or faulty wiring in the charging circuit (Chapter 5).
6    Short in vehicle wiring (Chapter 12).
7    Internally defective battery (Chapters 1 and 5).

## 20    Alternator light fails to go out

1    Faulty alternator or charging circuit (Chapter 5).
2    Drivebelt or tensioner defective (Chapter 1).

## 21    Alternator light fails to come on when key is turned on

1    Instrument cluster defective (Chapter 12).
2    Fault in the wiring harness (Chapter 12).

## Fuel system

## 22    Excessive fuel consumption

1    Dirty air filter element (Chapter 1).
2    Emissions system not functioning properly (Chapter 6).
3    Fuel injection system not functioning properly (Chapter 4).
4    Low tire pressure or incorrect tire size (Chapter 1).

## 23    Fuel leakage and/or fuel odor

1    Leaking fuel line (Chapters 1 and 4).
2    Tank overfilled.
3    Evaporative emissions control system problem (Chapters 1 and 6).
4    Problem with the fuel injection system (Chapter 4).

## Cooling system

## 24    Overheating

1    Insufficient coolant in system (Chapter 1).
2    Problem in circuit to electric coolant pump, or a faulty pump (Chapter 3).
3    Radiator core blocked or grille restricted (Chapter 3).
4    Thermostat faulty (Chapter 3).
5    Electric coolant fan inoperative or blades broken (Chapter 3).
6    Expansion tank cap not maintaining proper pressure (Chapter 3).

## 25    Overcooling

1    Faulty thermostat (Chapter 3).
2    Inaccurate temperature gauge sending unit (Chapter 3).

## 26    External coolant leakage

1    Deteriorated/damaged hoses; loose clamps (Chapters 1 and 3).
2    Water pump defective (Chapter 3).
3    Leakage from radiator core or coolant reservoir (Chapter 3).
4    Engine drain or water jacket core plugs leaking (Chapter 2).

## 27    Internal coolant leakage

1    Leaking cylinder head gasket (Chapter 2).
2    Cracked cylinder bore or cylinder head (Chapter 2).

## 28    Coolant loss

1    Too much coolant in reservoir (Chapter 1).
2    Coolant boiling away because of overheating (Chapter 3).
3    Internal or external leakage (Chapter 3).
4    Faulty expansion tank cap (Chapter 3).

## 29    Poor coolant circulation

1    Inoperative water pump (Chapter 3).
2    Restriction in cooling system (Chapters 1 and 3).
3    Drivebelt or tensioner defective (Chapter 1).
4    Thermostat sticking (Chapter 3).

## Clutch

### 30 Pedal travels to floor - no pressure or very little resistance

1   Master or release cylinder faulty (Chapter 8).
2   Hose/pipe burst or leaking (Chapter 8).
3   Connections leaking (Chapter 8).
4   No fluid in reservoir (Chapter 8).
5   If fluid level in reservoir rises as pedal is depressed, master cylinder center valve seal is faulty (Chapter 8).
6   If there is fluid on dust seal at master cylinder, piston primary seal is leaking (Chapter 8).
7   Broken release bearing or fork (Chapter 8).
8   Faulty pressure plate diaphragm spring (Chapter 8).

### 31 Fluid in area of master cylinder dust cover and on pedal

Rear seal failure in master cylinder (Chapter 8).

### 32 Fluid on release cylinder

Release cylinder plunger seal faulty (Chapter 8).

### 33 Pedal feels spongy when depressed

Air in system (Chapter 8).

### 34 Unable to select gears

1   Faulty transmission (Chapter 7).
2   Faulty clutch disc or pressure plate (Chapter 8).
3   Faulty release lever or release bearing (Chapter 8).
4   Faulty shift lever assembly or control cables (Chapter 8).

### 35 Clutch slips (engine speed increases with no increase in vehicle speed)

1   Clutch plate worn (Chapter 8).
2   Clutch plate is oil soaked by leaking rear main seal (Chapters 2 and 8).
3   Clutch plate not seated (Chapter 8).
4   Warped pressure plate or flywheel (Chapter 8).
5   Weak diaphragm springs (Chapter 8).
6   Clutch plate overheated. Allow to cool.

### 36 Grabbing (chattering) as clutch is engaged

1   Oil on clutch plate lining, burned or glazed facings (Chapter 8).
2   Worn or loose engine or transmission mounts (Chapter 2).
3   Worn splines on clutch plate hub (Chapter 8).
4   Warped pressure plate or flywheel (Chapter 8).
5   Burned or smeared resin on flywheel or pressure plate (Chapter 8).

### 37 Transmission rattling (clicking)

1   Release lever loose (Chapter 8).
2   Clutch plate damper spring failure (Chapter 8).

### 38 Noise in clutch area

1   Fork shaft improperly installed (Chapter 8).
2   Faulty bearing (Chapter 8).

### 39 Clutch pedal stays on floor

1   Clutch master cylinder piston binding in bore (Chapter 8).
2   Broken release bearing or fork (Chapter 8).

### 40 High pedal effort

1   Piston binding in bore (Chapter 8).
2   Pressure plate faulty (Chapter 8).
3   Incorrect size master or release cylinder (Chapter 8).

## Manual transmission

### 41 Knocking noise at low speeds

1   Worn driveaxle constant velocity (CV) joints (Chapter 8).
2   Worn side gear shaft counterbore in differential case (Chapter 7A).*

### 42 Noise most pronounced when turning

Differential gear noise (Chapter 7A).*

### 43 Clunk on acceleration or deceleration

1   Loose engine or transmission mounts (Chapter 2).
2   Worn differential pinion shaft in case.*
3   Worn side gear shaft counterbore in differential case (Chapter 7A).*
4   Worn or damaged driveaxle inboard CV joints (Chapter 8).

### 44 Clicking noise in turns

Worn or damaged outboard CV joint (Chapter 8).

### 45 Vibration

1   Rough wheel bearing (Chapter 10).
2   Damaged driveaxle (Chapter 8).
3   Out-of-round tires (Chapter 1).
4   Tire out of balance (Chapters 1 and 10).
5   Worn CV joint (Chapter 8).

### 46 Noisy in neutral with engine running

1   Damaged input gear bearing (Chapter 7A).*
2   Damaged clutch release bearing (Chapter 8).

### 47 Noisy in one particular gear

1   Damaged or worn constant mesh gears (Chapter 7A).*
2   Damaged or worn synchronizers (Chapter 7A).*
3   Bent reverse fork (Chapter 7A).*
4   Damaged fourth speed gear or output gear (Chapter 7A).*
5   Worn or damaged reverse idler gear or idler bushing (Chapter 7A).*

### 48 Noisy in all gears

1   Insufficient lubricant (Chapter 7A).
2   Damaged or worn bearings (Chapter 7A).*
3   Worn or damaged input gear shaft and/or output gear shaft (Chapter 7A).*

### 49 Slips out of gear

1   Worn or improperly adjusted linkage (Chapter 7A).
2   Shift linkage does not work freely, binds (Chapter 7A).
3   Input gear bearing retainer broken or loose (Chapter 7A).*
4   Worn or bent shift fork (Chapter 7A).*

### 50 Leaks lubricant

1   Side gear shaft seals worn (Chapter 7).
2   Excessive amount of lubricant in transmission (Chapters 1 and 7A).

3    Loose or broken input gear shaft bearing retainer (Chapter 7A).*
4    Input gear bearing retainer O-ring and/or lip seal damaged (Chapter 7A).*

## 51    Locked in gear

Lock pin or interlock pin missing (Chapter 7A).*

*Although the corrective action necessary to remedy the symptoms described is beyond the scope of this manual, the above information should be helpful in isolating the cause of the condition so that the owner can communicate clearly with a professional mechanic.*

## Automatic transmission
**Note:** *Due to the complexity of the automatic transmission, it is difficult for the home mechanic to properly diagnose and service this component. For problems other than the following, the vehicle should be taken to a dealer or transmission shop.*

## 52    Fluid leakage

1    Automatic transmission fluid is a deep red color. Fluid leaks should not be confused with engine oil, which can easily be blown onto the transmission by air flow.
2    To pinpoint a leak, first remove all built-up dirt and grime from the transmission housing with degreasing agents and/or steam cleaning. Then drive the vehicle at low speeds so air flow will not blow the leak far from its source. Raise the vehicle and determine where the leak is coming from. Common areas of leakage are:
a) *Transmission oil lines (Chapter 7).*
b) *Speed sensor (Chapter 6).*
c) *Driveaxle oil seals (Chapter 7).*

## 53    Transmission fluid brown or has a burned smell

Transmission fluid overheated (Chapter 1).

## 54    General shift mechanism problems

1    Chapter 7, Part B, deals with checking and adjusting the shift cable on automatic transmissions. Common problems which may be attributed to poorly adjusted cable are:
a) *Engine starting in gears other than Park or Neutral.*
b) *Indicator on shifter pointing to a gear other than the one actually being used.*
c) *Vehicle moves when in Park.*
2    Refer to Chapter 7B for the shift cable adjustment procedure.

## 55    Transmission slips, shifts roughly, is noisy or has no drive in forward or reverse gears

There are many probable causes for the above problems, but the home mechanic should be concerned with only one possibility - fluid level. Before taking the vehicle to a repair shop, check the level and condition of the fluid as described in Chapter 1. Correct the fluid level as necessary or change the fluid and filter if needed. If the problem persists, have a professional diagnose the cause.

## Driveaxles

## 56    Clicking noise in turns

Worn or damaged outboard CV joint (Chapter 8).

## 57    Shudder or vibration during acceleration

1    Excessive toe-in (Chapter 10).
2    Worn or damaged inboard or outboard CV joints (Chapter 8).
3    Sticking inboard CV joint assembly (Chapter 8).

## 58    Vibration at highway speeds

1    Out-of-balance front wheels and/or tires (Chapters 1 and 10).
2    Out-of-round front tires (Chapters 1 and 10).
3    Worn CV joint(s) (Chapter 8).

## Brakes
**Note:** *Before assuming that a brake problem exists, make sure that:*
a) *The tires are in good condition and properly inflated (Chapter 1).*
b) *The front end alignment is correct.*
c) *The vehicle is not loaded with weight in an unequal manner.*

## 59    Vehicle pulls to one side during braking

1    Incorrect tire pressures (Chapter 1).
2    Front end out of alignment (have the front end aligned).
3    Front, or rear, tire sizes not matched to one another.
4    Restricted brake lines or hoses (Chapter 9).
5    Malfunctioning caliper assembly (Chapter 9).
6    Loose suspension parts (Chapter 10).
7    Excessive wear of pad material or disc on one side (Chapter 9).
8    Contamination (grease or brake fluid) of brake pad material or disc on one side (Chapter 9).

## 60    Noise (grinding or high-pitched squeal when the brakes are applied)

Brake pads worn out. Replace pads with new ones immediately (Chapter 9).

## 61    Brake roughness or chatter (pedal pulsates)

1    Excessive lateral runout (Chapter 9).
2    Uneven pad wear (Chapter 9).
3    Defective disc (Chapter 9).

## 62    Excessive brake pedal effort required to stop vehicle

1    Malfunctioning power brake booster (Chapter 9).
2    Partial system failure (Chapter 9).
3    Excessively worn pads (Chapter 9).
4    Piston in caliper stuck or sluggish (Chapter 9).
5    Brake pads contaminated with oil or grease (Chapter 9).
6    Brake disc grooved and/or glazed (Chapter 9).

## 63    Excessive brake pedal travel

1    Partial brake system failure (Chapter 9).
2    Insufficient fluid in master cylinder (Chapters 1 and 9).
3    Air trapped in system (Chapter 9).

## 64    Dragging brakes

1    Incorrect adjustment of brake light switch (Chapter 9).
2    Master cylinder pistons not returning correctly (Chapter 9).
3    Caliper piston stuck (Chapter 9).
4    Restricted brakes lines or hoses (Chapter 9).
5    Incorrect parking brake adjustment (Chapter 9).

## 65    Grabbing or uneven braking action

1    Malfunction of proportioning valve (Chapter 9).
2    Binding brake pedal mechanism (Chapter 9).
3    Contaminated brake linings (Chapter 9).

## 66    Brake pedal feels spongy when depressed

1    Air in hydraulic lines (Chapter 9).
2    Master cylinder mounting bolts loose (Chapter 9).
3    Master cylinder defective (Chapter 9).

## 67 Brake pedal travels to the floor with little resistance

1    Little or no fluid in the master cylinder reservoir caused by leaking caliper piston(s) (Chapter 9).
2    Loose, damaged or disconnected brake lines (Chapter 9).

## 68 Parking brake does not hold

Parking brake improperly adjusted (Chapter 9).

## Suspension and steering systems

**Note:** *Before attempting to diagnose the suspension and steering systems, perform the following preliminary checks:*

a)  *Tires for wrong pressure and uneven wear.*
b)  *Steering universal joints from the column to the rack and pinion for loose connectors or wear.*
c)  *Front and rear suspension and the rack-and-pinion assembly for loose or damaged parts.*
d)  *Out-of-round or out-of-balance tires, damaged rims and loose and/or rough wheel bearings.*

## 69 Vehicle pulls to one side

1    Mismatched or uneven tires (Chapter 10).
2    Broken or sagging springs (Chapter 10).
3    Wheel alignment incorrect. Have the wheels professionally aligned.
4    Front brake dragging (Chapter 9).

## 70 Abnormal or excessive tire wear

1    Wheel alignment out-of-specification. Have the wheels aligned.
2    Sagging or broken springs (Chapter 10).
3    Tire out-of-balance (Chapter 10).
4    Worn strut damper (Chapter 10).
5    Overloaded vehicle.
6    Tires not rotated regularly.

## 71 Wheel makes a thumping noise

1    Blister or bump on tire (Chapter 10).
2    Improper strut damper or shock absorber action (Chapter 10).

## 72 Shimmy, shake or vibration

1    Tire or wheel out-of-balance or out-of-round (Chapter 10).
2    Worn wheel bearings (Chapter 10).
3    Worn tie-rod ends (Chapter 10).
4    Worn balljoints (Chapters 1 and 10).

5    Excessive wheel runout (Chapter 10).
6    Blister or bump on tire (Chapter 10).

## 73 Hard steering

1    Lack of lubrication at balljoints and/or tie-rod ends (Chapter 10).
2    Wheel alignment out-of-specifications. Have the wheels professionally aligned.
3    Low tire pressure(s) (Chapter 1).
4    Worn steering gear (Chapter 10).

## 74 Poor returnability of steering to center

1    Worn balljoints or tie-rod ends (Chapter 10).
2    Worn steering gear assembly (Chapter 10).
3    Wheel alignment out-of-specifications. Have the wheels professionally aligned.

## 75 Abnormal noise at the front end

1    Worn balljoints or tie-rod ends (Chapter 10).
2    Damaged strut/shock absorber mounting (Chapter 10).
3    Worn control arm bushings or tie-rod ends (Chapter 10).
4    Loose stabilizer bar (Chapter 10).
5    Loose wheel bolts (Chapter 1).
6    Loose suspension bolts (Chapter 10).

## 76 Wander or poor steering stability

1    Mismatched or uneven tires (Chapter 10).
2    Worn balljoints or tie-rod ends (Chapter 10).
3    Worn shock absorbers or strut assemblies (Chapter 10).
4    Loose stabilizer bar (Chapter 10).
5    Broken or sagging springs (Chapter 10).
6    Wheels out of alignment. Have the wheels professionally aligned.

## 77 Erratic steering when braking

1    Wheel bearings worn (Chapter 10).
2    Broken or sagging springs (Chapter 10).
3    Leaking wheel cylinder or caliper (Chapter 10).
4    Excessive brake disc runout (Chapter 9).

## 78 Excessive pitching and/or rolling around corners or during braking

1    Loose stabilizer bar (Chapter 10).
2    Worn strut dampers/shock absorbers or mounts (Chapter 10).

3    Broken or sagging springs (Chapter 10).
4    Overloaded vehicle.

## 79 Suspension bottoms

1    Overloaded vehicle.
2    Sagging springs (Chapter 10).

## 80 Cupped tires

1    Front wheel or rear wheel alignment out-of-specifications. Have the wheels professionally aligned.
2    Worn struts or shock absorbers (Chapter 10).
3    Wheel bearings worn (Chapter 10).
4    Excessive tire or wheel runout (Chapter 10).
5    Worn balljoints (Chapter 10).

## 81 Excessive tire wear on outside edge

1    Inflation pressures incorrect (Chapter 1).
2    Excessive speed in turns.
3    Wheel alignment incorrect (excessive toe-in). Have professionally aligned.
4    Suspension arm bent or twisted (Chapter 10).

## 82 Excessive tire wear on inside edge

1    Inflation pressures incorrect (Chapter 1).
2    Wheel alignment incorrect (toe-out). Have professionally aligned.
3    Loose or damaged steering components (Chapter 10).

## 83 Tire tread worn in one place

1    Tires out-of-balance.
2    Damaged wheel. Inspect and replace if necessary.
3    Defective tire (Chapter 1).

## 84 Excessive play or looseness in steering system

1    Wheel bearing(s) worn (Chapter 10).
2    Tie-rod end loose (Chapter 10).
3    Steering gear loose (Chapter 10).
4    Worn or loose steering intermediate shaft U-joint (Chapter 10).

## 85 Rattling or clicking noise in steering gear

1    Steering gear loose (Chapter 10).
2    Steering gear defective.

# Chapter 1
# Tune-up and routine maintenance

## Contents

## Specifications

### Recommended lubricants and fluids

**Note:** *Listed here are manufacturer recommendations at the time this manual was written. Manufacturers occasionally upgrade their fluid and lubricant specifications, so check with your local auto parts store for current recommendations.*

Engine oil
- Type .......................... API rating SM, BMW synthetic
- Viscosity .......................... SAE 5W-30 or 5W-40

Fuel .......................... Unleaded gasoline, 91 octane

Automatic transmission fluid
- 328i and 328xi models .......................... DEXRON VI automatic transmission fluid
- 325i, 325xi, 330i and 330xi models .......................... Shell M1375 automatic transmission fluid
- 8-speed models (GA8HP45Z, GA8HP70Z, GA8HP90Z, GA8P70H, GA8P75H) .......................... ATF-3, ATF-3+ or Shell oil L12108***

Manual transmission lubricant*
- GS6-17BG .......................... MTF-LT-3, BMW #83227533818 "lifetime" fluid
- GS6X-37BZ and GS6-53DZ (to 03/2007) .......................... MTF-LT-2, BMW #83220309031 "lifetime" fluid

Transfer case lubricant (AWD models) .......................... BMW part number 83220397244

Front differential lubricant (AWD models) .......................... SAF-XO synthetic lubricant

Rear differential lubricant .......................... SAF-XO synthetic lubricant

Brake (and clutch) fluid .......................... DOT 4 brake fluid or DOT 4 low-viscosity brake fluid

Engine coolant .......................... 50/50 mix of demineralized water and long-life, phosphate-free, nitrate-free and amino-free ethylene glycol antifreeze**

Power steering system .......................... ATF or CHF, as marked on reservoir cap

*Models requiring MTF-LT-2 fluid will have a yellow or green label next to the filler plug, while a blue label indicates MTF-LT-3 is required.*

**Caution:** *Do not mix coolants of different colors. Doing so might damage the cooling system and/or the engine. The manufacturer specifies either a green colored coolant or a yellow colored coolant to be used in these systems, depending on what was originally installed in the vehicle.*

***8-speed models are filled with ATF-3 lifetime fluid, in the event fluid must be added or replaced, only Shell oil L12108ATF can be mixed with the ATF-3. Do not mix ATF-3 with ATF-3+ or any other type of fluids*

## Capacities*

Engine oil (including filter)
| | |
|---|---|
| 2.0L engine ................................................................. | 5.3 qts (5.0 liters) |
| 3.0L engine ................................................................. | 6.9 qts (6.5 liters) |

Coolant

Manual transmission models
| | | |
|---|---|---|
| E90, E91, E92 and E93 chassis .................................. | 2.17 gallons | (8.2 liters) |

F30 chassis
| | | |
|---|---|---|
| 328i and 328i xDrive.................................................. | 1.84 gallons | (7.0 liters) |
| 320i and 320i xDrive.................................................. | 1.76 gallons | (6.7 liters) |

F31 chassis
| | | |
|---|---|---|
| 320i............................................................................ | 2.17 gallons | (8.2 liters) |
| 320i xDrive, 328i and 328i xDrive.............................. | 1.82 gallons | (6.9 liters) |

F34 chassis
| | | |
|---|---|---|
| 320i, 320i xDrive........................................................ | 1.87 gallons | (7.1 liters) |
| 328i............................................................................ | 1.90 gallons | (7.2 liters) |

Automatic transmission models

E90, E91, E92 and E93 chassis ......................................... 2.23 gallons    (8.4 liters)

F30 chassis
| | | |
|---|---|---|
| 328i, 328i xDrive, 320i and 320i xDrive.................... | 2.00 gallons | (7.6 liters) |

F31 chassis
| | | |
|---|---|---|
| 320i............................................................................ | 2.40 gallons | (9.1 liters) |
| 320i xDrive, 328i and 328i xDrive.............................. | 2.00 gallons | (7.6 liters) |

F34 chassis
| | | |
|---|---|---|
| 320i, 320i xDrive........................................................ | 2.03 gallons | (7.7 liters) |
| 328i............................................................................ | 1.98 gallons | (7.5 liters) |
| 328i xDrive ................................................................ | 2.00 gallons | (7.6 liters) |

Automatic transmission models (dry-fill)
| | | |
|---|---|---|
| 6 speed models.......................................................... | Up to 10.0 qts | (9.5 liters) |
| 8 speed models.......................................................... | Up to 9.3 qts | (8.8 liters) |

**Note:** *Since this is a dry-fill specification, the amount required during a routine fluid change will be substantially less. The best way to determine the amount of fluid to add during a routine fluid change is to measure the amount drained. Begin the refill procedure by initially adding 1/3rd of the amount drained. Then, with the engine running, add 1/2-pint at a time (cycling the shifter through each gear position between additions) until the level is correct on the dipstick (if equipped). It is important to not overfill the transmission (see Chapter 7B for more on checking fluid level and temperature).*

Manual transmission (fluid change)
| | |
|---|---|
| ZF GS6-17BG/DG......................................................... | 1.4 qts (1.3 liters) |
| ZF GS6-37BZ............................................................... | 1.6 qts (2.2 liters) |
| Transfer case (AWD models) ........................................... | 0.55 qts (0.52 liters) |
| Front differential (AWD models) ...................................... | 0.63 qts (0.6 liters) |
| Rear differential .............................................................. | 1.05 qts (1.0 liters) |

*All capacities approximate. Add as necessary to bring up to appropriate level.*

## Ignition system

Spark plug type
| | |
|---|---|
| 2.0L engine ................................................................. | Bosch 8165 |
| 3.0L engine ................................................................. | Bosch FR7NPP332 |

Spark plug gap
| | |
|---|---|
| 2.0L engine ................................................................. | 0.035 inch** |
| 3.0L engine ................................................................. | 0.040 inch |

Engine firing order
| | |
|---|---|
| 2.0L engine ................................................................. | 1-3-4-2 |
| 3.0L engine ................................................................. | 1-5-3-6-2-4 |

**Gap is preset from the factory. Do not adjust.*

## Brakes

| | |
|---|---|
| Disc brake pad lining thickness (minimum) ......................... | 3/32 inch (2.4 mm) |
| Parking brake initial adjustment....................................... | 8 to 9 clicks |
| Parking brake final adjustment ........................................ | See Chapter 9 |

## Torque specifications

**Note:** *One foot-pound (ft-lb) of torque is equivalent to 12 inch-pounds (in-lbs) of torque. Torque values below approximately 15 foot-pounds are expressed in inch-pounds, because most foot-pound torque wrenches are not accurate at these smaller values.*

| | Ft-lbs (unless otherwise indicated) | Nm |
|---|---|---|
| Engine oil drain plug*** | | |
|   2.0L engine | | |
|       With all-wheel drive | 18.5 | 25 |
|       Without all-wheel drive | 72 in-lbs | 8 |
|   3.0L engine | 18.5 | 25 |
| Automatic transmission drain plug | | |
|   With metal fluid pan | 106 in-lbs | 12 |
|   With plastic fluid pan | 71 in-lbs | 8 |
| Manual transmission drain plug | | |
|   GS6-17 transmission | 33 | 45 |
|   GS6-37 transmission | | |
|       M12 bolt | 18.5 | 25 |
|       M18 bolt | 26 | 35 |
| Front differential drain/fill plug (AWD) | 44 | 60 |
| Rear differential check/fill plug | 44 | 60 |
| Spark plugs | | |
|   2.0L engine | | |
|       M12 x 1.25 thread | 17 | 23 |
|       M14 x 1.25 thread | 22 | 30 |
|   3.0L engine | 18.5 | 25 |
| Drivebelt tensioner bolt(s) | | |
|   2.0L engine | 168 in-lbs | 19 |
|   3.0L engine | | |
|       Step 1 | 18.5 | 25 |
|       Step 2 | Tighten an additional 90 degrees | |
| Wheel bolts | | |
|   E90, E91, E92 and E93 chassis | 88.5 | 120 |
|   F30, F31 and F34 chassis | 103 | 140 |

*** *Always replace the plastic drain plug and sealing washers on non-plastic plugs*

# Notes

**Typical 3.0L engine compartment components**

| | | |
|---|---|---|
| 1 | Engine oil filler cap | |
| 2 | Oil filter cover | |
| 3 | Brake and clutch fluid reservoir (under cover) | |
| 4 | Air filter housing | |
| 5 | Coolant expansion tank | |
| 6 | Washer fluid reservoir | |
| 7 | Cabin air filter cover | |
| 8 | Engine electrical box (under cover) | |
| 9 | Strut tower braces | |
| 10 | Power steering fluid reservoir | |

**Typical engine underside components (splash shield removed)**

| | | | | | |
|---|---|---|---|---|---|
| 1 | Engine oil pan drain plug | 4 | Tension struts | 7 | Reinforcement frame |
| 2 | Catalytic converters | 5 | Steering tie-rod | 8 | Steering rack |
| 3 | Control arms | 6 | Stabilizer bar | 9 | Oil level sensor |

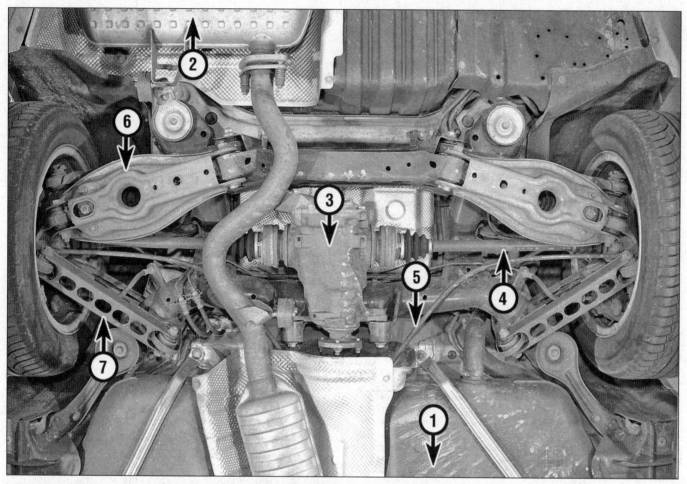

**Typical rear underside components**

1   Fuel tank
2   Muffler
3   Final drive unit

4   Driveshaft
5   Parking brake cable

6   Camber arm
7   Trailing arm

# 1 Maintenance schedule

The service intervals are tailored according to the operating conditions, driving style, time elapsed and mileage covered, instead of set distance/time limits. These factors are taken into account, and the maintenance requirements are calculated by the vehicle's on-board systems, then a symbol representing the item requiring attention is displayed in the instrument cluster. The urgency of the attention is indicated by a color-coding system - green, yellow or red. Consequently, the intervals listed below are guidelines, starting values/interval forecasts, or our recommendations. For more details, refer to the owner's manual supplied with the vehicle.

When the vehicle is new, it should be serviced by a dealer service department (or other shop recognized by the vehicle manufacturer as providing the same standard of service) in order to preserve the warranty. The vehicle manufacturer may reject warranty claims if you are unable to prove that servicing has been carried out properly and when specified, using only original equipment parts or parts certified to be of equivalent quality. In many cases, the initial maintenance check at the dealer is done at no cost to the owner.

The models covered in this manual have an on-board maintenance reminder system called Condition-Based Service (CBS) that stores information on various vehicle sensors, and displays warnings if necessary. For instance, if you are low on engine oil, a warning will come up on the display below the speedometer. To check an item monitored by the CBS system, toggle the small lever Up or Down on the turn signal lever, until the icon for the desired information is displayed, then press the square button on the lever to activate the system (see Section 4).

### Resetting the CBS

The reset feature of the CBS system allows the computer to record the mileage at which you have performed a scheduled maintenance task such as an oil change. This insures the accuracy of the reminders the system displays when a scheduled task is due. See Section 30 for the resetting procedure.

### I-Drive Information/Control system

Many models are equipped with an on-board program called I-Drive, which combines a number of functions formerly controlled by separate switches. I-Drive features a head-up LCD display at the center of the instrument panel that includes menu items such as: Climate Control, Communication, Entertainment, and Navigation. On the floor console is a knob and a menu button (just behind the shifter in the floor console) that operates the controller, with which the driver can call up various functions. One of the functions is called Central Information Display (CID), which will display the CBS maintenance information formerly seen in smaller view on the instrument panel of previous models. On 2009 and later models, this system has been upgraded, and renamed to the Car Information Computer (CIC) system.

## Every 250 miles or weekly, whichever comes first

Check the engine oil level (Section 4)
Check the engine coolant level (Section 4)
Check the brake and clutch fluid level (Section 4)
Check the windshield washer fluid level (Section 4)
Check the power steering fluid level (Section 4)
Check the tires and tire pressures (Section 5)

## Every 7500 miles or 6 months, whichever comes first

*All items listed above plus:*
Change the engine oil and oil filter (Section 6)*
**Note:** *This service interval is based on the CBS (Condition Based Service) system to monitor oil condition and display oil change information. However, under no circumstances should the oil change interval exceed 7,500 miles.*
Inspect (and replace, if necessary) the windshield wiper blades (Section 7)
Check and service the battery (Section 8)
Check the cooling system (Section 9)
Rotate the tires (Section 10)
Check the seat belts (Section 11)

## Every 15,000 miles or 12 months, whichever comes first

*All items listed above plus:*
Check all underhood hoses (Section 12)
Inspect the brake system (Section 13)*
Inspect the suspension and steering components (Section 14)*
Check the fuel system (Section 15)

Check the manual transmission lubricant level (Section 16)
Check the transfer case lubricant level (AWD models) (Section 17)
Check (and replace, if necessary) the cabin air filter (Section 18)*
Check the driveaxle boots (Section 19)
Check the engine drivebelt (Section 20)
Check the exhaust system (Section 21)
Reset the service interval display (Section 1)

## Every 30,000 miles or 30 months, whichever comes first

*All items listed above plus:*
Change the brake fluid (Section 22)*
Change the engine air filter (Section 23)*
Reset the service interval display (Section 1)

## Every 60,000 miles or 48 months, whichever comes first

Replace the engine drivebelt (Section 20)
Change the transfer case lubricant (AWD models) (Section 24)
Change the differential lubricant (Section 25)
Change the automatic transmission fluid (Section 26)*
Reset the service interval display (Section 1)

## Every 100,000 miles or 60 months, whichever comes first

**Note:** *These items have no specific recommendation concerning their inspection or replacement. However, we consider it prudent to carry out these tasks at least every 4 years.*
Flush the cooling system and replace the coolant (Section 27)
Replace the spark plugs (Section 28)

*\*This item is affected by "severe" operating conditions as described below. If your vehicle is operated under "severe" conditions, perform all maintenance indicated with an asterisk (\*) at 3000 mile/3 month intervals. Severe conditions are indicated if you mainly operate your vehicle under one or more of the following conditions:*
  *a) Operating in dusty areas*
  *b) Towing a trailer*
  *c) Idling for extended periods and/or low speed operation*
  *d) Operating when outside temperatures remain below freezing and when most trips are less than 4 miles*

*\*\* If operated under one or more of the following conditions, change the manual or automatic transmission fluid and differential lubricant every 15,000 miles:*
  *a) In heavy city traffic where the outside temperature regularly reaches 90-degrees F (32-degrees C) or higher*
  *b) In hilly or mountainous terrain*

## 2    Introduction

### General information

This Chapter is designed to help the home mechanic maintain his/her vehicle for safety, economy, long life and peak performance.

The Chapter contains a master maintenance schedule, followed by Sections dealing specifically with each task in the schedule. Visual checks, adjustments, component replacement and other helpful items are included. Refer to the **illustrations** for the location of most service points of the engine compartment and the underside of the vehicle.

Servicing your vehicle in accordance with the service indicator display and the following Sections will provide a planned maintenance program, which should result in a long and

reliable service life. This is a comprehensive plan, so maintaining some items but not others at the specified service intervals will not produce the same results.

As you service your vehicle, you will discover that many of the procedures can - and should - be grouped together, because of the particular procedure being performed, or because of the proximity of two otherwise-unrelated components to one another. For example, if the vehicle is raised for any reason, the exhaust can be inspected at the same time as the suspension and steering components.

The first step in this maintenance program is to prepare yourself before the actual work begins. Read through all the procedures you're planning to do, then gather up all the parts and tools needed. If it looks like you might run into problems during a particular job, seek advice from a mechanic or an experienced do-it-yourselfer.

### Owner's manual and VECI label information

Your vehicle owner's manual was written for your year and model and contains very specific information on component locations, specifications, fuse ratings, part numbers, etc. The owner's manual is an important resource for the do-it-yourselfer to have; if one was not supplied with your vehicle, it can generally be ordered from a dealer parts department.

Among other important information, the Vehicle Emissions Control Information (VECI) label contains specifications and procedures for applicable tune-up adjustments and, in some instances, spark plugs (see Chapter 6 for more information on the VECI label). The information on this label is the exact maintenance data recommended by the manufacturer. This data often varies by intended operating altitude, local emissions regulations, month of manufacture, etc.

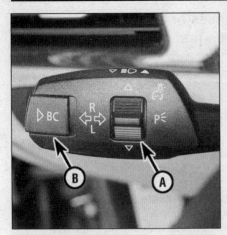

**4.4  Toggle the lever (A) on the turn signal arm, until the "OIL" icon is displayed on the instrument cluster, then press the square button (B) to activate the Condition Based Service (CBS) system**

**4.6  Oil level indicator icon display in the instrument cluster**

This Chapter contains procedural details, safety information and more ambitious maintenance intervals than you might find in manufacturer's literature. However, you may also find procedures or specifications in your owner's manual or VECI label that differ with what's printed here. In these cases, the owner's manual or VECI label can be considered correct, since it is specific to your particular vehicle.

---

**3   Tune-up general information**

The term tune-up is used in this manual to represent a combination of individual operations rather than one specific procedure.

If, from the time the vehicle is new, the routine maintenance schedule is followed closely and frequent checks are made of fluid levels and high wear items, as suggested throughout this manual, the engine will be kept in relatively good running condition and the need for additional work will be minimized.

More likely than not, however, there will be times when the engine may run poorly due to lack of regular maintenance. This is even more likely if a used vehicle, which has not received regular and frequent maintenance checks, is purchased. In such cases, an engine tune-up will be needed outside of the regular routine maintenance intervals.

The first step in any tune-up or diagnostic procedure to help correct a poor-running engine is a cylinder compression check. A compression check (see Chapter 2B) will help determine the condition of internal engine components and should be used as a guide for tune-up and repair procedures. If, for instance, a compression check indicates serious internal engine wear, a conventional tune-up will not improve the performance of the engine and would be a waste of time and money. Because of its importance, the compression check should be done by someone

with the right equipment and the knowledge to use it properly.

The following procedures are those most often needed to bring a generally poor running engine back into a proper state of tune.

## Minor tune-up

Check all engine related fluids (Section 4)
Clean, inspect and test the battery
  (Section 8)
Check the cooling system (Section 9)
Check all underhood hoses (Section 12)
Check the fuel system (Section 15)
Check the air filter (Section 23)

## Major tune-up

*All items listed under Minor tune-up, plus . . .*

Replace the air filter (Section 23)
Check the drivebelt (Section 20)
Replace the spark plugs (Section 28)

---

**4   Fluid level checks (every 250 miles or weekly)**

1   Fluids are an essential part of the lubrication, cooling, brake and windshield washer systems. Because the fluids gradually become depleted and/or contaminated during normal operation of the vehicle, they must be periodically replenished. See *Recommended lubricants and fluids* in this Chapter's Specifications before adding fluid to any of the following components. **Note:** *The vehicle must be on level ground when fluid levels are checked.*

## Engine oil

*Refer to illustrations 4.4, 4.6 and 4.7*
2   Frequent oil and filter changes are the most important preventative maintenance work which can be undertaken by the DIY owner. As engine oil ages, it becomes diluted and contaminated, which leads to premature engine wear. **Note:** *These engines do not have an oil-level dipstick. The oil level is checked by using the Condition-Based Service (CBS) of the iDrive (CID) and (CIC)*

systems on later models. If the level or temperature of the oil is out of range, a warning symbol will appear on the instrument panel.
3   There are two ways to check the oil level, static "engine not running" and dynamic "engine running.

### Static test "engine not running"

4   Turn the key to the "ON" position, but do not start the engine. Toggle the lever to the right of the square button Up or Down to scroll through the information display icons on the instrument cluster. Once the "OIL" icon is displayed, press the square button on the left end of the turn signal arm **(see illustration)**. The system will check to make sure there is enough oil to safely start the engine. **Note:** *On models equipped with CID system, use the iDrive controller on the center console and follow the on screen menu to check the engine oil. On 2009 and later models, use the CIC system controller on the center console and follow the on screen menu.*

### Dynamic test "engine running"

**Note:** *Always start with the static test before trying to do the dynamic test.*
5   Start the engine and allow the engine to fully warm up. With the engine running, toggle the lever to the right of the square button Up or Down to scroll through the information display icons on the instrument cluster until the "OIL" icon is displayed, press the square button on the left end of the turn signal arm **(see illustration 4.4)**.
6   Once the square button is pressed the system can take up to 5 minutes to give a reading. The readings include "OK" (no action required), "1, 2, 3-quarts" (add oil), "MAX" (overfilled) and "INACTIVE" (defective oil level sensor) **(see illustration)**.
7   To add oil, remove the filler cap from the valve cover **(see illustration)**. After adding oil, wait a few minutes to allow the level to stabilize, then check the level again. Add more oil if required. Install the filler cap and tighten it by hand only.

## Engine coolant

*Refer to illustrations 4.8 and 4.9*
**Warning:** *Do not allow antifreeze to come in contact with your skin or painted surfaces of the vehicle. Flush contaminated areas immediately with plenty of water. Don't store new coolant or leave old coolant lying around where it's accessible to children or pets - they're attracted by its sweet smell. Ingestion of even a small amount of coolant can be fatal! Wipe up garage floor and drip pan spills immediately. Keep antifreeze containers covered and repair cooling system leaks as soon as they're noticed.*
8   All vehicles covered by this manual are equipped with a pressurized coolant recovery system. A plastic expansion tank located at the front of the engine compartment is connected by a hose to the radiator **(see illustration)**. As the engine heats up during operation, the expanding coolant fills the tank.

**4.7 Remove the valve cover oil filler cap**

**4.8 Coolant recovery tank - do not remove the cap when the system is hot**

9   The coolant level in the tank should be checked regularly. **Warning:** *Do not remove the expansion tank cap to check the coolant level when the engine is warm!* The level in the tank varies with the temperature of the engine. When the engine is cold, remove the cap and inspect the float in the expansion tank. If the MAX mark on the float is level with the top of the threads on the tank filler neck, the coolant level is full, do not add coolant. If the MIN mark on the float is level with the top of the threads on the tank filler neck, remove the cap from the tank and add a 50/50 mixture of ethylene glycol based antifreeze and demineralized water **(see illustration).**

10   Drive the vehicle, let the engine cool completely then recheck the coolant level. Don't use rust inhibitors or additives. If only a small amount of coolant is required to bring the system up to the proper level, water can be used. However, repeated additions of water will dilute the antifreeze and water solution. In order to maintain the proper ratio of antifreeze and water, always top up the coolant level with the correct mixture. An empty plastic milk jug or bleach bottle makes an excellent container for mixing coolant.

11   If the coolant level drops consistently, there may be a leak in the system. Inspect the radiator, hoses, filler cap, drain plugs and water pump (see Section 9). If no leaks are noted, have the expansion tank cap pressure tested by a service station.

12   If you have to remove the expansion tank cap, wait until the engine has cooled completely, then wrap a thick cloth around the cap and unscrew it slowly, stopping if you hear a hissing noise. If coolant or steam escapes, let the engine cool down longer, then remove the cap.

13   Check the condition of the coolant as well. It should be relatively clear. If it's brown or rust colored, the system should be drained, flushed and refilled. Even if the coolant appears to be normal, the corrosion inhibitors wear out, so it must be replaced at the specified intervals.

## Brake and clutch fluid

*Refer to illustration 4.15*

14   The brake master cylinder is mounted on the front of the power booster unit in the engine compartment. The hydraulic clutch master cylinder used on manual transmission vehicles is located next to the brake master cylinder.

15   The brake master cylinder and the clutch master cylinder share a common reservoir. To check the fluid level of either system, release the clips and pull up the plastic cover in the left-rear corner of the engine compartment and look at the MAX and MIN marks on the brake fluid reservoir **(see illustration)**. The fluid level can also be checked with the CBS display on the instrument panel.

16   If the level is low, wipe the top of the reservoir cover with a clean rag to prevent contamination of the brake system before lifting the cover.

17   Add only the specified brake fluid to the reservoir (refer to *Recommended lubricants and fluids* in this Chapter's Specifications or to your owner's manual). Mixing different types of brake fluid can damage the system. Fill the brake master cylinder reservoir only to the MAX line. **Warning:** *Use caution when filling the reservoir - brake fluid can harm your eyes and damage painted surfaces. Do not use brake fluid that is more than one year old or has been left open. Brake fluid absorbs moisture from the air. Excess moisture can cause a dangerous loss of braking.*

18   While the reservoir cap is removed, inspect the master cylinder reservoir for contamination. If deposits, dirt particles or water droplets are present, the system should be drained and refilled.

19   After filling the reservoir to the proper level, make sure the lid is properly seated to prevent fluid leakage.

20   The fluid in the brake master cylinder will drop slightly as the brake pads at each wheel wear down during normal operation. If the master cylinder requires repeated replenishing to keep it at the proper level, this is an indication of leakage in the brake or clutch system, which should be corrected immediately. If the

**4.9 A float device in the coolant reservoir indicates the level of coolant - information on the tank describes proper level**

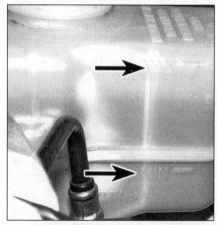

**4.15 Open the cover over the brake fluid reservoir to check the fluid level**

**4.22  Use only fluid designated for the purpose when filling the windshield washer tank**

**4.25  Power steering fluid reservoir**

**4.28  The fluid level is indicated on the marked dipstick attached to the cap**

brake system shows an indication of leakage, check all brake lines and connections, along with the calipers, wheel cylinders and booster (see Section 13 for more information). If the hydraulic clutch system shows an indication of leakage, check all clutch lines and connections, along with the clutch release cylinder (see Chapter 8 for more information).

21    If, upon checking the brake or clutch master cylinder fluid level, you discover the reservoir empty or nearly empty, the systems should be bled (see Chapters 8 and 9).

## Windshield washer fluid

*Refer to illustration 4.22*

22    Fluid for the windshield washer system is stored in a plastic reservoir located at the right rear corner of the engine compartment **(see illustration)**.

23    In milder climates, plain water can be used in the reservoir, but it should be kept no more than 2/3 full to allow for expansion if the water freezes. In colder climates, use windshield washer system antifreeze, available at any auto parts store, to lower the freezing point of the fluid. Mix the antifreeze with water in accordance with the manufacturer's directions on the container. **Caution:** *Do not use cooling system antifreeze - it will damage the vehicle's paint.*

## Power steering fluid

*Refer to illustrations 4.25 and 4.28*

24    Check the power steering fluid level periodically to avoid steering system problems, such as damage to the pump. **Caution:** *DO NOT hold the steering wheel against either stop (extreme left or right turn) for more than five seconds. If you do, the power steering pump could be damaged.*

25    The power steering reservoir, located at the left-rear corner of the engine compartment has a dipstick in the cap **(see illustration)**. There are two types of fluid for this reservoir - the color and label of the cap indicates the type to use for your vehicle.

26    Park the vehicle on level ground and apply the parking brake.

27    Run the engine until it has reached normal operating temperature. With the engine at idle, turn the steering wheel back and forth about 10 times to get any air out of the steering system. Shut the engine off with the wheels in the straight-ahead position.

28    Note the fluid level on the cap/dipstick. It should be between the two marks **(see illustration).**

29    Add small amounts of fluid until the level is correct. **Caution:** *Do not overfill the reservoir. If too much fluid is added, remove the excess with a clean syringe or suction pump.*

30    Check the power steering hoses and connections for leaks and wear.

## 5    Tire and tire pressure checks (every 250 miles or weekly)

*Refer to illustrations 5.2, 5.3, 5.4a, 5.4b and 5.8*

**Note:** *The covered vehicles have a Tire Pressure Monitoring (TPM) system that will flash a low-pressure warning on the instrument panel. However, there are other tire problems that can only be identified with a visual inspection, such as cuts, nails or other damage.*

1    Periodic inspection of the tires may spare you the inconvenience of being stranded with a flat tire. It can also provide you with vital information regarding possible problems in the steering and suspension systems before major damage occurs.

2    Cross-tread wear indicators will show up when the tread depth reaches 1/16-inch, at which point they can be considered worn out. Tread wear can be monitored with a simple, inexpensive device known as a tread-depth indicator **(see illustration)**.

3    Note any abnormal tread wear **(see illustration)**. Tread pattern irregularities such as cupping, flat spots and more wear on one side than the other are indications of front end

alignment and/or balance problems. If any of these conditions are noted, take the vehicle to a tire shop or service station to correct the problem.

4    Look closely for cuts, punctures and embedded nails or tacks. Sometimes a tire will hold air pressure for a short time or leak down very slowly after a nail has embedded itself in the tread. If a slow leak persists, check the valve stem core to make sure it is tight **(see illustration)**. Examine the tread for an object that may have embedded itself in the tire or for a plug that may have begun to leak (radial tire punctures are repaired with a plug that is installed in a puncture). If a puncture is suspected, it can be easily verified by spraying a solution of soapy water onto the puncture area **(see illustration)**. The soapy solution will bubble if there is a leak. Unless the puncture is unusually large, a tire shop or service station can usually repair the tire.

5    Carefully inspect the inner sidewall of each tire for evidence of brake fluid leakage. If you see any, inspect the brakes immediately.

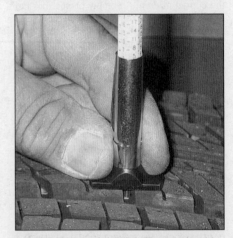

**5.2  A tire tread depth indicator should be used to monitor tire wear - they are available at auto parts stores and service stations and cost very little**

**UNDERINFLATION**

**CUPPING**

Cupping may be caused by:

• Underinflation and/or mechanical irregularities such as out-of-balance condition of wheel and/or tire, and bent or damaged wheel.

• Loose or worn steering tie-rod or steering idler arm.

• Loose, damaged or worn front suspension parts.

**OVERINFLATION**

**INCORRECT TOE-IN OR EXTREME CAMBER**

**FEATHERING DUE TO MISALIGNMENT**

5.3  This chart will help you determine the condition of your tires, the probable cause(s) of abnormal wear and the corrective action necessary

6    Correct air pressure adds miles to the life span of the tires, improves mileage and enhances overall ride quality. Tire pressure cannot be accurately estimated by looking at a tire, especially if it's a radial. A tire pressure gauge is essential. Keep an accurate gauge in the glove compartment. The pressure gauges attached to the nozzles of air hoses at gas stations are often inaccurate.

7    Always check tire pressure when the tires are cold. Cold, in this case, means the vehicle has not been driven over a mile in the three hours preceding a tire pressure check. A pressure rise of four to eight pounds is not uncommon once the tires are warm.

8    Unscrew the valve cap protruding from the wheel or hubcap and push the gauge firmly onto the valve stem **(see illustration)**.

5.4a  If a tire loses air on a steady basis, check the valve core first to make sure it's snug (special inexpensive wrenches are commonly available at auto parts stores)

5.4b  If the valve core is tight, raise the corner of the vehicle with the low tire and spray a soapy water solution onto the tread as the tire is turned slowly - slow leaks will cause small bubbles to appear

5.8  To extend the life of your tires, check the air pressure at least once a week with an accurate gauge (don't forget the spare!)

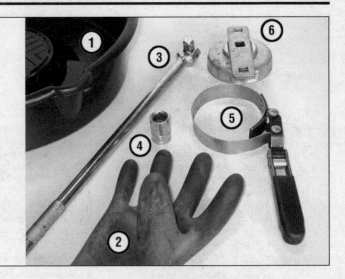

**6.2  These tools are required when changing the engine oil and filter**

1  **Drain pan** - It should be fairly shallow in depth, but wide in order to prevent spills

2  **Rubber gloves** - When removing the drain plug and filter, it is inevitable that you will get oil on your hands (the gloves will prevent burns)

3  **Breaker bar** - Sometimes the oil drain plug is pretty tight and a long breaker bar is needed to loosen it

4  **Socket** - To be used with the breaker bar or a ratchet (must be the correct size to fit the drain plug)

5  **Filter wrench** - This is a metal band-type wrench, which requires clearance around the filter to be effective

6  **Filter wrench** - This type fits on the top of the filter and can be turned with a ratchet or breaker bar (different size wrenches are available for different types of filters)

Note the reading on the gauge and compare the figure to the recommended tire pressure shown on the tire placard on the driver's side door. Be sure to reinstall the valve cap to keep dirt and moisture out of the valve stem mechanism. Check all four tires and, if necessary, add enough air to bring them up to the recommended pressure. The tire pressure for your model is listed on a decal on the door jamb.

9    Don't forget to keep the spare tire inflated to the specified pressure (refer to the pressure molded into the tire sidewall).

## 6    Engine oil and filter change (every 7500 miles or 6 months)

*Refer to illustrations 6.2, 6.6, 6.9, 6.12, 6.13, 6.14, 6.15, 6.18a and 6.18b*

1    Frequent oil changes are the most important preventive maintenance procedures that can be done by the home mechanic. As engine oil ages, it becomes diluted and contaminated, which leads to premature engine wear.

2    Make sure that you have all the necessary tools before you begin this procedure (**see illustration**). You should also have plenty of rags or newspapers handy for mopping up oil spills.

3    Access to the oil drain plug and filter will be improved if the vehicle can be lifted on a hoist, driven onto ramps or supported by jackstands. **Warning:** *Do not work under a vehicle supported only by a jack - always use jackstands!*

4    If you haven't changed the oil on this vehicle before, get under it and locate the oil drain plug. The exhaust components will be warm as you work, so note how they are routed to avoid touching them when you are under the vehicle.

5    Start the engine and allow it to reach normal operating temperature - oil and sludge will flow out more easily when warm. If new oil, a filter or tools are needed, use the vehicle to

go get them and warm up the engine/oil at the same time. Park on a level surface and shut off the engine when it's warmed up. Remove the oil filler cap from the valve cover.

6    Raise the vehicle and support it on jackstands. Make sure it is safely supported! Access to the oil pan drain plug is via a removable flap in the splash shield (**see illustration**).

7    Working in the engine compartment, locate the oil filter housing on the left-hand side of the engine, in front of the intake manifold.

8    Place a rag around the bottom of the housing to absorb any spilled oil.

9    Using a special oil filter removal tool or socket, unscrew and remove the cover complete with the filter cartridge (**see illustration**). The oil will drain from the housing back into the oil pan as the cover is removed

10    Pull the old filter element from the cover, and remove the O-rings from the cover.

11    Using a clean rag, wipe the mating faces of the housing and cover.

12    Install new O-rings on the cover (**see illustration**). New O-rings are normally sup-

plied with the new filter - check with your parts supplier.

13    Install the new filter cartridge in the cover (**see illustration**).

14    Smear a little clean engine oil on the O-rings, install the cover and tighten it to 18 ft-lbs (25 Nm) if using the special filter removal tool, or securely if using a strap wrench (**see illustration**).

15    Working under the vehicle, loosen the oil drain plug about half a turn (**see illustration**). Position the draining container under the drain plug, then remove the plug completely. If possible, try to keep the plug pressed into the sump while unscrewing it by hand the last couple of turns. **Warning:** *Wear eye protection and gloves while removing the plug the final few turns to avoid being scalded by hot oil.*

16    Discard the drain plug gasket.

17    Allow some time for the old oil to drain, noting that it may be necessary to reposition the container as the oil flow slows to a trickle.

18    After all the oil has drained, wipe off the drain plug with a clean rag. Install a new gasket (normally supplied with the new filter)

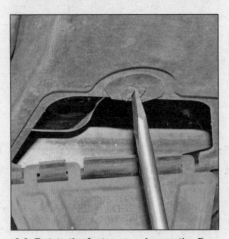

**6.6  Rotate the fastener and open the flap to access the oil drain plug**

**6.9  Unscrew the oil filter cover with a filter removal tool**

**6.12  Replace the filter cover O-rings – 3.0L engine shown, 2.0L engine similar**

**6.13  Slide the new filter element past the O-rings into the filter cover**

**6.14  Lubricate the O-rings with a little clean engine oil and reinstall the cover in the filter housing**

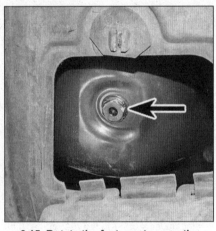

**6.15  Rotate the fastener to open the access flap and remove the oil pan drain plug**

**6.18a  Install a new washer or O-ring on the oil pan drain plug**

on the drain plug. Clean the area around the drain plug opening, then install and tighten the plug **(see illustrations)**.

19  Remove the old oil and all tools from under the vehicle, then lower the vehicle to the ground (if applicable).

20  Add a little less than the correct amount of oil to the engine through the oil filler cap orifice, using the correct grade and type of oil (see this Chapter's Specifications).

21  Start the engine and run it for 3 minutes; check for leaks around the oil filter seal and the drain plug. Note that there may be a delay of a few seconds before the oil pressure warning light goes out when the engine is first started, as the oil circulates through the engine oil galleries and the new oil filter before the pressure builds up.

22  Check the oil level (see Section 4, Steps 2 through 7), then reset the CBS display.

23  The old oil drained from the engine cannot be reused in its present state and should be disposed of. Check with your local auto parts store, disposal facility or environmental

agency to see if they will accept the oil for recycling. After the oil has cooled it can be drained into a container (capped plastic jugs, topped bottles, milk cartons, etc.) for transport to one of these disposal sites. Don't dispose of the oil by pouring it on the ground or down a drain!

---

## 7  Windshield wiper blade inspection and replacement (every 7500 miles or 6 months)

*Refer to illustrations 7.4a, 7.4b and 7.4c*

1  The windshield wiper and blade assembly should be inspected periodically for damage, loose components and cracked or worn blade elements.

2  Road film can build up on the wiper blades and affect their efficiency, so they should be washed regularly with a mild detergent solution.

3  If the wiper blade elements are cracked,

worn or warped, or no longer clean adequately, they should be replaced with new ones.

4  Lift the arm assembly away from the glass for clearance, press on the release

**6.18b  Reinstall the plug and tighten it to Specifications**

**7.4a  To remove the blade, pull the arm away until it locks, release the clip . . .**

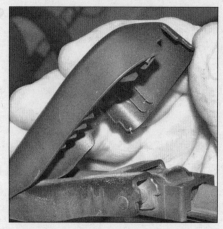

**7.4b  . . . and remove the plastic cover**

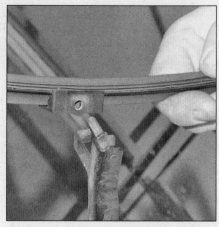

**7.4c  Rotate the blade 90-degrees and disengage it from the arm**

lever, then slide the wiper blade assembly out of the hook in the end of the arm **(see illustrations)**.

5    Attach the new wiper to the arm. Connection can be confirmed by an audible click.

## 8    Battery check, maintenance and charging (every 7500 miles or 6 months)

*Refer to illustrations 8.1a, 8.1b, 8.1c, 8.1d, 8.6, 8.7 and 8.8*

**Warning:** *Certain precautions must be followed when checking and servicing the battery. Hydrogen gas, which is highly flammable, is always present in the battery cells, so keep lighted tobacco and all other open flames and sparks away from the battery. The electrolyte inside the battery is actually diluted sulfuric acid, which will cause injury if splashed*

*on your skin or in your eyes. It will also ruin clothes and painted surfaces. When removing the battery cables, always detach the negative cable first and hook it up last!*
**Note:** *The battery on the covered models have a viewable condition indicator on top. A simple check of battery health means checking the color of the indicator. Green is OK, Black indicates a charge is required, and Yellow signifies the battery should be replaced.*

1    A routine preventive maintenance program for the battery in your vehicle is the only way to ensure quick and reliable starts. But before performing any battery maintenance, make sure that you have the proper equipment necessary to work safely around the battery **(see illustration)**. The battery is located under a cover in the rear of the trunk (see Chapter 5). Rotate the cover fasteners counterclockwise to release the cover **(see illustrations)**.

2    There are also several precautions that

should be taken whenever battery maintenance is performed. Before servicing the battery, always turn the engine and all accessories off and disconnect the cable from the negative terminal of the battery (see Chapter 5).

3    The battery produces hydrogen gas, which is both flammable and explosive. Never create a spark, smoke or light a match around the battery. Always charge the battery in a ventilated area.

4    Electrolyte contains poisonous and corrosive sulfuric acid. Do not allow it to get in your eyes, on your skin or on your clothes. Never ingest it. Wear protective safety glasses when working near the battery. Keep children away from the battery.

5    Note the external condition of the battery. If the positive terminal and cable clamp on your vehicle's battery is equipped with a rubber protector, make sure that it's not torn or damaged. It should completely cover the terminal. Look for any corroded or loose con-

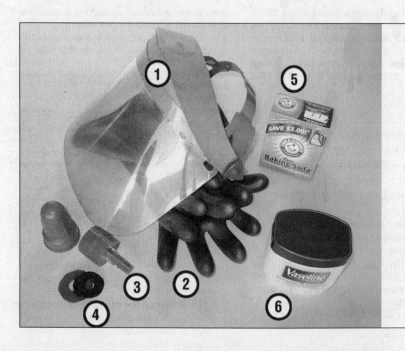

**8.1a  Tools and materials required for battery maintenance**

1   ***Face shield/safety goggles*** *- When removing corrosion with a brush, the acidic particles can easily fly up into your eyes*

2   ***Rubber gloves*** *- Another safety item to consider when servicing the battery; remember that's acid inside the battery*

3   ***Battery post/cable cleaner*** *- This wire brush cleaning tool will remove all traces of corrosion from the battery posts and cable clamps*

4   ***Treated felt washers*** *- Placing one of these on each post, directly under the cable clamps, will help prevent corrosion*

5   ***Baking soda*** *- A solution of baking soda and water can be used to neutralize corrosion*

6   ***Petroleum jelly*** *- A layer of this on the battery posts will help prevent corrosion*

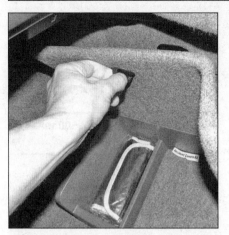

**8.1b   The battery is located in the right-rear corner of the luggage compartment - remove the padded cover**

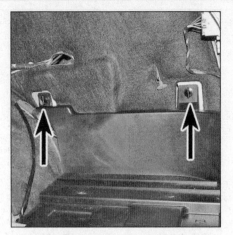

**8.1c   On Sedan models, release the clip and open the right-hand storage tray**

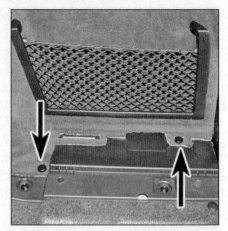

**8.1d   On Sports Wagon models, lift out the compartment floor panel, remove the side panel, then lift out the storage tray**

nections, cracks in the case or cover or loose hold-down clamps. Also check the entire length of each cable for cracks and frayed conductors.

6    If corrosion, which looks like white, fluffy deposits is evident, particularly around the terminals, the battery should be removed for cleaning **(see illustration)**. Loosen the cable clamp bolts with a wrench, being careful to remove the ground cable first, and slide them off the terminals. **Caution:** *Remove the negative cable first, then the positive.* To remove the battery, unbolt the metal retaining strap above the battery. Disconnect the hold-down clamp bolt and nut, remove the clamp and lift the battery from the rear of the trunk.

7    Clean the cable clamps thoroughly with a battery brush or a terminal cleaner and a solution of warm water and baking soda **(see illustration)**. Wash the terminals and the top of the battery case with the same solution, and make sure that the solution doesn't get into the battery. When cleaning the cables, terminals and battery top, wear safety goggles and rubber gloves to prevent any solu-

tion from coming in contact with your eyes or hands. Wear old clothes too - even diluted, sulfuric acid splashed onto clothes will burn holes in them. If the terminals have been extensively corroded, clean them up with a terminal cleaner. Thoroughly wash all cleaned areas with plain water.

8    Make sure that the battery tray is in good condition and the hold-down clamp fasteners are tight. If the battery is removed from the tray, make sure no parts remain in the bottom of the tray when the battery is reinstalled. When reinstalling the hold-down clamp bolts, do not overtighten them. You can prevent future corrosion on the terminals/posts by applying some petroleum jelly **(see illustration)**.

### Cleaning

9    Corrosion on the hold-down components, battery case and surrounding areas can be removed with a solution of water and baking soda. Thoroughly rinse all cleaned areas with plain water.

10    Any metal parts of the vehicle damaged

by corrosion should be covered with a zinc-based primer, then painted.

### Charging

**Warning:** *When batteries are being charged, hydrogen gas, which is very explosive and flammable, is produced. Do not smoke or allow open flames near a charging or a recently charged battery. Wear eye protection when near the battery during charging. Also, make sure the charger is unplugged before connecting or disconnecting the battery from the charger.*

**Note:** *The vehicle manufacturer recommends that your battery be recharged by a Vehicle Power Supply rather than a conventional transformer-type charger.*

11    Slow-rate charging is the best way to restore a battery that's discharged to the point where it will not start the engine. It's also a good way to maintain the battery charge in a vehicle that's only driven a few miles between starts. Maintaining the battery charge is particularly important in the winter when the battery must work harder to start the engine and

**8.6   Battery corrosion usually appears as light, fluffy powder**

**8.7   Remove the cable from the battery post and clean both terminal and post with this tool**

**8.8   Protect the cleaned terminals with petroleum jelly**

**Check for a chafed area that could fail prematurely.**

**Check for a soft area indicating the hose has deteriorated inside.**

**Overtightening the clamp on a hardened hose will damage the hose and cause a leak.**

**Check each hose for swelling and oil-soaked ends. Cracks and breaks can be located by squeezing the hose.**

**9.4  Hoses, like drivebelts, have a habit of failing at the worst possible time - to prevent the inconvenience of a blown radiator or heater hose, inspect them carefully as shown here**

electrical accessories that drain the battery are in greater use.

12   It's best to use a one or two-amp battery charger (sometimes called a "trickle" charger). They are the safest and put the least strain on the battery. They are also the least expensive. For a faster charge, you can use a higher amperage charger, but don't use one rated more than 1/10th the amp/hour rating of the battery. Rapid boost charges that claim to restore the power of the battery in one to two hours are hardest on the battery and can damage batteries not in good condition. This type of charging should only be used in emergency situations.

13   The average time necessary to charge a battery should be listed in the instructions that come with the charger. As a general rule, a trickle charger will charge a battery in 12 to 16 hours.

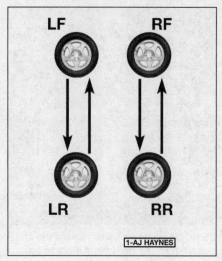

**10.2  Tire rotation pattern**

## 9   Cooling system check (every 7,500 miles or 6 months)

*Refer to illustration 9.4*

1   Many major engine failures can be traced to a faulty cooling system. Consistent checking could save expensive repairs.

2   The engine must be cold for the cooling system check, so perform the following procedure before the vehicle is driven for the day or after it has been shut off for at least three hours.

3   Remove the pressure-relief cap from the expansion tank at the right side of the engine compartment. Clean the cap thoroughly, inside and out, with clean water. The presence of rust or corrosion in the expansion tank means the coolant should be changed (see Section  27). The coolant inside the expansion tank should be relatively clean and transparent. If it's rust colored, drain the system and refill it with new coolant.

4   Carefully check the radiator hoses and the smaller diameter heater hoses (see Chapter 3). Inspect each coolant hose along its entire length, replacing any hose which is cracked, swollen or deteriorated **(see illustration)**. Cracks will show up better if the hose is squeezed. Pay close attention to hose clamps that secure the hoses to cooling system components. Hose clamps can pinch and puncture hoses, resulting in coolant leaks.

5   Make sure that all hose connections are tight. A leak in the cooling system will usually show up as white or rust colored deposits on the area adjoining the leak. If wire-type clamps are used on the hoses, it may be a good idea to replace them with screw-type clamps.

6   Clean the front of the radiator and air conditioning condenser with compressed air, if available, or a soft brush. Remove all bugs, leaves, etc. embedded in the radiator fins. Be

extremely careful not to damage the cooling fins or cut your fingers on them.

7   If the coolant level has been dropping consistently and no leaks are detectable, have the expansion tank cap and cooling system pressure checked at a service station.

## 10   Tire rotation (every 7,500 miles or 6 months)

*Refer to illustration 10.2*

**Note:** *The manufacturer does not recommend tire rotation for the covered vehicle. Check with your tire dealer for his advice before rotating your tires.*

1   If you decide to rotate your tires, they should be rotated at the regular intervals and whenever uneven wear is noticed. Since the vehicle will be raised and the tires removed anyway, check the brakes also (see Section 13).

2   Radial tires must be rotated in a specific pattern **(see illustration)**.

3   The vehicle must be raised on a hoist or supported on jackstands to get all four wheels off the ground. Make sure the vehicle is safely supported!

4   After the rotation procedure is finished, check and adjust the tire pressures as necessary and be sure to check the wheel bolt tightness.

## 11   Seat belt check (every 7,500 miles or 6 months)

1   Check seat belts, buckles, latch plates and guide loops for obvious damage and signs of wear.

2   See if the seat belt reminder light comes on when the key is turned to the Run or Start position. A chime should also sound.

3   The seat belts are designed to lock up during a sudden stop or impact, yet allow free movement during normal driving. Make sure the retractors return the belt against your chest while driving and rewind the belt fully when the buckle is unlatched.

4   If any of the above checks reveal problems with the seat belt system, replace parts as necessary.

## 12   Underhood hose check and replacement (every 15,000 miles or 12 months)

**Warning:** *Replacement of air conditioning hoses must be left to a dealer service department or air conditioning shop that has the equipment to depressurize the system safely. Never remove air conditioning components or hoses until the system has been depressurized and the refrigerant recovered.*

## General

1   High temperatures under the hood can cause deterioration of the rubber and plastic hoses used for engine, accessory and emission systems operation. Periodic inspection should be made for cracks, loose clamps, material hardening and leaks.

2   Information specific to the cooling system hoses can be found in Section 9.

3   Most (but not all) hoses are secured to the fittings with clamps. Where clamps are used, check to be sure they haven't lost their tension, allowing the hose to leak. If clamps aren't used, make sure the hose has not expanded and/or hardened where it slips over the fitting, allowing it to leak.

## Crankcase ventilation system hose

4   To reduce hydrocarbon emissions, crankcase blow-by gas is vented through hoses into the valve cover, to the crankcase oil separator mounted below the intake manifold, and to the intake manifold via rubber hoses on most models. The blow-by gases mix with incoming air in the intake manifold before being burned in the combustion chambers.

5   Check the ventilation hose for cracks, leaks and other damage. Disconnect it from the valve cover and the intake manifold and check the inside for obstructions. If it's clogged, clean it out with solvent.

## Vacuum hoses

6   It's quite common for vacuum hoses, especially those in the emissions system, to be color coded or identified by colored stripes molded into them. Various systems require hoses with different wall thickness, collapse resistance and temperature resistance. When replacing hoses, be sure the new ones are made of the same material.

7   Often the only effective way to check a hose is to remove it completely from the vehicle. If more than one hose is removed, be sure to label the hoses and fittings to ensure correct installation.

8   When checking vacuum hoses, be sure to include any plastic T-fittings in the check. Inspect the fittings for cracks and the hose where it fits over each fitting for distortion, which could cause leakage.

9   A small piece of vacuum hose (1/4-inch inside diameter) can be used as a stethoscope to detect vacuum leaks. Hold one end of the hose to your ear and probe around vacuum hoses and fittings, listening for the hissing sound characteristic of a vacuum leak. **Warning:** *When probing with the vacuum hose stethoscope, be careful not to come into contact with moving engine components such as drivebelts, the cooling fan, etc.*

## Fuel hose

**Warning:** *Gasoline is flammable, so take extra precautions when you work on any part of the fuel system. Don't smoke or allow open flames or bare light bulbs near the work area, and don't work in a garage where a gas-type*

appliance (such as a water heater or clothes dryer) is present. Since fuel is carcinogenic, wear fuel-resistant gloves when there's a possibility of being exposed to fuel, and, if you spill any fuel on your skin, rinse it off immediately with soap and water. Mop up any spills immediately and do not store fuel-soaked rags where they could ignite. The fuel system is under constant pressure, so, if any fuel lines are to be disconnected, the fuel pressure in the system must be relieved first (see Chapter 4 for more information). When you perform any kind of work on the fuel system, wear safety glasses and have a Class B type fire extinguisher on hand.*

10   The fuel lines are usually under pressure, so if any fuel lines are to be disconnected be prepared to catch spilled fuel. **Warning:** *Your vehicle is equipped with fuel injection and you must relieve the fuel system pressure before servicing the fuel lines.* Refer to Chapter 4 for the fuel system pressure relief procedure.

11   Check all flexible fuel lines for deterioration and chafing. Check especially for cracks in areas where the hose bends and just before fittings, such as where a hose attaches to the fuel pump, fuel filter and fuel injection unit.

12   When replacing a hose, use only hose that is specifically designed for your fuel injection system.

13   Spring-type clamps are sometimes used on fuel return or vapor lines. These clamps often lose their tension over a period of time, and can be sprung during removal. Replace all spring-type clamps with screw clamps whenever a hose is replaced. Some fuel lines use spring-lock type couplings, which require a special tool to disconnect. See Chapter 4 for more information on this type of coupling.

## Metal lines

14   Sections of metal line are often used for fuel line between the fuel pump and the fuel injection unit. Check carefully to make sure the line isn't bent, crimped or cracked.

15   If a section of metal fuel line must be replaced, use seamless steel tubing only, since copper and aluminum tubing do not have the strength necessary to withstand vibration caused by the engine.

16   Check the metal brake lines where they enter the master cylinder and brake proportioning unit (if used) for cracks in the lines and loose fittings. Any sign of brake fluid leakage calls for an immediate thorough inspection of the brake system.

## 13  Brake check (every 15,000 miles or 12 months)

**Warning:** *Dust created by the brake system is harmful to your health. Never blow it out with compressed air and don't inhale any of it. An approved filtering mask should be worn when working on brakes. Do not, under any circumstances, use petroleum-based solvents to clean brake parts. Use brake system cleaner only!*

**13.5  Inspect the thickness of the brake pads through the inspection hole - typical**

1   The brakes should be inspected every time the wheels are removed or whenever a defect is suspected. Indications of a potential brake system problem include the vehicle pulling to one side when the brake pedal is depressed, noises coming from the brakes when they are applied, excessive brake pedal travel, a pulsating pedal and leakage of fluid, usually seen on the inside of the tire or wheel. **Note:** *It is normal for a vehicle equipped with an Anti-lock Brake System (ABS) to exhibit brake pedal pulsations during severe braking conditions.*

## Disc brakes

*Refer to illustration 13.5*

2   Disc brakes can be visually checked without removing any parts except the wheels. Remove the hub caps (if applicable) and loosen the wheel bolts a quarter turn each.

3   Raise the vehicle and place it securely on jackstands. **Warning:** *Never work under a vehicle that is supported only by a jack!*

4   Remove the wheels. Now visible is the disc brake caliper which contains the pads. There is an outer brake pad and an inner pad. Both must be checked for wear. **Note:** *Usually the inner pad wears faster than the outer pad.* These vehicles have sensors in one front brake pad and one rear brake pad that keep the CBS (Condition Based Service) system informed of brake wear. If the system detects considerable wear in the pads, it will exhibit a warning on the instrument panel. However, if you are working on the vehicle and have one or more wheels removed, a visual inspection of the brakes is a good idea.

5   Measure the thickness of the outer pad at each end of the caliper and the inner pad through the inspection hole in the caliper body **(see illustration).** Compare the measurement with the limit given in this Chapter's Specifications; if any brake pad thickness is less than specified, then all brake pads must be replaced (see Chapter 9).

6   If you're in doubt as to the exact pad thickness or quality, remove them for measurement and further inspection (see Chapter 9).

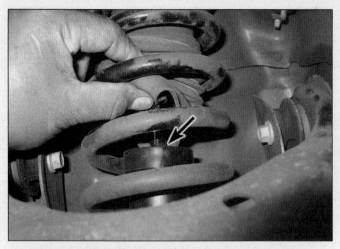

**14.6  Check the shocks for leakage at the indicated area**

**14.11  To check a balljoint for wear, try to pry the control arm up and down to make sure there is no play in the balljoint (if there is, replace it)**

7    Check the disc for score marks, wear and burned spots. If any of these conditions exist, the disc should be removed for servicing or replacement (see Chapter 9).

8    Before installing the wheels, check all the brake lines and hoses for damage, wear, deformation, cracks, corrosion, leakage, bends and twists, particularly in the vicinity of the rubber hoses and calipers.

9    Install the wheels, lower the vehicle and tighten the wheel bolts to the torque given in this Chapter's Specifications.

### Parking brake

10    Slowly pull up on the parking brake and count the number of clicks you hear until the handle is up as far as it will go. The adjustment is correct if you hear the specified number of clicks (see this Chapter's Specifications). If you hear more or fewer clicks, it's time to adjust the parking brake (see Chapter 9).

11    An alternative method of checking the parking brake is to park the vehicle on a steep hill with the engine running (so you can apply the brakes if necessary) with the parking brake set and the transmission in Neutral. If the parking brake cannot prevent the vehicle from rolling, it is in need of adjustment (see Chapter 9).

### 14   Steering and suspension check (every 15,000 miles or 12 months)

**Note:** *For detailed illustrations of the steering and suspension components, refer to Chapter 10.*

### Shock absorber check

*Refer to illustration 14.6*

1    Park the vehicle on level ground, turn the engine off and set the parking brake. Check the tire pressures.

2    Push down at one corner of the vehicle, then release it while noting the movement of the body. It should stop moving and come to rest in a level position within one or two bounces.

3    If the vehicle continues to move up-and-down or if it fails to return to its original position, a worn or weak shock absorber is probably the reason.

4    Repeat the above check at each of the three remaining corners of the vehicle.

5    Raise the vehicle and support it securely on jackstands.

6    Check the shock absorbers for evidence of fluid leakage **(see illustration)**. A light film of fluid is no cause for concern. Make sure that any fluid noted is from the shocks and not from some other source. If leakage is noted, replace the shocks as a set.

7    Check the shocks to be sure that they are securely mounted and undamaged. Check the upper mounts for damage and wear. If damage or wear is noted, replace the shocks as a set (front or rear).

8    If the shocks must be replaced, refer to Chapter 10 for the procedure.

### Steering and suspension check

*Refer to illustrations 14.11 and 14.12*

9    Check the tires for irregular wear patterns and proper inflation. See Section 5 in this Chapter for information regarding tire wear and Chapter 10 for information on wheel bearing replacement.

10    Inspect the universal joint between the steering shaft and the steering gear housing. Check the steering gear housing for lubricant leakage. Make sure that the dust boots are not damaged and that the boot clamps are not loose. Check the tie-rod ends for excessive play. Look for loose bolts, broken or disconnected parts and deteriorated rubber bushings on all suspension and steering components. While an assistant turns the steering wheel from side to side, check the steering components for free movement, chafing and binding. If the steering components do not seem to be reacting with the movement of the steering wheel, try to determine where the slack is located.

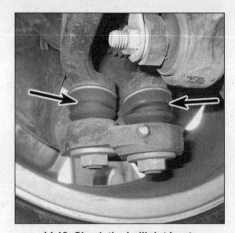

**14.12  Check the balljoint boots for damage**

11    Check the balljoints for wear by trying to move each control arm up and down with a prybar **(see illustration)** to ensure that its balljoint has no play. If any balljoint does have play, it's worn out. See Chapter 10 for the control arm replacement procedure (the balljoints aren't replaceable separately).

12    Inspect the balljoint boots for damage and leaking grease **(see illustration)**.

13    At the rear of the vehicle, inspect the suspension arm bushings for deterioration. Additional information on suspension components can be found in Chapter 10.

### 15   Fuel system check (every 15,000 miles or 12 months)

**Warning:** *Gasoline is flammable, so take extra precautions when you work on any part of the fuel system. Don't smoke or allow open flames or bare light bulbs near the work area, and don't work in a garage where a gas-type appliance (such as a water heater or clothes dryer) is present. Since fuel is carcinogenic, wear fuel-resistant gloves when there's a pos-*

16.1  Manual transmission check/fill plug

16.8  Automatic transmission check/fill plug

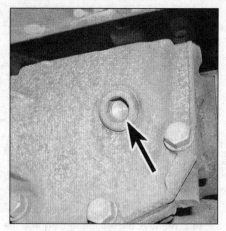

16.10  Rear differential check/fill plug

*sibility of being exposed to fuel, and, if you spill any fuel on your skin, rinse it off immediately with soap and water. Mop up any spills immediately and do not store fuel-soaked rags where they could ignite. When you perform any kind of work on the fuel system, wear safety glasses and have a Class B type fire extinguisher on hand. The fuel system is under constant pressure, so, before any lines are disconnected, the fuel system pressure must be relieved (see Chapter 4).*

1    If you smell gasoline while driving or after the vehicle has been sitting in the sun, inspect the fuel system immediately.

2    Remove the fuel filler cap and inspect if for damage and corrosion. The gasket should have an unbroken sealing imprint. If the gasket is damaged or corroded, install a new cap.

3    Inspect the fuel feed line for cracks. Make sure that the connections between the fuel lines and the fuel injection system and between the fuel lines and the fuel tank are tight. **Warning:** *Your vehicle is fuel injected, so you must relieve the fuel system pressure before servicing fuel system components. The fuel system pressure relief procedure is outlined in Chapter 4.*

4    Since some components of the fuel system - the fuel tank and part of the fuel feed line, for example - are underneath the vehicle, they can be inspected more easily with the vehicle raised on a hoist. If that's not possible, raise the vehicle and support it on jackstands.

5    With the vehicle raised and safely supported, inspect the gas tank and filler neck for punctures, cracks and other damage. The connection between the filler neck and the tank is particularly critical. Sometimes a rubber filler neck will leak because of loose clamps or deteriorated rubber. Inspect all fuel tank mounting brackets and straps to be sure that the tank is securely attached to the vehicle. **Warning:** *Do not, under any circumstances, try to repair a fuel tank (except rubber components). A welding torch or any open flame can easily cause fuel vapors inside the tank to explode.*

6    Carefully check all rubber hoses and metal lines leading away from the fuel tank.

Check for loose connections, deteriorated hoses, crimped lines and other damage. Repair or replace damaged sections as necessary (see Chapter 4).

7    The evaporative emission control system can also be a source of fuel odors. The function of the system is to store fuel vapors from the fuel tank in a charcoal canister until they can be routed to the intake manifold, where they mix with incoming air before being burned in the combustion chambers.

8    The most common symptom of a faulty evaporative emission system is a strong fuel odor coming from the area of the charcoal canister. If you have detected a fuel odor and have checked the areas described above, check the charcoal canister (see Chapter 6).

## 16   Transmission and differential lubricant level check (every 15,000 miles or 12 months)

### Manual transmission lubricant

*Refer to illustration 16.1*

1    Raise the vehicle and support it securely on jackstands. Remove the check/fill plug on the side of the transmission case **(see illustration)**. If the lubricant level is correct, it should be up to the lower edge of the hole.

2    If the level is not up to the hole, use a syringe or a gear oil pump to add more. Stop filling the transmission when the lubricant begins to run out of the hole.

3    Install the plug and tighten it securely. Drive the vehicle a short distance, then check for leaks.

### Automatic transmission fluid

*Refer to illustration 16.8*

4    The level of the automatic transmission fluid should be carefully maintained. Low fluid level can lead to slipping or loss of drive, while overfilling can cause foaming, loss of fluid and transmission damage.

5    The transmission fluid level should only be checked when the transmission is hot

(between 86 and 122 degrees F). **Caution:** *If the vehicle has just been driven for a long time at high speed or in city traffic in hot weather, or if it has been pulling a trailer, an accurate fluid level reading cannot be obtained. Allow the fluid to cool down for about 30 minutes.*

6    If the vehicle has not just been driven, park the vehicle on level ground, set the parking brake and start the engine. While the engine is idling, depress the brake pedal and move the selector lever through all the gear ranges, beginning and ending in Park.

7    There is no dipstick for checking fluid level on these vehicles. Connect a scan tool to the diagnostic connector (see Chapter 6), and set the tool to read fluid temperature. If the procedure is being performed at home, some other tool for checking the fluid temperature must be used (infrared tools are available at auto parts stores).

8    Remove the check/fill plug **(see illustration)**, and if a slight amount of fluid comes out of the hole, the fluid level is OK. If no fluid comes out, add some new fluid with a syringe until it starts to flow out of the hole. **Note:** *On GM manufactured transmissions, the check/fill plug is located on the back of the transmission case. On ZF manufactured transmissions, the check/fill plug is located on the side of the transmission case.*

9    Install a new sealing ring on the check/fill plug, then install the plug and tighten it securely.

### Differential lubricant

*Refer to illustration 16.10*

10    Raise the vehicle and support it securely on jackstands. Remove the check/fill plug on the differential case **(see illustration)**. If the lubricant level is correct, it should be up to the lower edge of the hole.

11    If the level is not up to the hole, use a syringe or a gear oil pump to add more. Stop filling the differential when the lubricant begins to run out of the hole.

12    Install the plug and tighten it securely. Drive the vehicle a short distance, then check for leaks.

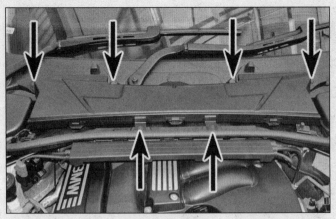

**18.2  Remove the mounting bolts and the cabin air filter cover**

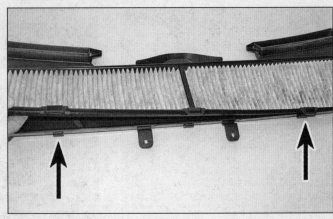

**18.3  Release the clips and lift out the cabin air filter element**

## 17   Transfer case lubricant level check (every 15,000 miles or 12 months)

1    Raise the vehicle and support it securely on jackstands at both ends, to keep the vehicle level.
2    Using a ratchet or breaker bar, unscrew the check/fill plug from the transfer case.
3    Use your little finger to reach inside the housing to feel the lubricant level. The level should be at or near the bottom of the plug hole. If it isn't, add the recommended lubricant through the plug hole with a syringe or squeeze bottle.
4    Install and tighten the plug. Check for leaks after the first few miles of driving.

## 18   Cabin air filter replacement (every 15,000 miles or 12 months)

*Refer to illustrations 18.2 and 18.3*
1    The cabin air filter is located in the cowl on the engine side of the firewall.
2    To replace the filter, remove the bolts and remove the upper section of the filter housing **(see illustration)**.
3    Release the clips at the front edge and remove the filter element **(see illustration)**.

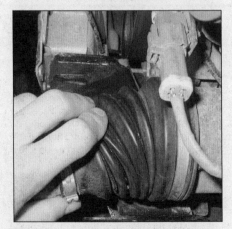

**19.2  Flex the driveaxle boots by hand to check for cracks and/or leaking grease**

4    Install the new filter element into the housing, ensuring it's correctly seated.
5    Install the upper housing and tighten the retaining bolts.

## 19   Driveaxle boot check (every 15,000 miles or 12 months)

*Refer to illustration 19.2*
1    The driveaxle boots are very important because they prevent dirt, water and foreign material from entering and damaging the constant velocity (CV) joints. Oil and grease can cause the boot material to deteriorate prematurely, so it's a good idea to wash the boots with soap and water. Because it constantly pivots back and forth following the steering action of the front hub, the outer CV boot wears out sooner and should be inspected regularly.
2    Inspect the boots for tears and cracks as well as loose clamps **(see illustration)**. If there is any evidence of cracks or leaking lubricant, they must be replaced (see Chapter 8). On AWD models, there are front driveaxles in addition to the driveaxles at the rear.

## 20   Drivebelt check and replacement

### *Check*
*Refer to illustrations 20.2a, 20.2b and 20.4*
1    Due to their function and construction, belts are prone to failure after a period of time, and should be inspected periodically to prevent problems.
2    The drivebelt on these models is used to drive the alternator, power steering pump and air conditioning compressor **(see illustration)**. The engine coolant pump and cooling fan are electrically powered, instead of being belt-driven.
3    The engine must be Off. Using your fingers (and a flashlight if necessary), move along the belt, checking for cracks and separation of the belt plies. Also check for fraying and glazing, which gives the belt a shiny appearance.
4    Both sides of the belts should be

inspected, which means the belt will have to be twisted to check the underside. If necessary, turn the engine using a wrench or socket on the crankshaft pulley bolt so that the whole belt can be inspected **(see illustration)**.

### *Replacement*
*Refer to illustrations 20.6 and 20.7*
5    If the drivebelt is to be re-used, before removal, mark the belt with an arrow to indicate the direction of rotation.
6    On 2.0L models, using a box-end wrench, or on 3.0L models, using a Torx bit or key, rotate the tensioner pulley clockwise to compress the tensioner, and slide the drivebelt from the pulleys **(see illustration)**.
7    If desired, to help in installation, the tensioner can be compressed fully and locked in position using a metal rod engaged with a hole in the tensioner and mounting plate **(see illustration)**. **Caution:** *The tensioner has a powerful spring, so a strong rod will be required.*
8    If the original belt is being installed,

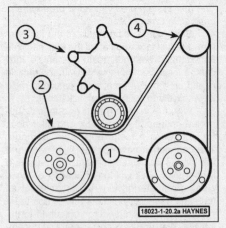

**20.2a  Drivebelt routing – 2.0L engine**

1    *Air conditioning compressor pulley*
2    *Crankshaft pulley*
3    *Tensioner assembly*
4    *Alternator pulley*

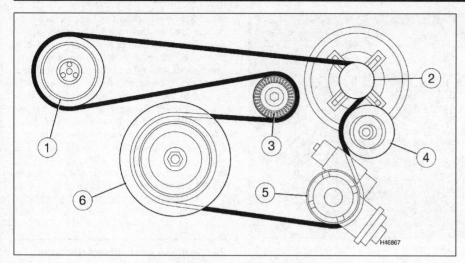

**20.2b  Drivebelt routing – 3.0L engine**

| | | | |
|---|---|---|---|
| 1 | Power steering pump pulley | 4 | Idler pulley |
| 2 | Alternator pulley | 5 | Air conditioning compressor pulley |
| 3 | Tensioner pulley | 6 | Crankshaft pulley |

**ACCEPTABLE**

Cracks Running Across "V" Portions of Belt

**20.4  Small cracks in the underside of a V-ribbed belt are acceptable - lengthwise cracks, or missing pieces that cause the belt to make noise, are cause for replacement**

1/2"

Missing Two or More Adjacent Ribs 1/2" or longer

**UNACCEPTABLE**

Cracks Running Parallel to "V" Portions of Belt

observe the rotational direction mark made before removal.

9   If the tensioner has not been locked in position, compress the tensioner and engage the belt with the pulleys, ensuring that it is routed as noted before removal **(see illustration 20.2)**. Make sure that the belt engages correctly with the grooves in the pulleys.

10   Where applicable, compress the tensioner until the locking rod can be removed, then withdraw the rod and release the tensioner.

11   Install the cooling fan and shroud (see Chapter 3).

## *Drivebelt tensioner replacement*

12   Remove the drivebelt (see Step 6).

13   On 2.0L models, remove the three drivebelt tensioner mounting bolts and on 3.0L models, remove the mounting bolt from the center of the tensioner.

14   Maneuver the tensioner out from the timing chain cover. **Note:** *The mounting bolt is aluminum and must be replaced.*

15   Installation is the reverse of removal.

## 21   Exhaust system check (every 30,000 miles or 24 months)

*Refer to illustration 21.2*

1   With the engine cold (at least three hours after the vehicle has been driven), check the complete exhaust system from the engine to the end of the tailpipe. Ideally, the inspection should be done with the vehicle on a hoist to permit unrestricted access. If a hoist isn't available, raise the vehicle and support it securely on jackstands.

2   Check the exhaust pipes and connections for evidence of leaks, severe corrosion and damage. Make sure that all brackets and hangers are in good condition and tight **(see illustration)**.

3   At the same time, inspect the underside of the body for holes, corrosion, open seams, etc. which may allow exhaust gases to enter the passenger compartment. Seal all body openings with silicone or body putty.

**20.6  Use a Torx bit or key in the socket of the tensioner housing**

**20.7  Insert a rod or drill bit into the holes to lock the tensioner in the compressed position – 3.0L engine shown**

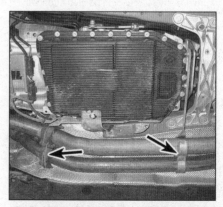

**21.2  Check the condition of the exhaust mounts, gaskets and fasteners**

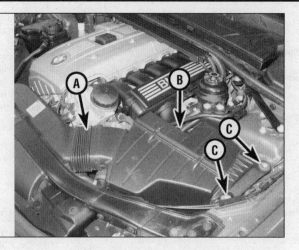

**23.1  Air filter housing details**

A   *Release the connection at the air intake duct*
B   *Loosen the clamp securing the MAF sensor hose*
C   *Remove the two mounting bolts*

clean from the back to the front surface with compressed air. Because it is a pleated-paper type filter, it cannot be washed or oiled. If it cannot be cleaned satisfactorily with compressed air, discard and replace it. While the cover is off, be careful not to drop anything down into the housing. **Caution:** *Never drive the vehicle with the air filter removed. Excessive engine wear could result and backfiring could even cause a fire under the hood.*
5     Wipe out the inside of the air filter housing.
6     Place the new filter into the air cleaner housing, making sure it seats properly.
7     Installation of the housing is the reverse of removal.

4     Rattles and other noises can often be traced to the exhaust system, especially the mounts and hangers. Try to move the pipes, muffler and catalytic converter. If the components can come in contact with the body or suspension parts, secure the exhaust system with new mounts.
5     Check the running condition of the engine by inspecting inside the end of the tail-pipe. The exhaust deposits here are an indication of engine state-of-tune. If the pipe is black and sooty or coated with white deposits, the engine may need a tune-up, including a thorough fuel system inspection and adjustment.

## 22   Brake fluid change (every 30,000 miles or 24 months)

**Warning:** *Brake fluid can harm your eyes and damage painted surfaces, so use extreme caution when handling or pouring it. Do not use brake fluid that has been standing open or is more than one year old. Brake fluid absorbs moisture from the air. Excess moisture can cause a dangerous loss of braking effectiveness.*
1     At the specified intervals, the brake fluid should be drained and replaced. Since the brake fluid may drip or splash when pouring it, place plenty of rags around the master cylinder to protect any surrounding painted surfaces.
2     Before beginning work, purchase the specified brake fluid (see *Recommended lubricants and fluids* in this Chapter's Specifications).
3     Remove the cap from the master cylinder reservoir.
4     Using a hand suction pump or similar device, withdraw the old fluid from the master cylinder reservoir.
5     Add new fluid to the master cylinder until it rises to the base of the filler neck.
6     Bleed the brake system as described in Chapter 9 at all four brakes until new and uncontaminated fluid is expelled from the bleeder screw. Be sure to maintain the fluid level in the master cylinder as you perform the bleeding process. If you allow the master cylinder to run dry, air will enter the system.

7     Refill the master cylinder with fluid and check the operation of the brakes. The pedal should feel solid when depressed, with no sponginess. **Warning:** *Do not operate the vehicle if you are in doubt about the effectiveness of the brake system.*

## 23   Air filter check and replacement (every 30,000 miles or 24 months)

*Refer to illustrations 23.1 and 23.3*

1     The air filter is located inside a housing at the left side of the engine compartment. To remove the air filter, loosen the clamp securing the inlet tube to the air filter cover **(see illustration)**.
2     Release the hose clamp that secures the MAF sensor at the rear of the housing, then remove the bolts securing the filter housing.
3     Lift the housing from the vehicle and turn it over to access the bolts securing the plate over the filter. Separate the housing halves and remove the air filter element **(see illustration)**.
4     Inspect the outer surface of the filter element. If it is dirty, replace it. If it is only moderately dusty, it can be reused by blowing it

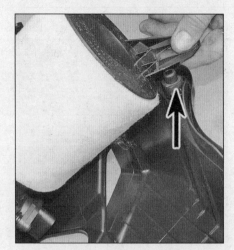

**23.3  Replace the air filter element - some models have a round filter, others a flat design**

## 24   Transfer case lubricant change (AWD models) (every 60,000 miles or 48 months)

**Note:** *The manufacturer does not suggest any scheduled changes of the transfer case lubricant.*
1     Drive the vehicle for at least 15 minutes to warm the lubricant in the case.
2     Raise the vehicle and support it securely on jackstands.
3     Remove the check/fill plug, then the drain plug and allow the old lubricant to drain completely.
4     After the lubricant has drained completely, reinstall the drain plug and tighten it securely.
5     Fill the case with the specified lubricant until it is level with the lower edge of the filler hole.
6     Install the check/fill plug and tighten it securely.
7     Drive the vehicle for a short distance, then check the drain and fill plugs for leakage.

## 25   Differential lubricant change (every 60,000 miles or 48 months)

**Note:** *All models have a rear differential, AWD models also have a front differential. The fluid checking or changing procedure is similar for both types and the maintenance interval is the same.*
1     This procedure should be performed after the vehicle has been driven so the lubricant will be warm and flow out of the differential more easily. To access the front differential filler plug, remove the splash shield under the engine, and the stiffening plate at the center-bottom of the subframe.
2     Raise the vehicle and support it securely on jackstands.
3     Remove the filler plug from the differential **(see illustration 16.10)**.
4     Remove the drain plug and allow the fluid to drain. Install a new sealing washer on the drain plug and reinstall it, tightening it securely.

**26.2  Automatic transmission pan drain plug (ZF transmission shown)**

**27.1  Use a hydrometer to check the strength of the antifreeze**

5    Use a hand pump, syringe or funnel to fill the differential housing with the specified lubricant until it's level with the bottom of the filler plug hole.

6    Install the fill plug and tighten it securely.

## 26   Automatic transmission fluid change (every 60,000 miles or 48 months)

*Refer to illustration 26.2*

**Warning:** *This procedure is potentially dangerous and is best left to a professional shop with a safe lifting apparatus. The vehicle must be kept level while being safely raised high enough for access to the check/fill plug. The engine must be running when checking or adding transmission fluid.*

1    Raise and safely support the vehicle in a level position.

2    Remove the splash shield for access, and remove the drain plug from the transmission fluid pan **(see illustration)**. Have a drain pan in position to collect the old fluid. **Warning:** *The transmission fluid is hot! Wear eye protection and gloves.*

3    Measure the amount of fluid that comes out, and add that amount of the recommended fluid in through the filler plug hole. A small transfer pump can be used to add the new fluid.

4    Check the fluid level as described in Section 16.

## 27   Cooling system servicing (draining, flushing and refilling) (every 100,000 miles or 60 months)

**Warning:** *Do not allow antifreeze to come in contact with your skin or painted surfaces of the vehicle. Rinse off spills immediately with plenty of water. Antifreeze is highly toxic if ingested. Never leave antifreeze lying around in an open container or in puddles on the floor; children and pets are attracted by its*

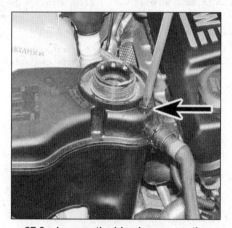

**27.2a  Loosen the bleed screw on the expansion tank . . .**

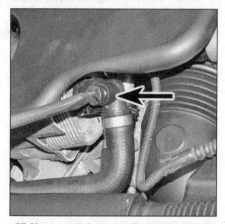

**27.2b  . . . and the one adjacent to the oil filter cap – 3.0L models shown**

*sweet smell and may drink it. Check with local authorities about disposing of used antifreeze. Many communities have collection centers which will see that antifreeze is disposed of safely. Never dump used antifreeze on the ground or pour it into drains.*

**Warning:** *On models equipped with lifetime coolant, never reuse the coolant. If the cooling system is partially drained, the corrosion protection effect of the coolant is significantly reduced. If a large quantity of coolant is removed, the entire cooling system must be drained and refilled with new coolant. If a small amount (under a quart), is drained, new fluid must be used to replace the coolant drained from the system.*

**Caution:** *Do not mix coolants of different colors. Doing so might damage the cooling system and/or the engine. The manufacturer specifies either a green colored coolant or a yellow colored coolant to be used in these systems. Read the warning label in the engine compartment for additional information.*

**Note:** *Non-toxic antifreeze is now manufactured and available at local auto parts stores, but even this type must be disposed of properly.*

**Note:** *Periodically, the cooling system should be drained, flushed and refilled to replenish the antifreeze mixture and prevent formation of*

*rust and corrosion, which can impair the performance of the cooling system and cause engine damage. When the cooling system is serviced, all hoses and the expansion tank cap should be checked and replaced if necessary.*

### Draining

*Refer to illustrations 27.1, 27.2a, 27.2b, 27.3a, 27.3b, 27.4 and 27.5*

1    With the engine completely cold, cover the expansion tank cap with a rag and slowly turn the cap counterclockwise to relieve the pressure in the cooling system (a hissing sound may be heard). Wait until any pressure in the system is released, then continue to turn the cap until it can be removed. The effectiveness of the coolant can easily be checked with an inexpensive hydrometer **(see illustration)**.

2    Unscrew the bleeder screw from the top of the expansion tank. 2.0L models, are equipped with two more bleeder screws; one at the radiator return hose and the other at the transmission cooler (automatic transmission models). Some 3.0L models are equipped with a bleed screw adjacent to the oil filler cap **(see illustrations)**.

3    Raise the front of the vehicle and sup-

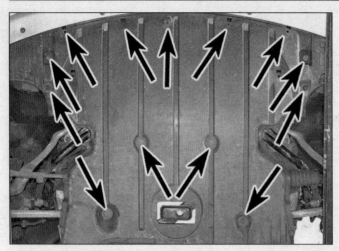

**27.3a  Remove the splash shield fasteners and splash shield**

**27.3b  Remove the radiator splash shield mounting bolts and the shield under the radiator**

port it securely on jackstands. Remove the retaining bolts/clips and the splash shields from beneath the engine and radiator **(see illustrations)**.

4    Position a suitable container beneath the drain plug on the left side of the radiator. Unscrew the drain plug and allow the coolant to drain into the container **(see illustration)**. On models without a radiator drain plug, release the clamp and disconnect the radiator lower hose.

5    To fully drain the system, also unscrew the coolant drain plug from the right-hand side of the cylinder block and allow the remainder of the coolant to drain into the container **(see illustration)**. Note that access to the drain plug is extremely limited.

6    If the coolant has been drained for a reason other than replacement, then it can be re-used, provided it is clean, though this is not recommended.

7    Once all the coolant has drained, install a new gasket or O-ring on the block drain plug and tighten it to the specified torque.

## Flushing

8    If coolant replacement has been neglected,

or if the antifreeze mixture has become diluted, then in time the cooling system may gradually lose efficiency, as the coolant passages become restricted due to rust, scale deposits, and other sediment. The cooling system efficiency can be restored by flushing the system clean.

9    The radiator should be flushed independently of the engine, to avoid unnecessary contamination.

### Radiator flushing

10    To flush the radiator, disconnect the top and bottom hoses and any other relevant hoses from the radiator (see Chapter 3).

11    Insert a garden hose into the radiator top inlet. Direct a flow of clean water through the radiator, and continue flushing until clean water emerges from the radiator bottom outlet.

12    If after a reasonable period the water still does not run clear, the radiator can be flushed with a good proprietary cooling system cleaning agent. It is important that the manufacturer's instructions are followed carefully. If the contamination is particularly bad, insert the hose in the radiator bottom outlet, and reverse-flush the radiator.

### Engine flushing

13    To flush the engine, remove the thermostat (see Chapter 3), then temporarily reinstall the thermostat cover.

14    With the top and bottom hoses disconnected from the radiator, insert a garden hose into the radiator top hose. Direct a clean flow of water through the engine, and continue flushing until clean water emerges from the radiator bottom hose.

15    On completion of flushing, reinstall the thermostat and reconnect the hoses (see Chapter 3).

## Filling

16    Before attempting to fill the cooling system, make sure that all hoses and clamps are in good condition, that the clamps are tight and the radiator and cylinder block drain plugs are securely tightened. **Note:** *Antifreeze mixture must be used all year round to prevent corrosion of the engine components.*

17    Loosen the bleed screw(s) **(see illustrations 27.2a and 27.2b)**.

18    Turn on the ignition (without starting the engine), and set the heater control to maximum temperature, with the fan speed set to low. This opens the heating valves.

19    Remove the expansion tank filler cap. Fill the system by pouring the coolant slowly into the expansion tank to prevent air pockets from forming. **Note:** *Both bleed screws should be open.*

20    If the coolant is being replaced, begin by pouring in new coolant (a 50/50 mix of water and antifreeze).

21    As soon as coolant emerges from the bleed screw(s) free from air bubbles, tighten the screw(s) securely.

22    Once the level in the expansion tank starts to rise, squeeze the radiator top and bottom hoses to help expel any trapped air in the system. Once all the air is expelled,

**27.4  Loosen the radiator drain plug**

**27.5  The cylinder block drain plug is located on the right-hand side**

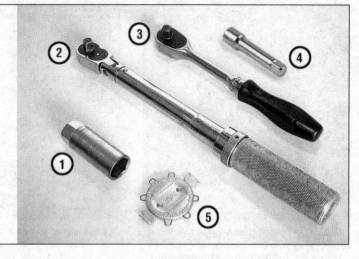

**28.4a  Tools required for spark plug removal, gap adjustment, and installation**

1   **Spark plug socket** - This will have special padding inside to protect the spark plug porcelain insulator
2   **Torque wrench** - Although not mandatory, use of this tool is the best way to ensure that the plugs are tightened properly
3   **Ratchet** - Standard hand tool to fit the plug socket
4   **Extension** - Depending on model and accessories, you may need special extensions and universal joints to reach one or more of the plugs
5   **Spark plug gap gauge** - This gauge for checking the gap comes in a variety of styles. Make sure the gap for your engine is included

top off the coolant level until the float in the expansion tank rises to indicate the maximum level, then install the expansion tank cap.

23   Start the engine and run it until it reaches normal operating temperature, then stop the engine and allow it to cool.

24   Check for leaks, particularly around disturbed components. Check the coolant level in the expansion tank, and top off if necessary. **Note:** *The system must be cold before an accurate level is indicated in the expansion tank. If the expansion tank cap is removed while the engine is still warm, cover the cap with a thick cloth, and unscrew the cap slowly to gradually relieve the system pressure (a hissing sound will normally be heard). Wait until any pressure remaining in the system is released, then continue to turn the cap until it can be removed.*

## 28   Spark plug check and replacement (every 100,000 miles or 60 months, whichever comes first)

*Refer to illustrations 28.4a, 28.4b, 28.10, and 28.12*

**Note:** *On vehicles manufactured before 03/2007, the spark plugs should be replaced after a maximum of 60,000 miles. The later platinum spark plugs have a longer life span.*

**Note:** *On 2.0L models, the gap is preset from the factory and not adjustable.*

1   The correct functioning of the spark plugs is vital for the correct running and efficiency of the engine. It is essential that the plugs installed are appropriate for the engine (see this Chapter's Specifications). If the correct type are used, and the engine is in good condition, the spark plugs should not need attention between scheduled replacement intervals.

2   Remove the mounting bolts and the engine cover for access to the ignition coils. Remove the individual ignition coils (see Chapter 5).

3   It is advisable to remove the dirt from the spark plug recesses, using a clean brush, vacuum cleaner or compressed air before removing the plugs, to prevent dirt dropping into the cylinders.

4   Unscrew the plugs using a spark plug socket and extension bar **(see illustrations)**. Keep the socket aligned with the spark plug - if it is forcibly moved to one side, the ceramic insulator may be broken off. As each plug is removed, examine it as follows.

5   Examination of the spark plugs will give a good indication of the condition of the engine (see the chart on the inside back cover of this manual). If the insulator nose of the spark plug is clean and white, with no deposits, this is indicative of a weak mixture or too hot a plug (a hot plug transfers heat away from the electrode slowly, a cold plug transfers heat away quickly).

6   If the tip and insulator nose are covered with hard black-looking deposits, then this is indicative that the mixture is too rich. Should the plug be black and oily, then it is likely that the engine is fairly worn.

7   If the insulator nose is covered with light tan to grayish-brown deposits, then the mixture is correct, and it is likely that the

engine is in good condition.

8   When buying new spark plugs, it is important to obtain the correct plugs for your specific engine (see this Chapter's Specifications).

9   The recommended spark plugs are of the multi-electrode type, and the gap between the center electrode and the ground electrodes cannot be adjusted. However, if single-electrode plugs are being installed, the gap between the ground and center electrode must be correct. If it is too large or too small, the size of the spark and its efficiency will be seriously impaired. The gap should be set to the value given by the spark plug manufacturer.

10   To set the gap on single-electrode plugs, measure it with a feeler gauge or wire gauge, then bend the outer plug electrode until the correct gap is achieved **(see illustration)**. The center electrode should never be bent, as this may crack the insulator and cause plug failure. If using feeler gauges, the gap is correct when the appropriate-size blade is a firm sliding fit.

11   Special spark plug electrode gap adjusting tools are available from most auto parts stores, or from some spark plug manufacturers.

**28.4b  Unscrew the spark plugs from the cylinder head**

**28.10  Measure the spark plug gap with a feeler gauge or a wire gauge**

**28.12  A length of rubber hose that fits a spark plug well can be used to get spark plugs started without cross-threading**

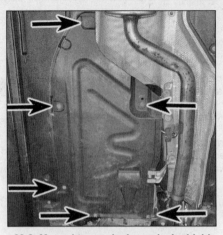

**29.2  Manual transmission splash shield mounting fastener locations**

**29.3  Location of the manual transmission lubricant check/fill plug**

12    Before installing the spark plugs, check that the plug exterior surfaces and threads are clean. It is often very difficult to insert spark plugs into their holes without cross-threading them. To avoid this possibility, put a short length of hose over the end of the spark plug **(see illustration)**.

13    Remove the rubber hose (if used), and tighten the plug to the specified torque (see this Chapter's Specifications) using the spark plug socket and a torque wrench. Install the remaining plugs in the same way.

14    Install the ignition coils as described in Chapter 5.

---

## 29  Manual transmission lubricant change (every 60,000 miles or 48 months)

*Refer to illustrations 29.2, 29.3 and 29.4*

**Note:** *New transmission oil drain plug and oil check/fill plug sealing rings may be required when reinstalling the plugs.*

1    The manual transmission oil should be drained with the transmission at normal operating temperature. If the vehicle has just been driven at least 20 miles, the transmission can be considered warm.

2    Immediately after driving the vehicle, park it on a level surface and apply the parking brake. If desired, raise the vehicle and support it securely on jackstands to improve access, but make sure that the vehicle is level. Remove the transmission splash shield, if equipped **(see illustration)**.

3    Unscrew the oil check/fill plug from the side of the transmission, and recover the

sealing ring, where applicable **(see illustration)**.

4    Loosen the transmission oil drain plug about half a turn **(see illustration)**. Position a draining container under the drain plug, then remove the plug completely. If possible, try to keep the plug pressed into the transmission while unscrewing it by hand the last couple of turns.

5    Reinstall the drain plug, using a new sealing ring where applicable, and tighten to the specified torque.

6    Fill the transmission through the check/fill plug hole with the specified quantity and type of oil until the oil overflows from the check/fill plug hole.

7    Install the check/fill plug, using a new sealing ring where applicable, and tighten to the specified torque.

8    Lower the vehicle. Reset the CBS display (see Section 30).

---

## 30  Resetting the Condition Based Service (CBS) display

1    Ensure that all electrical items are switched off, then turn on the ignition switch. **Note:** *Do not start the engine.*

2    Ensure the on-board time and date are correctly set in accordance with the instructions in the owner's manual.

3    Each service item that appears on the instrument cluster display can be reset. Note that it is only possible to reset an item if the service life of the item is below 80-percent.

4    Press the trip odometer button for approximately 10 seconds until the first CBS (Condition Based Service) item appears in the

**29.4  Location of the manual transmission lubricant drain plug**

instrument cluster display. Note that the most urgent item is displayed first. If this is not the item required, select the item to be reset by briefly pressing the button again.

5    When the required item is selected, press the button again until "Reset?" appears in the display. Note that if the button to confirm the reset is not pressed, the reset process will be cancelled, then the display will return to its normal state.

6    Press the button again for approximately 3 seconds to confirm the reset. Note that it is only possible to reset the brake pad display if the pad sensors are working properly.

7    Turn off the ignition switch.

# Chapter 2  Part A  3.0L six-cylinder engine

## Contents

## Specifications

### General

| | |
|---|---|
| Displacement.......................................................................... | 182 cubic inches (2996cc) |
| Bore........................................................................................ | 3.359 inches (85mm) |
| Stroke ..................................................................................... | 3.467 inches (88mm) |
| Direction of engine rotation..................................................... | Clockwise (viewed from front of vehicle) |
| No 1 cylinder location ............................................................. | Timing chain end |
| Firing order ............................................................................. | 1-5-3-6-2-4 |

### Camshafts

| | |
|---|---|
| Endplay.................................................................................... | 0.0008 to 0.006 inch (0.020 to 0.162 mm) |

### Lubrication system

| | |
|---|---|
| Minimum oil pressure at idle speed.......................................... | 21.7 psi (1.5 bar) |
| Regulated oil pressure............................................................. | 58.0 psi (4.0 bar) |

## Torque specifications

| | Ft-lbs (unless otherwise indicated) | Nm |
|---|---|---|

**Note:** *One foot-pound (ft-lb) of torque is equivalent to 12 inch-pounds (in-lbs) of torque. Torque values below approximately 15 foot-pounds are expressed in inch-pounds, because most foot-pound torque wrenches are not accurate at these smaller values.*

**Note:** *There are a number of aluminum fasteners used to prevent electrolysis between the different types of metals used. Whenever they are removed, they must be replaced with new aluminum fasteners. They are easily identified, since a magnet will not stick to them is it would on steel fasteners. Additionally, most aluminum fasteners are identified with a blue paint marking.*

| | Ft-lbs | Nm |
|---|---|---|
| Acoustic cover-to-valve cover* | | |
|     Step 1 | 36 in-lbs | 4 |
|     Step 2 | Tighten an additional 90-degrees | |
| Camshaft bearing cap bolts | | |
|     Step 1 | 72 in-lbs | 8 |
|     Step 2 | Tighten an additional 60-degrees | |
| Camshaft (intake) bearing cap | 84 in-lbs | 9 |
| Chain drive module-to-cylinder head | 72 in-lbs | 8 |
| Chain guide rail-to-cylinder block | 15 | 20 |
| Chain guide rail-to-cylinder head | 10 | 14 |
| Chain cover plugs | 18 | 25 |
| Chain tensioner-to-cylinder head | 37 | 50 |
| Crankshaft pulley hub bolt* | | |
|     Step 1 | 74 | 100 |
|     Step 2 | Tighten an additional 360-degrees | |
| Crankshaft vibration damper bolts | | |
|     N52 | 18 | 25 |
|     N52K | 26 | 35 |
| Cylinder head bolts* | | |
|     M7 bolts (N52 engine) | | |
|         Step 1 | 60 in-lbs | 7 |
|         Step 2 | Tighten an additional 90-degrees | |
|     M9 steel bolts | | |
|         Step 1 | 22 | 30 |
|         Step 2 | Tighten an additional 90-degrees | |
|         Step 3 | Tighten an additional 90-degrees | |
|     M9 aluminum bolts | | |
|         Step 1 | 84 in-lbs | 10 |
|         Step 2 | Tighten an additional 90-degrees | |
|     M10 bolts | | |
|         Step 1 | 22 | 30 |
|         Step 2 | Tighten an additional 90-degrees | |
|         Step 3 | Tighten an additional 90-degrees | |
|         Step 4 | Tighten an additional 45-degrees | |
| Valve cover bolts | | |
|     M6 bolts | 84 in-lbs | 10 |
|     M7 steel bolts | 132 in-lbs | 15 |
|     M7 aluminum bolts* | | |
|         N52 engine | | |
|             Step 1 | 60 in-lbs | 7 |
|             Step 2 | Tighten an additional 90-degrees | |
|         N52K engine | 84 in-lbs | 9 |
| Driveplate bolts* | 96 | 130 |
| Engine mounts | | |
|     Mount-to-subframe | | |
|         M8 | 21 | 28 |
|         M10 | 41 | 56 |
|     Mount-to-support arm | 41 | 56 |
|     Support arm-to-engine* | | |
|         Step 1 | 18 | 25 |
|         Step 2 | Tighten an additional 90-degrees | |
| Flywheel bolts* | 89 | 120 |
| Front subframe bolts* | | |
|     M10 | 35 | 47 |
|     M12 | 77 | 105 |
| Oil condition/level sensor | 84 in-lbs | 9 |
| Oil deflector-to-lower crankcase bolts* | | |
|     Step 1 | 36 in-lbs | 4 |
|     Step 2 | Tighten an additional 90-degrees | |
| Oil filter cap-to-housing | 18 | 25 |
| Oil filter housing and pipes on crankcase | | |
|     M8 | 16 | 22 |
|     M20 | 30 | 40 |

## Torque specifications

| | Ft-lbs (unless otherwise indicated) | Nm |
|---|---|---|
| Oil pressure switch/temperature sensor | | |
| Step 1 | 15 | 20 |
| Step 2 | Tighten an additional 16-degrees | |
| Oil pump chain module* | | |
| Step 1 | 36 in-lbs | 4 |
| Step 2 | Tighten an additional 90-degrees | |
| Oil pump pick-up pipe* | | |
| Step 1 | 36 in-lbs | 4 |
| Step 2 | Tighten an additional 100-degrees | |
| Oil pump sprocket | | |
| Step 1 | 15 | 20 |
| Step 2 | Tighten an additional 45-degrees | |
| Oil pump-to-lower crankcase (bedplate) | | |
| M8 x 123 mm* | | |
| Step 1 | 84 in-lbs | 10 |
| Step 2 | Tighten an additional 180-degrees | |
| M8 x 31 and 37 mm* | | |
| Step 1 | 84 in-lbs | 10 |
| Step 2 | Tighten an additional 90-degrees | |
| Oil spray nozzles | 84 in-lbs | 10 |
| Positioning motor-to-cylinder head bolts* | | |
| Step 1 | 36 in-lbs | 4 |
| Step 2 | Tighten an additional 90-degrees | |
| Oil pan oil drain plug | 18 | 25 |
| Oil pan | | |
| M8 x 24 and 26 mm | | |
| Step 1 | 72 in-lbs | 8 |
| Step 2 | Tighten an additional 90-degrees | |
| M8 x 92 and 112 mm | | |
| Step 1 | 72 in-lbs | 8 |
| Step 2 | Tighten an additional 180-degrees | |
| Strut tower supports* | | |
| M10 | | |
| Step 1 | 30 | 40 |
| Step 2 | Tighten an additional 90-degrees | |
| M12 | | |
| Step 1 | 74 | 100 |
| Step 2 | Tighten an additional 100-degrees | |
| Transmission cover plate-to-crankcase bolts* | | |
| Step 1 | 36 in-lbs | 4 |
| Step 2 | Tighten an additional 45-degrees | |
| Valvetronic settings | | |
| Eccentric shaft bearing cap-to-cylinder head* | 84 in-lbs | 10 |
| Eccentric shaft stop-screw-to-cylinder head | 84 in-lbs | 10 |
| Electric servo drive-to-cylinder head | 84 in-lbs | 10 |
| Electric servo drive-to-valve cover | 84 in-lbs | 10 |
| Guide block-to-cylinder head | 84 in-lbs | 10 |
| Oil spray nozzle-to-gate | 84 in-lbs | 10 |
| Return spring-to-cylinder head | 84 in-lbs | 10 |
| VANOS adjustment unit-to-camshafts* | | |
| Step 1 | 15 | 20 |
| Step 2 | Tighten an additional 180-degrees | |
| VANOS non-return valve-to-cylinder head | 120 in-lbs | 13 |
| VANOS solenoid valve | 84 in-lbs | 10 |

*Do not re-use, replace with new fasteners*

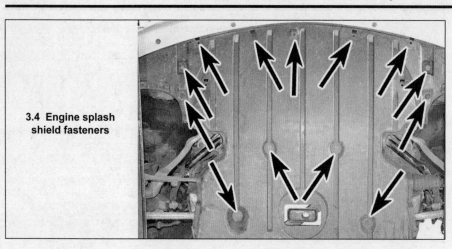

**3.4 Engine splash shield fasteners**

## 1 General information

### *How to use this Chapter*

This Part of Chapter 2 describes the repair procedures that can reasonably be carried out on the engine while it remains in the vehicle. If the engine has been removed from the vehicle and is being disassembled (see Chapter 2C), any preliminary disassembly procedures can be ignored.

**Note:** *While it may be possible physically to overhaul items such as the piston/connecting rod assemblies while the engine is in the vehicle, such tasks are not usually carried out as separate operations. Usually, several additional procedures are required (not to mention the cleaning of components and oilways); for this reason, all such tasks are classed as major overhaul procedures, and are described in Part C of this Chapter.*

Part C describes the removal of the engine/transmission from the vehicle, and the full overhaul procedures that can then be carried out.

### *Engine description*
#### General

These engines are of 6-cylinder double-overhead-cam design, mounted inline, with the transmission bolted to the rear of the engine.

The cylinder block and the camshaft cover are made from a magnesium-aluminum composite. Aluminum bolts are used extensively, as steel bolts/studs would react poorly with the magnesium. Aluminum bolts must never be re-used.

A timing chain from the crankshaft drives both the exhaust and intake camshafts. Hydraulic cam followers are installed between the camshafts and the valves. Each camshaft is supported by bearing caps bolted to the cylinder head.

The timing of both the exhaust and intake valves is variable by means of an adjustable hydraulic sprocket or "adjustment unit" on the end of each camshaft - BMW refers to this as a VANOS system. These units vary the relationship of the timing chain and sprockets to the camshafts. The duration and lift of the intake camshaft is also variable by means of an electric motor-driven eccentric shaft which effectively varies the pivot point of a lever acting between the camshaft and the rocker arm - BMW refers to this as a Valvetronic system. Engine load is controlled by varying valve lift and duration, rather than throttle valve position. This virtually eliminates pumping losses, improves engine output and reduces emissions.

The crankshaft rides on seven insert type main bearings. The endplay is controlled by thrust bearing shells located on the No. 4 main bearing.

The pistons are selected to be of matching weight, and incorporate fully-floating wrist pins retained by snap-rings.

The oil pump and vacuum pump are chain-driven from the front of the crankshaft.

### VANOS variable camshaft timing control

On all models, a variable camshaft timing control system, known as VANOS, is installed. The VANOS system uses data supplied by the ECM engine management system (see Chapter 6) to adjust the timing of both the intake and exhaust camshafts independently via a hydraulic control system (using engine oil as the hydraulic fluid). The camshaft timings are varied according to engine speed, retarding the timing (opening the valves later) at low speeds to improve low-speed driveability and high engine speeds for maximum power. At medium engine speeds, the camshaft timings are advanced (opening the valves earlier) to increase mid-range torque and to improve exhaust emissions.

## 2 Repair operations possible with the engine in the vehicle

Many major repair operations can be accomplished without removing the engine from the vehicle.

Clean the engine compartment and the exterior of the engine with some type of pressure washer before any work is done. A clean engine will make the job easier and will help keep dirt out of the internal areas of the engine.

Depending on the components involved, it may be necessary to remove the hood to improve access to the engine as repairs are performed (see Chapter 11 if necessary).

If vacuum, exhaust, oil or coolant leaks develop, indicating a need for gasket or seal replacement, the repairs can generally be made with the engine in the vehicle. The intake and exhaust manifold gaskets, valve cover gasket and cylinder head gasket are all accessible with the engine in place.

Exterior engine components such as the intake and exhaust manifolds, the water pump, the starter motor, the alternator and the fuel injection system can be removed for repair with the engine in place.

Since the cylinder head can be removed without pulling the engine, valve component servicing can also be accomplished with the engine in the vehicle.

The following operations can be carried out without having to remove the engine from the vehicle:

> *Removal and installation of the cylinder head.*
> *Removal and installation of the timing chain and sprockets.*
> *Removal and installation of the camshafts.*
> *Removal and installation of the oil pan.*
> *Removal and installation of the oil pump.*
> *Replacement of the engine/transmission mounts.*
> *Removal and installation of the flywheel/driveplate.*

## 3 Top Dead Center (TDC) for No 1 piston - locating

*Refer to illustrations 3.4, 3.6, 3.8, 3.10a and 3.10b*

1   Top Dead Center (TDC) is the highest point in the cylinder that each piston reaches as it travels up and down when the crankshaft turns. Each piston reaches TDC at the end of the compression stroke and again at the end of the exhaust stroke, but TDC generally refers to piston position on the compression stroke. The number one piston is at the timing chain end of the engine.

2   Positioning the number one piston at TDC is an essential part of many procedures, such as timing chain removal and camshaft removal.

3   Remove the valve cover (see Section 4).

4   Raise the front of the vehicle and support it securely on jackstands. Remove the fasteners and remove the engine splash shield **(see illustration)**.

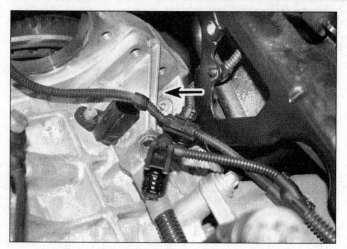

**3.6  Pull the blanking plug from the cylinder block**

**3.8  Insert the crankshaft setting tool through the timing hole into the indent in the flywheel/driveplate**

5    Using a socket or wrench on the crankshaft pulley bolt, turn the engine clockwise at least two complete revolutions until the tips of the front cam (number one cylinder) lobes on the intake camshaft begin pointing to the left-hand side.

6    Pull the plug (where installed) from the timing hole in the left-hand rear corner flange of the cylinder block **(see illustration)**.

7    To lock the crankshaft in position, a special tool will be required. BMW tool No 11 0 300 can be used, but alternatives are available.

8    Insert the tool through the timing hole. Turn the crankshaft clockwise until the rod enters the TDC hole in the flywheel/driveplate **(see illustration)**. **Note:** *On models equipped with an automatic transmission, it is possible to mistakenly insert the rod into a larger hole in the driveplate. Ensure that when the rod is inserted, it is not possible to rotate the crankshaft at all.*

9    The crankshaft is now locked in position with No 1 piston at TDC.

10    In this position, it should be possible to place BMW special tools No. 11 4 283, 11 4 282 and 11 4 281 (or equivalents) over the parallel flats of the camshafts. With the camshaft correctly positioned, the tools should contact the cylinder head upper surface with no clearance below them **(see illustrations)**. Essentially, these tools hold the flat-sided ends of the camshafts at exactly 90-degrees to the cylinder head upper gasket face. In this position, the lobes of No. 1 cylinder intake camshaft should be pointing upwards at an angle, the lobes of No. 6 cylinder exhaust camshaft should be pointing downwards at an angle, and the part number on the camshaft should be visible from above. Note that the square flanges on the rear of the camshafts should be positioned with the sides of the flanges exactly at right-angles to the top surface of the cylinder head.

11    **Do not** attempt to turn the engine with the flywheel/driveplate or camshaft locked in position, as engine damage may result.

---

**4    Valve cover - removal and installation**

**Note:** *The camshaft cover is made from magnesium alloy. Do not install steel bolts/studs into the cover, or excessive corrosion will result.*

## Removal

*Refer to illustrations 4.1, 4.3, 4.4, 4.5, 4.6, 4.7a, 4.7b, 4.7c, 4.10, 4.13 and 4.14*

1    Remove the plastic cap from the center of the cowl trim panel. Two different types of the cap are installed: one with a central slot, removed by rotating it 45-degrees counterclockwise, and one without a central slot,

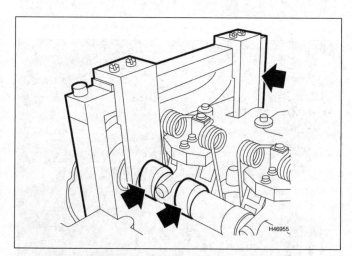

**3.10a  Fit the special tools over the parallel flats on the camshafts, touching the cylinder head upper surface - the intake camshaft lobes of No 1 cylinder should be pointing upwards**

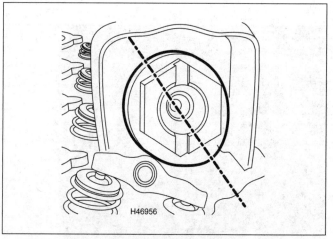

**3.10b  The No 6 cylinder exhaust camshaft lobes should be pointing downwards at an angle**

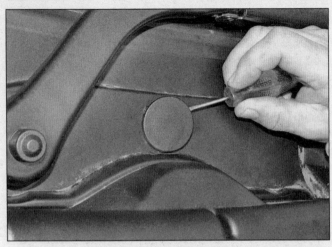

4.1 Pry out or rotate the plastic cap in the center of the cowl trim panel

4.3 Remove the bolt at the end of each support

which is pried out (see illustration). Note: If the cap or seal are damaged, they must be replaced. Failure to do so may result in a water leak.

2    Remove the bolt in the center of the cowl, exposed by the cap removal. Discard the bolt; a new one must be installed.

3    Remove the bolt at each outer end of the supports, then hold the rubber grommet in place and slide the supports outwards (see illustration). Do not allow the grommet to be displaced. Discard the bolts; new ones must be installed.

4    Working at the rear of the engine compartment, remove the cabin air filter cover bolts and remove the cover (see illustration). Slide the filter from the housing.

5    Release the clips and remove the left- and right-hand plastic covers from behind the strut tower on each side of the engine compartment. Unclip the hose from the left-hand cover (see illustration).

6    Depress the clips and pull the cable guide forwards from the cabin air filter lower housing (see illustration).

7    Release the catch and remove the bolt on each side, then slide the cabin air filter lower housing forwards and maneuver it out (see illustrations).

8    Remove the ignition coils (see Chapter 5).

9    Unclip the wiring harness for the fuel injectors. Ensure all wiring in the valve cover area is moved to one side. Note the installed positions of the various electrical connectors before disconnecting them.

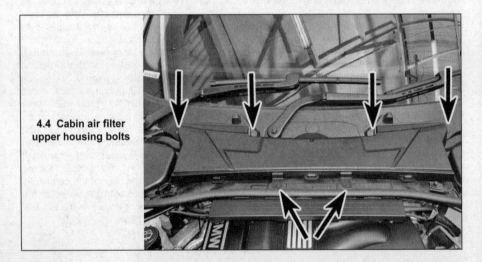

4.4 Cabin air filter upper housing bolts

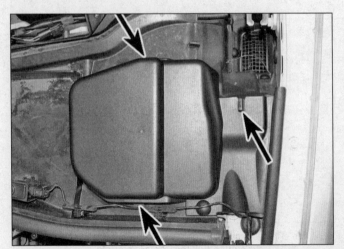

4.5 Release the clips and remove the plastic cover at each side

4.6 Release the clips and slide the cable guide forwards

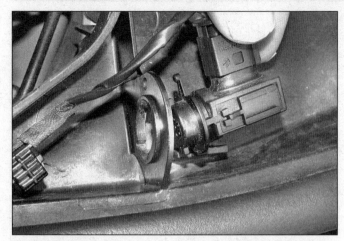

4.7a Rotate the temperature sensor and detach it from the bracket. Disconnect the hood switch on the passenger's side

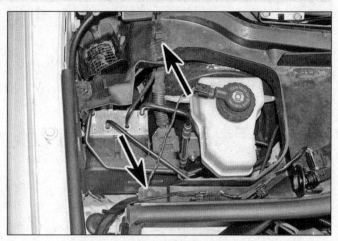

4.7b Remove the bolt and release the clip on each side

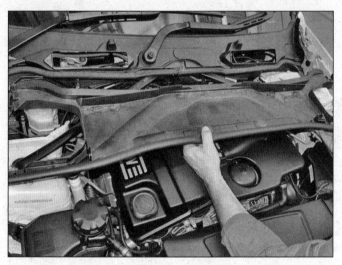

4.7c Slide the cabin air filter lower housing forwards

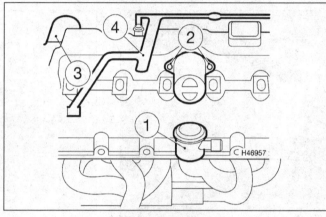

4.10 Valve cover details

1 Secondary air injection valve
2 Valvetronic servo motor bolts
3 Breather hose
4 Metal bracket

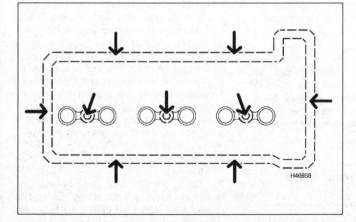

4.13 Loosen the outer bolts first, followed by the inner bolts

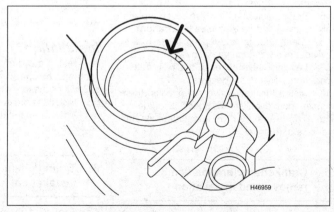

4.14 Replace the slotted sleeves

10 Disconnect the breather hose from the valve cover (see illustration).
11 Remove the bolts and the Valvetronic positioning motor.

12 Remove the nuts and the secondary air injection valve (where installed).
13 Remove the bolts and the valve cover (see illustration). Replace the gaskets. Dis-

card the bolts - new ones must be installed.
14 On some models, BMW states that the slotted sleeves for guiding the coils into the cylinder head must be replaced (see illustration).

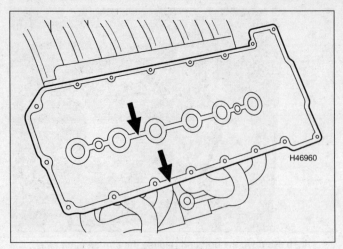

**4.15  Replace the seals**

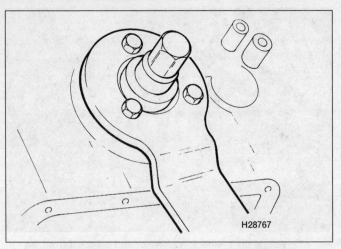

**6.8  BMW special tool used to hold the crankshaft pulley**

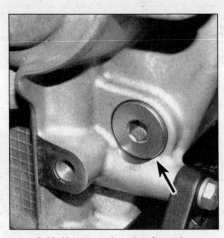

**6.11  Unscrew the plug from the left-hand corner**

**6.12  Unscrew the timing chain guide pins**

## Installation

*Refer to illustration 4.15*

15    Before installing the valve cover, replace all the seals and gaskets **(see illustration)**.
16    Clean the gasket/sealing faces of the cylinder head and the valve cover.
17    Lay the valve cover in position, taking care not to disturb the gaskets.
18    Install the new valve cover bolts, then tighten them evenly to the specified torque.
19    The remainder of installation is the reverse of removal.

## 5    Crankshaft vibration damper - removal and installation

## Removal

1    Raise the front of the vehicle and support it securely on jackstands. Release the fasteners and remove the engine splash shield (where installed) **(see illustration 3.4)**.
2    Remove the drivebelt(s) (see Chapter 1).

3    Unscrew the securing bolts, and remove the vibration damper/pulley from the hub. If necessary, hold the hub using a socket or wrench on the hub securing bolt.

## Installation

4    Install the damper securing bolts, and tighten to the specified torque. Again, hold the pulley if necessary when tightening the bolts.
5    Install the drivebelt(s) (see Chapter 1).
6    Where applicable, install the engine splash shield.

## 6    Timing chain - removal and installation

**Caution:** *The timing system is complex. Severe engine damage will occur if you make any mistakes. Do not attempt this procedure unless you are highly experienced with this type of repair. If you are at all unsure of your abilities, consult an expert. Double-check all your work and be sure everything is correct before you attempt to start the engine.*

## Removal

*Refer to illustrations 6.8, 6.11, 6.12, 6.14a and 6.14b*

1    Remove the valve cover (see Section 4).
2    Remove the crankshaft front oil seal (see Section 1).
3    Remove the drivebelt(s) (see Chapter 1).
4    Remove the retaining bolt and remove the auxiliary drivebelt tensioner. **Note:** *The bolt is aluminum and must be replaced.*
5    Secure the engine at TDC for No 1 cylinder (see Section 3).
6    Unscrew and remove the timing chain tensioner from the right-hand front corner of the cylinder head. **Note:** *A new sealing ring must be installed.*
7    The crankshaft pulley hub must now be released. This hub traps the crankshaft timing chain sprocket against the crankshaft shoulder. Once the hub bolt is loosened, the sprocket is free to rotate. Ensure the flywheel/driveplate and camshaft locking tools are in place. **Warning:** *The crankshaft pulley hub securing bolt is very tight. A tool will be required to hold the hub as the bolt is unscrewed. Do not attempt the job using poor quality tools, as injury or damage may result.*
8    Make up a tool to hold the pulley hub. A suitable tool can be fabricated using two lengths of steel bar, joined by a large pivot bolt. Bolt the holding tool to the pulley hub using the pulley-to-hub bolts. Alternatively, use special tool 11 9 280 available from BMW dealers or automotive tool specialists **(see illustration)**.
9    Using a socket and a long breaker-bar, loosen the pulley hub bolt. Note that the bolt is very tight. Unscrew the pulley hub bolt. Discard the bolt; a new one must be used on installation.
10    Withdraw the hub from the end of the crankshaft. If the hub is tight, use a puller to draw it off.
11    Unscrew the plugs from the top left-hand corner and the lower right-hand corner of the timing chain cover **(see illustrations)**.

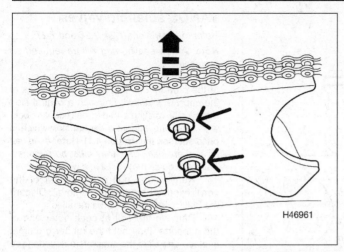

**6.14a Remove the bolts and pull the chain, tensioner blade, guide blade and crankshaft sprocket upwards as an assembly**

**6.14b Pull the timing chain up to trap the crankshaft sprocket against the guide**

12   Remove the two pins securing the timing chain guides now accessible through the plug apertures **(see illustration)**.

13   Remove the retaining bolts and remove the VANOS adjusting units (see Section 7).

14   Remove the central mounting bolts and lift up the timing chain module, complete with chain and crankshaft sprocket **(see illustrations)**. Note the orientation of the crankshaft sprocket (collar towards the crankshaft).

15   If required, disengage the chain from the sprocket and pull it upwards from the module.

## Installation

16   Ensure No 1 piston is still at TDC, with the crankshaft and camshafts locked in position (see Section 3).

17   Begin replacement by engaging the chain with the crankshaft sprocket. **Note:** *The collar on the sprocket must point towards the crankshaft side. Pull the chain upwards in the module to firmly trap the sprocket.*

18   Lower the timing chain and module in place, and feed the crankshaft pulley hub through the center of the sprocket.

19   Insert the new crankshaft pulley hub

retaining bolt. BMW tool No 11 5 200 must now be installed around the central bolt, and tightened onto the hub using the bolts provided. Tighten the hub central bolt to the specified torque. Counterhold the hub using the same method used during removal.

20   Remove the tool from the hub, and install a new oil seal (see Section 13).

21   Install the mounting bolts securing the timing chain guides, and install the cover plugs

22   Install the VANOS adjusting units to the ends of the camshafts (see Section 7).

23   Holding it upright, compress the tensioner a couple of times to empty any stored oil. Install and tighten the chain tensioner with a new sealing washer.

24   Remove the flywheel/driveplate and camshaft locking tools, then rotate the crankshaft two complete revolutions clockwise. Check that the flywheel/driveplate and camshaft locking tools can still be inserted. If not, repeat the VANOS adjusting units procedure.

25   The remainder of installation is the reverse of removal, noting the following points:

a)   *Replace all gaskets and seals.*
b)   *Replace all aluminum bolts.*
c)   *Tighten all fasteners to their specified torque where given.*
d)   *Install the drivebelt(s) (see Chapter 1).*

## 7   Variable valve timing system (VANOS) components - removal and installation

## *VANOS adjustment units*

**Note:** *To test the operation of the VANOS adjustment units, special equipment is required. Testing must therefore be entrusted to a BMW dealer.*

### Removal

*Refer to illustrations 7.3 and 7.4*

1   Position the crankshaft and camshafts at TDC for No 1 piston (see Section 3).

2   Unscrew the timing chain tensioner from the right-hand front corner of the cylinder head. Discard the sealing ring; a new one must be installed.

3   Remove the retaining bolt from the center of the VANOS adjustment unit **(see illustration)**.

4   Rotate the sensor gears so the cut-outs are pointing downwards (to facilitate removal), then pull the unit from the end of each camshaft **(see illustration)**.

5   Disengage the chains from the units as they are withdrawn.

### Installation

*Refer to illustrations 7.9 and 7.10*

6   Ensure that the crankshaft and camshafts are still at TDC on No 1 cylinder (see Section 3).

7   Position the VANOS units on the ends of the camshafts, paying attention to the identifying marks **(see illustration 7.5)**. Note that although the VANOS units are marked IN and EX, the sensor rings are identical.

**7.3 VANOS adjustment unit retaining bolt**

**7.5 The VANOS units are marked AUS/EX for exhaust and EIN/IN for intake**

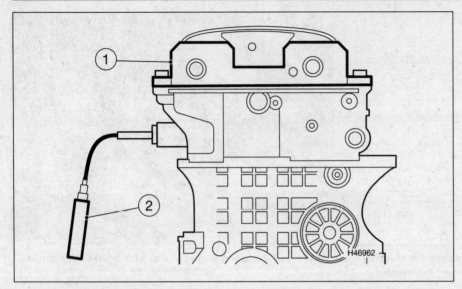

**7.9  Special BMW tool No 11 4 290 (1) and tensioner adjustment tool No 11 9 340 (2)**

8    Install the VANOS unit retaining bolt on each unit, and tighten them by hand until they just touch the sensor ring surface without any play.

9    Ensure that the timing chain rests correctly against the tensioner blade. Install BMW tool No 11 9 340 into the tension piston hole, then turn the adjuster screw on the tool until the end of the screw just touches the tensioner rail without tensioning the chain **(see illustration)**.

10    Attach BMW tool No 11 4 290 to the end of the cylinder head, ensuring that the locating pins of the tool engage correctly with the corresponding holes in the sensor ring gears **(see illustration)**. Screw the tool to the cylinder head using two old valve cover bolts.

11    Pre-tension the chain tensioner guide by screwing in the tool adjusting screw with a torque wrench to a value of 5.3 in-lbs (0.6

Nm). If no suitable torque wrench is available, turn in the adjusting screw by hand just enough to eliminate all freeplay in the chain.

12    Tighten both VANOS adjuster unit retaining bolts to the specified torque.

13    Remove the retaining bolts and remove tool No 11 4 290 from the end of the cylinder head.

14    Loosen the adjusting screw, and remove tool No 11 9 340 from the tensioner piston aperture.

15    Ensure the timing chain tensioner piston has been drained completely, then install it to the aperture in the cylinder head with a new sealing ring. Tighten it to the specified torque.

16    The remainder of installation is the reverse of removal, noting the following points:

 a)  *Install the valve cover (see Section 4).*
 b)  *Ensure the crankshaft locking tool is removed prior to starting the engine.*

### VANOS solenoid valves

*Refer to illustrations 7.24, 7.26 and 7.27*

**Note:** *A new sealing ring will be required on replacement.*

17    Remove the plastic cap from the center of the cowl trim panel. Two different types of the cap are installed: one with a central slot, removed by rotating it 45-degrees counterclockwise, and one without a central slot, which is pried out **(see illustration 4.1)**. **Note:** *If the cap or seal are damaged, they must be replaced. Failure to do so may result in a water leak.*

18    Remove the bolt in the center of the cowl, exposed by the cap removal. Discard the bolt; a new one must be installed.

19    Remove the bolt at each outer end of the supports, then hold the rubber grommet in place and slide the supports outwards **(see illustration 4.3)**. Do not allow the grommet to be dropped. Discard the bolts - new ones must be installed.

20    Working at the rear of the engine compartment, turn the fasteners 90-degrees counterclockwise and remove the cabin air filter cover. Slide the filter from the housing **(see illustration 4.4)**

21    Release the catches and remove the left- and right-hand plastic covers from behind the suspension turret on each side of the engine compartment. Unclip the hose from the left-hand cover **(see illustration 4.5)**.

22    Depress the clips and pull the cable guide forwards from the cabin air filter lower housing **(see illustration 4.6)**.

23    Release the catch and remove the bolt on each side, then slide the cabin air filter lower housing forwards and maneuver it out **(see illustrations 4.7a, 4.7b and 4.7c)**.

24    Remove the retaining screws and lift off the engine cover from the top of the engine **(see illustration)**. As the screws are aluminum, they must be replaced. **Note:** *Examine the screws carefully - on some engines they are fake - the screw heads are part of the plastic casting, and the cover can simply be pulled up.*

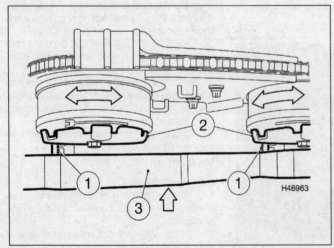

**7.10  Fit the special tool No 11 4 290 (3) to the cylinder head and engage the pins (1) with the corresponding holes in the sensor ring gears (2)**

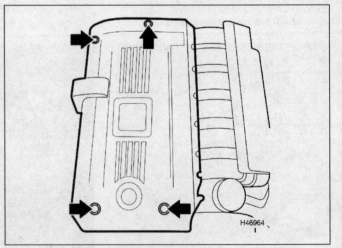

**7.24  Remove the bolts and remove the cover from the top of the engine**

25  Disconnect the solenoid valve wiring connectors. Note their positions; they must be installed to their original positions.

26  Remove the retaining brackets bolts and remove the solenoids **(see illustration)**. Replace the sealing rings.

27  Installation is the reverse of removal, but use new sealing rings. **Note:** *Prior to installation, hold the chain tensioner upright and compress the piston a few times to evacuate any oil* **(see illustration)**.

## 8  Camshafts and followers - removal, inspection and installation

**Note:** *Numerous special tools are required to safely complete the following procedures. Ensure suitable tools are available prior to beginning work.*

### *Removal*

1  Remove the VANOS adjustment units (see Section 7).

#### Intake camshaft

*Refer to illustrations 8.5, 8.6, 8.7, 8.9, 8.10, 8.11, 8.12, 8.13a and 8.13b*

2  In order to remove the intake camshaft, it's necessary to remove the Valvetronic intermediate levers as follows:

3  Using a wrench on the hexagonal section, rotate the eccentric shaft so the lobes are providing minimum lift.

4  Remove the banjo bolt and remove the oil spray nozzle from cylinder No 3.

5  Secure BMW special tool No 11 4 270 to the guide block with locking pliers **(see illustration)**.

6  Secure the bearing pins on the return spring by rotating the knurled wheel on the special tool **(see illustration)**.

7  Lift the handle of the special tool as far as it will go to hold the intermediate lever return spring in place, then remove the bolt securing the return spring **(see illustration)**. Gradually release the spring tension by low-

**7.26  VANOS solenoid wiring plugs and brackets**

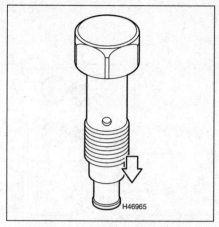

**7.27  Hold the tensioner upright and compress the piston a few times to evacuate the oil**

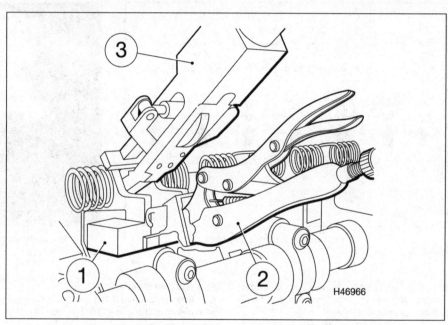

**8.5  Secure the special tool (3) to the guide block (1) with locking pliers (2)**

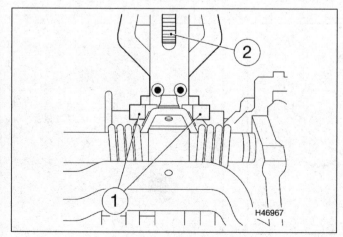

**8.6  Secure the bearing pins (1) on the return spring by rotating the tool wheel (2)**

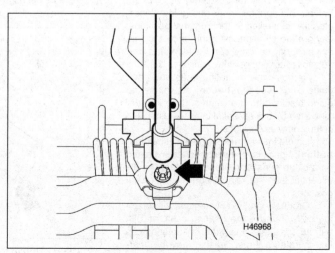

**8.7  Return spring retaining bolt**

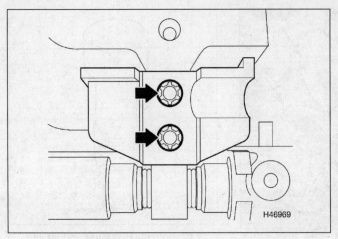

**8.9 Remove the bolts and remove the guide blocks**

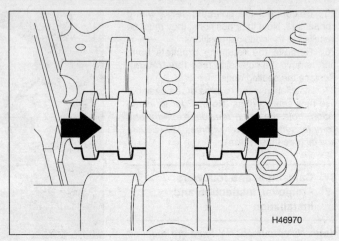

**8.10 Lift out the intermediate levers**

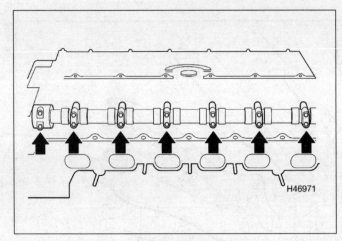

**8.11 Intake camshaft bearing caps**

**8.12 Press down one end of the ring, and pull up the other end**

ering the handle of the special tool. **Caution:** *Release the spring tension gradually as there is a risk of personal injury.*

8   Force the coils apart and remove the return springs. Repeat this procedure on all the return springs. It's absolutely vital that the Valvetronic springs, lever and guide blocks, etc, are reinstalled to their original positions. Lay out the components in order on a clean, dry surface, so they can be identified and reinstalled to their original positions.

9   Remove the mounting bolts and each guide block **(see illustration)**. Again, lay the guide blocks out on a clean surface in order (see Step 8). It is essential they are reinstalled in their original positions.

10   Lift out the intermediate levers **(see illustration)**. Again, lay the intermediate levers out on a clean surface in order (see Step 8). It's essential they are reinstalled to their original positions.

11   Gradually and evenly remove the retaining bolts, remove the bearing caps, and lift out the camshaft. Note that No 1 bearing cap incorporates a thrust washer. Lay the bearing caps out on a clean surface in order; it's essential they are reinstalled to their original

positions **(see illustration)**.

12   If required, remove the compression rings on the end of the camshaft, by pressing one end of the ring into the groove, pulling up the other ring, and unhooking it **(see illustration)**. Take care as the rings are easily broken.

13   Lift the rocker arms from their locations, and lay them out on a clean surface. Pull the hydraulic adjusters out and lay them on a clean surface. It is absolutely essential that the components are reinstalled to their original locations **(see illustrations)**.

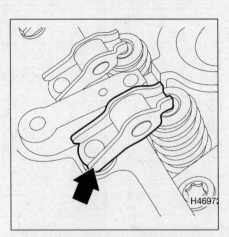

**8.13a Remove the rocker arms . . .**

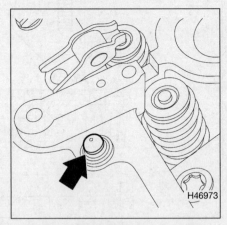

**8.13b . . . followed by the hydraulic adjusters**

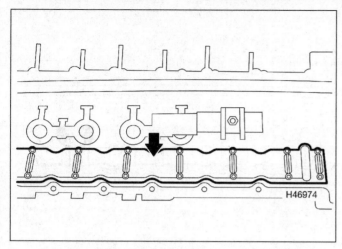

8.14 Remove the bolts and remove the upper casting

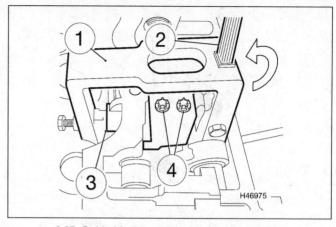

8.27 Guide block special tool mounting details

| | | | |
|---|---|---|---|
| 1 | Special tool No 11 4 450 | 3 | Bolt connection |
| 2 | Tool arm | 4 | Guide block bolts |

### Exhaust camshaft

*Refer to illustration 8.14*

14 Working from the outside inwards, gradually and evenly remove the bolts securing the upper and lower camshaft bearing castings **(see illustration)**. Lift out the castings and camshaft as an assembly.

15 Carefully separate the upper and lower castings, then remove the camshaft.

16 If required, remove the compression rings on the end of the camshaft, by pressing one end of the ring into the groove, pulling up the other ring, and unhooking it **(see illustration 8.12)**. Take care as the rings are easily broken.

17 Lift the rocker arms from their locations, and lay them out on a clean surface.

18 Pull the hydraulic adjusters out and lay them out on a clean surface. It's absolutely essential that the components are reinstalled in their original locations **(see illustrations 8.13a and 8.13b)**.

### Inspection

19 Clean all the components, including the bearing surfaces in the bearing castings and bearing caps. Examine the components carefully for wear and damage. In particular, check the bearing and cam lobe surfaces of the camshaft(s) for scoring and pitting. Examine the surfaces of the cam followers for signs of wear or damage. Replace components as necessary.

### *Installation*

#### Intake camshaft

*Refer to illustrations 8.27, 8.28, and 8.30*

20 Install the hydraulic adjusters and rocker arms in their original positions.

21 Ensure the flywheel/driveplate is still locked in the TDC position.

22 Lubricate the camshaft bearing surfaces with clean engine oil.

23 Install the camshaft so the lobes of No 1 cylinder are pointing upwards, and the part number on the camshaft is up. Install special tool No 11 4 821 on the camshaft (see Section 3).

24 Install the camshaft bearing caps to their original positions. Working evenly, tighten the retaining bolts to the specified torque.

25 Install the intermediate levers to their original positions.

26 Install the guide blocks to their original positions. Install the retaining bolts, tighten them by hand, then loosen them 90-degrees.

27 Attach special tool No 11 4 450 to the bolt connection of the Valvetronic eccentric shaft, and lift up the lever on the tool to tension the guide blocks **(see illustration)**. Tighten the block retaining bolts to their specified torque. Repeat this procedure on the remaining guide blocks. **Note:** *The guide block at cylinder No 3 can only be installed with one bolt until the return spring has been reinstalled later in the procedure.*

28 Install the return springs to their original locations. Ensure the springs engage correctly with the intermediate levers **(see illustration)**.

29 Secure special tool No 11 4 270 to the guide block, then secure the bearing pins in the return spring coils, and pull up the tool arm to tension the spring. Install the spring retaining bolt, and tighten it to the specified torque **(see illustration 8.5 and 8.6)**. Repeat this procedure on the remaining return springs.

30 Install the oil spray nozzle for cylinder No 3, and tighten the bolt to the specified torque. Ensure the nozzle points exactly at the quadrant teeth **(see illustration)**.

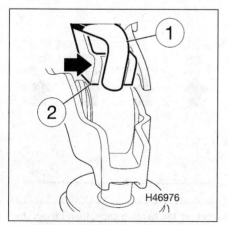

8.28 Check that the return spring (1) engages correctly with the intermediate lever (2)

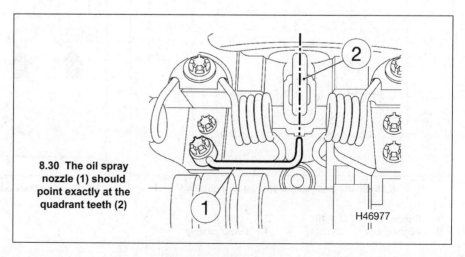

8.30 The oil spray nozzle (1) should point exactly at the quadrant teeth (2)

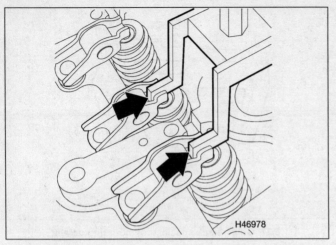

**8.32  Ensure the fingers of the tool contact the rocker arms**

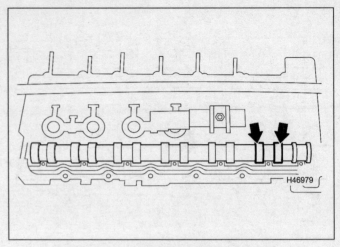

**8.34  Install the camshaft with the lobes at No 1 cylinder pointing upwards**

## Exhaust camshaft

*Refer to illustrations 8.32, 8.34 and 8.36*

31   Install the hydraulic adjusters and rocker arms to their original positions.

32   The exhaust valves of cylinder No 2 must be slightly depressed prior to replacement of the camshaft and bearing castings. Attach special tool No 11 4 462 to the cylinder head using the two special bolts provided. Ensure the fingers of the tool contact the rocker arms above the valves **(see illustration)**.

33   Carefully compress the rocker arms/ valves slightly by tightening the nut on the tool spindle.

34   Install the exhaust camshaft into the lower bearing casting. The lobes on the camshaft at cylinder No 1 must point upwards at an angle **(see illustration)**, and the part number on the camshaft must face upwards. Locate the casting/camshaft over the rocker arms.

35   Place the upper bearing casting over the camshaft. Insert the retaining bolts and tighten them to 72 in-lbs (8 Nm), then loosen all the retaining bolts 90-degrees.

36   The six milled surfaces along the length of the upper and lower bearing castings must be exactly aligned. Attach special tool No 11 4 461 to the milled surfaces as shown **(see illustration)**. Tighten the bolts finger-tight. **Note:** *The bolts should be on the inside, except on cylinder No 2 where the bolt must be on the outside.*

37   With the bearing castings securely clamped, tighten the casting retaining bolts gradually and evenly to the specified torque.

38   Remove the special tools clamping the castings, and the tool depressing the valves at No 2 cylinder.

## Both camshafts

39   Install the VANOS adjustment units (see Section 7).

## 9   Valvetronic components - removal and installation

### *Eccentric shaft*

#### Removal

*Refer to illustrations 9.3, 9.5 and 9.6*

1   Remove the intake valve intermediate levers (see Section 8, Steps 1 through 10).

2   Rotate the eccentric shaft by a wrench on the hexagonal section until its lobes are in the minimum lift position.

3   Remove the retaining bolts and remove the shaft bearing caps. Lay the caps out on a clean surface in order. It is essential they are reinstalled to their original positions **(see illustration)**. Discard the bolts; new ones must be installed.

4   Carefully maneuver the eccentric shaft from position.

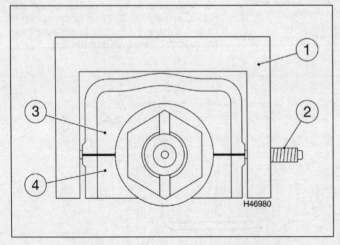

**8.36  Bearing alignment special tool details**

| 1 | Special tool No 11 4 461 | 3 | Upper casting |
| 2 | Aligning bolt | 4 | Lower casting |

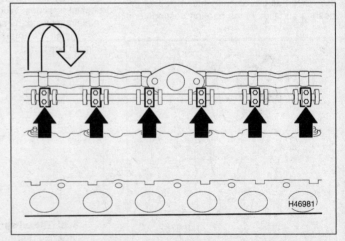

**9.3  Remove the bolts, remove the bearing caps, then lift out the eccentric shaft**

9.5 Remove the bolt and remove the magnetic sensor wheel

9.6 Carefully spread the bearing cage apart

5    If required, remove the bolt and remove the magnetic sensor wheel from the end of the shaft **(see illustration)**.

6    If required, carefully pull apart the bearing cages and remove the bearings from the shaft, then remove the shells from the bearing caps **(see illustration)**. Lay the caps/bearings out on a clean surface in order. Its essential they are reinstalled to their original positions. **Caution:** *Only spread the bearing cages just enough to remove them from the shaft - they are easily broken.*

### Installation

*Refer to illustration 9.7*

7    If removed, install the bearing shells into their original positions in the bearing caps. The inner shell must be installed with the pointed end facing downwards, and the outer shell with the pointed end upwards **(see illustration)**.

8    If removed, install the magnetic sensor wheel to the shaft and tighten the bolt securely.

9    If removed, install the bearings to their original positions on the eccentric shaft.

10    Lubricate the bearing surfaces with clean engine oil, then install the eccentric shaft in the minimum lift position.

11    Install the bearing caps and tighten the new retaining bolts to the specified torque.

12    Install the intermediate levers (see Section 8).

### *Positioning motor*

### Removal

13    Remove the two ignition coils on each side of the positioning motor (see Chapter 5).

14    Disconnect the wiring plug from the positioning motor.

15    Using an Allen bit and ratchet, rotate the end of the positioning motor shaft clockwise until the tension on the eccentric shaft has been relieved.

16    Remove the motor mounting bolts and the motor - note one of the mounting bolts is located under the motor. Discard the bolts - new ones must be installed.

### Installation

17    Position the motor in the aperture in the valve cover, then rotate the motor shaft counter-

clockwise with an Allen bit and draw the motor into position against the flange. Install the new bolts and tighten them to the specified torque.

18    The remainder of installation is the reverse of removal.

### *Position sensor*

*Refer to illustration 9.21*

19    Remove the valve cover (see Section 4).

20    Disconnect the sensor wiring plug.

21    Loosen the sensor retaining bolts **(see illustration)**. Note that the bolts are integral with the sensor - do not attempt to loosen them from the sensor. If fully unscrewed, the bolts *will* fall out.

22    Remove the sensor.

23    Installation is the reverse of removal.

---

### 10    Cylinder head - removal and installation

**Note:** *New cylinder head bolts and a new cylinder head gasket will be required on installation.*

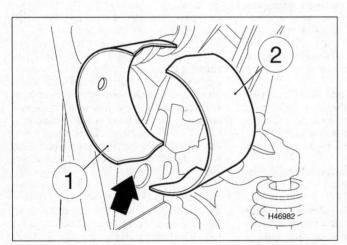

9.7 Install the inner shell (1) with the pointed end facing down, and the outer shell (2) with the pointed end facing upwards

9.21 Eccentric shaft position sensor bolts

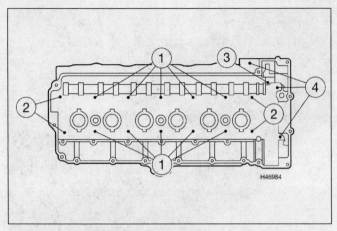

10.9  Cylinder head M10 bolts (1) and M9 bolts (2). Remove the M9 bolt (3) and M7 bolts (4) at the timing chain end of the engine

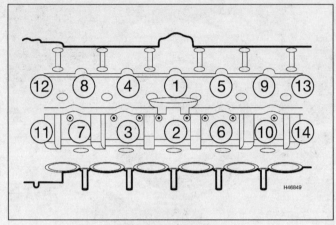

10.24  Cylinder head bolt tightening sequence

## Removal

*Refer to illustration 10.9*

1     Drain the cooling system (see Chapter 1).
2     Remove the intake and exhaust manifolds (see Chapter 4).
3     Note the installed positions of the clamps, then release them and disconnect the various cooling hoses from the cylinder head.
4     Remove the VANOS adjustment units (see Section 7).
5     Remove the retaining bolts, then unclip the timing chain module from the left-hand guide rail. Lift the module upwards to remove it **(see illustration 6.14a)**. Gently set the timing chain down in the cylinder block. It is imperative that the crankshaft is not rotated, as the timing chain will become trapped.
6     Remove the retaining bolts and pull the eccentric shaft position sensor forwards (see Section 9). Remove the retaining bolt and remove the magnetic sensor wheel from the end of the eccentric shaft **(see illustration 9.5)**. Take great care not to drop the bolt - retrieval would be difficult; the bolt is not magnetic.
7     Using a wrench on the hexagonal section, rotate the eccentric shaft so the lobes are pointing upwards, then remove the eccentric shaft M6 stop-screw between the 1st and 2nd cylinders.
8     Remove the M9 and M7 bolts at the timing chain end of the cylinder head.
9     Using suitable Torx driver bits, Remove the cylinder head bolts, working from the outside inward **(see illustration)**. *Note: There are M9 and M10 Torx bolts to remove. Keep track of the installed locations of the M9 bolts - they are different lengths.*
10   An assistant will now be required to help remove the cylinder head. Lift the cylinder head from the block - take care, as the cylinder head is heavy. As the cylinder head is removed, feed the timing chain through the opening in the front of the cylinder head, and support it from the cylinder block using wire.

**Caution:** *Do not set the cylinder head down on the sealing face. The valves protrude beyond the face, and may be damaged.*

11   Remove the cylinder head gasket, then seal the oil pump galley openings in the cylinder block sealing face with suitable-sized rubber/plastic plugs.

## Inspection

12   Cylinder head rebuilding requires special shop equipment. If the engine has over 100,000 miles on it and the heads have been removed for inspection or other work, the head should be brought to a competent engine machine shop, where it can be tested for coolant leaks, resurfaced if necessary and the valves and valve seats machined.
13   The mating faces of the cylinder head and block must be perfectly clean before installing the head. Use a plastic scraper to remove all traces of gasket and carbon, and also clean the tops of the pistons. Take particular care with the aluminum sealing faces, as the soft metal is easily damaged. Also make sure that debris is not allowed to enter the oil and water passages. Using adhesive tape and paper, seal the water, oil and bolt holes in the cylinder block. To prevent carbon entering the gap between the pistons and bores, smear a little grease in the gap.
14   Check the block and head for nicks, deep scratches and other damage. If very slight, they may be buffed out from the cylinder block. More serious damage, such as warpage, must be repaired with special shop equipment.
15   If warpage of the cylinder head is suspected, use a straight-edge to check it for distortion.
16   Clean out the bolt holes in the block using a pipe cleaner or thin rag and a screwdriver. Make sure that all oil and water is removed, otherwise there is a possibility of the block being cracked by hydraulic pressure

when the bolts are tightened.
17   Examine the bolt threads and the threads in the cylinder block for damage. If necessary, use the correct size tap to chase out the threads in the block.

## Installation

*Refer to illustration 10.24*

18   Ensure that the mating faces of the cylinder block and head are spotlessly clean, that the cylinder head bolt threads are clean and dry, and that they screw in and out of their locations.
19   Check that the cylinder head locating dowels are correctly positioned in the cylinder block.
20   Ensure the flywheel/driveplate is still locked in the TDC position (see Section 3).
21   Place a new cylinder head gasket on the block, locating it over the dowels. Make sure that it is the correct way up. **Note:** *Thicker-than-standard gaskets are available for use if the cylinder head-to-block surface has been machined.*
22   Lower the cylinder head onto the block, engaging it over the dowels.
23   Use new cylinder head bolts that have the threads pre-coated. Do not apply any lubricant to the bolts, or wipe away the coating. Insert the new bolts, complete with washers where necessary, and tighten the bolts as far as possible by hand. Ensure that the washers are correctly seated in their locations in the cylinder head. **Note:** *Do not install washers on any bolts which are installed in locations where there are already captive washers in the cylinder head. If a new cylinder head is installed (without captive washers), ensure that new washers are installed to all the bolts.*
24   Tighten the bolts in order to the Step 1 torque setting given in the Specifications **(see illustration)**. *Note: Suitable T50 and T60 Torx bits are available from BMW (part No 11 5 190 and 11 4 420).*

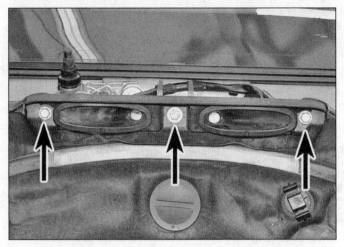

**11.5  Remove the bolts and remove the cowl housing**

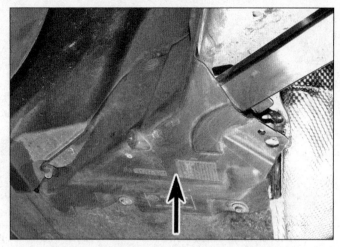

**11.8  Remove the underbody paneling at each side**

25  Tighten all cylinder head bolts to the Step 2 angle using an angle-measuring gauge.
26  Tighten bolts 1 through 10 to their Step 3 angle.
27  Tighten the M10 cylinder head bolts to the last angle setting.
28  Install the new M7 and M9 aluminum bolts in their proper locations at the timing chain end of the cylinder head and tighten them to their specified torque.
29  Install the eccentric shaft stop screw and tighten it to the specified torque.
30  Install the magnetic sensor wheel to the eccentric shaft and tighten the retaining bolt securely.
31  Install the eccentric shaft position sensor and tighten the bolts securely.
32  Using a length of wire as a hook, pull the timing chain up through the cylinder head, and install it into the timing chain module. Clip the module to the left-hand guide, insert the retaining bolts and tighten them to the specified torque.

33  Install the VANOS adjustment units (see Section 7).
34  The remainder of installation is the reverse of removal. Refill the cooling system (see Chapter 1).

## 11  Oil pan - removal and installation

### Removal

*Refer to illustrations 11.5, 11.8, 11.9a,11.9b, 11.10, 11.13a, 11.13b, 11.14 and 11.19*

1  Remove the strut support and the cabin air filter cover (see Section 4, Steps 1 through 7).
2  Disconnect the mass airflow sensor wiring plug, then release the clamp and disconnect the air intake hose.
3  Remove the air filter housing (see Chapter 4).
4  Remove the cover over the ignition coils.

5  Remove the mounting bolts and remove the cowl housing **(see illustration)**.
6  The engine must be supported in position using an engine hoist or engine support fixture. Attach the hoist or fixture to the engine lifting eyes at the front and rear of the engine. Take the weight off the engine mounts.
7  Loosen the nut at each side securing the engine mount support brackets to the mounts, then raise the engine approximately 1/2 inch (12 mm).
8  Remove the fasteners and the underbody paneling from each side in the area of the reinforcement brace under the subframe **(see illustration)**.
9  Remove the nuts/bolts and remove the reinforcement brace from each side under the front subframe **(see illustrations)**. Discard the nuts/bolts - new ones must be installed.
10  Remove the steering column lower universal joint pinch-bolt and lift the column shaft upwards from the steering gear

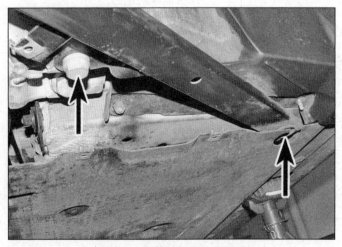

**11.9a  Remove the bolts at each end of the front reinforcement brace . . .**

**11.9b  . . . and the bolts in the center**

**11.10  Steering column lower joint pinch-bolt**

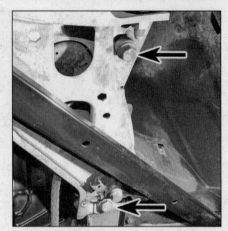

**11.13a  The front subframe is secured by two bolts at the rear on each side . . .**

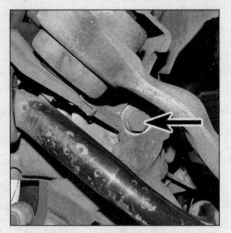

**11.13b  . . . and one at the front**

**(see illustration)**. Discard the pinch-bolt - a new one must be used. **Caution:** *Ensure the steering wheel/column is not rotated with the universal joint disconnected from the steering rack pinion. Damage to the column could result.*

11   Disconnect the wiring plugs from the ride height sensors (if installed), then disconnect the vacuum hoses from the engine mounts.

12   On models with electric power steering, cut the cable tie securing the wiring harness to the subframe.

13   Support the front subframe using a suitable jack and lengths of wood, then remove the mounting bolts at each side and carefully lower the subframe a maximum of 3.9 inches (10 cm) **(see illustrations)**. Pay attention to the power steering hoses/pipes as the subframe is being lowered - do not allow them to be bent or stretched. Note that the subframe bolts at the front are 3.5 inches (90 mm) long, the middle bolts are 5.7 inches (145 mm) long, and the rearmost bolts are 2 inches (53 mm) long. When installing, tighten down the front bolts first.

14   Disconnect the oil return hose(s) from the oil pan **(see illustration)**.

15   Note the installed positions of the various wiring plugs from the sensor(s) on the oil pan, then disconnect the sensors.

16   Loosen and remove the bolts securing the transmission casing to the oil pan.

17   Progressively loosen and remove the bolts securing the oil pan to the base of the cylinder block. Discard the bolts; new ones must be installed.

18   Break the oil pan joint by striking the oil pan with the palm of the hand, then lower the oil pan from the engine. Remove the gasket and discard it; a new one must be used on installation.

19   While the oil pan is removed, take the opportunity to check the oil pump intake pipe for signs of clogging or splitting. If necessary, unbolt the intake pipe, and remove it from the engine along with its gasket **(see illustration)**. The strainer can then be cleaned easily in solvent. Inspect the strainer mesh for signs of clogging or splitting and replace if necessary.

The bolts and sealing ring must be replaced.

20   Reinstall the oil pan gasket if it is not torn, otherwise use a new gasket.

## Installation

21   Thoroughly clean the mating surfaces of the oil pan and cylinder block.

22   Place the gasket in position on the oil pan flange.

23   Raise the oil pan up to the cylinder block, ensuring that the gasket stays in place, and install the new oil pan securing bolts, tightening them finger-tight only.

24   Tighten the oil pan-to-transmission and transmission-to-engine bolts to the specified torque.

25   Progressively tighten the oil pan-to-cylinder block bolts to the specified torque.

26   The remainder of installation is the reverse of removal, noting the following points:

a) *When raising the subframe into position, make sure that no pipes, hoses and/or wiring are trapped.*

b) *Use new subframe and reinforcement frame/plate bolts.*

c) *Tighten the engine mount nuts to the specified torque.*

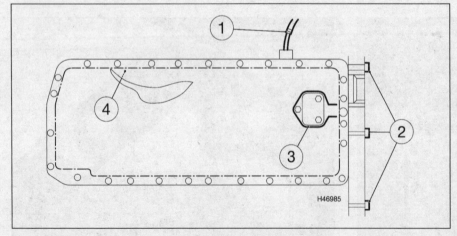

**11.14  Oil pan details**

| 1 | Oil return hose | 3 | Oil level sensor |
|---|---|---|---|
| 2 | Transmission-to-oil pan bolts | 4 | Oil pan retaining bolts |

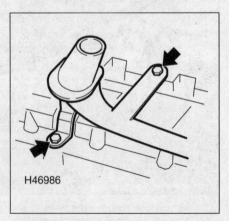

**11.19  Oil pump intake pipe retaining bolts**

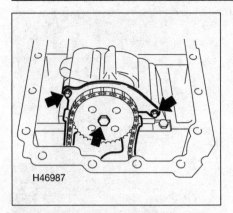

**12.4  Oil pump sprocket bolt and drive chain module bolts**

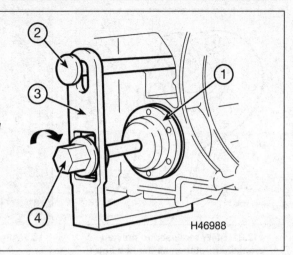

**12.9  Pump sealing cover removal details**

1    BMW tool No 11 9 200 - attached to the sealing cover using self-tapping screws
2    BMW tool No 11 4 362
3    BMW tool No 11 4 361
4    BMW tool No 11 4 364 - rotate clockwise to extract sealing cover

d)   On completion, refill the engine with oil (see Chapter 1).
e)   On automatic transmission models, check the transmission fluid level (see Chapter 1).

## 12  Oil pump and drive chain - removal and installation

### Oil pump

**Note:** *No separate parts are available for the pump. If defective, the complete pump must be replaced.*

#### Removal

*Refer to illustration 12.4*

1    Remove the oil pan and oil pick-up tube (see Section 11).
2    Remove the bolt securing the sprocket to the oil pump shaft, but leave the sprocket engaged in the drive chain.
3    Pull the sprocket and chain from the oil pump shaft.
4    Remove the mounting bolts securing the drive chain module to the pump **(see illustration)**.
5    Remove the retaining bolts and the oil

pump. **Note:** *Make a drawing or photo to indicate the location of the various-length bolts. Discard the bolts - new ones must be installed.*

#### Installation

6    Installation is the reverse of removal, noting the following points:
a)   *Replace all aluminum bolts.*
b)   *Tighten all fasteners to their specified torque where given.*

### Oil pump drive chain

#### Removal

*Refer to illustrations 12.9, 12.11, 12.13 and 12.21*

7    Remove the drivebelt (see Chapter 1).
8    Remove the bolt and remove the drive-belt tensioner.
9    The vacuum pump sealing cover must now be removed. BMW specifies the use of several special tools (No 11 9 200, 11 4 362, 11 4 361 and 11 4 364) to remove and install the cover **(see illustration)**. However, with care it is possible to pry the cover out using a screwdriver, and install a new cover without the use of special tools.

10   Rotate the crankshaft pulley bolt clockwise until the 3 holes in the vacuum pump drive sprocket align with the pump mounting bolts.
11   The pump sprocket must now be secured in position prior to removing the retaining bolt. BMW specifies the use of tools No 11 4 362 and 11 0 290 **(see illustration)**.
12   Remove the vacuum pump sprocket retaining bolt.
13   Use a screwdriver to push the drive chain tensioner to the right-hand side, and lock it in this position with a suitable rod or drill bit **(see illustration)**.
14   Pull the drive sprocket and chain from the vacuum pump shaft.
15   Remove the vibration damper (see Section 5).
16   Unscrew the bolt securing the sprocket to the oil pump shaft, but leave the sprocket engaged in the drive chain.
17   Pull the sprocket and chain from the oil pump shaft.
18   Remove the bolts securing the dive chain module to the pump **(see illustration 12.4)**.
19   Secure the engine at TDC on No 1 cylinder (see Section 3).

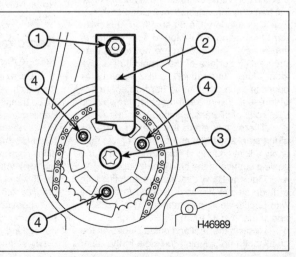

**12.11  Vacuum pump mounting details**

1    BMW tool No 11 4 362
2    BMW tool No 11 0 290
3    Sprocket retaining bolt
4    Pump mounting bolts

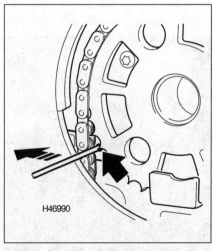

**12.13  Push the chain tensioner to the right-hand side and insert a 0.15 inch (4.0 mm) drill bit or rod**

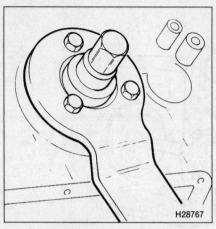

**12.21  BMW tool used to prevent crankshaft rotation as the hub bolt is loosened**

**13.5  Align the slots in the seal with the joints in the cylinder block**

**13.9  Inject sealing compound into the slot on each side**

20   The crankshaft pulley hub must now be released. This hub traps the crankshaft timing chain sprocket against the crankshaft shoulder. Consequently, once the hub bolt is loosened, the sprocket is free to rotate. Ensure the flywheel/driveplate and camshaft locking tools are in place. **Warning:** *The crankshaft pulley hub securing bolt is very tight. A tool will be required to counterhold the hub as the bolt is removed. Do not attempt the job using inferior or poorly-improvised tools, as injury or damage may result.*
21   Make up a tool to hold the pulley hub. A suitable tool can be fabricated using two lengths of steel bar, joined by a large pivot bolt. Bolt the holding tool to the pulley hub using the pulley-to-hub bolts. Alternatively use special tool 11 9 280 available from BMW dealers or automotive tool specialists **(see illustration)**.
22   Using a socket and a long swing-bar, loosen the pulley hub bolt. Note that the bolt is very tight. Unscrew the pulley hub bolt. Discard the bolt; a new one must be used on replacement.

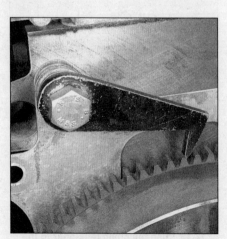

**14.2  Toothed tool used to lock the flywheel/driveplate in position**

23   Withdraw the hub from the end of the crankshaft. If the hub is tight, use a puller to draw it off.
24   Remove the plug from the timing chain cover, and unscrew the bolt securing the oil pump drive chain module to the cylinder block. Discard the bolt; a new one must be installed.

## Installation

25   Installation is the reverse of removal, noting the following points:
a) *Replace all aluminum bolts.*
b) *Tighten all fasteners to their specified torque where given.*

---

### 13   Oil seals - replacement

---

*Refer to illustrations 13.5 and 13.9*

1    To replace the crankshaft front oil seal, remove the crankshaft vibration damper (see Section 5). To replace the crankshaft rear oil seal, remove the flywheel/driveplate (see Section 14). While the flywheel/driveplate is off, this is a good time to check the clutch on manual transmission vehicles (see Chapter 8).
2    Carefully pry the oil seal from the cylinder block using a flat-bladed screwdriver or similar tool. Take great care not to damage the sealing surface of the crankshaft or cylinder block. Alternatively, drill 2 small holes opposite each other in the hard outer surface of the seal, insert 2 self-tapping screws, and use a pair of pliers to pull the seal out.
3    Thoroughly clean the sealing surfaces of the crankshaft hub and cylinder block, then apply a light coating of clean engine oil to the sealing surface of the crankshaft hub.
4    Genuine BMW seal kits are supplied with a guide sleeve already installed in the seal with Loctite sealing compound (No 128357) and primer (No 171000).
5    Position the seal and guide sleeve on the crankshaft hub, aligning the slots in the outer

circumference of the seal with the joint in the cylinder block **(see illustration)**.
6    Using the brush provided, coat both slots on the seal outer surface with the Loctite primer supplied. Allow the primer to dry for at least one minute before proceeding.
7    Using a suitable socket or piece of pipe, drive the oil seal into place as squarely as possible, until its outer edge is flush.
8    Using the brush provided, force Loctite primer as far as possible into the slot on each side of the seal.
9    Using the syringe provided in the kit, inject Loctite sealing compound into the slot on each side of the seal, then coat the surface of the sealing compound with primer **(see illustration)**.
10   Install the crankshaft vibration damper (see Section 5) or flywheel/driveplate (see Section 14).

---

### 14   Flywheel/driveplate - removal, inspection and installation

---

**Note:** *New flywheel/driveplate retaining bolts must be used on replacement.*

## Removal

*Refer to illustration 14.2*

1    On manual transmission models, remove the clutch assembly (see Chapter 8). On automatic transmission models, remove the transmission and torque converter (see Chapter 7B).
2    Prevent the flywheel/driveplate from turning by locking the ring gear teeth with a similar arrangement to that shown **(see illustration)**. Alternatively, bolt a strap between the flywheel/driveplate and the cylinder block/crankcase.
3    Loosen and remove the retaining bolts and remove the flywheel/driveplate, noting its locating dowel. **Caution:** *Be careful - the flywheel/driveplate is very heavy. Discard the*

**15.7  A ground strap is attached to the left-hand engine mounting bracket**

**16.3  Press the pilot bearing from the engine side of the flywheel**

bolts; they must be replaced whenever they are loosened or removed.

## Inspection

4    If the flywheel-to-clutch mating surface is deeply scored, cracked or otherwise damaged, then the flywheel must be replaced, unless it is possible to have it surface-ground. Seek the advice of a BMW dealer or engine reconditioning specialist.

5    If the ring gear is badly worn or has missing teeth, then it must be replaced. This job is best left to a BMW dealer or engine reconditioning specialist.

6    Manual transmission models are equipped with dual-mass flywheels. While the manufacturer does not publish any checking procedures, rotate the inner mass by hand counterclockwise, mark its position in relation to the outer mass, then rotate it by hand clockwise and measure the travel. As a general rule, if the movement is more than 1-3/16 inch (30 mm) or less than 19/32-inch (15 mm), consult a dealer or transmission specialist as to whether a new unit is needed.

## Installation

7    Clean the mating surfaces of the flywheel/driveplate and crankshaft and remove all traces of locking compound from the crankshaft threaded holes.

8    Install the flywheel/driveplate to the crankshaft, engaging it with the crankshaft locating dowel, and install the new retaining bolts. **Note:** *If the new bolts are not supplied pre-coated with locking compound, apply a few drops prior to installing the bolts.*

9    Lock the flywheel/driveplate using the method employed on removal, then tighten all the retaining bolts to the specified torque setting, in a diagonal sequence.

10   Install the clutch assembly (see Chapter 8) or the automatic transmission and torque converter (see Chapter 7B).

## 15   Engine mounts - check and replacement

## Check

1    Two engine mounts are used, one on either side of the engine.

2    If improved access is required, raise the front of the vehicle and support it securely on jackstands. Remove the fasteners and remove the engine splash shield.

3    Check the mount rubber to see if it is cracked, hardened or separated from the metal at any point. Replace the mount if any such damage or deterioration is evident.

4    Check that all the mount fasteners are securely tightened.

5    Using a large screwdriver or a crowbar, check for wear in the mount by carefully prying against it to check for freeplay. Where this is not possible, enlist the aid of an assistant to move the engine/transmission back-and-forth, or from side-to-side, while you observe the mounting. While some freeplay is to be expected, even from new components, excessive wear should be obvious. If excessive freeplay is found, first check that the fasteners are correctly secured, then replace any worn components as required.

## Replacement

*Refer to illustration 15.7*

6    Remove the towing hook from the tool kit in the trunk and thread it into the hole at the front of the engine, just inboard of the oil filter. Attach a hoist or engine support fixture to the towing hook, then take the weight off the mounts. Alternatively the engine can be supported from below with a jack and block of wood placed under the oil pan. Ensure that the engine is adequately supported before proceeding.

7    Remove the nuts securing the left and right engine mount brackets to the mount insulators, unbolt the mount brackets from the cylinder block, and remove the mounts. Disconnect any engine ground straps from the mounts (where installed) **(see illustration)**.

8    Remove the nuts securing the mounts to the subframe, then withdraw the mounts. Disconnect the vacuum hoses from the mounts as they are withdrawn (where applicable)

9    Installation is the reverse of removal. Tighten all fasteners to their specified torque where given.

## 16   Flywheel pilot bearing - inspection, removal and installation

## Inspection

1    The pilot bearing is installed into the center of the dual-mass flywheel, and provides support for the free end of the transmission input shaft on manual transmission vehicles. It can only be examined once the clutch has been removed (see Chapter 8). Using a finger, rotate the inner race of the bearing and check for any roughness, binding or looseness in the bearing. If any of these conditions are evident, the bearing must be replaced.

## Removal

*Refer to illustration 16.3*

2    Remove the flywheel (see Section 14).

3    The bearing must be pressed out using a hydraulic press with a drift that bears only on the inner bearing race. The bearing is pressed from the engine side of the flywheel and out of the clutch side **(see illustration)**. **Note:** *The act of pressing the bearing out will render it unusable - it must be replaced.*

**16.4a  Position the bearing . . .**

**16.4b  . . . and drive it into place**

## Installation

*Refer to illustrations 16.4a and 16.4b*

4    Using a suitable socket or piece of pipe, that bears only on the hard outer edge of the bearing, press the new bearing into the fly-wheel until it contacts the shoulder **(see illustrations)**.

5    Install the flywheel (see Section 14).

## 17  Oil pressure and level switches - removal and installation

## Oil pressure/temperature switch

*Refer to illustration 17.2*

1    The oil pressure switch is located on the left-hand side of the engine block behind the oil filter housing.

2    Disconnect the wiring plug, and unscrew the switch from the engine block **(see illustration)**. Be prepared for oil spillage.

3    Installation is the reversal of removal. Use a new sealing washer and tighten the switch to the specified torque. Check the engine oil level and add new oil if necessary.

## Oil condition/level switch

4    Drain the engine oil (see Chapter 1).

5    Remove the fasteners and the engine splash shield.

6    Disconnect the wiring plug, remove the three retaining nuts and remove the switch from the base of the oil pan.

7    Ensure that the oil pan mating surface is clean.

8    Install the switch with a new seal and apply a little thread-locking compound. Tighten the retaining nuts to the specified torque.

9    Install the engine splash shield, and refill the engine oil (see Chapter 1).

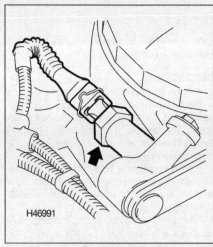

H46991

**17.2  The oil pressure switch is located behind the oil filter housing**

# Notes

# Notes

# Chapter 2  Part B
# 2.0L four-cylinder engine

## Contents

## Specifications

### General

| | |
|---|---|
| Displacement | 122 cubic inches (1999cc) |
| Bore | 3.307 inches (84mm) |
| Stroke | 3.527 inches (89.6mm) |
| Direction of engine rotation | Clockwise (viewed from front of vehicle) |
| No 1 cylinder location | Timing chain end |
| Firing order | 1-3-4-2 |
| Minimum compression pressure | 130 psi (9.0 bar) |
| Maximum deviation between cylinders | 29 psi (2.0 bar) |

### Camshafts

| | |
|---|---|
| Endplay | 0.003 to 0.005 inch (0.07 to 0.143 mm) |

### Lubrication system

| | |
|---|---|
| Minimum oil pressure at idle speed | 14.5 psi (1.0 bar) |
| Regulated oil pressure | 58.0 psi (4.0 bar) |

## Torque specifications

| | Ft-lbs (unless otherwise indicated) | Nm |
|---|---|---|

**Note:** *One foot-pound (ft-lb) of torque is equivalent to 12 inch-pounds (in-lbs) of torque. Torque values below approximately 15 foot-pounds are expressed in inch-pounds, because most foot-pound torque wrenches are not accurate at these smaller values.*

**Note:** *There are a number of aluminum fasteners used to prevent electrolysis between the different types of metals used. Whenever they are removed, they should be replaced with new aluminum bolts. They are easily identified, since a magnet will not stick to them as it would on steel fasteners.*

| | Ft-lbs | Nm |
|---|---|---|
| Camshaft bearing cap bolts | | |
|    Exhaust | 108 in-lbs | 12 |
|    Intake | 90 in-lbs | 10 |
| Camshaft sprocket-to-counterbalance shaft bolt* | | |
|    Step 1 | 15 | 20 |
|    Step 2 | 70 | 95 |
| Chain drive module-to-cylinder head | 90 in-lbs | 10 |
| Chain drive module-to-crankcase and oil pump | 90 in-lbs | 10 |
| Chain guide rail-to-cylinder block | 15 | 20 |
| Chain guide rail-to-cylinder head | 120 in-lbs | 14 |
| Chain cover plugs | 18 | 25 |
| Chain tensioner-to-cylinder head | 59 | 80 |
| Crankshaft vibration damper bolts | 26 | 35 |
| Counterbalance shafts module-to-bedplate bolts* | | |
|    Step 1 | 15 | 19 |
|    Step 2 | Rotate an additional 90-degrees | |
| Cylinder head bolts* | | |
|    M11 x 173 mm bolts | | |
|       Step 1 | 22 | 30 |
|       Step 2 | Rotate an additional 90-degrees | |
|       Step 3 | Rotate an additional 180-degrees | |
|    M9 x 173 mm bolts | | |
|       Step 1 | 22 | 30 |
|       Step 2 | Rotate an additional 90-degrees | |
|       Step 3 | Rotate an additional 180-degrees | |
|    M9 x 30 mm bolts | 16.5 | 22 |
|    M9 x 70 mm bolts | 16.5 | 22 |
| Engine mounts | | |
|    Mount-to-front axle support | 168 in-lbs | 19 |
|    Mount-to-support arm | | |
|       Left side mount | 41 | 56 |
|       Right side mount | | |
|          F30 chassis | 74 | 100 |
|          F31 and F34 chassis | 41 | 56 |
|    Support arm-to-engine | 28 | 38 |
| Driveplate/flywheel bolts* | | |
|    Step 1 | 44 | 60 |
|    Step 2 | Rotate an additional 45-degrees | |
| Front subframe bolts | | |
|    Front bolts (M12, 1.77 inches (45 mm) long) | 88.5 | 120 |
|    Middle bolts (M12, 6.4 inches (165 mm) long) | 88.5 | 120 |
|    Rear bolts (M14, 2.3 inches(60 mm) long) | 88.5 | 120 |
| Gear case plugs (M22 x 1.5) | 37 | 50 |
| High pressure fuel pump-to-valve cover bolts | 108 in-lbs | 12 |
| Oil condition/level sensor | 84 in-lbs | 9 |
| Oil filter cap-to-housing | 18 | 25 |
| Oil filter housing-to-cylinder head | 16 | 22 |
| Oil feed line-to-turbocharger | 90 in-lbs | 10 |
| Oil feed line from turbocharger-to-crankcase | 90 in-lbs | 10 |
| Oil return lines to turbocharger | 90 in-lbs | 10 |
| Oil return line from turbocharger-to-crankcase | 90 in-lbs | 10 |
| Oil pipe-to-cylinder head banjo bolt | 90 in-lbs | 10 |
| Oil pressure/temperature switch | 133 in-lbs | 15 |
| Oil pump hydraulic valve-to-crankcase bolts | 90 in-lbs | 10 |
| Oil pump pick-up pipe | 90 in-lbs | 10 |
| Oil pump-to-counterbalance shaft housing | 90 in-lbs | 10 |
| Oil spray nozzles | 108 in-lbs | 12 |

## Torque specifications (continued)

**Ft-lbs** (unless otherwise indicated)  **Nm**

**Note:** *One foot-pound (ft-lb) of torque is equivalent to 12 inch-pounds (in-lbs) of torque. Torque values below approximately 15 foot-pounds are expressed in inch-pounds, because most foot-pound torque wrenches are not accurate at these smaller values.*

**Note:** *There are a number of aluminum fasteners used to prevent electrolysis between the different types of metals used. Whenever they are removed, they should be replaced with new aluminum bolts. They are easily identified, since a magnet will not stick to them as it would on steel fasteners.*

| | Ft-lbs | Nm |
|---|---|---|
| Oil pan oil drain plug | | |
|     With all-wheel drive models (steel plug) | 18 | 25 |
|     Without all-wheel drive models (plastic plug) | 72 in-lbs | 8 |
| Oil level sensor-to-oil pan | 72 in-lbs | 8 |
| Oil pan | 90 in-lbs | 10 |
| Strut tower supports* | | |
|     Step 1 | 41 | 56 |
|     Step 2 | Rotate an additional 90-degrees | |
| Torsion damper hub-to-crankshaft (center bolt) | | |
|     Step 1 | 74 | 100 |
|     Step 2 | Rotate an additional 270-degrees | |
| Valvetronic settings | | |
|     Eccentric shaft bearing cap-to-cylinder head* | 84 in-lbs | 10 |
|     Eccentric shaft stop-screw-to-cylinder head | 84 in-lbs | 10 |
|     Electric servodrive-to-cylinder head | 84 in-lbs | 10 |
|     Electric servodrive-to-valve cover | 84 in-lbs | 10 |
|     Guide block-to-cylinder head | 84 in-lbs | 10 |
|     Oil spray nozzle-to-gate | 84 in-lbs | 10 |
|     Return spring-to-cylinder head | 84 in-lbs | 10 |
| Valve cover bolts | 84 in-lbs | 9 |
| VANOS solenoid valve-to-camshaft adjusters (center bolt) | | |
|     Step 1 | 40.5 | 55 |
|     Step 2 | Rotate an additional 55-degrees | |

*\* Do not re-use, replace with new fasteners*

## 1   General information

### *How to use this Chapter*

This Part of Chapter 2 describes the repair procedures that can reasonably be carried out on the engine while it remains in the vehicle. If the engine has been removed from the vehicle and is being disassembled (see Chapter 2C), any preliminary disassembly procedures can be ignored.

**Note:** *While it may be possible physically to overhaul items such as the piston/connecting rod assemblies while the engine is in the vehicle, such tasks are not usually carried out as separate operations. Usually, several additional procedures are required (not to mention the cleaning of components and oilways); for this reason, all such tasks are classed as major overhaul procedures, and are described in Part C of this Chapter.*

Part C describes the removal of the engine/transmission from the vehicle, and the full overhaul procedures that can then be carried out.

### *Engine description*
#### General

These engines are of 4-cylinder double-overhead-cam design, mounted inline, with the transmission bolted to the rear of the engine.

The cylinder block is made from an aluminum composite. Aluminum bolts are used extensively, and should never be re-used.

A timing chain from the crankshaft drives both the exhaust and intake camshafts. Hydraulic cam followers are installed between the camshafts and the valves. Each camshaft is supported by bearing caps bolted to the cylinder head.

The timing of both the exhaust and intake valves is variable by means of adjustable hydraulic sprocket or "adjustment unit" on the end of each camshaft - BMW refers to this as a VANOS system. These units vary the relationship of the timing chain and sprockets to the camshafts. The duration and lift of the intake camshaft is also variable by means of an electric motor-driven eccentric shaft which effectively varies the pivot point of a lever acting between the camshaft and the rocker arm - BMW refer to this as a Valvetronic system. Engine load is controlled by varying valve lift and duration, rather than throttle valve position. This virtually eliminates pumping losses, improves engine output and reduces emissions.

The crankshaft rides on six insert type main bearings. The endplay is controlled by thrust bearing shells located on the No. 4 main bearing.

The pistons are selected to be of matching weight, and incorporate fully-floating wristpins retained by snap-rings.

The oil pump and vacuum pump are chain-driven from the front of the crankshaft.

### VANOS variable camshaft timing control

On all models, a variable camshaft timing control system, known as VANOS, is installed. The VANOS system uses data supplied by the PCM/DME engine management system (see Chapter 6) to adjust the timing of both the intake and exhaust camshafts independently via a hydraulic control system (using engine oil as the hydraulic fluid). The camshaft timings are varied according to engine speed, retarding the timing (opening the valves later) at low speeds to improve low-speed driveability and high engine speeds for maximum power. At medium engine speeds, the camshaft timings are advanced (opening the valves earlier) to increase mid-range torque and to improve exhaust emissions.

## 2   Repair operations possible with the engine in the vehicle

Many major repair operations can be accomplished without removing the engine from the vehicle.

Clean the engine compartment and the exterior of the engine with some type of pressure washer before any work is done. A clean engine will make the job easier and will help keep dirt out of the internal areas of the engine.

Depending on the components involved, it may be necessary to remove the hood to improve access to the engine as repairs are performed (see Chapter 11 if necessary).

If vacuum, exhaust, oil or coolant leaks develop, indicating a need for gasket or seal replacement, the repairs can generally be made with the engine in the vehicle. The intake and exhaust manifold gaskets, valve cover gasket and cylinder head gasket are all accessible with the engine in place. Changing the oil pan gasket, however, requires virtually removing the engine to provide enough clearance for oil pan removal. Information on engine removal is in Part C.

Exterior engine components such as the intake and exhaust manifolds, the water pump, the starter motor, the alternator, the distributor and the fuel injection system can be removed for repair with the engine in place.

Since the cylinder head can be removed without pulling the engine, valve component servicing can also be accomplished with the engine in the vehicle.

The following operations can be carried out without having to remove the engine from the vehicle:

*Removal and installation of the
    cylinder head.
Removal and installation of the timing chain
    and sprockets.
Removal and installation of the camshafts.
Removal and installation of the oil pan.
Removal and installation of the connecting
    rod bearings, connecting rods,
    and pistons.\**

*Removal and installation of the oil pump.
Replacement of the engine/
    transmission mounts.
Removal and installation of the
    flywheel/driveplate.*

*\*Although it is possible to remove these components with the engine in place, for reasons of access and cleanliness it is recommended that the engine is removed.*

## 3   Top Dead Center (TDC) for No 1 piston - locating

1   Top Dead Center (TDC) is the highest point in the cylinder that each piston reaches as it travels up and down when the crankshaft turns. Each piston reaches TDC at the end of the compression stroke and again at the end of the exhaust stroke, but TDC generally refers to piston position on the compression stroke. The number one piston is at the timing chain end of the engine.

2   Positioning the number one piston at TDC is an essential part of many procedures, such as timing chain removal and camshaft removal.

3   Remove the air filter housing top and the spark plugs (see Chapter 1).

4   Remove the valve cover (see Section 4).

5   Raise the front of the vehicle and support it securely on jackstands (see *Jacking and towing*). Remove the fasteners and remove the engine splash shield.

6   Using a socket or wrench on the crankshaft center bolt, turn the engine clockwise at least two complete revolutions until the tips of the front cam (number one cylinder) lobes on the intake and exhaust camshafts are pointing upwards and slightly to the left-hand side.

7   Using a screwdriver, pull the seal plug from the timing hole in the left-hand rear corner flange of the cylinder block.

8   To lock the crankshaft in position, a special tool will be required. BMW tool No 2 219 548 can be used, but alternatives are available.

9   Lightly oil the tool then insert it through the timing hole. Turn the crankshaft clockwise until the rod enters the TDC hole in the flywheel/driveplate.

10   The crankshaft is now locked in position with No 1 piston at TDC.

11   In this position, it should be possible to place BMW special tool No. 83 30 2 212 830 (or equivalent) over the parallel flats of the camshafts. With the camshaft correctly positioned, the tools should contact the cylinder head upper surface with no clearance below them (see Chapter 2A, **illustration 3.10a**). Essentially, these tools hold the flat-sided ends of the camshafts at exactly 90-degrees to the cylinder head upper gasket face. In this position, the lobes of No. 1 cylinder intake camshaft should be pointing upwards at an angle.

12   **Do not** attempt to turn the engine with the flywheel/driveplate or camshaft locked in position, as engine damage may result.

## 4 Valve cover - removal and installation

**Note:** *The camshaft cover is made from magnesium alloy. Do not install steel bolts/studs into the cover, or excessive corrosion will result.*

### Removal

1 Disconnect the negative battery cable (see Chapter 5, Section 3).
2 Remove the engine cover, by lifting the front of the cover up and pulling it forwards.
3 Remove the strut tower crossbrace plastic push-pins and bolts then remove the brace.
4 Remove the sound insulator plastic retainers and lift the insulator off of the engine.
5 Remove the intake silencer (see chapter 4).
6 Loosen the clamps to the vent lines then disconnect the vent line from the valve cover.
7 Disconnect the electrical connectors to the variable camshaft control actuators, then remove the bolts and actuators from the valve cover (see Chapter 6).
8 Disconnect the fuel supply line quick-connect fitting (see Chapter 4), then remove the fuel line retaining brackets and remove the supply line to the fuel rail.
9 Remove and the high-pressure fuel pump line to the fuel rail, then remove the fuel rail and high-pressure fuel pump (see Chapter 4).
10 Remove the vacuum pump (see Chapter 9).
**Note:** *Discard the high-pressure fuel line – a new one must be used during installation.*
11 Unclip the oxygen sensor harness connector from the corner of the valve cover and place the harness out of the way.
12 Remove the servo flange bolts.
13 On N20 engine models, disconnect the electrical connector to the electro-pneumatic pressure converter then remove the mounting screws and place the converter out of the way.
14 Remove the ignition coils (see Chapter 5).
15 Remove the electrical harness cover then disconnect the positive battery cable nut and move the cable out of the way.
16 Remove the bolts in the reverse order of the tightening sequence **(see illustration 4.20)** and lift off the valve cover. Replace the gaskets. Discard the bolts - new ones must be installed.

### Installation

*Refer to illustration 4.20*

17 Before installing the valve cover, replace all the seals and gaskets.
18 Clean the gasket/sealing faces of the cylinder head and the valve cover.
19 Lay the valve cover in position, taking care not to disturb the gaskets.
20 Install the new valve cover bolts, then

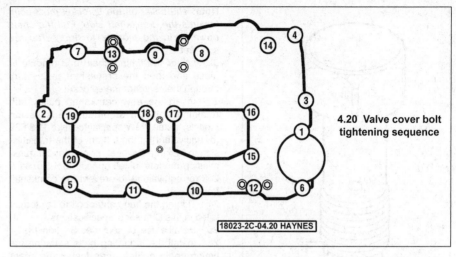

**4.20 Valve cover bolt tightening sequence**

18023-2C-04.20 HAYNES

tighten them evenly in sequence **(see illustration)** to the torque listed in this Chapter's Specifications.
21 The remainder of installation is the reverse of removal.

## 5 Crankshaft vibration damper - removal and installation

### Removal

1 Raise the front of the vehicle and support it securely on jackstands (see *Jacking and towing*). Release the fasteners and remove the engine splash shield (where installed).
2 Remove the drivebelt(s) (see Chapter 1).
3 Prevent the crankshaft from turning using special tool # 11 8 180 or 22 2 742 (or equivalent) that locks against the flywheel. Remove the six mounting bolts, and remove the vibration damper/pulley.
**Caution:** *Do not remove the crankshaft center bolt; if the center bolt is loosened or removed, the timing chain and oil pump sprockets will lose contact with the crankshaft, which will allow the intake and exhaust camshafts to turn independently of the crankshaft and severe engine damage will occur.*

### Installation

4 Install the damper mounting bolts and tighten the bolts to the torque listed in this Chapter's Specifications. Again, hold the pulley if necessary when tightening the bolts.
5 Install the drivebelt(s) (see Chapter 1).
6 Where applicable, install the engine splash shield.

## 6 Timing chain - removal and installation

**Caution:** *The timing system is complex. Severe engine damage will occur if you make any mistakes. Do not attempt this procedure unless you are highly experienced with this type of repair. If you are at all unsure of your*

*abilities, consult an expert. Double-check all your work and be sure everything is correct before you attempt to start the engine.*

### Removal

1 Remove the spark plugs (see Chapter 1).
2 Remove the valve cover (see Section 4).
3 Remove the crankshaft vibration damper (see Section 5).
4 Remove the crankshaft front oil seal (see Section 13).
5 Remove the drivebelt (see Chapter 1).
6 Remove the oil pan (see Section 11).
7 Secure the engine at TDC for No 1 cylinder (see Section 3).
8 Press the timing chain tensioner back using the timing chain guide the insert Special tool No. 11 4 120 (or equivalent) to lock the tensioner for the oil pump drive chain.
9 On automatic transmission models, install special tool No. 11 8 660 (or equivalent) at the bottom of the transmission to lock the flywheel and prevent the crankshaft from turning. On manual transmission models, install special tool No. 11 9 260 (or equivalent) to prevent the crankshaft from turning.
10 Remove the center bolt from the crankshaft. Discard the bolt; a new one must be used on installation.
**Caution:** *It will require 442 ft-lbs (600 Nm) of force to break the center bolt loose, a 3/4-inch-drive breaker bar and socket or air impact tool will have to be used.*
11 Remove the intake and exhaust camshaft VANOS adjusting units (see Section 7).
12 Remove the turbocharger wastegate vacuum unit bolts and move the unit back, slightly, to access the camshaft timing chain tensioner bolt head. Unscrew and remove the timing chain tensioner from the right-hand front corner of the cylinder head.
**Note:** *A new sealing ring must be installed.*
**Note:** *If the chain tensioner is going to be reused, its oil chamber must be drained. To drain the tensioner, place chain tensioner on a level surface and slowly compress the tensioner two times.*
13 The crankshaft pulley hub must now be released. Insert two vibration damper bolts

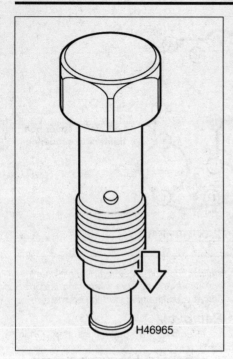

H46965

**6.28 Hold the tensioner upright and compress the piston a few times to evacuate the oil**

and pull the hub off the crankshaft.

**Caution:** *The crankshaft hub traps the crankshaft timing chain sprocket and oil pump drive gear against the crankshaft shoulder. Once the hub bolt is loosened, the sprockets are free to rotate. Ensure the flywheel/driveplate and camshaft locking tools are in place.*

14   Unscrew the large Allen-head plugs, one from the top right-hand corner and the two at the lower front section of the crankcase.

15   Remove the Torx screws for the timing chain module guides now accessible through the plug apertures.

16   Remove the timing chain module-to-cylinder head bolts and lift up the timing chain module, complete with chain and crankshaft sprocket. Note the orientation of the crankshaft sprocket (collar towards the crankshaft).

17   If required, disengage the chain from the sprocket and pull it upwards from the module.

## Installation

*Refer to illustration 6.28*

18   Ensure No 1 piston is still at TDC, with the crankshaft and camshafts locked in position (see Section 3).

19   Locate the plastic cap on the counterbalance shaft housing, next to the oil pump pick-up pipe mounting bolt, then remove the plastic cap on the top of the counterbalance shaft housing.

20   Install special tool No. 2 212 825 (or equivalent) into the hole the plastic cap was covering and lock the tool in place with a bolt. This will prevent the balance shaft from rotating out of time.

21   Engage the chain with the crankshaft sprocket.

**Note:** *The collar on the sprocket must point towards the crankshaft side. Pull the chain upwards in the module to firmly trap the sprocket.*

22   Lower the timing chain and module in place and feed the crankshaft pulley hub through the center of the sprocket.

23   Insert the **new** crankshaft pulley hub retaining bolt. On automatic transmission models, install BMW special tool No. 11 8 660 (or equivalent) at the bottom of the transmission to lock the flywheel, or on manual transmission models install special tool No. 11 9 260 (or equivalent) to prevent the crankshaft from turning.

24   Tighten the hub center bolt to the torque listed in this Chapter's Specifications.

25   Install a new oil seal (see Section 13).

26   Install the mounting bolts securing the timing chain guides, then install the cover plugs

27   Install the VANOS adjusters to the ends of the camshafts (see Section 7).

28   Holding it upright **(see illustration)**, compress the tensioner a couple of times to empty any stored oil. Install and tighten the chain tensioner with a new sealing washer.

29   Remove the flywheel/driveplate and camshaft locking tools, then rotate the crankshaft two complete revolutions clockwise. Check that the flywheel/driveplate and camshaft locking tools can still be inserted. If not, repeat the VANOS adjusting units procedure.

30   The remainder of installation is the reverse of removal, noting the following points:

a) *Replace all gaskets and seals.*
b) *Replace all aluminum bolts.*
c) *Tighten all fasteners to their specified torque values where given.*
d) *Install the drivebelt (see Chapter 1).*

---

## 7   Variable valve timing system (VANOS) components – removal and installation

### *VANOS intake and exhaust camshaft adjusters*

**Note:** *To test the operation of the VANOS intake and exhaust camshaft adjusters, special equipment is required. Testing must therefore be entrusted to a BMW dealer service department or other properly equipped repair facility.*

### Removal

1   Remove the valve cover (see Section 4).

2   Position the crankshaft and camshafts at TDC for the No 1 piston (see Section 3).

3   Remove the camshaft position (CMP) sensors from the cylinder head (see Chapter 6).

4   Remove the first camshaft cap lower mounting bolt for both camshafts, then install BMW special tool No. 83 30 2 212 831 (or equivalent) to the cylinder head and tighten

the tool down to lock the camshafts in place.

5   Starting with the exhaust camshaft adjuster, loosen the VANOS solenoid from the center of the VANOS adjuster unit, then loosen the intake camshaft adjuster VANOS solenoid.

**Note:** *The VANOS solenoid is also referred to as the solenoid center bolt.*

6   Remove the turbocharger wastegate vacuum unit bolts and move the unit back, slightly, to access the camshaft timing chain tensioner bolt head, then unscrew and remove the timing chain tensioner from the right-hand front corner of the cylinder head.

**Note:** *A new sealing ring must be installed.*

**Note:** *If the chain tensioner is going to be reused, its oil chamber must be drained. To drain the tensioner, place chain tensioner on a level surface and slowly compress the tensioner two times.*

7   Remove the VANOS solenoid valves (center bolt) from each camshaft adjuster unit, then slide the camshaft position (CMP) sensor wheel off of the adjusters. Be sure to keep them in order.

8   Slightly lift the timing chain up, then slide the exhaust camshaft adjuster forward while tilting it up, and remove the exhaust camshaft adjuster from the end of the exhaust camshaft.

9   Lift the timing chain up, slide the intake camshaft adjuster forward and remove the adjuster from the end of the intake camshaft.

### Installation

*Refer to illustrations 7.15 and 7.17*

10   Ensure that the crankshaft and camshafts are still at TDC on No 1 cylinder (see Section 3).

11   Position the camshaft VANOS units on the end of the camshafts, paying attention to the identifying marks. Note that although the VANOS units are marked IN and EX, the sensor rings are identical.

12   Install the camshaft position (CMP) sensor pulse rings on to the adjusters and set the timing chain on to the adjusters.

13   Place BMW special tool No. 83 30 2 212 830 (or equivalent) on end of the cylinder head. Starting with the intake camshaft adjuster, lift the chain up enough to rotate the adjuster until the alignment pin can be inserted from the special tool into the adjuster to lock it in place (approximately 2 o'clock position).

14   Place the timing chain over the intake camshaft adjuster, then lift the chain and rotate the exhaust adjuster until the alignment pin can be inserted into the adjuster to lock it in place (approximately 3 o'clock position) and lower the chain.

15   Mount BMW tool No. 83 30 2 212 830 (or equivalent) to the end of the cylinder head, ensuring that the locating pins of the tool engage correctly with the corresponding holes in the sensor ring gears **(see illustration)**. Screw the tool to the cylinder head using two old valve cover bolts.

16   Install the VANOS solenoid valve center bolt on each unit, and tighten them by hand

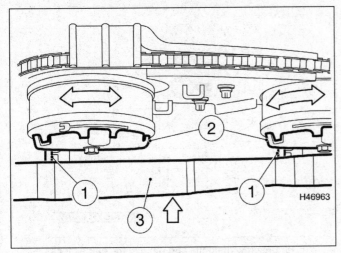

**7.15 Install special tool No 83 30 2 212 830 (or equivalent) (3) to the cylinder head and engage the pins (1) with the corresponding holes in the sensor ring gears (2)**

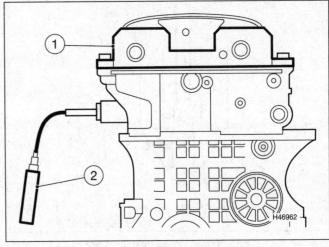

**7.17 Special BMW tool No 00 9 250 (1) and tensioner adjustment tool No 11 9 340 (2)**

until they just touch the sensor ring surface without any play.

17   Ensure that the timing chain rests correctly against the tensioner blade. Install BMW tool No 11 9 340 (or equivalent) into the tension piston hole, then turn the adjuster screw on the tool until the end of the screw just touches the tensioner rail without tensioning the chain **(see illustration)**.

18   Pre-tension the chain tensioner guide by screwing in the tool adjusting screw with a torque wrench to a value of 5.3 in-lbs (0.6 Nm). If no suitable torque wrench is available, turn in the adjusting screw by hand just enough to eliminate all freeplay in the chain.

19   Tighten both VANOS adjuster unit solenoid valves to the to the torque listed in this Chapter's Specifications.

20   Remove the retaining bolts and remove tool No 83 30 2 212 830 from the end of the cylinder head.

21   Loosen the adjusting screw, and remove tool No 11 9 340 from the tensioner piston aperture.

22   Ensure the timing chain tensioner piston has been drained completely, then install it to the aperture in the cylinder head with a new sealing ring. Tighten it to the torque listed in this Chapter's Specifications.

23   Remove BMW special tool No. 83 30 2 212 831 from the cylinder head

24   The remainder of installation is the reverse of removal, noting the following points:

a) *Camshaft cap bolts are installed and tighten to the torque listed in this Chapter's Specifications*

b) *Install the valve cover (see Section 4).*

c) *Ensure the crankshaft locking tool is removed prior to starting the engine.*

## VANOS actuators

**Note:** *The VANOS actuators are mounted at the end of the valve covers in front of each camshaft.*

25   Remove the engine cover, by lifting the front of the cover up and pulling it forwards.

26   Remove the strut tower crossbrace plastic push-pins and bolts then remove the brace.

27   Remove the sound insulator plastic retainers and lift the insulator off of the engine.

28   Remove the intake air duct (see Chapter 1, Section 23).

29   Disconnect the vacuum line holders and move he lines out of the way.

30   Working at the end of the cylinder head, disconnect the electrical connector to the VANOS intake or exhaust actuator.

31   Remove the actuator mounting bolts and pull the actuator(s) out of the valve cover.

32   Installation is the reverse of removal, making sure to replace he sealing ring on the actuator if it is damaged.

---

## 8   Camshafts and followers - removal, inspection and installation

**Caution:** *Numerous special tools are required to safely complete the following procedures. Ensure suitable tools are available prior to commencement.*

## Removal

1   Remove the VANOS adjuster units (see Section 7).

## Intake camshaft

*Refer to illustrations 8.15, 8.18 and 8.19*

2   In order to remove the intake camshaft, it's necessary to remove the Valvetronic intermediate levers as follows:

3   Remove the ignition coils (see Chapter 5).

4   Remove the fuel injectors (see Chapter 4), then remove the injector shaft tube fasteners and pull the shaft assemblies off the cylinder head. Once the shafts are out, remove the alignment dowels from the cylinder head.

5   Using an opened-end wrench on the slotted section, hold the shaft while adjusting the servo motor, using a 4 mm Allen wrench until the eccentric shaft is set to its lowest position (minimum lift).

6   Rotate the eccentric shaft so the lobes are in the middle between maximum and minimum stroke, insert a 6 mm Allen wrench into the Valvetronic servo motor located in the middle of the cylinder head, then remove the wrench from the eccentric shaft.

7   Remove the stop screw for the eccentric shaft from the cylinder head.

8   Remove the banjo bolt and remove the oil spray nozzle from cylinder No. 3.

9   Remove the minimum stroke stop from the cylinder head.

10   Place BMW special tool No 11 7 110 (or equivalent) over the return spring and against the cylinder head.

11   Rotating the knurled wheel on the special tool clockwise until both clamping arms in the tool lock the return spring in the gate of the tool.

12   The return spring is properly compressed when both clamping arms are parallel the top of the guide block.

13   Lift the first handle of the special tool,

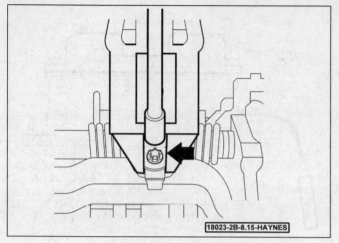

**8.15 Return spring retaining bolt**

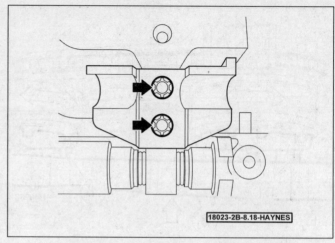

**8.18 Unscrew the bolts and remove the guide blocks**

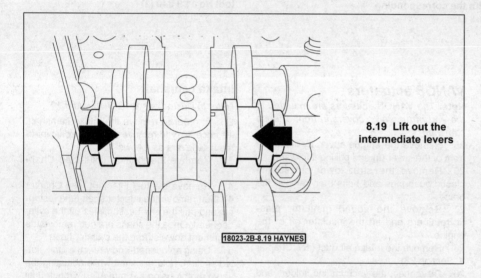

**8.19 Lift out the intermediate levers**

making sure both ends of the spring are in the lateral guides of the tool.

14 Rotate the second lever upwards, until the catch on the lever locks into the catch just below the first lever.

15 Remove the bolt securing the return spring to the cylinder head **(see illustration)**.

16 Compress the second lever slightly and unhook the catch the gradually release the spring tension by lowering the handle of the special tool.

**Caution:** *Release the spring tension gradually as there is a risk of personal injury.*

17 Force the coils apart and remove the return spring from the tool. Repeat this procedure on all the return springs. It's absolutely vital that the Valvetronic springs, lever and guide blocks, etc, are reinstalled to their original positions. Lay out the components in order on a clean, dry surface, so they can be identified and reinstalled to their original positions.

18 Remove the mounting bolts and each guide block **(see illustration)**. Again, lay the guide blocks out on a clean surface in order. It is essential they are reinstalled in their original positions.

19 Lift out the intermediate levers **(see illustration)**. Again, lay the intermediate levers out on a clean surface in order. It's essential they are reinstalled to their original positions.

20 Remove the PCM/DME control unit (see Chapter 6).

21 Gradually and evenly remove the retaining bolts, remove the bearing caps, and lift out the camshaft. Note that No 1 bearing cap incorporates a thrust washer. Lay the bearing caps out on a clean surface in order; it's essential they are reinstalled to their original positions. Check the camshaft bearing caps for identification marks. The caps are numbered from the timing chain end of the engine, and the marks can normally be read from the exhaust side of the engine. The intake camshaft caps are marked E1 to E7.

22 If required, remove the compression ring on the end of the camshaft by pressing one end of the ring into the groove, pulling up the other ring, and unhooking it. Take care as the ring is easily broken.

23 Lift the rocker arms from their locations and lay them out on a clean surface. Pull the hydraulic adjusters out and lay them on a clean surface. It is absolutely essential that the components are reinstalled to their original locations.

**Exhaust camshaft**

24 Remove the valve cover (see Section 4).

25 Check and adjust the valve timing if necessary (see Section 7).

26 Remove the timing chain module mounting bolts, the lift the chain module up and off of the cylinder head.

27 Remove the roller tappet from the center of the high-pressure fuel pump adapter then remove the pump adapter fasteners pump adapter from the cylinder head.

**Note:** *The bottom half of the high-pressure fuel pump adapter is the center two exhaust camshaft caps.*

28 Loosen the two remaining cap bolts a few turns at a time until the bolts are loose.

29 Working from the outside inwards, gradually and evenly remove the bolts securing the upper and lower camshaft bearing castings. Lift out the castings and camshaft as an assembly.

30 Carefully separate the upper and lower castings, then remove the camshaft.

31 If required, remove the compression ring on the end of the camshaft, by pressing one end of the ring into the groove, pulling up the other ring, and unhooking it. Take care as the ring is easily broken.

32 Lift the rocker arms from their locations, and lay them out on a clean surface. Pull the hydraulic adjusters out and lay them out on a clean surface. It's absolutely essential that the components are reinstalled in their original locations.

*Inspection*

33 Clean all the components, including the bearing surfaces in the bearing castings and bearing caps. Examine the components carefully for wear and damage. In particular, check the bearing and cam lobe surfaces of the camshaft(s) for scoring and pitting. Examine the surfaces of the cam followers for signs of wear or damage. Replace components as necessary.

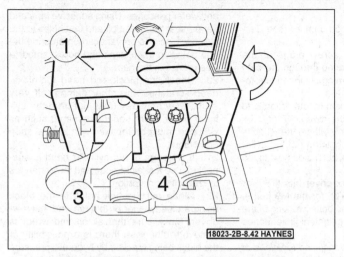

8.42  Guide block special tool mounting details

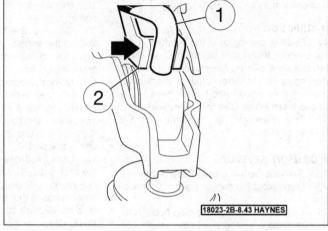

8.43  Check that the return spring (1) engages correctly with the intermediate lever (2)

(1)  Special tool No. 11 4 450        (3)  Bolt connection
(2)  Tool arm                          (4)  Guide block bolts

## Installation

### Intake camshaft

*Refer to illustrations 8.42 and 8.43*

34   Install the hydraulic adjusters and rocker arms in their original positions.
35   Ensure the flywheel/driveplate is still locked in the TDC position.
36   Lubricate the camshaft bearing surfaces with clean engine oil.
37   Install the intake so that the data code on the mounting flat is pointing upwards.
38   Position the camshaft so that the cam lobes point downward and slightly to the left as viewed from the back end of the camshaft. Install special tool No. 83 30 2 212 830 (or equivalent) on the camshaft (see Section 3).
39   Install the camshaft bearing caps to their original positions. Working evenly, tighten the retaining bolts to the specified torque listed in this Chapter's Specifications.
40   Install the intermediate levers to their original positions.
41   Install the guide blocks to their original positions. Install the retaining bolts, tighten them by hand, then loosen them 90-degrees.
42   Attach special tool No 11 4 450 (or equivalent) to the bolt connection of the Valvetronic eccentric shaft, and lift up the lever on the tool to tension the guide blocks **(see illustration)**. Tighten the block retaining bolts to their specified torque. Repeat this procedure on the remaining guide blocks.
**Note:** *The guide block at cylinder No 3 can only be installed with one bolt until the return spring has been reinstalled later in the procedure.*
43   Install the return springs to their original locations. Ensure the springs engage correctly with the intermediate levers **(see illustration)**.
44   Secure special tool No 11 7 110 (or equivalent) to the guide block, repeat Steps 10 through 14 and pull up the tool arm to tension the spring. Install the spring retaining

bolt, then tighten the bolt to the torque listed in this Chapter's Specifications. Repeat this procedure on the remaining return springs.
45   Install the oil spray nozzle for cylinder No 3, then tighten the bolt to the torque listed in this Chapter's Specifications. Ensure the nozzle points exactly at the actuator drive.

### Exhaust camshaft

46   Install the hydraulic adjusters and rocker arms to their original positions.
47   Install the exhaust camshaft into the lower bearing casting. The camshaft lobes for cylinder No. 4 must be pointing down towards the 4 o'clock position and the part number on the camshaft must face upwards.
48   Place the outer bearing caps over the camshaft ends then place the high-pressure fuel pump adapter over the middle of the camshaft. Insert the retaining bolts and tighten them finger-tight.
49   With the bearing caps seated, tighten the bolts gradually and evenly to the torque listed in this Chapter's Specifications.

### Both camshafts

50   Install the VANOS intake and exhaust adjuster units (see Section 7).

## 9    Valvetronic components - removal and installation

## *Eccentric shaft*

### Removal

1   Remove the intake valve intermediate levers (see Section 8, Steps 1 through 19).
2   Rotate the eccentric shaft with a wrench on the slotted section until its lobes are in the minimum lift position.
3   Remove the retaining bolts and remove the shaft bearing caps. Lay the caps out on a clean surface in order. It is essential they are

reinstalled to their original positions. Discard the bolts; new ones must be installed.
4   Carefully maneuver the eccentric shaft from position.
5   If required, carefully pull apart the bearing cages and remove the bearings from the shaft, then remove the shells from the bearing caps. Lay the caps/bearings out on a clean surface in order. Its essential they are reinstalled to their original positions.
**Caution:** *Only spread the bearing cages just enough to remove them from the shaft - they are easily broken.*

### Installation

7   If removed, install the bearing shells into their original positions in the bearing caps. The inner shell must be installed with the pointed end facing downwards, and the outer shell with the pointed end upwards.
8   If removed, install the magnetic sensor wheel to the shaft and tighten the bolt securely.
9   If removed, install the bearings to their original positions on the eccentric shaft.
10   Lubricate the bearing surfaces with clean engine oil, then install the eccentric shaft in the minimum lift position.
11   Install the bearing caps and tighten the new retaining bolts to the torque listed in this Chapter's Specifications.
12   Install the intermediate levers (see Section 8).

## *Servo motor*

### Removal

13   Disconnect the wiring plug from the positioning motor.
14   Remove the valve cover (see Section 4).
15   Using an Allen wrench, rotate the end of the positioning motor shaft clockwise until the tension on the eccentric shaft has been relieved.
16   Remove the motor mounting bolts and the motor - note one of the mounting bolts is

located under the motor. Discard the bolts - new ones must be installed.

## Installation

17 Position the motor in the aperture in the valve cover, then rotate the motor shaft counterclockwise with an Allen wrench and draw the motor into position against the flange. Install the new bolts and tighten them to the torque listed in this Chapter's Specifications.
18 The remainder of installation is the reverse of removal.

## *Position sensor*

19 Remove the valve cover (see Section 4).
20 Disconnect the sensor electrical connector.
21 Loosen the sensor retaining bolts. Note that the bolts are integral with the sensor - do not attempt to loosen them from the sensor. If fully unscrewed, the bolts *will* fall out.
22 Remove the sensor.
23 Installation is the reverse of removal.

---

## 10   Cylinder head - removal, inspection and installation

**Note:** *New cylinder head bolts and a new cylinder head gasket will be required on installation.*
**Caution:** *Do not remove the coating on the cylinder head bolts.*

## *Removal*

1 Drain the cooling system and engine oil (see Chapter 1).
2 Remove the intake plenum and exhaust module (see Chapter 4).
3 Remove the catalytic converter (see Chapter 4).
4 Note the installed positions of the clamps, then release them and disconnect the various cooling hoses from the cylinder head.
5 Remove the intake and exhaust VANOS adjustment units (see Section 7).
6 Remove the injectors (see Chapter 4), then remove the injector shaft tube fasteners and pull the shaft assemblies off the cylinder head. Once the shafts are out, remove the alignment dowels from the cylinder head.
7 Using an open-end wrench on the slotted section of the eccentric shaft, adjust the servo motor using a 4 mm Allen wrench until the eccentric shaft is at its lowest position (minimum lift).
8 Rotate the eccentric shaft so the lobes are in the middle between maximum and minimum stroke and insert a 6 mm Allen wrench into the valvetronic servomotor located in the middle of the cylinder head, then remove the wrench from the eccentric shaft.
9 Remove the stop screw for the eccentric shaft from the cylinder head.
10 Disconnect the electrical connectors to the cylinder head components, then remove the harness retainers and place the harness out of the way.
11 Remove the timing chain module-to-cyl-

inder head bolts.
12 Remove the vibration damper (see Section 5).
13 Remove the two screw plugs at the front of the engine. Working through the plug openings, release the timing chain module-to-crankcase bolts.
14 Move the timing chain module slightly to the side, then remove the reverse-Torx M9 x 30mm and M9 x 70mm cylinder head bolts from inside the timing chain end of the cylinder head and one on the outer side next to the first intake port.
15 Using suitable Torx driver bits (T60 for the M11 bolts, T50 or T55 for the M9 bolts), remove the cylinder head bolts, working in the order opposite that of the tightening sequence **(see illustration 10.30)**.
**Note:** *Keep track of the installed locations of the M9 bolts - they are different lengths.*
16 An assistant will now be required to help remove the cylinder head. Lift the cylinder head from the block - take care, as the cylinder head is heavy. As the cylinder head is removed, feed the timing chain through the opening in the front of the cylinder head, and support it from the cylinder block using wire.
**Caution:** *Do not set the cylinder head down on the sealing face. The valves protrude beyond the face and may be damaged.*
17 Remove the cylinder head gasket, then seal the oil pump galley openings in the cylinder block face with rubber/plastic plugs.

## *Inspection*

18 Cylinder head rebuilding requires special shop equipment. If the engine has over 100,000 miles on it and the heads have been removed for inspection or other work, the head should be brought to a competent automotive machine shop, where it can be tested for coolant leaks, resurfaced if necessary and the valves and valve seats machined.
19 The mating faces of the cylinder head and block must be perfectly clean before installing the head. Use a plastic scraper to remove all traces of gasket and carbon, and also clean the tops of the pistons. Take particular care with the aluminum sealing faces, as the soft metal is easily damaged. Also make sure that debris is not allowed to enter the oil

and water passages. Using adhesive tape and paper, seal the water, oil and bolt holes in the cylinder block. To prevent carbon entering the gap between the pistons and bores, smear a little grease in the gap.
20 Check the block and head for nicks, deep scratches and other damage. If very slight, they may be buffed out from the cylinder block. More serious damage, such as warpage, must be repaired with special shop equipment.
21 If warpage of the cylinder head is suspected, use a straight-edge and feeler gauges to check it for distortion.
22 Clean out the bolt holes in the block using a pipe cleaner or thin rag and a screwdriver. Make sure that all oil and water is removed, otherwise there is a possibility of the block being cracked by hydraulic pressure when the bolts are tightened.
23 Examine the bolt threads and the threads in the cylinder block for damage. If necessary, use the correct size tap to chase out the threads in the block.

## *Installation*

*Refer to illustration 10.30*
24 Ensure that the mating faces of the cylinder block and head are spotlessly clean, that the cylinder head bolt threads are clean and dry, and that they screw in and out of their locations.
25 Check that the cylinder head locating dowels are correctly positioned in the cylinder block.
26 Ensure the flywheel/driveplate is still locked in the TDC position (see Section 3).
27 Place a new cylinder head gasket on the block, locating it over the dowels. Make sure that it is the correct way up.
**Note:** *Thicker-than-standard gaskets are available for use if the cylinder head-to-block surface has been machined.*
28 With the help of an assistant, lower the cylinder head onto the block, engaging it over the dowels.
29 Use new cylinder head bolts that have the threads pre-coated. Do not apply any lubricant to the bolts, or wipe away the coating. Insert the new bolts, complete with washers where necessary, and tighten the bolts

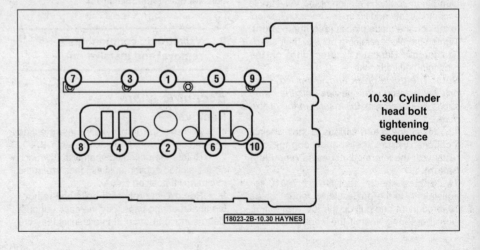

**10.30 Cylinder head bolt tightening sequence**

18023-2B-10.30 HAYNES

as far as possible by hand. Ensure that the washers are correctly seated in their locations in the cylinder head.

**Note:** *Do not install washers on any bolts which are installed in locations where there are already captive washers in the cylinder head. If a new cylinder head is installed (without captive washers), ensure that new washers are installed to all the bolts.*

30    Tighten the bolts in order to the Step 1 torque setting given in this Chapter's Specifications **(see illustration)**.

31    Tighten all cylinder head bolts to the Step 2 angle using an angle-measuring gauge.

32    Tighten bolts 1 through 10 to their Step 3 angle.

33    Install the reverse Torx M9 x 30 mm and M9 x 70 mm cylinder head bolts in their proper locations at the timing chain end of the cylinder head and tighten the bolts to the torque listed in this Chapter's Specifications.

34    Install the eccentric shaft stop screw and tighten it to the torque listed in this Chapter's Specifications.

35    Install the timing chain module (see Section 6). Clip the module to the left-hand guide, insert the retaining bolts tighten the bolts to torque listed in this Chapter's Specifications.

36    Install the VANOS adjustment units (see Section 7).

37    The remainder of installation is the reverse of removal. Refill the cooling system and engine oil, and install a new oil filter (see Chapter 1).

## 11    Oil pan - removal and installation

### *Removal*

1    Disconnect the negative battery cable (see Chapter 5, Section 3).

2    Remove the engine cover, by lifting the front of the cover up and pulling it forwards.

3    Remove the strut tower crossbrace plastic push-pins and bolts, then remove the brace.

4    Remove the sound insulator plastic retainers and lift the insulator off of the engine.

5    Remove the plastic wheelwell liner from each side (see Chapter 11, Section 10).

6    Drain the engine oil and engine coolant (see chapter 1).

7    Working under the vehicle, disengage the coolant hose retaining clips and disconnect the hoses from under the cooling fan shroud.

8    Disconnect the electrical connector to the steering gear then cut the cable tie securing the wiring harness to the subframe and move the electrical harness out from the subframe.

9    Remove the subframe outer bolts; nearest the front control arms then unclip the cable tie on the left side.

10    Remove the nuts/bolts and remove the left and right torsion struts from each side

under the front subframe. Discard the nuts/bolts - new ones must be installed.

11    Remove the steering column lower universal joint pinch-bolt and lift the column shaft upwards from the steering rack pinion. Discard the pinch-bolt - a new one must be used.

**Caution:** *Ensure the steering wheel/column is not rotated with the universal joint disconnected from the steering rack pinion. Damage to the column and airbag clockspring could result.*

12    The engine must be supported in position using an engine hoist or engine support fixture. Attach the hoist or fixture to the engine lifting eyes at the front and rear of the engine. Take the weight off the engine mounts.

13    With the help of an assistant, support the front subframe at four points, using a suitable transmission type jack with extendable arms or special jacking tool #00 2 030 and attachments 31 5 251, 253 and 255, then remove the mounting bolts at each side and carefully lower the subframe a maximum of 3.9 inches (10 cm). Pay attention to the power steering hoses/pipes as the subframe is being lowered - do not allow them to be bent or stretched.

**Note:** *The subframe bolts at the front are M12, 1.77 inches (45 mm) long, the middle bolts are M12, 6.4 inches (165 mm) long, and the rearmost bolts are M14, 2.3 inches (60 mm) long. When installing, tighten down the front bolts first.*

14    Disconnect the electrical connector to the oil level sensor.

15    Remove the bolts securing the transmission case to the oil pan.

16    Progressively loosen and remove the bolts securing the oil pan to the base of the cylinder block. Discard the bolts; new ones must be installed.

17    Break the oil pan joint by striking the oil pan with the palm of your hand, then lower the oil pan from the engine. Remove the gasket and discard it; a new one must be used on installation.

18    While the oil pan is removed, take the opportunity to check the oil pump intake pipe for signs of clogging or splitting. If necessary, unbolt the intake pipe, and remove it from the engine along with its gasket **(see illustration)**. The strainer can then be cleaned easily in solvent. Inspect the strainer mesh for signs of clogging or splitting and replace if necessary. The bolts and sealing ring must be replaced.

19    Reinstall the oil pan gasket if it is not torn, otherwise use a new gasket.

### *Installation*

20    Thoroughly clean the mating surfaces of the oil pan and cylinder block.

21    Place the gasket in position on the oil pan flange.

22    Raise the oil pan up to the cylinder block, ensuring that the gasket stays in place, and install the new oil pan securing bolts, tightening them finger-tight only.

23    Tighten the oil pan-to-transmission and transmission-to-engine bolts to the torque listed in this Chapter's Specifications.

24    Progressively tighten the oil pan-to-cylinder block bolts to the torque listed in  this Chapter's Specifications.

26    The remainder of installation is the reverse of removal, noting the following points:

a)    *When raising the subframe into position, make sure that no pipes, hoses and/or wiring are trapped.*

b)    *Use new subframe and reinforcement frame/plate bolts.*

c)    *Tighten the engine mount nuts to the torque listed in this Chapter's Specifications.*

d)    *On completion, refill the engine with oil and coolant (see Chapter 1).*

e)    *On automatic transmission models, check the transmission fluid level (see Chapter 1).*

## 12    Balance shafts, oil pump and drive chain - removal and installation

**Note:** *No separate parts are available for the balance shafts or oil pump. If defective, the complete pump must be replaced.*

### *Balance shafts and oil pump*

#### Removal

1    Remove the oil pan (see Section 11).

2    Install special tool No. 2 219 548 (or equivalent) into the timing hole to secure the crankshaft (see Section 3).

3    Remove the oil pump pick-up pipe bolt and remove the pipe.

4    Locate the plastic cap on the counterbalance shaft housing, next to the oil pump pick-up pipe, mounting bolt then remove the plastic cap on the top of the counterbalance shaft housing.

5    Install special tool No. 2 212 825 (or equivalent) into the hole the plastic cap was covering and lock the tool in place with a bolt. This will prevent the balance shaft from rotating out of time.

6    Install special tool No. 2 318 117 (or equivalent) to lock the balance shaft/oil pump sprocket in place.

7    Press the timing chain tensioner back until special tool No. 11 4 120 (or equivalent) can be inserted, then lock the tensioner in place.

8    Loosen the three timing chain module Torx screws a few turns then remove the oil pump drive shaft T60 Torx bolt securing the balance shaft/oil pump sprocket, but leave the sprocket engaged in the timing chain. Discard the bolt; a new one must be used on installation.

9    Remove the three chain module Torx screws and move the timing chain module and balance shaft/oil pump sprocket forward.

10    Remove the balance shaft and oil pump retaining bolts then lift them the assembly out.
**Note:** *Make a drawing or take a photo to indicate the location of the various-length bolts. Discard the bolts - new ones must be installed.*
11    Remove the balance shaft spacer bushings and check for damage; the balance shaft must be adjusted to fit correctly to the engine with the spacer bushings. Replace any that are damaged.
12    Remove the oil pump-to-balance shaft bolts and separate the oil pump from the balance shaft housing.

## Installation
13    Installation is the reverse of removal, noting the following points:
a) *Replace all aluminum bolts.*
b) *Tighten all fasteners to their specified torque where given.*
c) *Verify the valve timing (see Section 3).*

## Oil pump drive chain
### Removal
14    Remove the oil pump drive shaft bolt (see Steps 1 through 8).
15    On automatic transmission models, install special tool No. 11 8 660 (or equivalent) at the bottom of the transmission to lock the flywheel and prevent the crankshaft from turning. On manual transmission models install special tool No. 11 9 260 (or equivalent) to prevent the crankshaft from turning.
16    Remove the center bolt for the crankshaft hub. Discard the bolt; a new one must be used on installation.
**Caution:** *It will require 442 ft-lbs (600 Nm) of force to break the center bolt loose; a 3/4-inch breaker bar and socket or air impact tool will have to be used.*
17    The crankshaft hub must now be released. Insert two vibration damper bolts and pull the hub off the crankshaft.
18    Remove the chain module three Torx screws and remove the timing chain module with the sprocket.

### Installation
19    Check the camshaft gear flats for wear and the grip discs on the oil pump drive gear. The grip discs are welded on - if the discs are damaged, the oil pump drive gear must be replaced.
20    Press the timing chain tensioner back until special tool No. 11 4 120 (or equivalent) can be inserted and lock the tensioner in place.
21    On manual transmission models, install a grip disc to the crankshaft hub.
22    Install the oil pump drive module in first, then the camshaft drive module, if removed.
23    Insert the crankshaft hub through bolt modules.
24    Align the flats of the oil pump drive gear with the flats on the shaft, then install the module mounting bolts and tighten the bolts

to the torque listed in this Chapter's Specifications.
25    Install special tool No. 2 318 117 (or equivalent) to lock the balance shaft/oil pump sprocket in place.
26    Install the new oil pump drive shaft T60 Torx bolt and tighten the bolt to the torque listed in this Chapter's Specifications.
27    Install the new center bolt for the crankshaft hub. Secure the engine from rotating (see Step 15), then tighten the bolt to the torque listed in this Chapter's Specifications.
28    Installation is the reverse of removal, noting the following points:
a) *Replace all aluminum bolts.*
b) *Tighten all fasteners to their specified torque values where given.*
c) *Verify the valve timing (see Section 3).*

## 13   Oil seals - replacement

1    To replace the crankshaft front oil seal, remove the crankshaft vibration damper (see Section 5). To replace the crankshaft rear oil seal, remove the flywheel/driveplate (see Section 14), then remove the crankshaft position sensor (CKP) and magnet wheel (see Chapter 6).
**Note:** *While the flywheel is off, this is a good time to check the clutch on manual transmission vehicles (see Chapter 8).*
2    Carefully pry the oil seal from the cylinder block using a flat-bladed screwdriver or similar tool. Take great care not to damage the sealing face of the crankshaft or cylinder block. Another option is to drill two small holes opposite each other in the hard outer face of the seal, insert two self-tapping screws, and use a pair of pliers to pull the seal out.
3    Thoroughly clean the sealing surfaces of the crankshaft and cylinder block, then apply a light coating of clean engine oil to the sealing surface of the crankshaft.
4    Using a seal driver, a suitable socket or piece of pipe of the appropriate diameter, drive the oil seal into place as squarely as possible until its outer edge is flush.
5    Install the crankshaft vibration damper (see Section 5) or flywheel/driveplate (see Section 14) and crankshaft position sensor (see Chapter 6).

## 14   Flywheel/driveplate - removal, inspection and installation

**Note:** *New flywheel/driveplate retaining bolts must be used on installation.*

## Removal
1    On manual transmission models, remove the transmission (see Chapter 7A) and the clutch assembly (see Chapter 8). On automatic transmission models, remove the transmission and torque converter (see Chapter 7B).
2    Prevent the flywheel/driveplate from

turning by locking the ring gear teeth with a similar arrangement to that shown in Chapter 2A, **illustration 14.2.** Alternatively, bolt a strap between the flywheel/driveplate and the cylinder block/crankcase.
3    Loosen and remove the retaining bolts and remove the flywheel/driveplate, noting its locating dowel.
**Caution:** *Be careful - the flywheel/driveplate is very heavy.* Discard the bolts; they must be replaced with new ones whenever they are loosened or removed.

## Inspection
4    If the flywheel-to-clutch mating surface is deeply scored, cracked or otherwise damaged, then the flywheel must be replaced, unless it is possible to have it surface-ground. Seek the advice of a BMW dealer or engine reconditioning specialist.
5    If the ring gear is badly worn or has missing teeth, then it must be replaced. This job is best left to a BMW dealer or engine reconditioning specialist.
6    Manual transmission models are equipped with a dual-mass flywheel. While the manufacturer does not publish any checking procedures, rotate the inner mass by hand counterclockwise, mark its position in relation to the outer mass, then rotate it by hand clockwise and measure the travel. As a general rule, if the movement is more than one inch (30 mm) or less than half-inch (15 mm), consult a dealer or transmission specialist as to whether a new unit is needed.

## Installation
7    Clean the mating surfaces of the flywheel/driveplate and crankshaft and remove all traces of locking compound from the crankshaft threaded holes.
8    Install the flywheel/driveplate to the crankshaft, engaging it with the crankshaft locating dowel, and install the new retaining bolts.
**Note:** *If the new bolts are not supplied precoated with locking compound, apply a few drops prior to installing the bolts.*
9    Lock the flywheel/driveplate using the method employed on removal, then tighten all the retaining bolts to the specified torque setting, in a diagonal sequence.
10    Install the clutch assembly (see Chapter 8) and manual transmission (see Chapter 7A) or the automatic transmission and torque converter (see Chapter 7B).

## 15   Engine mounts - check and replacement

## Check
1    Two engine mounts are used, one on either side of the engine.
2    If improved access is required, raise the front of the vehicle and support it securely on jackstands. Remove the fasteners and remove the engine splash shield.

3    Check the mount rubber to see if it is cracked, hardened or separated from the metal at any point. Replace the mount if any such damage or deterioration is evident.

4    Check that all the mount fasteners are securely tightened.

5    Using a large screwdriver or a prybar, check for wear in the mount by carefully prying against it to check for freeplay. Where this is not possible, enlist the aid of an assistant to move the engine/transmission back-and-forth, or from side-to-side, while you observe the mount. While some freeplay is to be expected, even from new components, excessive wear should be obvious. If excessive freeplay is found, first check that the fasteners are tight, then replace any worn components as required.

## Replacement

6    Support the engine, either using a hoist or an engine support fixture connected to the engine lifting brackets (see Chapter 2C, Section 7), or by positioning a jack and a block of wood under the oil pan. Ensure that the engine is adequately supported before proceeding.

7    Remove the bolts/nuts securing the left and right engine mount brackets to the mount insulators, unbolt the mount brackets from the cylinder block, and remove the mounts. Disconnect any engine ground straps from the mounts (where installed).

8    Remove the bolt securing the mounts to the subframe, then withdraw the mounts.

9    Installation is the reverse of removal. Tighten all fasteners to the torque listed in this Chapter's Specifications.

## 16  Flywheel pilot bearing - inspection, removal and installation

This procedure is essentially the same as for the 3.0L six-cylinder engine. Refer to part A and follow the procedure outlined there However, use the flywheel bolt torque listed in this Chapter's Specifications.

## 17  Oil pressure and level switches - removal and installation

### Oil pressure/temperature switch

1    The oil pressure switch is located under the throttle body in the side of the engine block.

2    Disconnect the electrical connector and unscrew the switch from the engine block. Be prepared for oil spillage.

3    Installation is the reversal of removal. Use a new sealing washer and tighten the switch to the specified torque. Check the engine oil level and add new oil if necessary.

### Oil condition/level switch

4    Drain the engine oil (see Chapter 1).

5    Remove the fasteners and the engine splash shield.

6    Disconnect the wiring plug, Remove the three retaining bolts and remove the switch from the bottom corner of the oil pan.

7    Ensure that the oil pan mating surface is clean.

8 '   Install the switch with a new seal and apply a little thread-locking compound. Tighten the retaining nuts to the specified torque.

9    Install the engine splash shield, and refill the engine oil (see Chapter 1).

# Notes

# Chapter 2  Part C
# General engine overhaul procedures

## Contents

## Specifications

### General

2.0L (N20/N26) engine

| | |
|---|---|
| Displacement ................................................................ | 122 cubic inches (1986cc) |
| Bore ........................................................................ | 3.307 inches (84 mm) |
| Stroke ....................................................................... | 3.527 inches (89.6 mm) |
| Direction of engine rotation ....................................... | Clockwise (viewed from the front of the vehicle) |
| No 1 cylinder location................................................. | Timing chain end |
| Firing order................................................................. | 1-3-4-2 |
| Minimum compression pressure ................................. | 130 psi (9.0 bar) |
| Maximum deviation between cylinders ........................ | 29 psi (2.0 bar) |

3.0L (N52/N52K) engine

| | |
|---|---|
| Displacement................................................................ | 182 cubic inches (2996cc) |
| Bore ........................................................................ | 3.359 inches (85mm) |
| Stroke ....................................................................... | 3.467 inches (88mm) |
| Direction of engine rotation......................................... | Clockwise (viewed from the front of the vehicle) |
| No 1 cylinder location ................................................. | Timing chain end |
| Firing order ................................................................. | 1-5-3-6-2-4 |
| Minimum compression pressure.................................. | 130 psi (9.0 bar) |
| Maximum deviation between cylinders......................... | 29 psi (2.0 bar) |
| Camshaft endplay........................................................ | 0.0008 to 0.0060 inch (0.020 to 0.162 mm) |

### Lubrication system

Minimum oil pressure at idle speed

| | |
|---|---|
| 2.0L four-cylinder engine............................................. | 14.5 psi (1.0 bar) |
| 3.0L six-cylinder engine .............................................. | 21.7 psi (1.5 bar) |
| Regulated oil pressure.................................................. | 58.0 psi (4.0 bar) |

## Torque specifications

| | Ft-lbs (unless otherwise indicated) | Nm |
|---|---|---|

**Note:** *One foot-pound (ft-lb) of torque is equivalent to 12 inch-pounds (in-lbs) of torque. Torque values below approximately 15 foot-pounds are expressed in inch-pounds, because most foot-pound torque wrenches are not accurate at these smaller values.*

| | Ft-lbs (unless otherwise indicated) | Nm |
|---|---|---|
| Connecting rod cap bearing bolts | | |
| 2.0L engine | | |
| Step 1 | 15 | 20 |
| Step 2 | Rotate an additional 70-degrees | |
| Step 3 | Rotate an additional 70-degrees | |
| 3.0L | | |
| Step 1 | 15 | 20 |
| Step 2 | Tighten an additional 120 degrees | |
| Main bearing bedplate bolts | | |
| 2.0L engine | 16.5 | 22 |
| 3.0L engine | | |
| N52 | | |
| M8 | | |
| Step 1 | 84 in-lbs | 10 |
| Step 2 | Tighten an additional 90 degrees | |
| M10 | | |
| Step 1 | 132 in-lbs | 15 |
| Step 2 | Tighten an additional 90 degrees | |
| N52K | | |
| M8 x 37 mm | | |
| Step 1 | 72 in-lbs | 8 |
| Step 2 | Tighten an additional 90 degrees | |
| M10 x 100 mm | | |
| Step 1 | 15 | 20 |
| Step 2 | Tighten an additional 70 degrees | |
| M10 x 27 and 41 mm | | |
| Step 1 | 132 in-lbs | 15 |
| Step 2 | Tighten an additional 90 degrees | |
| Main bearing cap bolts* | | |
| 2.0L engine | | |
| Step 1 | 15 | 20 |
| Step 2 | Rotate an additional 90-degrees | |
| 3.0L engine | | |
| Step 1 | 15 | 20 |
| Step 2 | Tighten an additional 70 degrees | |

*\* Do not re-use.*

**Caution:** *All aluminum fasteners must be replaced with new ones whenever they are removed. If in doubt, try to attract it with a magnet (aluminum is not magnetic). Additionally, most aluminum fasteners are identified with a blue paint marking.*

**1.1  An engine block being bored. An engine rebuilder will use special machinery to recondition the cylinder bores**

**1.2  If the cylinders are bored, the machine shop will normally hone the engine on a machine like this**

## 1    General information - engine overhaul

*Refer to illustrations 1.1, 1.2, 1.3, 1.4, 1.5 and 1.6*

Included in this portion of Chapter 2 are general information and diagnostic testing procedures for determining the overall mechanical condition of your engine.

The information ranges from advice concerning preparation for an overhaul and the purchase of replacement parts and/or components to detailed, step-by-step procedures covering removal and installation.

The following Sections have been written to help you determine whether your engine needs to be overhauled and how to remove and install it once you've determined it needs to be rebuilt. For information concerning in-vehicle engine repair, see Chapter 2A or 2B.

The Specifications included in this Part are general in nature and include only those necessary for testing the oil pressure and checking the engine compression. Refer to Chapter 2A or 2B for additional engine Specifications.

It's not always easy to determine when, or if, an engine should be completely overhauled, because a number of factors must be considered.

High mileage is not necessarily an indication that an overhaul is needed, while low mileage doesn't preclude the need for an overhaul. Frequency of servicing is probably the most important consideration. An engine that's had regular and frequent oil and filter changes, as well as other required maintenance, will most likely give many thousands of miles of reliable service. Conversely, a neglected engine may require an overhaul very early in its service life.

Excessive oil consumption is an indication that piston rings, valve seals and/or valve guides are in need of attention. Make sure that oil leaks aren't responsible before deciding that the rings and/or guides are bad. Perform a cylinder compression check to deter-

**1.3  A crankshaft having a main bearing journal ground**

mine the extent of the work required (see Section 3). Also check the vacuum readings under various conditions (see Section 4).

Check the oil pressure with a gauge installed in place of the oil pressure sending unit and compare it to this Chapter's Specifications (see Section 2). If it's extremely low, the bearings and/or oil pump are probably worn out.

Loss of power, rough running, knocking or metallic engine noises, excessive valve train noise and high fuel consumption rates may also point to the need for an overhaul, especially if they're all present at the same time. If a complete tune-up doesn't remedy the situation, major mechanical work is the only solution.

An engine overhaul involves restoring the internal parts to the specifications of a new engine. During an overhaul, the piston rings are replaced and the cylinder walls are reconditioned (rebored and/or honed) **(see illustrations 1.1 and 1.2)**. If a rebore is done by an automotive machine shop, new oversize pistons will also be installed. The main bearings, connecting rod bearings and camshaft bearings are generally replaced with new ones and, if necessary, the crank-

**1.4  A machinist checks for a bent connecting rod, using specialized equipment**

shaft may be reground to restore the journals **(see illustration 1.3)**. Generally, the valves are serviced as well, since they're usually in less-than-perfect condition at this point. While the engine is being overhauled, other components, such as the starter and alternator, can be rebuilt or replaced as well. The end result should be similar to a new engine that will give many trouble free miles. **Note:** *Critical cooling system components such as the hoses, drivebelts, thermostat and water pump should be replaced with new parts when an engine is overhauled. The radiator should be checked carefully to ensure that it isn't clogged or leaking (see Chapter 3). If you purchase a rebuilt engine or short block, some rebuilders will not warranty their engines unless the radiator has been professionally flushed. Also, we don't recommend overhauling the oil pump - always install a new one when an engine is rebuilt.*

Overhauling the internal components on today's engines is a difficult and time-consuming task which requires a significant amount of specialty tools and is best left to a professional engine rebuilder **(see illustrations 1.4, 1.5 and 1.6)**. A competent engine

**1.5  A bore gauge being used to check the main bearing bore**

**1.6  Uneven piston wear like this indicates a bent connecting rod**

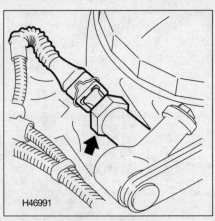

**2.3  The oil pressure sending unit is located behind the oil filter housing (six-cylinder engine)**

rebuilder will handle the inspection of your old parts and offer advice concerning the reconditioning or replacement of the original engine, never purchase parts or have machine work done on other components until the block has been thoroughly inspected by a professional machine shop. As a general rule, time is the primary cost of an overhaul, especially since the vehicle may be tied up for a minimum of two weeks or more. Be aware that some engine builders only have the capability to rebuild the engine you bring them while other rebuilders have a large inventory of rebuilt exchange engines in stock. Also be aware that many machine shops could take as much as two weeks time to completely rebuild your engine depending on shop workload. Sometimes it makes more sense to simply exchange your engine for another engine that's already rebuilt to save time.

## 2    Oil pressure check

*Refer to illustration 2.3*

1     Low engine oil pressure can be a sign of an engine in need of rebuilding. A low oil pressure indicator (often called an "idiot light") is not a test of the oiling system. Such indicators only come on when the oil pressure is dangerously low. Even a factory oil pressure gauge in the instrument panel is only a relative indication, although much better for driver information than a warning light. A better test is with a mechanical (not electrical) oil pressure gauge.

2     On 2.0L engines, the oil pressure switch is located on the side of the engine block, underneath the throttle body.

3     On 3.0L engines, the oil pressure sending unit is located on the engine block, near the oil filter housing **(see illustration)**.

4     Unscrew the oil pressure sending unit and screw in the hose for your oil pressure gauge. If necessary, install an adapter fitting. Use Teflon tape or thread sealant on the threads of the adapter and/or the fitting on the

end of your gauge's hose.

5     Connect an accurate tachometer to the engine, according to the tachometer manufacturer's instructions.

6     Check the oil pressure with the engine running (normal operating temperature) at the specified engine speed, and compare it to this Chapter's Specifications. If it's extremely low, the bearings and/or oil pump are probably worn out.

## 3    Cylinder compression check

1     A compression check will tell you what mechanical condition the upper end of your engine (pistons, rings, valves, head gaskets) is in. Specifically, it can tell you if the compression is down due to leakage caused by worn piston rings, defective valves and seats or a blown head gasket. **Note:** *The engine must be at normal operating temperature and the battery must be fully charged for this check.*

2     Begin by cleaning the area around the spark plugs before you remove them (compressed air should be used, if available). The idea is to prevent dirt from getting into the cylinders as the compression check is being done.

3     Remove all of the spark plugs from the engine (see Chapter 1).

4     Block the throttle wide open.

5     Disconnect the primary (low voltage) wires from the connectors at the ignition coils (see Chapter 5). Remove the fuel pump relay (see Chapter 4). The relays are located in the power distribution center in the engine compartment.

6     Install a compression gauge in the spark plug hole.

7     Crank the engine over at least seven compression strokes and watch the gauge. The compression should build up quickly in a healthy engine. Low compression on the first stroke, followed by gradually increasing pressure on successive strokes, indicates worn piston rings. A low compression reading on the first stroke, which doesn't build up during successive strokes, indicates leaking valves or a blown head gasket (a cracked head could

also be the cause). Deposits on the undersides of the valve heads can also cause low compression. Record the highest gauge reading obtained.

8     Repeat the procedure for the remaining cylinders and compare the results to this Chapter's Specifications.

9     Add some engine oil (about three squirts from a plunger-type oil can) to each cylinder, through the spark plug hole, and repeat the test.

10    If the compression increases after the oil is added, the piston rings are definitely worn. If the compression doesn't increase significantly, the leakage is occurring at the valves or head gasket. Leakage past the valves may be caused by burned valve seats and/or faces or warped, cracked or bent valves.

11    If two adjacent cylinders have equally low compression, there's a strong possibility that the head gasket between them is blown. The appearance of coolant in the combustion chambers or the crankcase would verify this condition.

12    If one cylinder is slightly lower than the others, and the engine has a slightly rough idle, a worn lobe on the camshaft could be the cause.

13    If the compression is unusually high, the combustion chambers are probably coated with carbon deposits. If that's the case, the cylinder head(s) should be removed and decarbonized.

14    If compression is way down or varies greatly between cylinders, it would be a good idea to have a leak-down test performed by an automotive repair shop. This test will pinpoint exactly where the leakage is occurring and how severe it is.

## 4    Vacuum gauge diagnostic checks

*Refer to illustrations 4.4 and 4.6*

1     A vacuum gauge provides inexpensive but valuable information about what is going on in the engine. You can check for worn rings or cylinder walls, leaking head or intake

**4.4 A simple vacuum gauge can be handy in diagnosing engine condition and performance**

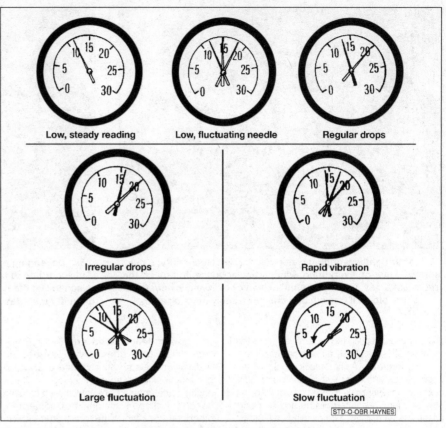

| Low, steady reading | Low, fluctuating needle | Regular drops |

| Irregular drops | Rapid vibration |

| Large fluctuation | Slow fluctuation |

STD-O-OBR HAYNES

**4.6 Typical vacuum gauge readings**

manifold gaskets, incorrect carburetor adjustments, restricted exhaust, stuck or burned valves, weak valve springs, improper ignition or valve timing and ignition problems.

2    Unfortunately, vacuum gauge readings are easy to misinterpret, so they should be used in conjunction with other tests to confirm the diagnosis.

3    Both the absolute readings and the rate of needle movement are important for accurate interpretation. Most gauges measure vacuum in inches of mercury (in-Hg). The following references to vacuum assume the diagnosis is being performed at sea level. As elevation increases (or atmospheric pressure decreases), the reading will decrease. For every 1,000 foot increase in elevation above approximately 2,000 feet, the gauge readings will decrease about one inch of mercury.

4    Connect the vacuum gauge directly to the intake manifold vacuum, not to ported (throttle body) vacuum **(see illustration)**. Be sure no hoses are left disconnected during the test or false readings will result.

5    Before you begin the test, allow the engine to warm up completely. Block the wheels and set the parking brake. With the transmission in Park, start the engine and allow it to run at normal idle speed. **Warning:** *Keep your hands and the vacuum gauge clear of the fans.*

6    Read the vacuum gauge; an average, healthy engine should normally produce about 17 to 22 in-Hg with a fairly steady needle **(see illustration)**. Refer to the following vacuum gauge readings and what they indicate about the engine's condition:

7    A low steady reading usually indicates a leaking gasket between the intake manifold and cylinder head(s) or throttle body, a leaky vacuum hose, late ignition timing or incorrect camshaft timing. Check ignition timing with a timing light and eliminate all other possible causes, utilizing the tests provided in this Chapter before you remove the timing chain cover to check the timing marks.

8    If the reading is three to eight inches below normal and it fluctuates at that low reading, suspect an intake manifold gasket

leak at an intake port or a faulty fuel injector.

9    If the needle has regular drops of about two-to-four inches at a steady rate, the valves are probably leaking. Perform a compression check or leak-down test to confirm this.

10    An irregular drop or down-flick of the needle can be caused by a sticking valve or an ignition misfire. Perform a compression check or leak-down test and read the spark plugs.

11    A rapid vibration of about four in-Hg vibration at idle combined with exhaust smoke indicates worn valve guides. Perform a leak-down test to confirm this. If the rapid vibration occurs with an increase in engine speed, check for a leaking intake manifold gasket or head gasket, weak valve springs, burned valves or ignition misfire.

12    A slight fluctuation, say one inch up and down, may mean ignition problems. Check all the usual tune-up items and, if necessary, run the engine on an ignition analyzer.

13    If there is a large fluctuation, perform a compression or leak-down test to look for a weak or dead cylinder or a blown head gasket.

14    If the needle moves slowly through a wide range, check for a clogged PCV system, incorrect idle fuel mixture, throttle body or intake manifold gasket leaks.

15    Check for a slow return after revving the engine by quickly snapping the throttle open until the engine reaches about 2,500 rpm and let it shut. Normally the reading should drop to near zero, rise above normal idle reading

(about 5 in-Hg over) and then return to the previous idle reading. If the vacuum returns slowly and doesn't peak when the throttle is snapped shut, the rings may be worn. If there is a long delay, look for a restricted exhaust system (often the muffler or catalytic converter). An easy way to check this is to temporarily disconnect the exhaust ahead of the suspected part and redo the test.

**5    Engine rebuilding alternatives**

The do-it-yourselfer is faced with a number of options when purchasing a rebuilt engine. The major considerations are cost, warranty, parts availability and the time required for the rebuilder to complete the project. The decision to replace the engine block, piston/connecting rod assemblies and crankshaft depends on the final inspection results of your engine. Only then can you make a cost effective decision whether to have your engine overhauled or simply purchase an exchange engine for your vehicle.

Some of the rebuilding alternatives include:

**Individual parts** - If the inspection procedures reveal that the engine block and most engine components are in reusable condition, purchasing individual parts and having a rebuilder rebuild your engine may be the most economical alternative. The block, crankshaft

**6.1  After tightly wrapping water-vulnerable components, use a spray cleaner on everything, with particular concentration on the greasiest areas, usually around the valve cover and lower edges of the block. If one section dries out, apply more cleaner**

**6.2  Depending on how dirty the engine is, let the cleaner soak in according to the directions and then hose off the grime and cleaner. Get the rinse water down into every area you can get at; then dry important components with a hair dryer or paper towels**

and piston/connecting rod assemblies should all be inspected carefully by a machine shop first.

**Short block** - A short block consists of an engine block with a crankshaft and piston/connecting rod assemblies already installed. All new bearings are incorporated and all clearances will be correct. The existing camshafts, valve train components, cylinder head and external parts can be bolted to the short block with little or no machine shop work necessary.

**Long block** - A long block consists of a short block plus an oil pump, oil pan, cylinder head, valve cover, camshaft and valve train components, timing sprockets and chain or gears and timing cover. All components are installed with new bearings, seals and gaskets incorporated throughout. The installation of manifolds and external parts is all that's necessary.

**6.3  Get an engine stand sturdy enough to firmly support the engine while you're working on it. Stay away from three-wheeled models: they have a tendency to tip over more easily, so get a four-wheeled unit**

**Low mileage used engines** - Some companies now offer low mileage used engines which is a very cost effective way to get your vehicle up and running again. These engines often come from vehicles which have been in totaled in accidents or come from other countries which have a higher vehicle turn over rate. A low mileage used engine also usually has a similar warranty like the newly remanufactured engines.

Give careful thought to which alternative is best for you and discuss the situation with local automotive machine shops, auto parts dealers and experienced rebuilders before ordering or purchasing replacement parts.

## 6   Engine removal - methods and precautions

*Refer to illustrations 6.1, 6.2, 6.3 and 6.4*

If you've decided that an engine must be removed for overhaul or major repair work, several preliminary steps should be taken. Read all removal and installation procedures carefully prior to committing to this job.

Locating a suitable place to work is extremely important. Adequate work space, along with storage space for the vehicle, will be needed. If a shop or garage isn't available, at the very least a flat, level, clean work surface made of concrete or asphalt is required.

Cleaning the engine compartment and engine before beginning the removal procedure will help keep tools clean and organized **(see illustrations 6.1 and 6.2)**.

An engine hoist will also be necessary. Make sure the hoist is rated in excess of the weight of the engine. Safety is of primary importance, considering the potential hazards involved in removing the engine from the vehicle.

If you're a novice at engine removal, get at least one helper. One person cannot easily do all the things you need to do to remove a big heavy engine from the engine compartment. Also helpful is to seek advice and assistance from someone who's experienced in engine removal.

Plan the operation ahead of time. Arrange for or obtain all of the tools and equipment you'll need prior to beginning the job **(see illustrations 6.3 and 6.4)**. Some of

**6.4  A clutch alignment tool is necessary if you plan to install a rebuilt engine mated to a manual transmission**

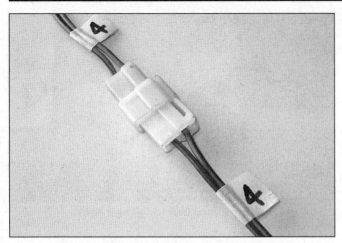

7.7a  Label both ends of each wire and hose before disconnecting them

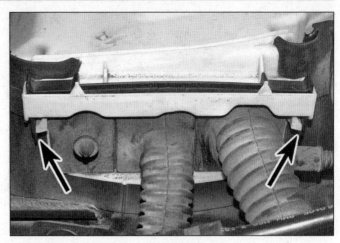

7.7b  Press out the retaining clips and pull up the black plastic locking catch at each end . . .

the equipment necessary to perform engine removal and installation safely and with relative ease are (in addition to an engine hoist) a heavy duty floor jack (preferably fitted with a transmission jack head adapter), complete sets of wrenches and sockets as described in the front of this manual, wooden blocks, plenty of rags and cleaning solvent for mopping up spilled oil, coolant and gasoline.

Plan for the vehicle to be out of use for quite a while. A machine shop can do the work that is beyond the scope of the home mechanic. Machine shops often have a busy schedule, so before removing the engine, consult the shop for an estimate of how long it will take to rebuild or repair the components that may need work.

---

### 7   Engine - removal and installation

**Warning:** *Gasoline is extremely flammable, so take extra precautions when you work on any part of the fuel system. Don't smoke or allow open flames or bare light bulbs near the*

*work area, and don't work in a garage where a gas-type appliance (such as a water heater or clothes dryer) is present. Since gasoline is carcinogenic, wear fuel-resistant gloves when there's a possibility of being exposed to fuel, and, if you spill any fuel on your skin, rinse it off immediately with soap and water. Mop up any spills immediately and do not store fuel-soaked rags where they could ignite. The fuel system is under constant pressure, so, if any fuel lines are to be disconnected, the fuel pressure in the system must be relieved first (see Chapter 4 for more information). When you perform any kind of work on the fuel system, wear safety glasses and have a Class B type fire extinguisher on hand.*
**Warning:** *The engine must be completely cool before beginning this procedure.*
**Note:** *This is an involved operation. Read through the procedure thoroughly before starting work, and ensure that adequate lifting tackle and jacking/support equipment is available. Make notes during disassembly to ensure that all wiring/hoses and brackets are correctly repositioned and routed during reassembly.*

### Removal

*Refer to illustrations 7.7a. 7.7b, 7.7c, 7.7d, 7.15a, 7.15b, 7.19 and 7.20*
1   Remove the hood (see Chapter 11).
2   Depressurize the fuel system (see Chapter 4), then disconnect the battery negative cable (see Chapter 5).
3   Drain the cooling system (see Chapter 1).
4   Drain the engine oil (see Chapter 1).
5   Remove the transmission (see Chapter 7A or 7B).
6   Remove the drivebelt (see Chapter 1), then unbolt the air conditioning compressor from the engine, release the pipes from the retaining clips, and support the compressor clear of the working area (see Chapter 3). **Warning:** *Do not disconnect the refrigerant lines refer to Chapter 3 for precautions to be taken.*
7   Make a note of their locations, then disconnect the engine wiring harness connectors from the electric box **(see illustrations)**.
8   Remove the fuel rail and injectors (see Chapter 4).
9   Remove the air filter housing and intake manifold.

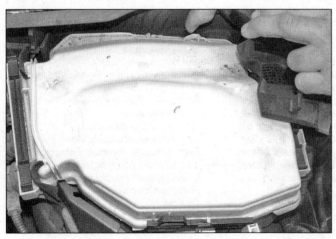

7.7c  . . . then slide the front and rear locking clip to the unlock position

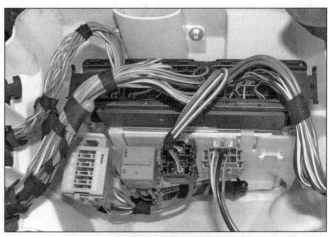

7.7d  Disconnect the engine wiring harness plugs

7.15a  Disconnect the ground strap from the mounting
to the body . . .

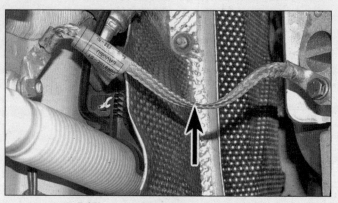

7.15b  . . . and from the cylinder head

7.19  Remove the reinforcement bolts
(center bolts shown)

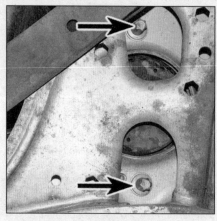

7.20  Remove the bolts securing the
mount to the subframe

## Installation

22   Installation is the reverse of removal, noting the following points:

a) *Tighten all fasteners to the specified torque where given.*

b) *Ensure that all wiring, hoses and brackets are positioned and routed as noted before removal.*

c) *Install the transmission as described in Chapter 7A or 7B.*

d) *On completion, refill the engine with oil, and refill the cooling system as described in Chapter 1.*

## 8   Engine overhaul - disassembly sequence

1   It's much easier to remove the external components if it's mounted on a portable engine stand. A stand can often be rented quite cheaply from an equipment rental yard. Before the engine is mounted on a stand, the flywheel/driveplate should be removed from the engine.

2   If a stand isn't available, it's possible to remove the external engine components with it blocked up on the floor. Be extra careful not to tip or drop the engine when working without a stand.

3   If you're going to obtain a rebuilt engine, all external components must come off first, to be transferred to the replacement engine. These components include:

*Clutch and flywheel (models with manual transmission)*

*Driveplate (models with automatic transmission)*

*Ignition system components*

*Emissions-related components*

*Engine mounts and mount brackets*

*Turbocharger (if, equipped)*

*Intake/exhaust manifolds*

*Fuel injection components*

*Oil filter*

*Ignition coils and spark plugs*

*Thermostat and housing assembly*

*Water pump*

10   Remove the radiator, cooling fan and shroud (see Chapter 3).

11   Disconnect the various coolant hoses from the engine and remove the coolant pump (see Chapter 3).

12   Disconnect the exhaust system and, on F-series chassis models, remove the catalytic converter (see Chapter 6).

13   Unbolt the power steering pump and move it to one side - there's no need to disconnect the fluid hoses (see Chapter 10).

14   Unless a hoist is available which is capable of lifting the engine out over the front of the vehicle with the vehicle raised, it will now be necessary to remove the jackstands and lower the vehicle to the ground. Ensure that the engine is adequately supported during the lowering procedure. **Note:** *On the F-series chassis, the manufacturer recommends removing the transmission to allow for easier removal and installation of the engine (see Chapter 7A or 7B).*

15   Unbolt the ground strap(s) from the engine mounting bracket(s), and from the cylinder head to the right-hand inner fender (where applicable) **(see illustrations)**.

16   Make a final check to ensure that all relevant hoses, pipes and wiring have been disconnected from the engine and moved clear to allow the engine to be lifted out.

17   Position the lifting tackle and hoist to support the engine from the lifting eye at the rear left-hand corner of the cylinder block. At the front left of the engine, just inboard of the oil filter, there is a threaded hole; install the towing hook (located in the tool kit in the trunk) into this hole and connect the other hoist chain to it.

18   Raise the hoist just enough to take the weight of the engine.

19   Remove the underbody protection panels to access the reinforcement frame bolts on each side. Unscrew the bolts and remove the frame **(see illustration)**. Discard the bolts; new ones must be installed.

20   Unscrew the nuts securing the left-hand engine mounting bracket to the mounting rubber/block, unbolt the mounting bracket from the cylinder block, then the mounting from the subframe, and remove the mounting bracket. Remove the bolts securing the right-hand mounting/block to the subframe **(see illustration)**. Unclip any hoses/pipes from the support brackets.

21   With the aid of an assistant, raise the hoist, and maneuver the engine from the engine compartment. Access is limited – take care not to damage any wiring, hoses, etc, as the engine is removed.

**Note:** *When removing the external components from the engine, pay close attention to details that may be helpful or important during installation. Note the installed position of gaskets, seals, spacers, pins, brackets, washers, bolts and other small items.*

4    If you're going to obtain a short block (assembled engine block, crankshaft, pistons and connecting rods), remove the timing chain, cylinder head, oil pan, oil pump pick-up tube, oil pump and water pump from your engine so that you can turn in your old short block to the rebuilder as a core. See *Engine rebuilding alternatives* for additional information regarding the different possibilities to be considered.

## 9    Pistons and connecting rods - removal and installation

### *Removal*

*Refer to illustrations 9.1, 9.3, 9.4a and 9.4b*

**Note:** *Prior to removing the piston/connecting rod assemblies, remove the cylinder head and oil pan (see Chapter 2A).*

1    Use your fingernail to feel if a ridge has formed at the upper limit of ring travel (about 1/4-inch down from the top of each cylinder). If carbon deposits or cylinder wear have produced ridges, they must be completely removed with a special tool **(see illustration)**. Follow the manufacturer's instructions provided with the tool. Failure to remove the ridges before attempting to remove the piston/connecting rod assemblies may result in piston breakage.

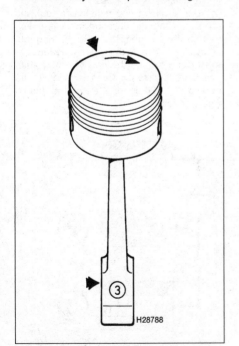

**9.4a  The cylinder number markings should be located on the exhaust manifold side of the connecting rod and the arrow on the piston crown should point towards the front of the engine**

**9.1  Before you try to remove the pistons, use a ridge reamer to remove the raised material (ridge) from the top of the cylinders**

2    After the cylinder ridges have been removed, turn the engine so the crankshaft is facing up.

3    Before the main bearing cap assembly and connecting rods are removed, check the connecting rod endplay with feeler gauges. Slide them between the first connecting rod and the crankshaft throw until the play is removed **(see illustration)**. Repeat this procedure for each connecting rod. The endplay is equal to the thickness of the feeler gauge(s). Check with an automotive machine shop for the endplay service limit (a typical end play limit should measure between 0.005 to 0.015 inch [0.127 to 0.369 mm]). If the play exceeds the service limit, new connecting rods will be required. If new rods (or a new crankshaft) are installed, the endplay may fall under the minimum allowable. If it does, the rods will have to be machined to restore it. If necessary, consult an automotive machine shop for advice.

4    Check the connecting rods and caps for identification marks. If they aren't plainly marked, use paint or marker to clearly identify each rod and cap (1, 2, 3, etc., depending on the cylinder they're associated with) **(see illustration)**.

**9.3  Checking the connecting rod endplay (side clearance)**

5    Loosen each of the connecting rod cap bolts 1/2-turn at a time until they can be removed by hand. **Note:** *New connecting rod cap bolts must be used when reassembling the engine, but save the old bolts for use when checking the connecting rod bearing oil clearance.*

6    Remove the number one connecting rod cap and bearing insert. Don't drop the bearing insert out of the cap.

7    Remove the bearing insert and push the connecting rod/piston assembly out through the top of the engine. Use a wooden or plastic hammer handle to push on the upper bearing surface in the connecting rod. If resistance is felt, double-check to make sure that all of the ridge was removed from the cylinder.

8    Repeat the procedure for the remaining cylinders.

9    After removal, reassemble the connecting rod caps and bearing inserts in their respective connecting rods and install the cap bolts finger tight. Leaving the old bearing inserts in place until reassembly will help prevent the connecting rod bearing surfaces from being accidentally nicked or gouged.

10    The pistons and connecting rods are now ready for inspection and overhaul at an automotive machine shop.

**9.4b  If the connecting rods and caps are not marked, use permanent ink or paint to mark the caps to the rods by cylinder number (for example, this would be the No. 4 connecting rod)**

**9.13 Install the piston ring into the cylinder then push it down into position using a piston so the ring will be square in the cylinder**

**9.14 With the ring square in the cylinder, measure the ring end gap with a feeler gauge**

## Piston ring installation

*Refer to illustrations 9.13, 9.14, 9.15, 9.18, 9.19a, 9.19b and 9.22*

11   Before installing the new piston rings, the ring end gaps must be checked. It's assumed that the piston ring side clearance has been checked and verified correct.

12   Lay out the piston/connecting rod assemblies and the new ring sets so the ring sets will be matched with the same piston and cylinder during the end gap measurement and engine assembly.

13   Insert the top (number one) ring into the first cylinder and square it up with the cylinder walls by pushing it in with the top of the piston **(see illustration)**. The ring should be near the bottom of the cylinder, at the lower limit of ring travel.

14   To measure the end gap, slip feeler gauges between the ends of the ring until a gauge equal to the gap width is found **(see illustration)**. The feeler gauge should slide between the ring ends with a slight amount of drag. A typical ring gap should fall between 0.010 and 0.020 inch [0.25 to 0.50 mm] for compression rings and up to 0.030 inch [0.76 mm] for the oil ring steel rails. If the gap is larger or smaller than specified, double-check to make sure you have the correct rings before proceeding.

15   If the gap is too small, it must be enlarged or the ring ends may come in contact with each other during engine operation, which can cause serious damage to the engine. If necessary, increase the end gaps by filing the ring ends very carefully with a fine file. Mount the file in a vise equipped with soft jaws, slip the ring over the file with the ends contacting the file face and slowly move the ring to remove material from the ends. When performing this operation, file only by pushing the ring from the outside end of the file towards the vise **(see illustration)**.

16   Excess end gap isn't critical unless it's greater than 0.040 inch (1.01 mm). Again, double-check to make sure you have the cor-

rect ring type.

17   Repeat the procedure for each ring that will be installed in the first cylinder and for each ring in the remaining cylinders. Remember to keep rings, pistons and cylinders matched up.

18   Once the ring end gaps have been checked/corrected, the rings can be installed on the pistons **(see illustration)**.

19   The oil control ring (lowest one on the piston) is usually installed first. It's composed of three separate components. Slip the spacer/expander into the groove **(see illustration)**. If an anti-rotation tang is used, make sure it's inserted into the drilled hole in the ring groove. Next, install the upper side rail in the same manner **(see illustration)**. Don't use a piston ring installation tool on the oil ring side rails, as they may be damaged. Instead, place one end of the side rail into the groove between the spacer/expander and the ring land, hold it firmly in place and slide a finger around the piston while pushing the rail into the groove. Finally, install the lower side rail, with its gap 120 degrees away from the upper side rail gap.

20   After the three oil ring components have been installed, check to make sure that both the upper and lower side rails can be rotated smoothly inside the ring grooves.

21   The number two (middle) ring is installed next. It's usually stamped with a mark which must face up, toward the top of the piston. Do not mix up the top and middle rings, as they have different cross-sections. **Note:** *Always follow the instructions printed on the ring package or box - different manufacturers may require different approaches.*

22   Use a piston ring installation tool and make sure the identification mark is facing the top of the piston, then slip the ring into the middle groove on the piston **(see illustration)**. Don't expand the ring any more than necessary to slide it over the piston. Rotate the end gap 120 degrees away from the oil expander gap.

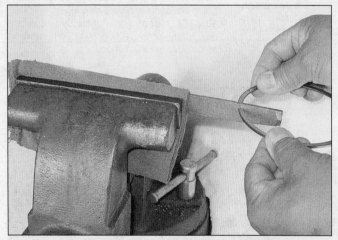

**9.15 If the ring end gap is too small, clamp a file in a vise as shown and file the piston ring ends - be sure to remove all raised material**

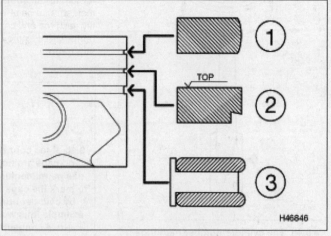

**9.18 Piston ring profiles**

1   *Top compression ring*           3   *Three-part oil control ring*
2   *2nd compression ring*

**9.19a Installing the spacer/expander in the oil ring groove**

**9.19b DO NOT use a piston ring installation tool when installing the oil control side rails**

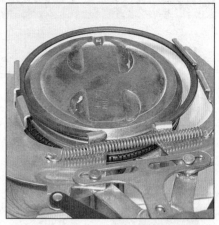

**9.22 Use a piston ring installation tool to install the number 2 and the number 1 (top) rings - be sure the directional mark on the piston ring(s) is facing toward the top of the piston**

23    Install the number one (top) ring in the same manner. Make sure the mark is facing up. Be careful not to confuse the number one and number two rings. Rotate the top ring so its gap is 120 degrees away from the second ring's gap. The three ring gaps should all be equally-spaced around the piston.

24    Repeat the procedure for the remaining pistons and rings.

## Installation

25    Before installing the piston/connecting rod assemblies, the cylinder walls must be perfectly clean, the top edge of each cylinder bore must be chamfered, and the crankshaft must be in place.

26    Remove the cap from the end of the number one connecting rod (refer to the marks made during removal). Remove the original bearing inserts and wipe the bearing surfaces of the connecting rod and cap with a clean, lint-free cloth. They must be kept spotlessly clean.

### Connecting rod bearing oil clearance check

*Refer to illustrations 9.35, 9.37 and 9.41*

27    Clean the back side of the new upper bearing insert, then lay it in place in the connecting rod.

28    Make sure the tab on the bearing fits into the recess in the rod. Don't hammer the bearing insert into place and be very careful not to nick or gouge the bearing face. Don't lubricate the bearing at this time.

29    Clean the back side of the other bearing insert and install it in the rod cap. Again, make sure the tab on the bearing fits into the recess in the cap, and don't apply any lubricant. It's critically important that the mating surfaces of the bearing and connecting rod are perfectly clean and oil free when they're assembled.

30    Position the piston ring gaps at 120-degree intervals around the piston.

31    Lubricate the piston and rings with clean engine oil and attach a piston ring compressor to the piston. Leave the skirt protruding about

1/4-inch to guide the piston into the cylinder. The rings must be compressed until they're flush with the piston.

32    Rotate the crankshaft until the number one connecting rod journal is at BDC (bottom dead center) and apply a liberal coat of engine oil to the cylinder walls.

33    With the mark on top of the piston facing the front (timing belt or chain end) of the engine, gently insert the piston/connecting rod assembly into the number one cylinder bore and rest the bottom edge of the ring compressor on the engine block.

34    Tap the top edge of the ring compressor to make sure it's contacting the block around its entire circumference.

35    Gently tap on the top of the piston with the end of a wooden or plastic hammer handle **(see illustration)** while guiding the end of the connecting rod into place on the crankshaft journal. The piston rings may try to pop out of the ring compressor just before entering the cylinder bore, so keep some downward pressure on the ring compressor. Work slowly, and if any resistance is felt as the piston enters the cylinder, stop immediately. Find out what's hanging

up and fix it before proceeding. Do not, for any reason, force the piston into the cylinder - you might break a ring and/or the piston.

36    Once the piston/connecting rod assembly is installed, the connecting rod bearing oil clearance must be checked before the rod cap is permanently installed.

37    Cut a piece of the appropriate size Plastigage slightly shorter than the width of the connecting rod bearing and lay it in place on the number one connecting rod journal, parallel with the journal axis **(see illustration)**.

38    Clean the connecting rod cap bearing face and install the rod cap. Make sure the mating mark on the cap is on the same side as the mark on the connecting rod **(see illustration 9.4)**.

39    Install the old rod bolts, at this time, and tighten them to the torque listed in this Chapter's Specifications. **Note:** *Use a thin-wall socket to avoid erroneous torque readings that can result if the socket is wedged between the rod cap and the bolt head. If the socket tends to wedge itself between the fastener and the*

**9.35 Use a plastic or wooden hammer handle to push the piston into the cylinder**

**9.37 Place Plastigage on each connecting rod bearing journal parallel to the crankshaft centerline**

# ENGINE BEARING ANALYSIS

## Debris

**Babbitt bearing embedded with debris from machinings**

**Microscopic detail of debris**

**Microscopic detail of gouges**

**Overplated copper alloy bearing gouged by cast iron debris**

**Aluminum bearing embedded with glass beads**

**Microscopic detail of glass beads**

**Damaged lining caused by dirt left on the bearing back**

## Misassembly

**Result of a lower half assembled as an upper - blocking the oil flow**

**Excessive oil clearance is indicated by a short contact arc**

**Polished and oil-stained backs are a result of a poor fit in the housing bore**

**Result of a wrong, reversed, or shifted cap**

## Overloading

**Damage from excessive idling which resulted in an oil film unable to support the load imposed**

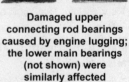

**Damaged upper connecting rod bearings caused by engine lugging; the lower main bearings (not shown) were similarly affected**

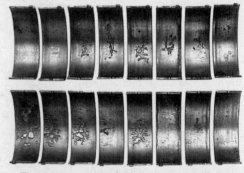

**The damage shown in these upper and lower connecting rod bearings was caused by engine operation at a higher-than-rated speed under load**

# Misalignment

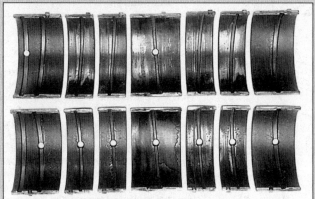

A warped crankshaft caused this pattern of severe wear in the center, diminishing toward the ends

A poorly finished crankshaft caused the equally spaced scoring shown

A tapered housing bore caused the damage along one edge of this pair

A bent connecting rod led to the damage in the "V" pattern

# Lubrication

Result of dry start: The bearings on the left, farthest from the oil pump, show more damage

Result of a low oil supply or oil starvation

Severe wear as a result of inadequate oil clearance

# Corrosion

Microscopic detail of corrosion

Corrosion is an acid attack on the bearing lining generally caused by inadequate maintenance, extremely hot or cold operation, or inferior oils or fuels

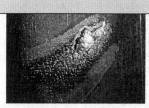

Microscopic detail of cavitation

Example of cavitation - a surface erosion caused by pressure changes in the oil film

Damage from excessive thrust or insufficient axial clearance

Bearing affected by oil dilution caused by excessive blow-by or a rich mixture

**9.41 Use the scale on the Plastigage package to determine the bearing oil clearance - be sure to measure the widest part of the Plastigage and use the correct scale; it comes with both standard and metric scales**

*cap, lift up on it slightly until it no longer contacts the cap. DO NOT rotate the crankshaft at any time during this operation.*

40    Remove the fasteners and detach the rod cap, being very careful not to disturb the Plastigage.

41    Compare the width of the crushed Plastigage to the scale printed on the Plastigage envelope to obtain the oil clearance **(see illustration)**. The connecting rod oil clearance is usually about 0.001 to 0.002 inch (0.025 to 0.05 mm). Consult an automotive machine shop for the clearance specified for the rod bearings on your engine.

42    If the clearance is not as specified, the bearing inserts may be the wrong size (which means different ones will be required). Before deciding that different inserts are needed, make sure that no dirt or oil was between the bearing inserts and the connecting rod or cap when the clearance was measured. Also, recheck the journal diameter. If the Plastigage was wider at one end than the other, the journal may be tapered. If the clearance still exceeds the limit specified, the bearing will have to be replaced with an undersize bearing. **Caution:** *When installing a new crankshaft always use a standard size bearing.*

### Final installation

*Refer to illustration 9.47*

43    Carefully scrape all traces of the Plastigage material off the rod journal and/or bearing face. Be very careful not to scratch the bearing - use your fingernail or the edge of a plastic card.

44    Make sure the bearing faces are perfectly clean, then apply a uniform layer of clean moly-base grease or engine assembly lube to both of them. You'll have to push the piston into the cylinder to expose the face of the bearing insert in the connecting rod.

45    Slide the connecting rod back into place

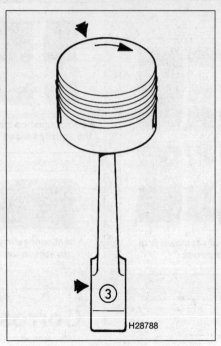

**9.47 The piston/connecting rods must be installed with the cylinder number markings on the exhaust manifold side of the engine, and the arrow on the piston crown pointing towards the front of the engine**

on the journal, install the rod cap, install the new bolts and tighten them to the torque listed in this Chapter's Specifications. **Caution:** *Install new connecting rod cap bolts. Do NOT reuse old bolts - they have stretched and cannot be reused.* Again, work up to the torque in three steps.

46    Repeat the entire procedure for the remaining pistons/connecting rods.

47    The important points to remember are:

a)  *Keep the back sides of the bearing inserts and the insides of the connecting rods and caps perfectly clean when assembling them.*

b)  *Make sure you have the correct piston/rod assembly for each cylinder.*

c)  *The mark on the piston must face the front (timing chain end) of the engine* **(see illustration)**.

d)  *Lubricate the cylinder walls liberally with clean oil.*

e)  *Lubricate the bearing faces when installing the rod caps after the oil clearance has been checked.*

48    After all the piston/connecting rod assemblies have been correctly installed, rotate the crankshaft a number of times by hand to check for any obvious binding.

49    As a final step, check the connecting rod endplay, as described in Step 3. If it was correct before disassembly and the original crankshaft and rods were reinstalled, it should still be correct. If new rods or a new crankshaft were installed, the endplay may be inadequate. If so, the rods will have to be removed and taken to an automotive machine shop for resizing.

## 10   Crankshaft - removal and installation

### Removal

*Refer to illustrations 10.1 and 10.3*

**Note:** *The crankshaft can be removed only after the engine has been removed from the vehicle. It's assumed that the flywheel or driveplate, crankshaft pulley, timing chain, oil pan, oil pump body, and piston/connecting rod assemblies have already been removed. The rear main oil seal retainer must be unbolted and separated from the block before proceeding with crankshaft removal.*

1    Before the crankshaft is removed, measure the endplay. Mount a dial indicator with the indicator in line with the crankshaft and just touching the end of the crankshaft as shown **(see illustration)**.

2    Pry the crankshaft all the way to the rear and zero the dial indicator. Next, pry the crankshaft to the front as far as possible and check the reading on the dial indicator. The distance traveled is the endplay. A typical crankshaft endplay will fall between 0.003 to 0.010 inch (0.076 to 0.254 mm). If it is greater than that, check the crankshaft thrust surfaces for wear after it's removed. If no wear is evident, new main bearings should correct the endplay.

3    If a dial indicator isn't available, feeler gauges can be used. Gently pry the crankshaft all the way to the front of the engine. Slip feeler gauges between the crankshaft and the front face of the thrust bearing or washer to determine the clearance **(see illustration)**.

4    Loosen the main bearing cap bolts and lower cylinder block (bedplate) bolts 1/4-turn at a time each, until they can be removed by hand. Loosen the bolts in the reverse of the tightening sequence **(see illustration 10.19)**

5    Gently tap the lower cylinder block with a soft-face hammer around its perimeter. Pull the lower cylinder block straight up and off the cylinder block. Try not to drop the bearing inserts if they come out with the assembly.

6    Carefully lift the crankshaft out of the engine. It may be a good idea to have an assistant available, since the crankshaft is quite heavy and awkward to handle. With the bearing inserts in place inside the engine block and main bearing caps or lower cylinder block, reinstall the main bearing caps or lower cylinder block onto the engine block and tighten the bolts finger tight. If you're working on a four-cylinder engine, make sure you install the caps with the arrows pointing towards the front (timing belt end) of the engine.

### Installation

7    Crankshaft installation is the first step in engine reassembly. It's assumed at this point that the engine block and crankshaft have been cleaned, inspected and repaired or reconditioned.

8    Position the engine block with the bottom facing up.

9    Remove the bolts and lift off the main

**10.1 Checking crankshaft endplay with a dial indicator**

**10.3 Checking the crankshaft endplay with feeler gauges at the thrust bearing journal**

bearing caps or lower cylinder block.

10   If they're still in place, remove the original bearing inserts from the block and from the main bearing cap assembly. Wipe the bearing surfaces of the block and main bearing cap assembly with a clean, lint-free cloth. They must be kept spotlessly clean. This is critical for determining the correct bearing oil clearance.

### Main bearing oil clearance check

*Refer to illustrations 10.17, 10.19a, 10.19b and 10.21*

11   Without mixing them up, clean the back sides of the new upper main bearing inserts (with grooves and oil holes) and lay one in each main bearing saddle in the engine block. Each upper bearing (engine block) has an oil groove and oil hole in it. **Caution:** *The oil holes in the block must line up with the oil holes in the upper bearing inserts.* **Note:** *The thrust bearing is located on the 4th or 6th journal on the lower cylinder block.* Clean the back sides of the lower main bearing inserts

and lay them in the corresponding location in the lower cylinder block/bridge. Make sure the tab on the bearing insert fits into the recess in the block or lower cylinder block. **Caution:** *Do not hammer the bearing insert into place and don't nick or gouge the bearing faces. DO NOT apply any lubrication at this time.*

12   Clean the faces of the bearing inserts in the block and the crankshaft main bearing journal bridge with a clean, lint-free cloth.

13   Check or clean the oil holes in the crankshaft, as any dirt here can go only one way - straight through the new bearings.

14   Once you're certain the crankshaft is clean, carefully lay it in position in the cylinder block.

15   Before the crankshaft can be permanently installed, the main bearing oil clearance must be checked.

16   Cut several strips of the appropriate size of Plastigage. They must be slightly shorter than the width of the main bearing journal.

17   Place one piece on each crankshaft main bearing journal, parallel with the journal axis as shown **(see illustration)**.

18   Clean the faces of the bearing inserts in the main bearing caps or the lower cylinder block. Hold the bearing inserts in place and install the caps or the lower cylinder block onto the crankshaft and cylinder block. DO NOT disturb the Plastigage.

19   Apply clean engine oil to all bolt threads prior to installation, then install all bolts finger-tight. Tighten the bolts in the sequence shown **(see illustrations)** progressing in steps, to the torque listed in this Chapter's Specifications. DO NOT rotate the crankshaft at any time during this operation.

**10.17 Place the Plastigage onto the crankshaft bearing journal as shown**

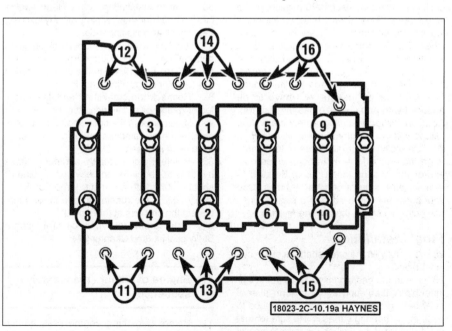

**10.19a 2.0L engine lower cylinder block/bedplate bolts and main bearing cap – TIGHTENING sequence**

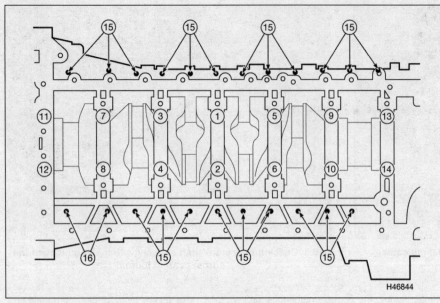

**10.19b  3.0L engine lower cylinder block/bedplate bolts and main cap bolts - TIGHTENING sequence**

**10.21  Use the scale on the Plastigage package to determine the bearing oil clearance - be sure to measure the widest part of the Plastigage and use the correct scale; it comes with both standard and metric scales**

20    Remove the bolts in the *reverse* order of the tightening sequence and carefully lift the caps and lower cylinder block straight up and off the block. Do not disturb the Plastigage or rotate the crankshaft.

21    Compare the width of the crushed Plastigage on each journal to the scale printed on the Plastigage envelope to determine the main bearing oil clearance **(see illustration)**. Check with an automotive machine shop for the oil clearance for your engine.

22    If the clearance is not as specified, the bearing inserts may be the wrong size (which means different ones will be required). Before deciding if different inserts are needed, make sure that no dirt or oil was between the bearing inserts and the cap assembly or block when the clearance was measured. If the Plastigage was wider at one end than the other, the crankshaft journal may be tapered. If the clearance still exceeds the limit specified, the bearing insert(s) will have to be replaced with an undersize bearing insert(s). **Caution:** *When installing a new crankshaft always install a standard bearing insert set.*

23    Carefully scrape all traces of the Plastigage material off the main bearing journals and/or the bearing insert faces. Be sure to remove all residue from the oil holes. Use your fingernail or the edge of a plastic card - don't nick or scratch the bearing faces.

### Final installation

24    Carefully lift the crankshaft out of the cylinder block.

25    Clean the bearing insert faces in the cylinder block, then apply a thin, uniform layer of moly-base grease or engine assembly lube to each of the bearing surfaces. Be sure to coat the thrust faces as well as the journal face of the thrust bearing.

26    Make sure the crankshaft journals are clean, then lay the crankshaft back in place in the cylinder block.

27    Clean the bearing insert faces and apply the same lubricant to them. Clean the mating surfaces of the engine block and lower cylinder block/bedplate thoroughly. The surfaces must be free of oil residue.

28    Squeeze a bead of BMW liquid sealant into the groove in the bottom of the block before installing and tightening the bedplate. Follow the sealant manufacturer's instructions.

29    Install the lower cylinder block onto the crankshaft and cylinder block.

30    Prior to installation, apply clean engine oil to all bolt threads, wiping off any excess, then install all bolts finger-tight.

31    Tighten the lower cylinder block bedplate and main cap bolts in the correct sequence **(see illustration 10.19)** to the torque listed in this Chapter's Specifications.

32    Recheck the crankshaft endplay with a feeler gauge or a dial indicator. The endplay should be correct if the crankshaft thrust faces aren't worn or damaged and if new bearings have been installed.

33    Rotate the crankshaft a number of times by hand to check for any obvious binding. It should rotate with a running torque of 50 in-lbs or less. If the running torque is too high, correct the problem at this time.

34    Install a new rear main oil seal using a BMW seal kit (see Chapter 2A).

### 11  Engine overhaul - reassembly sequence

1    Before beginning engine reassembly, make sure you have all the necessary new parts, gaskets and seals as well as the following items on hand:

   *Common hand tools*
   *A 1/2-inch drive torque wrench*
   *New engine oil*
   *Gasket sealant*
   *Thread-locking compound*

2    If you obtained a short block, it will be necessary to install the cylinder head, the oil pump and pick-up tube, the oil pan, the water pump, the timing chain and timing cover, and the valve cover (see Chapter 2A). In order to save time and avoid problems, the external components must be installed in the following general order:

   *Thermostat and housing cover*
   *Water pump*
   *Intake and exhaust manifolds*
   *Fuel injection components*
   *Emission control components*
   *Spark plugs*
   *Ignition coils*
   *Oil filter*
   *Turbocharger (if equipped)*
   *Engine mounts and mount brackets*
   *Clutch and flywheel (manual transmission)*
   *Driveplate (automatic transmission)*

### 12  Initial start-up and break-in after overhaul

**Warning:** *Have a fire extinguisher handy when starting the engine for the first time.*

1    Once the engine has been installed in the vehicle, double-check the engine oil and coolant levels.

2    With the spark plugs out of the engine and the ignition system and fuel pump disabled, crank the engine until oil pressure registers on the gauge or the light goes out.

3    Install the spark plugs, hook up the plug wires and restore the ignition system and fuel pump functions.

4    Start the engine. It may take a few

moments for the fuel system to build up pressure, but the engine should start without a great deal of effort.

5    After the engine starts, it should be allowed to warm up to normal operating temperature. While the engine is warming up, make a thorough check for fuel, oil and coolant leaks.

6    Shut the engine off and recheck the engine oil and coolant levels.

7    Drive the vehicle to an area with minimum traffic, accelerate from 30 to 50 mph, then allow the vehicle to slow to 30 mph with the throttle closed. Repeat the procedure 10 or 12 times. This will load the piston rings and cause them to seat properly against the cylinder walls. Check again for oil and coolant leaks.

8    Drive the vehicle gently for the first 500 miles (no sustained high speeds) and keep a constant check on the oil level. It is not unusual for an engine to use oil during the break-in period.

9    At approximately 500 to 600 miles, change the oil and filter.

10    For the next few hundred miles, drive the vehicle normally. Do not pamper it or abuse it.

11    After 2,000 miles, change the oil and filter again and consider the engine broken in.

# COMMON ENGINE OVERHAUL TERMS

## B

**Backlash** - The amount of play between two parts. Usually refers to how much one gear can be moved back and forth without moving the gear with which it's meshed.

**Bearing Caps** - The caps held in place by nuts or bolts which, in turn, hold the bearing surface. This space is for lubricating oil to enter.

**Bearing clearance** - The amount of space left between shaft and bearing surface. This space is for lubricating oil to enter.

**Bearing crush** - The additional height which is purposely manufactured into each bearing half to ensure complete contact of the bearing back with the housing bore when the engine is assembled.

**Bearing knock** - The noise created by movement of a part in a loose or worn bearing.

**Blueprinting** - Dismantling an engine and reassembling it to EXACT specifications.

**Bore** - An engine cylinder, or any cylindrical hole; also used to describe the process of enlarging or accurately refinishing a hole with a cutting tool, as to bore an engine cylinder. The bore size is the diameter of the hole.

**Boring** - Renewing the cylinders by cutting them out to a specified size. A boring bar is used to make the cut.

**Bottom end** - A term which refers collectively to the engine block, crankshaft, main bearings and the big ends of the connecting rods.

**Break-in** - The period of operation between installation of new or rebuilt parts and time in which parts are worn to the correct fit. Driving at reduced and varying speed for a specified mileage to permit parts to wear to the correct fit.

**Bushing** - A one-piece sleeve placed in a bore to serve as a bearing surface for shaft, piston pin, etc. Usually replaceable.

## C

**Camshaft** - The shaft in the engine, on which a series of lobes are located for operating the valve mechanisms. The camshaft is driven by gears or sprockets and a timing chain. Usually referred to simply as the cam.

**Carbon** - Hard, or soft, black deposits found in combustion chamber, on plugs, under rings, on and under valve heads.

**Cast iron** - An alloy of iron and more than two percent carbon, used for engine blocks and heads because it's relatively inexpensive and easy to mold into complex shapes.

**Chamfer** - To bevel across (or a bevel on) the sharp edge of an object.

**Chase** - To repair damaged threads with a tap or die.

**Combustion chamber** - The space between the piston and the cylinder head, with the piston at top dead center, in which air-fuel mixture is burned.

**Compression ratio** - The relationship between cylinder volume (clearance volume) when the piston is at top dead center and cylinder volume when the piston is at bottom dead center.

**Connecting rod** - The rod that connects the crank on the crankshaft with the piston. Sometimes called a con rod.

**Connecting rod cap** - The part of the connecting rod assembly that attaches the rod to the crankpin.

**Core plug** - Soft metal plug used to plug the casting holes for the coolant passages in the block.

**Crankcase** - The lower part of the engine in which the crankshaft rotates; includes the lower section of the cylinder block and the oil pan.

**Crank kit** - A reground or reconditioned crankshaft and new main and connecting rod bearings.

**Crankpin** - The part of a crankshaft to which a connecting rod is attached.

**Crankshaft** - The main rotating member, or shaft, running the length of the crankcase, with offset throws to which the connecting rods are attached; changes the reciprocating motion of the pistons into rotating motion.

**Cylinder sleeve** - A replaceable sleeve, or liner, pressed into the cylinder block to form the cylinder bore.

## D

**Deburring** - Removing the burrs (rough edges or areas) from a bearing.

**Deglazer** - A tool, rotated by an electric motor, used to remove glaze from cylinder walls so a new set of rings will seat.

## E

**Endplay** - The amount of lengthwise movement between two parts. As applied to a crankshaft, the distance that the crankshaft can move forward and back in the cylinder block.

## F

**Face** - A machinist's term that refers to removing metal from the end of a shaft or the face of a larger part, such as a flywheel.

**Fatigue** - A breakdown of material through a large number of loading and unloading cycles. The first signs are cracks followed shortly by breaks.

**Feeler gauge** - A thin strip of hardened steel, ground to an exact thickness, used to check clearances between parts.

**Free height** - The unloaded length or height of a spring.

**Freeplay** - The looseness in a linkage, or an assembly of parts, between the initial application of force and actual movement. Usually perceived as slop or slight delay.

**Freeze plug** - See Core plug.

## G

**Gallery** - A large passage in the block that forms a reservoir for engine oil pressure.

**Glaze** - The very smooth, glassy finish that develops on cylinder walls while an engine is in service.

## H

**Heli-Coil** - A rethreading device used when threads are worn or damaged. The device is installed in a retapped hole to reduce the thread size to the original size.

## I

**Installed height** - The spring's measured length or height, as installed on the cylinder head. Installed height is measured from the spring seat to the underside of the spring retainer.

## J

**Journal** - The surface of a rotating shaft which turns in a bearing.

## K

**Keeper** - The split lock that holds the valve spring retainer in position on the valve stem.

**Key** - A small piece of metal inserted into matching grooves machined into two parts fitted together - such as a gear pressed onto a shaft - which prevents slippage between the two parts.

**Knock** - The heavy metallic engine sound, produced in the combustion chamber as a result of abnormal combustion - usually detonation. Knock is usually caused by a loose or worn bearing. Also referred to as detonation, pinging and spark knock. Connecting rod or main bearing knocks are created by too much oil clearance or insufficient lubrication.

## L

**Lands** - The portions of metal between the piston ring grooves.

**Lapping the valves** - Grinding a valve face and its seat together with lapping compound.

**Lash** - The amount of free motion in a gear train, between gears, or in a mechanical assembly, that occurs before movement can begin. Usually refers to the lash in a valve train.

**Lifter** - The part that rides against the cam to transfer motion to the rest of the valve train.

# M

**Machining** - The process of using a machine to remove metal from a metal part.

**Main bearings** - The plain, or babbit, bearings that support the crankshaft.

**Main bearing caps** - The cast iron caps, bolted to the bottom of the block, that support the main bearings.

# O

**O.D.** - Outside diameter.

**Oil gallery** - A pipe or drilled passageway in the engine used to carry engine oil from one area to another.

**Oil ring** - The lower ring, or rings, of a piston; designed to prevent excessive amounts of oil from working up the cylinder walls and into the combustion chamber. Also called an oil-control ring.

**Oil seal** - A seal which keeps oil from leaking out of a compartment. Usually refers to a dynamic seal around a rotating shaft or other moving part.

**O-ring** - A type of sealing ring made of a special rubberlike material; in use, the O-ring is compressed into a groove to provide the sealing action.

**Overhaul** - To completely disassemble a unit, clean and inspect all parts, reassemble it with the original or new parts and make all adjustments necessary for proper operation.

# P

**Pilot bearing** - A small bearing installed in the center of the flywheel (or the rear end of the crankshaft) to support the front end of the input shaft of the transmission.

**Pip mark** - A little dot or indentation which indicates the top side of a compression ring.

**Piston** - The cylindrical part, attached to the connecting rod, that moves up and down in the cylinder as the crankshaft rotates. When the fuel charge is fired, the piston transfers the force of the explosion to the connecting rod, then to the crankshaft.

**Piston pin (or wrist pin)** - The cylindrical and usually hollow steel pin that passes through the piston. The piston pin fastens the piston to the upper end of the connecting rod.

**Piston ring** - The split ring fitted to the groove in a piston. The ring contacts the sides of the ring groove and also rubs against the cylinder wall, thus sealing space between piston and wall. There are two types of rings: Compression rings seal the compression pressure in the combustion chamber; oil rings scrape excessive oil off the cylinder wall.

**Piston ring groove** - The slots or grooves cut in piston heads to hold piston rings in position.

**Piston skirt** - The portion of the piston below the rings and the piston pin hole.

**Plastigage** - A thin strip of plastic thread, available in different sizes, used for measuring clearances. For example, a strip of plastigage is laid across a bearing journal and mashed as parts are assembled. Then parts are disassembled and the width of the strip is measured to determine clearance between journal and bearing. Commonly used to measure crankshaft main-bearing and connecting rod bearing clearances.

**Press-fit** - A tight fit between two parts that requires pressure to force the parts together. Also referred to as drive, or force, fit.

**Prussian blue** - A blue pigment; in solution, useful in determining the area of contact between two surfaces. Prussian blue is commonly used to determine the width and location of the contact area between the valve face and the valve seat.

# R

**Race (bearing)** - The inner or outer ring that provides a contact surface for balls or rollers in bearing.

**Ream** - To size, enlarge or smooth a hole by using a round cutting tool with fluted edges.

**Ring job** - The process of reconditioning the cylinders and installing new rings.

**Runout** - Wobble. The amount a shaft rotates out-of-true.

# S

**Saddle** - The upper main bearing seat.

**Scored** - Scratched or grooved, as a cylinder wall may be scored by abrasive particles moved up and down by the piston rings.

**Scuffing** - A type of wear in which there's a transfer of material between parts moving against each other; shows up as pits or grooves in the mating surfaces.

**Seat** - The surface upon which another part rests or seats. For example, the valve seat is the matched surface upon which the valve face rests. Also used to refer to wearing into a good fit; for example, piston rings seat after a few miles of driving.

**Short block** - An engine block complete with crankshaft and piston and, usually, camshaft assemblies.

**Static balance** - The balance of an object while it's stationary.

**Step** - The wear on the lower portion of a ring land caused by excessive side and back-clearance. The height of the step indicates the ring's extra side clearance and the length of the step projecting from the back wall of the groove represents the ring's back clearance.

**Stroke** - The distance the piston moves when traveling from top dead center to bottom dead center, or from bottom dead center to top dead center.

**Stud** - A metal rod with threads on both ends.

# T

**Tang** - A lip on the end of a plain bearing used to align the bearing during assembly.

**Tap** - To cut threads in a hole. Also refers to the fluted tool used to cut threads.

**Taper** - A gradual reduction in the width of a shaft or hole; in an engine cylinder, taper usually takes the form of uneven wear, more pronounced at the top than at the bottom.

**Throws** - The offset portions of the crankshaft to which the connecting rods are affixed.

**Thrust bearing** - The main bearing that has thrust faces to prevent excessive endplay, or forward and backward movement of the crankshaft.

**Thrust washer** - A bronze or hardened steel washer placed between two moving parts. The washer prevents longitudinal movement and provides a bearing surface for thrust surfaces of parts.

**Tolerance** - The amount of variation permitted from an exact size of measurement. Actual amount from smallest acceptable dimension to largest acceptable dimension.

# U

**Umbrella** - An oil deflector placed near the valve tip to throw oil from the valve stem area.

**Undercut** - A machined groove below the normal surface.

**Undersize bearings** - Smaller diameter bearings used with re-ground crankshaft journals.

# V

**Valve grinding** - Refacing a valve in a valve-refacing machine.

**Valve train** - The valve-operating mechanism of an engine; includes all components from the camshaft to the valve.

**Vibration damper** - A cylindrical weight attached to the front of the crankshaft to minimize torsional vibration (the twist-untwist actions of the crankshaft caused by the cylinder firing impulses). Also called a harmonic balancer.

# W

**Water jacket** - The spaces around the cylinders, between the inner and outer shells of the cylinder block or head, through which coolant circulates.

**Web** - A supporting structure across a cavity.

**Woodruff key** - A key with a radiused backside (viewed from the side).

# Notes

# Chapter 3
# Cooling, heating and air conditioning systems

## Contents

## Specifications

### General

| | |
|---|---|
| Expansion tank cap opening pressure | 29 psi ± 2.9 psi (1.4 ± 0.2 bar) |
| Air conditioning refrigerant capacity* | 21.2 ounces (590 ± 10g) |

*Refer to the underhood decal*

### Thermostat

| | |
|---|---|
| Opening temperatures | Not available |

### Torque specifications

**Note:** *One foot-pound (ft-lb) of torque is equivalent to 12 inch-pounds (in-lbs) of torque. Torque values below approximately 15 foot-pounds are expressed in inch-pounds, because most foot-pound torque wrenches are not accurate at these smaller values.*

| | Ft-lbs (unless otherwise indicated) | Nm |
|---|---|---|
| Air conditioning compressor mounting bolts | | |
| 2.0L engines | | |
| M8 bolts | 168 in-lbs | 19 |
| M10 bolts | 28 | 38 |
| 3.0L engines | | |
| M8 x 52 mm | | |
| Stage 1 | 84 in-lbs | 10 |
| Stage 2 | Tighten an additional 90 degrees | |
| M8 x 87 mm | | |
| Stage 1 | 84 in-lbs | 10 |
| Stage 2 | Tighten an additional 180 degrees | |

## Torque specifications (continued)

**Note:** *One foot-pound (ft-lb) of torque is equivalent to 12 inch-pounds (in-lbs) of torque. Torque values below approximately 15 foot-pounds are expressed in inch-pounds, because most foot-pound torque wrenches are not accurate at these smaller values.*

| | Ft-lbs (unless otherwise indicated) | Nm |
|---|---|---|
| Coolant pump | | |
|   2.0L engines | | |
|     Coolant pump-to-front axle support | 168 in-lbs | 19 |
|     Coolant pump-to-crankcase | 16.5 | 22 |
|   3.0L engines | | |
|     Stage 1 | 84 in-lbs | 10 |
|     Stage 2 | Tighten an additional 90 degrees | |
| Coolant temperature sensor | 120 in-lbs | 13 |
| Cooling fan viscous coupling-to-coolant pump (left-hand thread) | 30 | 40 |
| Instrument panel crossmember | | |
|   End nuts | 15 | 21 |
|   To steering column bracket | 168 in-lbs | 19 |
| Refrigerant line unions | 15 | 20 |
| Refrigerant line bolts | | |
|   M6 bolts | 71 in-lbs | 8 |
|   M8 bolts | 159 in-lbs | 18 |
| Thermostat cover bolts | 80 in-lbs | 9 |
| Thermostat housing | 84 in-lbs | 10 |

\* *Do not re-use*

**Caution:** *All aluminum fasteners must be replaced with new ones. If in doubt, try to attract the bolt/stud with a magnet. Aluminum is not magnetic.*

## 1   General information and precautions

The cooling system is of the pressurized type, comprising a pump, an aluminum cross-flow radiator, a cooling fan, and a thermostat. The system functions as follows: Cold coolant from the radiator passes through the hose to the coolant pump where it is pumped around the cylinder block and head passages. After cooling the cylinder bores, combustion surfaces and valve seats, the coolant reaches the underside of the thermostat, which is initially closed. The coolant passes through the heater and is returned through the cylinder block to the coolant pump.

When the engine is cold, the coolant circulates only through the cylinder block, cylinder head, expansion tank and heater. When the coolant reaches a predetermined temperature, the thermostat opens and the coolant passes through to the radiator. On some models, the thermostat opening and closing is controlled by the engine management PCM and a heating element within the wax capsule of the thermostat. This allows fine control of the engine running temperature, resulting in less emissions, and better fuel economy. As the coolant circulates through the radiator, it is cooled by the inrush of air when the vehicle is in forward motion. Airflow is supplemented by the action of the cooling fan. Upon reaching the radiator, the coolant is now cooled and the cycle is repeated.

Two different fan configurations are used, depending on model. On some engines, the fan is electrically-operated, and mounted on the engine side of the radiator. Others are equipped with a belt-driven cooling fan. The belt is driven by the crankshaft pulley via a viscous fluid coupling. The viscous coupling varies the fan speed, according to engine temperature. At low temperatures, the coupling provides very little resistance between the fan and pump pulley so only a slight amount of drive is transmitted to the cooling fan. As the temperature of the coupling increases, so does its internal resistance, increasing drive to the cooling fan.

The coolant pump is driven by an integral electric motor, which is under the control of the engine management PCM.

Refer to Section 10 for information on the air conditioning system.

**Warning:** *Do not attempt to remove the expansion tank filler cap or disturb any part of the cooling system while the engine is hot, as there is a high risk of scalding. If the expansion tank filler cap must be removed before the engine and radiator have fully cooled (even though this is not recommended), the pressure in the cooling system must first be relieved. Cover the cap with a thick layer of cloth, to avoid scalding, and slowly unscrew the filler cap until a hissing sound can be heard. When the hissing has stopped, indicating that the pressure has reduced, slowly unscrew the filler cap until it can be removed; if more hissing sounds are heard, wait until they have stopped before unscrewing the cap completely. Keep well away from the filler cap opening at all times.*

**Warning:** *Do not allow antifreeze to come into contact with skin or painted surfaces of the vehicle. Rinse off spills immediately with plenty of water. Never leave antifreeze lying around in an open container or in a puddle in the driveway or on the garage floor. Children and pets are attracted by its sweet smell. Antifreeze can be fatal if ingested.*

**Warning:** *Refer to Section 10 for precautions to be observed when working on models equipped with air conditioning.*

**Warning:** *On models equipped with lifetime coolant, never reuse the coolant. If the cooling system is partially drained, the corrosion protection effect of the coolant is significantly reduced. If a large quantity of coolant is removed, the entire cooling system must be drained and refilled with new coolant. If a small amount (under a quart), is drained, new fluid must be used to replace the coolant drained from the system.*

## 2   Cooling system hoses and expansion tank – removal and installation

### Cooling system hoses

*Refer to illustrations 2.3a and 2.3b*

**Warning:** *Refer to the Warnings given in Section 1 of this Chapter before proceeding.*

1   If the checks described in Chapter 1 reveal a faulty hose, it must be replaced as follows.

2   Drain the cooling system (see Chapter 1). If the coolant is not due for replacement, it may be re-used if it is collected in a clean container.

3   To disconnect a hose, pry up the wire retaining clip and pull the hose from its fitting **(see illustrations)**. Some hoses may be secured using traditional hose clamps. To disconnect these hoses, loosen the hose clamp adjusting screw, then move the clamp along the hose, until it is clear of the relevant inlet/outlet union. Carefully work the hose free. While the hoses can be removed with relative ease when new, or when hot, do not attempt to disconnect any part of the system while it is still hot. Some models have hoses retained by twist-on/twist-off clamps; rotate the clamps counterclockwise to remove them.

4   Note that the radiator inlet and outlet unions are fragile; do not use excessive force when attempting to remove the hoses. If a hose proves to be difficult to remove, try to release it by rotating the hose ends before

**2.3a  Pry up the wire locking clip**

**2.3b  Pull the hose from the fitting**

attempting to free it. If all else fails, carefully use a sharp knife to slit the hose and peel it from the radiator fitting. Do not gouge the radiator fitting.

5    To install a hose, simply push the end over the fitting until the retaining clip engages and locks the hose in place. Pull the hose to make sure it's locked in place. When installing a hose with traditional hose clips, first slide the clips onto the hose, then work the hose into position. If the hose is stiff, use a little soapy water as a lubricant, or soften the hose by soaking it in hot water. Continue to work the hose into position, checking that it is correctly routed, then slide each clip along the hose until it passes over the flared end of the relevant inlet/outlet union, before securing it in position with the retaining clip.

6    Refill the cooling system (see Chapter 1).

7    Check thoroughly for leaks as soon as possible after disturbing any part of the cooling system.

## Expansion tank

8    Remove the air intake duct (see chapter 4).

9    Disconnect the hoses to the expansion tank (see Step 5).

10    Remove the mounting bolts and pull the expansion tank back to unclip it from the bracket, then lift it up.

11    Disconnect the coolant level switch connector, then disconnect the remaining coolant hose and remove the tank.

12    Installation is the reverse of removal.

13    Refill the cooling system (see Chapter 1).

### 3  Radiator - removal, inspection and installation

**Warning:** *Refer to the* **Warnings** *given in Section 1 of this Chapter before proceeding.*

## Removal

*Refer to illustrations 3.2, 3.5a, 3.5b, 3.5c, 3.7a and 3.7b*

1    Drain the cooling system (see Chapter 1).

2    Remove the bolts and move the air intake duct rearwards and upwards **(see illustration)**.

3    Remove the air filter housing (see Chapter 4).

4    Remove the electric cooling fan and shroud (see Section 5).

5    Pry out the wire clips and disconnect the radiator upper and lower coolant hoses **(see illustrations)**. Where applicable, disconnect the coolant hose from the automatic transmission fluid cooler.

6    On E-series chassis models with an automatic transmission, remove the mounting bolt and detach the fluid cooler hoses from the radiator. On F-series chassis models with an automatic transmission, unlock the transmission oil cooler lines (see Section 2, Step 5) and disconnect the hose(s) from the radiator.

**3.2  Remove the bolts and the intake duct**

**3.5a  Pry up the clip and disconnect the upper . . .**

**3.5b  . . . and lower radiator hoses**

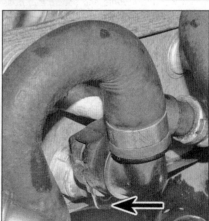

**3.5c  Pry out the clip and disconnect the coolant hose from the automatic transmission fluid cooler**

**3.7a  Remove the radiator retaining bolt in the left-hand upper corner . . .**

**3.7b  . . . and the right-hand upper corner**

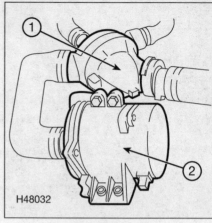

**4.3  Thermostat housing (1) and coolant pump 3.0L models (2)**

7    Remove the radiator upper mounting bolts, then pull the top of the radiator rearwards and upwards to remove it **(see illustrations)**.

## Inspection

8    If the radiator has been removed due to suspected blockage, reverse-flush it (see Chapter 1). Clean dirt and debris from the radiator fins, using a compressed air (in which case, wear eye protection) or a soft brush. Be careful, as the fins are easily damaged, and are sharp.
9    If necessary, a radiator specialist can perform a flow test on the radiator, to establish whether an internal blockage exists.
10   A leaking radiator must be referred to a specialist for permanent repair. Do not attempt to weld or solder a leaking radiator, as damage may result.
11   Inspect the radiator lower mounts for signs of damage or deterioration and replace if necessary.

## Installation

12   Installation is the reverse of removal, noting the following points:
a) *Lower the radiator into position, engage it with the mounts and secure it in position with the retaining bolts.*
b) *Ensure that the fan cowl is correctly located with the lugs on the radiator and secure it in position with the clips.*

c) *Reconnect the hoses and ensure the retaining clips engage securely.*
d) *Check the condition of the O-ring seals in the end of the radiator fittings. Replace any that are defective.*
e) *Refill the cooling system (see Chapter 1).*

## 4    Thermostat - removal and installation

**Warning:** *Refer to the* **Warnings** *given in Section 1 of this Chapter before proceeding.*
**Note:** *A new thermostat sealing ring and housing gasket/seal will be required on installation.*

## Removal

*Refer to illustration 4.3*

1    Remove the fasteners and the engine splash shield.
2    Drain the cooling system (see Chapter 1).
3    Release the clamps/pry out the clips and disconnect the four coolant hoses from the thermostat housing, which is located above the coolant pump at the front right-hand corner of the cylinder block **(see illustration)**.
4    Disconnect the electrical connector from the base of the thermostat housing.
5    Remove the mounting bolts and the ther-

mostat housing. **Note:** *The thermostat and housing are only available as a complete unit.*

## Installation

6    Installation is the reverse of removal, bearing in mind the following points.
a) *Replace the thermostat cover/housing O-ring seal.*
b) *Tighten the thermostat cover/housing bolts to the specified torque where given.*
c) *Refill the cooling system (see Chapter 1).*

## 5    Electric cooling fan and shroud - removal and installation

*Refer to illustrations 5.2a, 5.2b, 5.3, 5.4, 5.5a and 5.5b*

1    Remove the mounting bolts and the air intake hood from the center of the radiator support **(see illustration 3.2)**. Disconnect the intake hose as the air intake hood is withdrawn.
2    On automatic transmission models, release the fasteners and remove the engine splash shield. Remove the mounting bolt and detach the transmission cooler from the fan shroud **(see illustrations)**. There's no need to disconnect the hoses.

**5.2a  Remove the fasteners and remove the engine splash shield**

**5.2b  Transmission fluid cooler retaining bolt**

5.3  Release the power steering hoses from the fan shroud

5.4  Remove the bolt in the upper right-hand corner of the shroud

5.5a  Pull back the clip . . .

3    Disconnect the fan motor electrical connector and unclip the coolant hose and power steering lines from the top of the shroud **(see illustration)**.

4    Unclip the wiring harness, then remove the mounting bolt at the upper right-hand edge of the shroud **(see illustration)**.

5    Pull back and release the clip at the left-hand side, then lift the shroud out **(see illustrations)**.

6    Installation is the reverse of removal, ensuring the lugs on the lower edge of the shroud engage in the corresponding slots in the radiator edge.

## 6    Cooling system electrical switch/ sensor - testing, removal and installation

## *Testing*

1    Testing should be entrusted to a BMW dealer or suitably-equipped specialist.

## *Removal and installation*

**Warning:** *Refer to the* **Warnings** *given in Section 1 of this Chapter before proceeding.*

### Radiator outlet thermostatic switch

*Refer to illustration 6.5*

**Note:** *Not all models are equipped with a radiator outlet thermostatic switch.*

2    The switch is located in the radiator lower hose. The engine and radiator should be cold before removing the switch.

3    Disconnect the negative battery cable (see Chapter 5).

4    Either drain the cooling system to below the level of the switch (see Chapter 1), or have ready a suitable plug which can be used to plug the switch aperture in the radiator while the switch is removed. If a plug is used, take great care not to damage the radiator, and do not use anything which will allow foreign matter to enter the radiator.

5    Disconnect the electrical connector from the switch **(see illustration)**.

6    Release the retaining clip, and remove the switch and sealing washer.

7    Installation is the reverse of removal. Use a new sealing washer. Refill the cooling system (see Chapter 1).

8    Start the engine and run it until it reaches normal operating temperature, then continue to run the engine and check that the cooling fan comes on and functions correctly.

### Coolant temperature sensor

*Refer to illustration 6.12*

9    Either partially drain the cooling system to just below the level of the sensor (see Chapter 1), or have ready a suitable plug which can be used to plug the sensor aperture while it is removed. If a plug is used, take great care not to damage the sensor unit aperture, and do not use anything which will allow foreign matter to enter the cooling system.

10    Remove the mounting bolts and remove the air intake duct from the radiator support **(see illustration 3.2)**. Disconnect the intake hose as the duct is removed.

11    The sensor is screwed into the front side of the cylinder head. Release the clip and disconnect the wiring from the sensor.

12    Unscrew the sensor unit from the cylinder head **(see illustration)**.

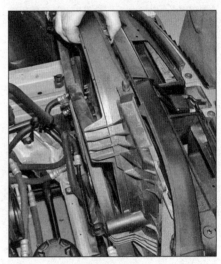

5.5b  . . . then lift out the fan and shroud

13    Apply a small amount of sealant to the sensor unit threads and install the sensor, tightening it to the specified torque.

14    Reconnect the wiring connector, then refill the cooling system (see Chapter 1). Check for leaks.

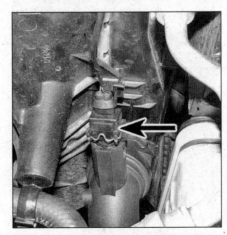

6.5  Radiator outlet thermostatic switch

6.12  Coolant temperature sensor location

### Coolant level sensor

*Refer to illustration 6.15*

15   The level sensor is mounted in the base of the coolant expansion tank. Disconnect the level sensor electrical connector **(see illustration)**.

16   Remove the retaining bolts and raise the coolant tank. There's no need to disconnect the hoses.

17   Tilt the expansion tank so the sensor is uppermost, then rotate the sensor counter-clockwise and pull it from the tank.

18   Installation is the reverse of removal. If necessary, add coolant (see Chapter 1).

### 7   Coolant pump - removal and installation

**Warning:** *Refer to the* **Warnings** *given in Section 1 of this Chapter before proceeding.* **Note:** *These models are equipped with an electric cooling pump.*

## Removal

1   Drain the cooling system (see Chapter 1).

### 2.0L engines

2   Raise the vehicle and support it securely on jackstands, then remove the lower splash shield.

3   Remove the coolant pump cover fasteners and cover, if equipped.

4   Remove the two lower pump bolts.
**Note:** *It may be necessary to slightly raise the engine to access the lower bolts.*

5   Remove the hose clamps, and disconnect the hoses. Be sure to note the locations of the clamps for installation purposes.
**Note:** *The hoses have clamp center line marks printed on them. The clamps must be placed on that center line to allow the clamp to be tightened correctly.*

6   Disconnect the electrical connector from the coolant pump, then remove the upper mounting bolt and detach the pump.

**Caution:** *If the coolant pump is being reused, it must be rotated one turn before installation, due to the breakaway torque at the impeller.*

7   Installation is the reverse of removal.

### 3.0L engine

8   Remove the thermostat (see Section 4).

9   Loosen the clamps and disconnect the coolant hoses from the rear of the pump, which is bolted to the right-hand front corner of the cylinder block **(see illustration 4.3)**.

10   Disconnect the electrical connector from the base of the pump.

11   Loosen and remove the pump retaining bolts and withdraw the pump. Discard the retaining bolts; new ones must be used.

## Installation

12   Position the pump against the cylinder block, then install the *new* retaining bolts, tightening them to their specified torque.

13   Reattach the hoses at the rear of the pump and tighten the clamps securely.

14   Reconnect the pump electrical connector.

15   Install the thermostat (see Section 4).

### 8   Heating and ventilation system - general information

1   The heating/ventilation system consists of a multi-speed blower motor, face-level vents in the center and at each end of the instrument panel, and air ducts to the front and rear footwells.

2   The control unit is located in the center of the instrument panel, and the controls operate flap valves to deflect and mix the air flowing through the various parts of the heating/ventilation system. The flap valves are contained in the air distribution housing, which acts as a central distribution unit, passing air to the various ducts and vents.

3   Cold air enters the system through the grille at the rear of the engine compartment. A cabin air filter is installed at the inlet to filter out

dust, spores and soot from the incoming air.

4   The airflow, which can be boosted by the blower, then flows through the various ducts, according to the settings of the controls. Stale air is expelled through ducts at the rear of the vehicle. If warm air is required, the cold air is passed through the heater core, which is heated by the engine coolant.

5   If necessary, the outside air supply can be closed off, allowing the air inside the vehicle to be recirculated. This can be useful to prevent unpleasant odors entering from outside the vehicle, but should only be used briefly, as the recirculated air inside the vehicle will soon deteriorate.

6   Certain models may have optional heated front seats. The heat is produced by electrically-heated mats in the seat and backrest cushions (see Chapter 12). The temperature is regulated automatically by a thermostat, and can be set at one of three levels, controlled by switches on the instrument panel.

### 9   Heater/ventilation components - removal and installation

## Heater/air conditioning/ ventilation control unit

*Refer to illustrations 9.2a and 9.2b*

1   Disconnect the negative battery cable (see Chapter 5).

2   Using a plastic trim tool, carefully pry the control unit from the instrument panel, releasing the clip on each side of the unit **(see illustrations)**. Noting their installed positions, disconnect the electrical connectors as the unit is withdrawn.

3   Carefully unclip the trim piece from the control unit.

4   Installation is the reverse of removal.
**Note:** *If a new control unit has been installed, it must be programmed using BMW test equipment at a BMW dealer or suitably-equipped specialist.*

**6.15  The level switch is located at the base of the expansion tank**

**9.2a  Carefully pry the control unit from the instrument panel**

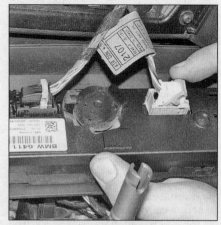

**9.2b  Squeeze the clips and disconnect the electrical connectors**

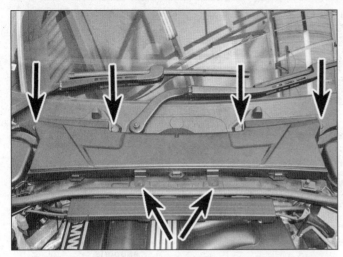

9.6  Remove the bolts and remove the cabin air filter cover

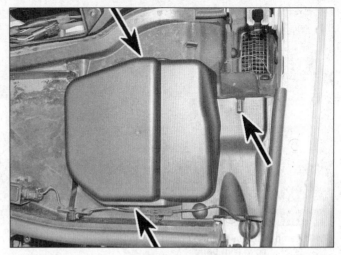

9.7  Release the clips and remove the plastic cover on each side

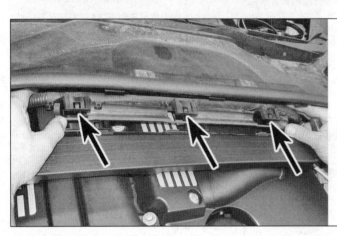

9.8  Release the clips and slide the cable guide forwards

9.9a  Rotate the temperature sensor and pull it from the bracket. On the passenger's side, disconnect the hood switch

## Heater assembly

*Refer to illustrations 9.6, 9.7, 9.8, 9.9a, 9.9b and 9.9c*

5    Have the air conditioning refrigerant discharged and recovered by an air conditioning shop.

6    Working at the rear of the engine compartment, remove the cabin air filter cover mounting bolts and cover **(see illustration)**. Slide the filter from the housing (see Chapter 1).

7    Release the catches and remove the left- and right-hand plastic covers from behind the strut tower on each side of the engine compartment. Unclip the wiring harness where applicable **(see illustration)**.

8    Depress the clips and pull the cable guide forwards from the cabin air filter lower housing **(see illustration)**.

9    Release the catch and remove the mounting bolt on each side, then slide the cabin air filter lower housing forwards and maneuver it out **(see illustrations)**.

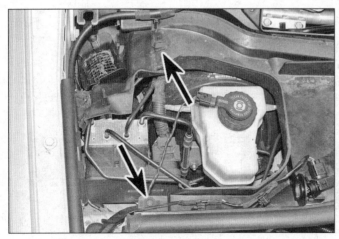

9.9b  Remove the bolt and release the clips on each side of the housing

9.9c  Pull the cabin air filter lower housing forwards

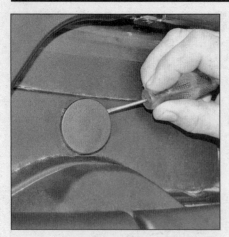

**9.10  Remove the cap in the center of the cowl trim panel**

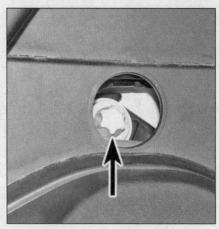

**9.11  Remove the bolt in the center . . .**

**9.12  . . . and the bolt at each end of the supports**

### Models with strut tower supports

*Refer to illustrations 9.10, 9.11 and 9.12*

10    Remove the plastic cap from the center of the cowl trim panel. Two different types of cap are used: one with a central slot, removed by rotating it 45 degrees counterclockwise,
and one without a central slot, which is pried out **(see illustration)**. **Note:** *If the cap or seal are damaged, they must be replaced. Failure to do so may result in water leaks.*

11    Remove the bolt in the center of the cowl **(see illustration)**. Discard the bolt; a new one must be installed.

12    Remove the bolt at each outer end of the
support, then hold the rubber grommet in place and slide the support outwards **(see illustration)**. Do not allow the grommets to fall. Discard the bolts; new ones must be installed.

### All models

*Refer to illustrations 9.13, 9.14, 9.16, 9.19a, 9.19b, 9.20, 9.22a through 9.22i and 9.23*

13    Remove the mounting bolts and detach the refrigerant lines from the expansion valve at the firewall **(see illustration)**. Discard the line seals; new ones must be installed.

14    Remove the mounting bolts, then remove the expansion valve **(see illustration)** and the plate behind the valve.

15    Remove the complete instrument panel (see Chapter 11).

16    Remove the plastic cap from the firewall, then remove the bolt **(see illustration)**.

17    Unclip the left- and right-hand footwell air ducts from the heater assembly.

18    Clamp both heater hoses as close to the firewall as possible to minimize coolant loss. Alternatively, drain the cooling system (see Chapter 1).

19    Disconnect the heater hoses at the firewall **(see illustrations)**. If possible, use compressed air applied to one of the heater

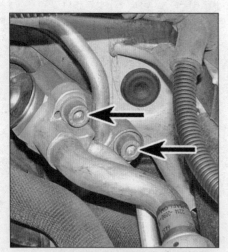

**9.13  Refrigerant line retaining bolts**

**9.14  Expansion valve retaining bolts**

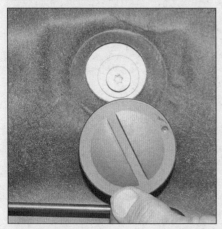

**9.16  Remove the cap and remove the bolt**

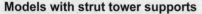

**9.19a  Squeeze together the tabs and release the upper hose clamp . . .**

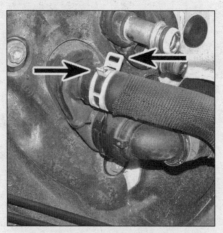

**9.19b  . . . pry out the wire clip and pull the lower hose from the line**

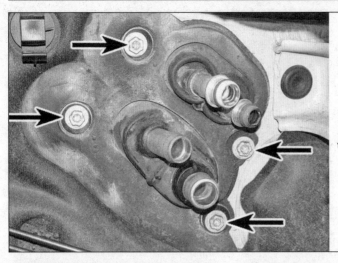

9.20  Remove the nuts, then remove the sealing plate and gasket

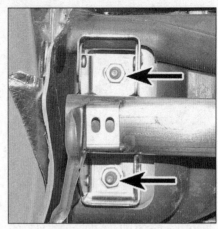

9.22a  The instrument panel crossmember is secured by two nuts at each end . . .

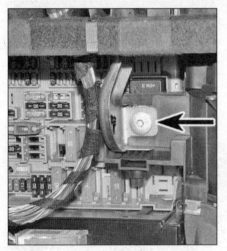

9.22b  . . . a bolt beside the fusebox . . .

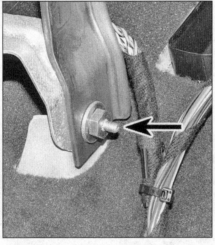

9.22c  . . . a bolt at the floor tunnel . . .

9.22d  . . . a bolt above the pedals . . .

core lines to evacuate coolant from the heater core.

20  Remove the fasteners securing the heater assembly in the area of the coolant hose connections, then carefully remove the sealing plate and gasket **(see illustration)**.

21  Noting their installed positions and routing, then unclip all wiring harnesses/cable ducts from the instrument panel crossmember.

22  Remove the various nuts and bolts and, with the help of an assistant, maneuver the

instrument panel crossmember from the passenger cabin **(see illustrations)**. **Caution:** *The instrument panel crossmember has a lot of sharp edges - it would be a good idea to wear gloves.*

23  Remove the heater assembly from the

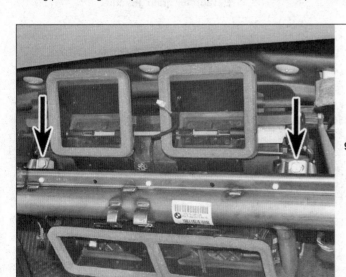

9.22e  . . . the bolts in the center . . .

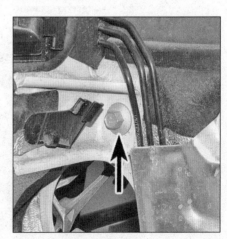

9.22f  . . . a bolt in the engine compartment above the steering column hole . . .

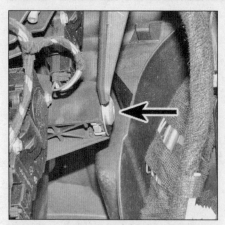

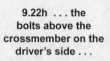

**9.22g** . . . a bolt on the right-hand side of the heater housing . . .

c) *Have the refrigerant recharged by the shop that recovered it.*
d) *Fill the cooling system (see Chapter 1).*

### Heater core

*Refer to illustrations 9.26a, 9.26b, 9.28a, 9.28b, 9.29, 9.30 and 9.31*

25 Remove the heater assembly as described previously in this Section.
26 Peel off the rubber grommet around the lines, and remove the screw securing the

**9.22h** . . . the bolts above the crossmember on the driver's side . . .

mounting plate around the lines **(see illustrations)**.
27 Disconnect the electrical connector from the air recirculation servo motor on the top of the heater blower motor housing, and release the wiring harness from the retaining clips.
28 Remove the mounting bolts and slide the heater blower motor housing upwards from the main heater housing **(see illustrations).**
29 Remove the core cover bolts and the cover **(see illustration)**.
30 Remove the fasteners securing the air

passenger's side. Note the evaporator drain grommet in the floor; make sure it is clear of dirt or debris **(see illustration)**.
24 Installation is the reverse of removal, noting the following points:

a) *Tighten all fasteners to their specified torque, where given.*
b) *Replace all seals and gaskets.*

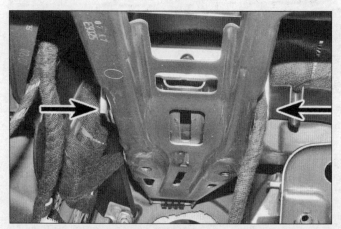

**9.22i** . . . and one on each side of the bracket above the steering column

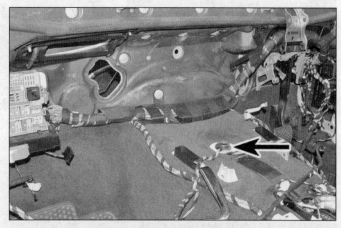

**9.23 Evaporator drain grommet**

**9.26a Peel off the grommet . . .**

**9.26b** . . . and remove the plate retaining screw

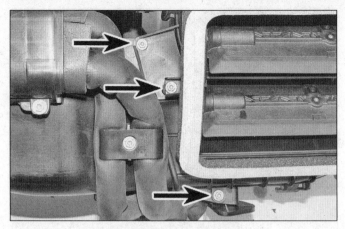

9.28a Remove the mounting bolts . . .

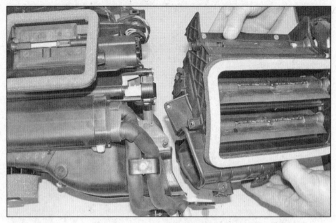

9.28b . . . and slide the blower motor housing upwards

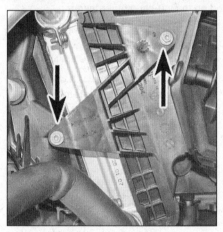

9.29 Core cover bolts

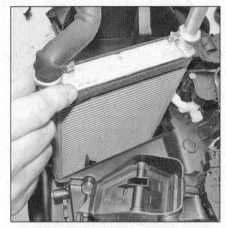

9.30 Slide the core from the housing

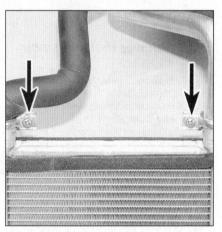

9.31 Loosen the line clamp bolts

conditioning evaporator line clamps, then slide the core and lines from the heater assembly **(see illustration)**. Be prepared for coolant spillage.

31 If necessary, loosen the clamp bolts and detach the lines from the core **(see illustration)**. Discard the sealing rings; new ones must be installed.

32 Installation is the reverse of removal, noting the following points:

a) *Use new sealing rings between the lines and the core.*

b) *When installing the core, the outlet con-*

*nection (slightly larger - marked with a black dot) must be at the top.*

c) *Refill the cooling system (see Chapter 1).*

### Heater blower motor

*Refer to illustrations 9.33, 9.35a and 9.35b*

33 Remove the mounting bolts, and slide the trim panel under the passenger's glove box downwards and rearwards **(see illus-**

tration). Disconnect the footwell light as the panel is withdrawn.

34 Disconnect the blower motor electrical connector.

35 Lift the retaining clip slightly, rotate the blower motor counterclockwise and slide it from the housing **(see illustrations)**.

36 Installation is the reverse of removal, making sure the motor is correctly clipped into the housing.

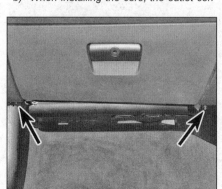

9.33 Panel retaining bolts

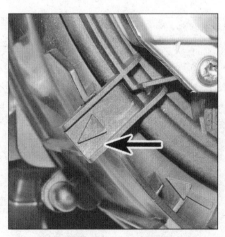

9.35a Lift the retaining clip . . .

9.35b . . . then rotate the blower motor counterclockwise and remove it

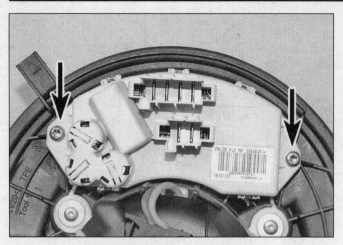

**9.38 Blower motor resistor screws**

**10.4a The refrigerant circuit service ports are located on the left-hand inner fender . . .**

## Heater blower motor resistor

*Refer to illustration 9.38*

37   Remove the heater blower motor (see Steps 33 through 35).
38   Remove the mounting fasteners and the resistor **(see illustration)**.
39   Installation is the reverse of removal, making sure the motor is correctly clipped into the housing.

## 10   Air conditioning system - general information and precautions

### General information

*Refer to illustrations 10.5a and 10.5b*

1   The cooling side of the system works in the same way as a domestic refrigerator. Refrigerant gas is drawn into a belt-driven compressor and passes into a condenser mounted in front of the radiator, where it loses heat and becomes liquid. The liquid passes through an expansion valve to an evaporator, where it changes from liquid under high pres-

sure to gas under low pressure. This change is accompanied by a drop in temperature, which cools the evaporator. The refrigerant returns to the compressor and the cycle begins again.
2   Air blown through the evaporator passes to the air distribution unit, where it is mixed with hot air blown through the heater core to achieve the desired temperature in the passenger compartment.
3   The operation of the system is controlled by the Powertrain Control Module, with a self-diagnosis system. Any problems with the system should be referred to a BMW dealer or air conditioning shop.
4   The air conditioning refrigerant circuit high-pressure and low-pressure service ports are located in the engine compartment **(see illustrations)**.

### Precautions

**Warning:** *The air conditioning system is under high pressure. DO NOT loosen any fittings or remove any components until after the system has been discharged. Air conditioning refrigerant must be properly discharged into an EPA-approved container at a dealer service department or an automotive air conditioning repair*

*facility. Always wear eye protection when disconnecting air conditioning system fittings.*

## 11   Air conditioning system components - removal and installation

**Warning:** *Refer to the precautions in Section 10.*

### Evaporator

*Refer to illustrations 11.3, 11.4a, 11.4b, 11.4c, 11.4d, 1 1.5a, 11.5b and 11.5c*

1   Have the air conditioning refrigerant discharged and recovered by a dealer or air conditioning shop. Remove the heater assembly (see Section 9).
2   Peel off the rubber grommet from the lines, and remove the screw securing the line clamp **(see illustration 9.26a and 9.26b)**.
3   Carefully cut through the foam seal at the top of the heater assembly **(see illustration)**.
4   Remove the upper heater housing mounting screws and housing **(see illustrations)**. Disconnect the positioning motor elec-

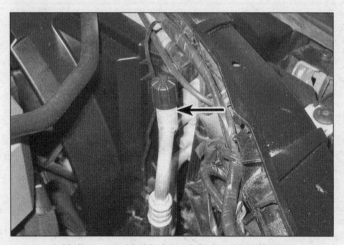

**10.4b . . . and behind the right-hand headlight**

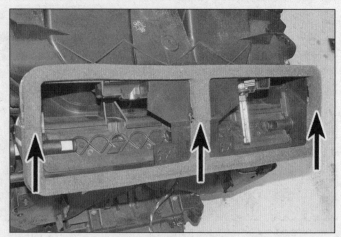

**11.3 Cut through the foam at the points indicated**

11.4a  Remove the mounting screws on the left-hand side . . .

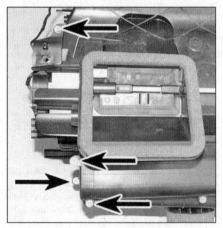

11.4c  . . . and right-hand side of the heater housing . . .

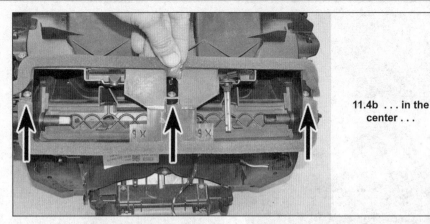

11.4b  . . . in the center . . .

11.4d  . . . then lift off the upper heater housing

11.5a  Lift out the plastic flap . . .

11.5b  . . . and remove the evaporator

11.5c  Recover the plastic cap from the lower edge

trical connectors and outlet temperature sensor plug as the housing is removed.

5    Lift out the plastic flap, then lift the evaporator from the housing. Recover the plastic cap from the lower edge of the evaporator (see illustrations).

6    Installation is the reverse of removal, but note that the receiver/drier should also be replaced. Have the refrigerant recharged by the shop that recovered it, and top-up the coolant level (see Chapter 1).

## Expansion valve

7    Have the air conditioning refrigerant discharged and recovered by a dealer or air conditioning shop.

### Models with strut tower braces

8    Remove the plastic cap from the center of the cowl trim panel. Two different types of the cap are installed: one with a central slot, removed by rotating it 45 degrees counterclockwise, and one without a central slot, which can be pried out (see illustration 9.10).
**Note:** If the cap or seal are damaged, they

must be replaced. Failure to do so may result in water leaks.

9    Remove the bolt in the center of the cowl (see illustration 9.11). Discard the bolt; a new one must be installed.

10    Remove the bolt at each outer end of the supports, then hold the rubber grommet in place and slide the supports out (see illustration 9.12). Do not allow the grommet to fall. Discard the bolts; new ones must be installed.

### All models

11    Working at the rear of the engine compartment, remove the bolts and remove the cabin air filter cover. Slide the filter from the housing (see illustration 9.6).

12    Release the catches and remove the left- and right-hand plastic covers from behind the strut towers on each side of the engine compartment. Unclip the hose from the left-hand cover (see illustration 9.7).

**11.20  Unscrew the cap**

**11.22  Remove the snap-ring and use an old bolt to extract the receiver/drier**

**11.23  Install the desiccant sack into the insert**

13   Depress the clips and pull the cable guide forwards from the cabin air filter lower housing **(see illustration 9.8)**.

14   Release the catch and remove the mounting bolt on each side, then slide the cabin air filter lower housing forwards and maneuver it out **(see illustrations 9.9a and 9.9b)**.

15   Remove the mounting bolts and detach the refrigerant lines from the expansion valve at the firewall **(see illustration 9.13)**. Discard the line seals; new ones must be installed.

16   Remove the mounting bolts and remove the expansion valve **(see illustration 9.14)**. Discard the O-ring seals; new ones must be installed.

17   Installation is the reverse of removal. Have the refrigerant recharged by the shop that recovered it, and top-off the coolant level (see Chapter 1).

## Receiver/drier

*Refer to illustrations 11.20, 11.22 and 11.23*

18   The receiver/drier should be replaced when:

> *There is dirt in the air conditioning system.*
> *The compressor has been replaced.*
> *The condenser or evaporator has been replaced.*
> *A leak has emptied the air conditioning system.*
> *The air conditioning system has been opened for more than 24 hours.*

**11.35  Evaporator temperature sensor**

19   Remove the condenser (see Steps 41 through 44).

20   Unscrew the cap from the condenser **(see illustration)**.

21   Remove the snap-ring securing the receiver/drier insert.

22   Using an old bolt, pull the insert from the receiver/drier **(see illustration)**.

23   Install the new desiccant sack into the new insert, and mount it to the condenser **(see illustration)**. The remainder of installation is the reverse of removal.

## Compressor

24   Have the air conditioning refrigerant discharged and recovered by a dealer or air conditioning shop.

25   On 3.0L engines, remove the thermostat (see Section 4).

26   Remove the mounting bolts and disconnect the air conditioning lines from the compressor. Discard the O-ring seals; new ones must be installed during assembly. Seal/plug the openings to prevent contamination.

27   Remove the drivebelt (see Chapter 1), then disconnect the electrical connector from the compressor.

28   Firmly apply the parking brake, then raise the front of the vehicle and support it securely on jackstands. Remove the mounting fasteners and remove the engine splash shield.

29   On 2.0L engines, remove the charge air inlet duct (see Chapter 4).

30   Working underneath the vehicle, remove the compressor mounting bolts and the compressor.

31   Installation is the reverse of removal, noting the following points:

a)   *Prior to installing the compressor, it is essential that the correct amount of refrigerant oil is added - refer to your dealer for the correct amount and specification.*

b)   *Always use new seals when reconnecting the refrigerant lines.*

c)   *Replace the receiver/drier.*

d)   *Have the refrigerant recharged by the shop that recovered it.*

## Sunlight sensor

32   Using a blunt, flat-bladed tool, carefully pry the sensor from the center of the instrument panel. Disconnect the electrical connector, and secure the harness from falling into the instrument panel with tape.

33   Installation is the reverse of removal.

## Evaporator temperature sensor

*Refer to illustration 11.35*

34   Remove the mounting bolts, then pull the trim panel under the passenger's side of the instrument panel downward and rearward **(see illustration 9.33)**. Disconnect the footwell light electrical connector as the panel is withdrawn.

35   Disconnect the sensor electrical connector, then withdraw the sensor from the heater housing **(see illustration)**.

36   Installation is the reverse of removal.

## Pressure sensor

**Note:** *The pressure sensor is located on the refrigerant line on the left-hand side of the engine compartment.*

37   Have the air conditioning refrigerant discharged by a BMW dealer or air conditioning shop.

38   Remove the mounting bolts and move the heat shield to one side.

39   Disconnect the sensor electrical connector and unscrew the sensor. Plug/seal the openings to prevent contamination.

40   Installation is the reverse of removal. Tighten the sensor securely and have the refrigerant recharged by a BMW dealer or air conditioning shop.

## Condenser

*Refer to illustrations 11.43 and 11.44*

**Note:** *The condenser is located in front of the radiator.*

41   Have the air conditioning refrigerant discharged and recovered by a dealer or air conditioning shop.

42   Remove the radiator (see Section 3).

43   Remove the mounting bolts and disconnect the refrigerant lines from the condenser **(see illustration)**. Discard the O-ring seals; new ones must be installed.

44   Remove the retaining bolt, pry out the retaining plate, and pull the right-hand side of the condenser rearward **(see illustration)**. Maneuver the condenser out.

45   Installation is the reverse of removal, noting the following points:

a) *Prior to installing the condenser it is essential that the correct amount of refrigerant oil is added - refer to your dealer for the correct amount and specification.*

b) *Always use new seals when reconnecting the refrigerant lines.*

c) *Replace the receiver/drier.*

d) *Have the refrigerant recharged by the shop that recovered it.*

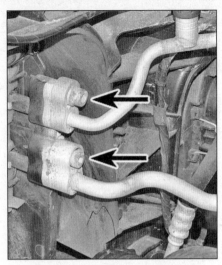

**11.43  Refrigerant line bolts**

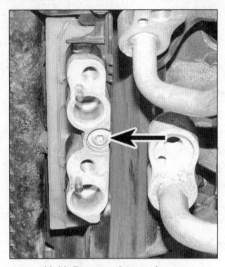

**11.44  Remove the condenser retaining bolt**

## 12   Radiator airflow control flaps and motor - removal and installation

*Refer to illustrations 12.2a, 12.2b, 12.3, 12.4a and 12.4b*

1   Remove the front bumper (see Chapter 11).

2   Pry up the center pins, pry out the pushpins, then remove the mounting bolts. Remove the intake ducting from the radiator support **(see illustrations)**.

3   Remove the Torx bolts and the bumper bar support **(see illustration)**.

4   Remove the Torx bolts, disconnect the electrical connector and pull the control flap

assembly forward from the vehicle **(see illustrations)**.

5   Installation is the reverse of removal.

**12.2b  Pry up the center pins and pry out the pushpins**

**12.2a  Remove the bolts and remove the plastic pushpins**

**12.3  Remove the Torx bolts and remove the bumper bar support**

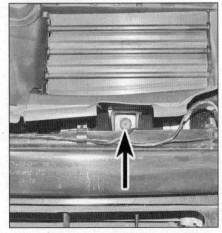

**12.4a  Remove the Torx bolt on each side . . .**

**12.4b  . . . and remove the control flap assembly**

# Notes

# Chapter 4
# Fuel and exhaust systems

## Contents

## Specifications

### Fuel system

| | |
|---|---|
| Fuel pump type | Electric, mounted in fuel tank |
| Fuel pressure regulator rating (in-tank) | 72 psi ± 0.3 psi (5.0 ± 0.02 bars) |
| Tank level sensor resistance | |
| Empty tank | 59 ohms |
| Full tank | 992 ohms |

### Torque specifications

**Note:** *One foot-pound (ft-lb) of torque is equivalent to 12 inch-pounds (in-lbs) of torque. Torque values below approximately 15 foot-pounds are expressed in inch-pounds, because most foot-pound torque wrenches are not accurate at these smaller values.*

| | Ft-lbs (unless otherwise indicated) | Nm |
|---|---|---|
| Camshaft position sensor bolt | 60 in-lbs | 7 |
| Coolant temperature sensor | 120 in-lbs | 13 |
| Crankshaft position sensor bolt* | | |
| Stage 1 | 24 in-lbs | 3 |
| Stage 2 | Tighten an additional 45-degrees | |
| Exhaust manifold nuts* - 3.0L engine | | |
| M6 nuts | 84 in-lbs | 10 |
| M7 nuts | 15 | 20 |
| M8 nuts | 16 | 22 |
| Fuel rail-to-intake manifold bolts | | |
| 2.0L engine | 71 in-lbs | 8 |
| 3.0L engine | 84 in-lbs | 10 |
| Fuel high-pressure sensor - 2.0L engine | 18 | 25 |
| Fuel injector coupling element bolts – 2.0L engine | 18 | 25 |
| Fuel injector pressure line unions – 2.0L engine | 133 in-lbs | 15 |
| Intake manifold - 3.0L engine | | |
| M6 | 84 in-lbs | 10 |
| M7 | 132 in-lbs | 15 |
| M8 | 16 | 22 |
| High pressure fuel pump feed line union - 2.0L engine | 22 | 30 |
| High pressure fuel pump-to-fuel rail line union - 2.0L engine | 22 | 30 |
| High pressure fuel pump bolts - 2.0L engine | 108 in-lbs | 12 |
| Exhaust module nuts-to-cylinder head - **(see illustration 13.23)** | | |
| Step 1 | 71 in-lbs | 8 |
| Step 2 | 115 in-lbs | 13 |
| Exhaust module heat shield bolts-to-cylinder head | 168 in-lbs | 19 |
| Wastegate vacuum unit bolts | 15 | 20 |
| Blow-off valve | 88 in-lbs | 10 |
| Intake plenum mounting nuts – 2.0L engine | 133 in-lbs | 15 |
| Engine compartment tension strut* | | |
| M10 | | |
| Stage 1 | 30 | 40 |
| Stage 2 | Tighten an additional 60-degrees | |
| M12 | | |
| Stage 1 | 74 | 100 |
| Stage 2 | Tighten an additional 90-degrees | |
| Transmission tunnel reinforcement plate | 18 | 24 |

* Do not re-use

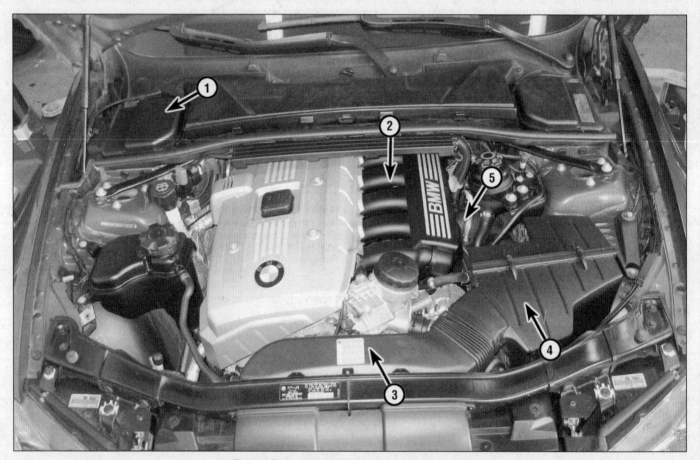

**Typical fuel system components – 3.0L engines**

| | | |
|---|---|---|
| 1 | Underhood fuse/relay box (under cover) | 2 | Intake manifold | 4 | Air filter housing |
| | | 3 | Intake air duct | 5 | Inlet hose to throttle body |

## 1   General information

### Fuel system warnings

Gasoline is extremely flammable and repairing fuel system components can be dangerous. Consider your automotive repair knowledge and experience before attempting repairs which may be better suited for a professional mechanic.

- Don't smoke or allow open flames or bare light bulbs near the work area
- Don't work in a garage with a gas-type appliance (water heater, clothes dryer)
- Use fuel-resistant gloves. If any fuel spills on your skin, wash it off immediately with soap and water
- Clean up spills immediately
- Do not store fuel-soaked rags where they could ignite
- Prior to disconnecting any fuel line, you must relieve the fuel pressure (see Section 3)
- Wear safety glasses
- Have a proper fire extinguisher on hand

### Fuel system

The fuel system consists of the fuel tank, electric fuel pump/fuel level sending unit (located in the fuel tank), fuel rail and fuel injectors. The fuel injection system is a multi-port system; multi-port fuel injection uses timed impulses to inject the fuel directly into the intake port of each cylinder. The Powertrain Control Module (PCM) controls the injectors. The PCM monitors various engine parameters and delivers the exact amount of fuel required into the intake ports.

Fuel is circulated from the fuel pump to the fuel rail through fuel lines running along the underside of the vehicle. Various sections of the fuel line are either rigid metal or nylon, or flexible fuel hose. The various sections of the fuel hose are connected either by quick-connect fittings or threaded metal fittings.

### Exhaust system

The exhaust system consists of the exhaust manifold(s), catalytic converter(s), muffler(s), tailpipe and all connecting pipes, flanges and clamps. The catalytic converters are an emission control device added to the exhaust system to reduce pollutants.

## 2   Troubleshooting

### Fuel pump

Refer to illustration 2.2

1   The fuel pump is located inside the fuel tank. Sit inside the vehicle with the windows closed, turn the ignition key to ON (not START) and listen for the sound of the fuel pump as it's briefly activated. You will only hear the sound for a second or two, but that sound tells you that the pump is working. Alternatively, have an assistant listen at the fuel filler cap.
**Note:** On F-series chassis, the fuel pump starts up automatically every time the door is opened.

2   If the pump does not come on, check the fuel pump fuse and relay **(see illustration)**. If the fuse and relay are okay, check the wiring back to the fuel pump. If the fuse, relay and wiring are okay, the fuel pump is probably defective. If the pump runs continuously with the ignition key in the ON position, the Powertrain Control Module (PCM) is probably defective. Have the PCM checked by a professional mechanic.

### Fuel injection system

Refer to illustration 2.9

**Note:** The following procedure is based on the assumption that the fuel pump is working and the fuel pressure is adequate (see Section 4).

3   Check all electrical connectors that are related to the system. Check the ground wire connections for tightness.

4   Verify that the battery is fully charged (see Chapter 5).

5   Inspect the air filter element (see Chapter 1).

6   Check all fuses related to the fuel system (see Chapter 12).

7   Check the air induction system between the throttle body and the intake manifold for air leaks. Also inspect the condition of all vacuum hoses connected to the intake manifold and to the throttle body.

8   Remove the air intake duct from the throttle body and look for dirt, carbon, varnish, or other residue in the throttle body, particularly around the throttle plate. If it's dirty, clean it with carb cleaner, a toothbrush and a clean shop towel.

9   With the engine running, place an automotive stethoscope against each injector, one at a time, and listen for a clicking sound that indicates operation **(see illustration)**. **Warning:** Stay clear of the drivebelt and any rotating or hot components.

10   If you can hear the injectors operating, but the engine is misfiring, the electrical circuits are functioning correctly, but the injectors might be dirty or clogged. Try a commercial injector cleaning product (available at auto parts stores). If cleaning the injectors doesn't help, replace the injectors.

11   If an injector is not operating (it makes no sound), disconnect the injector electrical connector and measure the resistance across the injector terminals with an ohmmeter. Compare this measurement to the other injectors. If the resistance of the non-operational injector is quite different from the other injectors, replace it.

12   If the injector is not operating, but the resistance reading is within the range of resistance of the other injectors, the PCM or the circuit between the PCM and the injector might be faulty.

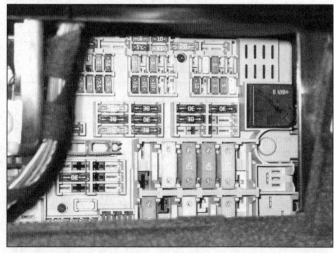

**2.2  The fuel pump fuse and relay are located in the interior fuse panel behind the glove box - use the cover legend to locate them**

**2.9  An automotive stethoscope is used to listen to the fuel injectors in operation**

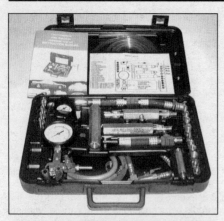

**4.1  This fuel pressure testing kit contains all the necessary fittings and adapters, along with the fuel pressure gauge, to test most automotive systems**

**6.1  A typical exhaust system hanger. Inspect regularly and replace at the first sign of damage or deterioration**

---

### 3    Fuel pressure relief procedure

**Warning:** *Gasoline is extremely flammable. See* **Fuel system warnings** *in Section 1.*
1    Remove the fuel filler cap to relieve any pressure built-up in the fuel tank.

#### 2.0L engine
2    Disconnect the electrical connector from the fuel pump (see Section 7).
3    Start the engine and allow it to run until it stalls.
**Warning:** *If you will be working on the high-pressure fuel pump, high-pressure fuel lines or fuel injectors, wait at least two hours before starting work.*
4    Disconnect the cable from the negative terminal of the battery (see Chapter 5).
5    Cover all fuel line connections with a rag before disconnecting them. Dispose of the rags properly.

#### 3.0L engine
6    Disconnect the cable from the negative terminal of the battery (see Chapter 5).
7    Locate the fuel pressure test port on the fuel rail, then unscrew the cap.
8    Surround and cover the test port with shop rags, then depress the Schrader valve inside the test port with a small screw-driver until the pressure in the fuel system is relieved. Properly dispose of the rags.

---

### 4    Fuel pressure - check

*Refer to illustration 4.1*
**Warning:** *Gasoline is extremely flammable. See* **Fuel system warnings** *in Section 1.*
**Note:** *The following procedure assumes that the fuel pump is receiving voltage and runs.*
1    2.0L models: Relieve the fuel system pressure (see Section 3). Raise the rear of the vehicle and support it securely on jackstands,

then remove the rear splash shield from under the vehicle. Remove the fuel line protective plate from the right rear of the vehicle, then disconnect the fuel feed line and using a T-fitting adapter, attach the fuel pressure gauge **(see illustration)**.
2    3.0L models: Locate the fuel pressure test port on the fuel rail, unscrew the cap and connect a fuel pressure gauge.
3    Start the engine and allow it to idle. Note the gauge reading as soon as the pressure stabilizes, and compare it with the pressure listed in this Chapter's Specifications.
4    If the fuel pressure is not within specifications, check the following:

   a)  *Check for a restriction in the fuel system (kinked fuel line, plugged fuel pump inlet strainer or clogged fuel filter, which is an integral part of the fuel pump module). If no restrictions are found, replace the fuel pump module (see Section 7).*
   b)  *If the fuel pressure is higher than specified, replace the fuel pump module (see Section 7).*

5    Turn off the engine. Fuel pressure should not fall more than 8 psi over five minutes. If it does, the problem could be a leaky fuel injector, fuel line leak, or faulty fuel pump module.
6    If you're working on a 2.0L model, relieve the fuel system pressure (see Section 3).
7    Disconnect the fuel pressure gauge. Wipe up any spilled gasoline.

---

### 5    Fuel lines and fittings - general information and disconnection

**Warning:** *Gasoline is extremely flammable. See* **Fuel system warnings** *in Section 1.*
1    Relieve the fuel pressure before servicing fuel lines or fittings (see Section 3), then disconnect the cable from the negative battery terminal (see Chapter 5) before proceeding.
2    The fuel supply line connects the fuel pump in the fuel tank to the fuel rail on the engine. The Evaporative Emission (EVAP)

system lines connect the fuel tank to the EVAP canister and connect the canister to the intake manifold.
3    Whenever you're working under the vehicle, be sure to inspect all fuel and evaporative emission lines for leaks, kinks, dents and other damage. Always replace a damaged fuel or EVAP line immediately.
4    If you find signs of dirt in the lines during disassembly, disconnect all lines and blow them out with compressed air. Inspect the fuel strainer on the fuel pump pick-up unit for damage and deterioration.

#### Steel tubing
5    It is critical that the fuel lines be replaced with lines of equivalent type and specification.
6    Some steel fuel lines have threaded fittings. When loosening these fittings, hold the stationary fitting with a wrench while turning the tube nut.

#### Plastic tubing
7    When replacing fuel system plastic tubing, use only original equipment replacement plastic tubing. **Caution:** *When removing or installing plastic fuel line tubing, be careful not to bend or twist it too much, which can damage it. Also, plastic fuel tubing is NOT heat resistant, so keep it away from excessive heat.*

#### Flexible hoses
8    When replacing fuel system flexible hoses, use only original equipment replacements.
9    Don't route fuel hoses (or metal lines) within four inches of the exhaust system or within ten inches of the catalytic converter. Make sure that no rubber hoses are installed directly against the vehicle, particularly in places where there is any vibration. If allowed to touch some vibrating part of the vehicle, a hose can easily become chafed and it might start leaking. A good rule of thumb is to maintain a minimum of 1/4-inch clearance around a hose (or metal line) to prevent contact with the vehicle underbody.

---

### 6    Exhaust system servicing - general information

*Refer to illustration 6.1*
**Warning:** *Allow exhaust system components to cool before inspection or repair. Also, when working under the vehicle, make sure it is securely supported on jackstands.*
1    The exhaust system consists of the exhaust manifolds, catalytic converter, muffler, tailpipe and all connecting pipes, flanges and clamps. The exhaust system is isolated from the vehicle body and from chassis components by a series of rubber hangers **(see illustration)**. Periodically inspect these hangers for cracks or other signs of deterioration, replacing them as necessary.

# Disconnecting Fuel Line Fittings

Two-tab type fitting; depress both tabs with your fingers, then pull the fuel line and the fitting apart

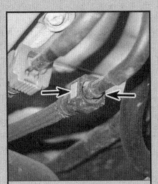

On this type of fitting, depress the two buttons on opposite sides of the fitting, then pull it off the fuel line

Threaded fuel line fitting; hold the stationary portion of the line or component (A) while loosening the tube nut (B) with a flare-nut wrench

Plastic collar-type fitting; rotate the outer part of the fitting

Metal collar quick-connect fitting; pull the end of the retainer off the fuel line and disengage the other end from the female side of the fitting . . .

. . . insert a fuel line separator tool into the female side of the fitting, push it into the fitting and pull the fuel line off the pipe

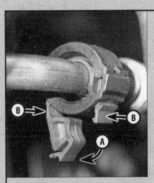

Some fittings are secured by lock tabs. Release the lock tab (A) and rotate it to the fully-opened position, squeeze the two smaller lock tabs (B) . . .

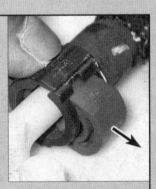

. . . then push the retainer out and pull the fuel line off the pipe

Spring-lock coupling; remove the safety cover, install a coupling release tool and close the tool around the coupling . . .

. . . push the tool into the fitting, then pull the two lines apart

Hairpin clip type fitting: push the legs of the retainer clip together, then push the clip down all the way until it stops and pull the fuel line off the pipe

2   Conduct regular inspections of the exhaust system to keep it safe and quiet. Look for any damaged or bent parts, open seams, holes, loose connections, excessive corrosion or other defects which could allow exhaust fumes to enter the vehicle. Do not repair deteriorated exhaust system components; replace them with new parts.

3   If the exhaust system components are extremely corroded, or rusted together, a cutting torch is the most convenient tool for removal. Consult a properly-equipped repair shop. If a cutting torch is not available, you can use a hacksaw, or if you have compressed air, there are special pneumatic cutting chisels that can also be used. Wear safety goggles to protect your eyes from metal chips and wear work gloves to protect your hands.

4   Here are some simple guidelines to follow when repairing the exhaust system:

a) *Work from the back to the front when removing exhaust system components.*

b) *Apply penetrating oil to the exhaust system component fasteners to make them easier to remove.*

c) *Use new gaskets, hangers and clamps.*

d) *Apply anti-seize compound to the threads of all exhaust system fasteners during reassembly.*

e) *Be sure to allow sufficient clearance between newly installed parts and all points on the underbody to avoid overheating the floor pan and possibly damaging the interior carpet and insulation. Pay particularly close attention to the catalytic converter and heat shield.*

## 7   Fuel pump/fuel level sensors - removal and installation

### *Removal*

1   There are two level senders installed in the fuel tank - one on each side. The pump is integral with the right-hand side sender, and at the time of writing, the pump and sender can only be replaced as an assembly. Check with a BMW dealer or parts specialist.

### Right-hand fuel level sender and fuel pump

*Refer to illustrations 7.5, 7.6a, 7.6b, 7.7, 7.8, 7.9 and 7.11*

2   Before removing the fuel level sender and fuel pump assembly, all fuel should be drained from the tank. Since a fuel tank drain plug is not provided, it is preferable to carry out the removal operation when the tank is nearly empty.

3   Remove the rear seat cushion (see Chapter 11).

4   Fold back the insulation material to expose the access cover.

5   Remove the mounting nuts, and remove the access cover from the floor **(see illustration)**.

6   Through the access hole, disconnect the electrical connectors, then depress the release button and disconnect the vent hose from the fuel level sensor and fuel pump cover **(see illustrations)**. Be prepared with a

container to collect fuel spillage.

7   Unscrew the fuel level sender and fuel pump assembly locking ring and remove it from the tank. Although a BMW tool (No 16 1 020) is available for this task, it can be accomplished using a large pair of pliers to push on two opposite raised ribs on the locking ring. Alternatively, a home-made tool can be fabricated to engage with the raised ribs of the locking ring. Turn the ring counterclockwise until it can be unscrewed by hand. Make an alignment mark between the collar and the tank to aid reassembly **(see illustration)**.

8   Carefully lift the fuel level sender and fuel pump assembly cover from the tank. Disconnect the vent hose and wiring plugs from the base of the cover. Note how the rods in the base of the cover are mounted in the assembly **(see illustration)**. Do not detach the black plastic wire connection between the cover and the pump unit - it's essential to stop the pump unit floating away during reassembly.

9   Noting their installed locations, disconnect the hoses from the assembly **(see illustration)**.

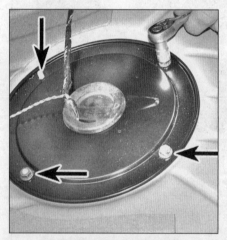

**7.5  Remove the access cover mounting nuts**

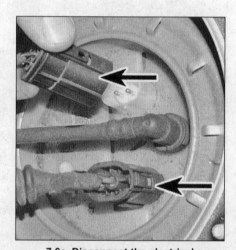

**7.6a  Disconnect the electrical connectors . . .**

**7.6b  . . . then depress the release button and disconnect the vent hose**

**7.7  Using a homemade tool to unscrew the locking ring**

**7.8  Disconnect the electrical connectors and vent hose**

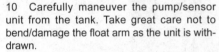

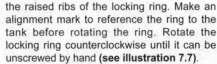

**7.9  Press in the button, disconnect the main hose, then unclip the remaining hoses**

**7.11  Release the clips and slide the level sensor upwards**

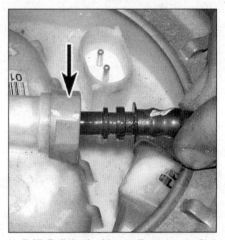

**7.15  Pull the locking collar away and disconnect the pipe**

10   Carefully maneuver the pump/sensor unit from the tank. Take great care not to bend/damage the float arm as the unit is withdrawn.

11   If required, the level sensor can be unclipped from the pump assembly **(see illustration)**. On full deflection, the sender resistance should read 993 ohms, and on zero deflection, the resistance should read 51 ohms.

### Left-hand fuel level sender

*Refer to illustrations 7.15, 7.17 and 7.18*

12   Remove the right-hand fuel level sensor and fuel pump (see Steps 2 through 11).

13   Fold back the insulation material to expose the access cover.

14   Remove the access cover mounting nuts and the cover from the floor **(see illustration 7.5)**.

15   Disconnect the wiring plug from the sensor unit cover, then pull the locking collar away and disconnect the fuel supply pipe **(see illustration)**.

16   Unscrew the fuel level sender locking ring and remove it from the tank. Although a BMW tool (No 16 1 020) is available for this task, it can be accomplished using a large pair of grips to push on two opposite raised ribs on the locking ring. Alternatively, a homemade tool can be fabricated to engage with

the raised ribs of the locking ring. Make an alignment mark to reference the ring to the tank before rotating the ring. Rotate the locking ring counterclockwise until it can be unscrewed by hand **(see illustration 7.7)**.

17   Tie a length of string or wire around the disconnected hoses accessible through the right-hand tank access hole, as these hoses will be removed with the left-hand fuel level sender **(see illustration)**. The idea is to pull the string or wire into the tank as the sender is removed, then leave it in place to facilitate installation.

18   Carefully lift the sender from the tank, and remove it **(see illustration)**. Untie the string or wire and leave it in place.

### Installation

*Refer to illustration 7.19*

19   Installation is the reverse of removal, noting the following points:

a) *Use a new sealing ring.*
b) *To allow the unit to pass through the aperture in the fuel tank, press the float arm against the fuel pick-up strainer.*
c) *When the unit is installed, the locating lug on the unit must engage with the corresponding slot in the fuel tank collar* **(see illustration)**.

d) *The locating rods of the right-hand sender unit cover must align with the corresponding holes in the pump/sender assembly.*
e) *The locking ring must be tightened until the notch on the ring aligns with the mark on the tank.*

**7.17  Tie string or wire around the hoses, then attach string to the main transfer hose to aid replacement**

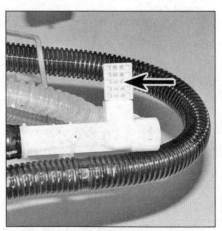

**7.18  The fuel pick-up pipe incorporates a coarse filter**

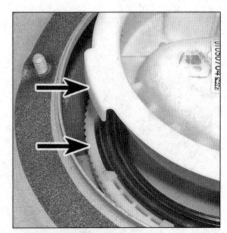

**7.19  The lug must engage with the slot on the tank collar**

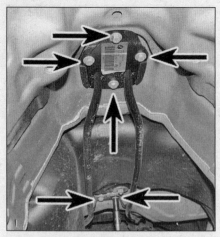

**8.7  Remove the bolts and the guide tubes**

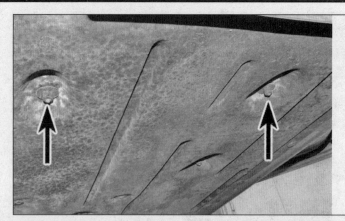

**8.9a  Remove the nuts and lower the panels in front of the tank**

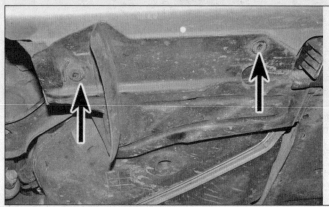

**8.9b  Remove the fasteners and remove the sill trim panels**

## 8　Fuel tank - removal and installation

*Refer to illustrations 8.7, 8.9a, 8.9b, 8.13 and 8.14*

1　Disconnect the negative battery cable (see Chapter 5).

2　Before removing the fuel tank, all fuel should be drained from the tank. Since a fuel tank drain plug is not provided, it is preferable to carry out the removal operation when the tank is nearly empty.

3　Remove the rear seat cushion (see Chapter 11).

4　Raise the rear of the vehicle and support it securely on jackstands. Remove the right rear wheel.

5　Remove the driveshaft (see Chapter 8).

6　Detach the parking brake cables from the lever (see Chapter 9).

7　Pull the parking brake cables from the guide tubes, then remove the guide tube mounting bolts and tubes **(see illustration)**.

8　The right wheelwell liner is retained by a combination of bolts, plastic nuts, and plastic pushpins. Remove these fasteners and maneuver the wheelwell liner from under the fender.

9　Working under the vehicle, pry up the center pins and remove the plastic expansion rivets. Release the clips, remove the trim panel mounting nuts and the panel from under the left-hand side of the tank **(see illustrations)**. Repeat this procedure on the right-hand side of the tank.

10　Working inside the vehicle, remove the fuel tank access cover mounting nuts from the left- and right-hand side of the floor panel beneath the rear seat cushion location.

11　Disconnect the wiring plug from the left-hand sender cover, then pull the locking collar away and disconnect the fuel feed pipe **(see illustration 7.15)**.

12　Disconnect the wiring plugs accessible through the right-hand sender/pump access hole. Depress the release button and disconnect the vent pipe from the sensor/pump unit cover **(see illustrations 7.6a and 7.6b)**.

13　Loosen the hose clip, then disconnect the fuel filler hose from the tank neck **(see illustration)**.

14　Working in the wheelwell area, release the connector, and unclip the vent hose from the filler pipe **(see illustration)**.

15　Support the fuel tank using a floorjack and a block of wood.

16　Remove the retaining nut in the center rear of the tank and the bolts securing the tank retaining straps. Lower the tank, and maneuver it out from under the vehicle.

17　Installation is the reverse of removal. Note that once the tank is installed, a minimum of 1.2 gallons (5 liters) of fuel must be added to allow the fuel system to function correctly.

## 9　Throttle body - removal and installation

### *Removal*

*Refer to illustrations 9.6, 9.7, 9.8, 9.9a, 9.9b, 9.9c and 9.11*

1　Disconnect the negative battery cable (see Chapter 5)

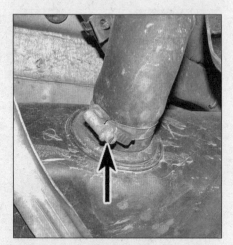

**8.13  Loosen the filler neck hose clip**

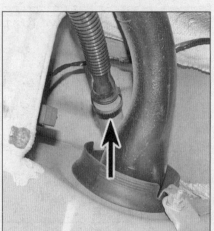

**8.14  Squeeze together the sides of the collar and disconnect the vent hose**

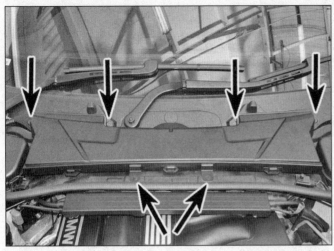

9.6 Remove the bolts and remove the cabin air filter cover

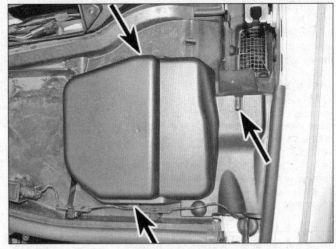

9.7 Release the clips and remove the plastic cover on each side behind the strut towers

9.8 Depress the clips and slide the cable guide(s) forward

9.9a Rotate the temperature sensor counterclockwise and pull it from the bracket on the lower cabin air filter cover

9.9b Release the catch and remove the bolt on each side . . .

## 2.0L engine

2   Remove the engine cover by lifting the front of the cover up and pulling it forwards.
3   Remove the strut tower crossbrace plastic push-pins and bolts, then remove the brace.
4   Remove the sound insulator plastic retainers and lift the insulator off the engine.
5   Remove the charge air duct to the throttle body.

## 3.0L engine

6   Remove the cabin air filter housing mounting bolts, and the housing (see illustration).
7   Release the clips and remove the plastic cover behind the left suspension strut tower in the engine compartment (see illustration). Repeat this procedure for the plastic cover behind the right hand strut tower.
8   Release the mounting clips and detach the cable guide from the front of the cabin air

filter lower housing (see illustration).
9   Remove the mounting bolt and release the clip on each side. Pull the lower section of the cabin air filter housing forwards and maneuver it out (see illustrations).
10   Remove the air filter housing (see Chapter 1).
11   Release the clamp and disconnect the air intake duct from the throttle body (see illustration).

9.9c . . . then pull the lower cabin air filter cover forwards

9.11 Intake duct clamp location

### All models

12   Unlock and disconnect the throttle body electrical connector and vent hose, if equipped. Remove the mounting bolts and the throttle body.

### *Installation*

13   Examine the throttle body-to-intake manifold O-ring seal. If it is in good condition, it can be re-used. Install the throttle body to the manifold, and tighten the mounting bolts securely.
14   The remainder of installation is the reverse of removal. Check for any diagnostic trouble codes and delete any stored fault codes (see Chapter 6).

---

### 10  Fuel rail and injectors - removal and installation

---

1   Disconnect the negative battery cable (see Chapter 5, Section 3).

### *2.0L engine*

#### Removal

2   Relieve the fuel system pressure (see

**10.17a Remove the Teflon seal from the injector using a sharp knife...**

Section 3).
3   Disconnect the cable from the negative terminal of the battery (see Chapter 5).
4   Remove the engine cover, by lifting the front of the cover up and pulling it forwards. Remove the strut tower crossbrace plastic push-pins and bolts then remove the brace. Remove the sound insulator plastic retainers and lift the insulator off of the engine.
5   Remove the ignition coils (see Chapter 5).
6   Remove and replace the high pressure fuel line to the high pressure pump (see Section 12).
7   Disconnect the electrical connector to the high pressure sensor at the end of the fuel rail.
8   Place clean rags to collect any fuel, then, starting with the unions on the fuel rail, loosen and pull up the high-pressure fuel pipe unions from the fuel rail to the injectors.
9   Loosen the fuel rail bolts, slowly and evenly, a 1/4-turn at a time until the rail is loose in the brackets.
10   Carefully rotate the fuel rail up, counterclockwise, until the fuel line unions to the injectors are clear of the injectors.
**Caution:** *Do not bend or distort the fuel lines at the injectors or at the fuel rail.*
11   Disconnect the electrical connectors from the injectors.
12   Loosen the ground wire retaining bolt just enough to remove the ground wire, then move the harness out of the way.
**Caution:** *The ground wire is held in place by one of the injector hold-down element bolts; if the bolts are not loosened and removed evenly, the hold-down element can tilt and damage the injector or injector threads.*
13   The hold-down elements are shaped like a "T;" loosen the bolt at the end of the T, first a little at a time, then the middle bolt, alternating between the bolts evenly until the hold-down element can be removed.
14   If necessary, use a vacuum cleaner to remove all dirt and debris from the area adjacent to the high-pressure pipes, injectors, etc. It's essential that these areas be completely clean.

**Caution:** *Do not allow fuel to contact the ignition coils, as the resistance of the silicone material used in the coils is significantly reduced by contact with fuel.*
15   Pull the injectors from the bores in the cylinder head. Place plastic caps over each injector fuel intake port and injection nozzle. Caps of various sizes are available from BMW dealers or automotive parts store.
**Caution:** *If the injectors are twisted with 53 in-lbs (6 Nm) of force or more while being removed, the injector(s) must be replaced.*
**Note:** *If the injector(s) are stuck, use BMW special tool No. 13 0 320 (or equivalent) to remove them.*
**Note:** *If the injectors are to be re-used, mark their positions. It's essential they be reinstalled to their original positions.*

### Installation

*Refer to illustrations 10.17a, 10.17b, 10.20a and 10.20b*

16   Use a small screwdriver to remove the coupling element from each injector. New ones must be installed.
17   Using a sharp razor knife (or the tools supplied in the BMW special tool kit) carefully cut the Teflon ring from the ends of the injectors. Take great care not to mark the metal of the injector nozzle **(see illustrations)**.
18   Clean the cylindrical part of each injector nozzle using clean, fluff-free rags – don't use any other cleaning agents/tools. Do not attempt to clean the nozzle tip.
19   New injectors are supplied with the Teflon ring already installed, and secured with plastic caps.
20   To replace the Teflon ring when reusing the original injectors, BMW technicians use a number of special tools (No. 13 0 190, 13 0 281, 13 0 282 and 13 0 283) which spreads the seal, pushes it into place, and compresses it into place afterwards (see illustrations). Equivalent tools may also available from specialist automotive tool manufacturers. If these tools are unavailable, the job should be left to a BMW dealer or specialist. Note that the seal must not be lubricated.

**10.17b... or the tools provided in the BMW kit**

**10.20a  Slide the new seal over the tapered installation tool . . .**

**10.20b . . . and into the groove on the injector**

10.39 Pull the plastic engine cover upwards - the bolt heads are fake

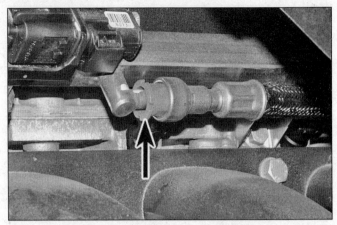

10.41 Press in the collar and disconnect the fuel feed pipe

21   When reusing the injectors, the coupling element must be replaced on each injector.

22   Use a nylon brush and a vacuum cleaner to thoroughly clean out the injector holes in the cylinder head. Take care not to let any debris fall into the combustion chamber.

23   If new injectors are being installed, their adjustment values must be programmed into the engine management ECM (DME) using dedicated diagnostic equipment/scanner. Make a note of the values on each injector before installing. They are printed on the injector body in a row; use the last 3-digits. If this equipment is not available, this should be done by a BMW dealer or BMW specialist.

**Note:** *It may be possible to drive the vehicle, with considerable reduced performance/increased emissions, to a dealer or BMW specialist for the numbers to be programmed, but the engine may run poorly or fail to start.*

24   Remove the plastic caps/compressing tool, and install each injector into its original position.

**Warning:** *The injectors must not be twisted with more than 53 in-lbs (6 Nm) of force while being installed or the injector(s) Teflon ring must be replaced.*

25   Place special tool No. 13 0 320 (or equivalent) over the injectors and install the coupling element bolts with a few turns. Screw the union sleeves of the tool onto the injectors. Tighten the knurled knobs on top of the union sleeves until all the play is gone.

26   Tighten the coupling element bolts to the torque listed in this Chapter's Specifications.

27   Using a torque wrench with a crows-foot adapter, turn the union sleeves counterclockwise until 9 in-lbs (2 Nm) is reached on the torque wrench.

28   Remove the special tool and install the coupling element between the injectors, with the curvatures facing downwards.

10.43 Fuel rail mounting bolts (two of four shown)

29   Install the bolts a little at a time to prevent the T-shaped coupling from binding until the bolts are hand tight.

30   Rotate the fuel injector pipes to the injectors, then reconnect the high-pressure pipe unions to their original locations on the injectors. It's essential that the pipes are installed without tension – it must be possible to screw on the union nuts easily by hand.

31   With each high-pressure pipe union tightened down by hand, tighten the injector clamp bolts to the torque listed in this Chapter's Specifications.

32   Tighten the T-shaped coupling element mounting bolts to the torque listed in this Chapter's Specifications.

33   Tighten the high-pressure fuel pipe unions to the torque listed in this Chapter's Specifications, using a crows-foot wrench.

34   Reconnect each injector electrical connector.

35   Install the high-pressure fuel pump lines (see Section 12).

36   Reinstall the ignition coils as described in Chapter 5.

37   The remaining installation is the reverse of removal.

10.44 Pry out the injector retaining clips

38   If new injectors have been installed, have their adjustment values entered into the PCM (DME) using BMW diagnostic equipment.

## 3.0L engine

### Removal

*Refer to illustrations 10.39, 10.41, 10.43 and 10.44*

39   Pull up and remove the plastic cover from the top of the engine **(see illustration)**.

40   Relieve the fuel system pressure (see Section 3).

41   Depress the locking collar, and disconnect the fuel feed pipe from the rail **(see illustration)**.

42   Unclip and remove the electrical connector strip from the injectors/fuel rail.

43   Remove the mounting bolts and pull out the fuel rail and injectors as an assembly **(see illustration)**.

44   To remove a fuel injector from the fuel rail, proceed as follows:

a)  *Pry off the metal securing clip, using a screwdriver* **(see illustration)**.

b)  *Pull the fuel injector from the fuel rail.*

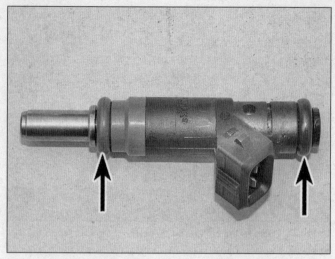

**10.45 Check the condition of the injector O-ring seals**

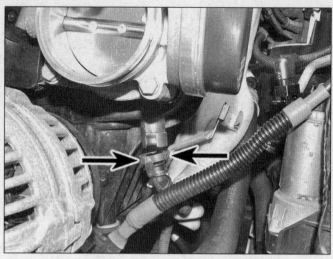

**11.17 Squeeze together the sides of the collar and disconnect the hose from the manifold**

**11.19 Press down the lower edge of the clips and pull the vent hose upwards**

## Installation

*Refer to illustration 10.45*

45   Lightly lubricate the fuel injector O-rings with petroleum jelly or clean engine oil **(see illustration)**.

46   Install the injectors to the fuel rail, and hold them in place with the clips pushed into the grooves.

47   The remainder of installation is the reverse of removal.

## 11   Manifolds - removal and installation

## *Intake manifold*

### 2.0L engines

1   Disconnect the negative battery cable (see Chapter 5, Section 3).

2   Remove the engine cover by lifting the front of the cover up and pulling it forwards.

3   Remove the strut tower crossbrace plastic push-pins and bolts then remove the brace.

4   Remove the sound insulator plastic retainers and lift the insulator off of the engine.

5   Disconnect the wiring harness clips and move the harness out of the way.

6   Remove the PCM "Digital Motor Electronics" (DME) control unit (see Chapter 6).

7   Release the quick-connectors for the fuel tank vent valve, then disconnect and cap the lines.

8   Disconnect the electrical connector to the fuel tank vent valve.

9   Disconnect the electrical connector to the throttle valve and sensors.

10   Remove the charge air cooler hose to the throttle body.

11   Remove the intake plenum mounting nuts and plenum.

12   Using new intake plenum gaskets, install the plenum. Tighten the nuts in several stages, working from the center out, to the torque listed in this Chapter's Specifications.

13   Installation is otherwise the reverse of removal.

### 3.0L engine

*Refer to illustrations 11.17 and 11.19*

14   Remove the fuel injectors (see Section 10).

15   Remove the air filter housing (see Chapter 1).

16   Noting their installed positions, disconnect all wiring plugs from the throttle body/manifold, and release the wiring harness/cables from the retaining clips/bolts on the manifold.

17   Squeeze together the sides of the locking collar and disconnect the breather hose from the manifold **(see illustration)**.

18   Remove the manifold retaining bolts and the bolts securing the manifold support bracket to the cylinder block (under the manifold). Lift the manifold approximately 3 to 4 inches.

19   Release the retaining clip and disconnect the hose on the base of the tank venting valve **(see illustration)**.

20   Tag and disconnect any hoses or wiring harness(s) from the retaining clips on the manifold and support bracket (under the manifold).

21   Remove the manifold from the cylinder head. Recover the seals.

22   Check the condition of the seals and replace if necessary.

23   Installation is the reverse of removal.

## *Exhaust manifolds – 3.0L engines*

*Refer to illustration 11.25*

24   Raise the front of the vehicle and support it securely on jackstands. Remove the fasteners and remove the engine splash shield.

25   Remove the nuts securing the manifold outlets to the exhaust system **(see illustration)**.

26   Trace the oxygen sensors' wiring back and disconnect the electrical connectors. Label them to ensure they are correctly reconnected later.

27    Remove the cover over the ignition coils (see Chapter 5).
28    Remove the coolant expansion tank (see Chapter 3).
29    Starting with the rear exhaust manifold, remove the mounting nuts and maneuver the manifold from the engine compartment. Take great care not to damage the oxygen sensor installed in the manifold. Discard the gasket.
30    Remove the nuts and the front exhaust manifold. Again take care not to damage the oxygen sensor. Discard the gasket.
31    Installation is the reverse of removal, noting the following points:
a)   *Apply anti-seize high-temperature grease to the manifold studs.*
b)   *Always replace the manifold gaskets.*
c)   *Tighten the manifold nuts to the specified torque.*

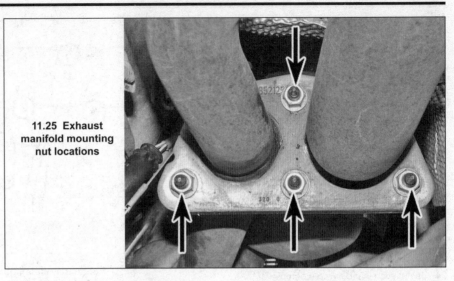

**11.25 Exhaust manifold mounting nut locations**

## 12   High-pressure fuel pump (2.0L engine) – removal and installation

**Warning:** *Gasoline is extremely flammable. See **Fuel system warnings** in Section 1.*
**Warning:** *Fuel pressure system is under extremely high pressure and cause skin and eye injuries. When removing the high-pressure fuel pump, once the pressure is relieved, let the vehicle sit for two hours with the battery disconnected before removing the pump.*

### Removal
1    Relieve the fuel system pressure (see Section 3).
2    Disconnect the negative battery cable (see Chapter 5, Section 3).
3    Remove the engine cover by lifting the front of the cover up and pulling it forwards.
4    Remove the strut tower crossbrace plastic push-pins and bolts then remove the brace.
5    Remove the sound insulator plastic retainers and lift the insulator off of the engine.
6    Remove the ignition coils (see Chapter 5).
7    Pull the sound insulator off of the pump, if equipped.
8    Using a flare-nut wrench, loosen and disconnect the high-pressure line pipe fittings.
**Caution:** *The manufacturer states that the pipe must be replaced if it has been removed.*
9    Using a flare-nut wrench, loosen then disconnect the feed pipe fitting on the high-pressure pump, but do not remove the line.
10    Disconnect the electrical connector from the high-pressure fuel pump.
11    Loosen the high-pressure fuel pump bolts 1/4-turn at a time until the bolts can be removed, then remove the pump. Always replace the bolts and O-ring.
**Caution:** *If the mounting bolts are loosened or tightened more than a 1/4-turn at a time, the high-pressure pump piston can break.*

**Caution:** *The bucket tappet can fall out when the high-pressure pump is being pulled off.*

### Installation
12    With the pump removed, rotate the engine by hand and make sure the camshaft lobe is at its Bottom Dead Center (BDC) base circle before trying to install the pump. To verify the camshaft is at (BDC), mount a dial indicator to fuel pump mounting flange and watch the needle movement until the (BDC) is reached.
13    Lubricate the bucket tappet with engine oil and install it.
14    Set the pump into the cylinder head and tighten the bolts evenly, no more than 1/4-turn at a time.
**Caution:** *If the mounting bolts are loosened or tightened more than 1/4-turn at a time, the high-pressure pump piston can break.*
**Note:** *As the pump bolts are tightened it will get harder to tighten the bolts until the spring in the pump is compressed.*
15    Tighten the bolts to the torque listed in this Chapter's Specifications.
16    Installation is the reverse of removal.
17    Reconnect the cable to the negative battery terminal (see Chapter 5), then start the engine and check for fuel leaks.

## 13   Exhaust module (turbocharger) – removal and installation

### Removal
**Note:** *The exhaust module consists of the exhaust manifold and exhaust turbocharger which must be removed and installed as an assembly.*
1    Disconnect the negative battery cable (see Chapter 5, Section 3).
2    Remove the engine cover by lifting the front of the cover up and pulling it forwards.
3    Remove the strut tower crossbrace plastic push-pins and bolts then remove the brace.

4    Remove the sound insulator plastic retainers and lift the insulator off of the engine.
5    Raise the vehicle and support it securely on jackstands, then remove the lower splash shield from under the vehicle.
6    Drain the engine oil and engine coolant (see chapter 1).
7    Remove the heat shield mounting bolts and heat shield form the exhaust manifold.
8    Disconnect the exhaust system from the turbocharger.
9    Disconnect the right side pipe of the charge air cooler (see Section 14).
10    Disconnect the vacuum line to the wastegate then disconnect the electrical connector to the blow-off valve.
11    Using a pair of needle-nose pliers, pull the wastegate linkage wire retaining clip down and out, then disconnect the linkage.
12    Remove the vacuum unit Torx head mounting screws and remove the vacuum unit.
13    Remove the harness from the harness routing brackets then remove the bracket bolts and brackets.
14    Remove the turbocharger support bracket bolts and support.
15    Remove the oil return pipe mounting bolts, then disconnect the pipe from the turbocharger. Be sure to replace the gasket.
16    Locate the mounting stud (across from the banjo bolt on the turbocharger) then remove the nut.
17    Remove the oil return line bolt, then pull the line from the cylinder block. Be sure to replace the O-ring.
18    Remove the coolant supply line mounting bolt and separate the coolant lines. Be sure to replace the O-ring.
19    Remove the oil feed line bolt from the rear of the cylinder block then pull the line from the cylinder block. Be sure to replace the sealing ring.
20    Remove the exhaust module mounting nuts, starting from the center, working in a circular pattern until all the bolts are removed, then remove the assembly. Always replace the mounting nuts.

**Note:** *Once the module assembly is removed the remaining oil supply line can be accessed and removed if necessary. Make sure to replace the O-ring.*

## Installation

*Refer to illustration 13.23*

22   Replace all of the graphite seal on the cylinder head, then place the module assembly onto the cylinder head and install two bolts hand tight to hold the assembly in place.

**Caution:** *The exhaust module assembly must be installed "stress free" make sure unit sits flush with the cylinder head before tightening any of the mounting bolts, or damage to the unit may occur.*

23   Install the mounting nuts and tighten in sequence **(see illustration)** to the torque listed in this Chapter's Specifications.

24   Installation is the reverse of removal.

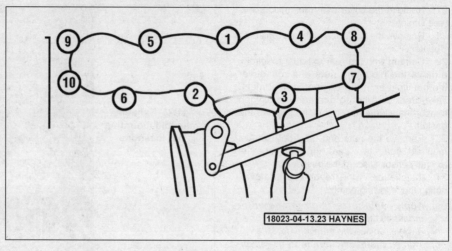

18023-04-13.23 HAYNES

**13.23  Exhaust module tightening sequence – 2.0L engines**

## 14   Charge air cooler – removal and installation

1   Remove the fan shroud (see Chapter 3).

2   Raise the vehicle and support it securely on jackstands, then remove the lower splash shield from under the vehicle.

3   Disconnect the left and right pressure hoses from the cooler. To disconnect the hoses, pry up the wire retaining clip and pull the hose off of the end of the cooler.

4   Remove the cooler mounting bolts and lower the cooler from the bottom of the engine compartment.

5   Installation is the reverse of removal. Be sure to lubricate the O-rings on the hoses (they will not slide onto the cooler without lubrication).

# Chapter 5
# Engine electrical systems

## Contents

## Specifications

### Alternator

| | |
|---|---|
| Regulated voltage | 13.5 to 14.2 volts (at 1500 rpm engine speed with no electrical equipment switched on) |

### Torque specifications

**Note:** *One foot-pound (ft-lb) of torque is equivalent to 12 inch-pounds (in-lbs) of torque. Torque values below approximately 15 foot-pounds are expressed in inch-pounds, because most foot-pound torque wrenches are not accurate at these smaller values.*

| | Ft-lbs (unless otherwise indicated) | Nm |
|---|---|---|
| Alternator mounting nut/bolts | | |
|    2.0L engine | 28 | 38 |
|    3.0L engine* | | |
|       Step 1 | 84 in-lbs | 10 |
|       Step 2 | Tighten an additional 180-degrees | |
| Alternator pulley retaining bolt | | |
|    Valeo alternator | 55 | 75 |
|    Bosch alternator | 48 | 65 |
| Starter motor nut/bolts | | |
|    2.0L engine | 28 | 38 |
|    3.0L engine | | |
|       Step 1 | 15 | 20 |
|       Step 2 | | |
|          M10 x 85 mm | Tighten an additional 180-degrees | |
|          M10 x 30 mm | Tighten an additional 90-degrees | |

*\* Do not re-use*

## 1 General information and precautions

The engine electrical system consists mainly of the charging and starting systems. Because of their engine-related functions, these components are covered separately from the body electrical devices such as the lights, instruments, etc (which are covered in Chapter 12).

The electrical system is of the 12 volt negative-ground type.

The battery is of the low maintenance or maintenance-free (sealed for life) type and is charged by the alternator, which is belt-driven from the crankshaft pulley.

The starter motor is of the pre-engaged type incorporating an integral solenoid. On starting, the solenoid moves the drive pinion into engagement with the ring gear on the flywheel/driveplate before the starter motor is energized. Once the engine has started, a one-way clutch prevents the motor armature being driven by the engine until the pinion disengages from the flywheel/driveplate.

### Precautions

Always observe the following precautions when working on the electrical system:

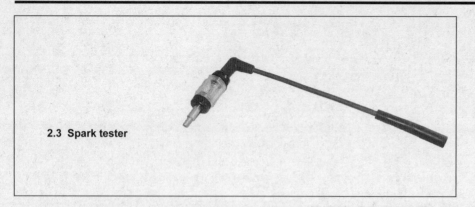

**2.3  Spark tester**

a)  Be extremely careful when servicing engine electrical components. They are easily damaged if checked, connected or handled improperly.

b)  Never leave the ignition switched on for long periods of time when the engine is not running.

c)  Never disconnect the battery cables while the engine is running.

d)  Maintain correct polarity when connecting battery cables from another vehicle during jump starting - see the "Jump starting" Section at the front of this manual.

e)  Always disconnect the cable from the negative battery terminal before working on the electrical system, but read the battery disconnection procedure first (see Section 3).

It's also a good idea to review the safety-related information regarding the engine electrical systems located in the *Safety first!* Section at the front of this manual before beginning any operation included in this Chapter.

If an audio unit with a built-in security code is installed, observe the following precautions: If the power source to the unit is cut, the anti-theft system will activate. Even if the power source is immediately reconnected, the audio unit will not function until the correct security code has been entered. Therefore, if you do not know the correct security code for the audio unit, do not disconnect the negative terminal of the battery or remove the audio unit from the vehicle.

## 2    Troubleshooting

### Ignition system

1    If a malfunction occurs in the ignition system, do not immediately assume that any particular part is causing the problem. First, check the following items:

a)  Make sure that the cable clamps at the battery terminals are clean and tight.

b)  Test the condition of the battery (see Steps 21 through 24). If it doesn't pass all the tests, replace it.

c)  Check the ignition coil or coil pack connections.

d)  Check any relevant fuses in the engine compartment fuse and relay box (see Chapter 12). If they're burned, determine the cause and repair the circuit.

### Check

*Refer to illustration 2.3*

**Warning:** *Because of the high voltage generated by the ignition system, use extreme care when performing a procedure involving ignition components.*

**Note 1:** *The ignition system components on these vehicles are difficult to diagnose. In the event of ignition system failure that you can't diagnose, have the vehicle tested at a dealer service department or other qualified auto repair facility.*

**Note 2:** *You'll need a spark tester for the following test. Spark testers are available at most auto supply stores.*

2    If the engine turns over but won't start, verify that there is sufficient ignition voltage to fire the spark plugs as follows.

3    On models with a coil-over-plug type ignition system, remove a coil and install the tester between the boot at the lower end of the coil and the spark plug **(see illustration)**. On models with spark plug wires, disconnect a spark plug wire from a spark plug and install the tester between the spark plug wire boot and the spark plug.

4    Crank the engine and note whether or not the tester flashes. **Caution:** *Do NOT crank the engine or allow it to run for more than five seconds; running the engine for more than five seconds may set a Diagnostic Trouble Code (DTC) for a cylinder misfire.*

### Models with a coil-over-plug type ignition system

5    If the tester flashes during cranking, the coil is delivering sufficient voltage to the spark plug to fire it. Repeat this test for each cylinder to verify that the other coils are OK.

6    If the tester doesn't flash, remove a coil from another cylinder and swap it for the one being tested. If the tester now flashes, you know that the original coil is bad. If the tester still doesn't flash, the PCM or wiring harness is probably defective. Have the PCM checked out by a dealer service department or other qualified repair shop (testing the PCM is beyond the scope of the do-it-yourselfer

because it requires expensive special tools).

7    If the tester flashes during cranking but a misfire code (related to the cylinder being tested) has been stored, the spark plug could be fouled or defective.

### Models with spark plug wires

8    If the tester flashes during cranking, sufficient voltage is reaching the spark plug to fire it.

9    Repeat this test on the remaining cylinders.

10    Proceed on this basis until you have verified that there's a good spark from each spark plug wire. If there is, then you have verified that the coils in the coil pack are functioning correctly and that the spark plug wires are OK.

11    If there is no spark from a spark plug wire, then either the coil is bad, the plug wire is bad or a connection at one end of the plug wire is loose. Assuming that you're using new plug wires or known good wires, then the coil is probably defective. Also inspect the coil pack electrical connector. Make sure that it's clean, tight and in good condition.

12    If all the coils are firing correctly, but the engine misfires, then one or more of the plugs might be fouled. Remove and check the spark plugs or install new ones (see Chapter 1).

13    No further testing of the ignition system is possible without special tools. If the problem persists, have the ignition system tested by a dealer service department or other qualified repair shop.

### Charging system

14    If a malfunction occurs in the charging system, do not automatically assume the alternator is causing the problem. First check the following items:

a)  Check the drivebelt tension and condition, as described in Chapter 1. Replace it if it's worn or deteriorated.

b)  Make sure the alternator mounting bolts are tight.

c)  Inspect the alternator wiring harness and the connectors at the alternator and voltage regulator. They must be in good condition, tight and have no corrosion.

d)  Check the fusible link (if equipped) or main fuse in the underhood fuse/relay box. If it is burned, determine the cause, repair the circuit and replace the link or fuse (the vehicle will not start and/or the accessories will not work if the fusible link or main fuse is blown).

e)  Start the engine and check the alternator for abnormal noises (a shrieking or squealing sound indicates a bad bearing).

f)  Check the battery. Make sure it's fully charged and in good condition (one bad cell in a battery can cause overcharging by the alternator).

g)  Disconnect the battery cables (negative first, then positive). Inspect the battery posts and the cable clamps for corrosion. Clean them thoroughly if necessary (see Chapter 1). Reconnect the cables (positive first, negative last).

**2.21  To test the open circuit voltage of the battery, touch the black probe of the voltmeter to the negative terminal and the red probe to the positive terminal of the battery; a fully charged battery should be at least 12.6 volts**

**2.23  Connect a battery load tester to the battery and check the battery condition under load following the tool manufacturer's instructions**

## Alternator - check

15   Use a voltmeter to check the battery voltage with the engine off. It should be at least 12.6 volts **(see illustration 2.21)**.

16   Start the engine and check the battery voltage again. It should now be approximately 13.5 to 15 volts.

17   If the voltage reading is more or less than the specified charging voltage, the voltage regulator is probably defective, which will require replacement of the alternator (the voltage regulator is not replaceable separately). Remove the alternator and have it bench tested (most auto parts stores will do this for you).

18   The charging system (battery) light on the instrument cluster lights up when the ignition key is turned to ON, but it should go out when the engine starts.

19   If the charging system light stays on after the engine has been started, there is a problem with the charging system. Before replacing the alternator, check the battery condition, alternator belt tension and electrical cable connections.

20   If replacing the alternator doesn't restore voltage to the specified range, have the charging system tested by a dealer service department or other qualified repair shop.

## Battery - check

*Refer to illustrations 2.21 and 2.23*

21   Check the battery state of charge. Visually inspect the indicator eye on the top of the battery (if equipped with one); if the indicator eye is black in color, charge the battery as described in Chapter 1. Next perform an open circuit voltage test using a digital voltmeter. **Note:** *The battery's surface charge must be removed before accurate voltage measurements can be made. Turn on the high beams for ten seconds, then turn them off and let the vehicle stand for two minutes.* With the engine and all accessories Off, touch the negative probe of the voltmeter to the negative termi-

nal of the battery and the positive probe to the positive terminal of the battery **(see illustration)**. The battery voltage should be 12.6 volts or slightly above. If the battery is less than the specified voltage, charge the battery before proceeding to the next test. Do not proceed with the battery load test unless the battery charge is correct.

22   Disconnect the negative battery cable, then the positive cable from the battery.

23   Perform a battery load test. An accurate check of the battery condition can only be performed with a load tester **(see illustration)**. This test evaluates the ability of the battery to operate the starter and other accessories during periods of high current draw. Connect the load tester to the battery terminals. Load test the battery according to the tool manufacturer's instructions. This tool increases the load demand (current draw) on the battery.

24   Maintain the load on the battery for 15 seconds and observe that the battery voltage does not drop below 9.6 volts. If the battery condition is weak or defective, the tool will indicate this condition immediately. **Note:** *Cold temperatures will cause the minimum voltage reading to drop slightly. Follow the chart given in the manufacturer's instructions to compensate for cold climates. Minimum load voltage for freezing temperatures (32 degrees F) should be approximately 9.1 volts.*

## *Starting system*

### The starter rotates, but the engine doesn't

25   Remove the starter (see Section 8). Check the overrunning clutch and bench test the starter to make sure the drive mechanism extends fully for proper engagement with the flywheel ring gear. If it doesn't, replace the starter.

26   Check the flywheel ring gear for miss-

ing teeth and other damage. With the ignition turned off, rotate the flywheel so you can check the entire ring gear.

### The starter is noisy

27   If the solenoid is making a chattering noise, first check the battery (see Steps 21 through 24). If the battery is okay, check the cables and connections.

28   If you hear a grinding, crashing metallic sound when you turn the key to Start, check for loose starter mounting bolts. If they're tight, remove the starter and inspect the teeth on the starter pinion gear and flywheel ring gear. Look for missing or damaged teeth.

29   If the starter sounds fine when you first turn the key to Start, but then stops rotating the engine and emits a zinging sound, the problem is probably a defective starter drive that's not staying engaged with the ring gear. Replace the starter.

### The starter rotates slowly

30   Check the battery (see Steps 21 through 24).

31   If the battery is okay, verify all connections (at the battery, the starter solenoid and motor) are clean, corrosion-free and tight. Make sure the cables aren't frayed or damaged.

32   Check that the starter mounting bolts are tight so it grounds properly. Also check the pinion gear and flywheel ring gear for evidence of a mechanical bind (galling, deformed gear teeth or other damage).

### The starter does not rotate at all

33   Check the battery (see Steps 21 through 24).

34   If the battery is okay, verify all connections (at the battery, the starter solenoid and motor) are clean, corrosion-free and tight. Make sure the cables aren't frayed or damaged.

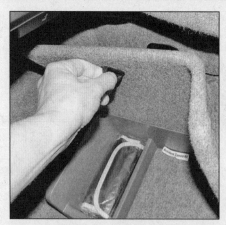

**4.2   Rotate the catch and lift out the panel (sedan models)**

**4.3a   Lift the handle and remove the floor panel (wagon models)**

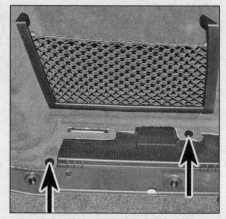

**4.3b   Rotate the fasteners 90-degrees . . .**

35   Check all of the fuses in the underhood fuse/relay box.
36   Check that the starter mounting bolts are tight so it grounds properly.
37   Check for voltage at the starter solenoid "S" terminal when the ignition key is turned to the start position. If voltage is present, replace the starter/solenoid assembly. If no voltage is present, the problem could be the starter relay, the Transmission Range (TR) switch (see Chapter 6) or clutch start switch (see Chapter 8), or with an electrical connector somewhere in the circuit (see the wiring diagrams at the end of Chapter 12). Also, on many modern vehicles, the Powertrain Control Module (PCM) and the Body Control Module (BCM) control the voltage signal to the starter solenoid; on such vehicles a special scan tool is required for diagnosis.

## 3   Battery - disconnection and reconnection

**Caution:** *Always disconnect the cable from the negative battery terminal FIRST and hook it up LAST or the battery may be shorted by the tool being used to loosen the cable clamps.*
**Note:** *On these models, the negative cable connector of the battery has an electrical monitor called the Intelligent Battery Sensor (IBS). Do not pry under the IBS, and do not attach any other ground wires to the negative cable end.*
   Some systems on the vehicle require battery power to be available at all times, either to maintain continuous operation (alarm system, power door locks, etc.), or to maintain control unit memory (radio station presets, Powertrain Control Module and other control units). When the battery is disconnected, the power that maintains these systems is cut. So, before you disconnect the battery, please note that on a vehicle with power door locks, it's a wise precaution to remove the key from the ignition and to keep it with you, so that it does not get locked inside if the power door locks should engage accidentally when the battery is reconnected!

   Devices known as "memory-savers" can be used to avoid some of these problems. Precise details vary according to the device used. The typical memory saver is plugged into the cigarette lighter and is connected to a spare battery. Then the vehicle battery can be disconnected from the electrical system. The memory saver will provide sufficient current to maintain audio unit security codes, PCM memory, etc. and will provide power to always hot circuits such as the clock and radio memory circuits. **Warning:** *Some memory savers deliver a considerable amount of current in order to keep vehicle systems operational after the main battery is disconnected. If you're using a memory saver, make sure that the circuit concerned is actually open before servicing it.* **Warning:** *If you're going to work near any of the airbag system components, the battery MUST be disconnected and a memory saver must NOT be used. If a memory saver is used, power will be supplied to the airbag, which means that it could accidentally deploy and cause serious personal injury.*

## Disconnection

   To disconnect the battery for service procedures requiring power to be cut from the vehicle, loosen the cable end bolt and disconnect the cable from the negative battery terminal. Isolate the cable end to prevent it from coming into accidental contact with the battery terminal.

## Reconnection

   After reconnecting the battery, several of the vehicle's electronic control modules will require time to relearn certain values. This will normally be complete within a normal driving pattern of 15 miles (approximately). In addition, several systems may require re-initialization as follows:

### Sunroof

*1)   With the battery reconnected and the ignition On, press the sunroof operating switch into the tilt position and hold it there.*
*2)   Once the sunroof has reached the fully-tilted position, hold the switch in that*

*position for approximately 20 seconds. Initialization is complete when the sunroof briefly lifts at the rear again.*

### Electric windows

*1)   Operate the button to fully close the window, then continue to hold the button for at least 1 second to normalize the auto stop function.*

## 4   Battery - removal and installation

**Note:** *When the battery is disconnected, any fault codes stored in the engine management PCM memory will be erased. If any faults are suspected, do not disconnect the battery until the fault codes have been read by a BMW dealer or specialist. If the vehicle is equipped with a code-protected audio unit, refer to your owner's manual.*
**Note:** *On these models, the negative cable connector of the battery has an electrical monitor called the Intelligent Battery Sensor (IBS). Do not pry under the IBS, and do not attach any other ground wires to the negative cable end.*
**Note:** *When a new battery is installed, there may be some electrical problems if the vehicle is not scanned at a dealership to alert the PCM that a new battery has been installed.*

## Removal

*Refer to illustrations 4.2, 4.3a, 4.3b, 4.3c, 4.3d, 4.3e, 4.4, 4.5, 4.6, 4.7a, 4.7b, 4.8a, 4.8b, 4.9, 4.10a and 4.10b*

1   The battery is located beneath a cover on the right-hand side of the trunk.
2   On sedan, coupe and convertible models, lift the catch and remove the right-hand side trunk side trim above the battery **(see illustration)**.
3   On wagon models, open the tailgate and lift out the rear floor panel, remove the fasteners and lift out the side panel, rotate the fasteners 90-degrees counterclockwise and lift out the trim above the battery **(see illustrations)**.

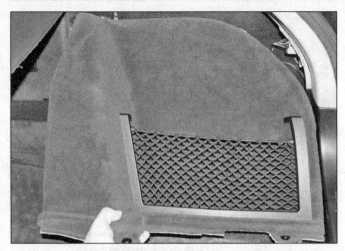

4.3c  . . . and lift the base of the panel inwards to remove it

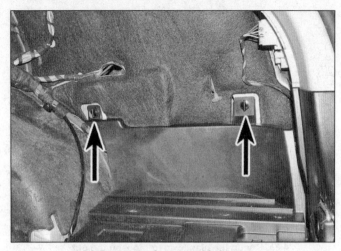

4.3d  Rotate the fasteners 90-degrees . . .

4.3e  . . . and lift the panel above
the battery

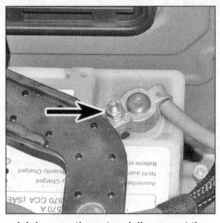

4.4  Loosen the nut and disconnect the
negative cable clamp

4.5  Remove the two bolts and the bracket
above the battery

4   Loosen the clamp nut, and disconnect the clamp from the battery negative (ground) terminal **(see illustration)**. Position the negative cable away from the battery, so there is no risk of accidental contact between it and the battery terminal. For extra protection, cover the disconnected cable clamp with a rag or rubber glove, etc.

5   Remove the support bracket mounting bolts and bracket, above the battery **(see illustration)**.

6   Pry up the plastic cover and remove the nut securing the connector assembly to the positive clamp **(see illustration)**.

7   Using a flat-bladed screwdriver, pry apart the retaining clip on each side and lift up the connector assembly from the top of the battery **(see illustrations)**. Position the connector assembly to one side.

8   Pry up the plastic cover, loosen the nut and pull the positive clamp assembly from the

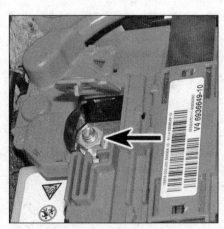

4.6  Pry up the cover and remove the nut

4.7a  Pry apart the retaining clip on
each side . . .

4.7b  . . . and lift off the
connector assembly

**4.8a  Pry up the plastic cover, loosen the nut . . .**

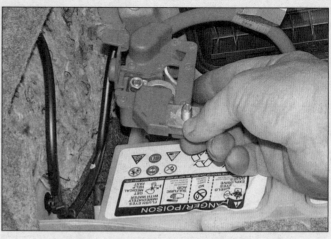

**4.8b  . . . and pull up the positive clamp**

terminal on the battery **(see illustrations)**.
9    Unscrew the bolt and remove the battery retaining clamp **(see illustration)**.
10   Lift the battery from its housing, disconnecting the vent hose as the battery is removed **(see illustrations)**. Take care as the battery is heavy.

**4.9   Remove the bolt and the battery retaining clamp**

### Installation

11   Installation is the reverse of removal. Connect the positive cable first, then the negative cable. Refer to Section 3 and perform the sunroof and power window initialization procedures.

### 5    Battery cables - replacement

1    When removing the cables, always disconnect the cable from the negative battery terminal first and hook it up last, or you might accidentally short out the battery with the tool you're using to loosen the cable clamps. Even if you're only replacing the cable for the positive terminal, be sure to disconnect the negative cable from the battery first.
2    Disconnect the old cables from the battery, then trace each of them to their opposite ends and disconnect them. Be sure to note the routing of each cable before disconnecting it to ensure correct installation.
3    If you are replacing any of the old cables, take them with you when buying new cables. It is vitally important that you replace the cables with identical parts.

4    Clean the threads of the solenoid or ground connection with a wire brush to remove rust and corrosion. Apply a light coat of battery terminal corrosion inhibitor or petroleum jelly to the threads to prevent future corrosion.
5    Attach the cable to the solenoid or ground connection and tighten the mounting nut/bolt securely.
6    Before connecting a new cable to the battery, make sure that it reaches the battery post without having to be stretched.
7    Installation is the reverse of removal. Connect the positive cable first, then the negative cable. Refer to Section 3 and perform the sunroof and power window initialization procedures.

### 6    Alternator - removal and installation

### Removal

*Refer to illustrations 6.4, 6.6a, 6.6b and 6.6c*

1    Disconnect the negative battery cable (see Section 3).

**4.10a  Pull the vent hose from the side of the battery . . .**

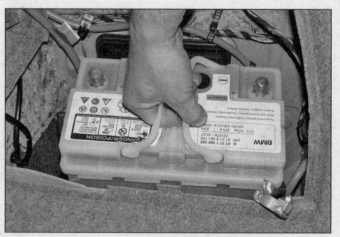

**4.10b  . . . and lift the battery out of the vehicle**

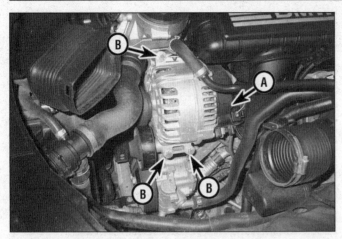

**6.4 Disconnect the electrical connectors (A) and remove the mounting bolts (B)**

**6.6a Insert the special tools into the alternator shaft and pulley center**

**6.6b Hold the alternator shaft and loosen the pulley center**

**6.6c Slide the pulley from the shaft**

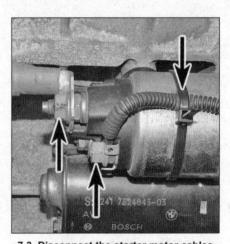

**7.3 Disconnect the starter motor cables and cut the clip securing them to the solenoid**

2    Remove the alternator drivebelt (see Chapter 1). On 2.0L models, remove the tensioner (see Chapter 1).

3    Remove the air cleaner housing (see Chapter 4).

4    Unlock and disconnect the electrical connector, remove the nut and disconnect the battery cable from the rear of the alternator **(see illustration)**.

5    Remove the upper and lower mounting bolts, then remove the alternator. **Note:** *Due to the magnesium crankcase, the alternator mounting bolts are made of aluminum, and cannot be re-used; install new bolts.*

6    On 3.0L models, to remove the alternator pulley on models with an over-running clutch, mount the alternator in a bench vise and pry off the plastic cap. The pulley can be removed by inserting BMW tool No 12 7 121 into the pulley center, and holding the alternator shaft with BMW tool No 12 7 122 **(see illustrations)**. Loosen the pulley center while holding the alternator shaft stationary. Suitable alternative tools are available from aftermarket tool manufacturers.

**Note:** *On 2.0L models, the alternator pul-*ley should not be removed. The pulley is not serviceable separately from the alternator; if there is a problem the alternator must be replaced as a complete unit.

## Installation

7    Installation is the reverse of removal, tightening all fasteners to their specified torque where given.

8    If the alternator is thought to be suspect, it should be removed from the vehicle and tested by a dealer service department or other qualified repair shop. However, check on the cost of repairs before proceeding, as it may prove more economical to obtain a new or exchange alternator.

---

**7    Starter motor - removal and installation**

---

## Removal

*Refer to illustrations 7.3 and 7.4*

1    Disconnect the battery negative cable (see Section 3).

2    Remove the intake manifold (see Chapter 4).

3    Noting their installed positions, remove the nuts and disconnect the leads from the starter solenoid **(see illustration)**.

4    Remove the bolts and the starter motor **(see illustration)**. **Note:** *Due to the magne-*

**7.4 Starter motor mounting bolts**

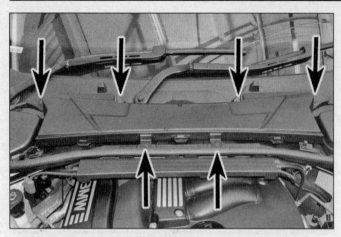

**9.1 Remove the mounting fasteners and the cabin air filter upper housing**

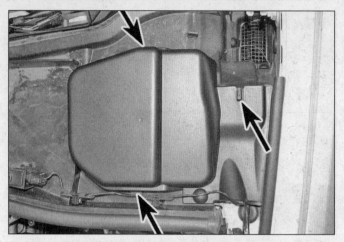

**9.2 Release the clips and remove the plastic cover on each side**

*sium crankcase, the starter mounting bolts are made of aluminum, and cannot be re-used; install new bolts.*

## Installation

5    Installation is the reverse of removal. Tighten the starter motor mounting bolts to the specified torque.

6    If the starter motor is thought to be suspect, it should be removed from the vehicle and tested by a dealer service department or other qualified repair shop. However, check on the cost of repairs before proceeding, as it may prove more economical to obtain a new or exchange starter.

## 8    Ignition system - general information and precautions

The ignition system is controlled by the engine management system (see Chapter 4), known as DME (Digital Motor Electronics). The DME system controls all ignition and fuel injection functions using a central PCM (Powertrain Control Module).

The ignition timing is based on inputs provided to the PCM by various sensors supplying information on engine load, engine speed, coolant temperature and inlet air temperature (see Chapter 6).

The engines are equipped with knock sensors to detect knocking (also known as pinging or pre-ignition). The knock sensors are sensitive to vibration and detect the knocking which occurs when a cylinder starts to pre-ignite. The knock sensor provides a signal to the PCM which in turn retards the ignition advance setting until the knocking ceases.

A distributorless ignition system is used, with a separate coil for each cylinder. The coils provide the high voltage signal directly to each spark plug.

The PCM uses the inputs from the various sensors to calculate the required ignition advance and the coil charging time.

Other than testing of the ignition coils (see Section 2), pinpoint diagnostics can only be performed with an advanced scan tool, at a dealership or other qualified shop.

## 9    Ignition coils - removal and installation

## All models

*Refer to illustrations 9.1, 9.2, 9.3, 9.4a, 9.4b, 9.6a and 9.6b*

1    Remove the engine cover by lifting the front of the cover up and pulling it forwards, once the cover is removed, starting at the rear of the engine compartment remove the cabin air filter cover mounting fasteners and cover. Slide the filter from the housing **(see illustration)**. If necessary, refer to Chapter 1.

2    Release the clips and remove the left and right plastic covers from behind the strut tower on each side of the engine compartment. Unclip the hose from the left-hand cover **(see illustration)**.

3    Depress the clips and pull the cable guide forwards from the cabin air filter lower housing **(see illustration)**.

4    Release the clip and remove the bolt at each side, then slide the cabin air filter lower housing forwards and maneuver it up and out **(see illustrations)**.

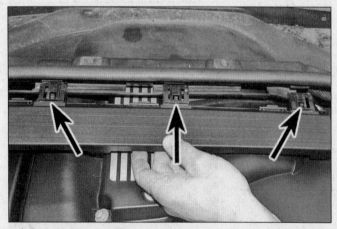

**9.3 Release the clips and slide the cable guide forward**

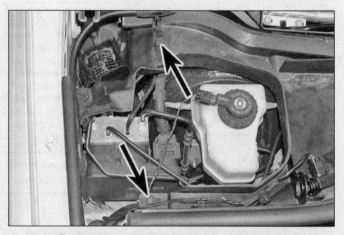

**9.4a Remove the mounting fastener and release the clip on each side**

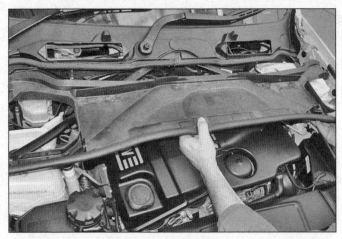

**9.4b  Slide the cabin air filter lower housing forward and out**

**9.6a  Lift the cover and disconnect the coil wiring plug**

**9.6b  Pull the coil from above the spark plug**

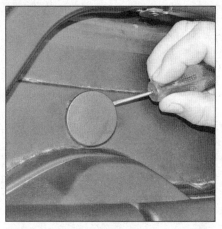

**9.8  Remove the cap from the center of the cowl trim panel . . .**

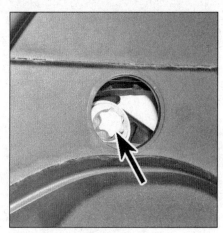

**9.9  . . . and remove the exposed bolt**

5    Unscrew the oil filler cap, then remove the bolts and the plastic cover from the top of the engine. Note that the camshaft cover is made from magnesium alloy and the plastic cover bolts are aluminum, and must not be re-used.

6    Pry up the right-hand edge of the plastic covers over the ignition coils (above the spark plugs), and disconnect the coil electrical connectors **(see illustrations)**. With the wiring plugs disconnected, pull the coils from the spark plugs. **Note:** *Keep track of which coils relate to which cylinders.*

7    Installation is the reverse of removal, but make sure that any ground leads and brackets are in position as noted before removal.

## *Models with strut tower supports*

*Refer to illustrations 9.8, 9.9 and 9.10*

8    Remove the plastic cap from the center of the cowl trim panel. Two different types of cap are used: one with a central slot, removed by rotating it 45-degrees counterclockwise,

and one without a central slot, which is pried out **(see illustration)**. **Note:** *If the cap or seal are damaged, they must be replaced. Failure to do so may result in water leaks.*

9    Remove the bolt in the center of the cowl **(see illustration)**. Discard the bolt; a new one must be used on reassembly.

10    Remove the bolt at each outer end of the supports, hold the rubber grommet in place and slide the supports outwards **(see illustration)**. Do not allow the grommet to be displaced. Discard the bolts; new ones must be installed.

11    Unscrew the oil filler cap, then remove the bolts and the plastic cover from the top of the engine. Note that the camshaft cover is made from magnesium alloy and the plastic cover bolts are aluminum, and must not be re-used.

12    Pry up the right-hand edge of the plastic covers over the ignition coils (above the spark plugs), and disconnect the coil electrical connectors **(see illustrations 9.6a and 9.6b)**. With the wiring plugs disconnected, pull the coils from the spark plugs. **Note:** *Keep track*

**9.10  Remove the mounting fastener at the end of each strut tower support**

*of which coils relate to which cylinders.*

13    Installation is the reverse of removal, but make sure that any ground wires and/or brackets are reinstalled where noted before removal.

# Notes

# Chapter 6
# Emissions and engine control systems

## Contents

## 1   General information

To prevent pollution of the atmosphere from incompletely burned and evaporating gases, and to maintain good driveability and fuel economy, a number of emission control systems are incorporated. They include the:

### Catalytic converter

A catalytic converter is an emission control device in the exhaust system that reduces certain pollutants in the exhaust gas stream. There are two types of converters: oxidation converters and reduction converters.

Oxidation converters contain a monolithic substrate (a ceramic honeycomb) coated with the semi-precious metals platinum and palladium. An oxidation catalyst reduces unburned hydrocarbons (HC) and carbon monoxide (CO) by adding oxygen to the exhaust stream as it passes through the substrate, which, in the presence of high temperature and the catalyst materials, converts the HC and CO to water vapor ($H_2O$) and carbon dioxide ($CO_2$).

Reduction converters contain a monolithic substrate coated with platinum and rhodium. A reduction catalyst reduces oxides of nitrogen (NOx) by removing oxygen, which in the presence of high temperature and the catalyst material produces nitrogen (N) and carbon dioxide ($CO_2$).

Catalytic converters that combine both types of catalysts in one assembly are known as "three-way catalysts" or TWCs. A TWC can reduce all three pollutants.

### Evaporative Emissions Control (EVAP) system

The Evaporative Emissions Control (EVAP) system prevents fuel system vapors (which contain unburned hydrocarbons) from escaping into the atmosphere. On warm days, vapors trapped inside the fuel tank expand until the pressure reaches a certain threshold. Then the fuel vapors are routed from the fuel tank through the fuel vapor vent valve and the fuel vapor control valve to the EVAP canister, where they're stored temporarily until the next time the vehicle is operated. When the conditions are right (engine warmed up, vehicle up to speed, moderate or heavy load on the engine, etc.) the PCM opens the canister purge valve, which allows fuel vapors to be drawn from the canister into the intake manifold. Once in the intake manifold, the fuel vapors mix with incoming air before being drawn through the intake ports into the combustion chambers where they're burned up with the rest of the air/fuel mixture. The EVAP system is complex and virtually impossible to troubleshoot without the right tools and training.

## Exhaust Gas Recirculation (EGR) system

The EGR system reduces oxides of nitrogen by recirculating exhaust gases from the exhaust manifold, through the EGR valve and intake manifold, then back to the combustion chambers, where it mixes with the incoming air/fuel mixture before being consumed. These recirculated exhaust gases dilute the incoming air/fuel mixture, which cools the combustion chambers, thereby reducing NOx emissions.

The EGR system consists of the Powertrain Control Module (PCM/DME), the EGR valve, the EGR valve position sensor and various other information sensors that the PCM/DMEuses to determine when to open the EGR valve. The degree to which the EGR valve is opened is referred to as "EGR valve lift." The PCM/DME is programmed to produce the ideal EGR valve lift for varying operating conditions. The EGR valve position sensor, which is an integral part of the EGR valve, detects the amount of EGR valve lift and sends this information

to the PCM/DME. The PCM/DME then compares it with the appropriate EGR valve lift for the operating conditions. The PCM/DME increases current flow to the EGR valve to increase valve lift and reduces the current to reduce the amount of lift. If EGR flow is inappropriate to the operating conditions (idle, cold engine, etc.) the PCM/DME simply cuts the current to the EGR valve and the valve closes.

## Secondary Air Injection (AIR) system

Some models are equipped with a secondary air injection (AIR) system. The secondary air injection system is used to reduce tailpipe emissions on initial engine start-up. The system uses an electric motor/pump assembly, relay, vacuum valve/solenoid, air shut-off valve, check valves and tubing to inject fresh air directly into the exhaust manifolds. The fresh air (oxygen) reacts with the exhaust gas in the catalytic converter to reduce HC and CO levels. The air pump and solenoid are controlled by the PCM/DME through the AIR relay. During initial start-up, the PCM energizes the AIR relay, the relay supplies battery voltage to the air pump and the vacuum valve/solenoid, engine vacuum is applied to the air shut-off valve which opens and allows air to flow through the tubing into the exhaust manifolds. The PCM/DME will operate the air pump until closed loop operation is reached (approximately four minutes).

During normal operation, the check valves prevent exhaust backflow into the system.

## Powertrain Control Module (PCM) or Digital Motor Electronics (DME) control unit

The Powertrain Control Module or Digital Motor Electronics control unit (DME) is the brain of the engine management system. It also controls a wide variety of other vehicle systems. In order to program the new PCM/DME, the dealer needs the vehicle as well as the new PCM/DME. If you're planning to replace the PCM/DME with a new one, there is no point in trying to do so at home because you won't be able to program it yourself.

## Positive Crankcase Ventilation (PCV) system

The Positive Crankcase Ventilation (PCV) system reduces hydrocarbon emissions by scavenging crankcase vapors, which are rich in unburned hydrocarbons. A PCV valve or orifice regulates the flow of gases into the intake manifold in proportion to the amount of intake vacuum available.

The PCV system generally consists of the fresh air inlet hose, the PCV valve or orifice and the crankcase ventilation hose (or PCV hose). The fresh air inlet hose connects the air intake duct to a pipe on the valve cover. The crankcase ventilation hose (or PCV hose) connects the PCV valve or orifice in the valve cover to the intake manifold.

# Information Sensors

**Accelerator Pedal Position (APP) sensor** - as you press the accelerator pedal, the APP sensor alters its voltage signal to the PCM in proportion to the angle of the pedal, and the PCM commands a motor inside the throttle body to open or close the throttle plate accordingly

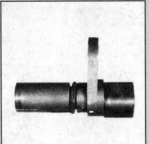

**Camshaft Position (CMP) sensor** - produces a signal that the PCM uses to identify the number 1 cylinder and to time the firing sequence of the fuel injectors

**Crankshaft Position (CKP) sensor** - produces a signal that the PCM uses to calculate engine speed and crankshaft position, which enables it to synchronize ignition timing with fuel injector timing, and to detect misfires

**Engine Coolant Temperature (ECT) sensor** - a thermistor (temperature-sensitive variable resistor) that sends a voltage signal to the PCM, which uses this data to determine the temperature of the engine coolant

**Fuel tank pressure sensor** - measures the fuel tank pressure and controls fuel tank pressure by signaling the EVAP system to purge the fuel tank vapors when the pressure becomes excessive

**Intake Air Temperature (IAT) sensor** - monitors the temperature of the air entering the engine and sends a signal to the PCM to determine injector pulse-width (the duration of each injector's on-time) and to adjust spark timing (to prevent spark knock)

**Knock sensor** - a piezoelectric crystal that oscillates in proportion to engine vibration which produces a voltage output that is monitored by the PCM. This retards the ignition timing when the oscillation exceeds a certain threshold

**Manifold Absolute Pressure (MAP) sensor** - monitors the pressure or vacuum inside the intake manifold. The PCM uses this data to determine engine load so that it can alter the ignition advance and fuel enrichment

**Mass Air Flow (MAF) sensor** - measures the amount of intake air drawn into the engine. It uses a hot-wire sensing element to measure the amount of air entering the engine

**Oxygen sensors** - generates a small variable voltage signal in proportion to the difference between the oxygen content in the exhaust stream and the oxygen content in the ambient air. The PCM uses this information to maintain the proper air/fuel ratio. A second oxygen sensor monitors the efficiency of the catalytic converter

**Throttle Position (TP) sensor** - a potentiometer that generates a voltage signal that varies in relation to the opening angle of the throttle plate inside the throttle body. Works with the PCM and other sensors to calculate injector pulse width (the duration of each injector's on-time)

*Photos courtesy of Wells Manufacturing, except APP and MAF sensors.*

**2.4a  Simple code readers are an economical way to extract trouble codes when the CHECK ENGINE light comes on**

**2.4b  Hand-held scan tools like these can extract computer codes and also perform diagnostics**

## 2  On Board Diagnosis (OBD) system

### General description

1    All models are equipped with the second generation OBD-II system. This system consists of an on-board computer known as the Powertrain Control Module (PCM/DME), and information sensors, which monitor various functions of the engine and send data to the PCM/DME. This system incorporates a series of diagnostic monitors that detect and identify fuel injection and emissions control system faults and store the information in the computer memory. This system also tests sensors and output actuators, diagnoses drive cycles, freezes data and clears codes.

2    The PCM/DME is the brain of the electronically controlled fuel and emissions system. It receives data from a number of sensors and other electronic components (switches, relays, etc.). Based on the information it receives, the PCM/DME generates output signals to control various relays, solenoids (fuel injectors) and other actuators. The PCM/DME is specifically calibrated to optimize the emissions, fuel economy and driveability of the vehicle.

3    It isn't a good idea to attempt diagnosis or replacement of the PCM/DME or emission control components at home while the vehicle is under warranty. Because of a federally-mandated warranty which covers the emissions system components and because any owner-induced damage to the PCM/DME, the sensors and/or the control devices may void this warranty, take the vehicle to a dealer service department if the PCM/DME or a system component malfunctions.

### Scan tool information

*Refer to illustrations 2.4a and 2.4b*

4    Because extracting the Diagnostic Trouble Codes (DTCs) from an engine management system is now the first step in trouble-shooting many computer-controlled systems and components, a code reader, at the very least, will be required **(see illustration)**. More powerful scan tools can also perform many of the diagnostics once associated with expensive factory scan tools **(see illustration)**. If you're planning to obtain a generic scan tool for your vehicle, make sure that it's compatible with OBD-II systems. If you don't plan to purchase a code reader or scan tool and don't have access to one, you can have the codes extracted by a dealer service department or an independent repair shop. **Note:** *Some auto parts stores even provide this service.*

## 3  Obtaining and clearing Diagnostic Trouble Codes (DTCs)

All models covered by this manual are equipped with on-board diagnostics. When the PCM/DME recognizes a malfunction in a monitored emission or engine control system, component or circuit, it turns on the Malfunction Indicator Light (MIL) on the dash. The PCM/DME will continue to display the MIL until the problem is fixed and the Diagnostic Trouble Code (DTC) is cleared from the PCM's memory. You'll need a scan tool to access any DTCs stored in the PCM/DME.

Before outputting any DTCs stored in the PCM/DME, thoroughly inspect ALL electrical connectors and hoses. Make sure that all electrical connections are tight, clean and free of corrosion. And make sure that all hoses are correctly connected, fit tightly and are in good condition (no cracks or tears).

### Accessing the DTCs

*Refer to illustration 3.1*

1    The Diagnostic Trouble Codes (DTCs) can only be accessed with a code reader or scan tool. Professional scan tools are expensive, but relatively inexpensive generic code readers or scan tools **(see illustrations 2.4a and 2.4b)** are available at most auto parts stores. Simply plug the connector of the scan tool into the diagnostic connector **(see illustration)**. Then follow the instructions included

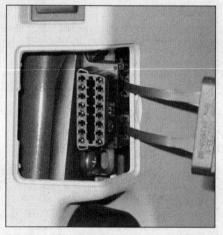

**3.1  To access the DLC in the driver's kick panel, remove the cover, then pull out the dust cover over the connector**

with the scan tool to extract the DTCs.

2    Once you have outputted all of the stored DTCs, look them up on the accompanying DTC chart.

3    After troubleshooting the source of each DTC, make any necessary repairs or replace the defective component(s).

### Clearing the DTCs

4    Clear the DTCs with the code reader or scan tool in accordance with the instructions provided by the tool's manufacturer.

### Diagnostic Trouble Codes

5    The accompanying tables are a list of the Diagnostic Trouble Codes (DTCs) that can be accessed by a do-it-yourselfer working at home (there are many, many more DTCs available to professional mechanics with proprietary scan tools and software, but those codes cannot be accessed by a generic scan tool). If, after you have checked and repaired the connectors, wire harness and vacuum hoses (if applicable) for an emission-related system, component or circuit, the problem persists, have the vehicle checked by a dealer service department or other qualified repair shop.

## OBD-II trouble codes

**Note:** *Not all trouble codes apply to all models.*
**Note:** *Cylinders 1 through 3 are referred to as Bank 1, and cylinders 4 through 6 are referred to as Bank 2.*

| Code | Probable cause |
| --- | --- |
| P0010 | Intake camshaft position actuator circuit open |
| P0011 | Intake camshaft position timing over-advanced |
| P0012 | Intake camshaft position timing over-retarded |
| P0013 | Exhaust camshaft position actuator circuit open |
| P0014 | Exhaust camshaft position timing over-advanced |
| P0015 | Exhaust camshaft position timing over-retarded |
| P0016 | Intake camshaft position sensor correlation |
| P0017 | Exhaust camshaft position sensor correlation |
| P0030 | Heated oxygen sensor, control circuit (Bank 1, sensor 1) |
| P0031 | Heated oxygen sensor, circuit low (Bank 1, sensor 1) |
| P0032 | Heated oxygen sensor, circuit high (Bank 1, sensor 1) |
| P0033 | Turbocharger bypass valve control circuit problem |
| P0034 | Turbocharger bypass valve control circuit - low |
| P0035 | Turbocharger bypass valve control circuit - high |
| P0036 | Heated oxygen sensor, control circuit (Bank 1, sensor 2) |
| P0037 | Heated oxygen sensor, circuit low (Bank 1, sensor 2) |
| P0038 | Heated oxygen sensor, circuit high (Bank 1, sensor 2) |
| P0040 | Upstream oxygen sensors swapped (crossed wiring harnesses) |
| P0041 | Downstream oxygen sensors swapped (crossed wiring harnesses) |
| P0050 | Oxygen sensor heater control circuit (Bank 2, sensor 1) |
| P0051 | Oxygen sensor heater control circuit low (Bank 2, sensor 1) |
| P0052 | Oxygen sensor heater control circuit high (Bank 2, sensor 1) |
| P0053 | Oxygen sensor heater, resistance (Bank 1, sensor 1) |
| P0056 | Oxygen sensor heater, control circuit  (Bank 2, sensor 2) |
| P0057 | Oxygen sensor heater control circuit low (Bank 2, sensor 2) |
| P0058 | Oxygen sensor heater control circuit high (Bank 2, sensor 2) |
| P0059 | Oxygen sensor heater, resistance (Bank 2, sensor 1) |
| P0070 | Ambient air temperature sensor, circuit |
| P0071 | Ambient air temperature sensor, circuit range/performance |
| P0072 | Ambient air temperature sensor, circuit low |
| P0073 | Ambient air temperature sensor, circuit high |
| P0090 | Fuel Pressure regulator 1,  control circuit open |
| P0091 | Fuel Pressure regulator 1,  control circuit low |
| P0092 | Fuel Pressure regulator 1,  control circuit high |
| P0100 | Mass Air Flow (MAF) or volume, A circuit |

## OBD-II trouble codes (continued)

**Note:** *Not all trouble codes apply to all models.*
**Note:** *Cylinders 1 through 3 are referred to as Bank 1, and cylinders 4 through 6 are referred to as Bank 2.*

| Code | Probable cause |
|------|----------------|
| P0101 | Mass Air Flow (MAF) or volume, A circuit range/performance |
| P0102 | Mass Air Flow (MAF) sensor circuit, low input |
| P0103 | Mass Air Flow (MAF) sensor circuit, high input |
| P0104 | Mass Air Flow (MAF) sensor circuit, intermittent failure |
| P0111 | Intake Air Temperature (IAT) sensor, bank 1, circuit low input |
| P0112 | Intake Air Temperature (IAT) sensor circuit, low input |
| P0113 | Intake Air Temperature (IAT) sensor circuit, high input |
| P0114 | Intake Air Temperature (IAT) sensor circuit, intermittent failure |
| P0116 | Engine Coolant Temperature (ECT) circuit range/performance problem |
| P0117 | Engine Coolant Temperature (ECT) sensor circuit, low input |
| P0118 | Engine Coolant Temperature (ECT) sensor circuit, high input |
| P0119 | Engine Coolant Temperature (ECT) sensor circuit, intermittent failure |
| P0121 | Throttle Position (TP) or APP sensor, circuit out of range or performance problem |
| P0122 | Throttle Position (TP) or APP sensor, circuit, low input |
| P0123 | Throttle Position (TP) or APP sensor circuit, high input |
| P0124 | Throttle position sensor/switch – circuit intermittent |
| P0125 | Insufficient coolant temperature for closed loop fuel control |
| P0128 | Coolant temperature below thermostat regulated temperature |
| P0131 | Upstream oxygen sensor circuit problem (Bank 1, sensor 1) |
| P0132 | Upstream oxygen sensor circuit, high voltage (Bank 1, sensor 1) |
| P0133 | Upstream oxygen sensor circuit, slow response (Bank 1, sensor 1) |
| P0134 | Upstream oxygen sensor circuit, no activity (Bank 1, sensor 1) |
| P0135 | Upstream oxygen sensor heater circuit problem (Bank 1) |
| P0136 | Downstream oxygen sensor circuit problem (Bank 2) |
| P0138 | Downstream oxygen sensor circuit, high voltage (Bank 2) |
| P0151 | Upstream oxygen sensor circuit, low voltage (Bank 2, sensor 1) |
| P0152 | Upstream oxygen sensor circuit, high voltage (Bank 2, sensor 1) |
| P0153 | Upstream oxygen sensor circuit, slow response (Bank 2, sensor 1) |
| P0155 | Upstream oxygen sensor heater circuit problem (Bank 2, sensor 1) |
| P0157 | Downstream oxygen sensor circuit, low voltage (Bank 2, sensor 2) |
| P0158 | Downstream oxygen sensor circuit, high voltage (Bank 2, sensor 2) |
| P0160 | Oxygen sensor circuit, no activity (Bank 2, sensor 2) |
| P0161 | Downstream oxygen sensor, heater circuit problem (Bank 2, sensor 2) |
| P0171 | System too lean (Bank 1) |
| P0172 | System too rich (Bank 1) |

| Code | Probable cause |
| --- | --- |
| P0174 | System too lean (Bank 2) |
| P0175 | System too rich (Bank 2) |
| P0190 | Fuel Rail Pressure (FRP) sensor, A circuit malfunction |
| P0192 | Fuel Rail Pressure (FRP) sensor circuit, low input |
| P0193 | Fuel Rail Pressure (FRP) sensor circuit, high input |
| P0196 | Engine Oil Temperature sensor circuit range/performance problem |
| P0197 | Engine Oil Temperature sensor circuit, low input |
| P0198 | Engine Oil Temperature sensor circuit, high input |
| P02AA | Cylinder number 5, fuel trim at maximum |
| P02AB | Cylinder number 5, fuel trim at minimum |
| P02AE | Cylinder number 6, fuel trim at maximum |
| P02AF | Cylinder number 6, fuel trim at minimum |
| P02A2 | Cylinder number 3, fuel trim at maximum |
| P02A3 | Cylinder number 3, fuel trim at minimum |
| P02A6 | Cylinder number 4, fuel trim at maximum |
| P02A7 | Cylinder number 4, fuel trim at minimum |
| P0201 | Injector no. 1 circuit malfunction |
| P0202 | Injector no. 2 circuit malfunction |
| P0203 | Injector no. 3 circuit malfunction |
| P0204 | Injector no. 4 circuit malfunction |
| P0205 | Injector no. 5 circuit malfunction |
| P0206 | Injector no. 6 circuit malfunction |
| P0221 | Throttle Position (TP) or APP sensor B circuit, range/performance problem |
| P0222 | Throttle Position (TP) or APP sensor B circuit, low input |
| P0223 | Throttle Position (TP) or APP sensor B circuit, high input |
| P0230 | Fuel pump primary circuit malfunction |
| P0234 | Engine overboost condition |
| P0261 | Cylinder 1 injector circuit low |
| P0262 | Cylinder 1 injector circuit high |
| P0264 | Cylinder 2 injector circuit low |
| P0265 | Cylinder 2 injector circuit high |
| P0267 | Cylinder 3 injector circuit low |
| P0268 | Cylinder 3 injector circuit high |
| P0270 | Cylinder 4 injector circuit low |
| P0271 | Cylinder 4 injector circuit high |
| P0273 | Cylinder 5 injector circuit low |
| P0274 | Cylinder 5 injector circuit high |

## OBD-II trouble codes (continued)

**Note:** *Not all trouble codes apply to all models.*
**Note:** *Cylinders 1 through 3 are referred to as Bank 1, and cylinders 4 through 6 are referred to as Bank 2.*

| Code | Probable cause |
|------|----------------|
| P0276 | Cylinder 6 injector circuit low |
| P0277 | Cylinder 6 injector circuit high |
| P0297 | Vehicle overspeed condition |
| P0298 | Engine oil over-temperature condition |
| P0300 | Random misfire detected |
| P0301 | Cylinder no. 1 misfire detected |
| P0302 | Cylinder no. 2 misfire detected |
| P0303 | Cylinder no. 3 misfire detected |
| P0304 | Cylinder no. 4 misfire detected |
| P0305 | Cylinder no. 5 misfire detected |
| P0306 | Cylinder no. 6 misfire detected |
| P0310 | Misfire detection monitor |
| P0315 | PCM unable to learn crankshaft pulse wheel tooth spacing |
| P0316 | Misfire occurred during first 1000 engine revolutions |
| P0320 | Ignition engine speed input circuit malfunction |
| P0325 | Knock sensor 1 circuit malfunction |
| P0326 | Knock sensor 1 circuit range/performance |
| P0330 | Knock sensor 2 circuit malfunction |
| P0331 | Knock sensor 2 circuit range/performance |
| P0340 | Camshaft Position (CMP) sensor A circuit performance (Bank 1, or single sensor) |
| P0341 | Camshaft Position (CMP) sensor A circuit intermittent (Bank 1, or single sensor) |
| P0350 | Ignition coil primary or secondary circuit malfunction |
| P0351 | Ignition coil A primary or secondary circuit malfunction |
| P0352 | Ignition coil B primary or secondary circuit malfunction |
| P0353 | Ignition coil C primary or secondary circuit malfunction |
| P0354 | Ignition coil D primary or secondary circuit malfunction |
| P0355 | Ignition coil E primary or secondary circuit malfunction |
| P0356 | Ignition coil F primary or secondary circuit malfunction |
| P0370 | Timing reference, high signal A resolution |
| P0373 | Timing reference, high signal A resolution erratic |
| P0420 | Catalyst system efficiency below threshold (Bank 1) |
| P0430 | Catalyst system efficiency below threshold (Bank 1) |
| P0440 | EVAP control system, incorrect flow |
| P0441 | EVAP control system, incorrect purge flow |
| P0442 | EVAP control system, small leak detected |

| Code | Probable cause |
| --- | --- |
| P0443 | EVAP control system, canister purge valve circuit open |
| P0444 | EVAP control system, canister purge valve circuit malfunction |
| P0445 | EVAP control system, canister purge valve circuit shorted |
| P0446 | EVAP control system canister vent solenoid circuit malfunction |
| P0451 | Fuel tank pressure sensor circuit out of range or performance problem |
| P0452 | Fuel tank pressure sensor circuit, low input |
| P0453 | Fuel tank pressure sensor circuit, high input |
| P0454 | Fuel tank pressure sensor circuit, noisy |
| P0455 | EVAP control system, big leak detected |
| P0456 | EVAP control system, very small leak detected |
| P0457 | EVAP control system, leak detected (fuel filler neck cap loose or off) |
| P0458 | EVAP control system, purge control valve circuit low |
| P0458 | EVAP control system, purge control valve circuit high |
| P0460 | Fuel level sensor circuit malfunction |
| P0461 | Fuel level sensor circuit range or performance problem |
| P0462 | Fuel level sensor circuit, low input |
| P0463 | Fuel level sensor circuit, high input |
| P0481 | High Fan Control (HFC) primary circuit failure |
| P0482 | Medium Fan Control (MFC) primary circuit failure |
| P0500 | Vehicle Speed Sensor (VSS) malfunction |
| P0501 | Vehicle Speed Sensor (VSS) range/performance problem |
| P0503 | Vehicle Speed Sensor (VSS), intermittent malfunction |
| P0505 | Idle Air Control (IAC) system malfunction |
| P0506 | Idle Air Control (IAC) rpm lower than expected |
| P0507 | Idle Air Control (IAC) rpm higher than expected |
| P0511 | Idle Air Control (IAC) circuit malfunction |
| P0512 | Starter request circuit |
| P0520 | Engine oil pressure switch, circuit |
| P0521 | Engine oil pressure switch, range/performance |
| P0522 | Engine oil pressure switch, circuit open |
| P0523 | Engine oil pressure switch, high |
| P0524 | Engine oil pressure switch, pressure too low |
| P0532 | Air conditioning pressure sensor circuit, low voltage |
| P0533 | Air conditioning pressure sensor circuit, high voltage |
| P0534 | Low air conditioning cycling period |
| P0537 | Air conditioning evaporator temperature circuit, low input |
| P0538 | Air conditioning evaporator temperature circuit, high input |

## OBD-II trouble codes (continued)

**Note:** *Not all trouble codes apply to all models.*

**Note:** *Cylinders 1 through 3 are referred to as Bank 1, and cylinders 4 through 6 are referred to as Bank 2.*

| Code | Probable cause |
|------|----------------|
| P0552 | Power Steering Pressure (PSP) sensor circuit malfunction |
| P0553 | Power Steering Pressure (PSP) sensor circuit malfunction |
| P0562 | System voltage low |
| P0563 | System voltage high |
| P0571 | Brake switch, A circuit |
| P0579 | Cruise control multifunction input A circuit range or performance problem |
| P0581 | Cruise control multifunction input A circuit, high |
| P0583 | Cruise control vacuum control circuit - high |
| P0597 | Thermostat heater control circuit, open |
| P0598 | Thermostat heater control circuit, low |
| P0599 | Thermostat heater control circuit, high |
| P0600 | Serial communication link (PCM) error |
| P0602 | Control module programming error |
| P0603 | Powertrain Control Module (PCM) Keep-Alive-Memory (KAM) test error |
| P0605 | Powertrain Control Module (PCM) Read-Only-Memory (ROM) error |
| P0606 | Powertrain Control Module (PCM) internal communication error |
| P0611 | Fuel injector control module performance |
| P0620 | Generator control circuit failure |
| P0622 | Generator field terminal circuit failure |
| P062F | Powertrain Control Module (PCM) EEPROM error |
| P0634 | PCM/PCM/TCM internal temperature too high |
| P0645 | Air conditioning clutch relay, primary circuit malfunction |
| P0646 | Air conditioning clutch relay, circuit low |
| P0647 | Air conditioning clutch relay, primary circuit high |
| P0660 | Intake manifold tuning valve control circuit open (Bank 1) |
| P0663 | Intake manifold tuning valve control circuit open (Bank 2) |
| P0668 | PCM/TCM internal temperature sensor, circuit too low |
| P0669 | PCM/TCM internal temperature sensor, circuit too high |
| P0668 | PCM/TCM internal temperature sensor, circuit too high |
| P0686 | PCM power relay, circuit low |
| P0691 | Fan 1 control, circuit low |
| P0692 | Fan 1 control, circuit high |
| P0700 | Transmission control system, MIL request |
| P0703 | Brake Pedal Position (BPP) switch circuit input malfunction |
| P0831 | Clutch pedal position switch malfunction, circuit low |
| P0832 | Clutch pedal position switch malfunction, circuit high |

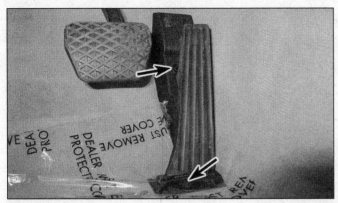

**4.3 Remove the bolts at the top and bottom of the accelerator pedal assembly**

**5.3 Depress the clip and disconnect the Camshaft Position (CMP) sensor electrical connector – 3.0L engine shown, 2.0L similar**

## 4 Accelerator Pedal Position (APP) sensor - replacement

*Refer to illustration 4.3*

1    The APP sensor is located at the upper end of, and is an integral component of, the accelerator pedal assembly. The APP sensor provides the PCM with a variable voltage signal that's proportional to the position (angle) of the accelerator pedal. The PCM uses this and other data to control the position of the throttle plate inside the electronically-controlled throttle body.

2    If a diagnostic scan tool test reveals there is a problem with the APP, the accelerator pedal and sensor must be replaced as a unit.

3    Remove the bolts securing the throttle pedal assembly, then disconnect the electrical connector **(see illustration)**.

4    Lift the throttle pedal assembly upwards, and disconnect the wiring plug. Note that the throttle pedal is only available as a complete assembly, which includes the position sensor. If defective, the complete assembly must be replaced.

5    Installation is the reverse of removal. After replacing the pedal and sensor, check with a scan tool and clear any DTCs.

## 5 Camshaft Position (CMP) sensors - replacement

*Refer to illustration 5.3*

1    Remove the air intake duct mounting bolts and duct (see Chapter 4). Disconnect the air hose as the duct is removed.

2    The CMP sensors are located in the front side of the cylinder head, under their respective camshaft ends. Ensure the ignition is switched off.

3    Squeeze together the locking lugs, and disconnect the sensor wiring plug **(see illustration)**.

4    Remove the retaining bolt and the sensor. Recover the seal.

5    Check the condition of the seal and

replace it if necessary.

6    Installation is the reverse of removal.

## 6 Crankshaft Position (CKP) sensor - replacement

### *2.0L engine*

1    On 2.0L engines, the CKP sensor has two connected parts: the connector housing mounted above the starter and the sensor end which is mounted underneath the starter and behind the flywheel.

2    Remove the starter (see Chapter 5).

3    Disconnect the electrical connector to the CKP housing, then remove the housing bolt.

4    Working through the starter opening, remove the sensor mounting bolt and pull the sensor from the crankcase.

5    Installation is the reverse of removal, making sure that the guide pin on the CKP sensor is inserted in the guiding groove on the crankcase.

### *3.0L engine*

*Refer to illustration 6.7*

6    On 3.0L engine models, the CKP sensor is located below the starter motor. For access,

remove the intake manifold (see Chapter 2A).

7    Disconnect the sensor electrical connector, then remove the retaining bolt and the sensor **(see illustration)**. **Note:** *The retaining bolt is aluminum, and must be replaced.*

8    Check the condition of the sealing ring and replace if necessary. Install the sensor and tighten the new retaining bolt to the specified torque.

9    Installation is the reverse of removal.

## 7 Engine Coolant Temperature (ECT) sensor - replacement

*Refer to illustration 7.2*

**Warning:** *Wait until the engine is completely cool before beginning this procedure.*

1    The PCM varies the intake air/fuel mixture, taking into account the input of the engine coolant temperature sensor and other sensors.

2    Disconnect the electrical connector at the ECT **(see illustration)**.

3    Use a wrench to unscrew the sensor.

4    Installation is the reverse of removal, with the exception of using a new copper washer.

5    Run the engine and check for coolant leakage, then check for any DTCs with a scan tool.

**6.7 On 3.0L engine, the Crankshaft Position (CKP) sensor is located below the starter**

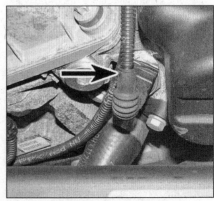

**7.2 Typical coolant temperature sensor location**

## 8   Mass Air Flow/Intake Air Temperature (MAF/IAT) sensor - replacement

*Refer to illustration 8.1*

1     The MAF/IAT sensor is located on top of the air duct/charge air cooler, near the air filter housing **(see illustration)**.

2     Disconnect the electrical connector from the MAF/IAT sensor.

3     Remove the screws securing the sensor and remove it slowly from the air duct. **Caution:** *Handle the sensor carefully, as it is fragile.*

4     Installation is the reverse of removal. Inspect the O-ring seals and replace if necessary.

## 9   Knock sensors - replacement

*Refer to illustrations 9.3a and 9.3b*

1     Disconnect the negative battery cable (see Chapter 5).

2     To access the knock sensors, remove the intake manifold (see Chapter 4A).

3     There are two knock sensors on the left side of the block **(see illustrations)**. Mark the mounting angle of the sensors.

4     Disconnect the electrical connector to the sensors.

5     Remove the mounting bolt at each sensor. These bolts are aluminum and must be discarded.

6     Installation is the reverse of removal, noting the following points:

a)  *Clean the block surface before installing the sensors*

b)  *Use new aluminum bolts*

c)  *Mount the sensors at the same angle as original*

d)  *Tighten bolts to 63 in-lbs, then an additional 90-degrees*

## 10   Oxygen sensors - replacement

*Refer to illustrations 10.2a and 10.2b*

1     On 2.0L engines there are two oxygen sensors: one upstream sensor (or "control sensor") and one downstream sensor (or "monitor sensor"). The sensors are located at each end of the catalytic converter. The sensor closest to the turbocharger is the upstream sensor and the sensor closest to the exhaust pipe is the downstream sensor.

2     On 3.0L engine models, there are four oxygen sensors - two for each cylinder bank - on all models. Each upstream oxygen sensor **(see illustration)** is located below the exhaust manifold flanges and above the catalytic converter. Each downstream oxygen sensor **(see illustration)** is located in the exhaust pipe, behind the converter. These are also referred to as catalyst monitor sensors. Use special

**8.1  Carefully remove the mounting screws and the MAF sensor from the air filter duct – 3.0L engine models shown**

care when servicing an oxygen sensor:

a)  *Oxygen sensors have a permanently attached pigtail and electrical connector that can't be removed from the sensor. Damage to or removal of the pigtail or the electrical connector will ruin the sensor.*

b)  *Keep grease, dirt and other contaminants away from the electrical connector and the louvered end of the sensor.*

c)  *Do not use cleaning solvents of any kind on an oxygen sensor or air/fuel ratio sensor.*

d)  *Do not drop or roughly handle an oxygen sensor or air/fuel ratio sensor.*

e)  *Be sure to install the silicone boot in the correct position to prevent the boot from melting and to allow the sensor to operate properly.*

3     Disconnect the cable from the negative battery terminal (see Chapter 5).

4     Raise the vehicle and place it securely on jackstands.

5     To remove the right upstream sensor on some models, it may be necessary to remove the exhaust heat shield, which is retained by two bolts.

6     Disconnect the oxygen sensor electrical connector. Using an oxygen sensor socket, remove the oxygen sensor **(see illustration 10.2a)**. If the sensor is difficult to loosen, spray some penetrant onto the sensor threads and allow it to soak in for the period of time specified by the penetrant manufacturer.

**Note:** *The sensor harness shields are color coded. Black for upstream sensor ("control sensor") and grey for downstream sensor ("monitor sensor").*

7     Apply a light coating of anti-seize compound to the threads of the new (or old) oxygen sensor to facilitate future removal. Do not get any anti-seize on the ceramic part of the sensor that goes into the pipe.

8     Installation is the reverse of removal. Be sure to tighten the sensor securely.

**9.3a  The front knock sensor is located on the block near the ECT sensor**

**9.3b  The rear knock sensor is mounted behind the starter motor**

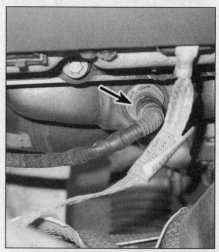

**10.2a  On 3.0L engines, the upstream oxygen sensors are located in the exhaust manifold, close to the engine**

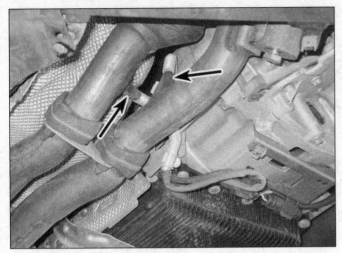

10.2b  On 3.0L engines, both downstream oxygen sensors are located in the exhaust pipes just behind the catalytic converters

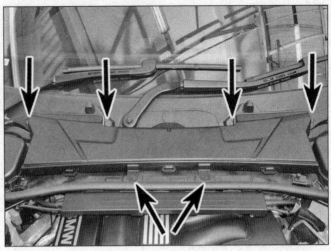

12.7  Remove the bolts and the cabin air filter cover

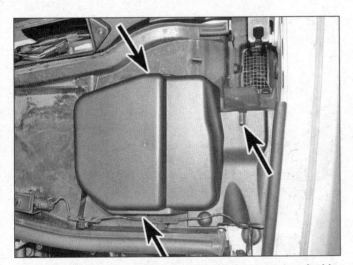

12.8  Release the clips and remove the plastic cover at each side of the cowl, behind the strut towers

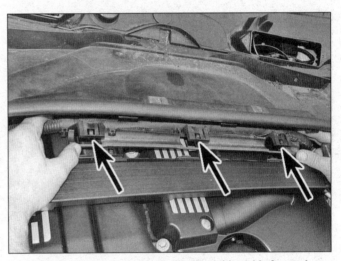

12.9  Depress the clips and slide the cable guide forward

## 11  Automatic transmission switches and sensors - general information

The automatic transmission is controlled by the Transmission Control Module, a large electro-hydraulic assembly inside the transmission which takes output from transmission sensors and sends signals to the transmission solenoids and the PCM. All of the communication to and from the TCM is in a wiring harness that can be disconnected to allow transmission removal from the vehicle.

Due to the complexity of the Mechatronic transmission control system, there are no serviceable components other than the fluid pan (see Chapter 1). The transmission should be diagnosed and repaired at a dealer or other qualified shop.

## 12  Powertrain Control Module (PCM) or Digital Motor Electronics (DME) control unit – removal and installation

*Refer to illustrations 12.7, 12.8, 12.9, 12.10a, 12.10b, 12.10c, 12.12a, 12.12b, 12.13 and 12.14*

1   Disconnect the negative battery cable (see Chapter 5). **Note:** *Disconnecting the battery will erase any fault codes stored in the PCM. It is recommended that prior to battery disconnection, the fault code memory of the module should be checked using a professional scan tool at a dealer or other qualified shop.*

### 2.0L engine

**Note:** *The Digital Motor Electronics (DME) control unit, is mounted in the engine compartment on top of the intake plenum.*

2   Remove the engine cover by lifting the

front of the cover up and pulling it forwards.

3   Remove the strut tower crossbrace plastic push-pins and bolts then remove the brace.

4   Remove the sound insulator plastic retainers and lift the insulator off of the engine.

5   Unlock and pull the electrical connectors from the DME control unit.

6   Remove the DME mounting screws and DME from the intake plenum.

### 3.0L engine

7   Remove the upper section of the cabin air filter housing **(see illustration)**.

8   Release the clips and remove the plastic cover behind the left-hand strut tower in the engine compartment **(see illustration)**. Repeat this procedure for the plastic cover behind the right-hand strut tower.

9   Release the clips and detach the cable guide from the front of the cabin air filter lower housing **(see illustration)**.

**12.10a  Rotate the temperature sensor counterclockwise and pull it from the bracket on the lower cabin air filter cover**

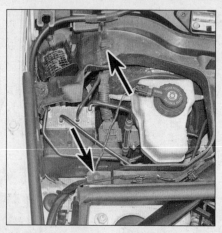

**12.10b  Release the catch and remove the bolt at each side . . .**

**12.10c . . . then pull the lower cabin air filter cover out from the cowl**

**12.12a  Squeeze together the clips and pull the black plastic clips upward**

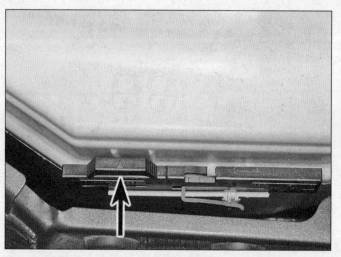

**12.12b  Slide the catch to the "unlock" position**

**12.13  Slide out the locking element**

10   Remove the bolt and release the clip on each side, then pull the lower section of the cabin air filter housing forward and maneuver it out **(see illustrations)**.

11   Remove the mounting bolts, loosen the nut, and lift out the heater end plate.

12   Working in the right corner of the engine compartment, release the locking clips and remove the cover from the electrical box **(see illustrations)**.

13   Slide out the locking elements, disconnect the module wiring plugs, then disconnect the plugs behind the PCM **(see illustration)**.

14   Release the retaining clips at the front, then slide the PCM upward from the vehicle **(see illustration)**.

### All models

15   Installation is the reverse of removal. After reconnecting the battery, the vehicle

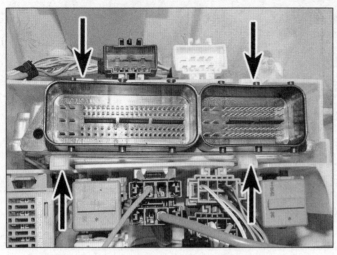

12.14  Release the clips and pull the PCM upward and out

14.4  Squeeze the sides of the collar and pull the hoses from the EVAP canister

must be driven for several miles so that the PCM/DME can learn its basic settings. If the engine still runs erratically, the basic settings may be reinstated by a BMW dealer or specialist using special diagnostic equipment. **Note:** *If a new module has been installed, it will need to be coded using special test equipment. Entrust this task to a dealer or other qualified shop.*

## 13   Catalytic converter - testing, precautions and replacement

### Testing

1   The performance of the catalytic converter is monitored by the oxygen sensors. When a change in readings occurs between the upstream and downstream sensors, a trouble code should be set that indicates the catalytic converter is not working efficiently.

2   Take the vehicle to a dealer or other qualified shop for analysis.

14.5  EVAP canister mounting bolts

### Precautions

3   The catalytic converter is a reliable and simple device which needs no maintenance in itself, but there are some facts an owner should be aware of if the converter is to function properly for its full service life.

a) *Always keep the ignition and fuel systems well-maintained in accordance with the manufacturer's schedule.*

b) *If the engine develops a misfire, do not drive the vehicle at all (or at least as little as possible) until the fault is corrected.*

c) *DO NOT push- or tow-start the vehicle - this will soak the catalytic converter in unburned fuel, causing it to overheat when the engine does start.*

d) *DO NOT switch off the ignition at high engine speeds.*

e) *DO NOT use fuel or engine oil additives - these may contain substances harmful to the catalytic converter.*

f) *DO NOT continue to use the vehicle if the engine burns oil to the extent of leaving a visible trail of blue smoke.*

g) *Remember that the catalytic converter operates at very high temperatures. DO NOT, therefore, park the vehicle in dry undergrowth, over long grass or piles of dead leaves after a long run.*

h) *Remember that the catalytic converter is FRAGILE - do not strike it with tools during servicing work.*

i) *In some cases a sulphurous smell (like that of rotten eggs) may be noticed from the exhaust. This is common to many catalytic converter-equipped cars and once the vehicle has covered a few thousand miles, the problem should disappear.*

j) *The catalytic converter, used on a well-maintained and well-driven vehicle, should last for between 50,000 and 100,000 miles - if the converter is no longer effective, it must be replaced.*

### Replacement

4   The catalytic converter is integral with the exhaust manifold, and they are replaced as a unit (see Chapter 4).

## 14   Evaporative Emissions Control (EVAP) system - component replacement

### Crankcase emission control

1   The components of this system require no attention other than to regularly check that the hose(s) are clear and undamaged.

### Evaporative emission control

#### Testing

2   If the system is thought to be faulty, disconnect the hoses from the EVAP canister and purge control valve and check that they are clear by blowing through them. Full testing of the system can only be carried out using a sophisticated scan tool connected to the OBD test port **(see illustration 3.1)**. If the purge control valve or EVAP canister is thought to be faulty, they must be replaced.

#### EVAP canister replacement

*Refer to illustrations 14.4 and 14.5*

3   The canister is located under the vehicle, just behind the right rear wheel. Raise the rear of the vehicle and support it securely on jackstands. Remove the inner wheelwell liner fasteners and pull the liner back.

4   Note the installed locations of the pipes. Squeeze together the sides of the collars and disconnect the lines from the canister **(see illustration)**.

5   Remove the canister mounting bolts and the canister **(see illustration)**.

6   Installation is the reverse of removal, ensuring the hoses are correctly and securely reconnected.

## Purge valve replacement

*Refer to illustration 14.7*

7   The valve is located on a bracket on the underside of the intake manifold **(see illustration)**.

8   On 3.0L models, loosen the clamp, disconnect the air intake hose from the throttle body, remove the throttle body mounting bolts and move the throttle body to one side (see Chapter 4 if necessary).

9   Ensure the ignition is switched off, and disconnect the electrical connector from the valve.

10   Disconnect the quick-release connector from the valve and release the hose.

11   Release the clip and slide the valve from the bracket.

12   Installation is the reverse of removal. Ensure the valve and hose are securely held by the retaining clips.

**14.7  The purge valve is located beneath the intake manifold (typical)**

# Chapter 7  Part A
# Manual transmission

## Contents

## Specifications

### Type

| | |
|---|---|
| 320i | GS6-17BG (Getrag) |
| 325i/328i | GS6-17BG (Getrag) |
| 325xi/328xi/330i/330xi | GS6X-37BZ (ZF) |

### Torque specifications

| | Ft-lbs (unless otherwise indicated) | Nm |
|---|---|---|
| Transmission crossmember-to-body bolts | | |
| E-series chassis | | |
| M8 bolt | 15 | 21 |
| M10 bolt | 31 | 42 |
| F-series chassis | 168 in-lbs | 19 |
| Transmission mount-to-transmission nut/bolts | | |
| E-series chassis | | |
| M8 bolt | 15 | 21 |
| M10 bolt | 31 | 42 |
| F-series chassis | 168 in-lbs | 19 |
| Transmission-to-engine bolts* | | |
| E-series chassis | | |
| Hex-head bolts | | |
| M8 | 18 | 25 |
| M10 | 36 | 49 |
| M12 | 55 | 74 |
| Torx-head bolts | | |
| M8 | 16 | 22 |
| M10 | 32 | 43 |
| M12 | 53 | 72 |
| F-series chassis | | |
| M8 bolt | 168 in-lbs | 19 |
| M10 bolt | 41 | 56 |
| Output flange-to-output shaft nut** | | |
| GS6-17 and GS6-37 transmissions | | |
| Stage 1 | 125 | 170 |
| Stage 2 | Fully loosen nut | |
| Stage 3 | 89 | 120 |
| Back-up light switch | 15 | 21 |

*_Do not re-use._

**Caution:** _All aluminum fasteners must be replaced with new ones whenever they are removed. If in doubt, try to attract it with a magnet (aluminum is not magnetic). Additionally, most aluminum fasteners are identified with a blue paint marking._

*** Coat the threads of the nut with thread-locking compound._

## 1   General information

The transmission is a 6-speed unit contained in an aluminum housing bolted to the rear of the engine.

Drive is transmitted from the crankshaft via the clutch to the input shaft, which has a splined extension to accept the clutch friction disc. The output shaft transmits the drive via the driveshaft to the rear differential.

The input shaft runs in line with the output shaft. The input shaft and output shaft gears are in constant mesh with the cluster-gear shaft. Selection of gears is by sliding synchromesh hubs, which lock the appropriate output shaft gears to the output shaft.

Gear selection is via a floor-mounted lever and selector mechanism or, depending on model, switches mounted on the steering wheel. A Sequential Manual Transmission (SMT) option is available for some models, where the gear changes can be performed sequentially using the floor-mounted lever,

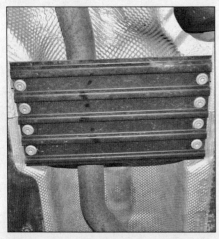

**2.2  Remove the reinforcement plate from below the exhaust system**

or the paddle shift switches on the steering wheel. On models so equipped, the gear changes can be performed automatically, with the Powertrain Control Module (PCM) controlling shifting and clutch operation (via hydraulic controls) dictated by driving style and road conditions. A launch control is available on some models, where at the press of a button, the PCM will control engine speed, clutch operation and shift functions, to achieve maximum acceleration - consult your owner's manual for further details.

The selector mechanism causes the appropriate selector fork to move its respective synchro-sleeve along the shaft, to lock the gear pinion to the synchro-hub. Since the synchro-hubs are splined to the output shaft, this locks the pinion to the shaft, so that drive can be transmitted. To ensure that shifting can be made quickly and quietly, a synchromesh system is fitted to all forward gears, consisting of synchro rings and spring-loaded fingers, as well as the gear pinions and synchro-hubs. The synchromesh cones are formed on the mating faces of the baulk rings and gear pinions.

The transmission is filled for life, and the manufacturer does not provide any fluid change specifications.

## 2   Shift lever assembly - removal and installation

*Refer to illustrations 2.2, 2.4, 2.6, 2.7 and 2.11*

**Note:** *A new shift lever bearing will be required on installation.*

1    Raise the vehicle and support it securely on jackstands. Remove the fasteners and the under-shield beneath the transmission (where equipped) (see Chapter 1, Section 29).

2    Remove the fasteners and the reinforcement plate from beneath the vehicle **(see illustration)**.

3    Remove the fasteners and the heat shield from beneath the driveshaft.

4    Starting at the front left-hand edge, push in the sides and free the shifter boot from the center console. On models manufactured 03/2007 and later, the shift boot is integral with the shift lever knob **(see illustration)**.

5    Support the transmission with a transmission jack, then remove the bolts/nuts and remove the crossmember and mount from the rear of the transmission.

6    Pry the securing clip from the end of the shift selector rod pin. Withdraw the selector rod pin from the eye on the end of the shift lever **(see illustration)**.

7    Release the shift lever lower bearing retaining ring from the shift selector arm. A special tool is available for this purpose, but two screwdrivers, with the tips engaged in opposite slots in the bearing ring, can be used instead. To unlock the bearing ring, turn it a quarter-turn counterclockwise **(see illustration)**.

8    The bearing can now be pushed up through the housing, and the shifter can be withdrawn from inside the vehicle.

9    If desired, the bearing can be removed from the shifter ball by pressing it downwards. To withdraw the bearing over the shifter eye, rotate the bearing until the eye passes through the slots provided in the bearing.

10   Install the new bearing in the reverse order of removal. Ensure that the bearing is pressed securely into position on the shifter ball.

11   Install the lever in the reverse order of removal, noting the following points:

a)  *Grease the bearing contact faces before installation.*

b)  *Lower the shifter into position, ensuring that the arrow on the shifter grommet points towards the front of the vehicle.*

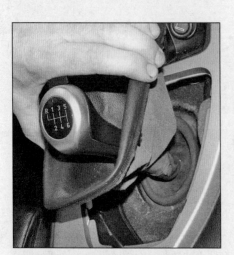

**2.4  Squeeze together the sides, and remove the shifter boot**

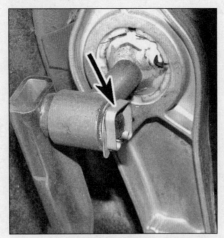

**2.6  Slide the retaining clip from the selector rod pin**

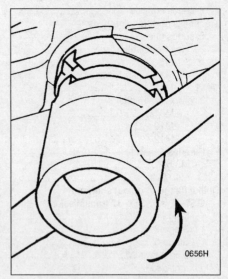

**2.7  Turn the bearing ring counterclockwise (special tool shown)**

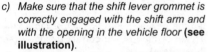

**2.11  Shifter grommet correctly engaged with the selector arm and vehicle floor**

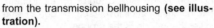

**3.3  Remove the bolts securing the release bearing guide sleeve**

**3.5  Drill a small hole in the oil seal**

c)  *Make sure that the shift lever grommet is correctly engaged with the shift arm and with the opening in the vehicle floor (see illustration).*

d)  *When engaging the bearing with the selector arm, make sure that the arrows or tabs (as applicable) on the top of the bearing point towards the rear of the vehicle.*

e)  *To lock the bearing in position in the selector arm, press down on the top of the bearing retaining tab locations until the tabs click into position.*

f)  *Grease the selector rod pin before engaging it with the shift lever eye.*

## 3   Oil seals - replacement

### Input shaft oil seal

*Refer to illustrations 3.3, 3.5 and 3.7*

1   Remove the transmission (see Section 5).

2   Remove the clutch release bearing and lever (see Chapter 8).

3   Unscrew the mounting bolts and withdraw the clutch release bearing guide sleeve

from the transmission bellhousing **(see illustration)**.

4   Note the installed depth of the now-exposed input shaft oil seal.

5   Drill one small hole in the oil seal (two small pilot holes should be provided at opposite points on the seal). Coat the end of the drill bit with grease to prevent any filings from the holes entering the transmission **(see illustration)**.

6   Using a small drift, tap one side of the seal (opposite to the hole) into the bellhousing as far as the stop.

7   Screw a small self-tapping screw into the opposite side of the seal, and use pliers to pull out the seal **(see illustration)**.

8   Clean the oil seal seating surface.

9   Lubricate the lips of the new oil seal with a little clean transmission oil, then carefully slide the seal over the input shaft into position in the bellhousing.

10   Tap the oil seal into the bellhousing to the previously-noted depth.

11   Install the guide sleeve to the transmission housing and tighten the retaining bolts securely, using a drop of locking compound on the threads of the bolts.

12   Install the clutch release lever and bear-

ing (see Chapter 8).

13   Install the transmission (see Section 5), then check the transmission oil level (see Chapter 1).

### Output flange oil seal

*Refer to illustrations 3.17, 3.18, 3.19 and 3.21*

**Note:** *Thread-locking compound will be required for installation of the transmission flange nut.*

14   Raise the vehicle and support securely on jackstands.

15   Disconnect the driveshaft from the transmission flange, and support it clear of the transmission using wire or string (see Chapter 8).

16   Where applicable, pry the transmission flange nut cover plate from the flange using a screwdriver. Discard the cover plate - it is not required on installation. If necessary, support the transmission and remove the transmission crossmember to improve access.

17   Counter-hold the transmission flange by bolting a forked or two-pin spanner tool to two of the flange bolt holes, then unscrew the flange securing nut using a deep socket and extension bar **(see illustration)**.

18   Using a puller, draw the flange from the

**3.7  Insert a self-tapping screw in to the hole, and pull the seal out with pliers**

**3.17  Hold the output flange and remove the nut using a deep socket**

**3.18  Use a three-legged puller to remove the output flange**

**3.19  Carefully pull the seal out**

**3.21  Tap the seal into place using a tubular spacer or socket which bears only on the hard outer edge of the seal**

end of the transmission output shaft **(see illustration)**. Be prepared to catch spilling oil.
19   Note the installed depth of the oil seal, then using an oil seal puller or remover (take care to avoid damage to the transmission output shaft), pull/pry the oil seal from the transmission casing **(see illustration)**.
20   Clean the oil seal seating surface.
21   Lubricate the lips of the new oil seal with a little clean transmission oil, then carefully tap the seal into the transmission casing to the previously-noted depth using a suitable tubular spacer or socket **(see illustration)**.
22   Install the flange to the output shaft.
**Note:** *To ease installation of the flange, immerse it in hot water for a few minutes, then install it on the shaft.*
23   Tighten the flange nut to step one of the torque setting, then loosen and remove the nut (step two). Coat the threads of the flange nut with thread-locking compound, then tighten the nut to the step three torque as specified. Counter-hold the flange as during removal.
24   If a flange nut cover plate was originally installed, discard it. There is no need to install a cover plate.
25   Reconnect the driveshaft to the trans-

mission flange (see Chapter 8), then check the transmission oil level (see Section 2), and lower the vehicle to the ground.

## Gear selector shaft oil seal

*Refer to illustration 3.31*
**Note:** *A new selector shaft eye securing roll-pin will be required on installation.*
26   Raise the vehicle and support securely on jackstands.
27   Disconnect the propeller shaft from the transmission flange, and support it clear of the transmission using wire or string (see Chapter 8). For improved access, support the transmission, and remove the transmission crossmember.
28   Slide back the locking collar, then slide out the pin securing the gear selector shaft eye to the end of the gear selector shaft.
29   Pull the gear selector shaft eye (as an assembly with the gear linkage) off the end of the selector shaft, and move the linkage clear of the selector shaft.
30   Using a small flat-bladed screwdriver, pry the selector shaft oil seal from the transmission casing.
31   Clean the oil seal seating surface, then

tap the new seal into position using a small socket or tube of the correct diameter **(see illustration)**.
32   Check the condition of the rubber washer in the end of the selector shaft eye and replace if necessary.
33   Push the selector shaft eye back onto the end of the selector shaft, then align the holes in the eye and shaft and secure the eye to the shaft using the pin.
34   Slide the locking collar into position over the roll-pin.
35   Reconnect the propeller shaft to the transmission flange (see Chapter 8).
36   Check the transmission oil level (see Section 2), then lower the vehicle.

---

**4     Back-up light switch - testing, removal and installation**

## Testing

1   The back-up light circuit is controlled by a plunger-type switch screwed into the right-hand side of the transmission case. If a fault develops in the circuit, first check that the circuit fuse has not blown.
2   To test the switch, disconnect the wiring connector, and use a multimeter (set to the resistance function) or a battery-and-bulb test circuit to check that there is continuity between the switch terminals only when reverse gear is selected. If this is not the case, and there are no obvious breaks or other damage to the wires, the switch is faulty, and must be replaced.

## Removal

*Refer to illustration 4.4*
3   Raise the vehicle and support securely on jackstands.
4   Disconnect the wiring connector, then unscrew the switch from the transmission casing **(see illustration)**.

**3.31  Tap the new selector shaft oil seal into position**

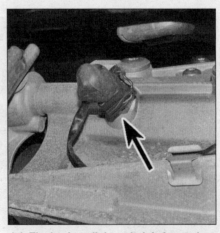

**4.4  The back-up light switch is located on the right-hand side of the transmission**

**5.6 Pry up the clips, and slide the pin at each side from the casing**

**5.10 Adapter plate retaining bolt**

## Installation

5    Screw the switch back into position in the transmission housing and tighten it securely. Reconnect the wiring connector, and test the operation of the circuit.

6    Lower the vehicle.

## 5    Manual transmission - removal and installation

**Note:** *This is an involved operation. Read through the procedure thoroughly before starting work, and ensure that adequate lifting and/ or jacking/support equipment is available.*

### Removal

*Refer to illustrations 5.6 and 5.10*

1    Disconnect the negative battery cable (see Chapter 5).

2    Raise the vehicle and support securely on jackstands. **Note:** *The vehicle must be raised sufficiently to allow clearance for the transmission to be removed from under the vehicle. Remove the bolts and remove the engine/transmission under-shields.*

3    Remove the starter motor (see Chapter 5).

4    Remove the driveshaft (see Chapter 8).

5    Remove the nut and remove the under-shield bracket from the side of the transmission.

6    Working under the vehicle, pry up the retaining clips and extract the pin securing the shift lever support bracket on each side to the transmission casing **(see illustration)**. Similarly, disconnect the selector rod pin from the end of the shift lever **(see illustration 2.6)**.

7    Working at the transmission bellhousing, remove the nuts and withdraw the clutch release cylinder from the studs on the bellhousing. Support the release cylinder clear of the working area, but do not strain the hose.

8    Noting their installed locations, disconnect all electrical connectors, and release any wiring harnesses from the transmission case.

9    On models so equipped, remove the exhaust mounting bracket from the rear of the transmission case.

10    Where applicable, unscrew the bolt securing the engine/transmission adapter plate to the right-hand side of the transmission bellhousing and/or remove the flywheel lower cover plate **(see illustration)**.

11    Place a suitable block of wood between the front of the engine oil pan and the steering gear. Once the transmission is removed, the engine will tend to tip forwards.

12    Place a transmission jack under the transmission casing, just behind the bellhousing. Use a block of wood to spread the load, then raise the jack to just take the weight of the transmission. **Caution:** *The transmission should be secured to the transmission jack with chains or heavy straps.*

13    Remove the crossmember and mounts from the rear of the transmission, and allow the transmission/engine assembly to lower slightly.

14    Remove the engine-to-transmission bolts. Discard all aluminum bolts; new ones must be used during installation.

15    Slide the transmission rearward to disengage the input shaft from the clutch. Take care during this operation to ensure that the weight of the transmission is not allowed to hang on the input shaft.

### Installation

16    Check that the clutch friction disc is centered (see Chapter 8).

17    Before installing the transmission, it is advisable to inspect the clutch release bearing and lever (see Chapter 8).

18    The remainder of installation is the reverse of removal, noting the following points:

a)    *Check that the transmission positioning dowels are securely in place at the rear of the engine.*

b)    *Tighten all fasteners to their specified torque.*

c)    *Lightly grease the gear selector arm pivot pin and the gear selector rod pin before installation.*

d)    *Reconnect the driveshaft to the transmission flange (see Chapter 8).*

e)    *Install the starter motor (see Chapter 5).*

## 6    Manual transmission overhaul - general information

Overhauling a manual transmission is a difficult and involved job for the home mechanic. In addition to disassembling and reassembling many small parts, clearances must be precisely measured and, if necessary, changed by selecting shims and spacers. Internal transmission components are also often difficult to obtain, and in many instances, extremely expensive. Because of this, if the transmission develops a fault or becomes noisy, the best course of action is to have the unit overhauled by a dealer or qualified transmission shop, or to obtain an exchange reconditioned unit. Be aware that some transmission repairs can be carried out with the transmission in the vehicle.

Nevertheless, it is not impossible for the more experienced mechanic to overhaul the transmission, provided the special tools are available, and the job is done in a deliberate step-by-step manner, so that nothing is overlooked.

The tools necessary for an overhaul include internal and external snap-ring pliers, bearing pullers, a slide hammer, a set of pin punches, a dial test indicator, and possibly a hydraulic press. In addition, a large, sturdy workbench and a vise will be required.

During disassembly of the transmission, make careful notes of how each component is installed, to make reassembly easier and more accurate.

Before disassembling the transmission, it will help if you have some idea what area is malfunctioning. Certain problems can be closely related to specific areas in the transmission, which can make component examination and replacement easier.

# Notes

# Chapter 7  Part B
# Automatic transmission

## Contents

## Specifications

### Transmission type

| | |
|---|---|
| 328i, 328xi | GA6L45R (GM) |
| 325i, 325xi, 330i, 330xi | GA6HP19Z (ZF) |
| 320i, 328i | GA8HP45Z (ZF) |

### Torque specifications

**Ft-lbs** (unless otherwise indicated)     **Nm**

**Note:** *One foot-pound (ft-lb) of torque is equivalent to 12 inch-pounds (in-lbs) of torque. Torque values below approximately 15 foot-pounds are expressed in inch-pounds, because most foot-pound torque wrenches are not accurate at these smaller values.*

**Note:** *On some applications different grades of bolt are used; the grade of each bolt is stamped on the bolt head. Ensure that each bolt is tightened to the correct torque for its grade.*

Transmission-to-engine bolts*
  6-speed models
    M10 x 30 mm

| | Ft-lbs | Nm |
|---|---|---|
|       Stage 1 | 15 | 20 |
|       Stage 2 | Tighten an additional 90-degrees | |
|     M10 x 85 mm | | |
|       Stage 1 | 15 | 20 |
|       Stage 2 | Tighten an additional 180-degrees | |
|     M12 | | |
|       Stage 1 | 18 | 25 |
|       Stage 2 | Tighten an additional 130-degrees | |
|   8-speed models | | |
|     M6 bolts | 80 in-lbs | 9 |
|     M10 x 8.8 bolts | 28 | 38 |
|     M10 x 10.9 bolts | 41 | 56 |
|     Steel Torx bolts M8 | 168 in-lbs | 19 |
|     Steel Torx bolts M12 | 50 | 66 |
| Output flange nut* | | |
|   Stage 1 | 140 | 190 |
|   Stage 2 | Loosen 360-degrees | |
|   Stage 3 | 89 | 120 |

*\* Do not re-use.*

**Caution:** *All aluminum fasteners must be replaced with new ones whenever they are removed. If in doubt, try to attract it with a magnet (aluminum is not magnetic). Additionally, most aluminum fasteners are identified with a blue paint marking.*

## Torque specifications

| | Ft-lbs (unless otherwise indicated) | Nm |
|---|---|---|

**Note:** *One foot-pound (ft-lb) of torque is equivalent to 12 inch-pounds (in-lbs) of torque. Torque values below approximately 15 foot-pounds are expressed in inch-pounds, because most foot-pound torque wrenches are not accurate at these smaller values.*

**Note:** *On some applications different grades of bolt can be used; the grade of each bolt is stamped on the bolt head. Ensure that each bolt is tightened to the correct torque for its grade.*

| | Ft-lbs (unless otherwise indicated) | Nm |
|---|---|---|
| Torque converter-to-driveplate bolts | | |
|     E-series chassis | | |
|         M8 | 19 | 26 |
|         M10 | | |
|             8.8 | 36 | 49 |
|             10.9 | 41 | 56 |
|     F-series chassis | | |
|         M10 x 10.9 bolt | 44 | 60 |
| Transmission crossmember-to-body bolts | | |
|     6-speed models | | |
|         M8 | 15 | 21 |
|         M10 | 31 | 42 |
|     8-speed models | 168 in-lbs | 19 |
| Transmission mount-to-transmission fasteners | | |
|     6-speed models | | |
|         M8 | 15 | 21 |
|         M10 | 31 | 42 |
|     8-speed models | | |
|         AWD models | 50 | 68 |
|         RWD models | 168 in-lbs | 19 |
| Transmission oil drain plug* | See Chapter 1 | |
| Transmission oil filler/level plug | See Chapter 1 | |

*\* Do not re-use.*

**Caution:** *All aluminum fasteners must be replaced with new ones whenever they are removed. If in doubt, try to attract it with a magnet (aluminum is not magnetic). Additionally, most aluminum fasteners are identified with a blue paint marking.*

## 1  General information

The six-speed and eight-speed automatic transmissions consist of a torque converter, an epicyclical geartrain and hydraulically operated clutches and brakes.

The torque converter provides a fluid coupling between the engine and transmission, which acts as a clutch, and also provides a degree of torque multiplication when accelerating.

The geartrain provides either six or eight forward, or one reverse gear ratio, according to which of its component parts are held stationary or allowed to turn. The components of the geartrain are held or released by brakes and clutches which are activated by a hydraulic control unit. A fluid pump within the transmission provides the necessary hydraulic pressure to operate the brakes and clutches.

Driver control of the transmission is by a four-position selector lever, incorporating a Steptronic function. The transmission has Park, Reverse, Neutral and Drive positions. An automatic kickdown facility shifts the transmission down a gear if the accelerator pedal is fully depressed.

Certain models are available with Steptronic gearchange that allows the driver to induce gearchanges with a simple movement of the shift lever - forward to upshift, and back to downshift.

Due to the complexity of the automatic transmission, any repair or overhaul work must be left to a dealer or specialist with the necessary special equipment for fault diagnosis and repair. The following Sections are limited to supplying general information, and any service information and instructions that can be used by the owner.

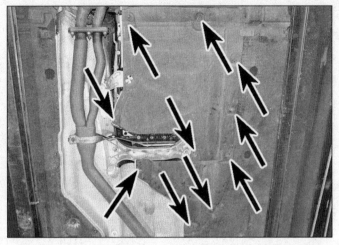

2.2  Remove the fasteners and the transmission splash shield

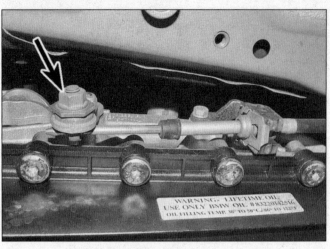

2.3  Remove the cable clamping nut

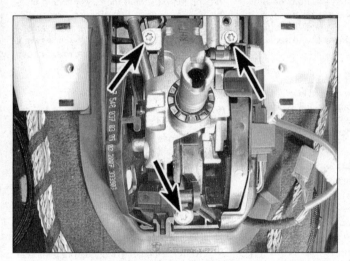

2.7  Remove the three bolts

3.2  Depress the catch to release the lever when the battery is disconnected

## 2  Shift lever - removal and installation

### Removal

#### 6-speed models

*Refer to illustrations 2.2, 2.3 and 2.7*

1  Raise the vehicle and support it securely on jackstands. Ensure the transmission is in Park.

2  Working underneath the vehicle, remove the splash shield fasteners and shield **(see illustration)**.

3  Loosen the selector cable clamping nut on the transmission lever **(see illustration)**.

4  Remove the locknut securing the selector outer cable and remove the cable from the support bracket on the transmission.

5  Remove the center console (see Chapter 11).

6  Noting their installed positions, disconnect any wiring plugs attached to the shift lever assembly.

7  Remove the mounting bolts securing the shift lever assembly to the floor and maneuver the assembly up from its location **(see illustration)**. Note: *The shift lever assembly is only available as a complete assembly with the selector cable and no further disassembly is recommended.*

### Installation

8  Installation is the reverse of removal, noting the following points:

a)  *Prior to installing the shift knob, push the boot down the shift lever until the locking groove in the lever is exposed.*

b)  *Adjust the shift cable (see Section 3).*

#### 8-speed models

**Note:** *On 8-speed transmissions, the shift lever is part of the Mechatronics system and it connected to the transmission by electrical wires - there is no linkage. If there is a problem with the shifter, it should be repaired by a BMW dealer or other BMW specialist.*

9  Remove the center console trim panels (see Chapter 11).

10  Remove the shift lever four mounting screws then lift the shifter up and disconnect the electrical connectors.

11  Installation is the reverse of removal.

## 3  Shift cable - removal, installation and adjustment

### Removal and installation

1  The shift cable can only be replaced as a unit with the shift lever assembly (see Section 2).

### Adjustment

*Refer to illustrations 3.2, 3.5a and 3.5b*

2  Move the shift lever to Park. To move the lever when the battery is disconnected, pry up the lever boot and depress the release catch **(see illustration)**.

3  If not already done, loosen the clamp nut securing the cable to the end fitting (the vehicle should be raised for access).

3.5a  Gently press the cable towards the bracket . . .

3.5b  . . . and tighten the clamping nut

4    Push the operating lever on the trans-mission away from the cable bracket on the transmission (towards the Park position).
5    Press the end of the cable in the oppo-site direction (towards the cable bracket), then release the cable, counter-hold the clamp and tighten the clamp nut **(see illustrations)**.
6    Check that the cable is correctly adjusted by starting the engine, applying the brakes firmly, and moving the shift lever through all the gear positions.

## 4    Fluid seals - replacement

### *Torque converter seal*
#### 6-speed models only
1    Remove the transmission and the torque converter (see Section 5).
2    Using a hooked tool, pry the old oil seal from the transmission bellhousing. Alterna-tively, drill a small hole, then screw a self-tap-ping screw into the seal and use pliers to pull out the seal.
3    Lubricate the lip of the new seal with clean transmission fluid, then carefully drive it into place using a large socket or tube.

4    Remove the old O-ring seal from the input shaft and slide a new one into place. Apply a smear of petroleum jelly to the new O-ring.
5    Install the torque converter and transmis-sion (see Section 5).

### *Output flange oil seal*
6    Replacement of the oil seal involves par-tial disassembly of the transmission, which is a complex operation. Oil seal replacement should be entrusted to a BMW dealer or specialist.

## 5    Automatic transmission - removal and installation

**Caution:** *On 8-speed transmissions, to pre-vent severe damage to the engine block, the section of bolt threads that protrude out of the transmission must be checked for damage or corrosion before trying to remove them. If there is corrosion, the corrosion must be removed and the threads completely cleaned before trying to remove them. If there was corrosion, replace the bolts once they have been removed.*
**Note:** *This is an involved operation. Read*

*through the procedure thoroughly before start-ing work, and ensure that adequate lifting tackle and/or jacking/support equipment is available. A suitable tool will be required to align the torque converter when installing the transmission, and new fluid pipe O-rings may be required.*

### *Removal*
*Refer to illustrations 5.8a, 5.8b, 5.9, 5.10, 5.11a, 5.11b, 5.12, 5.14, 5.15 and 5.18*
1    Disconnect the negative battery cable (see Chapter 5).
2    Raise the vehicle and support it securely on jackstands. Note that the vehicle must be raised sufficiently to allow clearance for the transmission to be removed from under the vehicle. Remove the bolts and remove the engine/transmission splash shield from the vehicle **(see illustration 2.2)**.
3    Remove the bolts and the front reinforce-ment brace/plate from under the transmission.
4    Remove the starter motor (see Chapter 5).
5    Remove the exhaust system and heat shield (see Chapter 4), then unbolt the exhaust mounting crossmember from under the vehicle.
6    Remove the driveshaft (see Chapter 8).
7    On 6-speed models, disconnect the shift

5.8a  Unclip the wiring harness and plugs . . .

5.8b  . . . then remove the cover plate mounting bolts and plate

**5.9 Remove the torque converter bolts**

**5.10 Remove the brackets adjacent to the transmission**

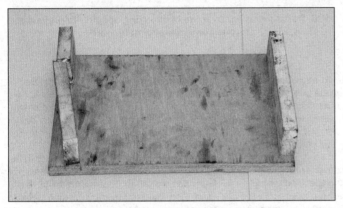

**5.11a Fashion a wooden platform . . .**

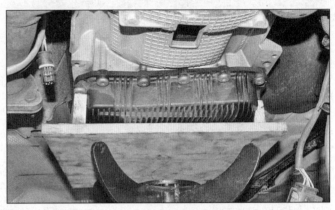

**5.11b . . . to support the transmission at the fluid pan flange on each side**

cable from the transmission (see Section 3).

8    Disconnect the wiring plugs under the front of the transmission bellhousing and unclip the wiring harness. Remove the cover plate mounting bolts and the plate **(see illustrations)**.

9    Mark the position of the torque converter to the driveplate, then unscrew the three torque converter bolts, turning the crankshaft with a wrench or socket on the pulley hub bolt to access each bolt in turn **(see illustration)**. **Note:** *On 8-speed models, special tool No. 2 222 741 (or equivalent) must be installed once all the torque converter bolts have been removed to prevent the converter from rotating.*

10    Remove the nuts and brackets from the

right-hand side of the transmission oil pan, then remove the heat shield mounting bolts and heat shield (where applicable) **(see illustration)**.

11    Support the transmission using a transmission jack and blocks of wood **(see illustrations)**. The transmission pan is plastic - ensure the transmission is supported around the edge of the pan. **Caution:** *The transmission is heavy, so ensure that it is adequately supported.*

12    Remove the crossmember mounting bolts/nuts and the crossmember from the rear of the transmission **(see illustration)**.

13    Place a suitable block of wood between the engine oil pan and the steering gear; once

the transmission is removed, the engine will be front-heavy.

14    Lower the transmission slightly, then rotate the electrical connector collar counterclockwise and pull the wiring plug from the transmission case **(see illustration)**; be sure to cover the opening with a plastic plug or tape. Release the wiring harness clips on the transmission case. **Caution:** *On 8-speed models, the transmission Mechatronics system can be destroyed by electrical static discharges. The contacts inside the connector or transmission opening must not be touched. Once the Mechatronics electrical connector is removed the opening and electrical connector should be covered.*

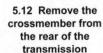

**5.12 Remove the crossmember from the rear of the transmission**

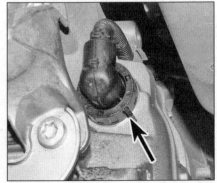

**5.14 Rotate the collar counterclockwise and pull the wiring plug from the case**

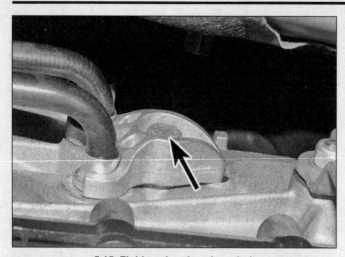

**5.15  Fluid cooler pipe clamp bolt**

**5.18  Bolt a metal bar over the bellhousing opening to prevent the torque converter sliding forward**

15   Unbolt the fluid cooler pipe brackets and clamps. Remove the fluid line clamp bolt and disconnect the fluid lines - be prepared for fluid to spill **(see illustration)**. Plug and seal the openings to prevent contamination.

16   Remove the engine-to-transmission bolts and washers, then slide the transmission rearwards. Ensure the torque converter comes away from the driveplate, and stays in place in the transmission.

17   Insert a suitable wooden or metal bar through the slot in the bottom of the bellhousing to hold the torque converter back. As the transmission is released from the engine, check to make sure that the engine is adequately supported, and no hoses remain connected.

18   Lower the transmission and carefully withdraw it from under the vehicle, making sure that the torque converter is held in position. If the transmission is to be removed for some time, ensure that the engine is adequately supported in the engine compartment. Take measures to ensure the torque converter is prevented from sliding forwards **(see illustration)**.

## Installation

19   Ensure that the transmission locating dowels are in position on the engine.

20   Before mating the transmission with the engine, it is essential that the torque converter is perfectly aligned with the driveplate.

21   Turn the driveplate to align one of the torque converter-to-driveplate bolt holes.

22   Ensure that the transmission is adequately supported, and maneuver it into position under the vehicle.

23   Install and tighten the engine-to-transmission bolts.

24   Install the torque converter-to-driveplate bolt. Tighten the bolt to the specified torque.

25   Turn the crankshaft for access to the remaining two torque converter-to-driveplate bolt locations (see Step 9). Install and tighten the bolts.

26   The remainder of installation is the reverse of removal, noting the following points.

    a)  *Tighten all fasteners to the specified torques, where applicable.*

    b)  *Check the condition of the transmission fluid pipe O-rings and replace them if necessary.*

    c)  *Install the driveshaft (see Chapter 8).*

    d)  *Install the starter motor (see Chapter 5).*

    e)  *Reconnect and adjust the shift cable (see Section 3).*

    f)  *Check the transmission fluid (see Chapter 1).*

## 6   Automatic transmission overhaul - general information

In the event of a fault occurring with the transmission, it is first necessary to determine whether it is of an electrical, mechanical or hydraulic nature, and to do this, special test equipment is required. It is therefore essential to have the work carried out by a dealer or qualified shop if a transmission fault is suspected.

Do not remove the transmission from the vehicle for possible repair before professional fault diagnosis has been carried out, since most tests require the transmission to be in the vehicle.

## 7   Electronic components/sensors - replacement

The turbine speed sensor, output speed sensor, transmission range switch and electronic control module (ECM) are all contained within the transmission case. Removal of the components involves removal of the transmission oil pan and partial disassembly of the transmission. Therefore, replacement of these components should be handled by a dealer or other qualified shop.

# Chapter 7 Part C  Transfer case

## Contents

## Specifications

### Torque specifications

**Ft-lbs** (unless otherwise indicated)          **Nm**

**Note:** *One foot-pound (ft-lb) of torque is equivalent to 12 inch-pounds (in-lbs) of torque. Torque values below approximately 15 foot-pounds are expressed in inch-pounds, because most foot-pound torque wrenches are not accurate at these smaller values.*

### Transfer case

| | Ft-lbs | Nm |
|---|---|---|
| Mounting bolts | 31 | 43 |
| Drain/fill plug | 44 | 60 |

### Driveshafts

**Note:** *On some installations different grades of bolt are used; the grade is stamped on the bolt head or marked under the bolt head. Ensure that each bolt is tightened to the correct torque for its grade.*

| | Ft-lbs | Nm |
|---|---|---|
| Front driveshaft (AWD models) | | |
| Mounting bolts* | | |
| Stage 1 | 15 | 20 |
| Stage 2 | Tighten an additional 45-degrees | |
| Rear driveshaft-to-transmission* | | |
| M10 bolts with 8.8 stamp | 48 | 35 |
| M10 bolts with 10.9 stamp | 64 | 47 |
| ZNS (external Torx) bolts/nuts | | |
| Step 1 | | |
| With M10 bolts | 15 | 20 |
| With M12 bolts with 10.9 stamp | 41 | 55 |
| Step 2 | Tighten an additional 90-degrees | |
| Rear driveshaft-to-rear differential | | |
| Step 1 | | |
| M10 bolts, with flex-disc | 15 | 20 |
| M12 bolts, with flex-disc | 41 | 55 |
| Step 2 | Tighten an additional 90-degrees | |
| M10 bolts, with universal joint | | |
| With ribbed teeth under bolt head | | |
| Step 1 | 30 | 40 |
| Step 2 | Tighten an additional 45-degrees | |
| Without ribbed teeth under bolt head | | |
| Step 1 | 15 | 20 |
| Step 2 | Tighten an additional 90-degrees | |
| Rear driveshaft center-bearing support bracket nuts/bolts | 15 | 21 |

*Do not reuse

## 1 General information

Models with an "x" in their designation, such as 325xi, are equipped with All Wheel Drive (AWD). These vehicles have two added components - the transfer case and the front differential. The transfer case is a group of gears in a housing attached to the rear of the transmission. The transfer case splits the power from the transmission to the front differential through a front driveshaft, and a rear driveshaft delivers power to the rear axle. The AWD feature is available with either a manual transmission or an automatic transmission.

The transfer case operates both differentials full-time. Some models are equipped with Active Torque Control (ATC), a traction management function that changes the delivery of torque from the transfer case, using an electronic clutch. Depending on the situation, the system may apply one or more brake calipers if wheelspin occurs, and differential output would go the opposite wheel.

## 2 Transfer case - removal and installation

**Warning:** *The engine and exhaust system should be allowed to cool thoroughly before beginning this procedure.*

**Note:** *There are no user-serviceable components within the transfer case, but if there is a problem with the unit, the transfer case can be removed, then taken to a dealer or other qualified shop.*

### *Removal*

1 Raise the vehicle and support it securely on jackstands.
2 Remove the bolts and the splash shield under the engine (see Chapter 2A).
3 Models with x-Drive have an extra reinforcement plate at the bottom of the subframe. Remove the bolts and the reinforcement plate.
4 Remove the exhaust heat shield and the exhaust system (see Chapter 4).
5 Make paint marks on the front driveshaft and the transfer case flange for later assembly. Remove the front driveshaft from the front differential and the transfer case (see Chapter 8).
6 Make paint marks on the rear driveshaft and the transfer case flange for later assembly. Remove the rear driveshaft from the transfer case and the rear differential (see Chapter 8). For the rear driveshaft to clear the flange on the transfer case, remove the driveshaft center support bearing bracket and have an assistant lower the middle of the driveshaft while you pull the flex-disc from the flange on the transfer case. **Caution:** *To avoid distortion, keep the flex-disc flat while removing the mounting bolts.*
7 Use a transmission jack to support the transmission, using chains or clamps to secure it to the jack.
8 Disconnect the electrical connectors at the transfer case, and disconnect and set aside the vent hose.
9 With the weight of the transmission held by the jack, remove the bolts securing the transmission crossmember to the rubber mounts and to the chassis. Remove the crossmember.
10 Have an assistant support the transfer case while you remove the transfer case-to-transmission bolts. Rock the transfer case and remove it from the vehicle.

### *Installation*

11 Installation is the reverse of removal, with the following precautions:

a) *Use new bolts where ZNS (external Torx) bolts were used.*

b) *Inspect the dowel pins and coat them lightly with anti-seize compound before installation.*

c) *If the transfer case input shaft utilized an O-ring, install a new one.*

d) *Fill the transfer case with new lubricant and check it again on level ground after driving 1/8-mile.*

# Chapter 8
# Clutch and driveline

## Contents

---

## Specifications

### Torque specifications

**Ft-lbs** (unless otherwise indicated)   **Nm**

**Note:** One foot-pound (ft-lb) of torque is equivalent to 12 inch-pounds (in-lbs) of torque. Torque values below approximately 15 foot-pounds are expressed in inch-pounds, because most foot-pound torque wrenches are not accurate at these smaller values.

**Note:** On some installations, different grades of bolts are used; the grade of each bolt is stamped on the bolt head. Ensure that each bolt is tightened to the correct torque for its grade.

#### Clutch

| | Ft-lbs | Nm |
|---|---|---|
| Clutch master cylinder mounting nuts | 80 in-lbs | 9 |
| Clutch pressure plate-to-flywheel bolts - new ZNS (external Torx) bolts | | |
| Step 1 | 132 in-lbs | 15 |
| Step 2 | Tighten an additional 90-degrees | |
| Clutch release cylinder | 16 | 22 |

#### Driveaxles

| | Ft-lbs | Nm |
|---|---|---|
| Driveaxle hub nut-(E-series chassis) | | |
| Front (AWD models) | 310 | 420 |
| Driveaxle hub bolt (F-series chassis)* | | |
| Step 1 | 154.5 | 210 |
| Step 2 | Tighten an additional 90 degrees | |
| Rear axle hub nut* | | |
| E-series chassis | | |
| M24 | 185 | 250 |
| M27 | 310 | 420 |
| F-series chassis | | |
| Step 1 | 107 | 145 |
| Step 2 | Tighten an additional 45 degrees | |
| Rear driveaxle-to-differential flange bolts-(E-series chassis) | | |
| M8 Torx | 39 | 52 |
| M10 Torx | 52 | 70 |
| M12 Torx | 89 | 120 |

## Torque specifications

**Note:** *One foot-pound (ft-lb) of torque is equivalent to 12 inch-pounds (in-lbs) of torque. Torque values below approximately 15 foot-pounds are expressed in inch-pounds, because most foot-pound torque wrenches are not accurate at these smaller values.*

**Note:** *On some installations, different grades of bolts are used; the grade of each bolt is stamped on the bolt head. Ensure that each bolt is tightened to the correct torque for its grade.*

| | **Ft-lbs** (unless otherwise indicated) | **Nm** |
|---|---|---|
| **Differential** | | |
| Front (AWD models) | | |
| Bearing pedestal-to-oil pan bolts | 20 | 27 |
| Front differential-to-oil pan bolts | 48 | 65 |
| Subframe reinforcement plate bolts | | |
| Step 1 | 41 | 56 |
| Step 2 | Tighten an additional 90-degrees | |
| Rear (all models) | | |
| Differential-to-subframe bolts | | |
| Front | 74 | 100 |
| Rear | 122 | 165 |
| Oil filler plug | 44 | 60 |
| Vibration damper on bracket (where equipped) | 50 | 68 |
| **Driveshafts** | | |
| Front driveshaft (AWD models) | | |
| Mounting bolts* | | |
| Stage 1 | 15 | 20 |
| Stage 2 | Tighten an additional 45-degrees | |
| Rear driveshaft-to-transmission* | | |
| M10 bolts with 8.8 stamp | 48 | 35 |
| M10 bolts with 10.9 stamp | 64 | 47 |
| ZNS (external Torx) bolts/nuts | | |
| Step 1 | | |
| With M10 bolts | 15 | 20 |
| With M12 bolts | 41 | 55 |
| Step 2 | Tighten an additional 90 degrees | |
| Rear driveshaft-to-rear differential | | |
| Flex-disc models | | |
| Step 1 | | |
| With M10 bolts, with flex-disc | 15 | 20 |
| With M12 bolts, with flex-disc | 41 | 55 |
| Step 2 | Tighten an additional 90 degrees | |
| Universal joint models | | |
| With ribbed teeth under bolt head | | |
| Step 1 | 30 | 40 |
| Step 2 | Tighten an additional 45 degrees | |
| Without ribbed teeth under bolt head | | |
| Step 1 | 15 | 20 |
| Step 2 | Tighten an additional 90 degrees | |
| Rear driveshaft center-bearing support bracket nuts/bolts | 15 | 21 |
| **Wheels** | | |
| Wheel bolts | See Chapter 1 | |

*Do not reuse

## 1  General information

Power is transmitted from the transmission to the rear axle by a two-piece driveshaft, joined behind the center bearing by a slip joint. The slip joint is a sliding, splined coupling that allows slight fore-and-aft movement of the driveshaft. The forward end of the driveshaft is attached to the output flange of the transmission by a flexible rubber coupling. On some models, a vibration damper is mounted between the front of the driveshaft and coupling. The middle of the rear driveshaft is supported by the center bearing, which is bolted to the vehicle body. Universal joints are located at the center bearing and at the rear end of the driveshaft, to compensate for movement of the transmission and differential on their mountings and for any flexing of the chassis.

The rear differential assembly includes the drive pinion, the ring gear, the differential housing and the output flanges. The drive pinion, which drives the ring gear, is also known as the differential input shaft and is connected to the driveshaft via an input flange. The differential is bolted to the ring gear and drives the rear wheels through a pair of driveaxles. E-series chassis models use a pair of output shaft flanges bolted to the driveaxles and F-series chassis models, the driveaxles inner joints are splined directly to the ring gear. Both Series use driveaxles with constant velocity (CV) joints at either end. The differential allows the wheels to turn at different speeds when cornering.

The driveaxles deliver power from the final drive unit output flanges to the rear wheels. The driveshafts are equipped with constant velocity (CV) joints at each end. The inner CV joints are bolted to the differential flanges, and the outer CV joints engage the splines of the wheel hubs, and are secured by a large nut.

Models with x-Drive (AWD) are equipped with a transfer case (see Chapter 7C) mounted to the rear of the transmission that splits power to the front and rear differentials, full-time. The front differential is mounted to the suspension subframe and delivers power to the front wheels via independent driveaxles.

Major repair work on the differential assembly components (drive pinion, ring-and-pinion and differential) requires many special tools and a high degree of expertise, and therefore should not be attempted by the home mechanic. If major repairs become necessary, we recommend that they be performed by a dealer service department or other qualified shop.

## 2  Clutch - description and check

### Description

All models are equipped with a single dry plate clutch, which consists of five main components; friction disc, pressure plate, dia-

phragm spring, covers and release bearing.

The friction disc is free to slide along the splines of the transmission input shaft, and is held in position between the flywheel and the pressure plate by the pressure exerted on the pressure plate by the diaphragm spring. Friction lining material is riveted to both sides of the friction disc. All models are equipped with a Self-Adjusting Clutch (SAC). The SAC uses a spring loaded wedge ring that rotates against the spring fingers within the pressure plate cover. As the friction lining material is worn, the wedge ring rotates under spring pressure, taking up the gap that is created as the friction lining material wears. This ensures a consistent clutch pedal feel over the life of the clutch.

The diaphragm spring is mounted on pins, and is held in place in the cover by annular fulcrum rings.

The release bearing is located on a guide sleeve at the front of the transmission, and the bearing is free to slide on the sleeve under the action of the release arm, which pivots inside the clutch bellhousing.

The clutch release system is hydraulically operated. The release system consists of the clutch pedal, the clutch master cylinder, the clutch release cylinder, the hydraulic line between the master cylinder and release cylinder, and the clutch release bearing.

When pressure is applied to the clutch pedal to release the clutch, the clutch master cylinder transmits this movement to the clutch release cylinder, which moves the clutch release lever. As the lever pivots, the shaft fingers push against the release bearing. The bearing pushes against the fingers of the diaphragm spring of the pressure plate assembly, which in turn releases the clutch plate.

Terminology can be a problem regarding the clutch components because common names have in some cases changed from that used by the manufacturer. For example, the clutch release cylinder is sometimes referred to as a slave cylinder, the driven plate is also called the clutch plate or disc, the pressure plate assembly is also known as the clutch cover, and the clutch release bearing is sometimes called a throw-out bearing.

**3.1  Driver's knee bolster panel mounting fasteners**

### Check

Other than replacing components that have obvious damage, some preliminary checks should be performed to diagnose a clutch system failure. Refer to the "Troubleshooting" Section at the beginning of this manual for diagnosis of clutch problems.

a) *Before proceeding, check and, if necessary, adjust clutch pedal freeplay and height (see Chapter 1).*

b) *To check clutch spin down time, run the engine at normal idle speed with the transaxle in Neutral (clutch pedal up - engaged). Disengage the clutch (pedal down), wait several seconds and shift the transaxle into Reverse. No grinding noise should be heard. A grinding noise would most likely indicate a problem in the pressure plate or the clutch disc.*

c) *To check for complete clutch release, run the engine (with the parking brake applied to prevent movement) and hold the clutch pedal approximately 1/2-inch from the floor. Shift the transaxle between 1st gear and Reverse several times. If the shift is not smooth, component failure is indicated.*

d) *Visually inspect the clutch pedal bushing at the top of the clutch pedal to make sure there is no sticking or excessive wear.*

e) *Under the vehicle, verify that the clutch release lever is solidly mounted on the ballstud.*

f) *Make sure that the hydraulic lines aren't leaking at either the master cylinder or the release cylinder (see Sections 3 and 4). Bleed the system if necessary (see Section 5).*

## 3  Clutch master cylinder - removal, inspection and installation

**Warning:** *Brake fluid is poisonous; wash off immediately and thoroughly in the case of skin contact, and seek immediate medical advice if any fluid is swallowed or gets into the eyes.*
**Caution:** *Don't allow brake fluid to come into contact with the paint as it will damage the finish.*

### Removal

*Refer to illustrations 3.1, 3.4, 3.5a, 3.5b and 3.6*

1    Release the fasteners and remove the trim panel above the driver's pedals **(see illustration)**. Disconnect any electrical connectors as the panel is withdrawn.

2    Release the clips, remove the plastic cover, then remove the brake fluid reservoir cap. Siphon out enough fluid so that the level is below the level of the reservoir fluid hose connection to the clutch master cylinder (the brake fluid reservoir feeds both the brake and clutch systems). **Note:** *Do not empty the reservoir, as this will draw air into the brake system.*

**3.4  Remove the mounting nuts and push the bolts out of the housing**

**3.5a  Pushrod pivot pin location**

3   Disconnect the clutch master cylinder hose from the brake fluid reservoir. Be prepared for fluid spillage, and plug the open end of the hose to prevent dirt entry.

4   Unscrew the mounting nuts and push back the bolts securing the master cylinder to the pedal bracket in the footwell **(see illustration)**.

5   Using an 8 mm socket, squeeze together the ends of the pin, then press out the master cylinder pushrod pivot pin from the clutch pedal **(see illustrations)**.

6   Using a small screwdriver, pry out the retaining clip and pull the hydraulic pressure line from the master cylinder **(see illustration)**. Withdraw the master cylinder and ease the fluid supply hose through the firewall grommet, taking care not to strain the pipe. Do not pull the hose completely through the grommet. Be prepared for fluid leaks.

7   Pull the supply hose from the top of the master cylinder, leaving the hose in place in the firewall grommet for reassembly. Be prepared for fluid spillage.

8   Depress the locking tab and disconnect the master cylinder switch wiring plug (if equipped). If required, carefully release the clips and detach the switch from the cylinder.

## Inspection

9   Inspect the master cylinder for fluid leaks and damage, and replace if necessary. At the time of writing, no spare parts were available for the master cylinder, and if faulty, the complete unit must be replaced. Check with your local dealer or parts supplier.

## Installation

10   Installation is the reverse of removal, noting the following points:

a) *Take care not to strain the master cylinder fluid pipe during installation.*

b) *Top-off the level in the brake fluid reservoir, then bleed the clutch hydraulic system (see Section 5).*

## 4    Clutch release cylinder - removal and installation

**Warning:** *Brake fluid is poisonous; wash off immediately and thoroughly in the case of skin contact, and seek immediate medical advice if any fluid is swallowed or gets into the eyes.*
**Caution:** *Don't allow brake fluid to come into contact with the paint as it will damage the finish.*

## Removal

1   Remove the brake fluid reservoir cap, and siphon out enough fluid so that the level is below the level of the reservoir fluid hose connection to the clutch master cylinder (the brake fluid reservoir feeds both the brake and clutch systems). Do NOT empty the reservoir, as this will draw air into the brake system.

2   To improve access, raise the vehicle and support it securely on jackstands.

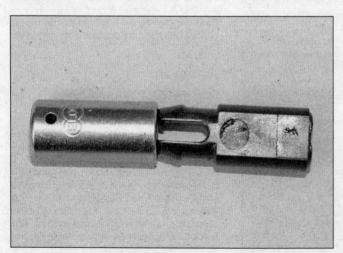

**3.5b  Push an 8mm socket onto the end of the pin to compress the retaining clips, then remove the pivot pin**

**3.6  Pry out the clip and detach the clutch fluid line**

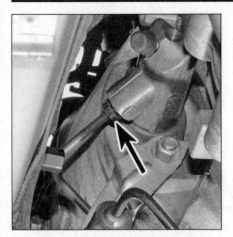

**4.4 Fluid pipe union nut (metal release cylinder)**

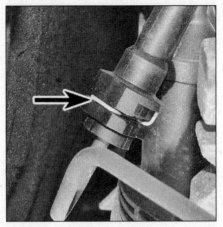

**4.7 Pry out the clip and separate the fluid line from the plastic release cylinder**

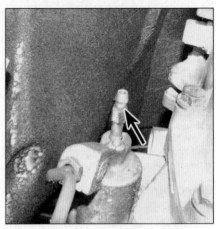

**5.7 Clutch release cylinder bleeder screw location**

3  Release the bolts and remove the splash shield (if equipped) for access to the transmission bellhousing.

### Metal release cylinder

*Refer to illustration 4.4*

4  Place a container beneath the hydraulic pipe connection on the clutch release cylinder to catch escaping brake fluid. Unscrew the union nut and disconnect the fluid line (see illustration).

5  Unscrew the securing nuts and withdraw the release cylinder from the mounting studs on the bellhousing.

### Plastic release cylinder

*Refer to illustration 4.7*

6  Remove the release cylinder mounting nuts and withdraw the release cylinder from the mounting studs on the transmission.

7  Pry out the retaining clip and disconnect the fluid line from the cylinder (see illustration).

## Inspection

8  Inspect the release cylinder for fluid leaks and damage, and replace if necessary. At the time of writing, no spare parts are available for the release cylinder, and if faulty, the complete unit must be replaced. Check with your dealer or specialist.

## Installation

9  On models with a plastic release cylinder, press the piston into the cylinder, then reconnect the fluid pipe. Refill the fluid reservoir, then extend and compress the piston in the cylinder five times while holding the cylinder vertical.

10  The remainder of installation is the reverse of removal, noting the following points:

a) *Before installation, clean and lightly grease the end of the release cylinder pushrod.*

b) *Tighten the mounting nuts to the specified torque.*

c) *Top-off the fluid level and bleed the clutch hydraulic system (see Section 5).*

## 5  Clutch hydraulic system - bleeding

**Warning:** *Brake fluid is poisonous; wash off immediately and thoroughly in the case of skin contact, and seek immediate medical advice if any fluid is swallowed or gets into the eyes.*
**Caution:** *Don't allow brake fluid to come into contact with the paint as it will damage the finish.*
**Note:** *Pressure-bleeding equipment is recommended for bleeding the clutch hydraulic system.*

## General information

*Refer to illustrations 5.7 and 5.8*

1  The hydraulic system should be bled of all air whenever any part of the system has been removed or if the fluid level has been allowed to fall so low that air has been drawn into the master cylinder. The procedure is similar to bleeding a brake system.

2  Only refill the system with new brake fluid (see *Recommended lubricants and fluids* in Chapter 1). **Caution:** *Do not re-use any of the fluid coming from the system during the bleeding operation or use fluid which has been inside an open container for an extended period of time.*

3  If the system has been filled with the incorrect fluid, the brake and clutch systems must be flushed completely with uncontaminated, correct fluid and new seals should be installed on the various components.

4  If fluid has been lost from the system, or air has entered because of a leak, ensure that the problem is corrected before proceeding.

5  To improve access, apply the parking brake, then raise the front of the vehicle, and support it securely on jackstands.

6  Remove the bolts and the splash shield

(where equipped) for access to the transmission bellhousing.

7  Check that the clutch system hoses and lines are secure, that the fittings are tight, and that the bleeder screw on the rear of the clutch release cylinder (mounted under the vehicle on the lower left-hand side of the transmission bellhousing) is closed. Clean any dirt from around the bleeder screw (see illustration).

8  Release the clips and remove the plastic cover over the reservoir (see illustration). Unscrew the brake fluid reservoir cap, and top the fluid up to the MAX level line; loosely reinstall the cap - remember to maintain the fluid level at least above the MIN level line throughout the procedure, or there is a risk of further air entering the system. Note that the brake fluid reservoir feeds both the brake and clutch hydraulic systems.

9  It is recommended that pressure-bleeding equipment is used to bleed the system. Alternatively, there is a number of one-man, do-it-yourself brake bleeding kits currently available at auto parts stores. These kits greatly simplify the bleeding operation, and

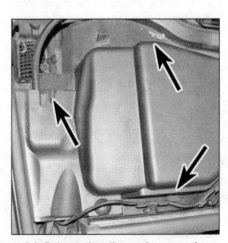

**5.8 Release the clips and remove the plastic cover from the left side of the engine compartment**

also reduce the risk of expelled air and fluid being drawn back into the system. If such a kit is not available, the basic (two-person) method must be used.

10   If pressure-bleeding equipment or a one-man kit is to be used, prepare the vehicle as described previously, and follow the equipment/kit manufacturer's instructions, as the procedure may vary slightly according to the type being used.

11   Whichever method is used, the same basic process must be followed to ensure the removal of all air from the system.

### *Bleeding*

#### Basic (two-person) method

12   You will need a clean glass jar, a length of plastic or rubber tubing which is a tight fit over the bleeder screw, and a box-end wrench to fit the screw. The help of an assistant will also be required.

13   Where applicable, remove the dust cap from the bleeder screw. Fit the wrench and tubing to the bleeder screw, place the other end of the tube in the jar, and pour in enough fluid to cover the end of the tube.

14   Ensure that the reservoir fluid level is maintained at least above the MIN level line throughout the procedure.

15   Have an assistant fully depress the clutch pedal and hold it in the depressed position.

16   While pedal pressure is maintained, loosen the bleeder screw (approximately one turn) and allow the compressed fluid and air to flow into the jar. Have your assistant maintain pedal pressure. When the flow stops, tighten the bleeder screw again, have your assistant release the pedal slowly, and recheck the reservoir fluid level.

17   Repeat Steps 15 and 16 until the fluid emerging from the bleeder screw is free from air bubbles.

18   When no more air bubbles appear, tighten the bleeder screw securely. Do not overtighten the bleeder screw.

19   Temporarily disconnect the bleed tube from the bleeder screw, and set the container of fluid aside.

20   Unscrew the two mounting nuts, and withdraw the release cylinder from the bellhousing, taking care not to strain the fluid hose.

21   Reconnect the bleed tube to the bleeder screw, and submerge the end of the tube in the container of fluid.

22   With the bleeder screw pointing vertically upwards, loosen the bleeder screw (approximately one turn), and slowly push the release cylinder pushrod into the cylinder until no more air bubbles appear in the fluid.

23   Hold the pushrod in position, then tighten the bleeder screw.

24   Slowly allow the pushrod to return to its rest position. Do not allow the pushrod to return quickly, as this will cause air to enter the release cylinder.

25   Remove the tube and wrench, and install the dust cap over the bleeder screw.

26   Install the release cylinder to the bell-

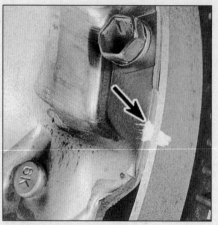

**6.2  Mark the relationship of the pressure plate to the flywheel if you are planning to reuse the pressure plate**

housing, and tighten the securing nuts to the specified torque.

#### Using a one-way valve kit

27   These kits consist of a length of tubing, with a one-way valve attached to prevent expelled air and fluid being drawn back into the system; some kits include a translucent container, which can be positioned so that the air bubbles can be more easily seen flowing from the end of the tube.

28   Connect the kit to the bleeder screw, then open the bleeder screw. Depress the clutch pedal with a smooth, steady stroke, and slowly release it; repeat this step until the expelled fluid is clear of air bubbles.

29   Remember to check the reservoir fluid level during the bleeding procedure; ensure that it is maintained at least above the MIN level mark at all times.

#### Using a pressure-bleeding kit

30   These kits are usually operated by the reservoir of pressurized air contained in a small chamber that can be metered. However, it will probably be necessary to reduce the pressure to a lower level than normal; refer to the instructions supplied with the pressure bleeder.

31   By connecting a pressurized, fluid-filled container to the fluid reservoir, bleeding can be carried out simply by opening the bleeder screw, and allowing the fluid to flow out until no more air bubbles can be seen in the expelled fluid.

32   This method provides an additional safeguard against air being drawn into the system during bleeding.

#### All methods

33   After bleeding, if it is suspected that air is still present in hydraulic system, remove the release cylinder (see Section 4). Without disconnecting the hydraulic lines, push the cylinder piston all the way in, and holding the cylinder so the bleeder screw is the highest point, bleed the system again. **Note:** *Make sure that the release cylinder piston is does not extend during the bleeding procedure. If*

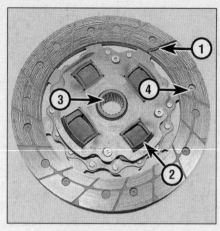

**6.6a  The clutch disc**

1   **Lining** - *this will wear down in use*
2   **Springs or dampers** - *check for cracking or deformation*
3   **Splined hub** - *the splines must not be worn and should slide smoothly on the transmission input shaft splines*
4   **Rivets** - *these secure the lining and will damage the flywheel and/or pressure plate if allowed to contact the surfaces*

*necessary, use a metal strip and two threaded bars to fabricate a tool to hold the piston in.*

34   When bleeding is complete and firm pedal feel is restored, wash off any spilled fluid. Check that the bleeder screw is tightened securely, and install the dust cap.

35   Check the fluid level in the reservoir, and top-off if necessary (see Chapter 1). Reinstall the plastic cover over the reservoir.

36   Discard any fluid that has been bled from the system; it can not be reused.

37   If the clutch feels at all spongy, air must still be present in the system, and further bleeding is required. If the system cannot be bled of all air after several attempts, it may be a sign of worn master or release cylinder seals.

38   Install the splash shield (where equipped) and lower the vehicle to the ground.

---

### 6   Clutch components - removal, inspection and installation

**Warning:** *Dust produced by clutch wear is hazardous to your health. DO NOT blow it out with compressed air and DO NOT inhale it. DO NOT use gasoline or petroleum-based solvents to remove the dust. Brake system cleaner should be used to flush the dust into a drain pan. After the clutch components are wiped clean with a rag, dispose of the contaminated rags and cleaner in a covered, marked container.*

### *Removal*

*Refer to illustration 6.2*

1   Remove the transmission (see Chapter 7A).

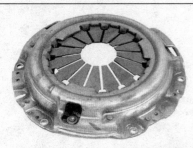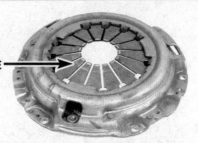

EXCESSIVE WEAR

**NORMAL FINGER WEAR**        **EXCESSIVE FINGER WEAR**        **BROKEN OR BENT FINGERS**

**6.6b  Replace the pressure plate if any of these conditions are noted**

2    If the original clutch is to be reinstalled, make alignment marks between the clutch pressure plate and the flywheel, so that the clutch can be installed in its original position **(see illustration)**.

3    Progressively and evenly loosen the clutch cover/pressure plate assembly-to-flywheel bolts in a criss-cross pattern, then remove the bolts and washers, if equipped.

4    Withdraw the clutch pressure plate from the flywheel. Be prepared to catch the clutch friction disc (which may drop out of the pressure plate as it is withdrawn), and note which way the friction disc is installed - the two sides of the disc are normally marked "Engine side" and "Transmission side." The greater projecting side of the hub faces away from the flywheel.

## Inspection

*Refer to illustrations 6.6a, 6.6b and 6.7*

5    With the clutch assembly removed, clean off all traces of dust using a dry cloth.

6    Inspect the lining on the clutch disc. BMW specifies a minimum friction material thickness of 1.0 mm above the heads of the rivets. Check for loose rivets, distortion, cracks, broken springs and other obvious damage

**(see illustration)**. Ordinarily the clutch disc is replaced as a matter of course, so if in doubt about the condition, replace it with a new one. The disc must also be replaced if the lining thickness has worn down to, or just above, the level of the rivet heads. Check the machined surface and the diaphragm spring fingers of the pressure plate **(see illustration)**.

7    Inspect the flywheel for cracks, heat checking, score marks and other damage. If the imperfections are slight, a machine shop can resurface it to make it flat and smooth. Refer to Chapter 2A for the flywheel removal procedure. If the surface of the pressure plate is grooved or otherwise damaged, replace the pressure plate assembly. Also check for obvious damage, distortion, cracking, etc. **(see illustration)**. Light glazing can be removed with emery cloth or sandpaper. If a new pressure plate is indicated, new or factory rebuilt units are available.

8    The release bearing should be replaced along with the clutch disc (see Section 7).

9    Check the bearing in the end of the crankshaft. Make sure that it turns smoothly and quietly. If the transmission input shaft contact face on the bearing is worn or damaged, install a new bearing (see Chapter 2A).

## Installation

*Refer to illustrations 6.12a, 6.12b, 6.13a, 6.13b, 6.13c, 6.13d, 6.14, 6.16 and 6.17*

10    If new clutch components are to be installed, ensure that all the anti-corrosion preservative coating is cleaned from the friction material on the disc and the contact surfaces of the pressure plate.

11    Carefully wipe the flywheel and pressure plate machined surfaces clean. It's important that no oil or grease is on these surfaces or the lining of the clutch disc. Handle these parts only with clean hands.

12    Position the disc on the flywheel, with the greater projecting side of the hub facing away from the flywheel (most friction discs will have an "Engine side" or "Transmission side" marking which should face the flywheel or transmission as applicable) **(see illustration)**. Using the proper BMW tool, or a suitable alternative tool available at your auto parts store, center the friction disc in the flywheel **(see illustration)**.

13    If the original pressure plate and cover is to be reinstalled, engage the legs of BMW tool 21 2 170 with the cover in the area of the adjusting springs. Screw down the knurled collar to lock the legs in place, then tighten down the spindle to compress the diaphragm

**6.7  Examine the pressure plate friction surface for score marks, cracks and evidence of overheating (blue spots)**

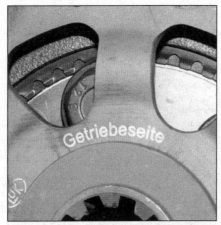

**6.12a  The friction disc may be marked "Getriebeseite," meaning "transmission side"**

**6.12b  Use a suitable tool to center the friction disc**

**6.13a  Use factory tool 21 2 170 to compress the diaphragm spring**

**6.13b  Push the adjustment ring thrust pieces fully counterclockwise . . .**

**6.13c  . . . and insert metal spacers between the thrust pieces and the cover**

**6.13d  A special factory tool is available to reset the adjustment ring thrust pieces**

**6.14  Ensure the cover locates over the flywheel dowel pins**

spring. Using a screwdriver, reset the self-adjusting mechanism by pushing the adjustment ring thrust pieces fully counterclockwise, while loosening the special tool spindle only enough to allow the adjustment ring to move. With the adjustment ring reset, tighten down

**6.16  Keep your fingers away when removing the metal spacers**

the special tool spindle to compress the spring fingers, while preventing the adjustment ring thrust pieces from moving by inserting metal spacers in the gap between the thrust pieces and the cover. Note that a special tool is available from BMW to reset the adjustment ring **(see illustrations).**

14    Install the clutch cover assembly, aligning the marks on the flywheel and clutch pressure plate if reinstalling the old clutch. Ensure that the clutch pressure plate locates over the dowels on the flywheel **(see illustration)**. Insert the mounting bolts and washers, and tighten them to the specified torque.

15    If a new pressure plate cover was installed, insert a 14 mm Allen key into the center of the diaphragm spring locking piece, turn it clockwise and remove it to release the spring.

16    If the original pressure plate cover was reinstalled, remove the spindle and knurled collar, then remove the compression tool from the cover. Pry out the metal spacers holding the adjustment ring thrust-pieces in place **(see illustration)**. **Caution:** *As the last spacer is withdrawn, the adjustment ring may spring into place. Make sure all fingers are clear of the area.*

17    If the BMW centering tool was used,

remove the tool by screwing a 10 mm bolt into its end and pulling using a pair of pliers **(see illustration)**.

18    Install the transmission (see Chapter 7A).

**7    Clutch release bearing and lever - removal, inspection and installation**

**Warning:** *Dust produced by clutch wear is hazardous to your health. DO NOT blow it out with compressed air and DO NOT inhale it. DO NOT use gasoline or petroleum-based solvents to remove the dust. Brake system cleaner should be used to flush the dust into a drain pan. After the clutch components are wiped clean with a rag, dispose of the contaminated rags and cleaner in a covered, marked container.*

**Removal**

*Refer to illustration 7.2*

1    Remove the transmission (see Chapter 7A).

2    Slide the release lever sideways to release it from the retaining spring clip and pivot, then pull the lever and bearing forwards

**6.17  Thread the bolt into the end of the centering tool and pull it out**

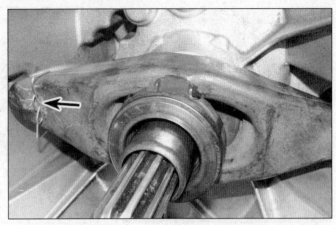

**7.2  Slide the release lever sideways to disengage it from the retaining clip**

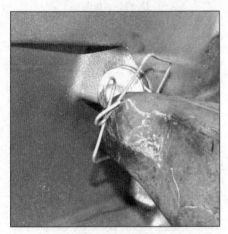

**7.8  Ensure the lever engages correctly with the retaining clip**

**8.9  There are two areas in the hub nut that can be staked - when removing the hub nut, use a hammer and punch to drive the staked area(s) outward**

from the guide sleeve **(see illustration)**.

3   Do not detach the release bearing from the lever. They are only available as a complete assembly.

## Inspection

4   Spin the release bearing, and check it for excessive roughness. Holding the outer race, attempt to move it laterally against the inner race. If any excessive movement or roughness is evident, replace the bearing. If a new clutch has been installed, it is wise to replace the release bearing as a matter of course.

5   Inspect the release bearing, pivot and release cylinder pushrod contact faces on the release lever for wear. Replace the lever if excessive wear is evident.

6   Check the release lever retaining spring clip, and replace if necessary. It is advisable to replace the clip as a matter of course.

## Installation

*Refer to illustration 7.8*

7   Clean the release bearing contact surfaces on the release lever and guide sleeve. Do not apply any grease or lubricant to the sliding surfaces of the bearing or guide sleeve.

8   Slide the release lever/bearing assembly into position over the guide sleeve, then push the end of the lever over the pivot, ensuring that the retaining spring clip engages correctly over the end of the release lever **(see illustration)**.

9   Install the transmission (see Chapter 7A).

---

## 8   Driveaxles - removal and installation

## *Front (AWD models only)*

### Removal

1   With the vehicle resting on its wheels, remove the wheel trim/hub cap (as applicable) and loosen the driveaxle retaining nut or bolt. Loosen the wheel bolts. **Note:** *Before loosening the driveaxle nut, use a hammer and punch to push out the staked portion of the nut* **(see illustration 8.9)**.
**Note:** *On F-series chassis models, always replace the driveaxle bolt and small compres-*

*sion spring whenever they are removed.*

2   Block the rear wheels, raise the front of the vehicle and support it securely on jackstands. Remove the relevant front wheel.

3   Remove the ABS wheel speed sensor and unbolt and set aside the brake caliper, but do not disconnect the brake fluid hose (see Chapter 9).

4   Disconnect the stabilizer bar link from the strut. Separate the tension strut and the control arm from the knuckle (see Chapter 10).

5   Use a puller to push the driveaxle stub through the hub, while pulling the steering knuckle outward until it is free of the driveaxle.

6   Use a suitable tool to pry the inboard CV joint away from the front differential housing. You will feel when the driveaxle is free.

7   When prying out the inner end of the right driveaxle, you should pry against the bearing bracket, not the differential.

### Installation

*Refer to illustration 8.9*

**Note:** *On F-series chassis models, always replace the driveaxle bolt and small compression spring whenever they are removed.*

8   Remove the snap-ring from the inboard end of the driveaxle, then install a new snap-ring before installation.

9   The remainder of installation is the reverse of removal, noting the following points:

a) *Lubricate the nut-to-wheel bearing contact area and tighten the nut to the specified torque. Do not oil the threads. If necessary, wait until the vehicle is lowered to the ground, then tighten the nut to the specified torque. Once tightened, use a hammer and punch to stake the nut* **(see illustration)**.

b) *Install new inner joint retaining bolts and plates (where equipped) and tighten to the specified torque.*

### *Rear*

**Note:** *On E-series chassis models new driveaxle-to-differential bolts will be required on installation.*

**8.14  Make alignment marks before removing the Torx bolts**

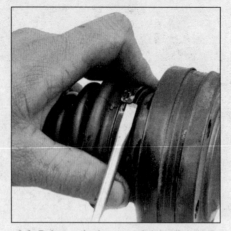

**9.3  Release the boot retaining clips and slide the boot down the driveaxle shaft**

**9.4  Carefully remove the sealing cover from the inner end of the joint (E-series only)**

## Removal

*Refer to illustration 8.14*

10   With the vehicle resting on its wheels, remove the wheel trim/hub cap (as applicable) and loosen the driveaxle retaining nut. Loosen the wheel bolts. **Note:** *Before loosening the driveaxle nut, use a hammer and punch to push out the staked portion of the nut* **(see illustration 8.9).**

11   Block the front wheels, raise the rear of the vehicle and support it securely on jackstands. Remove the relevant rear wheel.

### E-series chassis models

12   If the left driveaxle is to be removed, remove the exhaust system tailpipe to improve access (see Chapter 4).

13   Loosen and remove the left- and right-hand stabilizer bar mounts and pivot the bar downwards (see Chapter 10).

14   Make alignment marks, then loosen and remove the bolts securing the driveaxle constant velocity joint to the rear differential and the retaining plates (where applicable) **(see illustration)**. Position the driveaxle clear of the flange and tie it to the vehicle underbody using a piece of wire. **Note:** *Do not allow the driveshaft to hang under its own weight, as the CV joint may be damaged.*

15   Withdraw the driveaxle outer constant velocity joint from the hub assembly. The outer joint will be very tight; tap the joint out of the hub using a soft-faced mallet. If this fails to free it from the hub, the joint will have to be pressed out using a suitable tool that bolts to the hub.

16   Remove the driveshaft from underneath the vehicle.

### F-series chassis models

17   Remove the driveaxle nut and push the axle in slightly.

18   Support the rear differential then remove the mounting bolt/nuts (see Section 12) and lower the differential. Slightly rotate the unit until the axles have enough room to be removed, then secure the axles using a strap or wire.

19   Use a suitable tool to pry the inboard CV joint away from the rear differential housing. You will feel when the driveaxle is free.

20   Slide the driveaxle out of the differential and remove the axle from the vehicle. **Note:** *Have a drain pan ready to catch the rear differential lubricant that will spill out once the driveaxle has been removed.*

## Installation

21   Installation is the reverse of removal, noting the following points:

a)  *On E-series chassis models, install new inner joint retaining bolts and plates (where applicable) and tighten to the specified torque.*

b)  *On F-series chassis models, Check the dust plate and replace if needed. Replace the circlip on the end of the driveaxle making sure it is seated. into the groove on the axle, then coat the seal contact surface with differential oil. Slide the driveaxle into the rear differential until an audible click is heard and the driveaxle can't be easily pulled out. Reinstall the rear differential assembly (see Section 12) and refill the differential (see Chapter 1).*

**9.5  Remove the inner joint snap-ring from the driveaxle (E-series only)**

c)  *Lubricate the nut-to-hub flange contact area and tighten the nut to the specified torque. Do not oil the threads. If necessary, wait until the vehicle is lowered to the ground, then tighten the nut to the specified torque. Once tightened, use a hammer and punch to stake the nut* **(see illustration 8.9).**

## 9   Driveaxle boots - replacement

*Refer to illustrations 9.3, 9.4, 9.5, 9.6, 9.7, 9.20a and 9.20b*

**Note:** *If the CV joints are worn, indicating the need for an overhaul (usually due to torn boots and lost grease), explore all options before beginning the job. Complete rebuilt driveaxles are available on an exchange basis, which eliminates much time and labor.*

1   Remove the driveaxle (see Section 8).

2   Clean the driveaxle and mount it in a vise.

3   Release the two inner joint boot-retaining clips and free the boot and dust cover from the joint **(see illustration)**.

4   On E-series models pry off the sealing cover from the end of the inner constant velocity (CV) joint **(see illustration)**.

5   Scoop out excess grease and, on E-series models, remove the inner joint snap-ring from the end of the driveshaft **(see illustration)**.

6   On E-series models securely support the joint inner member and tap the driveaxle out of position using a hammer and drift **(see illustration)**. If the joint is a tight fit, a puller will be required to draw off the joint. Do not disassemble the inner joint. **Caution:** *On F-series chassis models, don't attempt to separate the inner CV joint from the shaft.*

7   With the joint removed, slide the inner boot and dust cover off from the end of the driveaxle **(see illustration)**.

8   Release the outer joint boot retaining clips, then slide the boot along the shaft and remove it.

**9.6  Support the inner joint member and tap out the driveaxle (E-series only)**

**9.7  Slide off the boot**

**9.20a  Fill the inner joint with the grease supplied with the boot kit**

9    Thoroughly clean the constant velocity joints using solvent, and dry thoroughly. Inspect the joints as follows.

10    Move the inner splined driving member from side-to-side to expose each ball in turn at the top of its track. Examine the balls for cracks, flat spots or signs of surface pitting.

11    Inspect the ball tracks on the inner and outer members. If the tracks have widened, the balls will no longer be a tight fit. At the same time, check the ball cage windows for wear or cracking between the windows.

12    If any of the constant velocity joint components are found to be worn or damaged, they must be replaced. The inner joint is available separately but if the outer joint is worn, it will be necessary to replace the complete joint and driveshaft assembly. If the joints are in satisfactory condition, obtain new boot repair kits which contain boots, retaining clips, an inner constant velocity joint snap-ring and the correct type and quantity of grease required.

13    Tape over the splines on the end of the driveaxle.

14    Slide the new outer boot onto the end of the driveaxle.

15    Pack the outer joint with the grease supplied in the boot kit. Work the grease well into the bearing tracks while twisting the joint, and fill the rubber boot with any excess.

16    Ease the boot over the joint and ensure that the boot lips are correctly located on both the driveshaft and constant velocity joint. Lift the outer sealing lip of the boot to equalize air pressure within the boot.

17    Fit the large metal retaining clip to the boot. Pull the retaining clip tight, then bend it back to secure it in position and cut off any excess. Secure the small retaining clip using the same procedure.

18    Engage the new inner boot with its dust cover and slide the assembly onto the driveaxle.

19    Remove the tape from the driveaxle splines and install the inner constant velocity joint. Press the joint fully onto the shaft and secure it in position with a new snap-ring.

20    Work the grease fully into the inner joint and fill the boot with any excess **(see illustrations)**.

21    Slide the inner boot into position and press the dust cover onto the joint, making sure the retaining bolt holes are correctly aligned. Lift the outer sealing lip of the boot to equalize air pressure within the boot, and secure it in position with the retaining clips.

22    Apply a smear of suitable sealant (BMW recommends BMW sealing gel) and press the new sealing cover fully onto the end of the inner joint.

23    Check that both constant velocity joints move freely and easily, then install the driveaxle (see Section 8).

## 10    Driveaxle oil seals - replacement

*Refer to illustrations 10.3, 10.5 and 10.7*
**Note:** *New driveaxle joint retaining bolts and a driveaxle flange snap-ring will be required.*

1    On E-series models, mark the relative positions of the driveaxle and the differential flange **(see illustration 8.14)**. Loosen and remove the bolts securing the driveshaft CV joint to the differential and the retaining plates (see Section 8). Position the driveaxle clear of the flange and tie it to the vehicle underbody using a piece of wire. **Note:** *Do not allow the driveaxle to hang under its own weight or the CV joint may be damaged.*

2    On F-series chassis models, remove the driveaxle (see Section 7).

3    On E-series models, carefully pry the driveaxle flange out from the differential, taking care not to damage the dust seal or case **(see illustration)**. Remove the flange and the dust seal. If the dust seal shows signs of damage, replace it.

4    Carefully pry the oil seal out from the rear differential. Wipe clean the oil-seal seating area.

**9.20b  Work the grease into the bearing tracks**

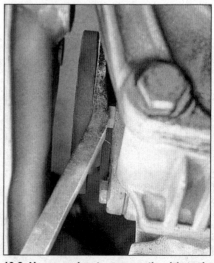

**10.3  Use a pry bar to remove the driveaxle flange from the differential**

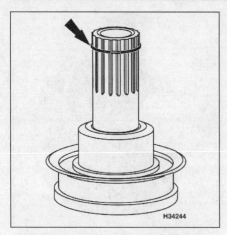

**10.5  Replace the output flange snap-ring**

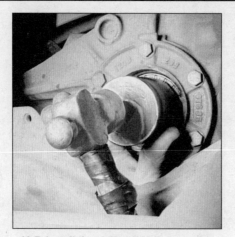

**10.7  Install the new seal using a socket that hits only on the hard outer edge of the seal**

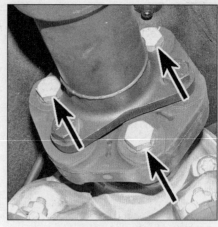

**11.3  Remove the driveshaft flange-to-transmission bolts/nuts**

5      With the flange or driveaxle removed, pry out the snap-ring from the end of the splined shaft **(see illustration)**.

6      Install a new snap-ring, making sure it is correctly located in the splined shaft groove.

7      Apply a little differential oil on the sealing lip of the new oil seal, then press it squarely into the casing until it reaches its stop. If necessary, the seal can be tapped into position using a metal tube which bears only on its hard outer edge **(see illustration)**.

8      Install the dust cover and insert the drive flange. Push the drive flange fully into position and check that it is securely retained by the snap-ring.

9      On E-series models, align the driveshaft with the flange and install the new retaining bolts and plates, tightening them to the specified torque.

10    On F-series chassis models, install the driveaxle (see Section 7).

11    Refill the differential with oil (see Chapter 1).

---

## 11  Driveshafts(s) - removal, inspection and installation

### *Rear driveshaft (all models)*
#### Removal
*Refer to illustrations 11.3, 11.4a, 11.4b and 11.5*

1      Block the front wheels. Raise the rear of the vehicle and support it securely on jackstands.

2      Remove the exhaust system and heat shield (see Chapter 4). Where necessary, unbolt the exhaust system mounting bracket(s) in order to gain the necessary clearance required to remove the driveshaft.

3      Make alignment marks between the shaft, transmission flange and rubber coupling (if equipped). Loosen and remove the nuts and bolts securing the coupling to the transmission **(see illustration)**. Discard the bolts and nuts; new ones should be used on installation.

4      Using paint or a suitable marker pen, make alignment marks between the driveshaft and differential flange. Unscrew the bolts securing the driveshaft to the rear differential and discard them; new fasteners must be used on installation **(see illustrations)**.

5      With the aid of an assistant, support the driveshaft, then unscrew the center support bearing bracket retaining bolts **(see illustration)**. Lower the center of the shaft and disengage it from the transmission (transfer case on x-Drive models) and rear differential. Remove the shaft from underneath the vehicle. **Note:** *Do not separate the two halves of the shaft without first making alignment marks. If the shafts are incorrectly joined, the driveshaft assembly may become imbalanced, leading to noise and vibration during operation.*

#### Inspection
6      Inspect the rubber coupling (if equipped), the support bearing shaft and universal joints. Inspect the transmission flange locating pin and driveshaft bushing for signs of wear or

**11.4a  Remove the bolts securing the driveshaft to the differential pinion flange**

**11.4b  On some models, a rubber coupling is installed between the driveshaft and the differential**

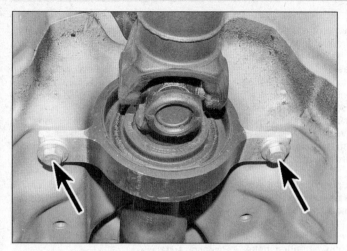

**11.5 The driveshaft center support bearing/bracket is secured by two bolts**

**11.9 Apply moly-based lubricant grease to the driveshaft centering pin on the transmission**

damage and replace as necessary.

7    Wear in the support bearing will lead to noise and vibration when the vehicle is driven. The bearing is best checked with the driveshaft removed. To gain access to the bearing with the shaft in position, remove the exhaust system and heat shields (see Chapter 4).

8    Rotate the bearing and check that it turns smoothly with no sign of freeplay; if it's difficult to turn, or if it has a gritty feeling, replace it. Also inspect the rubber portion. If it's cracked or deteriorated, replace it. If you have any doubts about the condition of the U-joints or center bearing, bring the complete driveshaft to a shop specializing in driveline repair for evaluation, repair or balancing.

### Installation

*Refer to illustration 11.9*

9    Apply a small amount of moly-based lubricant grease to the transmission pin and shaft bushing and maneuver the shaft into position **(see illustration)**.

10    Align the marks made prior to removal and engage the shaft bushing with the transmission and rear differential unit flanges. With the marks correctly aligned, install the bearing support bracket retaining bolts, tightening them only slightly at this stage.

11    Install new retaining bolts to the rear coupling of the driveshaft and tighten them to the specified torque.

12    Insert the new bolts and install the new retaining nuts. Tighten them to the specified torque, noting that the nut/bolt should only be rotated on the flange side to avoid stressing the rubber coupling.

13    Tighten the support bracket bolts to the specified torque.

14    Install the exhaust system and associated components (see Chapter 4).

### *Front (AWD models only)*

15    Block the rear wheels. Raise the front of the vehicle and support it securely on jackstands.

16    Remove the fasteners and the engine splash shield.

17    Remove the bolts and the front subframe reinforcement panel, if equipped.

18    Make match-marks on the front differential flange and the front of the driveshaft, as well as the rear of the driveshaft and the flange at the transfer case.

19    Remove the bolts securing the driveshaft front yoke to the differential flange.

20    Remove the bolts securing the driveshaft rear flange to the transfer case, and remove the driveshaft from the vehicle.

21    Installation is the reverse of removal, except that any ZNS bolts (zinc-plated aluminum) must be replaced.

### 12   Rear differential - removal and installation

**Note:** *New driveshaft rear coupling nuts and driveaxle retaining bolts will be required on installation.*

### *Removal*

1    Block the front wheels. Raise the rear of the vehicle and support it securely on jackstands. Remove both rear wheels.

2    Using paint or a marking pen, make alignment marks between the driveshaft and rear differential flange. Unscrew the bolts/nuts securing the driveshaft to the rear differential and discard them; new ones must be used on installation.

3    Remove the driveshaft (see Section 11). Disconnect the vent hose from the differential.

4    On E-series chassis models, remove the driveaxles (see Section 8). On F-series chassis models, the driveaxles must be removed once the rear differential is partially lowered. **Note:** *Do not allow the driveshaft to hang under its own weight as the CV joint may be damaged.* Discard the bolts; new ones should be used on installation.

5    Remove the nuts/bolts and the heat

shield panel from the left-hand end of the tension strut beneath the differential input-shaft flange.

6    Move a floor jack and block of wood into position and raise it so that it is supporting the weight of the differential.

7    Making sure the differential is safely supported, loosen and remove the bolts securing the front of the unit to the subframe and the single bolt securing the rear of the differential to the subframe.

8    Carefully lower the rear differential out of position and remove it from underneath the vehicle. Examine the differential mounts for signs of wear or damage and replace if necessary.

### *Installation*

9    Installation is the reverse of removal, noting the following:

a) *Raise the differential into position and engage it with the driveshaft rear joint, making sure the marks made prior to removal are correctly aligned.*

b) *Insert the differential front mounting bolts, then the rear bolt.*

c) *Tighten the front differential mounting bolts to the specified torque setting, followed by the rear bolt.*

d) *Install the new driveshaft joint bolts/nuts and tighten them to the specified torque.*

e) *Install the new driveshaft joint retaining bolts and plates and tighten them to the specified torque.*

f) *Refill/top-off the rear differential with oil (see Chapter 1).*

### 13   Front differential (AWD models) - removal and installation

**Note:** *This is a difficult procedure for the home mechanic, requiring an engine lifting device and a transmission jack.*

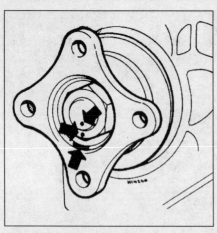

**14.2  Make alignment marks on the flange, the pinion shaft and nut to ensure proper assembly**

## Removal

1    Disconnect the negative battery cable (see Chapter 5).
2    Block the rear wheels. Raise the front of the vehicle and support it securely on jackstands.
3    Remove the fasteners, the engine splash shield and the shield below the radiator.
4    Remove the cabin air filter housing (see Chapter 1).
5    Remove the engine air filter housing.
6    Open the hood to the most upright position and attach an engine lift or engine support assembly to lifting points on the engine. **Note:** *The engine need only be raised enough to remove the weight from the engine mounts.*
7    On the left side, disconnect the tie-rod end, tension strut, control arm and the strut-to-steering knuckle pinch-bolt (see Chapter 10).
8    Remove the driveaxles (see Section 8).
9    Remove the bolts and the front subframe reinforcement panel, if equipped.
10   Disconnect the vent hose from the differ-

ential case.
11   Make match-marks on the front differential flange and the front of the driveshaft, as well as the rear of the driveshaft and the flange at the transfer case.
12   Remove the bolts securing the driveshaft front yoke to the differential flange.
13   Remove the bolts securing the driveshaft rear flange to the transfer case, and remove the driveshaft from the vehicle.
14   Remove one subframe mounting bolt and purchase new bolts that are 2.5 inches longer.
15   With a suitable support under the subframe (such as a transmission jack), replace each of the subframe mounting bolts with the longer bolts.
16   Lower the subframe two inches to access the differential-to-oil pan mounting bolts. Remove the differential from the vehicle.

## Installation

17   Installation is the reverse of removal, noting the following points:

   a)  *This is a good time to replace the drive-axle oil seals while the differential is out of the vehicle.*
   b)  *Use a new O-ring between the oil pan and the differential.*
   c)  *Use the original subframe bolts or new bolts of the same length as original.*
   d)  *Check and top-off the lubricant in the differential.*

---

## 14   Differential pinion seal - replacement

**Note:** *This procedure applies to the front (AWD models) and rear differential.*

## Removal

*Refer to illustration 14.2*

**Note:** *A new flange nut retaining plate will be required.*

1    Remove the driveshaft (see Section 11). Remove the exhaust system (see Chapter 4).
2    Remove the retaining plate and make alignment marks between the driveshaft flange nut, the differential pinion flange and pinion **(see illustration)**. Discard the retaining plate; a new one must be used on installation.
3    Hold the differential pinion flange stationary by bolting a length of metal bar to it. Unscrew the nut, noting the exact number of turns necessary to remove it.
4    Using a suitable puller, draw the differential pinion flange from the pinion and remove the dust cover. If the dust cover shows signs of wear, replace it.
5    Pry the oil seal from the differential case with a screwdriver. Wipe clean the oil-seal seating surface.

## Installation

6    Smear a little differential oil on the sealing lip of the new oil seal, then press it squarely into the differential case until it is flush with the outer face. If necessary, the seal can be tapped into position using a metal tube which bears only on its hard outer edge.
7    Install the dust cover and locate the differential pinion flange on the pinion, aligning the marks made on removal. Replace the flange nut, screwing it on by the exact number of turns counted on removal, so that all alignment marks align. **Caution:** *Do not over-tighten the flange nut. If the nut is overtightened, the collapsible spacer behind the flange will be deformed, necessitating its replacement. This is a complex operation requiring the rear differential to be disassembled.*
8    Secure the nut in position with the new retaining plate, tapping it squarely into position.

# Chapter 9   Brakes

## Contents

## Specifications

### Front brakes
| | |
|---|---|
| Caliper type | Teves, ATE floating caliper or Brembo |
| Brake pad friction material minimum thickness | 3/32 inch (2.4 mm) |
| Disc minimum thickness | Cast into disc |
| Maximum disc run-out | 0.008 inch (0.2 mm) |

### Rear disc brakes
| | |
|---|---|
| Brake pad friction material minimum thickness | 3/32 inch (2.4 mm) |
| Disc minimum thickness | Cast into disc |
| Maximum disc run-out | 0.008 inch (0.2 mm) |

### Parking brake
| | |
|---|---|
| Shoe friction material minimum thickness | 1/16 inch (1.5 mm) |

## Torque specifications

|  | **Ft-lbs** (unless otherwise indicated) | **Nm** |
|---|---|---|

**Note:** *One foot-pound (ft-lb) of torque is equivalent to 12 inch-pounds (in-lbs) of torque. Torque values below approximately 15 foot-pounds are expressed in inch-pounds, because most foot-pound torque wrenches are not accurate at these smaller values.*

| | Ft-lbs | Nm |
|---|---|---|
| ABS pressure sensors-to-master cylinder | 168 in-lbs | 19 |
| ABS wheel sensor retaining bolts | 72 in-lbs | 8 |
| Brake disc retaining bolt | 144 in-lbs | 16 |
| Brake hose unions | | |
|    M10 thread | 156 in-lbs | 17 |
|    M12 thread | 168 in-lbs | 19 |
| Front brake caliper | | |
|    Guide pins | | |
|    Socket head | | |
|       E90, E91, E92 and E93 chassis | 22 | 30 |
|       F30, F31 and F34 chassis | 20.5 | 28 |
|    Hexagon head | 26 | 35 |
|    Mounting bracket bolts | 81 | 110 |
|    Brake disc retaining bolt | 141 in-lbs | 16 |
| Master cylinder mounting nuts* | 16 | 22 |
| Rear brake caliper | | |
|    Guide pin bolts | | |
|    E90, E91, E92 and E93 chassis | | |
|       Socket head | 22 | 30 |
|       Hexagon head | 26 | 35 |
|    F30, F31 and F34 chassis | 20.5 | 28 |
|    Mounting bracket bolts | | |
|    E90, E91, E92 and E93 chassis | | |
|       M10 bolt | 48 | 65 |
|       M12 bolt | 81 | 110 |
|    F30, F31 and F34 chassis | | |
|       Step 1 | 22 | 30 |
|       Step 2 | Tighten an additional 90 degrees | |
| Wheel bolts | 89 | 120 |
| Power brake booster mounting nuts* | 16 | 22 |
| Vacuum pump drive sprocket bolt (E-series chassis) | 48 | 65 |

\* Do not re-use

## 1  General information

The braking system is of the servo-assisted, dual-circuit hydraulic type. Under normal circumstances, both circuits operate in unison. However, if there is hydraulic failure in one circuit, full braking force will still be available at two wheels.

All models are equipped with front and rear disc brakes. ABS is standard equipment on all models (refer to Section 19 for further information on ABS operation). **Note:** *On models equipped with Dynamic Stability Control (DSC), the ABS system also operates the traction-control side of the system.*

The front disc brakes are actuated by single-piston sliding type calipers, which ensure that equal pressure is applied to each disc pad.

All models are equipped with rear disc brakes, actuated by single-piston sliding calipers, while a separate drum brake arrangement is installed in the center of the brake disc to provide a separate means of parking brake application. **Note:** *When servicing any part of the system, work carefully and methodically; also observe scrupulous cleanliness when overhauling any part of the hydraulic system. Always replace components if in doubt about their condition, and use only genuine BMW parts, or equivalent.*

### *Precautions*

There are some general precautions and warnings related to the brake system:

a) *Use only brake fluid conforming to DOT 4 or DOT 4 low-viscosity specifications.*
b) *The brake pads and linings contain fibers which are hazardous to your health if inhaled. Whenever you work on brake system components, clean all parts with brake system cleaner. Do not allow the fine dust to become airborne. Also, wear an approved filtering mask.*
c) *Safety should be paramount whenever any servicing of the brake components is performed. Do not use parts or fasteners which are not in perfect condition, and be sure that all clearances and torque specifications are adhered to. If you are at all unsure about a certain procedure, seek professional advice. Upon completion of any brake system work, test the brakes carefully in a controlled area before putting the vehicle into normal service. If a problem is suspected in the brake system, don't drive the vehicle until it's fixed.*
d) *Used brake fluid is considered a hazardous waste and it must be disposed of in accordance with federal, state and local laws. DO NOT pour it down the sink, into septic tanks or storm drains, or on the ground.*
e) *Clean up any spilled brake fluid immediately and then wash the area with large amounts of water. This is especially true for any finished or painted surfaces.*

## 2  Brake hydraulic system - bleeding

**Warning:** *If the high-pressure hydraulic system linking the master cylinder, hydraulic (DSC) unit and (where equipped) accumulator has been disturbed, then bleeding of the brakes should be entrusted to a BMW dealer or other qualified brake shop. They will have access to the special service tester which is needed to operate the ABS modulator pump and bleed the high-pressure hydraulic system safely.*
**Warning:** *Wear eye protection when bleeding the brake system. If the fluid comes in contact with your eyes, immediately rinse them with water and seek medical attention.*
**Caution:** *Don't allow brake fluid to come into contact with the paint as it will damage the finish.*
**Note:** *Bleeding the brake system is necessary to remove any air that's trapped in the system when it's opened during removal and installation of a hose, line, caliper, wheel cylinder or master cylinder.*

### *General*

1   It will probably be necessary to bleed the system at all four brakes if air has entered the system due to low fluid level, or if the brake lines have been disconnected at the master cylinder.
2   During the bleeding procedure, add only clean, unused brake fluid of the recommended type (see Chapter 1); never re-use fluid that has already been bled from the system. Ensure that sufficient fluid is available before starting work.
3   If the system has been filled with the incorrect fluid, the brake system must be flushed completely with uncontaminated, correct fluid, and new seals should be installed to the various components.
4   If fluid has been lost from the system, or air has entered because of a leak, ensure that the problem is fixed before continuing.
5   Park the vehicle on level ground, switch off the engine and place the transmission in Park (automatic), or First or Reverse (manual). Block the wheels and release the parking brake.
6   Check that all hoses and lines are secure, unions tight and bleeder screws closed. Clean any dirt from around the bleeder screws.
7   Remove the master cylinder reservoir cap and fill the reservoir with brake fluid. Reinstall the cap. **Note:** *Check the fluid level often during the bleeding operation and add fluid as necessary to prevent the fluid level from falling low enough to allow air bubbles into the master cylinder.*
8   There are a number of one-man, do-it-yourself brake bleeding kits currently available from auto parts stores. It is recommended that one of these kits is used whenever possible, as they greatly simplify the bleeding operation, and reduce the risk of expelled air and fluid being drawn back into the system. If such a kit is not available, the basic (two-man)

method must be used.
9   If a kit is to be used, prepare the vehicle as described previously, and follow the kit manufacturer's instructions, as the procedure may vary slightly according to the type being used.
10   Whichever method is used, the same sequence must be followed (Steps 11 and 12) to ensure the removal of all air from the system.

### *Bleeding sequence*

11   If a brake line was disconnected only at a wheel, then only that caliper or wheel cylinder must be bled. If a brake line is disconnected at a fitting located between the master cylinder and any of the brakes, that part of the system served by the disconnected line must be bled.
12   If the complete system is to be bled, then it should be done in the following order:
   *Right rear brake*
   *Left rear brake*
   *Right front brake*
   *Left front brake*
**Warning:** *After bleeding the system on models with Dynamic Stability Control (DSC), the operation of the braking system should be checked by a BMW dealer or suitably-equipped specialist.*

### *Bleeding*
#### Basic (two-man) method

13   Have an assistant on hand, as well as a supply of new brake fluid, an empty clear plastic container, a length of plastic, rubber or vinyl tubing to fit over the bleeder valve and a wrench to open and close the bleeder valve.
14   Beginning at the right rear wheel, remove the dust cap and loosen the bleeder screw slightly, then tighten it to a point where it's snug but can still be loosened quickly and easily. Place one end of the tubing over the bleeder screw fitting and submerge the other end in brake fluid in the container.
15   Ensure that the master cylinder reservoir fluid level is maintained at least above the MIN level line throughout the procedure.
16   Have the assistant depress the brake pedal several times, then hold it in the depressed position.
17   While the pedal is held depressed, open the bleeder screw just enough to allow a flow of fluid to leave the valve. Watch for air bubbles to exit the submerged end of the tube. When the fluid flow slows after a couple of seconds, tighten the screw and have your assistant release the pedal. Recheck the reservoir level.
18   Repeat Steps 16 and 17 until no more air is seen leaving the tube, then tighten the bleeder. Be sure to check the fluid in the master cylinder reservoir frequently. If the master cylinder has been drained and refilled, and air is being bled from the first screw in the sequence, allow about 5 seconds between cycles for the master cylinder passages to refill.

**2.21 Bleeding a rear brake caliper using a one-way valve kit**

19   When no more air bubbles appear, tighten the bleeder screw securely, remove the tube and wrench, and reinstall the dust cap. Do not overtighten the bleeder screw.
20   Repeat the procedure on the remaining screws in the sequence, until all air is removed from the system and the brake pedal feels firm again.

### Using a one-way valve kit

*Refer to illustration 2.21*

21   These kits consist of a length of tubing, with a one-way valve attached to prevent expelled air and fluid being drawn back into the system; some kits include a translucent container, which can be positioned so that the air bubbles can be more easily seen flowing from the end of the tube **(see illustration)**.
22   Connect the kit to the bleeder screw, then open the bleeder screw. Depress the brake pedal with a smooth, steady stroke, and slowly release it; repeat this step until the expelled fluid is clear of air bubbles.
23   Remember to check the master cylinder reservoir fluid level; ensure that it is maintained at least above the MIN level line at all times.

### Using a pressure-bleeding kit

24   These kits are usually operated by the reservoir of pressurized air contained in a small chamber that can be metered. However, it will probably be necessary to reduce the pressure to a lower level than normal; refer to the instructions supplied with the pressure bleeder. **Note:** *BMW specifies that a pressure of 29 psi should not be exceeded in the brake hydraulic system.*
25   By connecting a pressurized, fluid-filled container to the master cylinder reservoir, bleeding can be carried out simply by opening each screw in turn (in the specified sequence), and allowing the fluid to flow out until no more air bubbles can be seen in the expelled fluid.
26   This method provides an additional safeguard against air being drawn into the system during bleeding.
27   Pressure-bleeding is particularly effective when bleeding difficult systems, or when

bleeding the complete system at the time of routine fluid replacement.

### All methods

28   When bleeding is complete, and firm pedal feel is restored, wash off any spilled fluid, tighten the bleeder screws securely, and install the dust caps.
29   Check the fluid level in the master cylinder reservoir, and top-off if necessary (see Chapter 1).
30   Discard any fluid that has been bled from the system; it is contaminated and cannot be reused.
31   Check the operation of the brakes. The pedal should feel solid when depressed, with no sponginess. If necessary, repeat the entire process. If the system cannot be bled of all air after several attempts, it may be a sign of worn master cylinder seals. **Warning:** *Do not operate the vehicle if you are in doubt about the effectiveness of the brake system. It is possible for air to become trapped in the anti-lock brake system hydraulic control unit, so, if the pedal continues to feel spongy after repeated bleedings or the BRAKE or ANTI-LOCK light stays on, have the vehicle towed to a dealer service department or other qualified shop to be bled with the aid of a scan tool.*

---

### 3   Brake hoses and lines - replacement

**Warning:** *If the high-pressure hydraulic system linking the master cylinder, hydraulic unit and (where equipped) accumulator has been disturbed, then bleeding of the brakes should be entrusted to a BMW dealer or other qualified brake shop. They will have access to the special service tester which is needed to operate the ABS modulator pump and bleed the high-pressure hydraulic system safely.*
**Warning:** *Wear eye protection when bleeding the brake system. If the fluid comes in contact with your eyes, immediately rinse them with water and seek medical attention.*
**Caution:** *Don't allow brake fluid to come into contact with the paint as it will damage the finish.*

1   About every six months, with the vehicle raised and placed securely on jackstands, the flexible hoses which connect the steel brake lines with the front and rear brake assemblies should be inspected for cracks, chafing of the outer cover, leaks, blisters and other damage. These are important and vulnerable parts of the brake system and inspection should be complete. A light and mirror will be needed for a thorough check. If a hose exhibits any of the above defects, replace it with a new one.

### Flexible hoses

2   Clean all dirt away from the ends of the hose.
3   To remove a brake hose, unscrew the tube nut with a flare-nut wrench, if available, to prevent rounding-off the corners of the nut,

then remove the bolt(s) or clip(s) securing the hose to the body (and any suspension components).
4   Disconnect the hose from the caliper, discarding the sealing washers on either side of the fitting.
5   Using new sealing washers, attach the new brake hose to the caliper. Tighten the banjo fitting bolt to the torque listed in this Chapter's Specifications.
6   Reverse the removal procedure to install the hose, making sure it isn't twisted.
7   Carefully check to make sure the suspension or steering components don't make contact with the hose. Have an assistant push down on the vehicle and also turn the steering wheel lock-to-lock during inspection.
8   Bleed the brake system (see Section 2). Test the brakes carefully before returning the vehicle to normal operation.

### Metal brake lines

9   When replacing brake lines, be sure to use the correct parts. Don't use copper tubing for any brake system components. Purchase steel brake lines from a dealer parts department or auto parts store.
10   Prefabricated brake line, with the tube ends already flared and fittings installed, is available at auto parts stores and dealer parts departments. These lines can be bent to the proper shapes using a tubing bender.
11   When installing the new line make sure it's well supported in the brackets and has plenty of clearance between moving or hot components.
12   After installation, check the master cylinder fluid level and add fluid as necessary. Bleed the brake system as outlined in Section 2 and test the brakes carefully before placing the vehicle into normal operation.

---

### 4   Front brake pads - replacement

**Warning:** *Disc brake pads must be replaced on both front wheels at the same time - never replace the pads on only one wheel. Also, the dust created by the brake system is harmful to your health. Never blow it out with compressed air and don't inhale any of it. An approved filtering mask should be worn when working on the brakes. Do not, under any circumstances, use petroleum-based solvents to clean brake parts. Use brake system cleaner only!*

1   Apply the parking brake, then loosen the front wheel bolts. Raise the front of the vehicle and support it securely on jackstands. Remove both front wheels.

### Teves and ATE (floating) calipers

*Refer to illustrations 4.2a through 4.2dd, 4.4a, 4.4b and 4.4c*

2   Follow **illustrations 4.2a through 4.2dd** for the actual pad replacement procedure. Be sure to stay in order and read the caption

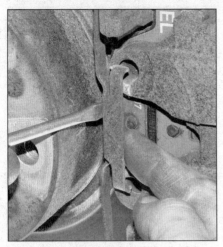

**4.2a  Pry the spring away from the hub, and out from the caliper (Teves caliper)**

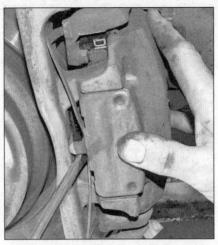

**4.2b  Pry the spring away from the hub, and out from the caliper (ATE caliper)**

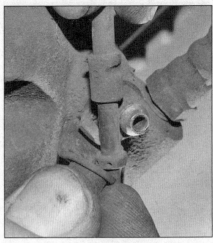

**4.2c  Release the pad wear sensor wiring from the rubber clip**

**4.2d  Open the junction box . . .**

**4.2e  . . . and disconnect the wear sensor wiring plug**

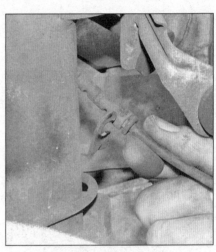

**4.2f  Pull the wiring from the bracket on the suspension strut**

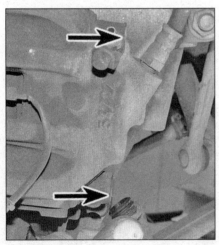

**4.2g  Pry out the rubber caps . . .**

**4.2h  . . . and unscrew the caliper guide pins**

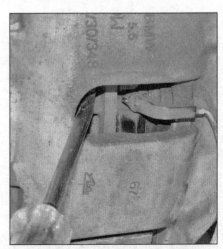

**4.2i  On ATE calipers, use a screwdriver to pry the caliper to the outside (which pushes the piston into the caliper body)**

4.2j  Pull the caliper rearwards

4.2k  On Teves calipers, pull the inner pad
from the piston. On all calipers, pull the
wear sensor from the pad

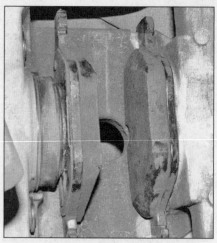

4.2l  On ATE calipers, both pads are
clipped into the caliper

4.2m  Suspend the caliper from the
suspension spring so no strain is placed
on the flexible hose

4.2n  On Teves calipers, remove the outer
pad from the caliper mounting bracket

4.2o  If new pads are installed, force the
piston back into the caliper body with a
piston retraction tool

4.2p  Use a wire brush to clean the pad
mounting surfaces - Teves calipers only

4.2q  Apply a small amount of anti-seize
compound to the pad mounting surfaces -
do not get any on the friction surfaces

4.2r  Press the inner pad into the caliper
piston - Teves calipers

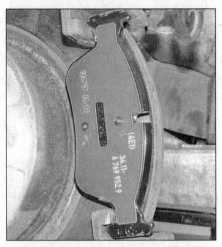

4.2s  On Teves calipers, install the outer pad to the mounting bracket - ensure the friction material is against the disc . . .

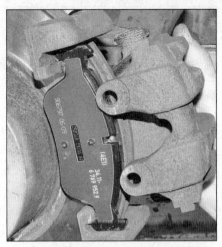

4.2t  . . . and slide the caliper into place, over the outer pad

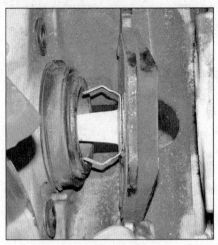

4.2u  On ATE calipers, clip the inner pad to the piston . . .

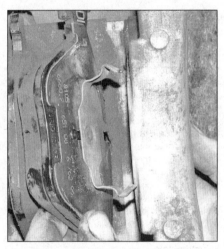

4.2v  . . . and the outer pad to the caliper body . . .

4.2w  . . . then slide the caliper into place

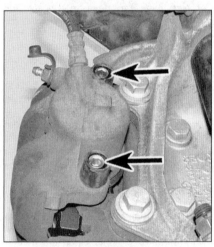

4.2x  Push the caliper guide pins into place, and tighten them to the specified torque

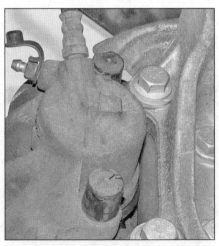

4.2y  Install the rubber caps over the guide pins

4.2z  Position the spring, lever it away from the hub, and push it into the caliper holes - Teves calipers

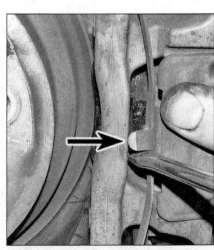

4.2aa  With the ends of the spring in place, pry the spring away from the hub, and engage the tab in the hole - ATE calipers

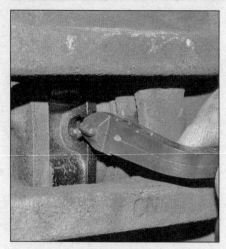

4.2bb   Press the new wear sensor . . .

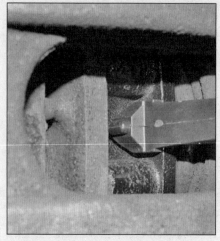

4.2cc   . . . into place in the inner pad

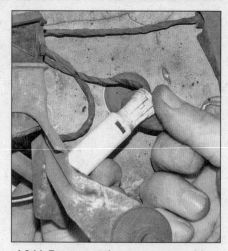

4.2dd   Reconnect the wear sensor wiring plug, and install it to the connection box on the inner wing. Don't forget to secure the wiring

under each illustration, and note the following points:

a) *New pads may have an adhesive foil on the back of the pad. Remove this foil prior to installation.*

b) *Thoroughly clean the caliper guide surfaces, and apply a little high-temperature brake assembly grease.*

c) *When pushing the caliper piston back to accommodate new pads, keep a close eye on the fluid level in the reservoir.*

d) *The manufacturer recommends that the brake pad wear sensor be replaced if it's been removed.*

3   Repeat the above procedure on the remaining front brake caliper.

4   When reinstalling the caliper, be sure to tighten the mounting bolts to the torque listed in this Chapter's Specifications. Before installing the wheels, use a wire brush or mildly abrasive cloth to clean the mating surfaces of the hub and wheel. Apply some anti-seize compound to the hub and wheel surface prior to installation **(see illustrations)**.

## Brembo (fixed) calipers

5   Disconnect the brake pad sensor harness connector, then detach the harness from the brackets.

6   Follow the harness to the sensor and press the clips together and pull the brake pad sensor forward the off on the inner pad.

7   To replace the front or rear pads, working from the large opening on the caliper, locate the two horizontal pad pins that go through the caliper and the brake pad backing plates. Using a small punch and hammer, drive out the top retaining pin.

8   Push the lower end of the cross-spring away from the bottom pad pin, then drive the pad pin out to the same side that the upper pin was removed. Remove the lower pad pin and the cross-spring.

**Note:** *The pad pins can only be driven out in one direction; they are removed towards the inboard side of the calipers.*

9   Using needle-nose pliers, pull the inboard (inner) brake pad from the caliper.

**Note:** *Note if special tool #34 1 050 is available (this is a tool that depresses the caliper pistons into their bores simultaneously), both*

pads may be removed at this time. If this tool is not available, remove only one pad during this step.

10   Using a small prybar or two screwdrivers, slowly push the caliper pistons into the bores on the inboard side. Front calipers have two pistons on each side of the caliper for a total of four. Rear calipers have one piston on each side. As a pistons are depressed to the bottom of the caliper bore, the fluid in the master cylinder reservoir will rise. Remove enough brake fluid so the reservoir is about half full. Continue to make sure that it doesn't overflow while pushing on all of the caliper pistons.

11   On front calipers, it's possible that one piston can be forced out of the caliper bore while the other is being pushed in on the same side. To prevent this, depress both pistons at the same time.

**Caution:** *Do not use grease on the back or sides of the brake pad surfaces; BMW specifies to use brake pad paste.*

12   Position the new inboard brake pad into

4.4a   Clean the corrosion from the hub surface . . .

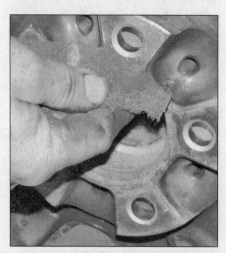

4.4b   . . . and the wheel center

4.4c   Apply a little anti-seize grease to the hub

the caliper.

13   Using needle-nose pliers, pull the outboard (outer) brake pad from the caliper.

14   Perform Step 10 on the outboard side of the caliper.

15   Position the new outboard brake pad into the caliper.

16   Install the top pad pin and place the cross-spring in position.

17   Press the bottom end of the cross-spring down and install the bottom pad pin.

18   Carefully drive the pins into the caliper until they are fully seated.

19   Install the wear sensor to the inboard brake pad.

20   Fully depress brake pedal several times so that brake pads contact brake discs.

21   Repeat the above procedure on the remaining caliper.

## All models

22   Install the wheels, then lower the vehicle to the ground and tighten the wheel bolts to the specified torque.

23   After the job has been completed, firmly depress the brake pedal a few times to bring the pads into contact with the disc. **Caution:** *New pads will not give full braking efficiency until they have seated-in. Be prepared for this, and avoid hard braking as far as possible for the first hundred miles or so after pad replacement*

24   Check the level of the brake fluid, adding some if necessary.

25   Turn the ignition key to the accessory position and leave it there for at least 30 seconds (don't start the engine) to turn the brake pad warning light off and to reset any associated trouble codes. If the light doesn't go off, refer to Chapter 1, Section 30 and reset the Condition Based Service (CBS) display.

26   Check the operation of the brakes carefully before placing the vehicle into normal service.

## 5   Rear brake pads - replacement

*Refer to illustrations 5.2a through 5.2q*

**Warning:** *Disc brake pads must be replaced* on both rear wheels at the same time - never replace the pads on only one wheel. Also, the dust created by the brake system is harmful to your health. Never blow it out with compressed air and don't inhale any of it. An approved filtering mask should be worn when working on the brakes. Do not, under any circumstances, use petroleum-based solvents to clean brake parts. Use brake system cleaner only!

**Note:** *This procedure applies to models with rear floating calipers only. On models with rear fixed (Brembo) calipers, refer to Section 4 for the pad replacement procedure.*

1   Apply the parking brake, then loosen the rear wheel bolts. Raise the rear of the vehicle and support it securely on jackstands. Remove both rear wheels.

2   See Steps 2 through 9 in Section 4 for brake pad replacement, but follow **illustrations 5.2a through 5.2q** for the rear brake pad replacement procedure. Be sure to stay in order and read the caption under each illustration.

**5.2a  Release the wear sensor wiring from the rubber strap attached to the bleed nipple**

**5.2b  Pull the wear sensor from the inner pad. BMW states that the sensor must be replaced**

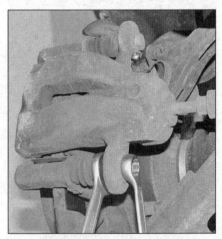

**5.2c  Remove the caliper lower guide pin bolt. Counter-hold the sleeve with a second wrench**

**5.2d  Pivot the caliper upwards to access the pads**

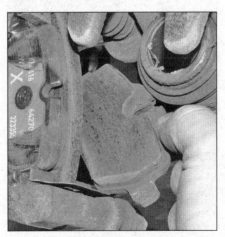

**5.2e  Pull out the inner pad . . .**

**5.2f  . . . followed by the outer pad**

5.2g  Remove the upper and
lower shims . . .

5.2h  . . . and clean the mounting surfaces
with a wire brush

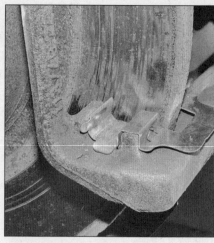

5.2i  Install the upper and lower shims

5.2j  If new pads are to be installed, push
the piston back into the caliper body
using a piston retraction tool

5.2k  Install the outer pad to the mounting
bracket. Ensure the friction material is
against the disc

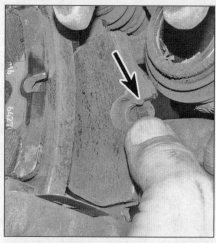

5.2l  Install the inner pad to the mounting
bracket. Note that the backing plate has a
fitting notch for the wear indicator

5.2m  Swing the caliper back down over
the pads

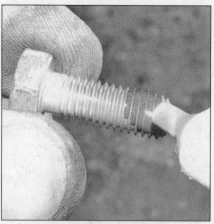

5.2n  Apply a little
thread-locking compound . . .

5.2o  . . . then insert the lower guide pin
bolt and tighten it to the specified torque

**5.2p  Open the connector box and swap the old sensor plug for the new one**

**5.2q  Press the wear sensor into the inner pad backing plate, and secure the wiring with the rubber strap**

**6.3  Measure the thickness of the disc with a micrometer**

## 6  Front brake disc - inspection, removal and installation

**Warning:** *Dust created by the brake system is harmful to your health. Never blow it out with compressed air and don't inhale any of it. An approved filtering mask should be worn when working on the brakes. Do not, under any circumstances, use petroleum-based solvents to clean brake parts. Use brake system cleaner only.*

### Inspection

*Refer to illustration 6.3*

**Note:** *If either disc requires replacement, BOTH should be replaced at the same time to ensure even and consistent braking. New brake pads should also be installed.*

1    Apply the parking brake, then raise the front of the vehicle and support it securely on jackstands. Remove the appropriate front wheel.

2    Visually inspect the disc surface for score marks and other damage. Light scratches and shallow grooves are normal after use and may not always be detrimental to brake operation, but deep scoring requires disc removal and refinishing by an automotive machine shop. Be sure to check both sides of the disc. If pulsating has been noticed during application of the brakes, suspect disc runout.

3    It's absolutely critical that the disc not be machined to a thickness under the specified minimum thickness. The minimum (or discard) thickness is cast or stamped into the hub of the disc. The disc thickness can be checked with a micrometer **(see illustration)**. If the disc has worn at any point to the specified minimum thickness or less, the disc must be replaced.

4    If the disc is thought to be warped, it can be checked for runout. Use a dial indicator set to zero and turn the disc. The indicator reading should not exceed the specified allowable runout limit. If it does, the disc should be refinished by an automotive machine shop.

**Note:** *Some professionals recommend that*

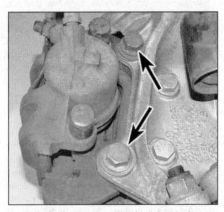

**6.6  Caliper mounting bracket bolts**

the discs be resurfaced regardless of the dial indicator reading (during brake pad replacement), as this will impart a smooth finish and ensure a perfectly flat surface, eliminating any brake pedal pulsation or other undesirable symptoms related to questionable discs. At the very least, if you elect not to have the discs resurfaced, remove the glaze from the surface with emery cloth or sandpaper, using a swirling motion.

5    Check the disc for cracks, especially around the wheel bolt holes, and any other wear or damage, and replace if necessary.

### Removal

*Refer to illustrations 6.6 and 6.7*

6    Unscrew the bolts securing the brake caliper mounting bracket to the hub carrier, then slide the caliper assembly off the disc **(see illustration)**. Using a piece of wire or string, tie the caliper to the front suspension coil spring, to avoid placing any strain on the hydraulic brake hose.

7    Use chalk or paint to mark the relationship of the disc to the hub. Remove the bolt securing the brake disc to the hub and remove the disc **(see illustration)**. If it is tight, lightly tap the rear face of the disc with a plastic mallet.

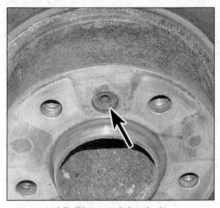

**6.7  Disc retaining bolt**

### Installation

8    Installation is the reverse of removal, noting the following points:

a) *Ensure that the mating surfaces of the disc and hub are clean and flat.*

b) *Align (if applicable) the marks made on removal, and tighten the disc retaining bolt to the specified torque.*

c) *If a new disc has been installed, use solvent to wipe any anti-corrosion preservative coating from the disc before installing the caliper. Ensure the disc mounting surface on the hub is free from dirt and corrosion.*

d) *Slide the caliper into position over the disc, making sure the pads slide past either side of the disc. Tighten the caliper mounting bolts to the specified torque.*

e) *Install the wheel, then lower the vehicle to the ground and tighten the wheel bolts to the specified torque.*

f) *Depress the brake pedal a few times to bring the brake pads into contact with the disc. Bleeding won't be necessary unless the brake hose was disconnected from the caliper. Check the operation of the brakes carefully before driving the vehicle.*

## 7 Rear brake disc - inspection, removal and installation

**Warning:** *Dust created by the brake system is harmful to your health. Never blow it out with compressed air and don't inhale any of it. An approved filtering mask should be worn when working on the brakes. Do not, under any circumstances, use petroleum-based solvents to clean brake parts. Use brake system cleaner only.*

### Inspection

**Note:** *If either disc requires replacement, BOTH should be replaced at the same time, to ensure even and consistent braking. New brake pads should also be installed.*

1    Firmly block the front wheels, then raise the rear of the vehicle and support it securely on jackstands. Remove the appropriate rear wheel. Release the parking brake.
2    Inspect the disc (see Section 6, Steps 2 through 5).

### Removal

3    Remove the brake pads (see Section 5).
4    Remove the bolts and remove the caliper mounting bracket. Discard the bolts; new ones must be installed.
5    Loosen and remove the brake disc retaining bolt **(see illustration 6.7)**.
6    It should now be possible to remove the brake disc from the stub axle by hand. If it is tight, lightly tap its rear face with a plastic mallet. If the parking brake shoes are binding, check that the parking brake is fully released.
7    Fully release the parking brake cable tension to obtain maximum freeplay in the cable (see Section 14).
8    Insert a screwdriver through one of the wheel bolt holes in the brake disc, and rotate the adjuster star wheel on the upper pivot to retract the shoes **(see illustration 14.6)**. The brake disc can then be removed.

### Installation

9    Installation is the reverse of removal, noting the following points:
a)  *Ensure that the mating surfaces of the disc and hub are clean and flat.*
b)  *Align (if applicable) the marks made on removal, and tighten the disc retaining bolt to the specified torque.*
c)  *If a new disc has been installed, use solvent to wipe any anti-corrosion preservative coating from the disc before installing the caliper. Ensure the disc mounting surface on the hub is free from dirt and corrosion.*
d)  *Slide the caliper into position over the disc, making sure the pads slide pass either side of the disc. Tighten the caliper mounting bolts to the specified torque.*
e)  *Install the wheel, then lower the vehicle to the ground and tighten the wheel bolts to the specified torque.*

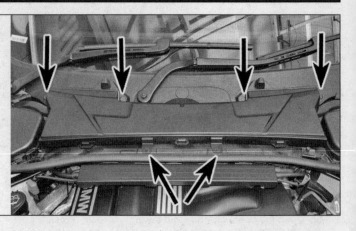

**10.1 Remove the cabin air filter cover mounting bolts and cover**

f)  *Adjust the parking-brake shoes and cable (see Section 14).*
g)  *Depress the brake pedal a few times to bring the brake pads into contact with the disc. Bleeding won't be necessary unless the brake hose was disconnected from the caliper. Check the operation of the brakes carefully before driving the vehicle. Recheck the parking brake.*

## 8 Front brake caliper - removal and installation

**Warning:** *Dust created by the brake system is harmful to your health. Never blow it out with compressed air and don't inhale any of it. An approved filtering mask should be worn when working on the brakes. Do not, under any circumstances, use petroleum-based solvents to clean brake parts. Use brake system cleaner only.*
**Caution:** *Don't allow brake fluid to come into contact with the paint as it will damage the finish.*
**Note:** *Always replace the calipers in pairs - never replace just one of them.*

### Removal

1    Apply the parking brake, then raise the front of the vehicle and support it securely on jackstands. Remove the appropriate wheel.
2    Clean the area around the brake hose fitting, then break loose the fitting from the caliper (but don't try to unscrew it yet - you'll twist the hose).
3    Remove the brake pads (see Section 4).
4    Unscrew the caliper from the end of the brake hose, then plug the hose and remove it from the vehicle.

### Installation

5    Screw the caliper fully onto the flexible hose fitting.
6    Install the brake pads (see Section 4).
7    Securely tighten the brake line fitting.
8    Remove the brake hose clamp and bleed the brake system according to the procedure in Section 2. Make sure there are no leaks from the hose connections.
9    Install the wheel, then lower the vehicle

to the ground and tighten the wheel bolts to the specified torque. Check the hydraulic fluid level (see Chapter 1). Test the brakes carefully before returning the vehicle to normal service.

## 9 Rear brake caliper - removal and installation

**Warning:** *Dust created by the brake system is harmful to your health. Never blow it out with compressed air and don't inhale any of it. An approved filtering mask should be worn when working on the brakes. Do not, under any circumstances, use petroleum-based solvents to clean brake parts. Use brake system cleaner only.*
**Caution:** *Don't allow brake fluid to come into contact with the paint as it will damage the finish.*
**Note:** *Always replace the calipers in pairs - never replace just one of them.*

### Removal

1    Block the front wheels, then raise the rear of the vehicle and support it securely on jackstands. Remove the relevant rear wheel.
2    Clean the area around the brake hose fitting, then break loose the fitting from the caliper (but don't try to unscrew it yet - you'll twist the hose).
3    Remove the brake pads (see Section 5).
4    Unscrew the caliper from the end of the flexible hose, then plug the hose.

### Installation

5    Screw the caliper fully onto the flexible hose fitting.
6    Install the brake pads (see Section 4).
7    Securely tighten the brake line fitting.
8    Remove the brake hose clamp and bleed the brake system according to the procedure in Section 2. Make sure there are no leaks from the hose connections.
9    Install the wheel, then lower the vehicle to the ground and tighten the wheel bolts to the specified torque. Check the hydraulic fluid level (see Chapter 1). Test the brakes carefully before returning the vehicle to normal service.
10    Check and, if necessary, adjust the parking brake (see Section 11).

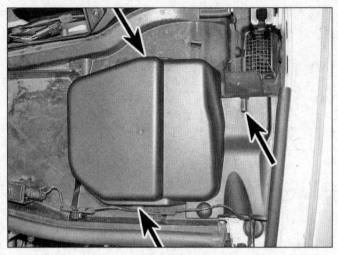

**10.2  Release the clips and remove the plastic cover from each side behind the strut towers**

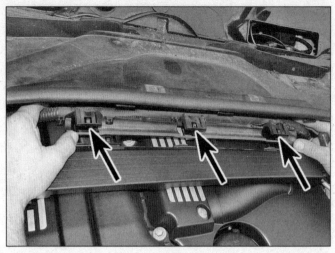

**10.3  Depress the clips and slide the cable guide(s) forwards**

## 10   Master cylinder - removal and installation

**Warning:** *Dust created by the brake system is harmful to your health. Never blow it out with compressed air and don't inhale any of it. An approved filtering mask should be worn when working on the brakes. Do not, under any circumstances, use petroleum-based solvents to clean brake parts. Use brake system cleaner only.*

**Caution:** *Don't allow brake fluid to come into contact with the paint as it will damage the finish.*

## *Removal*

*Refer to illustrations 10.1, 10.2, 10.3, 10.4a, 10.4b, 10.4c and 10.5*

**Warning:** *Although it is possible for the home mechanic to remove the master cylinder, if the brake lines are disconnected from the master cylinder, air will enter the high-pressure hydraulic system linking the master cylinder and (DSC) hydraulic unit. Bleeding of the high pressure system can only be safely carried out by a BMW dealer or specialist who has*

*access to the service tester (see Section 2). Once the master cylinder has been installed, the vehicle must be towed to a suitably-equipped BMW dealer or specialist.*

**Note:** *New master cylinder retaining nuts will be required on installation.*

1    Working at the rear of the engine compartment, remove the cabin air filter cover mounting bolts and cover **(see illustration)**. Slide the filter from the housing. If necessary, refer to Chapter 1.

2    Release the catches and remove the left- and right-hand plastic covers from behind the strut tower on each side of the engine compartment. Unclip the wiring where applicable **(see illustration)**.

3    Depress the clips and pull the cable guide forwards from the cabin air filter lower housing **(see illustration)**.

4    Release the catch and remove the bolt on each side, then slide the cabin air filter lower housing forwards and maneuver it out **(see illustrations)**.

5    Remove the master cylinder reservoir cap, and siphon the brake fluid from the reservoir. **Warning:** *Do not start the siphoning action by mouth! Use a siphoning kit available at most auto parts stores. To empty the*

reservoir without siphoning the fluid, open any convenient bleeder screw in the system, and gently pump the brake pedal to expel the fluid through a plastic tube connected to the screw until the level of fluid drops below that of the reservoir (see Section 2). Disconnect the wiring connector(s) from the brake fluid reservoir **(see illustration)**.

**10.4a  Rotate the temperature sensor counterclockwise and pull it from the bracket on the lower cabin air filter cover**

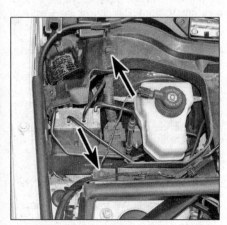

**10.4b  Release the catch and remove the bolt on each side . . .**

**10.4c  . . . then pull the lower cabin air filter cover forwards**

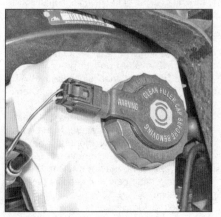

**10.5  Disconnect the wiring plug from the fluid level sensor**

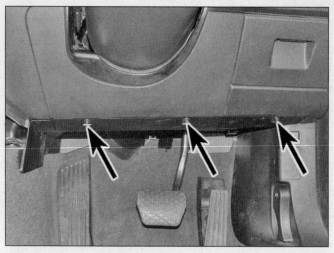

**11.7 Remove the three bolts securing the panel above the pedals**

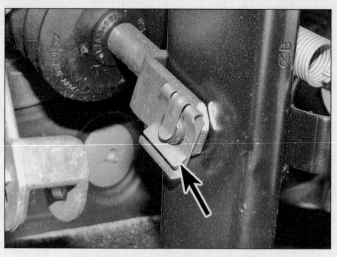

**11.8 Pushrod pin retaining clip location**

6   Disconnect the fluid hose(s) from the side of the reservoir, and plug the hoses to keep contaminants out of the brake system and to prevent losing any more brake fluid than is necessary.

7   Unclip and pull out the master cylinder reservoir locking pin.

8   Carefully ease the fluid reservoir out from the top of the master cylinder. Remove the reservoir seals, and plug the cylinder ports to prevent the entry of dirt or moisture.

9   Release the mounting fasteners and remove the driver's side trim panel above the pedals. Disconnect any electrical connectors as the panel is withdrawn.

10   Pry off the clip and remove the pin securing the pushrod to the brake pedal **(see illustration 11.8)**. The brake booster must be loosened so the master cylinder can be removed and installed.

11   Remove the brake booster retaining nuts; new ones must be installed during installation.

12   Clean the area around the brake line fittings on the lines from the master cylinder to the ABS modulator/hydraulic unit, and place rags beneath the line fittings to catch any spilled fluid. Make a note of the correct installed positions of the fittings, then unscrew the mounting nuts and carefully withdraw the lines. The brake lines must not be bent. Plug or tape over the line ends and master cylinder openings to keep contaminants out of the brake system and to prevent losing any more brake fluid than is necessary. Wash off any spilled fluid immediately with cold water.

13   Loosen and remove the nuts and washers securing the master cylinder to the brake booster, then withdraw the unit from the engine compartment. Remove the O-ring from the rear of the master cylinder. Discard the retaining nuts; new ones should be used on installation.

14   If the master cylinder is faulty, it must be replaced. Repair kits are not available from dealers, so the cylinder must be treated as a sealed unit. Replace the master cylinder O-ring seal and reservoir seals regardless of their apparent condition.

## Installation

15   Remove all traces of dirt from the master cylinder and brake booster mating surfaces, and install a new O-ring in the groove on the master cylinder body.

16   Install the master cylinder to the brake booster, ensuring that the booster pushrod is centered as it enters the master cylinder bore. Install new master cylinder retaining nuts and washers, and tighten them to the specified torque.

17   Wipe clean the brake line fittings, then install them to the master cylinder/hydraulic unit ports and tighten them securely.

18   Press the new reservoir seals firmly into the master cylinder ports, then ease the reservoir into position. Install the reservoir locking pin securely. Reconnect the fluid hose(s) to the reservoir, and reconnect the electrical connector(s).

19   The remainder of installation is the reverse of removal, noting the following points:

a) *Tighten all fasteners to their specified torque where given.*

b) *Have the vehicle towed to a dealer service department or other qualified repair shop to have the master cylinder and the remainder of the hydraulic system bled with the aid of a scan tool.*

c) *Test the operation of the brake system carefully before placing the vehicle into normal service.*

## 11   Brake pedal - removal and installation

### Manual transmission

1   Disconnect the clutch master cylinder pushrod from the clutch pedal, then remove the clutch master cylinder mounting bolts and push it to one side (see Chapter 8).

2   Remove the clutch pedal return spring and the pedal mounting clip, then slide the clutch pedal from the pivot.

3   Remove the brake light switch (see Section 18).

4   Slide off the retaining clip and remove the clevis pin securing the brake pedal to the servo unit pushrod.

5   Remove the mounting nuts and maneuver the brake pedal bracket assembly from under the instrument panel. Discard the self-locking nuts; new ones must be installed. If required, unhook the return spring and slide the pedal from the pivot.

6   Installation is the reverse of removal. Apply a smear of multipurpose grease to the pedal pivot and clevis pin.

### Automatic transmission

*Refer to illustrations 11.7, 11.8, 11.10a and 11.10b*

7   Working under the instrument panel, release the mounting fasteners and remove the driver's side trim panel above the pedals **(see illustration)**. Disconnect any electrical connectors as the panel is withdrawn.

8   Pry off the clip and remove the pin securing the brake booster pushrod to the brake pedal **(see illustration)**.

9   Remove the brake light switch (see Section 18).

10   Remove the mounting nuts and maneuver the pedal and bracket assembly from under the instrument panel **(see illustrations)**. Discard the self-locking nuts; new ones must be installed. Note that at the time of writing, the pedal was only available as part of the complete bracket assembly. Consult your dealer on parts availability.

11   Installation is the reverse of removal. Apply a smear of multipurpose grease to the pedal pivot and clevis pin.

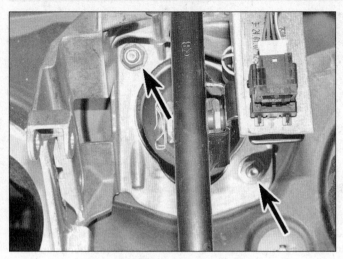

11.10a Pedal bracket lower nuts . . .

11.10b . . . and upper nut

## 12 Power brake booster - check

### Operating check

1    Depress the brake pedal several times with the engine off and make sure that there is no change in the pedal reserve distance.
2    Depress the pedal and start the engine. If the pedal goes down slightly, operation is normal.

### Airtightness check

3    Start the engine and turn it off after one or two minutes. Depress the brake pedal several times slowly. If the pedal goes down farther the first time but gradually rises after the second or third depression, the booster is airtight.
4    Depress the brake pedal while the engine is running, then stop the engine with the pedal depressed. If there is no change in the pedal reserve travel after holding the pedal for 30 seconds, the booster is airtight.

## 13 Power brake booster - removal and installation

Removal of the brake booster requires the removal of the ABS/DSC modulator/hydraulic unit. Due to the need for special diagnostic equipment, this task should only be carried out by a BMW dealer or suitably-equipped specialist.

## 14 Parking brake - adjustment

*Refer to illustrations 14.3, 14.4, 14.6 and 14.8*
1    Pull the parking brake lever to the fully-applied position, counting the number of clicks the lever travels. If adjustment is correct, there should be approximately 7 or 8 clicks before the parking brake is fully applied. If there are more than 10 clicks, adjust as follows.
2    Loosen and remove one wheel bolt from each rear wheel, block the front wheels, raise the rear of the vehicle and support it securely on jackstands.
3    Access to the parking brake cable adjuster can be gained by removing the parking brake lever boot from the center console **(see illustration)**. If greater access is required, the rear section of the center console will have to be removed (see Chapter 11).
4    Release the parking brake, then use a screwdriver to push the spring stop back until the retaining hook engages with the stop **(see illustration)**.
5    Starting with the right rear wheel, rotate the wheel so the adjuster wheel is visible through the hole.
6    Insert a screwdriver in through the bolt hole and fully expand the parking brake shoes by rotating the adjuster star wheel. When the wheel/disc can no longer be turned, back the adjuster wheel off by eight notches (for a 7.3 inch/185 mm diameter drum) or nine notches (for a 6.3 inch/160 mm diameter drum) so that

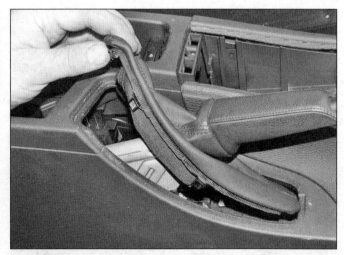

14.3 Squeeze the sides together and remove the parking brake lever boot from the center console

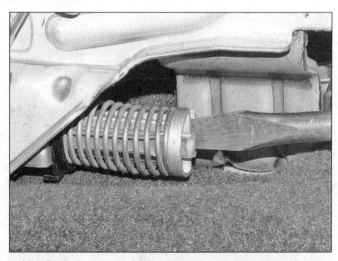

14.4 Push the spring stop back until it engages with the hook

**14.6  Rotate the adjuster star wheel (shown with the disc removed)**

**14.8  Pry the retaining hook from the cable stop**

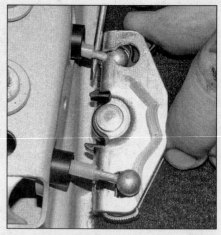

**15.4  Slide the cable end fittings up from the balance arm**

the wheel is free to rotate easily **(see illustration)**.

7    Repeat Steps 5 and 6 on the left rear wheel.

8    Unlock the cable adjuster unit by prying out the retaining hook from the spring stop with a screwdriver **(see illustration)**.

9    Fully release the parking brake lever and check that the wheels rotate freely. Slowly apply the parking brake, and check that the brake shoes start to contact the drums when the parking brake is set to the third notch of the ratchet mechanism. Check the adjustment by pulling the parking brake lever to the fully-applied position, counting the number of clicks the lever travels. Re-adjust the lever if necessary.

10   Once adjustment is correct, check the operation of the parking brake warning light switch, then install the center console section/parking brake lever boot (as applicable). Install the wheels, then lower the vehicle to the ground and tighten the wheel bolts to the specified torque. Verify the parking brake is actually holding the vehicle when applied.

## 15   Parking brake lever - removal and installation

*Refer to illustrations 15.4 and 15.5*

1    Remove the center console (see Chapter 11), then remove the airbag control unit (see Chapter 12).

2    Release the parking brake, then use a screwdriver to push the spring stop back until the retaining hook engages with the stop **(see illustration 14.4)**.

3    Disconnect the parking brake warning switch, then release the clips and move the cable guide/bracket to one side.

4    Press each cable retainer towards the center of the equalizer, on each side, and slide the ends of the parking brake cables upwards from the equalizer **(see illustration)**.

5    Remove the lever retaining nuts and lever **(see illustration)**.

6    Installation is the reverse of removal. Prior to installing the center console, adjust the parking brake (see Section 14).

## 16   Parking brake cables - removal and installation

### *Removal*

*Refer to illustration 16.3*

1    Detach the front ends of the cables from the lever equalizer arm (see Section 15).

2    Remove the rear brake discs (see Section 7).

3    Remove the cable retaining bracket bolt and the bracket from the rear hub assembly **(see illustration)**.

4    Rotate the wheel so the expander is visible through the hole (7 o'clock position). Press the release spring, in the expander, towards the rear of the vehicle, while pulling the cable from the backing plate and out of the expander.

5    Working back along the length of the cable and noting its correct routing, free it from all the relevant retaining clips.

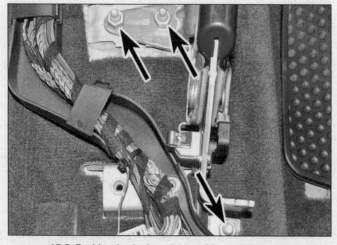

**15.5  Parking brake lever assembly retaining nuts**

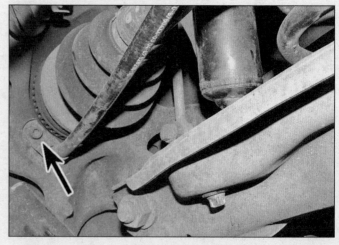

**16.3  Remove the cable retaining bracket bolt and the bracket**

**17.4a Using pliers, unhook and remove the parking brake shoe front return springs . . .**

**17.4b . . . and rear return springs**

## Installation

6 Insert the cable into the brake carrier/guard plate, and push it in up to the stop on the cable outer sleeve.

7 Grip the sleeve of the cable end, and push it into the expander until it snaps into place.

8 Installation is the reverse of removal. Prior to installing the center console, adjust the parking brake (see Section 14).

## 17 Parking brake shoes - removal and installation

## Removal

*Refer to illustrations 17.4a, 17.4b, 17.5a, 17.5b, 17.6 and 17.8*

1 Carefully pry up the parking brake lever boot from the center console. Remove the rear section of the center console if necessary for access (see Chapter 11).

2 Apply the parking brake, then use a screwdriver to push the spring stop back until the retaining hook engages with the stop **(see illustration 14.4)**.

3 Remove the rear brake disc (see Section 7), making a note of the installed position of all components.

4 Using a pair of pliers, carefully unhook and remove the parking brake shoe return springs **(see illustrations)**.

5 Release the shoe retaining pins using pliers by depressing them and rotating them through 90-degrees, then remove the pins and springs **(see illustrations)**.

6 Remove both parking brake shoes and the shoe adjuster mechanism, noting how it is installed **(see illustration)**.

7 Inspect the parking brake shoes for wear or contamination, and replace if necessary. It is recommended that the return springs are replaced as a matter of course.

8 While the shoes are removed, clean and inspect the condition of the shoe adjuster and expander mechanisms; replace them if

they show signs of wear or damage. Apply a fresh coat of high-temperature brake grease to the threads of the adjuster wheel

**17.5a Rotate the retainer pins through 90-degrees . . .**

**17.5b . . . then remove the pins, springs . . .**

**17.6 . . . and parking brake shoes**

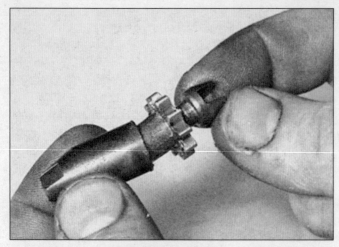

17.8 Clean the adjuster assembly and coat it with fresh brake assembly grease

17.11 Install the adjuster assembly, making sure it's correctly engaged with both parking brake shoes

18.4a Pull the switch from the switch mounting

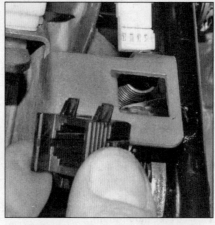

18.4b Press the retaining clips and remove the switch mounting

**(see illustration)** and sliding surfaces of the expander mechanism. Do not allow the grease to contact the shoe friction material.

## Installation

*Refer to illustration 17.11*

9    Prior to installation, clean the backing plate, and apply a thin smear of high-temperature brake grease to all those surfaces of the backing plate which bear on the shoes. Do not allow the grease to contact the shoe friction material.

10    Place the shoes in position and secure them with the retaining pins and springs.

11    Make sure the lower ends of the shoes are correctly engaged with the expander, then slide the adjuster mechanism into position between the upper ends of the shoes **(see illustration)**.

12    Check that all components are correctly installed, and install the upper and lower return springs using a pair of pliers.

13    Center the parking brake shoes and install the brake disc (see Section 7).

14    If removed from the expander, insert the parking brake cable end through the backing plate and into the expander.

15    Prior to installing the wheel, adjust the parking brake (see Section 14).

## 18    Brake light switch - removal and installation

## Removal

*Refer to illustrations 18.4a and 18.4b*

1    The brake light switch is located on the pedal bracket behind the instrument panel.

2    Loosen and remove the retaining bolts securing the driver's side knee bolster panel. Unclip the panel and remove it from the vehicle. Disconnect any electrical connectors as the panel is withdrawn.

3    Reach up behind the instrument panel and disconnect the wiring connector from the switch

4    Pull the switch from the mounting. If required, depress the clips and withdraw the switch mounting from the pedal bracket **(see illustrations)**.

## Installation

5    Fully depress the brake pedal and hold it down. Install the mount, then maneuver the switch into position. Push the switch fully into position, then slowly release the brake pedal and allow it to return to its stop. This will automatically adjust the switch. **Note:** *If the pedal is released too quickly, the switch will be incorrectly adjusted.*

6    Reconnect the electrical connector and check the operation of the brake lights. The lights should illuminate after the brake pedal has traveled approximately 3/16-inch (5 mm). If the switch is not functioning correctly, it is faulty and may need to be replaced; no other adjustment is possible.

7    Install the driver's side knee bolster panel.

## 19    Anti-lock Brake System (ABS) - general information

## General information

**Note:** *The ABS unit is a dual function unit, and controls both the Anti-lock Brake System (ABS) and traction control function of the Dynamic Stability Control (DSC) system.*

1    The anti-lock brake system is designed to maintain vehicle steerability, directional stability and optimum deceleration under severe braking conditions on most road surfaces. It does so by monitoring the rotational speed of each wheel and controlling the brake line pressure to each wheel during braking. This prevents the wheels from locking up.

2    The ABS system has three main components - the wheel speed sensors, the electronic control module (ECM) and the hydraulic unit (which consists of hydraulic solenoid valves and an electrically-drive return pump). Four wheel-speed sensors - one at each wheel - send a variable voltage signal to the ECM, which monitors these signals, compares them to its program and determines whether a wheel is about to lock up. When a wheel is about to lock up, the control unit signals the

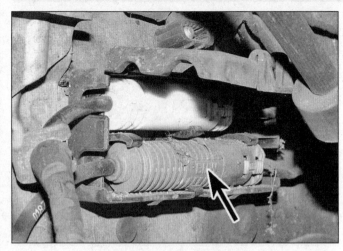

**20.3  Open the connector box on the inner fender and disconnect the ABS sensor wiring plug**

**20.4  Remove ABS sensor retaining bolt and pull the ABS sensor from the hub carrier**

hydraulic unit to reduce hydraulic pressure (or not increase it further) at that wheel's brake caliper. Pressure modulation is handled by electrically-operated solenoid valves. A brake pedal position sensor is integral with the power brake booster, and informs the ECM of brake pedal position.

3    If a problem develops within the system, an "ABS" warning light will glow on the dashboard. Sometimes, a visual inspection of the ABS system can help you locate the problem. Carefully inspect the ABS wiring harness. Pay particularly close attention to the harness and connections near each wheel. Look for signs of chafing and other damage caused by incorrectly routed wires. If a wheel sensor harness is damaged, the sensor must be replaced. **Warning:** *Do NOT try to repair an ABS wiring harness. The ABS system is sensitive to even the smallest changes in resistance. Repairing the harness could alter resistance values and cause the system to malfunction. If the ABS wiring harness is damaged in any way, it must be replaced.* **Caution:** *Make sure the ignition is turned off before unplugging or reattaching any electrical connections.*

4    An accumulator is also incorporated into the hydraulic system. As well as performing the ABS function as described above, the hydraulic unit also controls the traction/stability control side of the DSC system. If the ECM senses that the wheels are about to lose traction under acceleration, the hydraulic unit momentarily applies the rear brakes to prevent the wheel(s) spinning. If the system senses that the lateral acceleration/yaw rate of the vehicle is about to exceed a predetermined threshold - resulting in oversteer or understeer, the system can apply the brake of each individual wheel to maintain stability and prevent/control a skid.

5    The DSC system can also control the steering of the vehicle to maintain stability in an oversteer or understeer situation - known as Active steering. With conventional systems, the driver has to actively steer the vehicle in a straight line if the brakes are applied on a road

surface with varying traction levels. In these situations, the DSC control unit calculates the yaw rate with the brake pressure sensors on the front axle, then the DSC control unit transmits to the Active Steering control unit the yaw-moment compensation correction angle needed for stabilization.

6    Should a fault develop with the ABS/DSC system, the vehicle must be taken to a dealer or qualified shop for diagnosis.

### Diagnosis and repair

7    If a dashboard warning light comes on and stays on while the vehicle is in operation, the ABS system requires attention. Although special electronic ABS diagnostic testing tools are necessary to properly diagnose the system, you can perform a few preliminary checks before taking the vehicle to a dealer service department.

  a)  *Check the brake fluid level in the reservoir.*
  b)  *Verify that the computer electrical connectors are securely connected.*
  c)  *Check the electrical connectors at the hydraulic control unit.*
  d)  *Check the fuses.*
  e)  *Follow the wiring harness to each wheel and verify that all connections are secure and the wiring is undamaged.*

8    If the above preliminary checks do not rectify the problem, the vehicle should be diagnosed by a dealer service department or other qualified repair shop. Due to the complex nature of this system, all actual repair work must be done by a qualified automotive technician.

### 20  Anti-lock Brake System (ABS) components - removal and installation

### Accumulator/modulator/ hydraulic unit

1    Although it is possible for the home mechanic to remove the hydraulic unit, the

unit's self-diagnosis system must be tested and bled by BMW service test equipment. Removal and installation of the hydraulic unit should be entrusted to a BMW dealer or qualified brake shop.

### Electronic control module (ECM)

2    In order to remove the ECM, the hydraulic unit must first be removed, as the ECM is screwed to the side of the hydraulic unit. Removal and installation of the ECM should be entrusted to a BMW dealer or qualified brake shop.

### Front wheel speed sensor
#### Removal

*Refer to illustrations 20.3 and 20.4*

3    Block the rear wheels, then firmly apply the parking brake. Raise the front of the vehicle and support it securely on jackstands. Remove the appropriate front wheel. Trace the wiring back from the sensor to the connector, which is situated in a protective plastic box. Unclip the lid, then free the wiring connector and disconnect it from the main harness **(see illustration)**.

4    Loosen and remove the bolt securing the sensor to the hub carrier, then remove the sensor and lead assembly from the vehicle **(see illustration)**.

#### Installation

5    Apply a thin coat of multi-purpose grease to the sensor tip.

6    Ensure that the sensor and hub carrier sealing surfaces are clean, then install the sensor to the hub. Install the retaining bolt and tighten it to the specified torque.

7    Ensure that the sensor wiring is correctly routed and retained by all the necessary clips, then reconnect the sensor electrical connector. Install the sensor connector into the box and securely clip the lid in position.

8    Install the wheel, then lower the vehicle to the ground and tighten the wheel bolts to the specified torque.

**20.10 Fold back the inner fender liner, open the connector box, and disconnect the ABS sensor wiring plug**

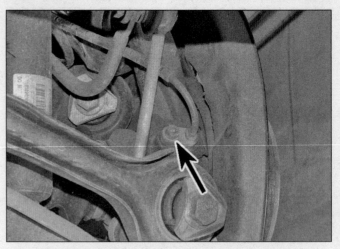

**20.11 Remove the mounting bolt and pull the sensor from the hub carrier**

## Rear wheel speed sensor

*Refer to illustrations 20.10 and 20.11*

9    Block the front wheels, then raise the rear of the vehicle and support it securely on jackstands. Remove the appropriate wheel.

10   Remove the sensor (see Steps 3 and 4). Note that the sensor wiring connector is located behind the inner wheel well liner. Remove the liner bolts and pull the rear section of the liner forwards to access the connector **(see illustration)**.

11   Install the sensor (see Steps 5 through 8) **(see illustration)**.

## Front reluctor rings

12   The front reluctor rings are fixed onto the rear of the wheel hubs. Examine the rings for damage such as chipped or missing teeth. If replacement is necessary, the complete hub assembly must be disassembled and the bearings replaced (see Chapter 10).

## Rear reluctor rings

13   The rear reluctor rings are pressed onto the driveshaft outer joints. Examine the rings for signs of damage such as chipped or missing teeth, and replace if necessary. If replacement is required, the driveaxle assembly must be replaced (see Chapter 8).

## 21 Vacuum pump - removal and installation

*Refer to illustrations 21.5 and 21.7*

**Note:** *Due to the Valvetronic system, very little vacuum is created in the intake manifold for the brake booster, creating the need for a vacuum pump. On 3.0L models, the vacuum pump is located on the left-hand face of the cylinder block, and is driven by a chain from the crankshaft sprocket. On 2.0L models, the vacuum pump is located at the rear of the valve cover, and is driven by the exhaust camshaft.*

## 3.0L models (E-series chassis)

1    Remove the drivebelt and drivebelt tensioner (see Chapter 1).

2    Remove the vacuum pump sealing cover. BMW specifies the use of several special tools (No 11 9 200, 11 4 362, 11 4 361 and 11 4 364) to remove and install the cover. However, it is possible to carefully pry the cover off using a screwdriver, and install a new cover without the use of special tools.

3    Remove the intake manifold (see Chapter 4).

4    Rotate the crankshaft pulley bolt clockwise until the three holes in the vacuum pump drive sprocket align with the pump mounting bolts.

5    Secure the pump sprocket in position prior to removing the retaining bolt. BMW specifies the use of tools No 11 4 362 and 11 0 290 **(see illustration)**.

6    Loosen the sprocket retaining bolt and the bolts securing the vacuum pump.

7    Use a screwdriver to push the drive chain tensioner to the right-hand side, and lock it in this position with a 4.0 mm rod or drill bit **(see illustration)**.

8    Fully unscrew the sprocket bolt and the pump mounting bolts, then pull out the pump. Replace the gasket between the pump and housing.

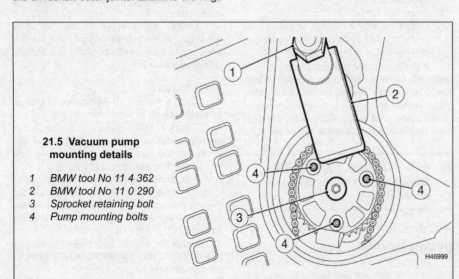

**21.5 Vacuum pump mounting details**

1   *BMW tool No 11 4 362*
2   *BMW tool No 11 0 290*
3   *Sprocket retaining bolt*
4   *Pump mounting bolts*

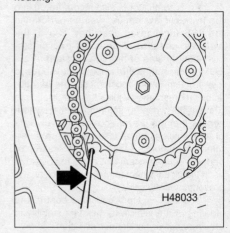

**21.7 Push the chain tensioner to the right-hand side and insert a 4.0 mm drill bit or rod**

9   Installation is the reverse of removal. Make sure the drive sprocket engages correctly with the pump shaft. Tighten the pump retaining bolts securely.

## 2.0L models (F-series chassis)

10   Turn the locks on the engine covers 90-degrees clockwise, then lift the covers up and off.

11   Remove the trailing link from the two strut towers by prying open the fastener covers the removing the bolts and link.

12   Remove the engine sound insulation cover plastic rivets and lift the insulation cover

off of the engine.

13   Disconnect both quick-connect ends of the vacuum line and remove the line.

14   Pull the positive battery cable out from the holder on the bottom of the vacuum pump.

15   Remove the turbocharger vacuum line screw at the pump and disconnect the line to the turbocharger control unit.

16   Remove the three mounting screws and pull the pump off of the cover.

17   If necessary, replace the vacuum pump O-ring.

18   Lubricate the O-ring on the pump, then

make sure the slot in the vacuum pump is aligned with the gear on the exhaust camshaft.

19   Slowly install the vacuum pump while rotating and pushing the pump into the exhaust camshaft gear.

**Note:** *Do not force the vacuum pump on to the gear, if the gear is not aligned properly the pump will not fully seat against the valve cover.*

20   Install the vacuum pump screws and tighten them securely.

21   The remainder of installation is the reverse of removal.

---

## 22   Troubleshooting

| PROBABLE CAUSE | CORRECTIVE ACTION |
|---|---|

### No brakes - pedal travels to floor

| PROBABLE CAUSE | CORRECTIVE ACTION |
|---|---|
| 1  Low fluid level<br>2  Air in system | 1 and 2  Low fluid level and air in the system are symptoms of another problem - a leak somewhere in the hydraulic system. Locate and repair the leak |
| 3  Defective seals in master cylinder | 3  Replace master cylinder |
| 4  Fluid overheated and vaporized due to heavy braking | 4  Bleed hydraulic system (temporary fix). Replace brake fluid (proper fix) |

### Brake pedal slowly travels to floor under braking or at a stop

| PROBABLE CAUSE | CORRECTIVE ACTION |
|---|---|
| 1  Defective seals in master cylinder | 1  Replace master cylinder |
| 2  Leak in a hose, line, caliper or wheel cylinder | 2  Locate and repair leak |
| 3  Air in hydraulic system | 3  Bleed the system, inspect system for a leak |

### Brake pedal feels spongy when depressed

| PROBABLE CAUSE | CORRECTIVE ACTION |
|---|---|
| 1  Air in hydraulic system | 1  Bleed the system, inspect system for a leak |
| 2  Master cylinder or power booster loose | 2  Tighten fasteners |
| 3  Brake fluid overheated (beginning to boil) | 3  Bleed the system (temporary fix). Replace the brake fluid (proper fix) |
| 4  Deteriorated brake hoses (ballooning under pressure) | 4  Inspect hoses, replace as necessary (it's a good idea to replace all of them if one hose shows signs of deterioration) |

### Brake pedal feels hard when depressed and/or excessive effort required to stop vehicle

| PROBABLE CAUSE | CORRECTIVE ACTION |
|---|---|
| 1  Power booster faulty | 1  Replace booster |
| 2  Engine not producing sufficient vacuum, or hose to booster clogged, collapsed or cracked | 2  Check vacuum to booster with a vacuum gauge. Replace hose if cracked or clogged, repair engine if vacuum is extremely low |
| 3  Brake linings contaminated by grease or brake fluid | 3  Locate and repair source of contamination, replace brake pads or shoes |
| 4  Brake linings glazed | 4  Replace brake pads or shoes, check discs and drums for glazing, service as necessary |
| 5  Caliper piston(s) or wheel cylinder(s) binding or frozen | 5  Replace calipers or wheel cylinders |
| 6  Brakes wet | 6  Apply pedal to boil-off water (this should only be a momentary problem) |
| 7  Kinked, clogged or internally split brake hose or line | 7  Inspect lines and hoses, replace as necessary |

**Troubleshooting (continued)**
**PROBABLE CAUSE**                                          **CORRECTIVE ACTION**

### Excessive brake pedal travel (but will pump up)

| | |
|---|---|
| 1  Drum brakes out of adjustment | 1  Adjust brakes |
| 2  Air in hydraulic system | 2  Bleed system, inspect system for a leak |

### Excessive brake pedal travel (but will not pump up)

| | |
|---|---|
| 1  Master cylinder pushrod misadjusted | 1  Adjust pushrod |
| 2  Master cylinder seals defective | 2  Replace master cylinder |
| 3  Brake linings worn out | 3  Inspect brakes, replace pads and/or shoes |
| 4  Hydraulic system leak | 4  Locate and repair leak |

### Brake pedal doesn't return

| | |
|---|---|
| 1  Brake pedal binding | 1  Inspect pivot bushing and pushrod, repair or lubricate |
| 2  Defective master cylinder | 2  Replace master cylinder |

### Brake pedal pulsates during brake application

| | |
|---|---|
| 1  Brake drums out-of-round | 1  Have drums machined by an automotive machine shop |
| 2  Excessive brake disc runout or disc surfaces out-of-parallel | 2  Have discs machined by an automotive machine shop |
| 3  Loose or worn wheel bearings | 3  Adjust or replace wheel bearings |
| 4  Loose lug nuts | 4  Tighten lug nuts |

### Brakes slow to release

| | |
|---|---|
| 1  Malfunctioning power booster | 1  Replace booster |
| 2  Pedal linkage binding | 2  Inspect pedal pivot bushing and pushrod, repair/lubricate |
| 3  Malfunctioning proportioning valve | 3  Replace proportioning valve |
| 4  Sticking caliper or wheel cylinder | 4  Repair or replace calipers or wheel cylinders |
| 5  Kinked or internally split brake hose | 5  Locate and replace faulty brake hose |

### Brakes grab (one or more wheels)

| | |
|---|---|
| 1  Grease or brake fluid on brake lining | 1  Locate and repair cause of contamination, replace lining |
| 2  Brake lining glazed | 2  Replace lining, deglaze disc or drum |

### Vehicle pulls to one side during braking

| | |
|---|---|
| 1  Grease or brake fluid on brake lining | 1  Locate and repair cause of contamination, replace lining |
| 2  Brake lining glazed | 2  Deglaze or replace lining, deglaze disc or drum |
| 3  Restricted brake line or hose | 3  Repair line or replace hose |
| 4  Tire pressures incorrect | 4  Adjust tire pressures |
| 5  Caliper or wheel cylinder sticking | 5  Repair or replace calipers or wheel cylinders |
| 6  Wheels out of alignment | 6  Have wheels aligned |
| 7  Weak suspension spring | 7  Replace springs |
| 8  Weak or broken shock absorber | 8  Replace shock absorbers |

**Troubleshooting (continued)**

**PROBABLE CAUSE**

**CORRECTIVE ACTION**

## Brakes drag (indicated by sluggish engine performance or wheels being very hot after driving)

| PROBABLE CAUSE | CORRECTIVE ACTION |
|---|---|
| 1  Brake pedal pushrod incorrectly adjusted | 1  Adjust pushrod |
| 2  Master cylinder pushrod (between booster and master cylinder) incorrectly adjusted | 2  Adjust pushrod |
| 3  Obstructed compensating port in master cylinder | 3  Replace master cylinder |
| 4  Master cylinder piston seized in bore | 4  Replace master cylinder |
| 5  Contaminated fluid causing swollen seals throughout system | 5  Flush system, replace all hydraulic components |
| 6  Clogged brake lines or internally split brake hose(s) | 6  Flush hydraulic system, replace defective hose(s) |
| 7  Sticking caliper(s) or wheel cylinder(s) | 7  Replace calipers or wheel cylinders |
| 8  Parking brake not releasing | 8  Inspect parking brake linkage and parking brake mechanism, repair as required |
| 9  Improper shoe-to-drum clearance | 9  Adjust brake shoes |
| 10  Faulty proportioning valve | 10  Replace proportioning valve |

## Brakes fade (due to excessive heat)

| PROBABLE CAUSE | CORRECTIVE ACTION |
|---|---|
| 1  Brake linings excessively worn or glazed | 1  Deglaze or replace brake pads and/or shoes |
| 2  Excessive use of brakes | 2  Downshift into a lower gear, maintain a constant slower speed (going down hills) |
| 3  Vehicle overloaded | 3  Reduce load |
| 4  Brake drums or discs worn too thin | 4  Measure drum diameter and disc thickness, replace drums or discs as required |
| 5  Contaminated brake fluid | 5  Flush system, replace fluid |
| 6  Brakes drag | 6  Repair cause of dragging brakes |
| 7  Driver resting left foot on brake pedal | 7  Don't ride the brakes |

## Brakes noisy (high-pitched squeal)

| PROBABLE CAUSE | CORRECTIVE ACTION |
|---|---|
| 1  Glazed lining | 1  Deglaze or replace lining |
| 2  Contaminated lining (brake fluid, grease, etc.) | 2  Repair source of contamination, replace linings |
| 3  Weak or broken brake shoe hold-down or return spring | 3  Replace springs |
| 4  Rivets securing lining to shoe or backing plate loose | 4  Replace shoes or pads |
| 5  Excessive dust buildup on brake linings | 5  Wash brakes off with brake system cleaner |
| 6  Brake drums worn too thin | 6  Measure diameter of drums, replace if necessary |
| 7  Wear indicator on disc brake pads contacting disc | 7  Replace brake pads |
| 8  Anti-squeal shims missing or installed improperly | 8  Install shims correctly |

**Note:** *Other remedies for quieting squealing brakes include the application of an anti-squeal compound to the backing plates of the brake pads, and lightly chamfering the edges of the brake pads with a file. The latter method should only be performed with the brake pads thoroughly wetted with brake system cleaner, so as not to allow any brake dust to become airborne.*

## Brakes noisy (scraping sound)

| PROBABLE CAUSE | CORRECTIVE ACTION |
|---|---|
| 1  Brake pads or shoes worn out; rivets, backing plate or brake shoe metal contacting disc or drum | 1  Replace linings, have discs and/or drums machined (or replace) |

**Troubleshooting (continued)**

| PROBABLE CAUSE | CORRECTIVE ACTION |
|---|---|

### Brakes chatter

| PROBABLE CAUSE | CORRECTIVE ACTION |
|---|---|
| 1  Worn brake lining | 1  Inspect brakes, replace shoes or pads as necessary |
| 2  Glazed or scored discs or drums | 2  Deglaze discs or drums with sandpaper (if glazing is severe, machining will be required) |
| 3  Drums or discs heat checked | 3  Check discs and/or drums for hard spots, heat checking, etc. Have discs/drums machined or replace them |
| 4  Disc runout or drum out-of-round excessive | 4  Measure disc runout and/or drum out-of-round, have discs or drums machined or replace them |
| 5  Loose or worn wheel bearings | 5  Adjust or replace wheel bearings |
| 6  Loose or bent brake backing plate (drum brakes) | 6  Tighten or replace backing plate |
| 7  Grooves worn in discs or drums | 7  Have discs or drums machined, if within limits (if not, replace them) |
| 8  Brake linings contaminated (brake fluid, grease, etc.) | 8  Locate and repair source of contamination, replace pads or shoes |
| 9  Excessive dust buildup on linings | 9  Wash brakes with brake system cleaner |
| 10  Surface finish on discs or drums too rough after machining (especially on vehicles with sliding calipers) | 10  Have discs or drums properly machined |
| 11  Brake pads or shoes glazed | 11  Deglaze or replace brake pads or shoes |

### Brake pads or shoes click

| PROBABLE CAUSE | CORRECTIVE ACTION |
|---|---|
| 1  Shoe support pads on brake backing plate grooved or excessively worn | 1  Replace brake backing plate |
| 2  Brake pads loose in caliper | 2  Loose pad retainers or anti-rattle clips |
| 3  Also see items listed under Brakes chatter | |

### Brakes make groaning noise at end of stop

| PROBABLE CAUSE | CORRECTIVE ACTION |
|---|---|
| 1  Brake pads and/or shoes worn out | 1  Replace pads and/or shoes |
| 2  Brake linings contaminated (brake fluid, grease, etc.) | 2  Locate and repair cause of contamination, replace brake pads or shoes |
| 3  Brake linings glazed | 3  Deglaze or replace brake pads or shoes |
| 4  Excessive dust buildup on linings | 4  Wash brakes with brake system cleaner |
| 5  Scored or heat-checked discs or drums | 5  Inspect discs/drums, have machined if within limits (if not, replace discs or drums) |
| 6  Broken or missing brake shoe attaching hardware | 6  Inspect drum brakes, replace missing hardware |

### Rear brakes lock up under light brake application

| PROBABLE CAUSE | CORRECTIVE ACTION |
|---|---|
| 1  Tire pressures too high | 1  Adjust tire pressures |
| 2  Tires excessively worn | 2  Replace tires |
| 3  Defective proportioning valve | 3  Replace proportioning valve |

### Brake warning light on instrument panel comes on (or stays on)

| PROBABLE CAUSE | CORRECTIVE ACTION |
|---|---|
| 1  Low fluid level in master cylinder reservoir (reservoirs with fluid level sensor) | 1  Add fluid, inspect system for leak, check the thickness of the brake pads and shoes |
| 2  Failure in one half of the hydraulic system | 2  Inspect hydraulic system for a leak |
| 3  Piston in pressure differential warning valve not centered | 3  Center piston by bleeding one circuit or the other (close bleeder valve as soon as the light goes out) |
| 4  Defective pressure differential valve or warning switch | 4  Replace valve or switch |
| 5  Air in the hydraulic system | 5  Bleed the system, check for leaks |
| 6  Brake pads worn out (vehicles with electric wear sensors - small probes that fit into the brake pads and ground out on the disc when the pads get thin) | 6  Replace brake pads (and sensors) |

**Troubleshooting (continued)**

| PROBABLE CAUSE | CORRECTIVE ACTION |
|---|---|

## *Brakes do not self adjust*

### Disc brakes

| | |
|---|---|
| 1  Defective caliper piston seals | 1  Replace calipers. Also, possible contaminated fluid causing soft or swollen seals (flush system and fill with new fluid if in doubt) |
| 2  Corroded caliper piston(s) | 2  Same as above |

### Drum brakes

| | |
|---|---|
| 1  Adjuster screw frozen | 1  Remove adjuster, disassemble, clean and lubricate with high-temperature grease |
| 2  Adjuster lever does not contact star wheel or is binding | 2  Inspect drum brakes, assemble correctly or clean or replace parts as required |
| 3  Adjusters mixed up (installed on wrong wheels after brake job) | 3  Reassemble correctly |
| 4  Adjuster cable broken or installed incorrectly (cable-type adjusters) | 4  Install new cable or assemble correctly |

## *Rapid brake lining wear*

| | |
|---|---|
| 1  Driver resting left foot on brake pedal | 1  Don't ride the brakes |
| 2  Surface finish on discs or drums too rough | 2  Have discs or drums properly machined |
| 3  Also see Brakes drag | |

# Notes

# Chapter 10
# Suspension and steering systems

## Contents

## Specifications

### Front suspension

Type........................................................................................... Independent, with MacPherson struts incorporating coil springs and telescopic shock absorbers. Stabilizer bar installed on all models

### Rear suspension

Type........................................................................................... Independent, trailing arms located by upper and lower control arms with coil springs and shock absorbers. Stabilizer bar installed on all models

### Steering

Type........................................................................................... Rack and pinion. Power assistance standard on all models

## Torque specifications

**Ft-lbs** (unless otherwise indicated) **Nm**

**Note:** *One foot-pound (ft-lb) of torque is equivalent to 12 inch-pounds (in-lbs) of torque. Torque values below approximately 15 ft-lbs are expressed in inch-pounds, since most foot-pound torque wrenches are not accurate at these smaller values.*

**Note:** *On some fasteners, different grades of bolt are used; the grade of each bolt is stamped on the bolt head. Ensure that each bolt is tightened to the correct torque for its grade.*

### Front suspension

| | Ft-lbs | Nm |
|---|---|---|
| Stabilizer bar connecting link nuts* | 43 | 58 |
| Stabilizer bar mounting clamp nuts* | 20.5 | 28 |
| Control arm balljoint nut* | 122 | 165 |
| Control arm-to-subframe nut* | | |
|   M12 | | |
|     8.8 | | |
|       Step 1 | 50 | 68 |
|       Step 2 | Tighten an additional 90-degrees | |
|     12.9 | | |
|       Step 1 | 74 | 100 |
|       Step 2 | Tighten an additional 90-degrees | |

### Front suspension

| | Ft-lbs | Nm |
|---|---|---|
| DSC sensor bolts | 72 in-lbs | 8 |
| Hub/bearing assembly bolts* | | |
|   E90, E91, E92 and E93 chassis | 81 | 110 |
|   F30, F31 and F34 chassis | | |
|     Step 1 | 59 | 80 |
|     Step 2 | Tighten an additional 90-degrees | |
| Strut piston rod nut* | 47 | 64 |
| Strut-to-hub carrier nut* | | |
|   E90, E91, E92 and E93 chassis | | |
|     M8 | 33 | 45 |
|     M10 | 60 | 81 |
|   F30, F31 and F34 chassis | | |
|     Step 1 | 32 | 44 |
|     Step 2 | Tighten an additional 90-degrees | |
| Strut-to-body nuts* | | |
|   E90, E91, E92 and E93 chassis | 25 | 34 |
|   F30, F31 and F34 chassis | | |
|     M8 | | |
|       Step 1 | 20.5 | 28 |
|       Step 2 | Tighten an additional 90-degrees | |
|     M10 | | |
|       Step 1 | 41 | 56 |
|       Step 2 | Tighten an additional 90-degrees | |
| Tension strut balljoint nut* | | |
|   E90, E91, E92 and E93 chassis | 122 | 165 |
|   F30, F31 and F34 chassis | 129 | 175 |
| Tension strut balljoint nut* | 122 | 165 |
| Tension strut-to-subframe nut* | | |
|   M12 | | |
|     8.8 | | |
|       Step 1 | 50 | 68 |
|       Step 2 | Tighten an additional 90-degrees | |
|     10.9 | | |
|       Step 1 | 74 | 100 |
|       Step 2 | Tighten an additional 90-degrees | |

## Torque specifications (continued)

**Ft-lbs** (unless otherwise indicated) **Nm**

**Note:** *One foot-pound (ft-lb) of torque is equivalent to 12 inch-pounds (in-lbs) of torque. Torque values below approximately 15 ft-lbs are expressed in inch-pounds, since most foot-pound torque wrenches are not accurate at these smaller values.*

**Note:** *On some fasteners, different grades of bolt are used; the grade of each bolt is stamped on the bolt head. Ensure that each bolt is tightened to the correct torque for its grade.*

### Rear suspension

| | Ft-lbs | Nm |
|---|---|---|
| Stabilizer bar link nuts* | | |
|     E90, E91, E92 and E93 chassis | 15 | 21 |
|     F30, F31 and F34 chassis | 20.5 | 28 |
| Stabilizer bar link | | |
|     E90, E91, E92 and E93 chassis | | |
|         Bolt | 15 | 21 |
|         Nut* | 43 | 58 |
|     F30, F31 and F34 chassis | | |
|         Bolt | 20.5 | 28 |
|         Nut* | 41 | 56 |
| Camber arm-to-hub carrier nut* | 122 | 165 |
| Camber arm-to subframe nut* | 122 | 165 |
| Control arm-to-hub carrier bolt* | | |
|     Step 1 | 74 | 100 |
|     Step 2 | Tighten an additional 90-degrees | |
| Control arm-to-subframe nut* | 74 | 100 |
| Shock absorber | | |
|     E90, E91, E92 and E93 chassis | | |
|         Upper mounting nut* | | |
|             M10 | 20 | 27 |
|             M14 | 27 | 37 |
|         Lower mounting bolt* | | |
|             M10 | 44 | 60 |
|             M12 | 74 | 100 |
|         Lower mounting nut* | 27 | 37 |
|     F30, F31 and F34 chassis | | |
|         Upper mounting bolts | 20.5 | 28 |
|         Lower mounting bolt/nut* | | |
|             Step 1 | 74 | 100 |
|             M12 | Tighten an additional 90-degrees | |
| Subframe | 80 | 108 |
| Toe arm-to-hub carrier | 74 | 100 |
| Toe arm-to-subframe nut* | 74 | 100 |
| Traction strut-to-hub carrier bolt:* | | |
|     Step 1 | 74 | 100 |
|     Step 2 | Tighten an additional 90-degrees | |
| Traction strut-to-subframe nut* | 74 | 100 |
| Trailing arm-to-hub carrier nut* | 74 | 100 |
| Trailing arm-to-subframe nut* | 74 | 100 |

### Steering

| | Ft-lbs | Nm |
|---|---|---|
| Lateral acceleration sensor | 72 in-lbs | 8 |
| Power steering pipe union bolts | | |
|     M10 union bolt | 108 in-lbs | 12 |
|     M14 union bolt | 26 | 35 |
|     M16 union bolt | 30 | 40 |
|     M18 union bolt | 33 | 45 |
| Power steering pump bolts | | |
|     Step 1 | 15 | 20 |
|     Step 2 | Tighten an additional 90-degrees | |
| Steering column bolts/nuts | 16 | 22 |
| Steering column universal joint clamp/pinch-bolt* | 16 | 22 |
| Steering gear mounting bolts/nuts* | | |
|     E90, E91, E92 and E93 chassis | | |
|         Step 1 | 41 | 56 |
|         Step 2 | Tighten an additional 90-degrees | |
|     F30, F31 and F34 chassis | 41 | 56 |

* Do not re-use

## Torque specifications

**Ft-lbs** (unless otherwise indicated) **Nm**

**Note:** *One foot-pound (ft-lb) of torque is equivalent to 12 inch-pounds (in-lbs) of torque. Torque values below approximately 15 ft-lbs are expressed in inch-pounds, since most foot-pound torque wrenches are not accurate at these smaller values.*

**Note:** *On some fasteners, different grades of bolt are used; the grade of each bolt is stamped on the bolt head. Ensure that each bolt is tightened to the correct torque for its grade.*

| | Ft-lbs | Nm |
|---|---|---|
| Steering wheel | 46 | 63 |
| Track rod end balljoint retaining nut* | | |
|    E90, E91, E92 and E93 chassis | 122 | 165 |
|    F30, F31 and F34 chassis | 129 | 175 |
| Track rod end clamp bolt* | | |
|    E90, E91, E92 and E93 chassis | 30 | 40 |
|    F30, F31 and F34 chassis | 23.5 | 32 |
| Track rod to steering gear | | |
|    E90, E91, E92 and E93 chassis | 81 | 110 |
|    F30, F31 and F34 chassis | 77 | 105 |

## Wheels

| | |
|---|---|
| Wheel bolts | See Chapter 1 |

* *Do not re-use*

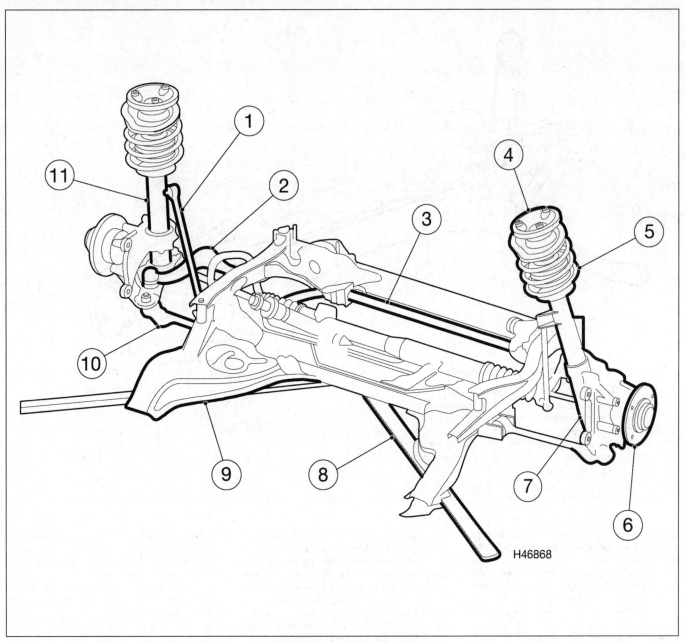

**1.1  Front suspension details**

| | | | | | | |
|---|---|---|---|---|---|---|
| 1 | Stabilizer bar link | 5 | Coil spring | 9 | Front subframe |
| 2 | Tension strut | 6 | Wheel bearing | 10 | Control arm |
| 3 | Front stabilizer bar | 7 | Hub carrier | 11 | Shock absorber strut |
| 4 | Strut top mounting | 8 | Reinforcement strut/brace | | |

## 1  General information

*Refer to illustrations 1.1 and 1.2*

The independent front suspension is of the MacPherson strut type, incorporating coil springs and integral telescopic shock absorbers. The MacPherson struts are located by transverse lower suspension arms, which use rubber inner mount bushings, and incorporate a balljoint at the outer ends. The front hub carriers, which carry the brake calipers and the hub/disc assemblies, are bolted to the MacPherson struts and connected to the lower arms through balljoints. A front stabilizer bar is installed on all models. The stabilizer bar is rubber-mounted and is connected to both suspension struts/lower arms (as applicable) by connecting links **(see illustration)**.

The rear suspension is of the fully independent type consisting of trailing arms, which are linked to the rear axle carrier by various control arms/struts. Coil springs are installed between the upper control arms and vehicle body, and shock absorbers are connected to the vehicle body and trailing arms. A rear stabilizer bar is installed on all models. The stabi-

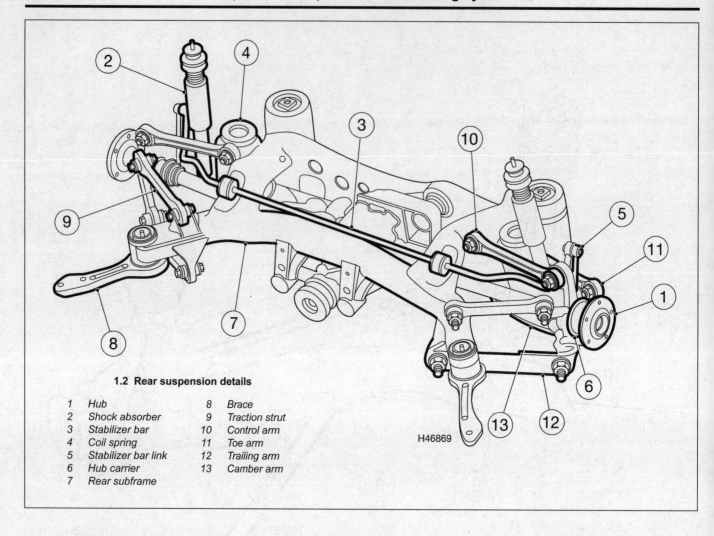

**1.2  Rear suspension details**

| | | | |
|---|---|---|---|
| 1 | Hub | 8 | Brace |
| 2 | Shock absorber | 9 | Traction strut |
| 3 | Stabilizer bar | 10 | Control arm |
| 4 | Coil spring | 11 | Toe arm |
| 5 | Stabilizer bar link | 12 | Trailing arm |
| 6 | Hub carrier | 13 | Camber arm |
| 7 | Rear subframe | | |

H46869

lizer bar is rubber-mounted, and is connected to the upper control arms by connecting links **(see illustration)**.

The steering column is connected to the steering gear by an intermediate shaft, which incorporates a universal joint.

The steering gear is mounted onto the front subframe, and is connected by two tie-rods to the steering arms projecting forwards

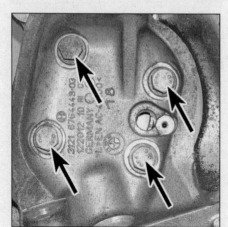

**2.2  Front hub retaining bolts**

from the hub carriers. The tie-rod ends are threaded, to facilitate adjustment.

Power-assisted steering is standard equipment on all models. The hydraulic steering system is powered by a belt-driven pump, which is driven off the crankshaft pulley. On some models, a fully-electronic system is available, which has a rack-mounted electric motor to provide the power assistance.
**Note:** *The information contained in this Chapter is applicable to the standard suspension set-up. On models with M-Technic sports suspension, slight differences will be found. Refer to your BMW dealer for details.*

## 2  Front hub assembly - removal and installation

### Removal
*Refer to illustration 2.2*

1    Remove the front brake disc (see Chapter 9). If you're working on an all-wheel drive model, unstake and remove the driveaxle hub nut (see Chapter 8).
2    Remove the four retaining bolts and the

hub-and-bearing assembly **(see illustration)**. If you're working on an all-wheel drive model, draw the hub-and-bearing assembly off of the end of the driveaxle with a puller. Discard the bolts; new ones must be installed. **Note:** *The hub and bearing are only available as a complete assembly.*

### Installation
3    Ensure the mating surfaces of the hub and hub carrier are clean, then position the hub on the carrier.
4    Install the new retaining bolts and tighten them to the specified torque.
5    Reinstall the brake disc (see Chapter 9).
6    If you're working on an all-wheel drive model, install the driveaxle hub nut (see Chapter 8 for installation details and the proper torque setting).

## 3  Front hub carrier - removal and installation

**Note:** *New suspension strut-to-hub, tension strut balljoint and control arm balljoint nuts will be required on installation.*

**3.1  Remove the bolts and the engine under-shield**

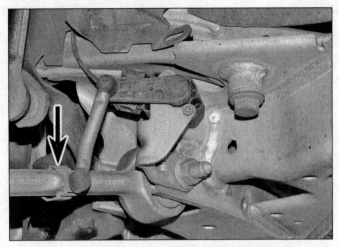

**3.4  Release the clamp and detach the sensor rod**

## Removal

*Refer to illustrations 3.1, 3.4, 3.5, 3.8a and 3.8b*

1  Firmly apply the parking brake, then raise the front of the vehicle and support it securely on jackstands. Remove the relevant front wheel, then remove the fasteners and remove the engine under-shield **(see illustration)**.

2  Remove the hub assembly (see Section 2).

3  Remove the ABS wheel speed sensor (see Chapter 9).

4  On models with Xenon headlights, release the clamp and detach the ride height sensor rod from the control arm **(see illustration)**.

5  Loosen the bolt securing the control arm to the front subframe **(see illustration)**. This will prevent damage to the mount bushings as the hub carrier is removed.

6  Detach the control arm and tension strut from the hub carrier (see Section 5).

7  Remove the nut and detach the tie-rod end from the hub carrier (see Section 25).

8  Loosen and remove the bolt securing the suspension strut to the hub carrier. **Note:** *The bolt is inserted from the front.* Slide the hub

carrier down and off from the end of the strut. Discard the nut; a new one must be installed. To ease removal, insert a large screwdriver or Allen key into the slot on the back of the hub carrier and slightly spread the hub carrier clamp **(see illustrations)**. Take care to spread the carrier clamp only as much as absolutely necessary, as excessive force will cause damage.

9  Examine the hub carrier for signs of wear or damage, and replace if necessary.

## Installation

*Refer to illustration 3.11*

10  Clean the threads of the strut-to-hub carrier bolt hole by running a tap of the correct thread size and pitch down it.

11  Position the hub carrier correctly with the suspension strut, ensuring that the locating pins on the strut slide into the slot in the hub carrier clamp **(see illustration)**. Slide the hub carrier up until it contacts the stop on the strut. Install the bolt from the front and tighten the new nut to the specified torque.

12  Engage the hub carrier with the control-arm balljoint stud, and install the new retaining

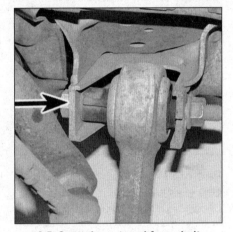

**3.5  Control arm-to-subframe bolt**

nut. Tighten the nut to the specified torque.

13  Engage the tension strut balljoint with the hub carrier. Install the new nut and tighten it to the specified torque.

14  Engage the tie-rod balljoint in the hub carrier. Install a new retaining nut and tighten it to the specified torque.

**3.8a  The hub carrier bolt is inserted from the front**

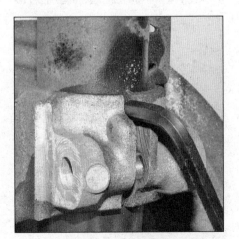

**3.8b  Use an Allen key to slightly spread the hub carrier clamp**

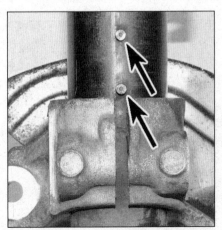

**3.11  Ensure the locating pins slide into the slot**

**4.8  Counterhold the balljoint, and remove
the stabilizer bar link nut**

**4.10  Remove the cap from the center of
the cowl trim panel**

**4.12  Remove the bolts at the end
of the braces**

15   Install the new hub assembly (see Section 2) where applicable.
16   On models where the hub was not disturbed, install the ABS wheel speed sensor and disc (see Chapter 9).
17   Install the wheel and the under-shield, then lower the vehicle to the ground and tighten the wheel bolts to the specified torque.

## 4   Front strut - removal, overhaul and installation

### *Removal*

*Refer to illustration 4.8*

1   Block the rear wheels, apply the parking brake, then raise the front of the vehicle and support it securely on jackstands. Remove the appropriate wheel. Remove the fasteners and remove the engine under-shield.
2   Remove the brake disc (see Chapter 9).
3   Trace the wiring back to the connectors, and disconnect the ABS wheel speed sensor and the brake pad wear sensor. Unclip the wiring from any retaining clips.
4   Release the clamp and detach the ride height sensor rod from the control arm (see

illustration 3.4), if equipped.
5   Loosen the bolt/nut securing the control arm to the front subframe **(see illustration 3.5)**. This will prevent damage to the mount bushings as the hub carrier is removed.
6   Detach the control arm and tension strut from the hub carrier (see Section 5).
7   Undo the nut and detach the tie-rod end from the hub carrier (see Section 25).
8   Counterhold using the flats on the balljoint shank, then remove the nut securing the stabilizer bar link to the strut **(see illustration)**. Discard the nut; a new one must be installed. **Note:** *The brake hose bracket is also retained by the nut.*
9   Place a floor jack under the hub carrier to prevent it falling as the upper mounting nuts are removed.

### Models with strut tower braces

*Refer to illustrations 4.10 and 4.12*

10   Remove the plastic cap from the center of the cowl trim panel. Two different types of the cap are used: one with a central slot, removed by rotating it 45-degrees counter-clockwise, and one without a central slot, which is pried out **(see illustration)**. **Note:** *If the cap or seal are damaged, they must be*

replaced. Failure to do so may result in water leaks.
11   Remove the bolt in the center of the cowl, exposed by the cap removal. Discard the bolt; a new one must be installed.
12   Remove the bolt at each outer end of the braces, then hold the rubber grommet in place and slide the braces outwards **(see illustration)**. Do not allow the grommet to be displaced. Discard the bolts; new ones must be installed.

### All models

*Refer to illustrations 4.13a, 4.13b and 4.13c*

13   From within the engine compartment, unscrew the strut upper mounting nuts, then carefully lower the strut assembly out from underneath the fender. **Note:** *On some models, a centering pin fixed to the strut upper mounting plate aligns with a corresponding hole in the body* **(see illustration)**. *On models where no centering pin is installed, make alignment marks between the mounting plate and vehicle body. It is essential that the mounting plate is installed in its original location to preserve the strut camber angle. Remove the sealing washer and mounting shim from between the strut and the fender* **(see illustrations)**.

**4.13a  Centering pin location**

**4.13b  Remove the sealing washer . . .**

**4.13c  . . . and mounting shim**

**4.16  Compress the spring until the upper seat is no longer under tension**

**4.17a  Pry off the cap**

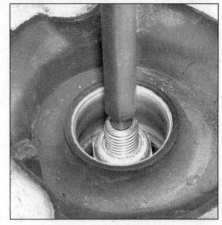

**4.17b  Use an Allen bit to prevent the piston rod rotating . . .**

## Overhaul

*Refer to illustrations 4.16, 4.17a, 4.17b, 4.17c, 4.24a, 4.24b, 4.25, 4.26a, 4.26b, 4.26c and 4.26d*

**Warning:** *Before attempting to disassemble the front suspension strut, a suitable tool to hold the coil spring in compression must be obtained. Adjustable coil spring compressors are readily available, and are recommended for this operation. Any attempt to disassemble the strut without such a tool is likely to result in damage or personal injury.*

14   With the strut removed from the vehicle, clean away all external dirt, then mount it upright in a vise.

15   Loosen and remove the bolt securing the suspension strut to the hub carrier. Remove the ABS sensor wiring bracket, then slide the hub carrier down and off from the end of the strut. Discard the nut; a new one must be installed. To ease removal, insert a suitably-sized Allen key into the slot on the back of the hub carrier and slightly spread the hub carrier clamp **(see illustrations 3.8a and 3.8b)**. Take care to spread the carrier clamp only as much as absolutely necessary, as excessive force will cause damage.

16   Install the spring compressor, and compress the coil spring until all tension is relieved from the upper spring seat **(see illustration)**.

17   Remove the cap from the top of the strut to gain access to the strut upper mount retaining nut. Loosen the nut while retaining the strut piston with a suitable Allen bit **(see illustrations)**.

18   Remove the mounting nut, and lift off the mounting plate, thrust bearing, shim, washer and supporting ring/seat as an assembly.

19   Lift off the coil spring, followed by the bump stop, boot and lower spring seat.

20   With the strut assembly now completely disassembled, examine all the components for wear, damage or deformation, and check the upper mounting bearing for smoothness of operation. Replace any of the components as necessary.

21   Examine the strut for signs of fluid leakage. Check the strut piston for signs of pitting along its entire length, and check the strut body for signs of damage.

22   If any doubt exists about the condition of the coil spring, carefully remove the spring compressors and check the spring for distortion and signs of cracking. Replace the spring if it is damaged or distorted, or if there is any

**4.17c  . . . then remove the nut using a socket and a box-end wrench**

doubt as to its condition.

23   Inspect all other components for damage or deterioration, and replace any that are suspect.

24   Install the lower spring seat, and slide the bump stop and boot onto the strut piston **(see illustrations)**.

**4.24a  Install the lower spring seat . . .**

**4.24b  . . . followed by the boot and bump stop**

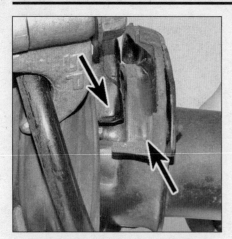

**4.25 Ensure the spring end and seat are correctly positioned**

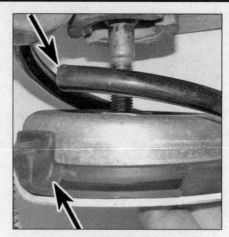

**4.26a Install the support ring/seat, aligning the spring end with the seat**

**4.26b Install the shim . . .**

25   Install the coil spring onto the strut, making sure the rubber seat and spring are correctly positioned **(see illustration)**.
26   Install the support ring/seat, shim, washer and upper mounting plate, so that the spring end is against the seat stop **(see illustrations)**.
27   Install the new mounting plate nut and tighten it to the specified torque.
28   Ensure the spring ends and seats are correctly positioned, then carefully release the compressor and remove it from the strut. Reinstall the cap to the top of the strut.

## Installation

29   Installation is the reverse of removal, noting the following points:

a)  *Tighten all fasteners to their specified torque where given.*
b)  *Replace all self-locking nuts.*
c)  *We recommend the front wheel alignment is checked at the earliest opportunity. On models with active steering, have the steering angle sensor calibration checked using BMW diagnostic*

equipment. Entrust this task to a dealer or qualified suspension shop.

---

## 5   Front suspension arms - removal, overhaul and installation

**Note:** *New control arm front balljoint nuts will be required on installation.*

## *Removal*

1   Block the rear wheels, firmly apply the parking brake, then raise the front of the vehicle and support it securely on jackstands. Remove the appropriate front wheel. Remove the fasteners and remove the engine undershield **(see illustration 3.1)**.

### Control arm

*Refer to illustrations 5.3a and 5.3b*
2   On models equipped with suspension ride-height sensors, release the clamp and disconnect the sensor link bracket from the arm.

3   Unscrew the control arm balljoint nut to the point where the edge of the nut is flush with the end of the balljoint shank, then release the arm from the hub carrier by gently tapping the end of the balljoint shank with a soft-faced hammer **(see illustrations)**. There is no need to use a balljoint separator.
4   Remove the nut and pull the inner mounting bolt from the control arm **(see illustration 3.5)**. **Note:** *The bolt is inserted from the rear.* Discard the nut; a new one must be installed.
5   Remove the lower arm assembly from underneath the vehicle. **Note:** *The balljoint may be a tight fit in the crossmember and may need to be tapped to release it.*

### Tension strut

*Refer to illustrations 5.6 and 5.7*
6   Remove the tension strut balljoint nut. If necessary, use a Torx bit in the end of the balljoint shank to counter-hold the nut, then release the arm from the hub carrier by gently tapping the end of the balljoint shank with a soft-faced hammer **(see illustration)**. There is no need to use a balljoint separator.

**4.26c . . . washer . . .**

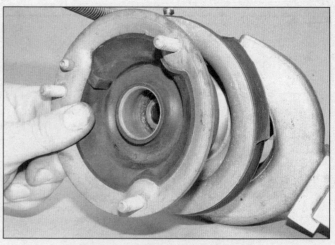

**4.26d . . . and upper mounting plate**

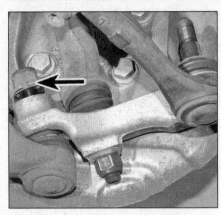

**5.3a  Remove the control arm balljoint nut . . .**

**5.3b  . . . and tap the balljoint from the hub carrier**

**5.6  Use a Torx bit to counter-hold the tension-strut balljoint shank while removing the nut**

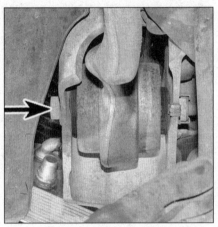

**5.7  Tension strut-to-subframe bolt**

**7.2  Use a second wrench to counterhold the stabilizer bar balljoint stud**

7    Remove the inner mounting bolt and remove the strut from the subframe **(see illustration)**. Discard the nut; a new one must be installed.

## Overhaul

8    Thoroughly clean the arm or strut and the area around the mounts, removing all traces of dirt and undercoating if necessary, then check carefully for cracks, distortion or any other signs of wear or damage, paying particular attention to the mount bushings and balljoint. **Note:** *The balljoints are integral with both the arm and the strut. If the tension strut bushing requires replacement, the strut should be taken to a dealer or qualified shop. A hydraulic press and suitable spacers are required to press the bushing out of position and install the new one.*

## Installation

### Control arm

9    Locate the inner end of the control arm with the subframe, insert the bolt from the rear, then install the new nut - do not tighten the nut yet. On models with height sensors, install the bracket before installing the retaining nut.

10    Ensure the balljoint studs and mounting holes are clean and dry, then move the control arm into position and engage the balljoint with the hub carrier. If necessary, press the inner balljoint stud into position using a jack positioned beneath the arm.

11    Install a new nut to the outer balljoint stud, and tighten it to the specified torque setting.

12    On models equipped with suspension ride-height sensors, install the sensor link bracket to the control arm and secure the clamp.

13    Raise the front suspension with a floor jack to simulate normal ride height, then tighten the control arm inner bolt/nut to the specified torque.

14    Install the engine under-shield.

15    Install the wheel, then lower the vehicle to the ground and tighten the wheel bolts to the specified torque.

16    On models with active steering, it may be necessary to have the steering angle sensor calibration carried out using BMW diagnostic equipment.

17    We recommend that the front wheel alignment be checked at the earliest opportunity. On models with active steering, have the steering angle sensor calibration checked

using BMW diagnostic equipment. Entrust this task to a dealer.

### Tension strut

18    Position the inner end of the strut in the subframe bracket, then insert the bolt and install the new nut - do not tighten the nut yet.

19    Engage the strut balljoint with the hub carrier, install the new nut and tighten it to the specified torque.

20    Raise the front suspension with a floor jack to simulate normal ride height, then tighten the strut inner bolt/nut to the specified torque.

21    Install the engine under-shield.

22    Install the wheel, then lower the vehicle to the ground and tighten the wheel bolts to the specified torque.

## 6    Front arm balljoint - replacement

The balljoints on both the tension strut and control arm are integral, and cannot be replaced separately. If defective, the complete arm or tension strut must be replaced (see Section 5).

## 7    Front stabilizer bar - removal and installation

## Removal

*Refer to illustrations 7.2 and 7.3*

**Note:** *On F-series chassis models, the front subframe must be lowered (see Chapter 2B, Section 11) to allow the stabilizer bar to be removed.*

1    Block the rear wheels, firmly apply the parking brake, then raise the front of the vehicle and support it securely on jackstands. Remove the fasteners and the engine undershield, then remove both front wheels.

2    Unscrew the retaining nuts, and free the connecting link from each end of the stabilizer bar using a second wrench to counterhold the balljoint stud **(see illustration)**.

3    Make alignment marks between the

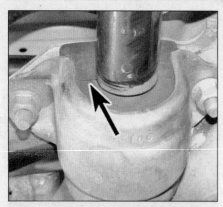

**7.3 The split-side of the stabilizer bar bushing is at the rear**

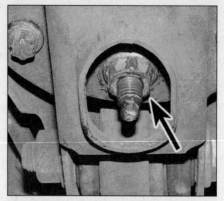

**11.4 Rear shock absorber lower mounting nut**

mount bushings and the stabilizer bar, then loosen the stabilizer bar mounting clamp retaining nuts **(see illustration)**.

4    Remove the nuts and both clamps from the subframe, and maneuver the stabilizer bar out from underneath the vehicle. Remove the mount bushings from the bar. Discard the self-locking nuts; new ones must be installed.

5    Carefully examine the stabilizer bar components for signs of wear, damage or deterioration, paying particular attention to the mount bushings. Replace worn components as necessary.

## Installation

6    Install the rubber mount bushings to the stabilizer bar, aligning them with the marks made prior to removal. Rotate each bushing so that its flat surface is at the top, and the split side on the rear.

7    Maneuver the stabilizer bar it into position. Install the mounting clamps and the new retaining nuts. Ensure that the bushing markings are still aligned with the marks on the bars, then tighten the mounting clamp retaining nuts to the specified torque.

8    Engage the stabilizer bar connecting links with the bar. Make sure the flats on the balljoint shank are correctly located against the lugs on the bar, then install the new retaining nuts and tighten them to the specified torque.

9    Install the brackets to the center of the stabilizer bar and tighten the bolts securely.

10   Install the under-shield, then install the wheels, lower the vehicle to the ground and tighten the wheel bolts to the specified torque.

## 8   Front stabilizer bar connecting link - removal and installation

**Note:** *New connecting link nuts will be required on installation.*

1    Firmly apply the parking brake, then raise the front of the vehicle and support it securely on jackstands.

2    Unscrew the retaining nut, then free the

connecting link from the stabilizer bar using a second wrench to counter-hold the link balljoint stud.

3    Loosen and remove the nut securing the link to the suspension strut, using a second wrench to counter-hold the link balljoint stud **(see illustration 4.8)**.

4    Check the connecting link balljoints for signs of wear. Check that each balljoint is free to move easily, and that the rubber boots are undamaged. If necessary, replace the connecting link.

5    Installation is the reverse of removal, using new nuts and tightening them to the specified torque setting.

## 9   Rear hub assembly - removal and installation

**Note:** *The hub assembly should not be removed unless it, or the hub bearing, is to be replaced. The hub is a press-fit in the bearing inner race, and removal of the hub will damage the bearings. If the hub is to be removed, be prepared to replace the hub bearing at the same time.*

**Note:** *A long bolt or length of threaded bar and suitable washers will be required for this procedure.*

## Removal

1    Remove the relevant driveaxle (see Chapter 8).

2    Remove the brake disc (see Chapter 9).

3    Bolt a slide hammer to the hub surface, and use the hammer to draw the hub out from the bearing. If the bearing inner race stays attached to the hub, a puller will be required to draw it off.

4    With the hub removed, replace the bearing (see Section 10).

## Installation

5    Apply a smear of oil to the hub surface, and position it in the bearing inner race.

6    Draw the hub into position using a long bolt or length of threaded rod and two nuts. Fit a large washer to either end of the bolt, so the inner one bears against the bearing inner race, and the outer one against the hub.

Slowly tighten the nut(s) until the hub is pulled fully into position. **Note:** *Do not be tempted to knock the hub into position with a hammer and drift, as this will almost certainly damage the bearing.*

7    Remove the bolt/threaded rod and washers (as applicable), and check that the hub bearing rotates smoothly and easily.

8    Install the brake disc (see Chapter 9).

9    Install the driveaxle (see Chapter 8).

## 10   Rear hub bearings - replacement

1    Remove the rear hub (see Section 9).

2    Remove the hub bearing retaining snapring from the trailing arm.

3    Tap the hub bearing out from the hub carrier using a hammer and suitable punch.

4    Thoroughly clean the hub carrier bore, removing all traces of dirt and grease, and polish away any burrs or raised edges which might hinder reassembly. Replace the snapring if there is any doubt about its condition.

5    On reassembly, apply a light film of clean engine oil to the bearing outer race to aid installation.

6    Place the bearing in the hub carrier and tap it fully into position, ensuring that it enters the carrier squarely, using a suitable tubular spacer which bears only on the bearing outer race.

7    Secure the bearing in position with the snap-ring, making sure it is correctly positioned in the hub carrier groove.

8    Install the rear hub (see Section 9).

## 11   Rear shock absorber - removal, inspection and installation

## Removal

*Refer to illustrations 11.4, 11.5a, 11.5b, 11.6a and 11.6b*

1    Block the front wheels, then raise the rear of the vehicle and support it securely on jackstands. To improve access, remove the rear wheel.

2    On E-series chassis models, remove the luggage compartment side trim panel (see Chapter 11).

3    Position a floojack underneath the hub carrier, then raise the jack so that it is supporting the weight of the carrier. This will prevent the hub carrier from dropping when the shock absorber is unbolted.

### E90, E91, E92 and E93 chassis

4    Loosen and remove the nut securing the shock absorber to the lower mount **(see illustration)**. Counterhold the shock absorber shaft with a wrench.

5    From within the luggage compartment, pry up the rubber cap, then unscrew the upper mounting nut, counter-holding the shock absorber shaft with a wrench **(see illustrations)**. Lower the shock absorber out from underneath the vehicle.

**11.5a  When installing the rubber cap above the shock absorber mounting, the arrow must point upward**

**11.5b  Rear shock absorber upper mounting nut**

**11.6a  Remove the shock absorber mounting bolts . . .**

6    If required, remove the two bolts and remove the mounting from the suspension arm **(see illustrations)**.

### F30, F31 and F34 chassis

7    Remove the cover from the camber arm, then loosen the shock absorber lower bolt/ nut.
8    Remove the three mounting bolts from the top of the shock absorber, then lower the jack and remove the shock absorber through the wheelwell.

## Inspection

9    Remove the trim cap, bump stop and protective tube.
10    Examine the shock absorber for signs of fluid leakage. Check the piston for signs of pitting along its entire length, and check the body for signs of damage. While holding it in an upright position, test the operation of the shock absorber by moving the piston through a full stroke, then through short strokes of two to four inches (50 to 100 mm). In both cases, the resistance felt should be smooth and continuous. If the resistance is jerky, or uneven, or if there is any visible sign of wear or damage, replacement is necessary. **Note:** *Shock absorbers should only be replaced in pairs.*
11    Inspect all other components for signs of damage or deterioration, and replace any that are suspect.
12    Slide the tube, bump stop and cap onto the shock absorber.

## Installation

### E90, E91, E92 and E93 chassis

13    If removed, install the lower mounts to the suspension arm and tighten the bolts to the specified torque.
14    Ensure the upper mount and body contact surfaces are clean and dry.
15    Maneuver the shock absorber into position, and install the new upper mounting nut.
16    Engage the lower end of the shock absorber with the mount, then install the nut, tightening it to the specified torque.
17    Tighten the upper mounting nut to the

specified torque setting, then install the rubber cap over the upper mounting, noting that the arrow must point upwards.
18    Install the luggage compartment trim panel.
19    Install the wheel and lower the vehicle to the ground. Tighten the wheel bolts to the torque listed in this Chapter's Specifications.

### F30, F31 and F34 chassis

20    Installation is the reverse of removal, making sure to tighten the lower shock absorber bolt/nut at the normal ride height position.

---

**12    Rear coil spring - removal and installation**

---

## Removal

1    Block the front wheels, then raise the rear of the vehicle and support it securely on jackstands. Remove the relevant wheel.
2    The coil spring must be removed using special BMW tool Nos 33 5 011/ 012/013/014/015/016. Do not attempt to remove the coil spring without these tools.
3    Insert the lower collar of the special tool (No 33 5 012) above the lowest coil of the spring, ensuring it makes the maximum contact with the spring, and is positioned correctly.
4    Insert the guide spindles (Nos 33 5 013, 33 5 014 and 33 5 015) through the base of the spring and up through the lower collar.
5    Insert the upper collar of the special tool No. 33 5 011, or equivalent (E-series chassis models) or No. 2 241 788, or equivalent (F-series chassis models) below the highest coil of the spring, ensuring it makes the maximum contact with the spring, and locates correctly with the upper end of the guide spindles.
6    Fit tool No 33 5 016 over the lower end of the guide spindles, then tighten the spindles and compress the spring just enough to remove it. Do not fully compress the spring, or it will be damaged.
7    Inspect the spring closely for signs of

**11.6b  . . . and maneuver the mount from the control arm**

damage, such as cracking, and check the spring seats for signs of wear. Replace worn components as necessary.

## Installation

8    Maneuver the compressed spring into place, ensuring the ends of the coils and the seats are correctly aligned.
9    Gradually release the tension on the spring, ensuring it is positioned correctly with the spring seats as it extends.
10    Install the wheel, then lower the vehicle to the ground. Tighten the wheel bolts to the specified torque.

---

**13    Rear hub carrier - removal, overhaul and installation**

---

## Removal

*Refer to illustration 13.8*

1    Block the front wheels, then raise the rear of the vehicle and support it securely on jackstands. Remove the relevant wheel.
2    Remove the relevant driveaxle (see Chapter 8).
3    Remove the brake disc and ABS wheel speed sensor (see Chapter 9).

**13.8  Stabilizer bar link bolt location**

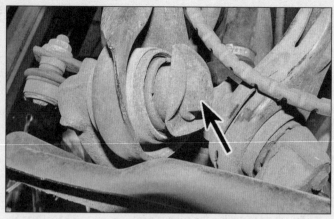

**14.2  Control arm-to-hub carrier bolt location**

4    Disconnect the parking brake cable from the rear wheel (see Chapter 9).
5    Remove the coil spring (see Section 12).
6    Position a jack underneath the hub carrier to support the weight of the arm.
7    Loosen and remove the shock absorber lower mounting nut, then remove the 2 bolts and remove the shock absorber mounting (see Section 11).
8    Remove the bolt and detach the stabilizer bar link from the hub carrier **(see illustration)**.
9    Disconnect the trailing arm, traction strut, tow arm, control arm and camber arm from the hub carrier (see Section 14) then remove the hub carrier.

## Overhaul

10   Thoroughly clean the hub carrier and the area around the carrier mountings, removing all traces of dirt and undercoating if necessary. Check carefully for cracks, distortion or any other signs of wear or damage, paying particular attention to the mount bushings and balljoint. If either the bushings or balljoint require replacement, the hub carrier should be taken to a dealer or suitably-equipped garage. A hydraulic press and suitable spacers are

required to press the bushings/balljoints out of position and install the new ones. Inspect the pivot bolts for signs of wear or damage and replace as necessary.

## Installation

11   Installation is the reverse of removal, noting the following points:

 a) *Replace all self-locking nuts.*
 b) *Only tighten the trailing arm, traction strut, toe arm, control arm and camber arm bolts/nuts when the rear suspension has been raised with a floor jack to simulate normal ride height.*
 c) *Tighten all fasteners to their specified torque where given.*
 d) *Have the rear wheel alignment checked at the earliest opportunity.*

---

## 14   Rear suspension arms - removal, overhaul and installation

---

## Removal

1    Block the front wheels, then raise the

rear of the vehicle and support it securely on jackstands. Remove the relevant wheel.

### Control arm

*Refer to illustrations 14.2 and 14.3*
2    Remove the bolt securing the control arm to the hub carrier **(see illustration)**. Discard the bolt; a new one must be installed.
3    Remove the nut, and pull out the bolt securing the arm to the rear subframe **(see illustration)**. Note that the bolt is inserted from the front. Discard the nut; a new one must be installed.

### Trailing arm

*Refer to illustration 14.4*
4    Remove the bolts and detach the trailing arm from the hub carrier and rear subframe **(see illustration)**. Note that the inner bolt is inserted from the rear, while the outer bolt is inserted from the front. Discard the nuts; new ones must be installed.

### Camber arm

*Refer to illustrations 14.8a and 14.8b*
5    Remove the rear coil spring (see Section 12).

**14.3  Control arm-to-subframe bolt location**

**14.4  Remove the bolts and remove the trailing arm**

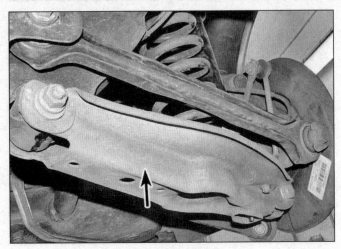

14.8a  Camber arm location

14.8b  Make alignment marks between the eccentric bolt head and the arm

6    Remove the two bolts and the shock absorber lower mount from the camber arm **(see illustration 11.6a)**. **Note**: *The nuts must be replaced.*
7    Support the hub carrier with a floor jack.
8    Make alignment marks between the camber arm and the inner eccentric bolt head, then remove the nuts and the arm-retaining bolts **(see illustrations)**. **Note:** *The inner bolt is inserted from the front, while the outer bolt is inserted from the rear. Replace the self-locking nuts.*
9    Maneuver the camber arm out of the vehicle.

### Traction strut

*Refer to illustrations 14.11 and 14.12*

10    Remove the bolt and detach the stabilizer bar link from the hub carrier **(see illustration 13.8)**.
11    Remove the bolt securing the traction strut to the hub carrier **(see illustration)**. Discard the bolt; a new one must be installed. Note that the tapered side of the strut bushing must fit against the hub carrier.
12    Remove the nut and pull the inner mount-

ing bolt from the bracket **(see illustration)**. Discard the nut; a new one must be installed.
13    Maneuver the traction strut from the vehicle.

### Toe arm

*Refer to illustration 14.15*

14    Make alignment marks between the toe arm inner eccentric bolt head and the subframe.
15    Remove the bolt securing the toe arm to the hub carrier **(see illustration)**.
16    Remove the nut, then pull the inner eccentric bolt from the subframe. On some models, it's necessary to unclip the plastic cover from the bolt head. **Note:** *The bolt is inserted from the front. Discard the self-locking nut; a new one must be installed.*

### *Overhaul*

17    Thoroughly clean the arms/strut and the area around the mounts, removing all traces of dirt and undercoating if necessary. Check for cracks, distortion or any other wear or damage, paying particular attention to the mount bushings. If the bushings require replacement, the arm/strut should be taken to

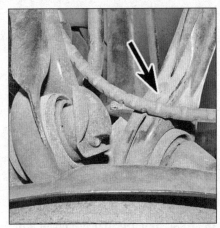

14.11  Hub carrier end of the traction strut

a BMW dealer or suitably-equipped garage. A hydraulic press and suitable spacers are required to press the bushings out of position and install the new ones.
18    Inspect the pivot bolts for signs of wear or damage, and replace as necessary.

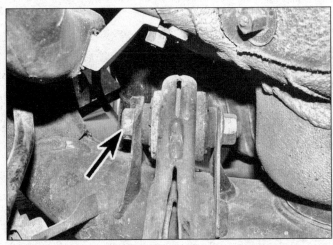

14.12  Traction strut-to-subframe bolt location

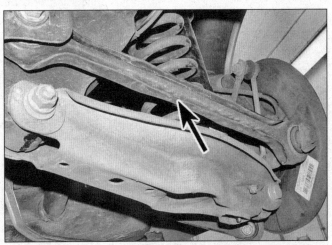

14.15  Toe arm location

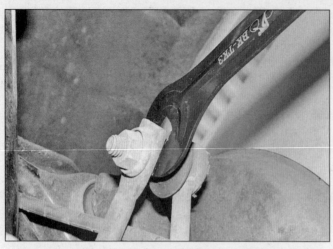

15.3  Use a slim wrench to counterhold the stabilizer bar link balljoint shank

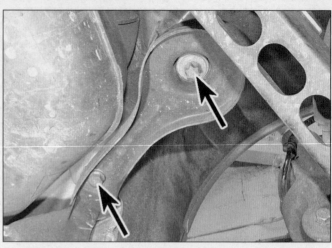

15.6  Remove the bolts and remove the brace from each side

## Installation

19  Installation is the reverse of removal, noting the following points:

a) *Replace all self-locking nuts.*
b) *The trailing arm, traction strut, toe arm, control arm and camber arm bolts/nuts should only be tightened when the rear suspension has been raised with a floor jack to simulate normal ride height.*
c) *Tighten all fasteners to their specified torque where given.*
d) *Have the rear wheel alignment checked at the earliest opportunity.*

## 15  Rear stabilizer bar - removal and installation

### Removal

*Refer to illustrations 15.3, 15.6, 15.7, 15.8 and 15.9*

1  Remove both rear coil springs (see Section 12).
2  Remove the control arm from the left-hand side and both traction struts (see Section 14).
3  Remove the nuts and detach both stabilizer bar links from the stabilizer bar (see illustration).
4  Lower the rear subframe slightly to enable the stabilizer bar to be removed. Remove the rear exhaust section mounts and heat shield.
5  Disconnect the wiring for the rear ABS sensors and brake pad wear sensors at the junction on the rear subframe.
6  Remove the bolts from the braces at each side securing the front of the subframe to the vehicle body (see illustration).
7  Use clamps on the rear brake flexible hoses, then disconnect the hoses from the rigid pipes (see illustration).
8  Support the rear subframe with a floor jack and suitable sections of wood. Loosen the subframe mounting bolts and lower the subframe as much as possible without placing any strain on the brake hoses (see illustration).
9  Make alignment marks between the mount bushings and stabilizer bar, then loosen the stabilizer bar mounting clamp retaining

bolts (see illustration).
10  Remove both clamps from the subframe and maneuver the stabilizer bar out from underneath the vehicle. Remove the mount bushings from the bar.
11  Carefully examine the stabilizer bar components for signs of wear, damage or deterioration, paying particular attention to the mount bushings. Replace any worn components as necessary.

### Installation

12  Install the rubber mount bushings to the stabilizer bar, aligning them with the marks made prior to removal.
13  Raise the stabilizer bar and maneuver it into position.
14  Install the mounting clamps and the bolts. Ensure that the bushing markings are still aligned with the marks on the bars, then securely tighten the mounting clamp retaining bolts.
15  Installation is the reverse of removal, noting the following points:

a) *Replace all self-locking nuts.*

15.7  Clamp the flexible hoses

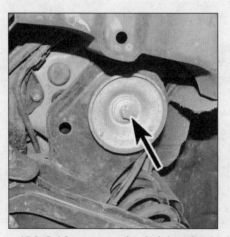

15.8  Subframe mounting bolt location

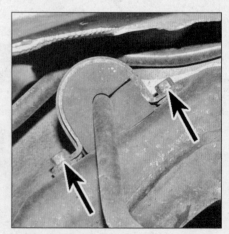

15.9  Stabilizer bar clamp bolt locations

b) The traction strut and control arm bolts/ nuts should only be tightened when the rear suspension has been raised with a floor jack to simulate normal ride height.

c) Tighten all fasteners to their specified torque where given.

d) Reconnect the brake hoses and bleed the hydraulic system (see Chapter 9).

e) Have the rear wheel alignment checked at the earliest opportunity.

## 16  Steering wheel - removal and installation

**Warning:** *These models are equipped with a Supplemental Restraint System (SRS), more commonly known as airbags. Always disable the airbag system before working in the vicinity of any airbag system component to avoid the possibility of accidental deployment of the airbag(s), which could cause personal injury (see Chapter 12).*

**Warning:** *Do not use a memory saving device to preserve the PCM or radio memory when working on or near airbag system components.*

### Removal

*Refer to illustrations 16.3 and 16.4*

1   Set the front wheels in the straight-ahead position, and set the steering lock.

2   Remove the airbag unit from the center of the steering wheel (see Chapter 12).

3   Loosen and remove the steering wheel retaining bolt. Disconnect the steering wheel electrical connector(s) **(see illustration)**.

4   Mark the steering wheel and steering column shaft in relation to each other, then lift the steering wheel off the column splines. If it is tight, tap it up near the center, using the palm of your hand, or twist it from side-to-side, while pulling upwards to release it from the shaft splines **(see illustration)**. The airbag clockspring will automatically be locked in position as the wheel is removed; do not attempt to rotate it while the wheel is removed.

**16.3  Remove the steering wheel retaining bolt**

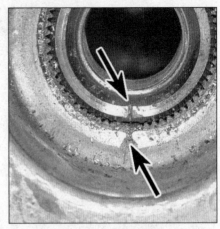

**16.4  Make alignment marks between the steering wheel and the shaft**

### Installation

5   Installation is the reverse of removal, noting the following points:

a) If the clockspring has been rotated with the wheel removed, center it by pressing down on the white button and rotating its center fully counterclockwise. From this position, rotate the center back through three complete rotations in a clockwise direction.

b) Engage the wheel with the column splines, aligning the marks made on removal, and tighten the steering wheel retaining bolt to the specified torque.

c) Install the airbag unit (see Chapter 12).

## 17  Steering column - removal, inspection and installation

**Warning:** *These models are equipped with a Supplemental Restraint System (SRS), more commonly known as airbags. Always disable the airbag system before working in the vicinity of any airbag system component to avoid the possibility of accidental deployment of the airbag(s), which could cause personal injury (see Chapter 12).*

**Warning:** *Do not use a memory saving device to preserve the PCM or radio memory when working on or near airbag system components.*

**Note:** *New steering column shear-bolts and an intermediate shaft clamp bolt/nut will be required on installation.*

### Removal

*Refer to illustrations 17.2, 17.3, 17.5a, 17.5b, 17.6a, 17.6b, 17.7, 17.8, 17.9a, 17.9b and 17.9c*

1   Disconnect the negative battery cable (see Chapter 5).

2   Remove the three Torx bolts and the driver's knee bolster panel below the steering wheel **(see illustration)**. Disconnect any electrical connectors as the panel is withdrawn.

3   Reach up behind the instrument panel and pull the footwell heating duct downwards from the driver's side. Detach the duct from the heater distribution housing **(see illustration)**. Release the wiring harness from the duct as it's withdrawn.

**17.2  Remove the 3 bolts and the panel (driver's knee bolster) above the pedals**

**17.3  Unclip the driver's side footwell heating duct**

**17.5a  Unclip the column upper shroud**

**17.5b  Squeeze together the clips and detach the upper shroud from the boot**

**17.6a  Disconnect the switch gear electrical connectors . . .**

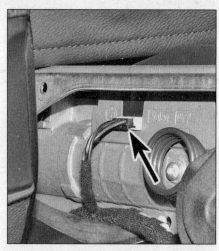

**17.6b  . . . and the connector on the top of the column**

4    Fully extend the steering wheel, and set it in the lowest position. Remove the steering wheel (see Section 16).

5    Using a blunt, flat-bladed tool, carefully pry the column upper cover from the lower cover. Set the column in the highest position, then press the retaining clip on each side outwards slightly, and pull the lower column cover downward. If required, unclip the upper cover from the gap cover **(see illustrations)**.

6    Tag and disconnect the electrical connectors from the column switches and free the harness from its retaining clips on the column **(see illustrations)**. Don't overlook the connector on the top side of the column.

7    Slide up the rubber boot at the base of the column **(see illustration)**.

8    Loosen and remove the clamp bolt, then disengage the shaft from the column **(see illustration)**. Discard the bolt; a new one must be installed.

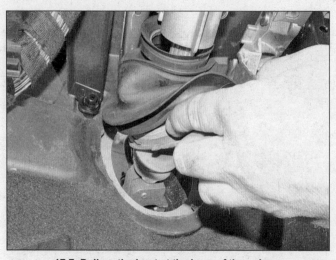

**17.7  Pull up the boot at the base of the column**

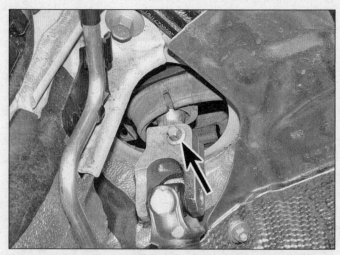

**17.8  Remove the clamp bolt (viewed from the engine compartment)**

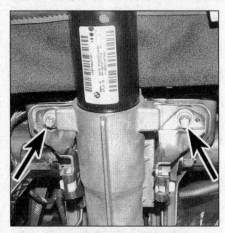

**17.9a  Remove the upper mounting bolts . . .**

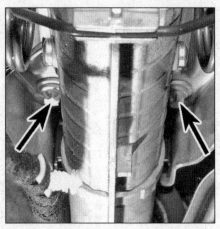

**17.9b  . . . and the lower mounting bolts**

**17.9c  Maneuver the column rearward**

9    Remove the four mounting bolts/nuts and pull the column to the rear **(see illustrations)**.

## Inspection

10    The steering column incorporates a telescopic safety feature. In the event of a front-end crash, the shaft collapses and prevents the steering wheel injuring the driver. Before installing the steering column, examine the column and mountings for damage and deformation, and replace as necessary.

11    Check the steering shaft for signs of free-play in the column bushings. If any damage or wear is found on the steering column bushings, the column should be overhauled. Overhaul of the column is a complex task requiring several special tools, and should be entrusted to a BMW dealer.

## Installation

12    Maneuver the column into position and engage it with the intermediate shaft splines, aligning the marks made prior to removal.

13    Move the column into position and screw in the mounting bolts, tightening them to the specified torque.

14    Reconnect the electrical connectors to the ignition switch and column switches. Secure the wiring to the column, ensuring it is correctly routed.

15    Ensure the intermediate shaft and column marks are correctly aligned and insert the column into the shaft. Install the new clamp bolt and tighten it to the specified torque.

16    Install the rubber boot to the bulkhead at the base of the column.

17    Install the lower and upper steering column covers.

18    Install the steering wheel (see Section 16).

19    Install the footwell air duct.

20    Reconnect the negative battery cable (see Chapter 5).

21    If a new column has been installed, it will be necessary to recalibrate the steering angle sensor using BMW diagnostic equipment. Entrust this task to a dealer or other qualified shop.

## 18   Steering column lock - general information

At the time of writing, the electrically-operated steering column lock is only available as a complete unit with the steering column. Check with a dealer or parts specialist.

## 19   Steering column intermediate shaft - removal and installation

**Warning:** *These models are equipped with a Supplemental Restraint System (SRS), more commonly known as airbags. Always disable the airbag system before working in the vicinity of any airbag system component to avoid the possibility of accidental deployment of the airbag(s), which could cause personal injury (see Chapter 12).*

**Warning:** *Do not use a memory saving device to preserve the PCM or radio memory when working on or near airbag system components.*

## Removal

1    Block the rear wheels, firmly apply the parking brake, then raise the front of the vehicle and support it securely on jackstands. Set the front wheels in the straight-ahead position. Remove the bolts and the engine under-shield **(see illustration 3.1)**.

2    Remove the fasteners and the driver's knee bolster panel **(see illustration 17.2)**.

3    Pry the rubber boot upwards from the base of the column **(see illustration 17.7)**.

4    Using paint or a marking pen, make alignment marks between the intermediate shaft universal joint and the steering column, the shaft and flexible coupling, and the flexible coupling and the steering gear pinion **(see illustration 17.8)**.

5    Loosen and remove the clamp bolts, then slide the two halves of the shaft together and remove the shaft assembly from the vehicle.

6    Inspect the intermediate shaft universal

joint for signs of roughness in its bearings and ease of movement. Also examine the shaft rubber coupling for signs of damage or deterioration, and check that the rubber is securely bonded to the flanges. If the universal joint or rubber coupling are suspect, the complete intermediate shaft should be replaced.

## Installation

7    Check that the front wheels are still in the straight-ahead position, and that the steering wheel is correctly positioned.

8    Align the marks made on removal, and engage the intermediate shaft joint with the steering column and the coupling with the steering gear.

9    Insert the new clamp bolts, and tighten them to the specified torque setting.

10    The remainder of installation is the reverse of removal. If a new shaft has been installed, it will be necessary to recalibrate the steering angle sensor using BMW diagnostic equipment. Entrust this task to a dealer or other qualified shop.

## 20   Steering gear - removal, inspection and installation

**Warning:** *These models are equipped with a Supplemental Restraint System (SRS), more commonly known as airbags. Always disable the airbag system before working in the vicinity of any airbag system component to avoid the possibility of accidental deployment of the airbag(s), which could cause personal injury (see Chapter 12).*

**Warning:** *Do not use a memory saving device to preserve the PCM or radio memory when working on or near airbag system components.*

## Removal

*Refer to illustration 20.3a, 20.3b and 20.5*

1    Block the rear wheels, firmly apply the parking brake, then raise the front of the vehicle and support it securely on jackstands.

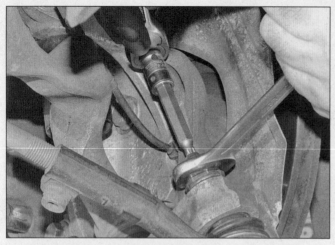

20.3a  Counterhold the tie-rod end shank with a Torx bit

20.3b  Remove the nut and tap the tie-rod end from the steering knuckle

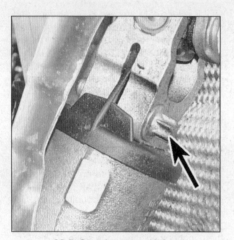

20.5  Steering gear pinion coupling pinch-bolt

Remove both front wheels, then remove the fasteners and the engine under-shield.

2   Set the steering in the straight-ahead position and engage the steering lock. On models with electric power steering, disconnect the negative battery cable (see Chapter 5).

3   Remove the nuts securing the outer tie-rod ends to the steering knuckles. Unscrew them until the edge of the nuts are flush with the ends of the balljoint shanks. Release the balljoints by gently tapping the ends of the shanks with a soft-faced hammer (see illustrations). There is no need to use a universal balljoint separator.

4   Using paint or a marking pen, make alignment marks between the intermediate shaft coupling and the steering gear pinion. Note: *On some models, an alignment mark is already provided on the pinion flange, which aligns with a mark cast into the pinion housing.*

5   Loosen and remove the coupling pinch-bolt (see illustration).

## Conventional power steering

*Refer to illustration 20.6*

6   Using brake hose clamps, clamp both the supply and return hoses near the power steering fluid reservoir to minimize fluid loss. Mark the unions to ensure they are correctly positioned on reassembly. Loosen and remove the feed and return pipe union bolts from the steering gear pinion housing, and remove the sealing washers - remove the heat shield if necessary. Be prepared for fluid spillage, and position a suitable container beneath the pipes while unscrewing the bolts (see illustration). Plug the pipe ends and steering gear orifices to prevent fluid leakage and to keep dirt out of the hydraulic system.

7   Release the power steering pipes from the retaining clips on the steering gear.

## Electric power steering

*Refer to illustration 20.8*

8   Release the steering gear wiring harness from the cable ties, then disconnect the wiring plug from the motor (see illustration).

## All types

*Refer to illustration 20.9*

9   Loosen and remove the steering gear mounting bolts, and remove the steering gear

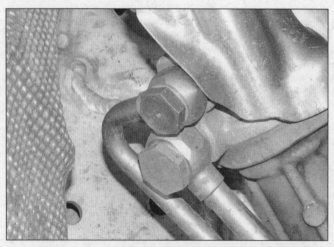

20.6  Remove the bolts and detach the pipes from the steering gear

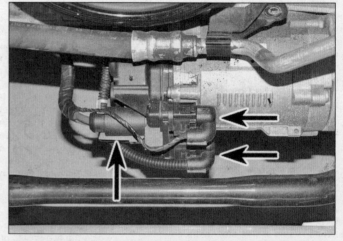

20.8  Disconnect the electrical connectors from the electric power steering gear

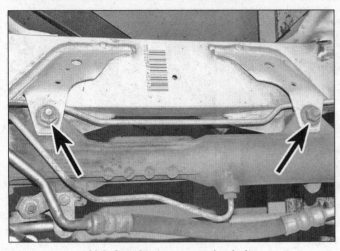

**20.9  Steering gear mounting bolts**

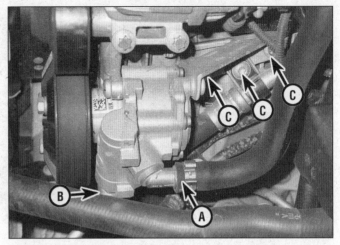

**21.5  Disconnect the return hose (A) and the pressure line (B), then remove the power steering pump mounting bolts (C)**

from underneath the vehicle **(see illustration)**. Discard the nuts and bolts; new ones must be installed.

## Inspection

10   Examine the steering gear assembly for signs of wear or damage, and check that the rack moves freely throughout the full length of its travel, with no signs of roughness or excessive freeplay between the steering gear pinion and rack. It is not possible to overhaul the steering gear assembly housing components; if it is faulty, the assembly must be replaced. The only components which can be replaced individually are the steering gear boots (see Section 24), the outer tie-rod ends (see Section 25) or the tie-rod shafts.

## Installation

11   Position the steering gear and insert the mounting bolts. Use new nuts and bolts, and tighten them to the specified torque.
12   On models with conventional power steering, position a new sealing washer on each side of the pipe hose unions and install the union bolts. Tighten the union bolts to the specified torque.
13   On models with electric power steering, reconnect the motor electrical connector and secure the harness in its original position using cable ties.
14   Align the marks made on removal and connect the intermediate shaft coupling to the steering gear. Insert the new clamp bolt, then tighten it to the specified torque.
15   Insert the outer tie-rod ends into the steering knuckles. Install new nuts and tighten them to the specified torque.
16   Install the wheels and the engine undershield, then lower the vehicle to the ground and tighten the wheel bolts to the specified torque.

### Conventional power steering

17   Bleed the hydraulic system (see Section 22).
18   The front wheel alignment should be checked at the earliest opportunity. On mod-

els with active steering, have the steering angle sensor calibration checked using BMW diagnostic equipment. Entrust this task to a dealer or other qualified shop.

### Electric power steering

19   If a new steering gear has been installed, it must be programmed/calibrated using BMW diagnostic equipment. Entrust this task to a dealer or other qualified shop.
20   We recommend that the front wheel alignment be checked at the earliest opportunity. On models with active steering, have the steering angle sensor calibration checked using BMW diagnostic equipment. Entrust this task to a dealer or other qualified shop.

## 21   Power steering pump - removal and installation

**Note:** *This procedure applies only to models with conventional power steering. On models with electric power steering, the motor is integral with the rack assembly. Consult a dealer or parts specialist with regard to parts availability.*

## Removal

*Refer to illustration 21.5*
1   Block the rear wheels, then raise the front of the vehicle and support it securely on jackstands. Remove the fasteners and the engine under-shield.
2   Remove the air cleaner assembly (see Chapter 4).
3   Release the drivebelt tension and unhook the drivebelt from the pump pulley (see Chapter 1).
4   Using a brake hose clamp, clamp the return hose near the power steering fluid reservoir. This will minimize fluid loss during subsequent operations. With a drain pan in place under the pump, remove the banjo bolt securing the pressure hose. Collect the old fluid and dispose of it properly.
5   Remove the bolt securing the air con-

ditioning pipe to the power steering pump bracket, then remove the two bolts securing the pump bracket to the engine **(see illustration)**. **Note:** *The mounting bolts are aluminum and must be replaced.*
6   If the power steering pump is faulty, seek the advice of your dealer or auto parts store as to the availability of new or remanufactured pumps.

## Installation

7   Where necessary, transfer the rear mounting bracket to the new pump, and securely tighten its mounting bolts.
8   Prior to installation, ensure that the pump is primed by injecting the specified type of fluid in through the supply hose union and rotating the pump shaft.
9   Maneuver the pump into position and install the pivot bolts, tightening them to the specified torque.
10   Position a new sealing washer on each side of the pressure hose banjo fitting and install the banjo bolt. Tighten the banjo bolt to the specified torque.
11   Install the return hose to the pump and tighten the hose clamp.
12   Install and tension the drivebelt (see Chapter 1).
13   Install the air cleaner assembly (see Chapter 4).
14   Lower the vehicle to the ground and bleed the hydraulic system (see Section 22).

## 22   Power steering system - bleeding

1   With the engine stopped, fill the fluid reservoir to the top with the specified type of fluid.
2   With the engine running, slowly move the steering from lock-to-lock twice to purge out the trapped air, then stop the engine and top-off the level in the fluid reservoir. Repeat this procedure until the fluid level in the reservoir does not drop any further.

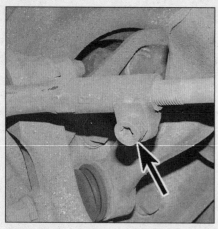

**24.2  Remove the tie-rod end clamp bolt**

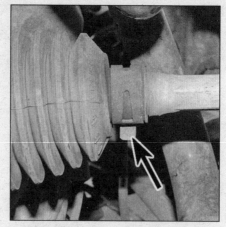

**24.3  Release the boot outer clamp**

**24.5  Release the clamp securing the boot to the steering gear**

3    If, when turning the steering, an abnormal noise is heard from the fluid lines, it indicates that there is still air in the system. Check this by turning the wheels to the straight-ahead position and switching off the engine. If the fluid level in the reservoir rises, then air is present in the system and further bleeding is necessary.

## 23  Active steering control unit - removal and installation

1    Disconnect the negative battery cable (see Chapter 5).
2    Release the fasteners and remove the rear section of the left front wheelwell liner.
3    Remove the bolt securing the ground cable to the bracket, then disconnect the electrical connectors from the control unit.
4    Remove the mounting nut and bolt, then maneuver the control unit from the vehicle.
5    Installation is the reverse of removal. **Note:** *If a new unit is installed, it must be programmed/coded using BMW diagnostic equipment. Entrust this task to a dealer or other qualified shop.*

## 24  Steering gear boots - replacement

*Refer to illustrations 24.2, 24.3 and 24.5*

1    Raise the front of the vehicle and support it securely on jackstands. Remove the fasteners and remove the engine under-shield.
2    Remove the tie-rod end clamp bolt **(see illustration)**. Discard the bolt; a new one must be installed.
3    Release the clamp securing the rubber boot to the tie-rod **(see illustration)**. Note the installed position of the boot on the tie-rod.
4    Mark the position of the tie-rod end on the threaded portion of the tie-rod, or count the number of turns and unscrew the tie-rod end from the tie-rod.
5    Release the clamp securing the boot to

the steering gear, and pull the boot over the tie-rod **(see illustration)**.
6    Thoroughly clean the tie-rod and the steering gear housing, using fine abrasive paper to polish off any corrosion, burrs or sharp edges which might damage the new boot's sealing lips on installation. Scrape off all the grease from the old boot, and apply it to the tie-rod inner balljoint. This assumes that grease has not been lost or contaminated as a result of damage to the old boot. Use fresh grease if in doubt - consult a dealer or parts store.
7    Apply a little grease to the tie-rod so the boot will slide, then carefully slide the new boot (with the retaining clips in place) over the tie-rod, and position it on the steering gear housing. Position the outer edge of the boot on the tie-rod.
8    Secure the boot with the retaining clamp.
9    Thread the tie-rod into the tie-rod end, aligning the marks made previously, or counting the number of turns, so the tie-rod and end are in their original positions.
10    Insert the new tie-rod end clamp bolt and tighten it to the specified torque.
11    Ensure the outer end of the boot is still in the correct position, then secure it with the retaining clip.
12    Install the engine under-shield and lower the vehicle to the ground.
13    It is recommended that the front wheel alignment be checked at the earliest opportunity. On models with active steering, have the steering angle sensor calibration checked using BMW diagnostic equipment. Entrust this task to a dealer or other qualified shop.

## 25  Tie-rod ends - removal and installation

### Removal

1    Apply the parking brake, then raise the front of the vehicle and support it securely on jackstands. Remove the appropriate front wheel.

2    Make a mark on the tie-rod and measure the distance from the mark to the center of the tie-rod end. Record this measurement, as it will be needed to ensure the wheel alignment remains correctly set when the balljoint is installed.
3    Unscrew the tie-rod end clamp bolt **(see illustration 24.2)**. Discard the bolt; a new one must be installed.
4    Remove the nut securing the tie-rod end to the steering knuckle, and unscrew it until the edge of the nut is flush with the end of the shank. Release the balljoint by gently tapping the end of the shank with a soft-faced hammer **(see illustration 20.3a and 20.3b)**. There is no need to use a balljoint separator tool - a new one must be installed.
5    Unscrew the tie-rod end from the tie-rod, counting the exact number of turns required.
6    Carefully clean the tie-rod end and the threads. Replace the tie-rod end if its movement is sloppy or too stiff, if excessively worn, or if damaged in any way; carefully check the stud taper and threads. If the balljoint boot is damaged, the complete balljoint assembly must be replaced; the boot is not available separately. **Note:** *Tie-rod ends should be replaced only in pairs.*

### Installation

7    Screw the tie-rod end onto the tie-rod by the number of turns noted on removal. This should position the tie-rod end close to the relevant distance from the tie-rod mark noted prior to removal.
8    Install the tie-rod end to the steering knuckle, then install a new retaining nut and tighten it to the specified torque.
9    Insert the new tie-rod end clamp bolt, and tighten it to the specified torque.
10    Install the wheel, then lower the vehicle to the ground and tighten the wheel bolts to the specified torque.
11    It is recommended that the front wheel alignment be checked at the earliest opportunity. On models with active steering, have the steering angle sensor calibration checked using BMW diagnostic equipment. Entrust this task to a BMW dealer or other qualified shop.

## 26  Tie-rods - replacement

1    Remove the steering gear boots (see Section 24).
2    Disconnect the tie-rod ends from the steering knuckles (see Section 25).
3    Move the rack in as far as possible, then loosen and remove the large inner tie-rod nut from the end of the steering gear. Remove the tie-rod and inner tie-rod nut.
4    Position the new inner tie-rod end/tie-rod on the rack, start the threads and tighten the retaining nut to the specified torque. **Note:** *The tie-rods should only be replaced as a pair.*
5    Install the steering boots (see Section 24).

## 27  Dynamic Stability Control - general information and component replacement

### *General information*

1    Dynamic Stability Control (DSC) is standard on most models, and available as an option on all other models. DSC includes ABS and Traction control, but this Section is concerned with Cornering Brake Control (CBC). By monitoring steering wheel movements, suspension ride heights, road speed and lateral acceleration the system controls the pressure in the brake lines to each of the four brake calipers during braking, reducing the possibility of understeer or oversteer. The suspension ride height sensors also provide information to the Adaptive Headlight Control Module, which corrects headlight aiming according to load and vehicle attitude.

### *Component replacement*

#### Steering angle sensor

2    The steering angle sensor is integral with the steering column switch module (see Chapter 12).

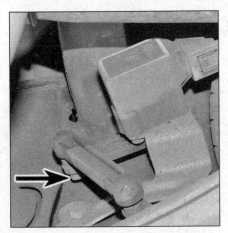

**27.6  A nut secures the rod to the sensor arm**

**27.3  Remove the nut securing the rod to the arm**

#### Front ride height sensor

*Refer to illustrations 27.3 and 27.4*

3    Remove the nut securing the control rod to the sensor arm **(see illustration)**.
4    Remove the two retaining bolts and withdraw the ride sensor **(see illustration)**. Disconnect the electrical connector as the sensor is removed.
5    Installation is the reverse of removal. Have the headlight alignment checked on completion.

#### Rear ride height sensor

*Refer to illustration 27.6*

6    Remove the nut securing the jointed rod to the sensor **(see illustration)**.
7    Remove the bolt securing the sensor mounting bracket to the subframe, then disconnect the sensor wiring plug.

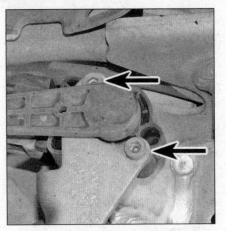

**27.4  Ride height sensor retaining bolt locations**

8    If required, remove the 2 bolts and separate the sensor from the mounting bracket.
9    Installation is the reverse of removal.

#### DSC control unit

10   The DSC control unit is integral with the ABS control unit. Replacement of the control unit should be handled at a dealer or other qualified shop.

## 28  Wheels and tires - general information

*Refer to illustration 28.1*

1    All vehicles covered by this manual are equipped with metric-sized fiberglass or steel belted radial tires **(see illustration)**. Use of other size or type of tires may affect the ride

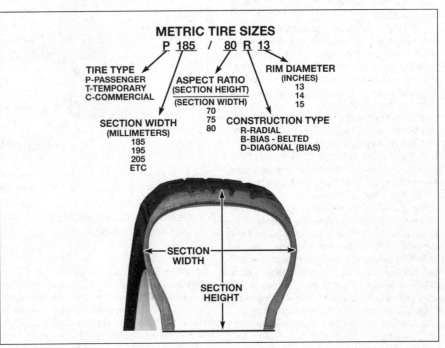

**28.1  Metric tire size code**

and handling of the vehicle. Don't mix different types of tires, such as radials and bias belted, on the same vehicle as handling may be seriously affected. It's recommended that tires be replaced in pairs on the same axle, but if only one tire is being replaced, be sure it's the same size, structure and tread design as the other.

2    Because tire pressure has a substantial effect on handling and wear, the pressure on all tires should be checked at least once a month or before any extended trips (see Chapter 1).

3    Wheels must be replaced if they are bent, dented, leak air, have elongated bolt holes, are heavily rusted, out of vertical symmetry or if the wheel bolts won't stay tight. Wheel repairs that use welding or peening are not recommended.

4    Tire and wheel balance is important in the overall handling, braking and performance of the vehicle. Unbalanced wheels can adversely affect handling and ride characteristics as well as tire life. Whenever a tire is installed on a wheel, the tire and wheel should be balanced by a shop with the proper equipment.

## 29    Wheel alignment - general information

*Refer to illustration 29.1*

A wheel alignment refers to the adjustments made to the wheels so they are in proper angular relationship to the suspension and the ground. Wheels that are out of proper alignment not only affect vehicle control, but also increase tire wear. The front end angles normally measured are camber, caster and toe-in **(see illustration)**. Toe-in and camber are adjustable; if the caster is not correct, check for bent components. Rear toe-in is also adjustable.

Getting the proper wheel alignment is a very exacting process, one in which complicated and expensive machines are necessary to perform the job properly. Because of this, you should have a technician with the proper equipment perform these tasks. We will, however, use this space to give you a basic idea of what is involved with a wheel alignment so you can better understand the process and deal intelligently with the shop that does the work.

Toe-in is the turning in of the wheels. The purpose of a toe specification is to ensure parallel rolling of the wheels. In a vehicle with zero toe-in, the distance between the front edges of the wheels will be the same as the distance between the rear edges of the wheels. The actual amount of toe-in is normally only a fraction of an inch. On the front end, toe-in is controlled by the tie-rod end position on the tie-rod. On the rear end, it's controlled by a cam at the inner end of the control arm. Incorrect toe-in will cause the tires to wear improperly by making them scrub against the road surface.

Camber is the tilting of the wheels from vertical when viewed from one end of the vehicle. When the wheels tilt out at the top, the camber is said to be positive (+). When

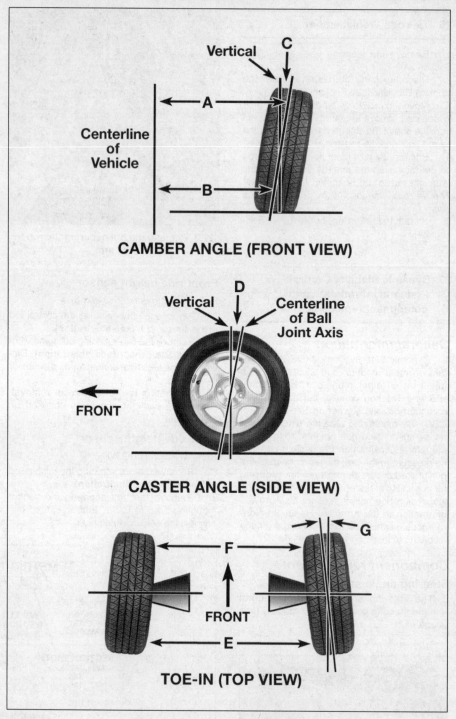

**29.1 Camber, caster and toe-in angles**

A minus B = C (degrees camber)
D = degrees caster

E minus F = toe-in (measured in inches)
G = toe-in (expressed in degrees)

the wheels tilt in at the top the camber is negative (-). The amount of tilt is measured in degrees from vertical and this measurement is called the camber angle. This angle affects the amount of tire tread which contacts the road and compensates for changes in the suspension geometry when the vehicle is cornering or traveling over an undulating surface.

On the front end it is adjusted by altering the position of the strut upper mount in the strut tower. On the rear end, it's adjusted by a cam at the inner end of the camber arm.

Caster is the tilting of the front steering axis from the vertical. A tilt toward the rear is positive caster and a tilt toward the front is negative caster.

# Chapter 11  Body

## Contents

## Specifications

### Torque specifications

**Note:** *One foot-pound (ft-lb) of torque is equivalent to 12 inch-pounds (in-lbs) of torque. Torque values below approximately 15 foot-pounds are expressed in inch-pounds, because most foot-pound torque wrenches are not accurate at these smaller values.*

| | Ft-lbs (unless otherwise indicated) | Nm |
|---|---|---|
| Fender mounting bolts | 67 in-lbs | 7.5 |
| Seat belt | | |
| Front anchorage mounting bolts | 32 | 44 |
| All other mountings | 27 | 36 |
| Seat mounting bolts | 30 | 40 |

## 1  General information

**Warning:** *The models covered by this manual are equipped with Supplemental Restraint Systems (SRS), more commonly known as airbags. Always disable the airbag system before working in the vicinity of any airbag system components to avoid the possibility of accidental deployment of the airbags, which could cause personal injury (see Chapter 12).*

Certain body components are particularly vulnerable to accident damage and can be unbolted and repaired or replaced. Among these parts are the hood, doors, tailgate, liftgate, bumpers and front fenders.

Only general body maintenance practices and body panel repair procedures within the scope of the do-it-yourselfer are included in this Chapter.

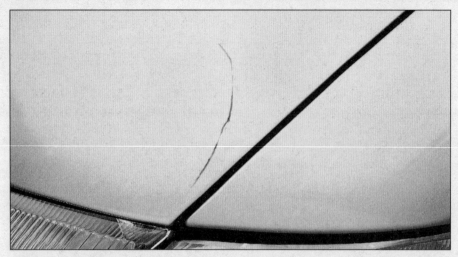

Make sure the damaged area is perfectly clean and rust free. If the touch-up kit has a wire brush, use it to clean the scratch or chip. Or use fine steel wool wrapped around the end of a pencil. Clean the scratched or chipped surface only, not the good paint surrounding it. Rinse the area with water and allow it to dry thoroughly

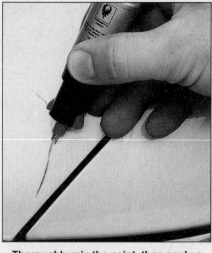

Thoroughly mix the paint, then apply a small amount with the touch-up kit brush or a very fine artist's brush. Brush in one direction as you fill the scratch area. Do not build up the paint higher than the surrounding paint

## 2   Repair minor paint scratches

No matter how hard you try to keep your vehicle looking like new, it will inevitably be scratched, chipped or dented at some point. If the metal is actually dented, seek the advice of a professional. But you can fix minor scratches and chips yourself. Buy a touch-up paint kit from a dealer parts department or an auto parts store. To ensure that you get the right color, you'll need to have the specific make, model and year of your vehicle and, ideally, the paint code, which is located on a special metal plate under the hood or in the door jamb.

## 3   Body repair - minor damage

### *Plastic body panels*

The following repair procedures are for minor scratches and gouges. Repair of more serious damage should be left to a dealer service department or qualified auto body shop. Below is a list of the equipment and materials necessary to perform the following repair procedures on plastic body panels.

*Wax, grease and silicone removing solvent*
*Cloth-backed body tape*
*Sanding discs*
*Drill motor with three-inch disc holder*
*Hand sanding block*
*Rubber squeegees*
*Sandpaper*
*Non-porous mixing palette*
*Wood paddle or putty knife*
*Curved-tooth body file*
*Flexible parts repair material*

### **Flexible panels (bumper trim)**

1    Remove the damaged panel, if necessary or desirable. In most cases, repairs can be car-

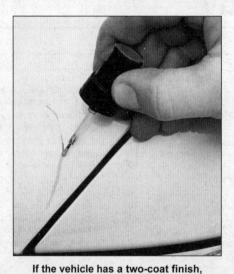

If the vehicle has a two-coat finish, apply the clear coat after the color coat has dried

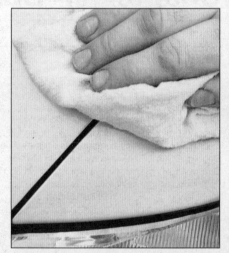

Wait a few days for the paint to dry thoroughly, then rub out the repainted area with a polishing compound to blend the new paint with the surrounding area. When you're happy with your work, wash and polish the area

ried out with the panel installed.
2    Clean the area(s) to be repaired with a wax, grease and silicone removing solvent applied with a water-dampened cloth.
3    If the damage is structural, that is, if it extends through the panel, clean the backside of the panel area to be repaired as well. Wipe dry.
4    Sand the rear surface about 1-1/2 inches beyond the break.
5    Cut two pieces of fiberglass cloth large enough to overlap the break by about 1-1/2 inches. Cut only to the required length.
6    Mix the adhesive from the repair kit according to the instructions included with the kit, and apply a layer of the mixture approximately 1/8-inch thick on the backside of the panel. Overlap the break by at least 1-1/2 inches.
7    Apply one piece of fiberglass cloth to the adhesive and cover the cloth with additional adhesive. Apply a second piece of fiberglass

cloth to the adhesive and immediately cover the cloth with additional adhesive in sufficient quantity to fill the weave.
8    Allow the repair to cure for 20 to 30 minutes at 60-degrees to 80-degrees F.
9    If necessary, trim the excess repair material at the edge.
10    Remove all of the paint film over and around the area(s) to be repaired. The repair material should not overlap the painted surface.
11    With a drill motor and a sanding disc (or a rotary file), cut a "V" along the break line approximately 1/2-inch wide. Remove all dust and loose particles from the repair area.
12    Mix and apply the repair material. Apply a light coat first over the damaged area; then continue applying material until it reaches a level

slightly higher than the surrounding finish.

13 Cure the mixture for 20 to 30 minutes at 60-degrees to 80-degrees F.

14 Roughly establish the contour of the area being repaired with a body file. If low areas or pits remain, mix and apply additional adhesive.

15 Block sand the damaged area with sandpaper to establish the actual contour of the surrounding surface.

16 If desired, the repaired area can be temporarily protected with several light coats of primer. Because of the special paints and techniques required for flexible body panels, it is recommended that the vehicle be taken to a paint shop for completion of the body repair.

## Steel body panels

*See photo sequence*

### Repair of dents

17 When repairing dents, the first job is to pull the dent out until the affected area is as close as possible to its original shape. There is no point in trying to restore the original shape completely as the metal in the damaged area will have stretched on impact and cannot be restored to its original contours. It is better to bring the level of the dent up to a point that is about 1/8-inch below the level of the surrounding metal. In cases where the dent is very shallow, it is not worth trying to pull it out at all.

18 If the backside of the dent is accessible, it can be hammered out gently from behind using a soft-face hammer. While doing this, hold a block of wood firmly against the opposite side of the metal to absorb the hammer blows and prevent the metal from being stretched.

19 If the dent is in a section of the body which has double layers, or some other factor makes it inaccessible from behind, a different technique is required. Drill several small holes through the metal inside the damaged area, particularly in the deeper sections. Screw long, self-tapping screws into the holes just enough for them to get a good grip in the metal. Now pulling on the protruding heads of the screws with locking pliers can pull out the dent.

20 The next stage of repair is the removal of paint from the damaged area and from an inch or so of the surrounding metal. This is easily done with a wire brush or sanding disk in a drill motor, although it can be done just as effectively by hand with sandpaper. To complete the preparation for filling, score the surface of the bare metal with a screwdriver or the tang of a file or drill small holes in the affected area. This will provide a good grip for the filler material. To complete the repair, see the Section on filling and painting.

### Repair of rust holes or gashes

21 Remove all paint from the affected area and from an inch or so of the surrounding metal using a sanding disk or wire brush mounted in a drill motor. If these are not available, a few sheets of sandpaper will do the job just as effectively.

22 With the paint removed, you will be able to determine the severity of the corrosion and decide whether to replace the whole panel, if possible, or repair the affected area. New body panels are not as expensive as most people think and it is often quicker to install a new panel than to repair large areas of rust.

23 Remove all trim pieces from the affected area except those which will act as a guide to the original shape of the damaged body, such as headlight shells, etc. Using metal snips or a hacksaw blade, remove all loose metal and any other metal that is badly affected by rust. Hammer the edges of the hole to create a slight depression for the filler material.

24 Wire-brush the affected area to remove the powdery rust from the surface of the metal. If the back of the rusted area is accessible, treat it with rust inhibiting paint.

25 Before filling is done, block the hole in some way. This can be done with sheet metal riveted or screwed into place, or by stuffing the hole with wire mesh.

26 Once the hole is blocked off, the affected area can be filled and painted. See the following subsection on filling and painting.

### Filling and painting

27 Many types of body fillers are available, but generally speaking, body repair kits which contain filler paste and a tube of resin hardener are best for this type of repair work. A wide, flexible plastic or nylon applicator will be necessary for imparting a smooth and contoured finish to the surface of the filler material. Mix up a small amount of filler on a clean piece of wood or cardboard (use the hardener sparingly). Follow the manufacturer's instructions on the package, otherwise the filler will set incorrectly.

28 Using the applicator, apply the filler paste to the prepared area. Draw the applicator across the surface of the filler to achieve the desired contour and to level the filler surface. As soon as a contour that approximates the original one is achieved, stop working the paste. If you continue, the paste will begin to stick to the applicator. Continue to add thin layers of paste at 20-minute intervals until the level of the filler is just above the surrounding metal.

29 Once the filler has hardened, the excess can be removed with a body file. From then on, progressively finer grades of sandpaper should be used, starting with a 180-grit paper and finishing with 600-grit wet-or-dry paper. Always wrap the sandpaper around a flat rubber or wooden block, otherwise the surface of the filler will not be completely flat. During the sanding of the filler surface, the wet-or-dry paper should be periodically rinsed in water. This will ensure that a very smooth finish is produced in the final stage.

30 At this point, the repair area should be surrounded by a ring of bare metal, which in turn should be encircled by the finely feathered edge of good paint. Rinse the repair area with clean water until all of the dust produced by the sanding operation is gone.

31 Spray the entire area with a light coat of primer. This will reveal any imperfections in the surface of the filler. Repair the imperfections with fresh filler paste or glaze filler and once more smooth the surface with sandpaper. Repeat this spray-and-repair procedure until you are satisfied that the surface of the filler and the feathered edge of the paint are perfect. Rinse the area with clean water and allow it to dry completely.

32 The repair area is now ready for painting. Spray painting must be carried out in a warm, dry, windless and dust free atmosphere. These conditions can be created if you have access to a large indoor work area, but if you are forced to work in the open, you will have to pick the day very carefully. If you are working indoors, dousing the floor in the work area with water will help settle the dust that would otherwise be in the air. If the repair area is confined to one body panel, mask off the surrounding panels. This will help minimize the effects of a slight mismatch in paint color. Trim pieces such as chrome strips, door handles, etc., will also need to be masked off or removed. Use masking tape and several thickness of newspaper for the masking operations.

33 Before spraying, shake the paint can thoroughly, then spray a test area until the spray painting technique is mastered. Cover the repair area with a thick coat of primer. The thickness should be built up using several thin layers of primer rather than one thick one. Using 600-grit wet-or-dry sandpaper, rub down the surface of the primer until it is very smooth. While doing this, the work area should be thoroughly rinsed with water and the wet-or-dry sandpaper periodically rinsed as well. Allow the primer to dry before spraying additional coats.

34 Spray on the top coat, again building up the thickness by using several thin layers of paint. Begin spraying in the center of the repair area and then, using a circular motion, work out until the whole repair area and about two inches of the surrounding original paint is covered. Remove all masking material 10 to 15 minutes after spraying on the final coat of paint. Allow the new paint at least two weeks to harden, then use a very fine rubbing compound to blend the edges of the new paint into the existing paint. Finally, apply a coat of wax

---

## 4   Body repair - major damage

1 Major damage must be repaired by an auto body shop specifically equipped to perform body and frame repairs. These shops have the specialized equipment required to do the job properly.

2 If the damage is extensive, the frame must be checked for proper alignment or the vehicle's handling characteristics may be adversely affected and other components may wear at an accelerated rate.

3 Due to the fact that all of the major body components (hood, fenders, etc.) are separate and replaceable units, any seriously damaged components should be replaced rather than repaired. Sometimes the components can be found in a wrecking yard that specializes in used vehicle components, often at considerable savings over the cost of new parts.

These photos illustrate a method of repairing simple dents. They are intended to supplement *Body repair - minor damage* in this Chapter and should not be used as the sole instructions for body repair on these vehicles.

1  If you can't access the backside of the body panel to hammer out the dent, pull it out with a slide-hammer-type dent puller. Tap with a hammer near the edge of the dent to help 'pop' the metal back to its original shape, about 1/8-inch below the surface of the surrounding metal

2  Using coarse-grit sandpaper, remove the paint down to the bare metal. Clean the repair area with wax/silicone remover.

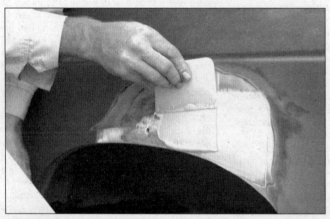

3  Following label instructions, mix up a batch of plastic filler and hardener, then quickly press it into the metal with a plastic applicator. Work the filler until it matches the original contour and is slightly above the surrounding metal

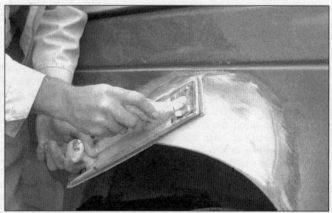

4  Let the filler harden until you can just dent it with your fingernail. File, then sand the filler down until it's smooth and even. Work down to finer grits of sandpaper - always using a board or block - ending up with 360 or 400 grit

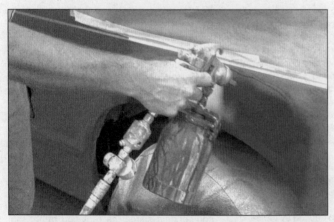

5  When the area is smooth to the touch, clean the area and mask around it. Apply several layers of primer to the area. A professional-type spray gun is being used here, but aerosol spray primer works fine

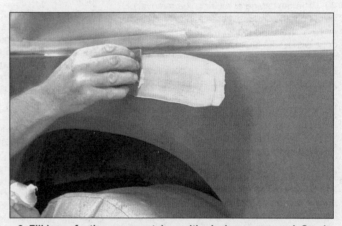

6  Fill imperfections or scratches with glazing compound. Sand with 360 or 400-grit and re-spray. Finish sand the primer with 600 grit, clean thoroughly, then apply the finish coat. Don't attempt to rub out or wax the repair area until the paint has dried completely (at least two weeks)

## 5 Upholstery, carpets and vinyl trim - maintenance

### Upholstery and carpets

1 Every three months remove the floormats and clean the interior of the vehicle (more frequently if necessary). Use a stiff whiskbroom to brush the carpeting and loosen dirt and dust, then vacuum the upholstery and carpets thoroughly, especially along seams and crevices.

2 Dirt and stains can be removed from carpeting with basic household or automotive carpet shampoos available in spray cans. Follow the directions and vacuum again, then use a stiff brush to bring back the "nap" of the carpet.

3 Most interiors have cloth or vinyl upholstery, either of which can be cleaned and maintained with a number of material-specific cleaners or shampoos available in auto supply stores. Follow the directions on the product for usage, and always spot-test any upholstery cleaner on an inconspicuous area (bottom edge of a backseat cushion) to ensure that it doesn't cause a color shift in the material.

4 After cleaning, vinyl upholstery should be treated with a protectant. **Note:** *Make sure the protectant container indicates the product can be used on seats - some products may make a seat too slippery.* **Caution:** *Do not use protectant on vinyl-covered steering wheels.*

5 Leather upholstery requires special care. It should be cleaned regularly with saddle-soap or leather cleaner. Never use alcohol, gasoline, nail polish remover or thinner to clean leather upholstery.

6 After cleaning, regularly treat leather upholstery with a leather conditioner, rubbed in with a soft cotton cloth. Never use car wax on leather upholstery.

7 In areas where the interior of the vehicle is subject to bright sunlight, cover leather seating areas of the seats with a sheet if the vehicle is to be left out for any length of time.

### Vinyl trim

8 Don't clean vinyl trim with detergents, caustic soap or petroleum-based cleaners. Plain soap and water works just fine, with a soft brush to clean dirt that may be ingrained. Wash the vinyl as frequently as the rest of the vehicle.

9 After cleaning, application of a high-quality rubber and vinyl protectant will help prevent oxidation and cracks. The protectant can also be applied to weather-stripping, vacuum lines and rubber hoses, which often fail as a result of chemical degradation, and to the tires.

## 6 Fastener and trim removal

*Refer to illustrations 6.3 and 6.4*

1 There is a variety of plastic fasteners used to hold trim panels, splash shields and other parts in place in addition to typical screws, nuts and bolts. Once you are familiar with them, they can usually be removed without too much difficulty.

2 The proper tools and approach can prevent added time and expense to a project by minimizing the number of broken fasteners and/or parts.

3 The following illustration shows various types of fasteners that are typically used on most vehicles and how to remove and install them **(see illustration)**. Replacement fasteners are commonly found at most auto parts stores, if necessary.

# Fasteners

This tool is designed to remove special fasteners. A small pry tool used for removing nails will also work well in place of this tool

A Phillips head screwdriver can be used to release the center portion, but light pressure must be used because the plastic is easily damaged. Once the center is up, the fastener can easily be pried from its hole

Here is a view with the center portion fully released. Install the fastener as shown, then press the center in to set it

This fastener is used for exterior panels and shields. The center portion must be pried up to release the fastener. Install the fastener with the center up, then press the center in to set it

This type of fastener is used commonly for interior panels. Use a small blunt tool to press the small pin at the center in to release it . . .

. . . the pin will stay with the fastener in the released position

Reset the fastener for installation by moving the pin out. Install the fastener, then press the pin flush with the fastener to set it

This fastener is used for exterior and interior panels. It has no moving parts. Simply pry the fastener from its hole like the claw of a hammer removes a nail. Without a tool that can get under the top of the fastener, it can be very difficult to remove

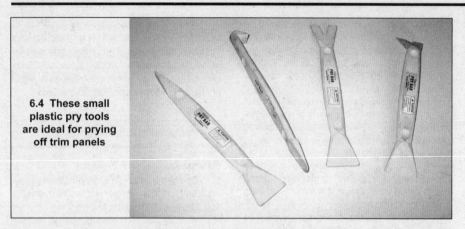

**6.4   These small plastic pry tools are ideal for prying off trim panels**

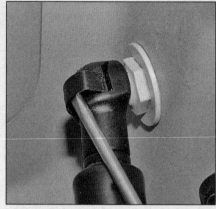

**7.2   Pry out the clip securing the hood support strut**

4   Trim panels are typically made of plastic and their flexibility can help during removal. The key to their removal is to use a tool to pry the panel near its retainers to release it without damaging surrounding areas or breaking-off any retainers. The retainers will usually snap out of their designated slot or hole after force is applied to them. Stiff plastic tools designed for prying on trim panels are available at most auto parts stores **(see illustration)**. Tools that are tapered and wrapped in protective tape, such as a screwdriver or small pry tool, are also very effective when used with care.

## 7   Hood - removal, installation and adjustment

### *Removal*

*Refer to illustrations 7.2 and 7.3*

1   Open the hood and have an assistant support it. Using a pencil or felt tip pen, mark the outline of each hood hinge relative to the hood to use as a guide on installation, then disconnect any electrical connectors and washer hose lines.

2   With the aid of an assistant, support the hood in the open position, then remove the retaining clips and detach the support struts from the hood **(see illustration)**.

3   Loosen and remove the left and right-hand rear hinge-to-hood bolts and loosen the front bolts **(see illustration)**. Slide the hood forward to disengage it from the hinges and remove it from the vehicle. Remove any shims which are in between the hinge and hood.

4   Disconnect the ground strap attached to the left hinge.

5   Inspect the hood hinges for signs of wear and freeplay at the pivots, and replace the hinges if necessary. Each hinge is secured to the body by two bolts. Mark the position of the hinge on the body, then remove the hinge mounting bolts and the hinge.

### *Installation and adjustment*

6   Install the shims (if equipped) to the hinge and, with the aid of an assistant, engage the hood with the hinges. Install the rear bolts and tighten them by hand only. Align the hinges with the marks made on removal, then tighten the retaining bolts securely. Reattach the ground strap.

7   Close the hood, and check for alignment with the adjacent panels. If necessary, loosen the hinge bolts and re-align the hood to suit. Ideally, the gap at each fender and the gap at the cowl should all be similar in width. Once the hood is correctly aligned, securely tighten the hinge bolts and check that the hood fastens and releases satisfactorily.

## 8   Hood latches and release cable - removal and installation

### *Latches*

#### *Removal*

*Refer to illustrations 8.1 and 8.4*

1   Remove the fasteners securing the connection housing to the inner fender. Pry open the housing and disconnect the inner and outer cables **(see illustration)**.

2   Remove the mounting bolts at the top edge of the bumper **(see illustration 9.3)**.

3   Make alignment marks between the latch and radiator support panel to aid installation.

4   Loosen and remove the latch mounting bolts, then lift the latch from the radiator support panel. Release the outer cable from the latch, then detach the inner cable from the latch **(see illustration)**. Remove the lock from the vehicle.

**Note:** *On F-series chassis models, there are four screws in two rows next to each hood latch, but only two are for the latch. When facing the engine, on the right side, remove the first row outer and the second row inner screw. On the left side, remove the first row inner and the second row outer screw.*

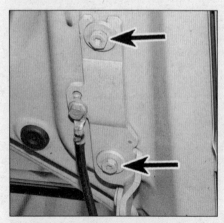

**7.3   Remove the lower hinge bolt and loosen the upper bolt**

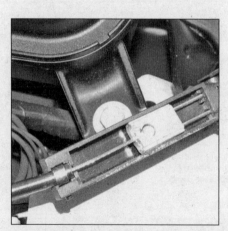

**8.1   Pry open the housing and disconnect the cables**

**8.4   Remove the bolts securing the hood latch**

**8.11  Remove the driver's knee bolster panel mounting bolts and the panel**

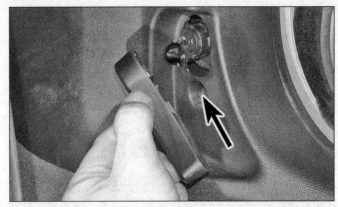

**8.12  Remove the release handle bolt, then remove the kick panel mounting bolt**

## Installation

5    Locate the hood release inner cable in the latch and reconnect the outer cable to the lever. Seat the latch on the radiator support panel.
6    Align the latch with the marks made prior to removal. Install the bolts and tighten them securely.
7    Check that the latch operates smoothly when the release lever is moved, without any sign of resistance. Check that the hood fastens and releases satisfactorily.
8    Once the latches are operating correctly, install the bumper bolts.

## *Cable*

### Removal

9    The hood release cable is in three sections; the main cable from the release lever to the connection at the right-hand side inner fender (next to the windshield washer reservoir), the second from the connection to the right-hand hood lock, and the third linking the two hood latches.

### Release lever-to-connecting cable

*Refer to illustrations 8.11, 8.12, 8.13a, 8.13b, 8.14, 8.15, 8.16, 8.17a, 8.17b and 8.17c*

10    Open the driver's door, and carefully pull up the door sill trim panel.
11    Remove the fasteners and the driver's knee bolster panel above the pedals (**see**

**8.13a  Remove the bolts . . .**

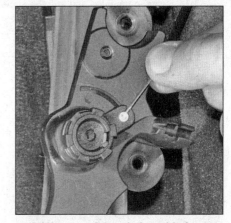

**8.13b  . . . and detach the cable from the lever**

**illustration**). Disconnect any electrical connectors as the panel is withdrawn.
12    Remove the hood release handle mounting bolt and handle, then remove the kick panel mounting bolt and kick panel (**see illustration**).
13    Remove the release lever assembly mounting bolts and pull the assembly from the A-pillar, then separate the cable inner end fitting from the release lever (**see illustrations**).
14    Remove the upper section of the cabin

air filter housing mounting bolts and the housing (**see illustration**).
**Note:** *On F-series chassis models, the cable is routed along the radiator support and is held in place by two clips. To access the clips remove the air intake duct (see Chapter 1).*
15    Release the catches and remove the left and right plastic covers from behind the strut tower on each side of the engine compartment. Unclip the hose from the left-hand cover (**see illustration**).

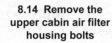

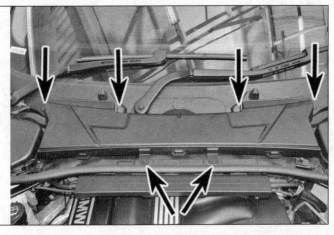

**8.14  Remove the upper cabin air filter housing bolts**

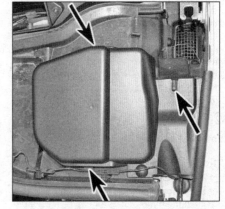

**8.15  Release the clips and remove the plastic cover on each side**

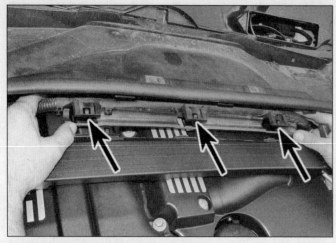

8.16 **Release the clips and pull the cable guide forwards**

8.17a **Rotate the temperature sensor counterclockwise and detach it from the bracket**

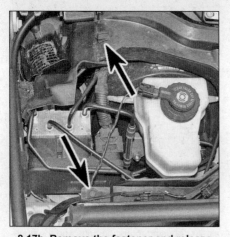

8.17b **Remove the fastener and release the clip on each side . . .**

8.17c **. . . then slide the cabin air filter lower housing forward**

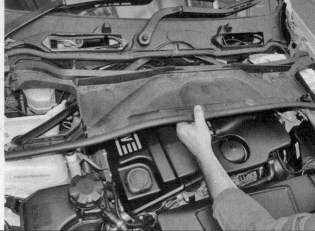

16   Depress the clips and pull the cable guide forwards from the cabin air filter lower housing **(see illustration)**.

17   Release the catch and remove the bolt at each side, then slide the cabin air filter lower housing forward and maneuver it out **(see illustrations)**.

18   Remove the plastic expansion rivet and nut, then remove the water channel on the right-hand side.

19   Push/pull the outer release cable grommet from the engine compartment firewall, and pull the cable into the engine compartment.

20   Unclip the connection housing from the inner fender. Pry open the connection housing and disconnect the inner and outer cables **(see illustration 8.1)**.

### Connection cable-to-hood lock cable

21   Unclip the connection housing from the inner fender. Pry open the housing and disconnect the inner and outer cables **(see illustration 8.1)**.

22   Remove the hood latch (see Steps 1

through 4). To improve access, remove the intake hood from the radiator support panel.

### Installation

23   Installation is the reverse of removal, ensuring that the cable is correctly routed, and secured to all the relevant retaining clips. Check that the hood latch operates correctly before closing the hood.

## 9   Bumper covers - removal and installation

**Note:** *These vehicles have urethane bumper covers, behind which are steel protective bumper beams with impact-absorbing units.*

### Front

*Refer to illustrations 9.2, 9.3, 9.4, 9.5 and 9.6*

1   Apply the parking brake, raise the front of the vehicle and support it securely on jackstands, then remove the engine splash

shield fasteners and shield from under the vehicle.

2   On models with headlight washers, pull the washer jet covers forwards. Gently pull the retaining clips apart slightly, and remove the covers **(see illustration)**.

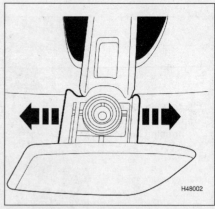

9.2 **Pull out the retaining clips and remove the cover**

9.3  Remove the mounting fasteners, then remove the rubber sealing strip

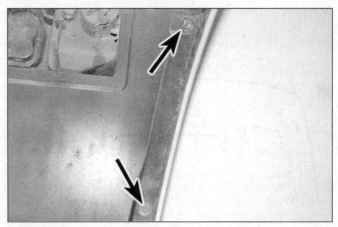

9.4  Remove the mounting bolts securing the wheelwell liner

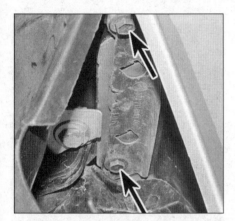

9.5  Remove the mounting bolts securing the bumper to the fender on each side

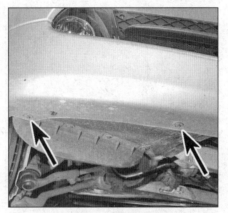

9.6  Remove the mounting bolts at the lower edge of the bumper (right-side bolts shown)

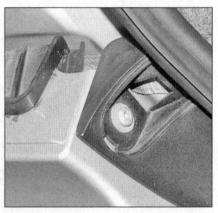

9.12  Pry out the cap and remove the bolt on each side of the trunk lid/tailgate opening

3    On F-series chassis models, remove the plastic trim cover from the radiator support and, on all models, remove the mounting bolts at the upper edge of the bumper, then pull up the rubber sealing strip from the edges, if equipped (see illustration).
Note: *On F-series chassis models, once all eight upper bolts are removed, there are four clips that must be removed before the upper edge is released.*
4    Remove the mounting bolts at each side securing the wheelwell liner to the bumper (see illustration).
5    Pull back the wheelwell liner and remove the mounting bolts at each side securing the bumper to the fender (see illustration).
6    Remove the mounting bolts on the underside of the bumper (see illustration).
7    Pull the rear edges of the bumper out slightly, then pull the bumper forward a little. Noting their installed locations, disconnect the various electrical connectors.
Note: *On models equipped with aerodynamic trim, there are two bars that lock into the bumper cover from behind. They are located to the inside of the fog lights and must be unclipped before the bumper can be removed.*
8    With the help of an assistant, pull the bumper forward and away from the vehicle.
9    Installation is the reverse of removal.

### Rear

*Refer to illustrations 9.12, 9.13, 9.14, 9.15, 9.16a and 9.16b*

10   To improve access, block the front wheels, then raise the rear of the vehicle and support it securely on jackstands. An assistant is also helpful.
11   Remove the body-mounted rear light units (see Chapter 12).

12   Pry out the caps and remove the bolts in the front corners of the trunk lid/tailgate opening (see illustration).
13   Remove the bolts securing the wheelwell liner to the bumper (see illustration).
14   Pull the wheelwell liner forward and remove the bolt at each side securing the bumper to the rear quarter-panel (see illustration).
15   Remove the fasteners at the lower edges

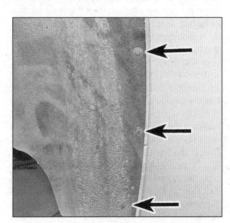

9.13  Remove the bolts securing the wheelwell liner to the bumper

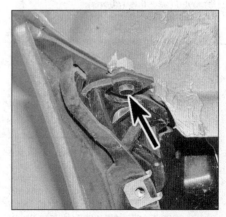

9.14  Remove the fastener on each side securing the bumper to the fender

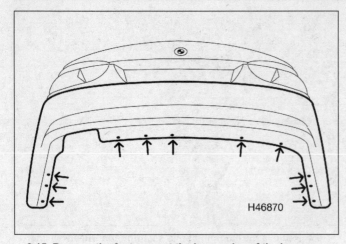

**9.15  Remove the fasteners at the lower edge of the bumper –
E-series shown, F-series similar**

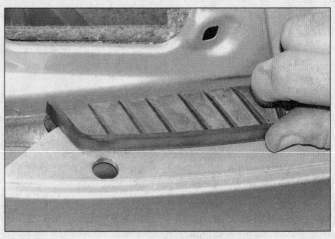

**9.16a  Pry up the plastic holders slightly . . .**

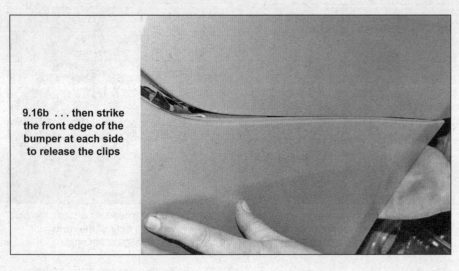

**9.16b  . . . then strike
the front edge of the
bumper at each side
to release the clips**

**11.2  Door stop strut Torx bolt location**

of the bumper **(see illustration)**.

16    Gently pry up the black plastic holders
in the rear light openings, and with the help
of an assistant, push the bumper rearward
to release the retaining clips. Strike the front
edge of the bumper on each side with the
palm of your hand to help release the clips.
Disconnect the parking sensor electrical connectors (where applicable) as the bumper is
removed **(see illustrations)**.

17    Installation is the reverse of removal,
ensuring that the bumper ends are correctly
engaged with their slides. Apply thread-locking compound to the bumper mounting bolts
and tighten them securely.

### 10   Front fender - removal and installation

1    Block the rear wheels, then raise the
front of the vehicle and support it securely
with jackstands. Remove the front wheels
and open the hood. Measure the gap between
the rear of the fender and the front edge
of the door to aid installation. Before opening the hood, note the gap between the
fender and the hood.

2    Disengage the inner fenderwell liner by
removing the plastic fasteners. These can be
removed with a small round gasket punch.
Use a hammer to cut out the center of the
fasteners with the punch. New fasteners,
available at auto parts stores, will be used for
installation.

3    The wheelwell liner is in two sections;
remove the rear section, then the front section
(which is secured by screws and nuts).

4    Remove the fender mounting bolts along
the top of the fender.

5    On Sports Wagon and Sedan models,
remove the bolts in the door jamb area (one
at the rear bottom of the fender, and one at
the front edge).

6    On Convertible and Coupe models,
remove the mounting bolts in the door jamb
area (two at the rear bottom of the fender, and
one at the front).

7    Use masking tape along the front of the
door to prevent scratches there. Make sure
to disengage any cables, hoses or electrical
harnesses that may be clipped or tied to the
fender.

8    Carefully pull the fender up and off the
vehicle.

9    Installation is the reverse of removal.
Install all mounting bolts somewhat loosely,
then position the fender to achieve the correct
fender-to-door gap. Tighten the bolts to the
torque listed in this Chapter's Specifications.

### 11   Door - removal, installation and adjustment

## Removal

*Refer to illustrations 11.2 and 11.3*

1    Disconnect the negative battery cable
(see Chapter 5).

2    Remove the Torx bolt securing the door
stop strut to the pillar **(see illustration)**. Use
masking tape at the panels adjoining the door
to protect the paint.

3    Unscrew the hinge nuts from both the
upper and lower door hinges **(see illustration)**. **Note:** *It is helpful to have a floor jack
positioned under the middle of the door (with
a padded length of wood used to protect the
paint) to support the door while removing the
hinge nuts.*

4    Have an assistant support the door while

**11.3  Remove the hinge nuts**

**12.1  Carefully pry the decorative trim from the panel**

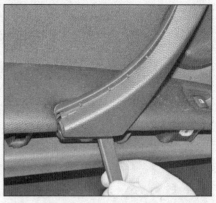

**12.2  Pry the interior door handle trim from the passenger's door panel**

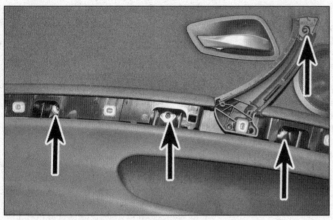

**12.3  Remove the bolts securing the door panel**

**12.4  Pull the panel inwards, before lifting it over the locking knob**

you remove the retaining bolt and withdraw the door electrical connector from the pillar. Pull out the locking element and unplug the connector as the door is withdrawn. If necessary, the hinge pins can be unscrewed from the hinges.

### *Installation*

5    Maneuver the door into position and reconnect the electrical connector. Push the connector into the pillar and secure it in place with the bolt.
6    Engage the hinges with the studs on the door, and tighten the nuts loosely. Make minor movements of the door (with an assistant) to achieve the proper alignment, then tighten the nuts. If necessary, the position of the door can be adjusted by inserting or removing shims between the hinge and the door (available from BMW dealers).
7    Align the door stop strut with the body, then install and tighten the securing bolt.

### *Adjustment*

8    Close the door and check the door alignment with the surrounding body panels. Slight adjustment of the door position can be made by loosening the hinge retaining nuts and repositioning the hinge/door as necessary. Once the door is correctly positioned, securely tighten the hinge nuts. If the paint

work around the hinges has been damaged, paint the affected area with a suitable touch-in brush to prevent corrosion.

---

### 12   Door inner trim panel - removal and installation

---

### *Removal*

#### Front door

*Refer to illustrations 12.1, 12.2, 12.3, 12.4 and 12.5*

1    On E-series chassis models, use a plastic trim tool (see Section 6), carefully pry the decorative trim from the door panel starting at the front of the trim, then unhook it from the rear **(see illustration)**.
2    Carefully pry out the interior door handle trim starting at the lower edge **(see illustration)**, then on F-series chassis models, use a screwdriver to disengage the switch cover lock from the opening. Use a plastic trim tool to disengage the switch assembly clips and lift the switch assembly from the door panel enough to disconnect the electrical connector and remove the switch assembly.
3    On E-series chassis models, remove the Torx bolts securing the door trim **(see illustration)**.

4    Release the door trim panel clips, carefully prying between the panel and door with a plastic trim tool. Work around the outside of the panel, including the top edge. When all the studs are released, ease the panel away from the top of the door, then lift it over the locking knob **(see illustration)**.
5    Holding the panel away from the door, disconnect the interior handle release cable from the door lock **(see illustration)**.
**Note:** *On F-series chassis models, disconnect the cable from the support first, then the release handle.*

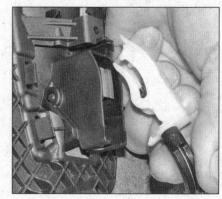

**12.5  Unclip the rear edge, and disconnect the release handle cable - E-series shown**

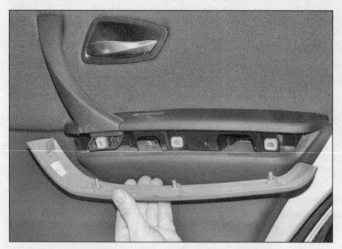

**12.8  Pry the decorative trim from the panel**

**12.9  Pry the cover from the door handle . . .**

6    Disconnect the various electrical connectors as the panel is removed. An assistant
is helpful.
7    If required, carefully peel the watershield
away from the door. Use a putty knife to cut
through the sealant, if necessary.

### Rear door

*Refer to illustrations 12.8, 12.9 and 12.10*

8    Using a plastic trim tool (see Section 6),
carefully pry the decorative trim from the door
panel starting at the front of the trim, then
unhook it **(see illustration)**.
**Note:** *On F-series chassis models, The decorative trim and door handle cover have been
combined into one piece, which is pried off.*
9    Using a trim tool, carefully pry the cover
from the door pull handle, starting at the base
of the trim **(see illustration)**.
10   Remove the panel-retaining Torx bolts
**(see illustration)**.
11   Release the door trim panel clips, carefully prying between the panel and door with
a plastic trim tool. Work around the outside

of the panel, including the top edge. When all
the studs are released, ease the panel away
from the top of the door, then lift it over the
locking knob **(see illustration 12.4)**.
12   Holding the panel away from the door,
disconnect the interior handle release cable
from the door lock **(see illustration 12.5)**.
13   Disconnect the various electrical connectors as the panel is removed. An assistant
is helpful.
14   If required, carefully peel the watershield
away from the door. Use a putty knife to cut
through the sealant, if necessary.

## *Installation*

15   Installation is the reverse of removal.
Before installation, check whether any of
the trim panel retaining clips were broken
during removal, and replace them as necessary. If the watershield was removed, be
sure it is returned to its original location. If the
watershield is damaged on removal, it may
be repairable with duct tape to keep the inner
door waterproofed.

## 13  Door handle and latch components - removal and installation

## *Removal*

### Interior door handle

*Refer to illustration 13.3*

1    Remove the interior door trim panel (see
Section 12).
2    Release the interior handle lever, pry out
the locking clip and detach the cable from the
handle **(see illustration 12.5)**.
3    Remove the retaining bolt, release the
clips and remove the handle from the door
trim **(see illustration)**.

### Front door latch assembly

*Refer to illustrations 13.7a, 13.7b, 13.8, 13.9a
and 13.9b*

4    Remove the window regulator assembly
(see Section 14). **Note:** *It isn't necessary to
completely remove the window - slide it to the*

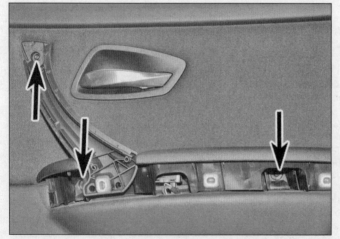

**12.10  . . . and remove the panel retaining bolts - typical E-series
chassis models, F-series similar**

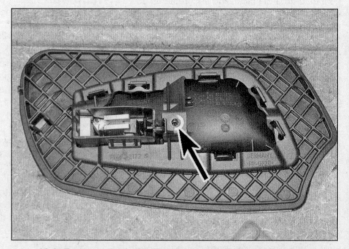

**13.3  Remove the bolt, then release the clips around the
circumference and pull the handle from the panel**

**13.7a  Pull the outer cable from the bracket and disengage the inner cable**

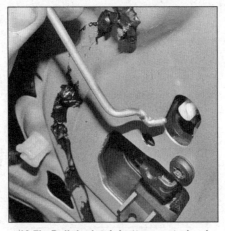

**13.7b  Pull the latch button control rod from the lock**

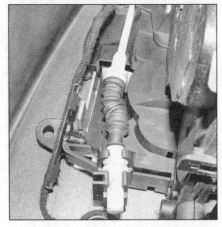

**13.8  Pull the release cable from the door latch**

*top of the channel and secure it in place with duct tape.*

5    If working on the driver's door, remove the lock cylinder (see Steps 13 and 14).

6    Release the latch assembly wiring retaining clips and disconnect the wiring connector(s).

7    Disconnect the interior release cable from the latch, then unclip the latch-button control rod from the latch **(see illustrations)**.

8    Unclip the release cable from the door latch by pulling the cable from the clips. Note the routing of the cable; it must be installed in the original position **(see illustration)**.

9    Loosen and remove the latch assembly retaining screws, then maneuver the assembly from the door **(see illustrations)**.

### Front door exterior handle

*Refer to illustrations 13.11 and 13.12*

10    If working on the driver's door, remove the lock cylinder (see Steps 13 and 14). If working on the passenger's door, pry out the grommet in the door end panel to expose the outer handle rear cover retaining bolt - remove the bolt, and pull out the cover. **Note:** *On models with handle lighting, lift out the lighting*

**13.9a  Remove the door latch bolts . . .**

**13.9b  . . . and maneuver the latch from the door**

*element and position it in the handle opening to prevent accidental damage as the handle is removed.*

11    Pull the outer handle rearward, then outward to disengage the front locator **(see illustration)**.

12    To remove the handle operating frame,

remove the door latch, then remove the rubber gasket from the front handle mount **(see illustration)**. Remove the Torx bolt and pull the frame forward and off. Disconnect any electrical connectors as the frame is removed.

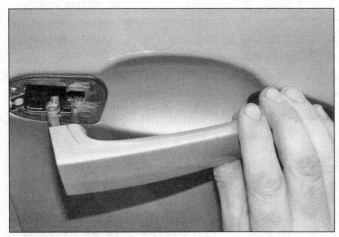

**13.11  Pull the handle rearwards, then outwards**

**13.12  Remove the rubber gaskets and the retaining bolt**

**13.14  Pull the lock cylinder from the door**

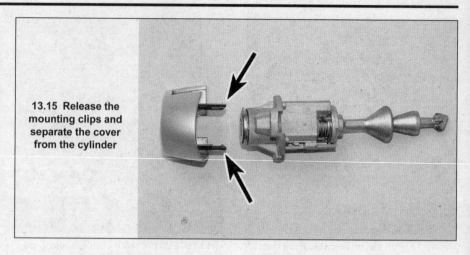

**13.15  Release the mounting clips and separate the cover from the cylinder**

### Front door lock cylinder

*Refer to illustrations 13.14 and 13.15*

13   Pry out the rubber plug from the end of the door opening to expose the lock cylinder retaining bolt.
**Note:** *On models equipped with handle lighting, lift out the lighting element and position it in the handle opening to prevent accidental damage as the handle is removed* (**see illustration 13.21**).
14   Remove the lock cylinder retaining bolt, insert the key, and pull the lock cylinder from the door (**see illustration**).
15   If required, release the retaining clips and separate the cylinder from the plastic cover (**see illustration**).

### Rear door latch

16   Remove the door inner trim panel and watershield (see Section 12). Disconnect the door latch electrical connector(s).
17   Disconnect the release cable from the latch, then unclip the lock-button control rod (**see illustrations 13.7a and 13.7b**).
18   Unclip the outer handle release cable from the door latch. Note the routing of the cable; it must be installed in the original position (**see illustration 13.8**).
19   Loosen and remove the latch assembly retaining Torx bolts, release the wiring harness

from the retaining clips, then maneuver it from the door (**see illustrations 13.9a and 13.9b**).

### Rear door exterior handle

*Refer to illustrations 13.20a, 13.20b and 13.21*

20   Pry out the grommet in the door end panel to expose the outer handle rear cover retaining bolt. Remove the rear cover mounting fastener and cover from the outer handle (**see illustrations**).
21   Pull the outer handle rearward, then outward to disengage the front guide (**see illustration**). **Note:** *On models with handle lighting, lift out the lighting element and position it in the handle opening to prevent accidental damage as the handle is removed.*
22   To remove the handle operating frame, remove the door latch (see Steps 16 through 19), then remove the rubber gasket from the front handle mounting (**see illustration 13.12**). Remove the Torx bolt and pull the frame forward and off. Disconnect any electrical connectors as the frame is removed.

### *Installation*

#### Interior door handle

23   Clip the door handle into the trim and install the retaining bolt.
24   Reconnect the release cable to the handle.

25   Install the door trim panel (see Section 12).

### Front door latch assembly

26   Ensure that the seal on the door latch is undamaged.
27   Maneuver the latch assembly into position. Install the bolts, but don't tighten them at this stage.
28   Force the latch fully into the corner of the door frame. The latch seal must fully contact the door frame to prevent water entering. Tighten the retaining bolts securely.
29   Reconnect the release cable and electrical connectors to the latch.
30   Clip the latch-button control rod and interior release cable into place on the latch.
31   On the driver's door, install the lock cylinder (see Steps 39 and 40).
32   Install the window regulator assembly (see Section 14).
33   Do not close the door until the operation of the latch has been reset and checked as follows:

a)  *With the door open, use a screwdriver to close the door latch by pushing in the latch lever.*
b)  *With the door open, use the key and unlock the door.*
c)  *With the door open, use the outside handle and open the latch.*

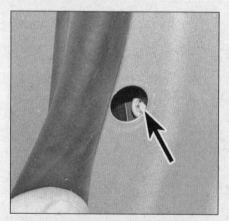

**13.20a  Remove the retaining bolt . . .**

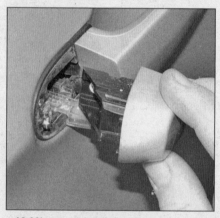

**13.20b  . . . and pull the rear cover from the door**

**13.21  Place the handle lighting element in the opening to prevent damage**

**13.34  Position the latch lever so the retaining clip holds it outward**

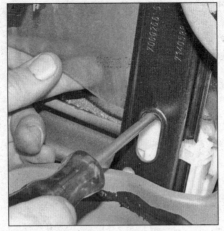

**14.5a  Use a screwdriver . . .**

**14.5b  . . . to push out the window catch**

## Front door exterior handle

*Refer to illustration 13.34*

34   Ensure that the latch lever is positioned as shown **(see illustration)**. If not, pull the lever outwards until it engages with the retaining clip.

35   Insert the front of the handle into the corresponding hole in the door, followed by the rear of the handle. Hold the handle gently against the door and push it forward until it clicks into place.

36   If installing the driver's door handle, install the lock cylinder (see Steps 39 and 40). If installing the passenger's handle, fit the outer handle rear cover into place, and tighten the retaining bolt securely. Install the grommet to the door end panel.

37   Do not close the door until the operation of the latch has been reset and checked (see Step 33).

## Front door lock cylinder

38   If separated, clip the plastic cover back onto the cylinder.

39   Lubricate the outside of the lock cylinder with a suitable grease.

40   Install the lock cylinder into the door latch, and tighten the retaining bolt securely. Install the plastic grommet into the door end panel. Do not close the door until the opera-

tion of the latch has been reset and checked (see Step 33).

## Rear door latch

41   Ensure that the seal on the door latch is undamaged.

42   Maneuver the latch assembly into position. Install the bolts, but don't tighten them at this stage.

43   Force the latch fully into the corner of the door frame. The latch seal must fully contact the door frame to prevent water entering. Tighten the retaining bolts securely.

44   Reconnect the release cable and electrical connectors to the latch.

45   Clip the latch button control rod into place on the latch.

46   Do not close the door until the operation of the latch has been reset and checked (see Step 33).

47   Reseal the plastic watershield to the door. Install the trim panel (see Section 12).

## Rear door exterior handle

48   Ensure that the lock lever is positioned as shown in **illustration 13.34**. If not, pull the lever outwards until it engages with the retaining clip.

49   Insert the front of the handle into the corresponding hole in the door, followed by the

rear of the handle. Hold the handle gently against the door and push it forward until it clicks into place.

50   Install the outer handle rear cover into place, and tighten the retaining bolt securely. Install the grommet on the door end panel.

51   Do not close the door until the operation of the latch has been set up and checked (see Step 33).

## 14   Door window glass and regulator - removal and installation

## *Removal*

### Front door window

*Refer to illustrations 14.5a, 14.5b and 14.6*

1   Fully open the window, then raise it approximately 4.5 inches (105 mm) on E-series chassis models and 5.7 inches (145 mm) on F-series chassis models, (measured at the rear of the glass), to access the window fasteners.

2   Disconnect the battery negative cable (see Chapter 5).

3   Remove the inner trim panel and the watershield (see Section 12).

4   Starting at the rear using a wide, flat-bladed tool such as a putty knife, carefully pry up the window inner sealing strip from the base of the window.

5   Pry out the window catches, and slide the window upwards **(see illustrations)**.
**Caution:** *Do not push the catches too far or they will snap and the regulator will have to be replaced.*

6   Lifting the rear first, remove the window from the vehicle **(see illustration)**.

### Front door window regulator

*Refer to illustrations 14.9a, 14.9b and 14.10*

7   Release the door window from the catches (see Steps 1 through 5). There is no need to remove the window from the door, sim-

**14.6  Lift the rear first, then remove the window**

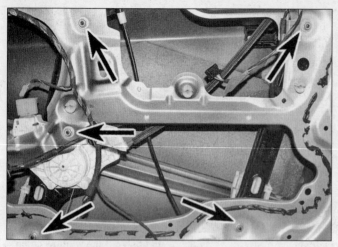

14.9a   Remove the regulator mounting nuts . . .

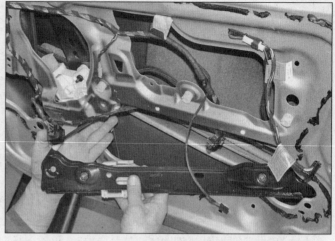

14.9b   . . . and maneuver the regulator from the door

14.10   Window motor retaining bolts

14.12   Pry up the inner sealing strip from the door

14.13a   Pull the rubber strip from the front edge of the door

ply use duct tape or rubber wedges to secure the window in the full Up position.

8   Disconnect the window motor electrical connector.

9   Remove the regulator mounting nuts, release any retaining clips, and maneuver the regulator from the door **(see illustrations)**.

10   Where applicable, remove the retaining bolts and separate the motor from the regulator **(see illustration)**.

### Rear door window

*Refer to illustrations 14.12, 14.13a, 14.13b, 14.13c, 14.16 and 14.17*

11   Fully lower the window, then remove the door inner trim panel and watershield (see Section 12).

12   Using a wide, flat-bladed tool, carefully pry up the window inner sealing strip from the door skin **(see illustration)**.

13   Carefully pull the rubber weatherstrip from the front edge of the door window frame, then pull the plastic window frame trim from the front of the frame. Peel back the window sealing strip from the front edge of the window opening to gain access to the window trim panel bolts. Remove the retaining bolts, and lift the panel from the door **(see illustrations)**.

14   Fully close the window, then lower it approximately 4-3/4 inches (120 mm), measured at the front edge.

15   Disconnect the battery negative cable (see Chapter 5).

16   Press the window catch outwards, and slide the window upwards **(see illustration)**.

17   Lifting the rear first, remove the window from the vehicle **(see illustration)**.

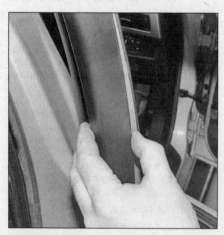

14.13b   Pull the plastic trim from the front of the frame

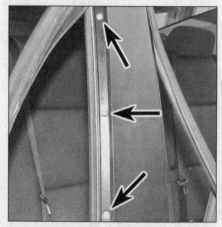

14.13c   Pry the sealing strip from the front of the window opening and remove the mounting bolts

**14.16 Press the window catch outwards . . .**

**14.17 . . . and lift the window from the door**

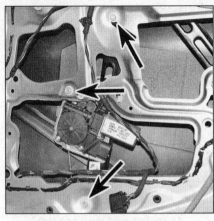

**14.21 Window regulator retaining nuts**

### Rear door/rear side fixed windows

18    The rear door/rear side fixed windows are bonded in place. Replacement should be handled by a dealer or automotive glass specialist.

### Rear door window regulator

*Refer to illustrations 14.21 and 14.22*

19    Release the door window from the clamp catches (see Steps 1 through 5), slide it upwards and secure it in position with adhesive tape.

20    Disconnect the regulator motor electrical connector, and release the harness from any retaining clips.

21    Remove the regulator mounting nuts, release any retaining clips, lift out the lower end of the assembly, and maneuver it from the door **(see illustration)**.

22    Where applicable, remove the motor retaining bolts, and separate the motor from the regulator **(see illustration)**.

## Installation

### Door window glass

23    Installation is the reverse of removal. Replace the window catches if they are damaged.

### Door window regulators

24    Installation is the reverse of removal. Once the regulator has been installed, operate the window switch to fully close the window, then continue to hold the button for at least one second to normalize the auto stop function.

---

## 15    Trunk lid/tailgate and support struts - removal and installation

## *Trunk lid*

### Removal

*Refer to illustration 15.1*

1    Open the trunk, pry up the center pins slightly and remove the plastic expanding rivets. Remove the trim panel from the trunk lid **(see illustration)**.

2    Disconnect the wiring connectors from the license plate lights and trunk lid lock, and tie a piece of string to the end of the wiring.

Noting the correct routing of the wiring harness, release the harness rubber grommets from the trunk lid and withdraw the wiring. When the end of the wiring appears, untie the string and leave the string in position in the trunk lid; it can then be used to draw the wiring into position during installation.

3    Draw around the outline of each hinge with a marking pen. Loosen the hinge upper bolt, remove the lower bolt and remove the trunk lid from the vehicle.

4    Inspect the hinges for signs of wear or damage and replace if necessary. The hinges are secured to the vehicle by bolts.

### Installation

5    Installation is the reverse of removal, aligning the hinges with the marks made before removal. Have an assistant to help hold the trunk lid while you install the fasteners.

6    Close the trunk lid and check its alignment with the surrounding panels. If necessary, slight adjustment can be made by loosening the retaining bolts and repositioning the trunk lid on its hinges. Ideally, the gap around the trunk lid should be the same all around. If the paint work around the hinges has been damaged, paint the affected area with a suitable touch-up brush to prevent corrosion.

## *Tailgate*

7    Open the tailgate and remove the trim from the left and right sides **(see illustration 16.10)**, and also at the top of the tailgate.

8    Disconnect the electrical connectors and washer hose.

9    Detach the support struts from the tailgate.

10    Use a felt-tip pen to mark the position of the tailgate hinges on the body.

11    With the help of two assistants, remove the tailgate hinge bolts, then remove the tailgate.

12    Installation is the reverse of removal.

## *Support struts*

13    Support the trunk lid/tailgate in the open position. Using a small flat-bladed screwdriver, raise the spring clip, and pull the support strut off its upper mounting **(see illustration 7.2)**. Repeat the procedure on the lower strut mounting and remove the strut from the vehicle. When one strut has been removed, install the new strut before removing the strut from the other side.

14    Installation is the reverse of removal, ensuring that the struts are securely retained by their retaining clips.

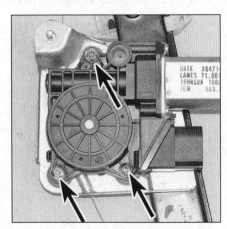

**14.22 Regulator motor retaining bolts**

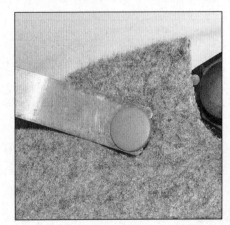

**15.1 Pry out the center pins and the plastic expansion rivets**

**16.3a Trunk lid latch retaining bolt locations**

**16.3b Slide the outer fitting from the bracket, and slide the end fitting from the lever**

**16.4a Release the clip and slide off the outer cable fitting . . .**

## 16 Trunk lid/tailgate latch components - removal and installation

### *Removal*

#### Trunk lid latch

*Refer to illustrations 16.3a, 16.3b, 16.4a, 16.4b and 16.4c*

1    Open the trunk, pry up the center pins and remove the plastic expanding rivets. Remove the trim panel from the trunk lid (see Section 15).

2    Disconnect the latch electrical connector.

3    Remove the mounting fasteners, and maneuver the latch from the trunk lid. Disconnect the cable from the lock cylinder as the latch is removed **(see illustrations)**.

4    To disconnect the operating cable, release the clip and slide off the plastic outer cable fitting. Pry up the center pin and detach the inner cable end fitting **(see illustrations)**.

#### Trunk lid lock cylinder

*Refer to illustration 16.7*

5    Remove the trim panel from the trunk lid (see Section 15).

6    Disconnect the operating cable from the

**16.4b . . . pry out the center pin . . .**

lock cylinder **(see illustration 16.3b)**.

7    Remove the mounting fasteners, then pull the lock cylinder from the panel **(see illustration)**.

#### Trunk lock release button

*Refer to illustration 16.9*

8    Remove the trim panel (see Section 15).

9    Reach up behind the button, squeeze the sides and push out the assembly **(see**

**16.4c . . . and pry the inner cable end fitting from the lever**

**illustration)**. Disconnect the electrical connector as the button is removed.

#### Tailgate latch

*Refer to illustrations 16.10, 16.12a, 16.12b, 16.13, 16.14, 16.15 and 16.16*

10    Pull the rear window side trims inward to release the retaining clips, and disengage them from the upper trim **(see illustration)**.

**16.7 Lock cylinder retaining bolt locations**

**16.9 Squeeze together the sides and push the button from the lid**

**16.10 Pull the side trims inwards to release the clips**

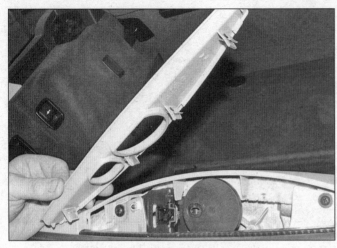

**16.12a Pull the plastic trim rearwards . . .**

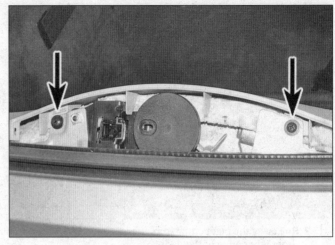

**16.12b . . . and remove the mounting bolts**

11   Release the mounting clips, then fold down and remove the trim insert on the tailgate rear panel.

12   Open the rear window, pull the plastic trim at the top of the rear panel rearward to release the clips, then remove the mounting bolts at the top of the panel (**see illustrations**).

13   Pry out the cover, then remove the bolt in each side of the handle recess (**see illustration**).

14   Pull the rear trim panel away from the tailgate to release the retaining clips (**see illustration**). Disconnect the trunk compartment light as the panel is removed.

15   Remove the mounting bolts and slide the latch from the tailgate (**see illustration**).

16   Disconnect the release cable and electrical connector as the latch is removed (**see illustration**).

### Rear window latch

*Refer to illustration 16.19*

17   Remove the tailgate lower trim panel (see Steps 10 through 14).

18   Disconnect the latch electrical connector.

**16.13 Pry out the cover and remove the bolt at each side**

19   Remove the mounting bolts and withdraw the latch from the tailgate (**see illustration**).

## Installation

20   Installation is the reverse of removal, noting the following points:

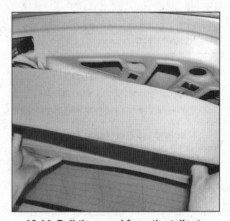

**16.14 Pull the panel from the tailgate**

a)   *Reconnect all electrical connectors, and secure the wiring harnesses using the retaining clips (where applicable).*

b)   *Match-up any previously-make alignment marks.*

c)   *Check the operation of the latches/lock cylinders before installing the trim panels.*

d)   *Tighten all fasteners securely.*

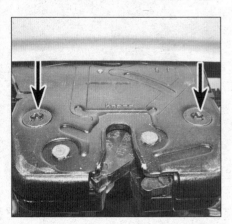

**16.15 Remove the mounting bolts and the tailgate latch**

**16.16 Slide the outer cable fitting from the bracket and disconnect the release cable**

**16.19 Tailgate window latch bolts**

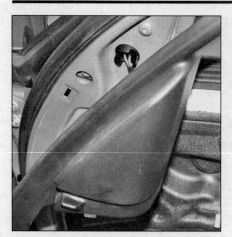

**17.2  Pull away the plastic trim from the front inner edge of the door**

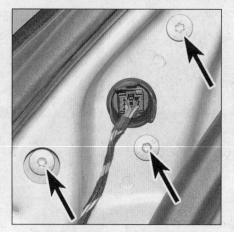

**17.3  Exterior mirror retaining bolts**

**17.6  Carefully pry the mirror from the housing**

## 17  Mirrors and associated components - removal and installation

### *Exterior mirror assembly*

*Refer to illustrations 17.2 and 17.3*

1    Remove the door inner trim panel (see Section 12).
2    Carefully pull the plastic trim away from the front inner edge of the door frame **(see illustration)**.
3    Disconnect the mirror electrical connector, then remove the retaining Torx bolts and remove the mirror from the door **(see illustration)**. Remove the rubber seal between the door and mirror; if the seal is damaged it must be replaced.
4    Installation is the reverse of removal, tightening the mirror bolts securely.

### *Exterior mirror glass*

*Refer to illustration 17.6*

**Caution:** *Wear gloves when prying the mirror glass out.*
**Note:** *If the mirror glass is removed when the*

mirror is cold, the retaining clips are likely to break.
5    Tilt the mirror glass fully inward.
6    Insert a wide plastic or wooden wedge in between the outer edge of the mirror glass and mirror housing and carefully pry the glass from the motor **(see illustration)**. Take great care when removing the glass; do not use excessive force, as the glass is easily broken.
7    Remove the glass from the mirror and, where necessary, disconnect the wiring connectors from the mirror heating element.
8    On installation, reconnect the wiring to the glass and clip the glass onto the motor, taking great care not to break it.

### *Exterior mirror switch*

9    Refer to Chapter 12.

### *Exterior mirror motor*

*Refer to illustration 17.11*

10    Remove the mirror glass (see Steps 5 through 7).
11    Remove the single retaining bolt and pull the motor from the mirror housing **(see illustration)**. Disconnect the electrical connector as the motor is removed.

12    Installation is the reverse of removal. Reconnect the wiring to the glass and clip the glass onto the motor, taking great care not to break it.

### *Exterior mirror housing cover*

*Refer to illustrations 17.14a and 17.14b*

13    Remove the mirror glass (see Steps 5 through 7).
14    Release the mounting clips and remove the mirror housing cover **(see illustrations)**.
15    Installation is the reverse of removal.

### *Interior mirror*

16    There are two different types of mirror arms and mountings. One type has a plastic cover over the plug connection, and the other type has a mirror arm which splits in two to reveal the electrical connector.

#### Plastic cover type arm

17    Carefully pry out the plastic cover, then disconnect the mirror electrical connector (where applicable).
18    Strike the lower part of the mirror forwards with the palm of your hand to unclip the arm from the mounting. **Caution:** *Do not twist*

**17.11  Remove the motor mounting bolt and the motor**

**17.14a  Release the mounting clips . . .**

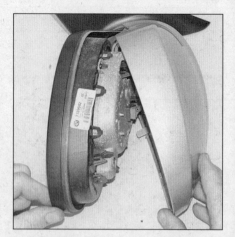

**17.14b  . . . and remove the cover**

*the arm while attempting removal, as the clip will be damaged. Do not pull the arm to the rear, as the windshield may be damaged.*

### Split cover mirror arm

*Refer to illustrations 17.19 and 17.21*

19   Pry apart the two sides of the mirror base cover **(see illustration)**.

20   Noting their installed positions, disconnect the various electrical connectors from the mirror and rain sensor (if equipped).

21   Rotate the mirror arm 60-degrees counterclockwise and remove it **(see illustration)**.

### All types

22   To install the mirrors, position the mirror arm over the mount at an angle of 60-degrees to the vertical. Push the arm up and check that it engages correctly. Where applicable, install the covers and reconnect the electrical connector(s).

## 18   Windshield and fixed glass - general information

Replacement of the windshield and fixed glass requires the use of special fast setting adhesive/caulk materials. These operations should be left to a dealer or a shop specializing in glass work.

## 19   Sunroof - general information, motor replacement and initialization

### General information

1   Due to the complexity of the sunroof mechanism, considerable expertise is needed to repair, replace or adjust the sunroof components successfully. Removal of the roof requires removal of the headliner, which is a complex and tedious operation. Therefore, any problems with the sunroof (except motor replacement) should be referred to a dealer or other qualified shop.

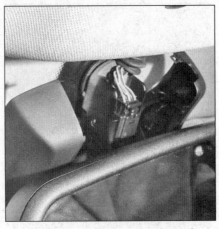

**17.19  Pry apart the two halves of the cover**

2   On models with an electric sunroof, if the sunroof motor fails to operate, first check the relevant fuse. If the fault cannot be traced and rectified, the sunroof can be opened and closed manually using an Allen key to turn the motor spindle (a key is supplied with the vehicle tool kit). To gain access to the motor, unclip the cover from the headliner. Remove the Allen key from the tool kit and insert it into the motor spindle. Disconnect the motor wiring connector and rotate the key to move the sunroof to the required position.

### Motor replacement

*Refer to illustrations 19.5a, 19.5b and 19.6*

3   Disconnect the negative battery cable (see Chapter 5).

4   Starting at the front edge, carefully pry the interior light lens unit from between the sun visors.

5   Release the clips at the front edge and remove the interior light unit from the headliner between the sun visors **(see illustrations)**. Disconnect the electrical connector(s) as the unit is removed.

6   Remove the mounting bolts and pull the motor out. Disconnect the electrical connector as the motor is removed **(see illustration)**.

**17.21  Rotate the mirror arm 60-degrees counterclockwise**

7   Installation is the reverse of removal, but carry out the initialization procedure as described in Step 8.

### Initialization

8   Initialize the sunroof as follows:

a) *Press and hold the switch in the tilt position.*

b) *After reaching the end of tilt position, keep the switch pressed for another 30 seconds. The normalization is complete when the sunroof rear end lifts briefly.*

c) *Keep the switch pressed in the tilt position, after approximately 5 seconds, the sunroof will move to the closed position, back to the open position, then finally back to the closed position.*

d) *Release the switch.*

## 20   Seats - removal and installation

### Front seat removal

*Refer to illustrations 20.3, 20.4, 20.6 and 20.7*

**Warning:** *These vehicles are equipped with side-impact airbags in the outer edges of the*

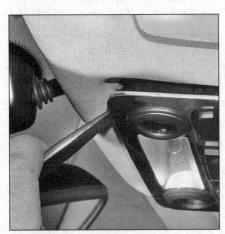

**19.5a  Use a flat-bladed tool to release the clips . . .**

**19.5b  . . . at the front edge of the interior light unit**

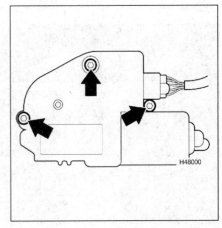

**19.6  Sunroof motor retaining bolts**

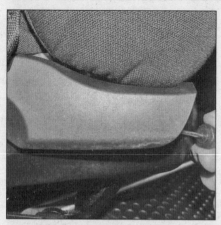

**20.3  Release the clip at the front edge and remove the trim**

**20.4  Remove the seat belt retaining bolt**

## Sports wagon models

*Refer to illustrations 20.16, 20.17 and 20.18*

13    Pull up on the front of the seat cushion to release the left and right retaining clips, and remove it forward.

14    Remove the center seat belt lower anchorage bolt and lift the cushion out of the vehicle. Disconnect the seat heating wiring connectors (where applicable) as the seat is withdrawn.

15    Release the rear seat back, and fold it forward.

16    The trim panel between the seat back and the door opening must be removed. Pull the top of the trim forward to release the retaining clip, then pull the trim panel upward to remove it **(see illustration)**. Repeat this procedure on the opposite trim panel.

17    Remove the bolt on each side, securing the seat back outer brackets to the vehicle body **(see illustration)**.

18    Lift each seat back assembly at the outer edges, and pull outward to disengage the center mounting **(see illustration)**. Maneuver the seats from the vehicle.

## Fixed rear seat removal

*Refer to illustrations 20.20 and 20.21*

19    Pull up on the front edge of the seat cushion to release the left and right retaining clips, then remove the seat cushion from the vehicle.

20    Remove the mounting bolts at the center, lower edge of the backrest **(see illustration)**.

21    On E-series chassis models, working in the trunk compartment, use a large flat-bladed screwdriver to release the catches, then slide the seat upwards to release its lower retaining pins and remove it from the vehicle **(see illustration)**.

22    On F-series chassis models, lift the seat back up and out, making sure the wire locking guides on each end of the seat back are out of their channels.

## Installation

### Front seat

23    Installation is the reverse of removal, noting the following points.

a)  *On manually-adjusted seats, install the seat-retaining bolts and tighten them by*

---

front seat backs. Be sure to disarm the airbag system before beginning this procedure (see Chapter 12).

**Warning:** *The seat belt tensioners are part of the Supplemental Restraint System and are triggered by a frontal impact above a predetermined force. When the system is triggered, a pyrotechnic (explosive) device is detonated which acts on the seat belt anchorage, and keeps the occupant in position in the seat. Once the tensioner has been triggered, the seat belt will be permanently locked and the assembly must be replaced. There is a risk of injury if the system is triggered inadvertently when working on the vehicle. Before working on the seats or seat belts, disable the airbag system (see Chapter 12).*

1    Slide the seat fully forwards and raise the seat cushion fully.

**Note:** *Remove the headrest from the top of the seat to make it easier to get the seat out of the vehicle.*

2    Disconnect the negative battery cable (see Chapter 5).

3    Starting at the rear, carefully pry the seat belt anchorage trim from the seat cushion side **(see illustration)**.

**Note:** *On F-series chassis models, the seat belt anchorage trim center section must be pried out then up to access the seat belt retaining bolt.*

4    Remove the retaining bolt and detach the seat belt from the seat **(see illustration)**.

5    Loosen and remove the bolts securing the rear of the seat rails to the floor.

6    Slide the seat fully backwards, then loosen and remove the bolts at the front **(see illustration)**.

7    Working under the front of the seat, slide out the locking element and disconnect the seat electrical connector **(see illustration)**.

8    Lift the seat out from the vehicle.

## Folding rear seat removal

### Sedan models

9    The trim panel between the seat back and the door opening must be removed. Pull the top of the trim forward to release the retaining clip, then pull the trim panel upwards to remove it. Repeat this procedure on the opposite trim panel.

10    Pull up on the front of the seat cushion to release the left and right retaining clips, then remove it forward and out of the vehicle. Disconnect the seat heating wiring connectors (where applicable) as the seat is withdrawn.

11    Release the rear seat back, and fold it forward.

12    Remove the mounting bolt on each side at the outer hinges, then pull the seat back from the center mountings.

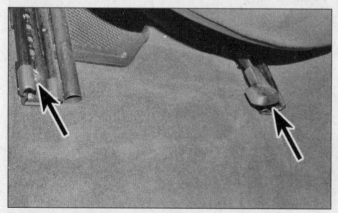

**20.6  Remove the mounting bolts at the front**

**20.7  Slide out the locking element and disconnect the electrical connector**

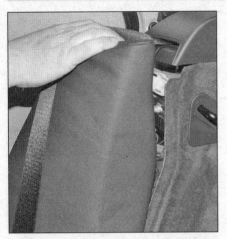

20.16  Pull the top edge forward, then lift the trim panel upwards

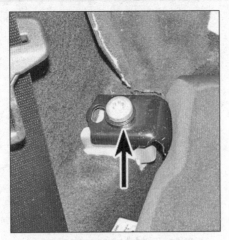

20.17  Remove the fastener on each side . . .

20.18  . . . then pull the cushions outwards to disengage the center mounting

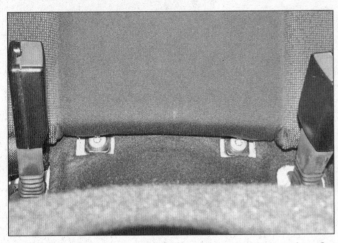

20.20  Remove the mounting bolts at the center, lower edge of the backrest

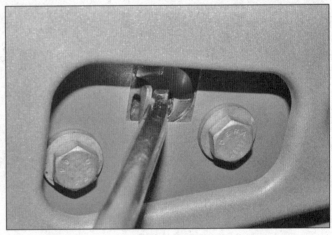

20.21  Use a screwdriver to release the catches in the trunk interior

hand only. Slide the seat fully forwards, then slide it back by two stops of the seat locking mechanism. Rock the seat to ensure that the seat locking mechanism is correctly engaged, then tighten the mounting bolts securely.

b)  *On electrically-adjusted seats, ensure that the wiring is connected and correctly routed, then tighten the seat mounting bolts securely.*

c)  *Tighten the seat belt mounting bolt to the specified torque.*

d)  *Reconnect the negative battery cable (see Chapter 5).*

### Folding rear seat

24   Installation is the reverse of removal. Tighten the seat belt lower mounting bolts to the specified torque setting.

### Fixed rear seat

25   Installation is the reverse of removal, making sure the seat back lower locating pegs or wire locking sides are correctly engaged with the body, and the seat belt buckles and lap belt are fed through the correct openings.

## 21   Seat belt components - removal and installation

**Warning:** *The seat belt tensioners are part of the Supplemental Restraint System and are triggered by a frontal impact above a predetermined force. When the system is triggered, a pyrotechnic (explosive) device is detonated which acts on the seat belt anchorage, and keeps the occupant in position in the seat. Once the tensioner has been triggered, the seat belt will be permanently locked and the assembly must be replaced. There is a risk of injury if the system is triggered inadvertently when working on the vehicle. Before working on the seats or seat belts, disable the airbag system (see Chapter 12).*

### Front seat belt removal

*Refer to illustrations 21.5 and 21.6*

1   Remove the B-pillar trim panel (see Section 22).

2   Pry the belt anchorage trim from the seat **(see illustration 20.3)**.

3   Remove the belt anchorage bolt from the

seat frame, and detach the belt.

4   Remove the seat belt guide mounting and separate the seat belt guide from the pillar.

5   Remove the bolt securing the upper seat belt mounting **(see illustration)**.

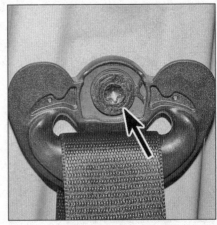

21.5  Seat belt upper mounting bolt location

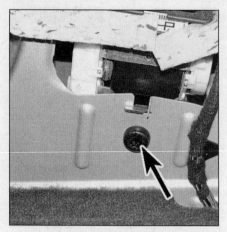

**21.6  Seat belt inertia reel retaining bolt location**

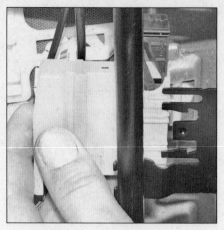

**21.9a  Slide the connector from the bracket . . .**

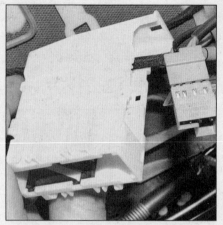

**21.9b  . . . and pry out the electrical connectors until the relevant plug is released**

**21.10  Remove the buckle assembly retaining bolt**

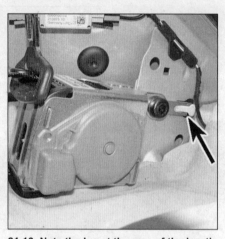

**21.13  Note the lug at the rear of the inertia reel bracket**

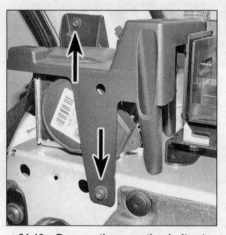

**21.18a  Remove the mounting bolts at the front . . .**

6    Remove the inertia-reel retaining bolt and remove the seat belt from the door pillar **(see illustration)**.
7    If equipped, remove the retaining bolts and the height adjustment mechanism from the door pillar.

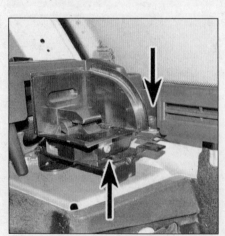

**21.18b  . . . and the mounting fasteners at the rear**

### *Front seat belt buckle removal*

*Refer to illustrations 21.9a, 21.9b and 21.10*

8    Remove the seat (see Section 20).
9    Release the tensioner wiring harness from the retaining clips, slide the connector from the mounting bracket, then release the clips/cable tie and pry out the electrical connectors one at a time until the relevant plug is released **(see illustrations)**.
10    Loosen and remove the buckle-assembly retaining bolt and remove the assembly from the side of the seat **(see illustration)**. **Note:** *The bolt must be replaced.*

### *Rear side seat belt removal*

#### Sedan models

*Refer to illustration 21.13*

11    Remove the rear seat (see Section 20).
12    Remove the package tray (see Section 22).
13    Remove the retaining bolt and remove the inertia reel unit. Note how the mounting bracket engages with the lug on the pillar **(see illustration)**.

14    Remove the seat belt lower mounting bolt.

#### Sports wagon models

*Refer to illustrations 21.18a, 21.18b and 21.19*

15    Remove the rear seat (see Section 20).
16    Remove the D-pillar trim panel (see Section 22).
17    Remove the trunk interior side panel (see Section 22).
18    Remove the 4 bolts and remove the cover over the inertia reel **(see illustrations)**.
19    Loosen and remove the Torx bolt securing the lower end of the belt to the body **(see illustration)**.
20    The inertia reel is secured by one Torx bolt. Loosen and remove the bolt and washer.
21    Maneuver the assembly from the mounting bracket and withdraw it from the vehicle.

### *Rear seat belt buckle removal*

*Refer to illustrations 21.23a and 21.23b*

22    Remove the rear seat cushion (see Section 20).

**21.19 Inertia reel retaining bolt location**

**21.23a Pry up the locking catch and disconnect the electrical connector**

**21.23b Seat belt buckle mounting bolt location**

23 Disconnect the electrical connector (where applicable) then loosen and remove the bolt and washer. Remove the buckle from the vehicle. Note the mounting bracket locating pin **(see illustrations)**.

### Rear center belt and buckle removal

#### Sedan models
*Refer to illustrations 21.25 and 21.26*

24 Remove the rear seat (see Section 20).
25 Remove the retaining bolt and remove the inertia reel unit **(see illustration)**.
26 Remove the seat belt lower mounting bolt **(see illustration)**.

#### Sports wagon models
27 The center belt inertia-reel unit is not available separately from the backrest. Check with your dealer or parts specialist.

### Installation
28 Installation is the reverse of removal, ensuring that all fasteners are tightened to their specified torque where given. Apply thread-locking compound to the mounting bolts.

## 22 Interior trim - removal and installation

**Warning:** *These models are equipped with a Supplemental Restraint System (SRS), more commonly known as airbags. Always disable the airbag system before working in the vicinity of any airbag system component to avoid the possibility of accidental deployment of the airbag(s), which could cause personal injury (see Chapter 12).*
**Warning:** *Do not use a memory saving device to preserve the PCM or radio memory when working on or near airbag system components.*
1 The interior trim panels are secured using either bolts or various types of trim fasteners, usually studs or clips.
2 Check that there are no other panels overlapping the one to be removed; usually there is a sequence that has to be followed that will become obvious on close inspection.
3 Remove all obvious fasteners, such as bolts. If the panel will not come free, it is held by hidden clips or fasteners. These are usually situated around the edge of the panel and can be pried up to release them; note that clips and fasteners can break quite eas-

ily, so have a supply of new ones on hand. The best way of releasing such clips without the correct type of tool (see Section 6) is to use a large flat-bladed screwdriver or putty knife.
4 Some panels are secured by plastic expanding rivets, where the center pin must be pried up before the rivet can be removed. **Note:** *In many cases the adjacent sealing strip must be pried back to release a panel.*
5 When removing a panel, never use excessive force or the panel may be damaged; always check carefully that all fasteners have been removed or released before attempting to withdraw a panel.

### A-pillar trim
*Refer to illustrations 22.8 and 22.9*

6 Disable the airbag system (see Chapter 12).
7 Pull the rubber weatherstrip from the door pillar in the area of the pillar trim.
8 Using a pry tool, carefully pry out the trim insert from the A-pillar trim **(see illustration)**.
9 Remove the retaining Torx bolt, and pull the trim to the center of the vehicle, starting at

**21.25 Rear center belt inertia reel bolt location**

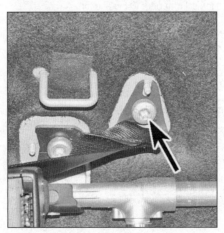

**21.26 Rear center belt lower mounting bolt location**

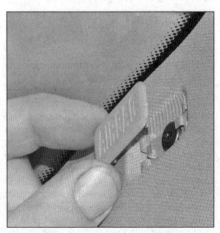

**22.8 Pry out the insert and remove the bolt**

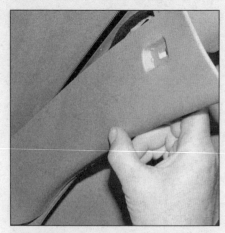

**22.9  Note how the base of the A-pillar trim engages with the instrument panel**

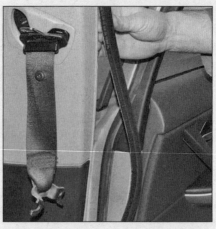

**22.12  Pull away the weatherstrip at each side of the B-pillar**

**22.13  Pull the lower edge of the trim panel inwards**

**22.14a  Pull the lower edge of the trim inwards to release the clips**

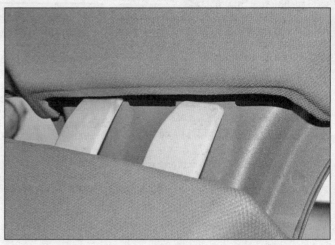

**22.14b  The two lugs of the upper trim engage with the headliner**

the top **(see illustration)**.

10   Installation is the reverse of removal; secure the fasteners by pressing them firmly into place and ensure that all disturbed components are correctly secured.

## B-pillar trim

*Refer to illustrations 22.12, 22.13, 22.14a and 22.14b*

11   Carefully pry up the front door sill trim panel from its retaining clips.

12   Pull away the rubber weatherstrip on each side of the B-pillar **(see illustration)**.

13   The lower edge of the lower trim is secured by plastic clips. Pull the lower edge of the trim inwards, then pull it downwards to disengage it from the upper trim panel **(see illustration)**. Note how the trim engages with the rear door sill trim panel.

14   Pull the lower edge of the upper trim inwards to release the retaining clips, then pull it downwards. Note how the upper edge of the trim engages with the headliner molding **(see illustrations)**. Feed the seat belt through the trim panel as it's withdrawn.

15   Installation is the reverse of removal; secure the fasteners by pressing them firmly into place and ensure that all disturbed components are correctly secured. Pry the retaining clips from the door sill and install them on the sill trim prior to installation.

## C-pillar trim

### Sedan models

*Refer to illustration 22.17*

16   Pull the door weatherstrip away from the area adjacent to the pillar trim.

17   Pry out the cap at the top edge of the trim and remove the Torx bolt beneath **(see illustration)**.

18   Pull the pillar trim upward from the pillar.

19   Installation is the reverse of removal; secure the fasteners by pressing them firmly into place and ensure that all disturbed components are correctly secured.

### Sports wagon models

*Refer to illustration 22.20*

20   Pry out the cap and remove the bolt

beneath **(see illustration)**.

21   Pull the trim panel upwards and inwards to release the clips.

22   Installation is the reverse of removal.

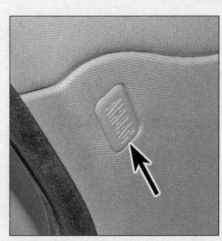

**22.17  Pry out the cap and remove the bolt beneath**

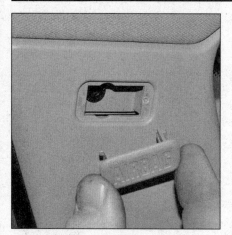

**22.20 Pry out the cap and remove the mounting bolt**

**22.25 Pry out the clip at the front edge of the upper pillar trim**

**22.28a Pry up the center pins and remove the plastic expansion rivets**

## *D-pillar trim*

*Refer to illustration 22.25*

23   Lift out the luggage compartment floor panel, then rotate the fastener counterclockwise and lift out the side panel above the battery.

24   Remove the C-pillar trim panel (see Steps 20 and 21).

25   Pry out the clip at the front edge, then pull the upper pillar trim panel downwards to release the retaining clips **(see illustration)**.

26   Remove the mounting bolts, then pull the lower pillar trim panel inwards to release the retaining clips. Disconnect any electrical connectors as the trim is removed.

27   Installation is the reverse of removal.

## *Trunk area trim panel*

### Sedan models

*Refer to illustrations 22.28a, 22.28b, 22.29, 22.30, 22.31a and 22.31b*

28   Lift out the trunk compartment floor panel, pry up the center pins, pry out the plastic expansion rivets, then pry out the caps. Remove the mounting bolts and remove the

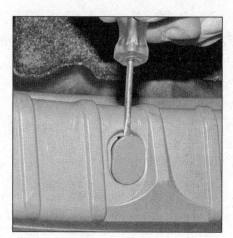

**22.28b Pry up the caps and remove the mounting bolts beneath**

trunk lid sill trim panel **(see illustrations)**.

29   Remove the warning triangle from the holders (where applicable), then rotate the holders counterclockwise and remove them **(see illustration)**.

**22.29 Remove the warning triangle holder**

30   Remove the Torx bolt securing the anchor point **(see illustration)**.

31   Pry up the center pin and pry out the retaining clips **(see illustrations)**.

32   Remove the panel.

33   Installation is the reverse of removal.

**22.30 Remove the Torx bolt securing the storage anchor**

**22.31a Pry up the center pins . . .**

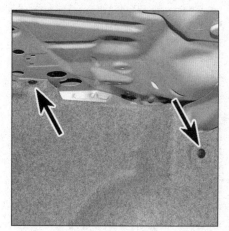

**22.31b . . . and remove the plastic expansion rivets**

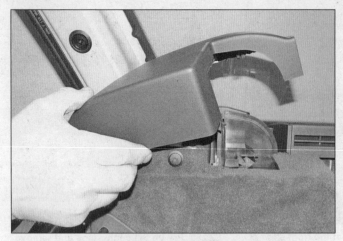

**22.36 Pull up the cover over the inertia reel**

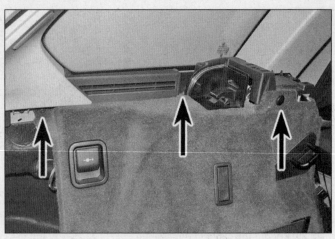

**22.38 Remove the mounting bolts and pry out the plastic expansion rivet**

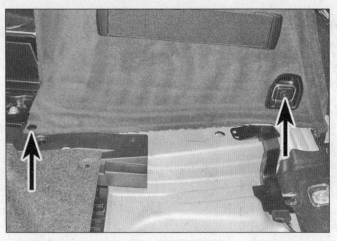

**22.39 Remove the storage hook bolt and pry out the plastic expansion rivet**

**22.41 Pry out the expansion rivets and remove the hook bolt**

## Sports wagon models

*Refer to illustration 22.36*

34    Fold the rear seat cushion forwards.

35    Remove the trunk compartment floor panel.

36    Pull up the plastic cover over the seat belt inertia reel, and feed the seat belt though the slot **(see illustration)**.

### Left panel

*Refer to illustrations 22.38 and 22.39*

37    Operate the release handle, open the access panel in front of the rear lights, and lift the handle out.

38    Remove the mounting bolts, and pry out the expansion rivet at the top edge of the side trim panel **(see illustration)**.

39    Disconnect the power outlet electrical connector (where applicable), pry out the expansion rivet and remove the bolt securing the hook **(see illustration)**. Lift out the panel.

### Right panel

*Refer to illustrations 22.41 and 22.42*

40    Rotate the fasteners counterclockwise and lift out the panel above the battery.

41    Pry up the center pin and remove the plastic expansion rivet. Remove the Torx bolt from the hook at the lower section of the side panel **(see illustration)**.

42    Remove the mounting bolts at the top of the panel, pry up the center pin and remove the plastic expansion rivet **(see illustration)**.

43    Lift out the side panel.

### Both sides

44    Installation is the reverse of removal.

## *Glovebox and cupholders*

*Refer to illustrations 22.45, 22.46 and 22.47*

45    Using a blunt, flat-bladed tool, carefully pry the decorative trim strip above the glove-

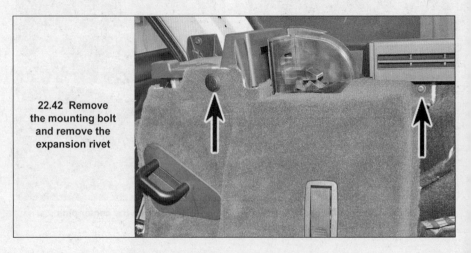

**22.42 Remove the mounting bolt and remove the expansion rivet**

22.45 Using a blunt, flat-bladed tool, carefully pry the cup holder surround trim from the instrument panel

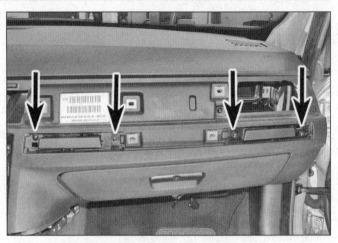

22.46 Cup holder retaining bolt locations

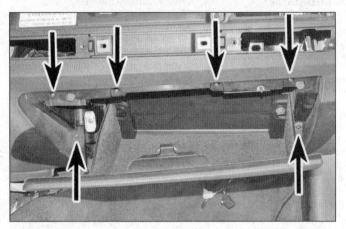

22.47 Remove the mounting bolts and withdraw the glovebox

22.51 Pry up the speaker grille

box from the instrument panel **(see illustration)**.

46   Remove the retaining bolts and remove the cup holder assemblies above the glovebox **(see illustration)**, if equipped.

47   On F-series chassis models, disable the airbag system (see chapter 12), then remove the instrument panel end caps (see Steps 71 and 72), lower trim panel (see Steps 60 and 61) to access the glovebox lower mounting screws. On all models open the glovebox, remove the retaining bolts, the glovebox, hinge and bracket as an assembly **(see illustration)**.

**Note:** *If the glovebox damper needs to be replaced, pry the damper locking tabs back and pull the damper off of the retaining bracket.*

## Package tray

*Refer to illustrations 22.51, 22.53 and 22.56*

49   Remove the rear seats (see Section 20).
50   Remove both C-pillar trim panels (see Steps 16 through 18).
**Note:** *On Sports wagon models, remove the D-pillar trim panels (see Steps 23 through 27).*
51   Pry up the grille, then remove the bolts

and remove the speakers from the rear package tray **(see illustration)**. Disconnect the speaker electrical connectors as they are withdrawn.

52   Remove the bolts and detach the seat belt lower anchors (see Section 21).

53   Pry up the center pins, and remove the plastic expansion rivets at the front edge of the package tray **(see illustration)**.

54   On models with folding rear seats,

remove the side cushion on each side by pulling the top edge forwards, then lifting it out.

55   Pry up the trims around the seat belts where they pass through the package tray.

56   Pull the package tray forwards and remove it **(see illustration)**. Feed the seat belts through the package tray as it's withdrawn.

57   Installation is the reverse of removal.

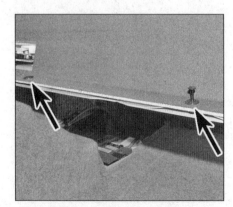

22.53 Pry up the center pins and remove the plastic expansion rivets

22.56 Pull the package tray forwards and feed the seat belts through

### Kick panel

58  Pull away the rubber weatherstrip in the area of the trim panel.
59  Pull the door sill trim panel upwards to release the clips at the front.

#### Passenger's side

*Refer to illustration 22.60*

60  Remove the mounting bolts and pull the lower fascia panel rearward **(see illustration)**. Disconnect the electrical connectors as the panel is withdrawn.
61  Pull the kick panel inward to release the retaining clips.

#### Driver's side

62  On F-series chassis models, disable the airbag system (see Chapter 12). Remove the bolts and remove the panel above the pedals **(see illustration 8.11)**. Disconnect any electrical connectors as the panel is withdrawn.
63  Remove the bolt and pull the hood release handle out **(see illustration 8.12)**.
64  Remove the retaining bolt, then pull the kick panel inwards/rearwards to release the retaining clips. Disconnect any electrical connectors as the panel is withdrawn.

#### Both sides

65  Installation is the reverse of removal.

### Sun visors

*Refer to illustrations 22.66 and 22.67*

66  To remove the sun visor, remove the Torx bolts securing the outer mounting **(see illustration)**. Disconnect the vanity mirror switch electrical connector as the sun visor is withdrawn.
67  To remove the inner mounting, pry open the plastic cover and remove the mounting Torx bolt **(see illustration)**.
68  Installation is the reverse of removal.

### Grab handles

69  Pry down the plastic covers and remove the retaining Torx bolts to remove the handles.

**22.60  Remove the trim panel mounting bolts and pull the trim panel rearwards**

70  Installation is the reverse of removal.

### Instrument panel end caps

71  To remove an end cap, simply pry it off.
72  Installation is the reverse of removal. Make sure the locating pins are not broken and align them with their respective slots.

### Driver's side storage compartment

73  Pry out the driver's side vent trim panel.
74  Open the storage compartment door and remove the two screws at the top.
75  Remove the storage compartment holder from the back side of the instrument panel through the vent opening.
76  Carefully pull the storage compartment out through the front of the instrument panel.
**Note:** *The storage compartment is mounted to the holder and both are fastened to each other on the back side of the instrument panel.*
77  Installation is the reverse of removal.

---

### 23  Radiator grille - removal and installation

---

1  Open the hood.
2  Remove the fasteners securing the air

duct to the top of the radiator **(see illustration 9.3)**.
3  Carefully remove the sealing strip.
4  Reach through the openings to access the back of the radiator to release the clips securing the grille.
5  Take care not to scratch the surrounding paint on the front bumper cover when removing/installing the grille. **Caution:** *Wear gloves when reaching through the openings.*
6  Installation is the reverse of removal.

---

### 24  Center console - removal and installation

---

### Removal

*Refer to illustrations 24.1, 24.2a, 24.2b, 24.2c, 24.3, 24.5, 24.6a, 24.6b, 24.7a, 24.7b, 24.8a, 24.8b and 24.9*

1  On manual transmission models, carefully squeeze the sides of the shift lever boot inward, then pull it upwards from the center console trim **(see illustration)**.
2  On 6-speed automatic transmission models, pull the selector lever knob from the lever with a sharp pull straight up. **Caution:** *Do not twist the knob or the mechanism will be damaged.* Squeeze the sides of the gear

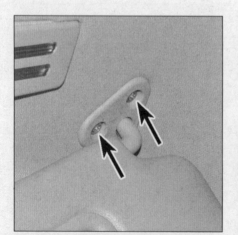

**22.66  Sun visor outer mounting bolt locations**

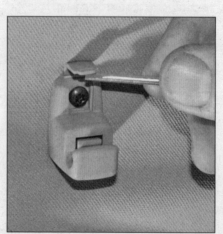

**22.67  Pry open the cover and remove the inner mounting bolt**

**24.1  Squeeze together the sides and pull up the shift lever boot**

**24.2a Pull the shift lever knob sharply upwards**

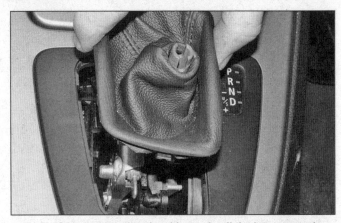

**24.2b Squeeze together the sides and pull the boot upwards**

lever boot inwards, pull it upward from the center console trim, then pry up the shift boot trim. Disconnect the electrical connector as the trim is removed **(see illustrations)**.

**Note:** *On models equipped with iDrive controllers, place a piece of tape between controller panel and the instrument panel and carefully pry the iDrive controller trim panel up until the electrical connectors can be disconnected, then remove the controller panel and iDrive controller.*

3    Remove the trim screw, if equipped, then using a plastic trim tool (see Section 6), carefully pry up the trim from the top of the center console **(see illustration)**. Disconnect any electrical connectors as the trim is removed.

4    On 8-speed automatic transmission models, remove the shift lever four mounting screws then lift the shifter up and disconnect the electrical connectors.

5    Pry out the caps and remove the bolts at the front of the console **(see illustration)**.

6    Carefully release the clips at the rear/ sides of the console, then pull the rear section away to release the clips at the top **(see illustrations)**. Disconnect any electrical connectors as it is withdrawn.

**24.2c Pry up the boot surround trim**

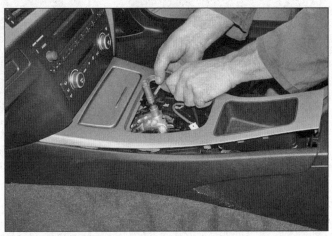

**24.3 Pry up the trim from the top of the center console**

**24.5 Remove the caps and remove the mounting bolts**

**24.6a Release the clips on each side at the lower part of the rear section (shown from the inside of the console) . . .**

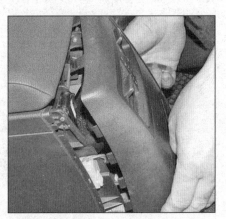

**24.6b . . . and pull the rear section out**

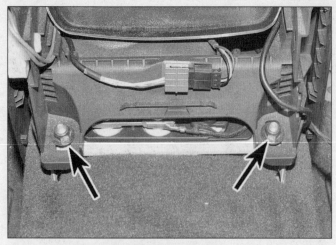

24.7a Remove the nuts . . .

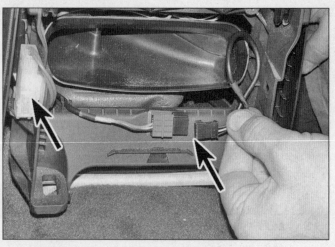

24.7b . . . and disconnect the electrical connectors

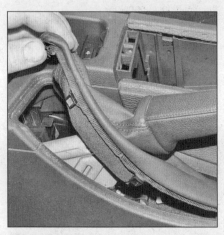

24.8a Squeeze in the sides and remove
the parking brake lever boot from
the console

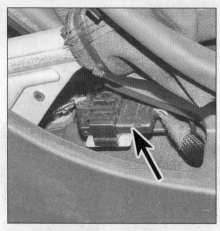

24.8b Rotate the locking lever, and
disconnect the electrical connector in
the opening

7 Remove the nuts securing the rear of the console **(see illustrations)**. Disconnect any electrical connectors accessible through the rear section.

8 Carefully pry the parking brake lever boot from the console, and disconnect the electrical connectors below **(see illustrations)**. To

improve access, cut the cable tie and pull the boot from the lever. Ensure the parking brake lever is fully raised.

9 Remove the mounting screws at the front and middle of the console, raise the rear of the console, then pull it rearwards a little to disengage the guides at the front **(see illustration)**. Noting their installed locations, discon-

nect any electrical connectors as the console is withdrawn. Maneuver the center console over the parking brake lever.

### *Installation*

10 Maneuver the center console over the parking brake lever, and ensure the front guides and vent engage correctly. The remainder of installation is the reverse of removal, making sure all fasteners are securely tightened.

---

### 25 Instrument panel assembly - removal and installation

---

**Warning:** *These models are equipped with a Supplemental Restraint System (SRS), more commonly known as airbags. Always disable the airbag system before working in the vicinity of any airbag system component to avoid the possibility of accidental deployment of the airbag(s), which could cause personal injury (see Chapter 12).*

**Caution:** *There are sharp edges on sheetmetal panels behind the instrument panel and at the ends of the instrument panel crossmember. Wear gloves.*

**Note:** *This is a difficult procedure for the home mechanic. There are many hard-to-access fasteners and numerous electrical connectors to tag and disconnect.*

### *Removal*

*Refer to illustrations 25.8, 25.10a, 25.10b, 25.13, 25.14a, 25.14b, 25.15, 25.17a, 25.17b and 25.17c*

1 Remove the center console (see Section 24).

2 Disconnect the negative battery cable (see Chapter 5).

3 Remove the steering column (see Chapter 10).

4 Remove both A-pillar trim panels (see Section 22).

5 Remove the mounting fasteners and remove the lower trim panel from the passenger's side **(see illustration 22.60)**. Discon-

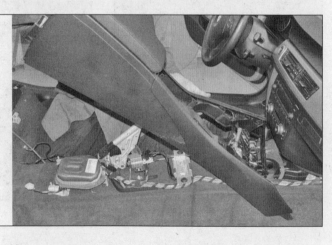

24.9 Raise the rear
of the console and
maneuver it over the
parking brake lever

**25.8  Carefully pry the decorative trim panel from the instrument panel**

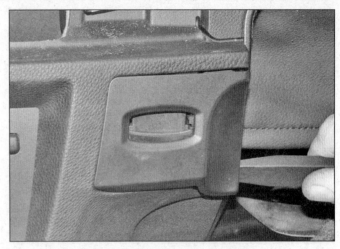

**25.10a  Pry the surround trim away . . .**

nect any electrical connectors as the panel is withdrawn.

6    Remove the instrument cluster (see Chapter 12).

7    Remove the light control unit/switch (see Chapter 12).

8    Using a blunt, flat-bladed tool, carefully pry the decorative trim panel from the passenger's side of the instrument panel **(see illustration)**. Disconnect any electrical connectors as the panel is removed.

9    Remove the heating/air conditioning control panel (see Chapter 3).

10    Using a blunt, flat-bladed tool, carefully pry the surround trim from the driver's side of the instrument panel, then remove the mounting bolts and remove the ignition switch **(see illustrations)**. Disconnect any electrical connectors as the switch is removed.

11    Remove the audio unit from the instrument panel (see Chapter 12).

12    Remove the passenger's side glovebox and end caps (see Section 22).

13    Disconnect the passenger's side airbag electrical connectors (see Chapter 12).

**25.10b  . . . and remove the ignition switch bolts**

Remove the fastener securing the airbag support bracket to the instrument panel **(see illustration)**.

14    If equipped, remove the center speaker

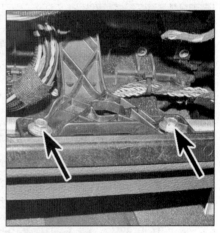

**25.13  Airbag support bracket bolts**

from the instrument panel (see Chapter 12). On models without a speaker, pry up the vent grille and remove the bolts below **(see illustrations)**.

15    Carefully pry the solar sensor from the

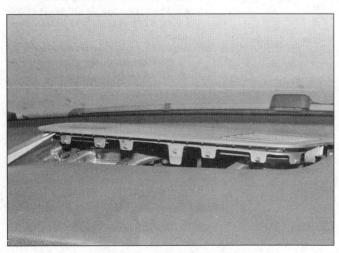

**25.14a  Pry up the center grille . . .**

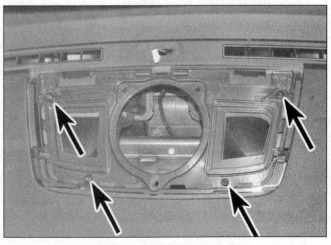

**25.14b  . . . and remove the bolts**

**25.15 Push the solar sensor from the instrument panel**

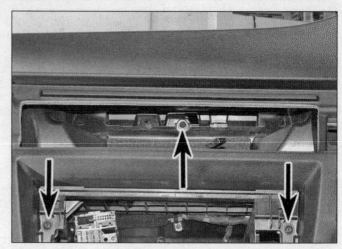

**25.17a The instrument panel is secured by mounting fasteners in the center . . .**

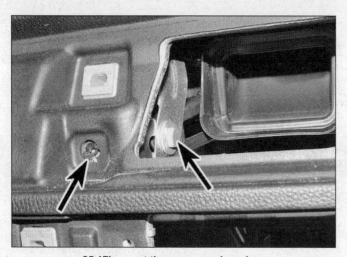

**25.17b . . . at the passenger's end . . .**

**25.17c . . . and the driver's end**

center of the fascia, and disconnect the electrical connector **(see illustration)**.

16   Pull the rear cabin center vent duct from the lower instrument panel.

17   The instrument panel is now secured by bolts at the center and the ends. Remove the bolts, and with the aid of an assistant, pull the instrument panel rearward. Noting their installed positions, disconnect any electrical connectors as necessary. Maneuver the instrument panel from the passenger cabin **(see illustrations)**. **Caution:** *To avoid damage to the instrument panel when removing* *the last mounting bolts, have an assistant support the instrument panel. You'll also need an assistant's help when installing the instrument panel and these bolts.*

## Installation

18   Installation is the reverse of removal, noting the following points:

a)   *Maneuver the instrument panel into position and ensure that the wiring is correctly routed and securely retained by its clips.*

b)   *Clip the instrument panel back into position, making sure the locating lugs at the front edge engage correctly and all the wiring connectors are fed through their respective openings. Install all the instrument panel fasteners and tighten them securely.*

c)   *Reconnect the battery and check that all the electrical components and switches function correctly.*

# Notes

# Notes

# Chapter 12
# Chassis electrical system

## Contents

## 1  General information

The electrical system is a 12-volt, negative ground type. Power for the lights and all electrical accessories is supplied by a lead/acid-type battery that is charged by the alternator.

This Chapter covers repair and service procedures for the various electrical components not associated with the engine. Information on the battery, alternator, ignition system and starter motor can be found in Chapter 5.

It should be noted that when portions of the electrical system are serviced, the negative cable should be disconnected from the battery to prevent electrical shorts and/or fires.

## 2  Electrical troubleshooting - general information

*Refer to illustrations 2.5a, 2.5b, 2.6 and 2.9*

A typical electrical circuit consists of an electrical component, any switches, relays, motors, fuses, fusible links or circuit breakers related to that component and the wiring and connectors that link the component to both the battery and the chassis. To help you pinpoint an electrical circuit problem, wiring diagrams are included at the end of this Chapter.

Before tackling any troublesome electrical circuit, first study the appropriate wiring diagrams to get a complete understanding of what makes up that individual circuit. Trouble spots, for instance, can often be narrowed down by noting if other components related to the circuit are operating properly. If several components or circuits fail at one time, chances are the problem is in a fuse or ground connection, because several circuits are often routed through the same fuse and ground connections.

Electrical problems usually stem from simple causes, such as loose or corroded connections, a blown fuse, a melted fusible link or a failed relay. Visually inspect the condition of all fuses, wires and connections in a problem circuit before troubleshooting the circuit.

If test equipment and instruments are going to be utilized, use the diagrams to plan ahead of time where you will make the necessary connections in order to accurately pinpoint the trouble spot.

The basic tools needed for electrical troubleshooting include a circuit tester or voltmeter (a 12-volt bulb with a set of test leads can also be used), a continuity tester, which includes a bulb, battery and set of test leads, and a jumper wire, preferably with a circuit breaker incorporated, which can be used to bypass electrical components (see illustrations). Before attempting to locate a problem with test instruments, use the wiring diagram(s) to decide where to make the connections.

### Voltage checks

Voltage checks should be performed if a circuit is not functioning properly. Connect one lead of a circuit tester to either the negative battery terminal or a known good ground. Connect the other lead to a connector in the circuit being tested, preferably nearest to the

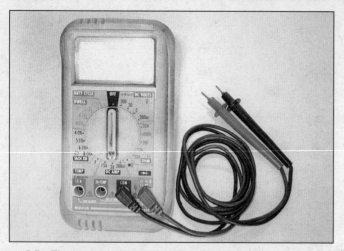

**2.5a  The most useful tool for electrical troubleshooting is a digital multimeter that can check volts, amps, and test continuity**

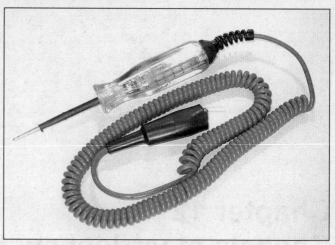

**2.5b  A test light is a very handy tool for checking voltage**

battery or fuse **(see illustration)**. If the bulb of the tester lights, voltage is present, which means that the part of the circuit between the connector and the battery is problem free. Continue checking the rest of the circuit in the same fashion. When you reach a point at which no voltage is present, the problem lies between that point and the last test point with voltage. Most of the time the problem can be traced to a loose connection. **Note:** *Keep in mind that some circuits receive voltage only when the ignition key is in the Accessory or Run position.*

### Finding a short

One method of finding shorts in a circuit is to remove the fuse and connect a test light or voltmeter in place of the fuse terminals. There should be no voltage present in the circuit. Move the wiring harness from side-to-side while watching the test light. If the bulb goes on, there is a short to ground somewhere in that area, probably where the

insulation has rubbed through. The same test can be performed on each component in the circuit, even a switch.

### Ground check

Perform a ground test to check whether a component is properly grounded. Disconnect the battery and connect one lead of a continuity tester or multimeter (set to the ohms scale), to a known good ground. Connect the other lead to the wire or ground connection being tested. If the resistance is low (less than 5 ohms), the ground is good. If the bulb on a self-powered test light does not go on, the ground is not good.

### Continuity check

A continuity check is done to determine if there are any breaks in a circuit - if it is passing electricity properly. With the circuit off (no power in the circuit), a self-powered continuity tester or multimeter can be used to check the circuit. Connect the test leads to both ends

of the circuit (or to the power end and a good ground), and if the test light comes on the circuit is passing current properly **(see illustration)**. If the resistance is low (less than 5 ohms), there is continuity; if the reading is 10,000 ohms or higher, there is a break somewhere in the circuit. The same procedure can be used to test a switch, by connecting the continuity tester to the switch terminals. With the switch turned On, the test light should come on (or low resistance should be indicated on a meter).

### Finding an open circuit

When diagnosing for possible open circuits, it is often difficult to locate them by sight because the connectors hide oxidation or terminal misalignment. Merely wiggling a connector on a sensor or in the wiring harness may correct the open circuit condition. Remember this when an open circuit is indicated when troubleshooting a circuit. Intermittent problems may also be caused by oxidized or loose connections.

**2.6  In use, a basic test light's lead is clipped to a known good ground, then the pointed probe can test connectors, wires or electrical sockets - if the bulb lights, the part being tested has battery voltage**

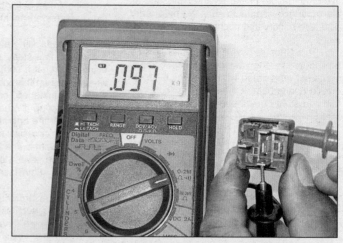

**2.9  With a multimeter set to the ohms scale, resistance can be checked across two terminals - when checking for continuity, a low reading indicates continuity, a high reading indicates lack of continuity**

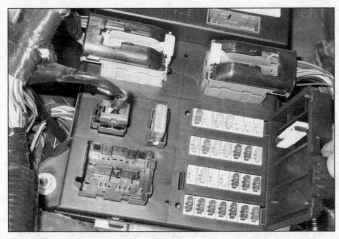

**3.1a  Some relays are located in the electrical box in the left-hand corner of the engine compartment**

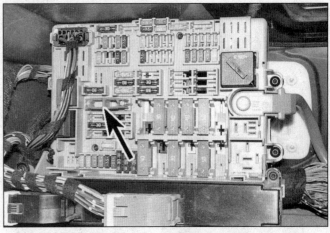

**3.1b  The fusebox is located behind the glove box. Note the tweezers for removing the fuses**

Electrical troubleshooting is simple if you keep in mind that all electrical circuits are basically electricity running from the battery, through the wires, switches, relays, fuses and fusible links to each electrical component (light bulb, motor, etc.) and to ground, from which it is passed back to the battery. Any electrical problem is an interruption in the flow of electricity to and from the battery.

## 3   Fuses and fusible links - general information

### Fuses

*Refer to illustrations 3.1a, 3.1b and 3.3*

The electrical circuits of the vehicle are protected by a combination of fuses, circuit breakers and fusible links. The main fuse/relay panel is in the engine compartment **(see illustration)**, while the interior fuse/relay panel is located inside the passenger compartment **(see illustration)**. Each of the fuses is designed to protect a specific circuit, and the various circuits are identified on the fuse panel itself.

Several sizes of fuses are employed in the fuse blocks. There are small, medium and large sizes of the same design, all with the same blade terminal design. The medium and large fuses can be removed with your fingers, but the small fuses require the use of pliers or the small plastic fuse-puller tool found in most fuse boxes.

If an electrical component fails, always check the fuse first. The best way to check the fuses is with a test light. Check for power at the exposed terminal tips of each fuse. If power is present at one side of the fuse but not the other, the fuse is blown. A blown fuse can also be identified by visually inspecting it **(see illustration)**.

Be sure to replace blown fuses with the correct type. Fuses (of the same physical size) of different ratings may be physically interchangeable, but only fuses of the proper rating should be used. Replacing a fuse with one of a higher or lower value than specified is not recommended. Each electrical circuit needs a specific amount of protection. The amperage value of each fuse is molded into the top of the fuse body.

If the replacement fuse immediately fails, don't replace it again until the cause of the problem is isolated and corrected. In most cases, this will be a short circuit in the wiring caused by a broken or deteriorated wire.

### Fusible links

Some circuits are protected by fusible links. The links are used in circuits which are not ordinarily fused, or which carry high current, such as the circuit between the alternator and the starter motor. Fusible links, which are usually several wire gauges smaller in size than the circuit that they protect, are designed to melt if the circuit is subjected to more current than it was designed to carry. If you have to replace a blown fusible link, make sure that you replace it with one of the same specification. If the replacement fusible link blows in the same circuit, make sure that you troubleshoot the circuit in which the fusible link melted BEFORE installing another fusible link.

## 4   Circuit breakers - general information

Circuit breakers protect certain circuits, such as the power windows or heated seats. Depending on the vehicle's accessories, there may be one or two circuit breakers, located in the fuse/relay box in the engine compartment.

Because the circuit breakers reset automatically, an electrical overload in a circuit breaker-protected system will cause the circuit to fail momentarily, then come back on. If the circuit does not come back on, check it immediately.

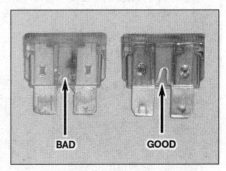

**3.3  When a fuse blows, the element between the terminals melts**

For a basic check, pull the circuit breaker up out of its socket on the fuse panel, but just far enough to probe with a voltmeter. The breaker should still contact the sockets. With the voltmeter negative lead on a good chassis ground, touch each end prong of the circuit breaker with the positive meter probe. There should be battery voltage at each end. If there is battery voltage only at one end, the circuit breaker must be replaced.

Some circuit breakers must be reset manually.

## 5   Relays - general information

Several electrical accessories in the vehicle, such as the fuel injection system, horns, starter, and fog lamps use relays to transmit the electrical signal to the component. Relays use a low-current circuit (the control circuit) to open and close a high-current circuit (the power circuit). If the relay is defective, that component will not operate properly. Most relays are mounted in the engine compartment and interior fuse/relay boxes **(see illustrations 3.1a and 3.1b)**.

# Electrical connectors

Most electrical connectors have a single release tab that you depress to release the connector

Some electrical connectors have a retaining tab which must be pried up to free the connector

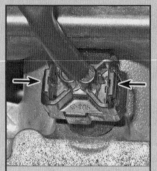

Some connectors have two release tabs that you must squeeze to release the connector

Some connectors use wire retainers that you squeeze to release the connector

Critical connectors often employ a sliding lock (1) that you must pull out before you can depress the release tab (2)

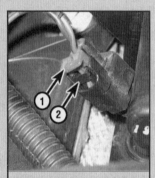

Here's another sliding-lock style connector, with the lock (1) and the release tab (2) on the side of the connector

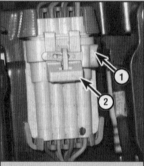

On some connectors the lock (1) must be pulled out to the side and removed before you can lift the release tab (2)

Some critical connectors, like the multi-pin connectors at the Powertrain Control Module employ pivoting locks that must be flipped open

## 6  Electrical connectors - general information

Most electrical connections on these vehicles are made with multiwire plastic connectors. The mating halves of many connectors are secured with locking clips molded into the plastic connector shells. The mating halves of some large connectors, such as some of those under the instrument panel, are held together by a bolt through the center of the connector.

To separate a connector with locking clips, use a small screwdriver to pry the clips apart carefully, then separate the con-nector halves. Pull only on the shell, never pull on the wiring harness as you may damage the individual wires and terminals inside the connectors. Look at the connector closely before trying to separate the halves. Often the locking clips are engaged in a way that is not immediately clear. Additionally, many connectors have more than one set of clips.

Each pair of connector terminals has a male half and a female half. When you look at the end view of a connector in a diagram, be sure to understand whether the view shows the harness side or the component side of the connector. Connector halves are mirror images of each other, and a terminal shown on the right side end-view of one half will be on the left side end-view of the other half.

It is often necessary to take circuit voltage measurements with a connector connected. Whenever possible, carefully insert a small straight pin (not your meter probe) into the rear of the connector shell to contact the terminal inside, then clip your meter lead to the pin. This kind of connection is called "backprobing." When inserting a test probe into a terminal, be careful not to distort the terminal opening. Doing so can lead to a poor connection and corrosion at that terminal later. Using the small straight pin instead of a meter probe results in less chance of deforming the terminal connector.

# Bulb removal

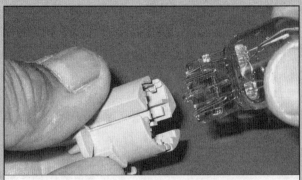

To remove many modern exterior bulbs from their holders, simply pull them out

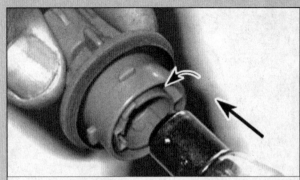

On bulbs with a cylindrical base ("bayonet" bulbs), the socket is spring-loaded; a pair of small posts on the side of the base hold the bulb in place against spring pressure. To remove this type of bulb, push it into the holder, rotate it 1/4-turn counterclockwise, then pull it out

If a bayonet bulb has dual filaments, the posts are staggered, so the bulb can only be installed one way

To remove most overhead interior light bulbs, simply unclip them

## 7  Bulbs - replacement

1    Whenever a bulb is replaced, note the following points:

a) *Remember that if the light has just been in use, the bulb may be extremely hot.*

b) *With the battery disconnected, always check the bulb contacts and holder, ensuring that there is clean metal-to-metal contact between the bulb and its contacts in the socket. Clean off any corrosion or dirt before installing a new bulb.* **Caution:** *If the battery is not disconnected, the exposed contacts have power at the contact which will shock if the contact is touched.*

c) *Wherever bayonet-type bulbs are installed ensure that the contact(s) bear firmly against the bulb contact.* **Caution:** *If the battery is not disconnected, the exposed contacts have power at the contact which will shock if the contact is touched.*

d) *Always ensure that the new bulb is of the correct rating and that it is completely clean before installing it; this applies particularly to headlight/fog light bulbs.*

## *Exterior lights*
### Xenon (HID) headlights

**Warning:** *Some models use High Intensity Discharge (HID) bulbs instead of halogen bulbs. These can be identified by the high voltage warning sticker on the headlight housing. According to the manufacturer, the high voltages produced by this system can be fatal in the event of shock. Also, the voltage can remain in the circuit even after the headlight switch has been turned to OFF and the ignition key has been removed. Therefore, for your safety, we don't recommend that you try to replace one of these bulbs yourself. Instead, have this service performed by a qualified repair shop.*

### Halogen headlights
#### High-beam bulbs

*Refer to illustrations 7.2 and 7.4*

2    On E-series chassis models, unclip the cover from the rear of the headlight **(see illustration)**, and on F-series chassis models, push the locking tabs down on the access cover and remove the cover. With the outer cover removed, rotate the large round protec-tive cap counterclockwise and remove the cap.

3    Pull the electrical connector from the bulb.

4    Release the retaining clip and pull the

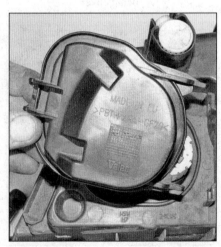

**7.2  Pull the inner edge of the cover rearwards to unclip it**

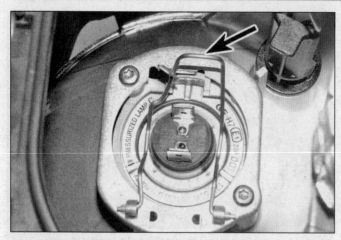

**7.4  Press the top of the clip forwards, the move it to the side to release it**

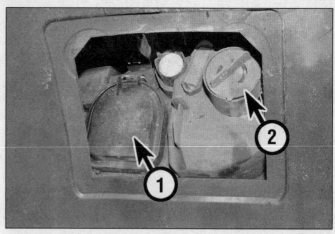

**7.9  Rotate the fasteners and remove the flap to access the low beam cover (1) or indicator bulbholder (2)**

bulb from the reflector **(see illustration)**.

5    When handling the new bulb, avoid touching the glass with your fingers; moisture and grease from the skin can cause blackening and rapid failure of this type of bulb. If the glass is accidentally touched, wipe it clean with rubbing alcohol.

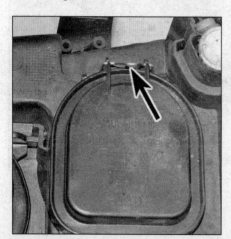

**7.10  Release the clip at the top of the low beam cover**

6    Push the new bulb into the reflector, ensuring that the bulb's locating lugs align with the corresponding slots in the reflector.

7    Secure the bulb in place with the retaining clip, and reconnect the electrical connector.

8    Install the cover to the rear of the headlight.

### Low-beam bulbs

*Refer to illustrations 7.9 and 7.10*

9    The low beam bulb is accessed through a flap in the inner fender liner. Turn the wheel inwards and locate the flap, then use a coin to rotate the fasteners counterclockwise and open the flap **(see illustration)**.

10    Two different types of covers are installed on the rear of the headlight to access the low beam. Either unclip the cover, or rotate it counterclockwise to remove it **(see illustration)**.

11    Perform Steps 3 through 8.

12    Close the flap in the inner fender liner, then rotate the fastener clockwise to secure it.

### Front side marker light bulbs

*Refer to illustration 7.14*

13    Remove the plastic cover from the rear of the main beam bulb **(see illustration 7.2)**.

14    Pull the bulb holder from the headlight unit. The bulb is of the capless type and is a push-fit in the holder **(see illustration)**.

15    Installation is the reverse of removal.

### Front turn signal light bulbs

*Refer to illustration 7.18*

**Note:** *On early F-series chassis models, the side-turn light is accessed through the headlight bulb hole opening (see Step 2). On later models the turn signals have been incorporated into the side view mirror and use a LED light strip. On these models, if defective, the complete light unit must be replaced.*

16    The indicator bulb is accessed through a flap in the inner fender liner. Turn the wheel inwards, then use a coin to rotate the fasteners and open the flap **(see illustration 7.9)**.

17    Twist the bulb holder counterclockwise to remove it from the light unit.

18    The bulb is a bayonet fitting in the holder. Push the bulb in slightly, then rotate it counterclockwise and pull it from the holder **(see illustration)**.

19    Installation is a reverse of the removal.

**7.14  Pull out the side marker bulb holder then pull the capless bulb from the holder**

**7.18  Push the indicator bulb in slightly, then rotate it counterclockwise**

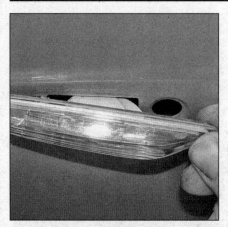

**7.20 Push the side marker lens rearwards and pull out the front edge**

**7.25 The fog light bulb is integral with the holder**

**7.27 Fog light aim adjustment bolt**

### Front side-turn light bulbs

**Note:** *On early F-series chassis models, the side-turn light is incorporated into the headlight housing. On later models, the turn signals have been incorporated into the side view mirror and use a LED light strip. On these models, if defective, the complete light unit must be replaced.*

*Refer to illustration 7.20*

20   On E-series chassis models, using finger pressure, push the side lens housing gently rearwards. Pull out the front edge of the lens and withdraw it from the fender (see illustration).

21   Rotate the bulb holder counterclockwise and pull it from the lens, then pull the capless bulb from the holder.

22   Installation is the reverse of removal.

### Front fog light bulbs

*Refer to illustrations 7.25 and 7.27*

23   Remove the front section of the inner fender liner.

24   Disconnect the electrical connector, then rotate the bulbholder counterclockwise and

remove it from the light.

25   The bulb is integral with the bulbholder (see illustration).

26   When handling the new bulb, avoid touching the glass with your fingers; moisture and grease from the skin can cause blackening and rapid failure of this type of bulb. If the glass is accidentally touched, wipe it clean with rubbing alcohol.

27   Installation is the reverse of removal. If necessary, adjust the aim of the light by rotating the adjusting screw adjacent to the lens (see illustration).

### Body-mounted rear lights

#### Sedan E-series chassis models

*Refer to illustrations 7.28a and 7.28b*

28   Working inside the trunk compartment, release the retaining clip or fastener to open the access panel. Release the retaining clip and separate the bulb holder from the light housing (see illustrations).

#### Sedan F-series chassis models

29   Remove the rear taillight housing (see Section 8).

30   Disengage the socket holder clips and separate the holder from the housing.

#### All models

31   Press down on the bulb and rotate the bulb counterclockwise and remove it. Installation is the reverse of removal.

#### Sports wagon models

*Refer to illustration 7.33*

32   Open the flap in the rear tailgate to expose the bulbholder (left-hand lights) or lift out the floor panel, remove the fasteners and lift out the side panel (right-hand lights).

33   Release the retaining clip and pull the bulbholder assembly from the rear of the light (see illustration).

34   Press the relevant bulb in slightly, twist it counterclockwise, and remove it from the bulbholder.

35   Installation is the reverse of removal.

### Trunk lid-mounted rear light bulbs

*Refer to illustrations 7.36 and 7.37*

36   Pry out the center pins and the expansion clips, then partially release the trunk lid

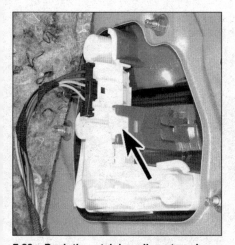

**7.28a Push the retaining clip outwards . . .**

**7.28b . . . and pull the bulbholder from the light unit**

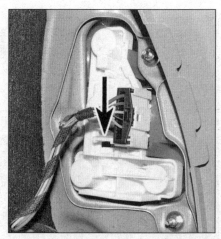

**7.33 Depress the clip and pull the bulbholder from the light unit, then press in the bulb, rotate it counterclockwise and remove it**

7.36  Pry up the center pins from the expansion clips

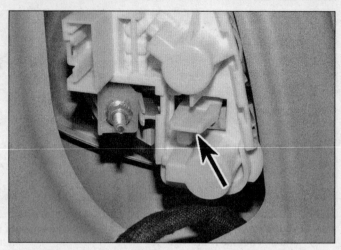

7.37  Press the retaining clip up and pull the bulbholder from the trunk lid

trim panel behind the light cluster **(see illustration)**.

37　Release the retaining clip, and remove

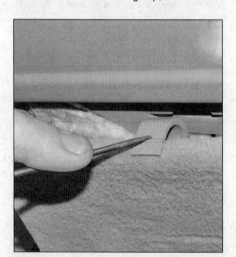

7.40  Release the mounting clips and fold down the tailgate panel

the bulbholder from the trunk lid **(see illustration)**.

38　Press the relevant bulb in slightly, twist it counterclockwise, and remove it from the bulbholder.

39　Installation is the reverse of removal.

### Tailgate-mounted rear light bulbs

*Refer to illustrations 7.40 and 7.41*

40　Open the tailgate. Carefully release the retaining clips at the lower edge of the tailgate trim panel and fold the panel downwards **(see illustration)**.

41　Release the retaining clip and remove the bulbholder from the tailgate **(see illustration)**.

42　Press the relevant bulb in slightly, twist it counterclockwise, and remove it from the bulbholder.

43　Installation is the reverse of removal.

### High-mounted brake light

44　The high-mounted brake light is an LED light strip. **Note:** *LED (Light Emitting Diode) high-mount brake lights have no replaceable*

bulbs. *On these models, if defective, the complete light unit must be replaced.*

### License plate light bulbs

*Refer to illustrations 7.45 and 7.46*

45　Using a small screwdriver in the slot provided, push the light unit to the right and pull it out **(see illustration)**.

46　The bulb can be pried out from the contacts. **Note:** *Later models are equipped with LED (Light Emitting Diode) license plate lights, which have no replaceable elements* **(see illustration)**. *On these models, if defective, the complete light unit must be replaced.*

47　Installation is the reverse of removal, making sure the bulb is securely held in position by the contacts.

## *Interior lights*

### Center light unit bulbs

*Refer to illustrations 7.48a and 7.48b*

48　Push the light unit rearwards, then pull down the front edge. Rotate the bulbholder

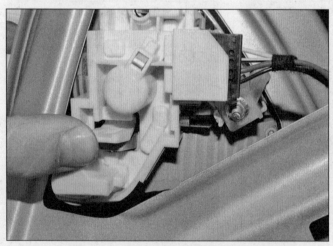

7.41  Lift the retaining clip and pull the bulbholder from the tailgate

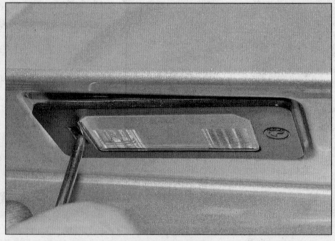

7.45  Push the license plate light unit to the right to compress the clip

**7.46  LED type license plate light**

**7.48a  Push the light unit rearwards, and pull down the front edge**

counterclockwise, and pull the capless bulb from the holders (**see illustrations**).

49   Push the new bulb(s) into the holder(s), and install them in to the light unit. Install the light unit. Note that the front edge of the light unit must be installed first, followed by the rear edge.

### Front light unit bulbs

*Refer to illustrations 7.50, 7.51a and 7.51b*

50   Using a blunt, flat-bladed tool, carefully pry out the light lens (**see illustration**).

51   Using the same tool, depress the clips at the front edge, and pull the unit downwards. The clips are exactly in line with the center line of each reading light (**see illustrations**).

52   Rotate the bulb holder counterclockwise and pull the capless bulb from the holder.

53   Push the new bulb(s) into the holder(s), and install them in to the light unit. Clip the lens back into place before installing the light unit. Note that the rear edge of the light unit must be installed first, followed by the front edge.

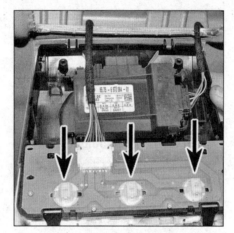

**7.48b  Rotate the bulb holders counterclockwise and pull the capless bulb from the holder**

### Footwell light bulbs

54   Carefully pry the light out from the panel. Disconnect the electrical connector as the light unit is withdrawn.

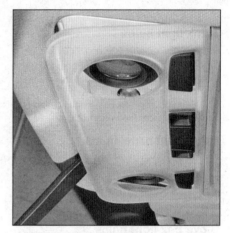

**7.50  Carefully pry the lens from the light unit**

55   Release the catch, remove the cover and remove the bulb.

56   Install the new bulb into position, install the cover, and install the light to the panel.

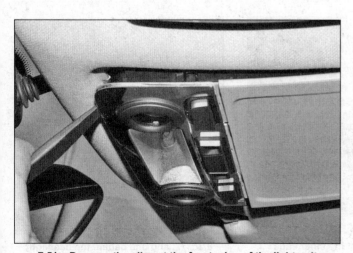

**7.51a  Depress the clips at the front edge of the light unit**

**7.51b  Use a blunt tool to press the clips rearwards**

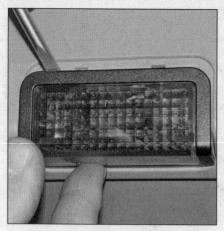

7.57  Carefully pry out the light

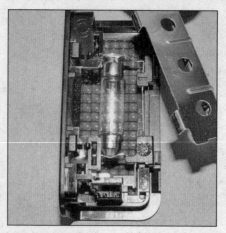

7.58  Remove the cover to access the bulb

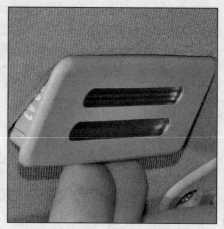

7.64  Pull down the front edge of the vanity light and pull the bulb from the contacts

## Trunk light bulbs

*Refer to illustrations 7.57 and 7.58*

57   Carefully pry the light out from the panel **(see illustration)**. Disconnect the electrical connector as the light unit is withdrawn.
58   Slide out the lens cover and pull the bulb from the contacts **(see illustration)**.

## Instrument panel lights

59   The instrument panel is illuminated by a series of LEDs *(Light Emitting Diode)*, which are not replaceable. If a fault develops, have the system checked by a BMW dealer or suitably-equipped specialist.

## Glove box light bulbs

60   Open the glove box. Using a small flat-bladed screwdriver, carefully pry the top of the light assembly and withdraw it. Release the bulb from its contacts.
61   Install the new bulb, ensuring it is securely held in position by the contacts, and clip the light unit back into position.

## Heater/air conditioning control panel light

62   The control panel is illuminated by LEDs *(Light Emitting Diode)* which are not serviceable. If a fault develops, have the system checked by a BMW dealer or suitably-equipped specialist.

## Switch illumination bulbs

63   All of the switches are illuminated by LEDs *(Light Emitting Diode)*; these LED lights are an integral part of the switch assembly and cannot be obtained separately. LED replacement will therefore require the replacement of the complete switch assembly.

## Vanity lights bulbs

*Refer to illustration 7.64*

64   Pry down the front edge of the light unit, and pull the bulb from the contacts **(see illustration)**.

## 8   Exterior light housings - removal and installation

### *Headlight housing*

*Refer to illustrations 8.3a, 8.3b and 8.3c*

1   Remove the front bumper cover (see Chapter 11).
2   Where equipped, carefully pry out the headlight washer nozzle from the trim below the headlamp, and pull it out to its stop. With a sharp tug, separate the nozzle from the washer tube.
3   Remove the mounting bolts and pull the headlight forward slightly **(see illustrations)**.
4   Noting their installed positions, disconnect all electrical connector(s) from the rear of the headlight.
5   Remove the headlight unit from the vehicle.
6   Installation is the reverse of removal. Once the light unit is correctly positioned,

8.3a  Remove the bolts at the top of the headlight . . .

8.3b  . . . two bolts at the inner edge . . .

8.3c  . . . and one behind the headlight

securely tighten the retaining bolts and check the headlight beam alignment (see Section 9).

### Turn signal indicator

7    The front turn signal indicators are integral with the headlight housing. If the turn signal indicator is faulty, the headlight housing must be replaced. On later F-series chassis models, the side turn signals have been incorporated into the side view mirror and use a LED light strip. On these models, if defective, the complete light unit must be removed (see Chapter 11) to disassemble the mirror, then remove the light strip fastener and light strip.

### Turn signal side marker

8    Using finger pressure, gently push the side marker lens rearward. Pull out the front edge of the lens and withdraw it from the fender **(see illustration 7.20)**. Disconnect the electrical connector as the unit is withdrawn.
9    Installation is the reverse of removal.

### Front fog light

*Refer to illustration 8.12*

10   Remove the fasteners and pull back the front section of the inner fender liner (see Chapter 11).
11   Disconnect the fog light electrical connector.
12   Remove the mounting bolts and pull the fog light from the bumper **(see illustration)**.
13   Installation is the reverse of removal.

### Body-mounted rear lights

#### Sedan models

##### E-series chassis models

*Refer to illustration 8.16*

14   From inside the trunk compartment, pry open the access panel behind the rear lights.
15   Disconnect the electrical connector, release the clip and pull the bulbholder assembly from the rear light **(see illustrations 7.29a and 7.29b)**.
16   Remove the retaining nuts and remove the cluster from the fender **(see illustration)**.
17   Installation is the reverse of removal.

##### F-series chassis models

18   Open the trunk lid and remove the trim panel fastener on the side of the taillight housing, then use a trim tool to slide the panel up and off to expose the housing mounting nuts.
19   Remove the mounting nuts, then grip the taillight housing and pull it straight out and away from the body. Disconnect the electrical connector and remove the housing.
20   Installation is the reverse of removal.

#### Sports wagon models

*Refer to illustration 8.23*

21   Operate the release catch and lift out the access panel for the left-hand rear lights, or for the right-hand rear lights, lift out the floor panel, remove the fasteners and lift out the panel in front of the rear lights. To improve access to the left-hand light, remove the warning triangle.

22   Disconnect the electrical connector, release the retaining clip, and pull the bulbholder assembly from the rear light **(see illustration 7.33)**.
23   Remove the retaining nuts, and remove the light cluster **(see illustration)**.
24   Installation is the reverse of removal. Note how the outer light unit guide engages with the pin on the vehicle body.

### Trunk lid-mounted rear lights

*Refer to illustration 8.27*

25   Pry up the center pins, then pry out the clips and partially release the trunk lid trim panel behind the light cluster **(see illustration 7.36)**.
26   Disconnect the electrical connector, release the retaining clip, and remove the bulbholder from the trunk lid **(see illustration 7.37)**.
27   Remove the securing nut and remove the plastic retainer, then remove the light cluster **(see illustration)**. Note that the edge of the light unit wraps around the edge of the trunk lid.
28   Installation is the reverse of removal.

**8.12  Fog light retaining bolt locations**

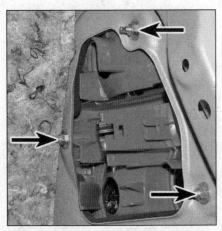

**8.16  Rear light retaining nut locations - Sedan models**

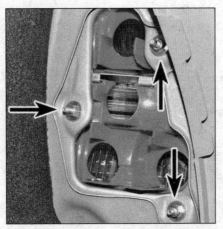

**8.23  Rear light retaining nut locations - Sports wagon models**

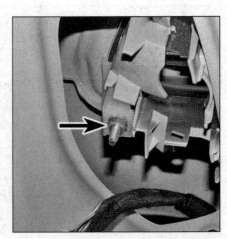

**8.27  Remove the nut, then remove the plastic retainer**

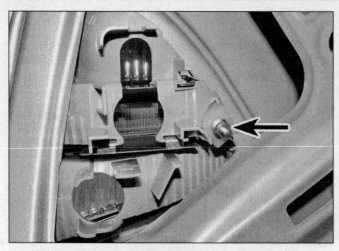

8.32  Loosen the retaining nut

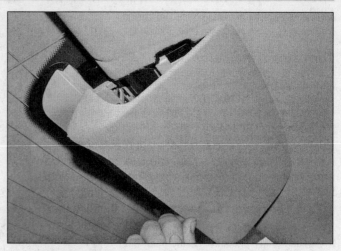

8.34  Pull down the rear edge of the brake light cover

## Tailgate-mounted rear lights

*Refer to illustration 8.32*

29   Release the mounting clips and fold down the tailgate trim panel behind the rear lights **(see illustration 7.40)**.
30   Pull away the section of insulation behind the rear lights.
31   Disconnect the rear light cluster electrical connector, release the retaining clip and remove the bulb holder **(see illustration 7.41)**.
32   Loosen the securing nut, press the clamping lever in the direction of the light cluster and remove it **(see illustration)**.
33   Installation is the reverse of removal.

## High-mounted brake light
### Sedan models

*Refer to illustrations 8.34 and 8.35*

34   Pull down the rear edge of the cover in front of the high-mounted brake light **(see illustration)**.
35   Disconnect the electrical connector, pull out the locking catches and remove the light unit **(see illustration)**.
36   Installation is the reverse of removal.

### Sports wagon models

37   Removal of the high-mounted brake light involves removal of the rear spoiler. This is a complex task requiring special tools and experience. Any attempt to remove the spoiler without the necessary equipment is very likely to result in damage. We recommend this procedure is handled by a BMW dealer or other qualified shop.

### License plate light

38   Remove the light unit **(see illustration 7.45)**. Disconnect the electrical connector as the unit is withdrawn.
39   Installation is the reverse of removal.

## 9   Headlights - adjustment

**Warning:** *The headlights must be aimed correctly. If adjusted incorrectly, they could temporarily blind the driver of an oncoming vehicle and cause an accident or seriously reduce your ability to see the road. The headlights should be checked for proper aim every 12 months and any time a new headlight is installed or front-end bodywork is performed. The following procedure is only intended to provide temporary adjustment until you can have the headlights professionally adjusted by a dealer service department.*
**Note:** *All covered models have halogen bulbs for the high beam. On earlier models, the low-beam bulb is also a halogen type. On later models, the low-beam bulb is a Xenon type, also called High Intensity Discharge (HID).*
**Note:** *Some models have an electrically-operated headlight beam adjustment system*

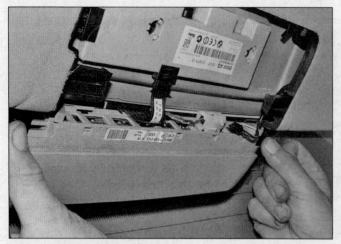

8.35  Slide out the catches and remove the light unit

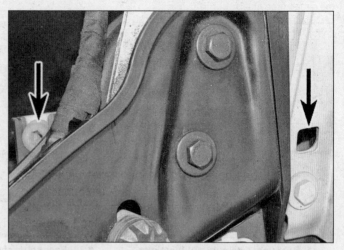

9.1  The headlight vertical adjustment screw is accessed from behind the headlight, while the horizontal screw (if equipped) is accessed through a hole in the inner fender

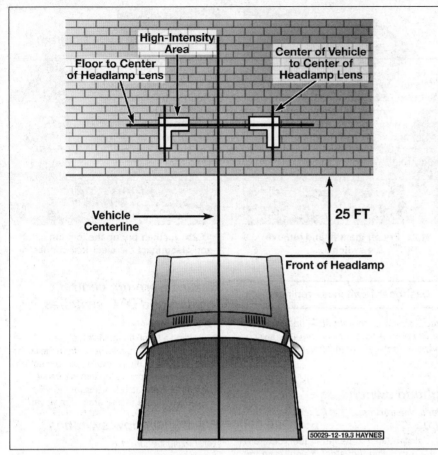

**9.2  Headlight adjustment details**

**High-Intensity Area**

**Floor to Center of Headlamp Lens**

**Center of Vehicle to Center of Headlamp Lens**

**Vehicle Centerline**

**25 FT**

**Front of Headlamp**

50029-12-19.3 HAYNES

5    Adjustment should be made with the vehicle parked 25 feet from the wall, sitting level, the gas tank full and no unusually heavy load in the vehicle.

6    The high intensity zone should be vertically centered with the exact center about three inches below the horizontal line.

7    Have the headlights adjusted by a qualified technician at the earliest opportunity.

## Fog lights

8    Park the vehicle 25 feet from the wall.

9    Tape a horizontal line on the wall that represents the height of the fog lights and tape another line four inches below that line.

10    Using the adjusting screw on each fog light, adjust the pattern on the wall so that the top of the fog light beam meets the lower line on the wall.

**Note:** *The adjustment screw on F-series chassis models is accessed through a small hole in the fog light fascia in the bumper cover.*

## 10   Instrument cluster - removal and installation

*Refer to illustrations 10.3a, 10.3b and 10.4*

**Note:** *At the time of writing, no individual components were available for the instrument cluster. If there is a fault with one of the instruments, remove the cluster as described below and take it to your BMW dealer for testing.*

1    Disconnect the negative battery cable (see Chapter 5).

2    Move the steering column down as far as it will go, and extend it completely.

3    Loosen and remove the retaining Torx bolts from the top of the instrument panel, then carefully pull the top of the cluster from the instrument panel **(see illustrations)**.

4    Pry up the retaining catches, then disconnect the wiring connectors and remove the instrument cluster from the vehicle **(see illustration)**.

5    Installation is the reverse of removal, making sure the wiring is correctly reconnected and securely held in position by any retaining clips. Reconnect the battery and

which is controlled through the switch in the instrument panel. On these models ensure that the switch is set to the off position before adjusting the headlight aim.

## Headlights

*Refer to illustrations 9.1 and 9.2*

1    Each headlight has an adjusting screw for vertical adjustment **(see illustration)**. There is no horizontal adjustment screw.

2    There are several ways to adjust the headlights. The simplest method requires an open area with a blank wall and a level floor **(see illustration)**.

3    Position masking tape vertically on the wall in reference to the vehicle centerline and the centerlines of both headlights.

4    Position a horizontal tape line in reference to the centerline of the headlights. **Note:** *It might be easier to position the tape on the wall with the vehicle parked only a few inches away.*

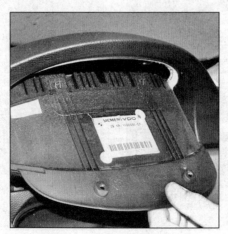

**10.3a  Remove the mounting bolts ...**

**10.3b  ... and pull the top of the instrument cluster rearwards**

**10.4  Pry up the retaining catches to disconnect the electrical connectors**

**11.1  Pry the decorative trim strip/air vent from the instrument panel**

**11.2a  Pry off the trim and remove the switch . . .**

**11.2b  . . . then pry up the locking catch and disconnect the electrical connector**

check the operation of the warning lights to ensure that they are functioning correctly. **Note:** *If the instrument cluster has been replaced, the new unit must be coded to match the vehicle. This can only be carried out by a dealer or other qualified shop.*

**11.3  Release the clips and detach the switch from the panel**

## 11  Dashboard switches - replacement

**Note:** *Disconnect the negative battery cable (see Chapter 5) before removing any switch, and reconnect the cable after installing the switch.*

### Lighting switch

*Refer to illustrations 11.1, 11.2a, 11.2b and 11.3*

1    Using a blunt, flat-bladed tool, carefully pry the decorative trim strip/air vent from the left-hand side of the instrument panel **(see illustration)**. Disconnect any electrical connectors as the trim is removed.
2    Carefully pry the switch and surrounding trim from the instrument panel. Unlock and disconnect the electrical connector from the switch as it's withdrawn **(see illustrations)**.
3    If required, release the catches and detach the switch from the trim **(see illustration)**.
4    Installation is the reverse of removal.

### Hazard warning, central locking and DTC switches

*Refer to illustration 11.5*

5    Using a blunt, flat-bladed tool, carefully pry the decorative trim strip/air vents from the instrument panel **(see illustration)**. Disconnect any electrical connectors as the trim is removed.
6    Press the switch block from the strip.
7    Installation is the reverse of removal.

### Electric window switches

*Refer to illustration 11.8*

8    Using a blunt, flat-bladed tool, carefully pry the switch panel from the armrest **(see illustration)**. If necessary, use a piece of cardboard to protect the armrest material.
**Note:** *On F-series chassis models, the inner door handle trim panel must be removed (see Chapter 11) and the switch cover lock disengaged before trying to pry the switch panel out of the armrest.*
9    Disconnect the electrical connectors as the switch panel is removed.
10   Installation is the reversal of removal.

**11.5  Carefully pry the decorative trim strip from the instrument panel**

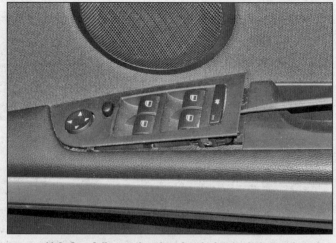

**11.8  Carefully pry the electric window switch panel from the armrest**

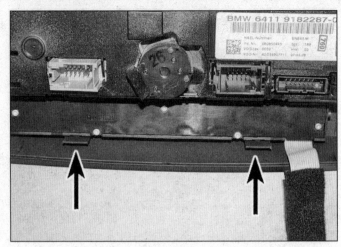

**11.17 Release the clips and detach the switch cluster**

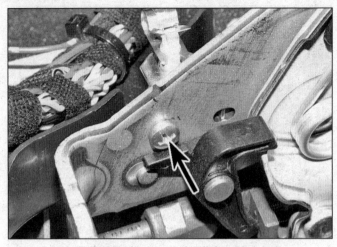

**11.21 Parking brake warning light switch bolt**

## Exterior mirror switches

11   The mirror adjustment switch is integral with the electric window switch (see Steps 8 through 10).

## Clutch pedal position switch

12   Remove the driver's side lower instrument panel retaining bolts, then unclip the panel and remove it from the vehicle. Noting their installed positions, disconnect any electrical connectors as the panel is withdrawn.
13   Disconnect the electrical connector from the switch.
14   Using a screwdriver, unclip the switch from the side of the master cylinder.
15   Installation is the reverse of removal.

## Central instrument panel switch cluster

*Refer to illustration 11.17*

16   Remove the heating/air conditioning/climate control panel (see Chapter 3).
17   Disconnect the electrical connector, then release the clips and detach the switch cluster from the control panel **(see illustration)**.
18   Installation is the reverse of removal.

## Heated rear window/blower/air conditioning switches

19   The switches are an integral part of the control unit and cannot be replaced. If a switch is faulty, seek the advice of a BMW dealer or parts specialist.

## Parking brake warning light switch

*Refer to illustration 11.21*

20   Remove the center console (see Chapter 11) to gain access to the parking brake lever.
21   Disconnect the wiring connector from the warning light switch, then remove the bolt and

remove the switch **(see illustration)**.
22   Installation is the reverse of removal. Check the operation of the switch before installing the center console; the warning light should illuminate between the first and second clicks of the ratchet mechanism.

## Brake light switch

23   Refer to Chapter 9.

## Courtesy light switches

24   The courtesy light switches are a function of the door/trunk lid/tailgate lock assemblies. To remove the relevant lock, refer to Chapter 11.

## Sunroof/interior light switches

25   Using a blunt, flat-bladed tool, carefully pry out the interior light lens **(see illustration 7.50)**.
26   Release the clips, and pry the switch/panel assembly from the headliner **(see illustrations 7.51a and 7.51b)**. Disconnect the electrical connectors as the panel is withdrawn.
27   No further disassembly is recommended. The switches are not available separately. Consult a dealer or parts specialist.
28   Installation is the reverse of removal. If a new switch/panel assembly has been installed, the switch module for the sunroof will need to be programmed using BMW diagnostic equipment. Entrust this task to a BMW dealer or suitably-equipped specialist.
29   Initialize the sunroof as follows:
a)   *Press and hold the switch in the tilt position.*
b)   *After reaching the end of the tilt position, keep the switch pressed for another 30 seconds. The normalization is complete when the sunroof rear end lifts briefly.*
c)   *Keep the switch pressed in the tilt position, and after approximately 5 seconds, the sunroof will move to the closed position, back to the open position, then finally back to the closed position.*
d)   *Release the switch.*

## Trunk lid/tailgate release switches

30   Unclip the diagnostic plug socket cover on the driver's side kick panel.
31   Push the release switch from the panel. Disconnect the electrical connector as the switch is removed.
32   Installation is the reverse of removal.

## iDrive controller

33   Remove the center console (see Chapter 11).
34   Carefully pry the controller knob upwards from the assembly.
35   Remove the mounting bolts and detach the controller from the console.
36   Installation is the reverse of removal.

## Automatic transmission s hift paddles

37   Remove the driver's airbag (see Section 21).
38   Disconnect the shift paddle electrical connectors, remove the mounting bolts and pull the paddles from the steering wheel.
39   Installation is the reverse of removal.

## 12   Audio unit and speakers - removal and installation

**Note:** *This Section applies to the range of audio units which BMW installs as standard equipment. Removal and installation procedures of non-standard units will differ slightly.*

## Instrument panel-mounted unit
### E-series chassis models

*Refer to illustrations 12.1a, 12.1b, 12.3, 12.4a and 12.4b*

1   Using a blunt, flat-bladed tool, carefully pry the decorative trim from the passenger's side of

**12.1a Carefully pry the decorative trim . . .**

**12.1b . . . from the passenger's side of the instrument panel**

**12.3 Audio unit retaining bolts**

**12.4a Pry up the locking catch and disconnect the main electrical connector . . .**

the instrument panel **(see illustrations)**. Disconnect any electrical connectors as the trim is removed. Replace any damaged trim clips.

2   Remove the heater/air conditioning/climate control panel (see Chapter 3).

**12.4b . . . followed by the antenna connection**

3   Remove the mounting bolts and pull the unit slightly from the instrument panel **(see illustration)**.

4   Noting their installed positions, disconnect the electrical connectors from the rear of the unit (slide out the locking element on the main plug) **(see illustrations)**.

5   Installation is the reverse of removal.

## F-series chassis models

6   Using a trim tool, pry out the decorative center trim panel and vents from the face of the instrument panel, disconnecting any electrical connectors as the trim panel is removed.

**Note:** *The trim panel is long - it covers the full face of the instrument panel - be sure to disengage all the fasteners before trying to remove the panel.*

7   Using a thin plastic trim tool, carefully pry out the small cover just below heater and air conditioning controller, then disconnect the electrical connector for the light to the panel.

8   Remove the four mounting screws and pull the radio/heater/air conditioning controller

forward until the electrical connectors can be disconnected, then remove the unit.

9   Remove the radio controller mounting screws and separate the units.

10   Installation is the reverse of removal.

## CD changer

### E-series chassis models

11   Disconnect the negative battery cable (see Chapter 5).

12   Remove the left-hand side trunk compartment trim panel (see Chapter 11).

13   Remove the mounting bolts, and lift the unit from position. Disconnect the electrical connectors as the unit is withdrawn.

14   Installation is the reverse of removal.

### F-series chassis models

15   Remove the radio/heater/air conditioning controller (see Steps 6 through 10)

16   Remove the CD changer mounting screws, pull forward until the electrical connectors can be disconnected, then remove the unit from the instrument panel.

17   Installation is the reverse of removal.

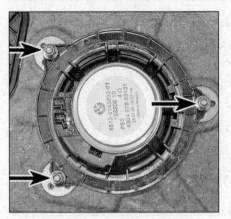

**12.23  Door speaker retaining nut locations**

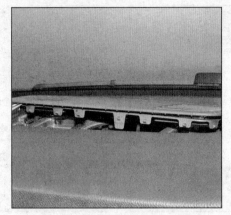

**12.31  Pry up the instrument panel speaker grille**

**12.34  Pry up the rear package tray speaker grille**

## Amplifier

18   Disconnect the negative battery cable (see Chapter 5).

19   The amplifier (where equipped) is located behind the left-hand side trunk compartment trim panel. Open the flap and lift out the storage tray.

20   Disconnect the amplifier electrical connectors, remove the retaining bolts and remove the unit. Note that on Sedan models, the amplifier is located below the CD changer (where equipped).

21   Installation is the reverse of removal.

## Speakers

### Door panel speaker(s)

*Refer to illustration 12.23*

22   Remove the door inner trim panel (see Chapter 11).

23   Unscrew the mounting nuts and remove the speaker from the door trim **(see illustration)**.

24   Where installed, unscrew the large retaining collar and remove the small speaker from the trim panel.

25   Installation is the reverse of removal.

### Door upper speaker

26   Remove the door inner trim panel (see Chapter 11).

27   Carefully unclip the plastic panel from the front inner edge of the door.

28   Remove the foam wedge from the door frame.

29   Disconnect the speaker electrical connector, release the catches and remove the speaker.

30   Installation is the reverse of removal.

### Instrument panel speaker

*Refer to illustration 12.31*

31   Carefully pry up the speaker grille from the instrument panel **(see illustration)**.

32   Remove the retaining bolts, pull the speaker out, and disconnect the electrical connector.

33   Installation is the reverse of removal.

### Rear speaker

*Refer to illustrations 12.34 and 12.35*

34   Carefully pry the speaker grille out from the rear package tray **(see illustration)**.

35   Remove the retaining bolts and lift the speaker **(see illustration)**. Disconnect the electrical connector as the speaker is withdrawn.

36   Installation is the reverse of removal.

### Floor speakers

*Refer to illustrations 12.39 and 12.40*

37   The floor speakers are located under the front seats. Remove the relevant front seat (see Chapter 11).

38   Pull the front door sill trim panel upward to release the retaining clips.

39   Remove the mounting bolts and remove the speaker grille **(see illustration)**.

40   Fold back the carpet, disconnect the electrical connector, remove the mounting nuts and lift out the speaker assembly **(see illustration)**.

41   If required, remove the bolts and detach the speaker from the housing.

42   Installation is the reverse of removal. Pry the retaining clips from the door sill and attach them to the sill trim panel prior to installation.

---

## 13   Antenna - removal and installation

### Roof-mounted antenna

The roof-mounted antenna is bonded onto the panel. Replacement requires special

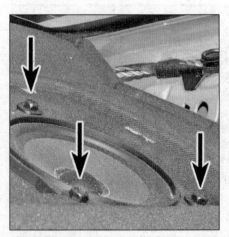

**12.35  Remove the speaker retaining bolts**

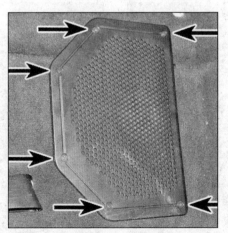

**12.39  Remove the bolts and the speaker grille**

**12.40  Speaker assembly retaining nut locations**

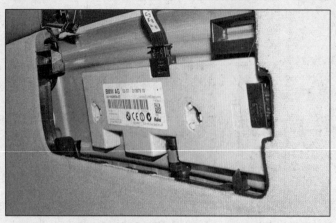

**13.3  Roof-mounted antenna amplifier**

**14.2  Pry the switch surround from the instrument panel**

tools and the experience to use them. We recommend this task is handled by a dealer or
specialist.

## Amplifier

*Refer to illustration 13.3*

An amplifier is installed to boost the signal to the radio unit. On sedan models, the
amplifier is located above the high-mounted
brake light. On Sports wagon models, the
amplifier is located under the rear spoiler.

To remove the amplifier on sedan models, remove the brake light (see Section 8),
then disconnect the antenna lead and wiring.
Remove the retaining bolts and remove the
amplifier **(see illustration)**. Installation is the
reverse of removal.

Amplifier replacement on Sports wagon
models requires removal of the spoiler, which
is a complex task requiring special tools and
experience. Any attempt to remove the spoiler
without the necessary equipment is very likely
to result in damage. We recommend this procedure is handled by a BMW dealer or other
qualified shop.

## Rear window antenna

The antenna is a printed grid type and

is located in the rear window. An amplifier,
located in front of the high-mounted brake
light, boosts the signal to the radio unit. The
only way to replace the antenna or amplifier is
to replace the rear window.

## 14  Ignition switch and engine start/ stop switch - replacement

### Ignition switch

*Refer to illustrations 14.2 and 14.3*

1    The covered models use a coded fob
instead of a traditional metal key. Inserting
the fob into the switch allows the use of the
engine start/stop switch, which actually starts
the engine.
2    Carefully pry off the switch trim **(see
illustration)**.
3    Remove the mounting bolts and pull the
switch from the instrument panel **(see illustration)**. Disconnect the electrical connector
as the switch is withdrawn.
4    Installation is the reverse of removal.

### Engine start/stop switch
### E-series chassis models

*Refer to illustration 14.6*

5    Using a blunt, flat-bladed tool, carefully
pry the decorative trim strip/air vents from the
instrument panel **(see illustration 11.5)**. Disconnect any electrical connectors as the trim
is removed.
6    Squeeze together the clips and push the
engine start/stop switch from the trim **(see
illustration)**.
7    Installation is the reverse of removal.

### F-series chassis models

8    Using a trim tool, pry out the switch from
the instrument panel, then disconnect the
electrical connector.
9    Installation is the reverse of removal.

## 15  Steering column switches - replacement

### Steering column switch module

*Refer to illustrations 15.3a, 15.3b, 15.3c, 15.4
and 15.6*

1    Place the steering column in the fully

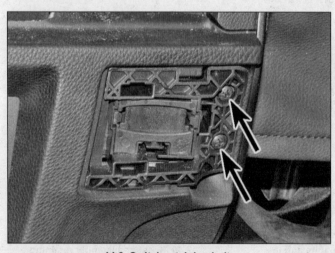

**14.3  Switch retaining bolts**

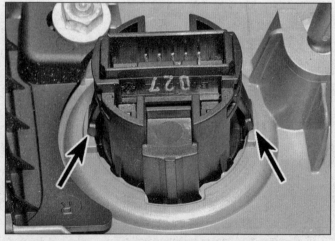

**14.6  Squeeze together the clips and push the start switch
from the trim**

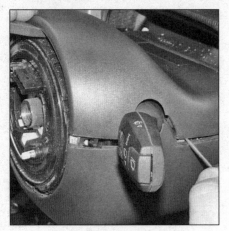

15.3a  Unclip the column upper shroud . . .

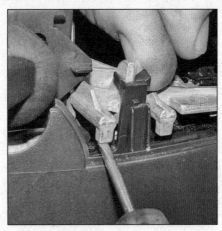

15.3b  . . . and lower column shroud . . .

15.3c  . . . if required, squeeze together the clips and detach the upper shroud from the boot

15.4  Remove the switch module retaining bolts

15.6  Release the clips around the outer edge of the clockspring (upper clips shown)

lowered and extended position. Remove the steering wheel (see Chapter 10).

2    Note that as the steering wheel is removed, the clockspring is automatically locked to prevent any accidental rotation.

3    Unclip the upper and lower steering column covers **(see illustrations)**.

4    Remove the mounting bolts and slide the module up the steering column **(see illustration)**.

5    Disconnect the various electrical connectors from the module as it's withdrawn. **Note:** *The steering column switch module has very few mechanical elements, as the operating components are optical switches. The module also incorporates the steering angle sensor. Handle the module with great care.*

6    If required, release the clips and separate the clockspring **(see illustration)**. No further disassembly of the module is recommended.

7    Installation is the reverse of removal, ensuring that the wiring is correctly routed. **Note:** *If a new module has been installed, it must be coded/calibrated using BMW diag-* nostic equipment. Entrust this task to a dealer or other qualified shop.

## Steering wheel switches

**Note:** *Two different types of steering wheels are used on the 3-Series range; either a Multifunction steering wheel, or a Sports steering wheel.*

8    Remove the driver's airbag (see Section 21).

### Multifunction steering wheel

*Refer to illustration 15.10*

9    Disconnect the switch electrical connector from the center of the steering wheel. **Note:** *The switches are wired together.*

10   Carefully pry the switches from the steering wheel **(see illustration)**. Note that the horn switch is integral with the airbag unit.

11   Installation is the reverse of removal.

### Sports steering wheel

*Refer to illustration 15.13*

12   Remove the retaining bolts on the front face of the steering wheel (two securing the upper section and one securing the lower section), and unclip the switch carrier panel from

15.10  Pry the switch block from the steering wheel (multifunction steering wheel)

15.13  Each steering wheel switch is
secured by a bolt

16.3  Horn retaining nut

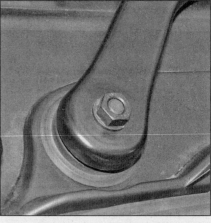

17.3a  Remove the wiper arm spindle nut

the steering wheel. Disconnect the electrical
connector as the panel is withdrawn.
13   If required, remove the bolts and detach
the switches from the panel **(see illustration)**.
14   Installation is the reverse of removal.

---

## 16   Horn(s) - removal and installation

*Refer to illustration 16.3*

1   The horn(s) is/are located behind the left
and right ends of the front bumper.
2   To gain access to the horn(s) from
below, apply the parking brake and raise the
front of the vehicle and support it securely on
jackstands. Remove the retaining bolts and
remove the lower front section of the inner
fender liner. Unclip and remove the brake disc
cooling duct (where applicable).
3   Remove the retaining nut and remove
the horn, disconnecting its wiring connectors

as they become accessible **(see illustration)**.
4   Installation is the reverse of removal.

---

## 17   Wiper arms, motor and linkage -
removal and installation

### Wiper arms

*Refer to illustrations 17.3a, 17.3b and 17.4*

1   Operate the wiper motor, then switch it
off so that the wiper arms return to the at rest
position.
2   Stick a piece of masking tape to the
windshield or rear window along the edge of
the wiper blade(s) to use as an alignment aid
on installation.
3   Pry off the wiper-arm-spindle nut cover,
then loosen and remove the spindle nut. Lift
the blade off the windshield and pull the wiper
arm off its spindle. If necessary, the arm can be
pried off the spindle using a flat-bladed screwdriver or puller **(see illustrations)**. **Note:** *If
both windshield wiper arms are to be removed*

*at the same time, mark them for identification;
the arms are not interchangeable.*
4   Ensure that the wiper arm and spindle
splines are clean and dry, then install the arm
to the spindle, aligning the wiper blade with the
tape on the windshield. **Note:** *If the splined-
tapered sleeves on the arms are loose, they
must be replaced.* Install the spindle nut, tightening it to the specified torque setting, and clip
the nut cover back in position. If the wipers are
being installed on a new windshield, position
the wiper arms as shown **(see illustration)**.

### Wiper motor and linkage
#### Front wiper motor

*Refer to illustrations 17.6, 17.7, 17.8a, 17.8b,
17.18c, 17.10a, 17.10b, 17.12a, 17.12b,
17.12c and 17.14*

5   Working at the rear of the engine compartment, remove the bolts and remove the
cabin air filter cover (see Chapter 1). Slide the
filter from the housing.
6   Release the catch at each side and
remove the left and right plastic covers from

17.3b  If using a puller, install the nut so
it's level with the end of the spindle to
prevent thread damage

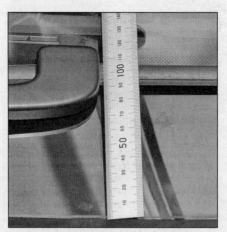

17.4  The distance from the windshield
surround trim to the lower edge of the
arm-to-blade pivot point is 88 ± 3 mm
(driver's side) or 95 ± 3 mm
(passenger's side)

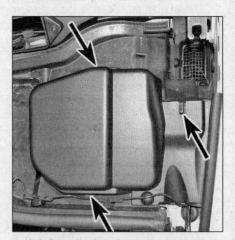

17.6  Release the clips and remove the
plastic covers behind the strut towers

**17.7  Release the clips and pull the cable guide forwards**

**17.8a  On the driver's side, rotate the air temperature sensor and detach it from the panel. On the passenger's side, disconnect the hood switch**

behind the strut tower at each side of the engine compartment. Unclip the hose from the right-hand cover **(see illustration)**.

7    Depress the clips and pull the cable guide forwards from the cabin air filter lower housing **(see illustration)**.

8    Release the catch and remove the bolt at each side, then slide the cabin air filter lower housing forwards and maneuver it from the cowl **(see illustrations)**.

9    Remove the wiper arms (see Steps 1 through 3).

10    Disconnect the washer hose, pull away the sealing strip and pull the cowl trim panel upwards from the base of the windshield.

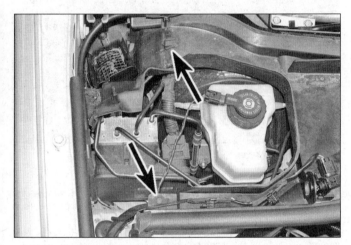

**17.8b  Remove the bolt, and release the clip on each side . . .**

**17.8c  . . . then pull the lower cabin air filter housing forwards**

**17.10a  Pull the cowl trim panel upward from the base of the windshield**

**17.10b  Disconnect the heated washer nozzle electrical connector**

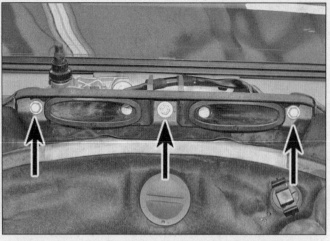

17.12a  Remove the bolts and remove the firewall center panel

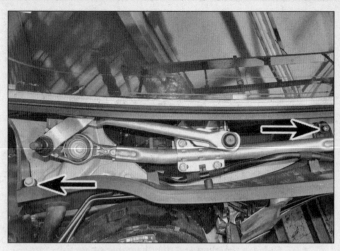

17.12b  Remove the nut/bolt . . .

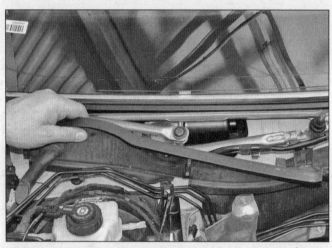

17.12c  . . . and remove the right-hand panel

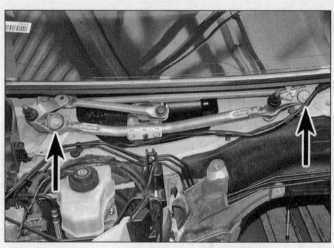

17.14  Wiper linkage retaining bolt locations

Maneuver the cowl trim panel from the vehicle (see illustrations). Disconnect the heated washer nozzle electrical connectors as the panel is withdrawn.

11   On models with strut supports, loosen the center bolt, remove the outer bolts and carefully remove both supports from the cowl. Note that new bolts must be installed upon reassembly (see Chapter 10). Take care not to move the support's grommets.

12   Remove the bolts/nut and remove the firewall center and right-hand panels (see illustrations).

13   Unclip the wiring harness from the linkage bracket.

14   Remove the wiper linkage retaining bolts, and lift the linkage assembly from the cowl (see illustration). Disconnect the wiper motor electrical connector as it's withdrawn.

15   No further disassembly is recommended. **Note:** *The motor and linkage are only available as a complete assembly.* Installation is the reverse of removal.

### Rear wiper motor

*Refer to illustrations 17.16, 17.18, 17.19, 17.20, 17.22 and 17.23*

16   Pull the rear window side trims inward to release the retaining clips, and disengage them from the upper trim (see illustration).

17   Release the mounting clips, then fold down and remove the trim insert on the tailgate rear panel (see illustration 7.40).

18   Open the rear window, pull the plastic trim at the top of the rear panel rearward to

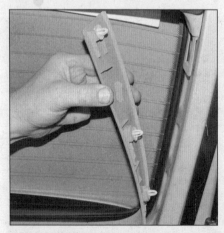

17.16  Pull the window side trims inwards to release the clips

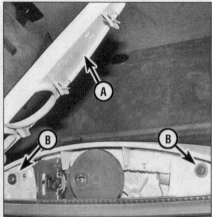

17.18  Pull the plastic trim panel (A) rearwards, then remove the mounting bolts (B)

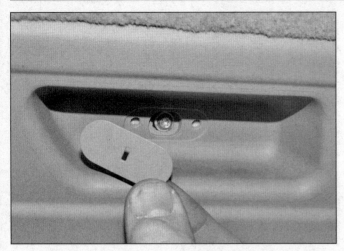

**17.19  Pry out the cover in each handle recess, and remove the bolt**

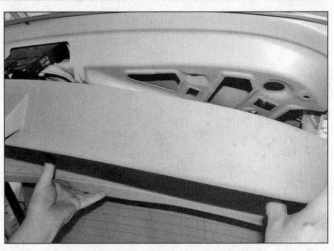

**17.20  Pull the panel from the tailgate**

release the clips, then remove the mounting bolts at the top of the panel **(see illustration)**.

19   Pry out the cover, then remove the bolt in the handle recess on each side **(see illustration)**.

20   Pull the rear trim panel away from the tailgate to release the retaining clips **(see illustration)**. Disconnect the trunk compartment light as the panel is withdrawn.

21   Disconnect the wiper motor electrical connector.

22   Remove the retaining bolts and remove the wiper motor **(see illustration)**.

23   If required, the window lock can be separated from the wiper motor by removing the retaining bolts **(see illustration)**. Installation is the reverse of removal.

## Rear wiper arm spindle and housing

*Refer to illustrations 17.25, 17.26 and 17.27*

24   Remove the rear wiper arm (see Steps 1 through 3).

**17.22  Remove the bolts and remove the wiper motor**

25   Open the tailgate, pry out the two plastic caps, and remove the nuts securing the plastic cover over the spindle **(see illustration)**. Remove the cover.

**17.23  Tailgate lock bolt locations**

26   On the outside of the rear window, loosen and remove the wiper-arm spindle nut and any washers **(see illustration)**.

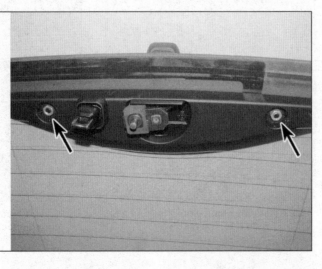

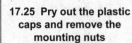

**17.25  Pry out the plastic caps and remove the mounting nuts**

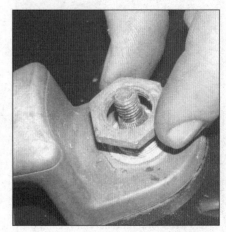

**17.26  Loosen and remove the wiper spindle nut**

**17.27  Remove the nut and remove the housing and spindle as an assembly**

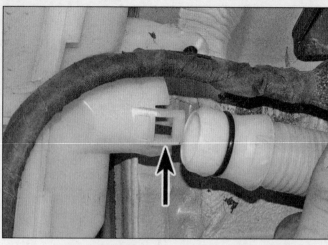

**18.2  Release the clips and detach the filler hose**

27    On the inside of the rear window, disconnect the rear window-button electrical connector, remove the retaining nut, and maneuver the housing and spindle out **(see illustration)**. No further disassembly is recommended.
28    Installation is the reverse of removal.

## 18   Windshield/headlight washer system components - removal and installation

### Washer reservoir

*Refer to illustrations 18.2 and 18.3*

1    The reservoir is located behind the right front wheelwell. Remove the inner fender liner (see Chapter 11).
2    Unclip the wiring harness and hose from the reservoir clips, then disconnect the filler hose **(see illustration)**. Be prepared for fluid spillage.
3    Remove the bolt and maneuver the reservoir from the fenderwell **(see illustration)**.

Noting their installed positions, disconnect the electrical connectors and hoses from the reservoir components.
4    Installation is the reverse of removal. Make sure the locating lugs on the rear edge of the reservoir engage correctly with the corresponding slots in the inner fender. Refill the reservoir and check for leakage.

### Washer pumps

*Refer to illustration 18.6*

5    Remove the reservoir (see Steps 1 through 3). On Sports wagon models, two pumps are used - one for the windshield and one for the rear window.
6    Disconnect the wiring connector(s) and hose(s) from the washer pump(s). Carefully rotate the pump(s) clockwise, and pull them up from the reservoir. Inspect the pump sealing grommet(s) for signs of damage or deterioration and replace if necessary **(see illustration)**.
7    Installation is the reverse of removal, using a new sealing grommet if the original one

shows signs of damage or deterioration. Make sure the locating lugs on the rear edge of the reservoir engage correctly with the corresponding slots in the inner fender. Refill the reservoir and check the pump grommet for leaks.

### Washer reservoir level switch

*Refer to illustration 18.9*

8    Remove the reservoir (see Steps 1 through 3).
9    Rotate the level switch counterclockwise and remove it from the reservoir **(see illustration)**.
10    Installation is the reverse of removal, using a new sealing grommet if the original one shows signs of damage or deterioration. Make sure the locating lugs on the rear edge of the reservoir engage correctly with the corresponding slots in the inner fender. Refill the reservoir and check for leaks.

### Washer nozzles

**Windshield**

11    Working at the rear of the engine com-

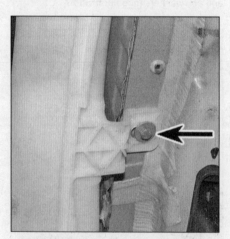

**18.3  Washer fluid reservoir retaining bolt location**

**18.6  Rotate the pump clockwise and pull it up from the reservoir**

**18.9  Rotate the level switch counterclockwise and pull it from the reservoir**

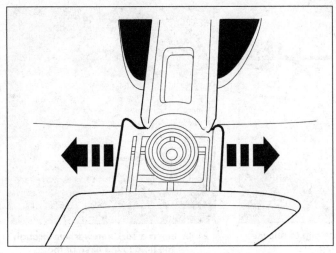

**18.16  Spread the clips and detach the cover**

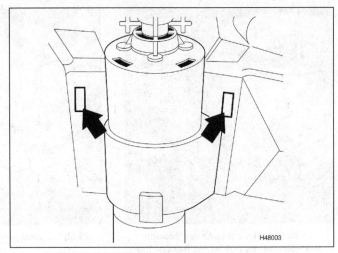

**18.20  Release the clips on the underside of the nozzle**

partment, remove the bolts and remove the cabin air filter cover. Slide the filter from the housing **(see illustration 17.5)**.

12   Reaching through the openings, disconnect the hoses and, where applicable, the heated nozzle electrical connectors **(see illustration 17.10b)**.

13   Press the washer nozzle rearward, pull up the front edge, and maneuver it from the panel.

14   Installation is the reverse of removal.

### Headlight

*Refer to illustrations 18.16 and 18.20*

15   Using a wooden or plastic lever, carefully pry out the washer nozzle cover from below the headlight, and pull it out to its stop.

16   Pull out the clips and detach the cover from the nozzle **(see illustration)**.

17   Remove the front bumper (see Chapter 11).

18   Where applicable, disconnect the nozzle heater electrical connector.

19   Disconnect the hose from the nozzle. Be prepared for fluid spillage.

20   Release the mounting clips and maneuver the nozzle from the vehicle **(see illustration)**.

21   Installation is the reverse of removal.

### Rear window

22   Remove the high-mounted brake light (see Section 8).

23   Release the clip, disconnect the hose and pull the nozzle from the high-mounted brake light.

24   Installation is the reverse of removal. Aim the nozzle to an area 4 inches (100 mm) from the top, and 12.6 inches (320 mm) from the edge of the window.

### *Wiper/washer system control module*

25   The wiper/washer system is controlled

by the central control module assembly, integral with the main fusebox (see Section 3).

---

## 19   Cruise control system - information and component replacement

### *Information*

1   The cruise control function is incorporated into the engine management ECM/DME. The only serviceable external component is the clutch pedal switch. Problems with the system can be diagnosed with a professional scan tool at a dealer or other qualified shop.

### *Switch replacement*

2   The clutch switch is attached to the side of the clutch master cylinder (see Chapter 9).

3   The cruise control switch is integral to the steering column multi-function switch (see Section 15).

---

## 20   Airbag system - general information and precautions

The models covered by this manual are equipped with a driver's airbag mounted in the center of the steering wheel, a passenger's airbag located behind the instrument panel, two side curtain airbags located in each A-pillar/headliner, and two side impact airbags located in each front seat. The airbag system is comprised of the airbag units, impact sensors, the control unit and a warning light in the instrument panel.

The airbag system is triggered in the event of a heavy frontal or side impact above a predetermined force, depending on the point of impact. The airbag(s) is inflated within milliseconds and forms a safety cushion between the cabin occupants and the cabin interior,

and therefore greatly reduces the risk of injury. The airbag then deflates almost immediately.

Every time the ignition is switched on, the airbag control unit performs a self-test. The self-test takes approximately 2 to 6 seconds and during this time the airbag warning light on the instrument panel is illuminated. After the self-test has been completed the warning light should go out. If the warning light fails to come on, remains illuminated after the initial period or comes on at any time when the vehicle is being driven, there is a fault in the airbag system. The vehicle should be taken to your dealer immediately for service.

### *Precautions*

**Warning:** *Failure to follow these precautions could result in accidental deployment of the airbag and personal injury.*

**Warning:** *Never install a memory-saver device, used to preserve PCM memory and radio station presets, when working on or around any of the airbag system components.*

Whenever working in the vicinity of the steering wheel, instrument panel or any of the other SRS system components, the system must be disarmed. To disarm the system:

a)  *Point the wheels straight ahead and turn the ignition key to the LOCK position.*

b)  *Disconnect the cable from the negative terminal of the battery.*

c)  *Wait at least two minutes for the back-up power supply capacitor to be depleted.*

Whenever handling an airbag module, always keep the airbag opening (trim side) pointed away from your body. Never place the airbag module on a bench or other surface with the airbag opening facing the surface. Always place the airbag module in a safe location with the airbag opening (trim side) facing up.

Never measure the resistance of any SRS component. An ohmmeter has a built-in battery supply that could accidentally deploy the airbag.

21.3a  Insert a screwdriver through the hole/depression in the front of the steering wheel . . .

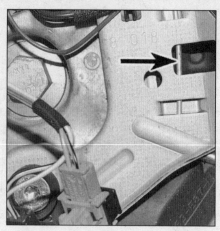

21.3b  . . . and push the clip to release the airbag

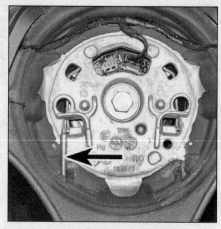

21.4a  Insert a Torx screwdriver through the hole in the base of the steering wheel . . .

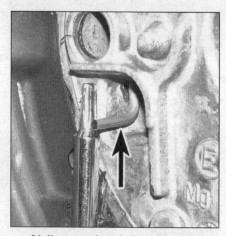

21.4b  . . . and push the spring clip towards the center of the wheel

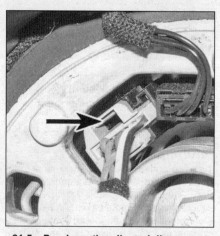

21.5a  Pry down the clip and disconnect the airbag electrical connector (standard) steering wheel

21.5b  Pry up the locking clip . . .

Never use electrical welding equipment on a vehicle equipped with an airbag without first disconnecting the negative battery cable.

Never dispose of a live airbag module. Return it to your dealer for safe deployment, using special equipment, and disposal.

**21  Airbag system components - removal and installation**

**Warning:** *Refer to the precautions in Section 20 before carrying out the following operations.*
1    Disconnect the negative battery cable (see Chapter 5) and wait two minutes before proceeding. **Warning:** *Isolate the negative battery cable to prevent accidental contact between the cable and the battery.*

### Driver's side airbag

2    Two different types of driver's airbags may be installed: a Sports steering wheel airbag, or normal steering wheel airbag.

### Sports steering wheel
*Refer to illustrations 21.3a and 21.3b*
3    To release the spring clip, with the steering wheel in the straight-ahead position, insert a T25 Torx screwdriver 0.6 inch (1.5 cm) through the hole in the front-side of the steering wheel, at 90 degrees to the steering column. Pull that side of the airbag away from the wheel **(see illustrations)**. Repeat this process on the other side of the wheel.

### Standard steering wheel
*Refer to illustrations 21.4a and 21.4b*
4    To release the spring clip, with the steering wheel in the straight-ahead position, insert a T20 Torx screwdriver straight up, approximately 2 inches (5.5 cm) through the hole in the base of the steering wheel, at 90 degrees to the steering column. Pull that side of the airbag away from the wheel **(see illustrations)**. Repeat this process on the other side of the wheel.

### Both steering wheels
*Refer to illustrations 21.5a, 21.5b and 21.5c*
5    Disconnect the airbag electrical

connector(s) **(see illustrations)**. Whenever handling an airbag module, always keep the airbag opening (trim side) pointed away from

21.5c  . . . and disconnect the airbag electrical connector (sports steering wheel)

**21.8  Pry up the locking catch and disconnect the passenger's airbag electrical connector(s)**

**21.9  Passenger's airbag retaining nut locations**

your body. Never place the airbag module on a bench or other surface with the airbag opening facing the surface. Always place the airbag module in a safe location with the airbag opening (trim side) facing up.

6    On installation, reconnect the electrical connectors, making sure they are locked in place. Note that the connectors are color-coded to ensure correct installation. The connector plugs into the socket of the same color. Position the airbag on the wheel and push the unit until it locks in place. Reconnect the battery negative cable.

### Passenger's side airbag

*Refer to illustrations 21.8 and 21.9*

7    Remove the glove box (see Chapter 11).
8    Pry up the locking catch and disconnect the airbag electrical connector(s) **(see illustration)**. **Note:** *On models manufactured from 03/2006, there is an electrical connector at each end of the airbag.*
9    Remove the retaining nuts and remove the airbag **(see illustration)**.

10    Installation is the reverse of removal. Tighten the airbag retaining nuts to the specified torque, and reconnect the negative battery cable (see Chapter 5).

### Side impact airbags

11    The side impact airbags are incorporated into the side of the front and rear seats. Removal of the units requires the seat upholstery to be removed. This is a specialized procedure, which we recommend should be handled by a dealer or other qualified shop.

### Side curtain airbags

12    Replacement of the side curtain airbags requires removal of the headliner. This is a specialized procedure, and should be handled by a dealer or other qualified shop.

### Airbag control unit

*Refer to illustrations 21.14a and 21.14b*

13    Remove the center console (see Chapter 11).
14    Remove the insulation cover, remove the

retaining nuts and bolts, then lift the module. Note the ground strap retained by one of the mounting nuts. Disconnect the electrical connector as the unit is withdrawn **(see illustrations)**.

15    Installation is the reverse of removal. **Note:** *The control unit must be installed with the arrow pointing towards the front of the vehicle, and the ground strap must be placed under one of the module mounting nuts. If a new control unit is installed, it must be programmed using BMW diagnostic equipment. This procedure should be handled by a dealer or other qualified shop.*

### Impact sensors

16    There may be two impact sensors on each side of the vehicle (one in each front door, one at the base of the B-pillars), and a sensor built into the control unit.

### Door sensors

**Note:** *Not installed on all models.*

17    Remove the door inner trim panel and

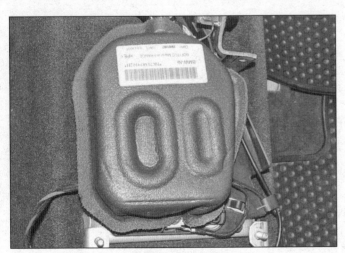

**21.14a  Remove the insulation cover**

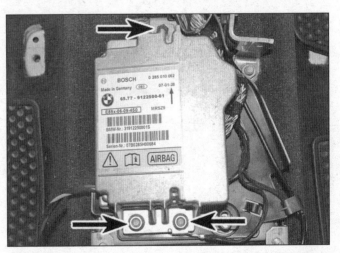

**21.14b  Remove the nuts/bolts and remove the airbag control unit**

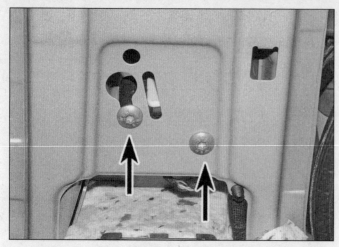

**21.20a  Loosen the upper bolt, and remove the lower bolt**

**21.20b  Depress the clip and disconnect the sensor electrical connector**

sound insulation material (see Chapter 11).
18   Remove the two retaining bolts, and remove the sensor. Disconnect the electrical connector as the sensor is withdrawn.

## B-pillar sensors

*Refer to illustrations 21.20a and 21.20b*
19   Remove the B-pillar trim panel (see Chapter 11).
20   Loosen the upper bolt and remove the lower bolt, then maneuver the sensor from position. Disconnect the electrical connector as the sensor is withdrawn **(see illustrations)**.

## All sensors

21   Installation is the reverse of removal. Tighten the fasteners to their specified torque.

## 22   Wiring diagrams - general information

Since it isn't possible to include all wiring diagrams for every year covered by this manual, the following diagrams are those that are typical and most commonly needed.

Prior to troubleshooting any circuits, check the fuse and circuit breakers (if equipped) to make sure they're in good condition. Make sure the battery is properly charged and check the cable connections (see Chapter 1).

When checking a circuit, make sure that all connectors are clean, with no broken or loose terminals. When unplugging a connector, do not pull on the wires. Pull only on the connector housings themselves.

## BMW 3 Series wiring diagrams

Diagram 1

 **WARNING:** This vehicle is equipped with a supplemental restraint system (SRS) consisting of a combination of driver (and passenger) airbag(s), side impact protection airbags and seatbelt pre-tensioners. The use of electrical test equipment on any SRS wiring systems may cause the seatbelt pre-tensioners to abruptly retract and airbags to explosively deploy, resulting in potentially severe personal injury. Extreme care should be taken to correctly identify any circuits to be tested to avoid choosing any of the SRS wiring in error.

**For further information see airbag system precautions in body electrical systems chapter.**

**Note:** The SRS wiring harness can normally be identified by yellow and/or orange harness or harness connectors.

## Key to symbols

| | | |
|---|---|---|
| Solenoid actuator | Bulb | Wire splice, soldered joint, or unspecified connector |
| Ground point and location | Switch | Connecting wires |
| Wire color (blue with red tracer) | Fuse/Fusible link | Diode |
| | BL/RT | |
| | Resistor | Light-emitting diode |
| Dashed outline denotes part of a larger item, containing in this case an electronic or solid state device (pins 31 and 32 of a connector X14270). | Variable resistor | Item number |
| | | Motor/pump |
| | Variable resistor | Heating element |

## Typical luggage comp. fusebox 7

(models to 03/2007)

| Fuse | Rating | Circuit protected |
|---|---|---|
| F104 | – | Battery sensor |
| F105 | 100A | Electric power steering |
| F106 | 100A | Auxiliary heater |
| F106 | 100A | Electric auxiliary heater |
| F108 | 250A | Junction box |
| F203 | 100A | B+ terminal, starter, battery |

(models from 03/2007)

| Fuse | Rating | Circuit protected |
|---|---|---|
| F101 | 250A | Junction box |
| F102 | 100A | B+ terminal, starter, battery |
| F103 | 100A | Electric power steering |
| F104 | 100A | Auxiliary heater |
| F105 | | Intelligent battery sensor |
| F106 | 100A | Electric auxiliary heater |

## Typical engine comp. fusebox 29

| Fuse | Rating | Circuit protected |
|---|---|---|
| F01 | 30A | Ignition coils |
| F02 | 30A | Coolant thermostat, coolant pump, camshaft sensors, VANOS solenoids |
| F03 | 20A | Crankshaft sensor, engine control unit, mass air flow sensor, fuel tank vent valve, oil condition sensor, variable intake manifold controllers |
| F04 | 30A | Oxygen sensor heater, crankcase breather heater |
| F05 | 30A | Fuel injector relay |
| F06 | 10A | EAC sensor, engine compartment fusebox fan, exhaust fan, passenger compartment fusebox, secondary air injection mass airflow sensor, exhaust flap |
| F07 | 40A | Valvetronic relay |
| F09 | 30A | Electric cooling pump |
| F010 | 5A | Crankcase breather heating relay |

## Ground locations

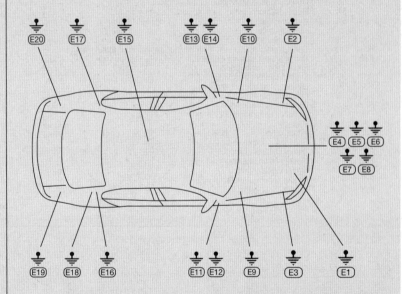

| | |
|---|---|
| E1 | Engine bay, RH lower engine block |
| E2 | Engine bay, LH front inner fender |
| E3 | Engine bay, RH front inner fender |
| E4 | Engine bay, top of cylinder head |
| E5 | Engine bay, top of cylinder head |
| E6 | Engine bay, top of cylinder head |
| E7 | Engine bay, top of cylinder head |
| E8 | Engine bay, top of cylinder head |
| E9 | Engine bay, RH strut tower |
| E10 | Engine bay, LH rear of engine compartment |
| E11 | Passenger compartment, RH footwell |
| E12 | Passenger compartment, RH footwell |
| E13 | Passenger compartment, LH footwell |
| E14 | Passenger compartment, LH footwell |
| E15 | Passenger compartment, under center console |
| E16 | Passenger compartment, below RH rear seat bolster |
| E17 | Passenger compartment, below LH rear seat bolster at C-pillar |
| E18 | Passenger compartment, below rear seat backrest, lower RH |
| E19 | Luggage compartment, RH side |
| E20 | Luggage compartment, LH side |

## BMW 3 Series wiring diagrams

Diagram 2

### Typical passenger comp. fusebox 18

(models to 03/2007)

| Fuse | Rating | Circuit protected |
|---|---|---|
| F1 | - | Not used |
| F2 | 5A | Antenna |
| F3 | 20A | Heated passenger seat |
| F4 | 5A | Car access system |
| F5 | 7.5A | Roof function control |
| F6 | 15A | Transmission control unit |
| F7 | 20A | Auxiliary heater control unit |
| F8 | 5A | CD changer, antenna |
| F9 | 10A | Cruise control |
| F10 | - | Not used |
| F11 | 10A | Audio system |
| F12 | 20A | Convertible roof/sunroof, roof function control unit |
| F13 | 5A | iDrive controller |
| F14 | - | Not used |
| F15 | 5A | Automatic air conditioner sensor |
| F16 | 15A | Horn |
| F17 | 5A | Telephone |
| F18 | 5A | CD changer |
| F19 | 7.5A | Comfort access control unit, front door outer handle control units, alarm |
| F20 | 5A | Dynamic stability control, transfer case control unit |
| F21 | 7.5A | Driver's door switch cluster |
| F22 | 10A | Longitudinal dynamics management, tow hitch release speaker |
| F23 | 10A | Digital tuner, satellite radio |
| F24 | 5A | Tire pressure control |
| F25 | 10A | Front seat belt positioner control units |
| F26 | 10A | Shift selector lighting, telephone |
| F27 | 5A | Driver's door switch cluster, telephone |
| F28 | 5A | Roof function control centre, park distance control |
| F29 | 5A | Automatic air conditioning sensor, front seat heating control units |
| F30 | 20A | 12v sockets, front cigar lighter |
| F31 | 20A | Car communication control unit/audio system control unit |
| F32 | 30A | Driver's seat heating control unit, driver's seat control unit |
| F33 | 30A | Front seat control unit |
| F34 | 30A | Sound system amplifier |
| F35 | 30A | Dynamic stability control |
| F36 | 30A | Footwell control unit |
| F37 | 30A | Driver's seat control unit |
| F38 | 30A | Transfer case control unit |
| F39 | 30A | Wipers |
| F40 | 20A | Fuel pump |
| F41 | 30A | Footwell control unit |
| F42 | 30A | Trailer control unit |
| F43 | 30A | Headlight washer pump |
| F44 | 30A | Trailer control unit |
| F45 | 40A | Active steering system |
| F46 | 30A | Heated rear window |

| Fuse | Rating | Circuit protected |
|---|---|---|
| F47 | 20A | Trailer socket |
| F48 | 20A | Rear wash/wipe control unit |
| F49 | 30A | Passenger seat heater |
| F50 | 40A | Active steering system |
| F51 | 50A | Car access system |
| F52 | 50A | Footwell control unit |
| F53 | 50A | Footwell control unit |
| F54 | 60A | B+ potential distributor |
| F55 | - | Not used |
| F56 | 15A | Central locking |
| F57 | 15A | Central locking |
| F58 | 5A | Instrument cluster, diagnostic socket (OBDII) |
| F59 | 5A | Steering column switch cluster |
| F60 | 7.5A | Air conditioning and heating system |
| F61 | 10A | Luggage compartment lights, central info. display, glove box light |
| F62 | 30A | Electric windows |
| F63 | 30A | Electric windows |
| F64 | 30A | Electric windows |
| F65 | 40A | Dynamic stability control |
| F66 | 50A | Diesel fuel heater |
| F67 | 50A | Blower control |
| F68 | 50A | Vacuum pump relay |
| F69 | 50A | Engine cooling fan |
| F70 | 50A | Secondary air injection pump |
| F71 | 20A | Trailer socket |
| F72 | - | Not used |
| F73 | - | Not used |
| F74 | - | Not used |
| F75 | - | Not used |
| F76 | - | Not used |
| F77 | 30A | Fuel injectors, ignition coils |
| F78 | - | Not used |
| F79 | - | Not used |
| F80 | - | Not used |
| F81 | - | Not used |
| F82 | - | Not used |
| F83 | - | Not used |
| F84 | - | Not used |
| F85 | - | Not used |
| F86 | - | Not used |
| F87 | - | Not used |
| F88 | - | Not used |

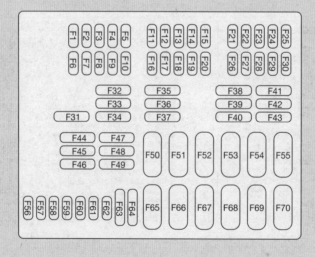

H47037

## BMW 3 Series wiring diagrams

**Diagram 3**

### Typical passenger comp. fusebox 18

(models 03/2007 to 09/2007)

| Fuse | Rating | Circuit protected |
|------|--------|-------------------|
| F1 | 10A | Roll over protection control unit |
| F2 | 5A | Instrument cluster, on board diagnostics (OBDII) |
| F3 | 20A | Heated passenger seat |
| F4 | 5A | Car access system |
| F5 | - | Not used |
| F6 | 15A | Transmission control unit |
| F7 | 20A | Auxiliary heater control unit |
| F8 | 20A | Audio amplifier |
| F9 | 10A | Cruise control |
| F10 | 15A | Trailer control unit |
| F11 | 10A | Audio system |
| F12 | 20A | Convertible roof/sunroof, roof function control unit |
| F13 | 5A | iDrive controller, tire pressure control |
| F14 | - | Not used |
| F15 | 5A | Automatic air conditioner sensor |
| F16 | 15A | Horn |
| F17 | 5A | Telephone |
| F18 | 5A | Antenna (convertible), interior rear view mirror (not convertible), shift selector lighting |
| F19 | 7.5A | Alarm |
| F20 | 5A | Dynamic stability control, transfer case control unit |
| F21 | 7.5A | Driver's door switch cluster, electric mirrors |
| F22 | 10A | Longitudinal dynamics management |
| F23 | 10A | Digital tuner, satellite radio |
| F24 | 5A | DC converter, fan cut-out relay |
| F25 | 10A | Front seat belt positioner control units |
| F26 | 10A | Telephone |
| F27 | 5A | Driver's door switch cluster, telephone |
| F28 | 5A | Roof function control centre, park distance control |
| F29 | 5A | Front seat heating control units |
| F30 | 20A | 12v sockets, front cigar lighter |
| F31 | 20A | Car communication control unit/audio system control unit |
| F32 | 30A | Driver's seat control unit |
| F33 | 5A | Comfort access control unit, front door outer handles control unit |
| F34 | 5A | CD changer, antenna |
| F35 | 30A | Dynamic stability control |
| F36 | 30A | Footwell control unit |
| F37 | 10A | Driver's seat control unit |
| F38 | 30A | Transfer case control unit |
| F39 | 30A | Wipers |
| F40 | 7.5A | Roof function control unit |
| F41 | 30A | Footwell control unit |
| F42 | 40A | Footwell control unit |
| F43 | - | Not used |
| F44 | 30A | Trailer control unit |
| F45 | 40A | Active steering system |
| F46 | 30A | Heated rear window |
| F47 | 20A | Trailer socket |

| Fuse | Rating | Circuit protected |
|------|--------|-------------------|
| F48 | 20A | Rear wash/wipe control unit |
| F49 | 30A | Passenger seat heater |
| F50 | 10A | Engine control unit |
| F51 | 40A | Car access system |
| F52 | 20A | Driver's heated seat |
| F53 | 20A | Passenger's heated seat |
| F54 | 30A | Trailer control unit |
| F55 | - | Not used |
| F56 | 15A | Central locking |
| F57 | 15A | Central locking |
| F58 | 5A | Instrument cluster |
| F59 | 5A | Steering column switch cluster |
| F60 | 5A | Central information display |
| F61 | 10A | Luggage compartment lights, central info. display, glove box light |
| F62 | 30A | Electric windows |
| F63 | 30A | Electric windows |
| F64 | 30A | Electric windows, diagnostic socket (OBDII) |
| F65 | 10A | Selector lever illumination, longitudinal dynamics management |
| F66 | 50A | Diesel fuel heater |
| F67 | 40A | Blower control |
| F68 | 40A | Footwell control unit |
| F69 | 50/60A | Engine cooling fan |
| F70 | 40A | Secondary air injection pump |
| F71 | 20A | Trailer socket |
| F72 | - | Not used |
| F73 | - | Not used |
| F74 | 10A | Engine control unit, exhaust flap, fuel tank leakage diagnostic unit, nitrogen oxide sensor |
| F75 | 10A | EAC sensor, engine fusebox fan, engine control unit, secondary air pump relay |
| F76 | 30A | Crankshaft sensor, fuel tank vent valve, mass air flow sensor, oil condition sensor, variable intake manifold sensor, volume control valve |
| F77 | 30A | Fuel injectors, ignition coils |
| F78 | 30A | Camshaft sensors, thermostat, coolant pump, engine control unit, VANOS valves, waste gate valves |
| F79 | 30A | Crankcase breather heater, oxygen sensor heater |
| F80 | 40A | Electric coolant pump (non turbo) |
| F81 | 30A | Trailer control unit |
| F82 | - | Not used |
| F83 | 40A | Footwell control unit |
| F84 | - | Not used |
| F85 | - | Not used |
| F86 | - | Not used |
| F87 | - | Not used |
| F88 | 20A | Fuel pump |

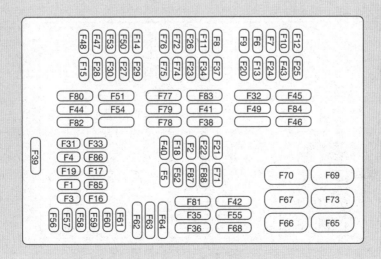

## BMW 3 Series wiring diagrams

Diagram 4

### Typical passenger comp. fusebox ⓲

(models from 09/2007)

| Fuse | Rating | Circuit protected |
|---|---|---|
| F1 | 10A | Rear wash/wipe |
| F2 | 5A | Instrument cluster, on board diagnostics (OBDII) |
| F3 | 20A | Heated passenger seat |
| F4 | 10A | Engine control unit |
| F5 | - | Not used |
| F6 | 5A | Automatic air conditioner sensor, DC converter |
| F7 | 20A | Roof function control, park distance control |
| F8 | 20A | Cigar lighters, 12 volt sockets |
| F9 | 5A | Driver's door switch cluster, telephone |
| F10 | 5A | Front seat heating |
| F11 | 20A | Crankshaft sensor, engine control unit, fuel tank vent valve, mass air flow sensor, oil condition sensor, variable intake manifold sensor, fuel volume control valve |
| F12 | 15A | Vacuum pump relay |
| F13 | 5A | Telephone, USB hub |
| F14 | 10A | Audio |
| F15 | 20A | Audio amplifier |
| F16 | 10A | EAC sensor, engine fusebox fan, engine control unit, radiator shutter control, secondary air pump relay |
| F17 | 10A | Engine control unit, exhaust flap, fuel tank leakage diagnostic control unit |
| F18 | 10A | Digital tuner, satellite radio |
| F19 | 5A | CD changer, antenna (convertible) |
| F20 | 10A | Seat control |
| F21 | 10A | Cruise control |
| F22 | 15A | Automatic transmission control unit |
| F23 | 20A | Auxiliary heater control |
| F24 | 15A | Towing control unit |
| F25 | 20A | Convertible top control unit, roof control unit |
| F26 | 5A | Dynamic stability control, transfer case control unit |
| F27 | 5A | iDrive controller, tire pressure control |
| F28 | 5A | Cooling fan cut-out relay, DC converter |
| F29 | 5A | Sunroof |
| F30 | 10A | Seat belt positioner controllers |
| F31 | 30A | Trailer control unit |
| F32 | 30A | Trailer control unit |
| F33 | 40A | Electric coolant pump |
| F34 | 5A | CD changer, antenna |
| F35 | 30A | Dynamic stability control |
| F36 | 40A | Car access system |
| F37 | 10A | Camshaft sensors, thermostat, coolant pump, engine control unit, VANOS valves, waste gate valves |
| F38 | 30A | Crankcase breather heater, engine control unit, oxygen sensor heater |
| F39 | 30A | Fuel injectors, ignition coils |
| F40 | 30A | Transfer case control unit |
| F41 | 30A | Footwell control unit |
| F42 | 40A | Footwell control unit |
| F43 | 30A | Headlight washer pump |
| F44 | 30A | Trailer control unit |
| F45 | 30A | Passenger seat control unit |
| F46 | 30A | Driver's seat control unit |

| Fuse | Rating | Circuit protected |
|---|---|---|
| F47 | 30A | Heated rear window |
| F48 | 30A | Headlight washer, rear wash/wipe control |
| F49 | 40A | Passenger seat control unit |
| F50 | 30A | Wipers |
| F51 | 40A | Car access system |
| F52 | - | Not used |
| F53 | 10A | Roll-over protection |
| F54 | 7.5A | Alarm |
| F55 | 5A | Car access system |
| F56 | 20A | Car communication control unit/audio system control unit |
| F57 | 15A | Horns |
| F58 | 5A | Instrument cluster, diagnostic socket (OBDII) |
| F59 | 5A | Telephone |
| F60 | 5A | Central information display |
| F61 | 5A | Comfort access control unit, dual remote control receive, front door handle control unit |
| F62 | 7.5A | Roof function control unit |
| F63 | 5A | Antenna, electrochromic rear view mirror, selector lever illumination |
| F64 | 5A | Diagnostic socket (OBDII) |
| F65 | 10A | Selector lever illumination, longitudinal dynamics management |
| F66 | 7.5A | Driver's door switch cluster, passenger electric mirror |
| F67 | 20A | Dynamic stability control |
| F68 | 20A | Driver's seat heater control unit |
| F69 | - | Not used |
| F70 | 20A | Fuel pump |
| F71 | 20A | Trailer control unit |
| F72 | 15A | Central locking |
| F73 | 15A | Central locking |
| F74 | 5A | Instrument cluster |
| F75 | 5A | Passenger seat control unit |
| F76 | 5A | Audio |
| F77 | 10A | Glovebox light, heating and air conditioning, luggage compartment light |
| F78 | 30A | Window control |
| F79 | 30A | Wiper control |
| F80 | 30A | Window control |
| F81 | 30A | Footwell control unit |
| F82 | 30A | Dynamic stability control control unit |
| F83 | 40A | Footwell control unit |
| F84 | 40A | Footwell control unit |
| F85 | 30A | Car access system |
| F86 | 40A | Footwell control unit |
| F87 | - | Not used |
| F88 | 40A | Blower |
| F89 | 40A | Secondary air pump relay |
| F90 | 40A | Dynamic stability control control unit |
| F91 | - | Not used |
| F92 | 50/60A | Engine cooling fan |

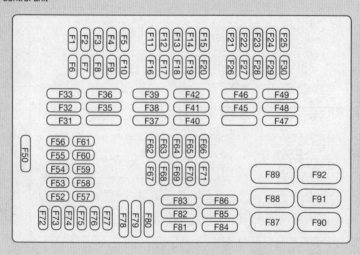

H47039

### Color codes

| | | | |
|---|---|---|---|
| WS | White | RT | Red |
| BL | Blue | GN | Green |
| GR | Grey | VI | Violet |
| GE | Yellow | SW | Black |
| BR | Brown | OR | Orange |

\* From 03/2007
\*\* From 09/2007

### Key to items

1 Battery
2 B+ terminal luggage compartment
3 Jump start terminal point
4 Starter motor
5 Alternator
6 Battery sensor
7 Luggage compartment fusebox
8 Engine management control unit
9 Car access system
10 Slide-in compartment
11 Stop-start button
12 Electric steering lock
13 Stop light switch
14 Clutch switch control unit
15 Automatic transmission control unit
16 Gear indicator lighting
17 Dynamic stability control unit
18 Passenger compartment fusebox
19 Tire pressure control unit
20 LH front wheel module
21 RH front wheel module
22 LH rear wheel module
23 RH rear wheel module
24 LH front wheel transmitter
25 RH front wheel transmitter
26 LH rear wheel transmitter
27 RH rear wheel transmitter
28 Diagnostic connector

**Diagram 5**

H47040

**Typical starting & charging**

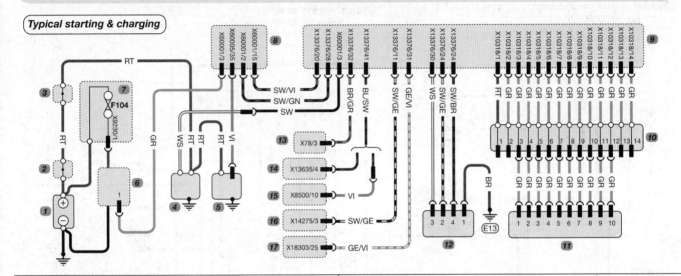

**Typical tire pressure control**

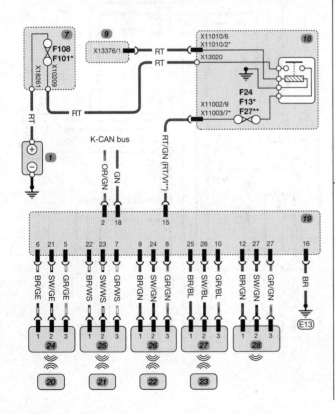

**Typical diagnostic socket (OBDII) (up to 03/2007)**

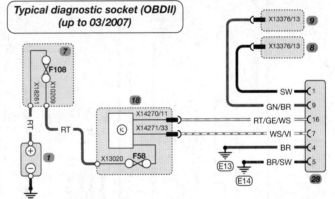

**Typical diagnostic socket (OBDII) (from 03/2007)**

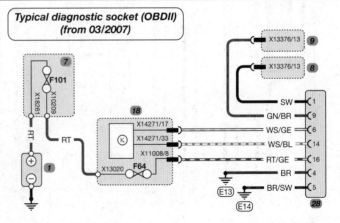

## Color codes

| | | | |
|---|---|---|---|
| **WS** | White | **RT** | Red |
| **BL** | Blue | **GN** | Green |
| **GR** | Grey | **VI** | Violet |
| **GE** | Yellow | **SW** | Black |
| **BR** | Brown | **OR** | Orange |

\* From 03/2007
\*\* From 09/2007

## Key to items

1 Battery
7 Luggage compartment fusebox
8 Engine management control unit
9 Car access system
18 Passenger compartment fusebox
29 Engine compartment fusebox
30 Engine management relay
31 Engine cooling fan

32 Engine coolant pump
33 Radiator outlet temperature sensor
34 Engine coolant temperature sensor
35 Characteristic map thermostat
36 B+ potential distributor
37 Radiator shutter motor
38 Radiator shutter solenoid
39 Engine cooling fan cut-out relay

**Diagram 6**

H47041

**Typical engine cooling fan (up to 03/2007)**

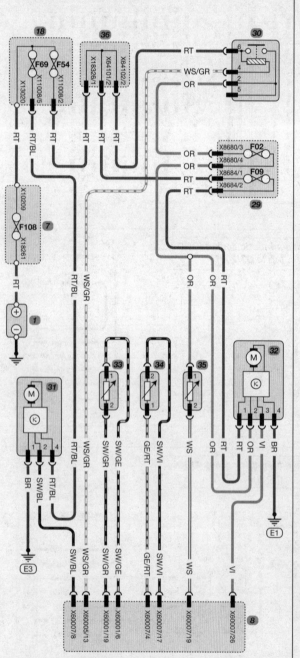

**Typical engine cooling fan (from 03/2007)**

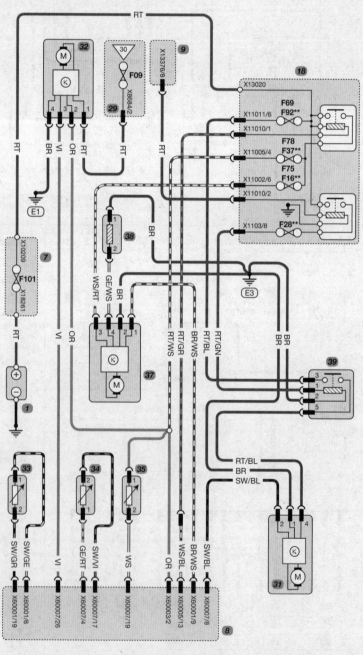

## Color codes

| | | | |
|---|---|---|---|
| **WS** | White | **RT** | Red |
| **BL** | Blue | **GN** | Green |
| **GR** | Grey | **VI** | Violet |
| **GE** | Yellow | **SW** | Black |
| **BR** | Brown | **OR** | Orange |

## Key to items

8 Engine management control unit
9 Car access system
13 Stop light switch
18 Passenger compartment fusebox
42 Footwell control unit
43 Light switch control unit
44 Steering column switch cluster
45 License plate light
46 LH headlight unit
  a = side light
  b = low beam
  c = high beam
  d = direction indicator
  e = xenon light unit
  f = xenon control unit

47 RH headlight unit
  a = side light
  b = low beam
  c = high beam
  d = direction indicator
  e = xenon light unit
  f = xenon control unit
48 LH outer rear light unit
  a = tail light
  b = stop light
  c = direction indicator
49 LH inner rear light unit
  a = tail light
  b = reversing lights
  c = fog light

50 RH outer rear light unit
  a = tail light
  b = stop light
  c = direction indicator
51 RH inner rear light unit
  a = tail light
  b = reversing lights
  c = fog light
52 Suppressor
53 High level brake light
54 LH front foglight
55 RH front foglight
56 LH indicator side repeater
57 RH indicator side repeater
58 Reversing light switch

59 Hazard warning switch/
  central locking switch

**Diagram 7**

H47042

*Typical exterior lighting*

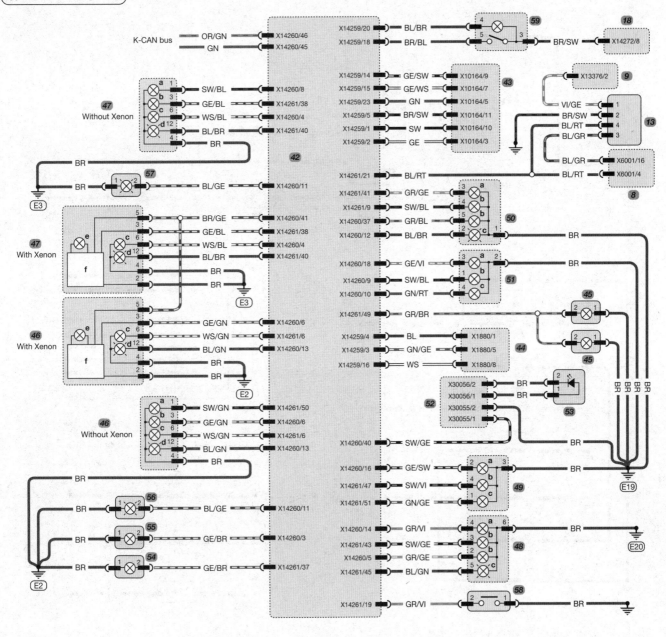

## Color codes

| | | | |
|---|---|---|---|
| **WS** | White | **RT** | Red |
| **BL** | Blue | **GN** | Green |
| **GR** | Grey | **VI** | Violet |
| **GE** | Yellow | **SW** | Black |
| **BR** | Brown | **OR** | Orange |

## Key to items

1 Battery
7 Luggage compartment fusebox
9 Car access system
18 Passenger compartment fusebox
42 Footwell control unit
65 Driver's door courtesy light
66 RH rear door courtesy light
67 Passenger's door courtesy light
68 LH rear door courtesy light
69 Driver's footwell light
70 Passenger's footwell light

71 Driver's exit light
72 Passenger's exit light
73 Roof function control unit
74 Rear interior light
75 LH vanity mirror light
76 LH vanity mirror light switch
77 RH vanity mirror light
78 RH vanity mirror light switch
79 Glove compartment light
80 Luggage compartment light
81 Tailgate lock motor

**Diagram 8**

\*   From 03/2007
\*\*   From 09/2007

H47043

**Typical interior lighting**

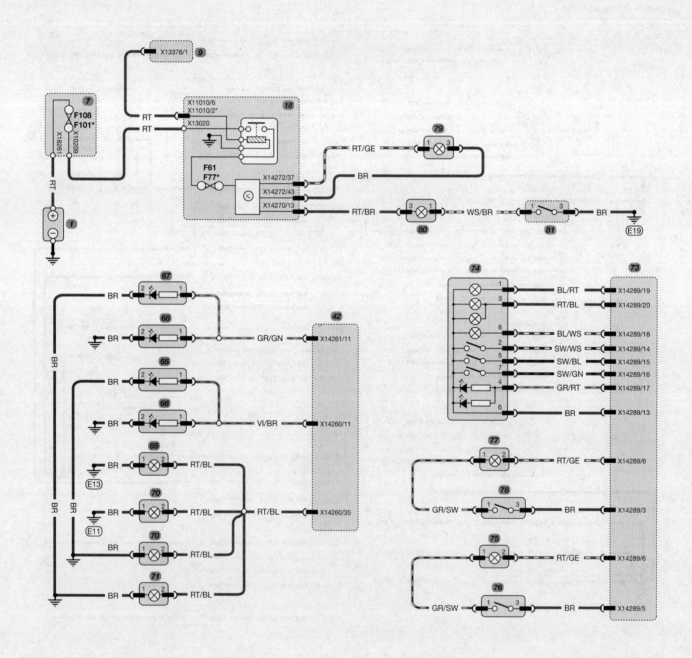

### Color codes

| | | | |
|---|---|---|---|
| **WS** | White | **RT** | Red |
| **BL** | Blue | **GN** | Green |
| **GR** | Grey | **VI** | Violet |
| **GE** | Yellow | **SW** | Black |
| **BR** | Brown | **OR** | Orange |

\*   From 03/2007
\*\* From 09/2007

### Key to items

**Diagram 9**

1   Battery
7   Luggage compartment fusebox
18  Passenger compartment fusebox
73  Roof function control unit
85  Rain/light sensor
87  Front wiper motor
88  Rear wiper motor
89  Front washer pump
90  Rear washer pump
91  Headlight washer pump
92  Outside air temperature sensor
93  LH heated washer jet
94  RH heated washer jet

H47044

**Typical wash/wipe**

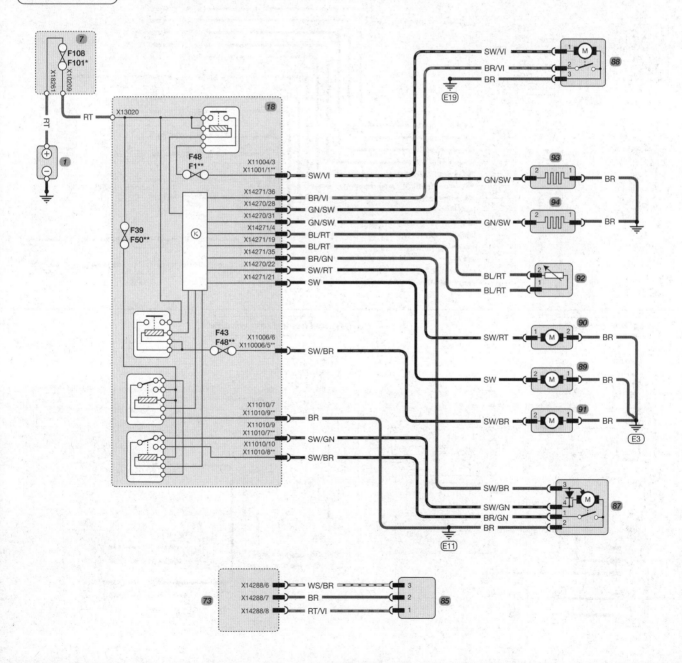

## Color codes

| | | | |
|---|---|---|---|
| **WS** | White | **RT** | Red |
| **BL** | Blue | **GN** | Green |
| **GR** | Grey | **VI** | Violet |
| **GE** | Yellow | **SW** | Black |
| **BR** | Brown | **OR** | Orange |

## Key to items

1   Battery
7   Luggage compartment fusebox
9   Car access system
18   Passenger compartment fusebox
97   Instrument cluster control unit
98   Outside air temp. sensor
99   LH fuel tank sensor
100   RH fuel tank sensor/fuel pump
101   Washer fluid level switch
102   Handbrake switch
103   Coolant level switch
104   Heating and air conditioning control unit
105   Heater blower output stage
106   Heater blower
107   Heated rear window
108   Heated rear window lockout circuit

\*   From 03/2007
\*\*   From 09/2007

**Diagram 10**

H47045

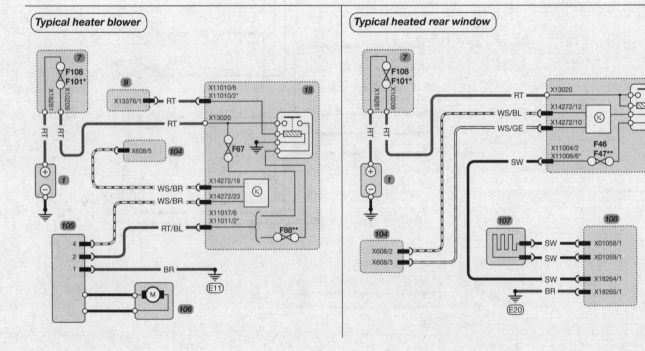

**Typical instruments & indicator lights**

**Typical heater blower**

**Typical heated rear window**

## Color codes

| | | | |
|---|---|---|---|
| **WS** | White | **RT** | Red |
| **BL** | Blue | **GN** | Green |
| **GR** | Grey | **VI** | Violet |
| **GE** | Yellow | **SW** | Black |
| **BR** | Brown | **OR** | Orange |

\*   From 03/2007
\*\*  From 09/2007

## Key to items

1   Battery
7   Luggage compartment fusebox
9   Car access system
18  Passenger compartment fusebox
42  Footwell control unit
109 Driver's door lock assembly
110 Passenger's door lock assembly
111 Driver's switch cluster
112 Driver's window motor
113 Passenger's window motor
114 LH rear window motor
115 RH rear window motor
116 Passenger window switch
117 LH rear window switch
118 RH rear window switch

**Diagram 11**

H47046

**Typical electric windows**

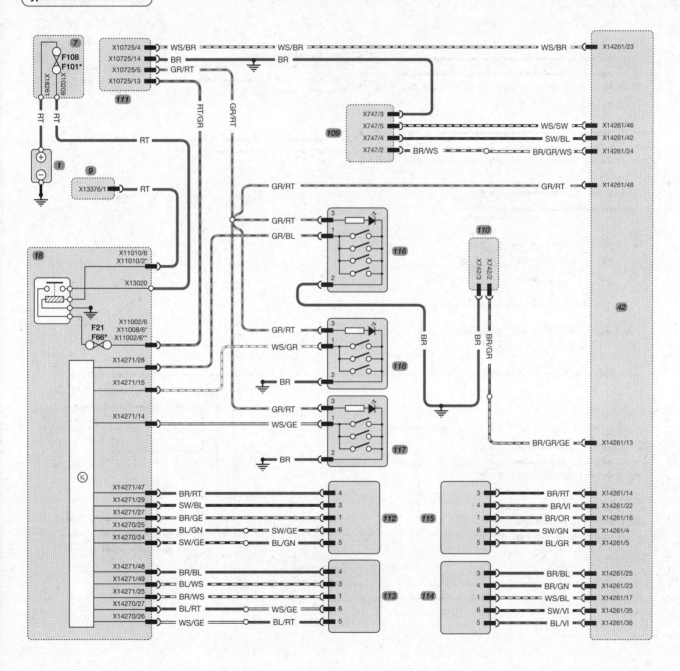

## Color codes

| | | | |
|---|---|---|---|
| **WS** | White | **RT** | Red |
| **BL** | Blue | **GN** | Green |
| **GR** | Grey | **VI** | Violet |
| **GE** | Yellow | **SW** | Black |
| **BR** | Brown | **OR** | Orange |

## Key to items

9   Car access system
18   Passenger compartment fusebox
42   Footwell control unit
59   Hazard warning switch/central locking switch
81   Tailgate lock motor
109   Driver's door lock assembly
110   Passenger's door lock assembly
120   Trunk/tailgate button
121   Fuel filler flap lock
122   Antenna module
123   Trunk/tailgate release switch

124   LH rear door lock assembly
125   RH rear door lock assembly

**Diagram 12**

H47047

**Typical central locking**

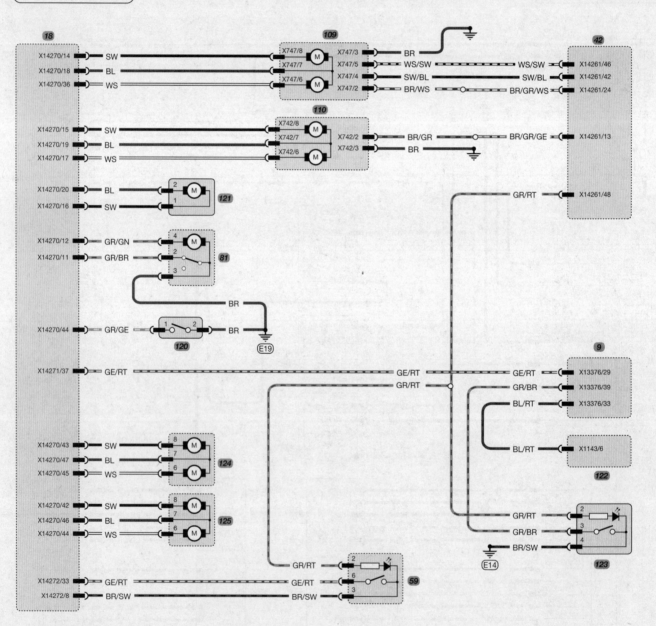

# Index

# E

# V

# W

# Notes

# Haynes Automotive Manuals

*NOTE: If you do not see a listing for your vehicle, consult your local Haynes dealer for the latest product information.*

## ACURA

12020 **Integra** '86 thru '89 **& Legend** '86 thru '90
12021 **Integra** '90 thru '93 **& Legend** '91 thru '95
**Integra** '94 thru '00 *- see HONDA Civic (42025)*
**MDX** '01 thru '07 *- see HONDA Pilot (42037)*
12050 **Acura TL** all models '99 thru '08

## AMC

**Jeep CJ** *- see JEEP (50020)*
14020 **Mid-size models** '70 thru '83
14025 **(Renault) Alliance & Encore** '83 thru '87

## AUDI

15020 **4000** all models '80 thru '87
15025 **5000** all models '77 thru '83
15026 **5000** all models '84 thru '88
**Audi A4** '96 thru '01 *- see VW Passat (96023)*
15030 **Audi A4** '02 thru '08

## AUSTIN-HEALEY

**Sprite** *- see MG Midget (66015)*

## BMW

18020 **3/5 Series** '82 thru '92
18021 **3-Series** incl. Z3 models '92 thru '98
18022 **3-Series** incl. Z4 models '99 thru '05
18023 **3-Series** '06 thru '10
18025 **320i all 4 cyl models** '75 thru '83
18050 **1500 thru 2002** except Turbo '59 thru '77

## BUICK

19010 **Buick Century** '97 thru '05
**Century (front-wheel drive)** *- see GM (38005)*
19020 **Buick, Oldsmobile & Pontiac Full-size (Front-wheel drive)** '85 thru '05 **Buick** Electra, LeSabre and Park Avenue; **Oldsmobile** Delta 88 Royale, Ninety Eight and Regency; **Pontiac** Bonneville
19025 **Buick, Oldsmobile & Pontiac Full-size (Rear wheel drive)** '70 thru '90 **Buick** Estate, Electra, LeSabre, Limited, **Oldsmobile** Custom Cruiser, Delta 88, Ninety-eight, **Pontiac** Bonneville, Catalina, Grandville, Parisienne
19030 **Mid-size Regal & Century** all rear-drive models with V6, V8 and Turbo '74 thru '87
**Regal** *- see GENERAL MOTORS (38010)*
**Riviera** *- see GENERAL MOTORS (38030)*
**Roadmaster** *- see CHEVROLET (24046)*
**Skyhawk** *- see GENERAL MOTORS (38015)*
**Skylark** *- see GM (38020, 38025)*
**Somerset** *- see GENERAL MOTORS (38025)*

## CADILLAC

21015 **CTS & CTS-V** '03 thru '12
21030 **Cadillac Rear Wheel Drive** '70 thru '93
**Cimarron** *- see GENERAL MOTORS (38015)*
**DeVille** *- see GM (38031 & 38032)*
**Eldorado** *- see GM (38030 & 38031)*
**Fleetwood** *- see GM (38031)*
**Seville** *- see GM (38030, 38031 & 38032)*

## CHEVROLET

10305 **Chevrolet Engine Overhaul Manual**
24010 **Astro & GMC Safari Mini-vans** '85 thru '05
24015 **Camaro V8** all models '70 thru '81
24016 **Camaro** all models '82 thru '92
24017 **Camaro & Firebird** '93 thru '02
**Cavalier** *- see GENERAL MOTORS (38016)*
**Celebrity** *- see GENERAL MOTORS (38005)*
24020 **Chevelle, Malibu & El Camino** '69 thru '87
24024 **Chevette & Pontiac T1000** '76 thru '87
**Citation** *- see GENERAL MOTORS (38020)*
24027 **Colorado & GMC Canyon** '04 thru '10
24032 **Corsica/Beretta** all models '87 thru '96
24040 **Corvette** all V8 models '68 thru '82
24041 **Corvette** all models '84 thru '96
24045 **Full-size Sedans** Caprice, Impala, Biscayne, Bel Air & Wagons '69 thru '90
24046 **Impala SS & Caprice and Buick Roadmaster** '91 thru '96
**Impala** '00 thru '05 *- see LUMINA (24048)*
24047 **Impala & Monte Carlo** all models '06 thru '11
**Lumina** '90 thru '94 *- see GM (38010)*
24048 **Lumina & Monte Carlo** '95 thru '05
**Lumina APV** *- see GM (38035)*
24050 **Luv Pick-up** all 2WD & 4WD '72 thru '82
**Malibu** '97 thru '00 *- see GM (38026)*
24055 **Monte Carlo** all models '70 thru '88
**Monte Carlo** '95 thru '01 *- see LUMINA (24048)*
24059 **Nova** all V8 models '69 thru '79
24060 **Nova and Geo Prizm** '85 thru '92
24064 **Pick-ups** '67 thru '87 - Chevrolet & GMC
24065 **Pick-ups** '88 thru '98 - Chevrolet & GMC
24066 **Pick-ups** '99 thru '06 - Chevrolet & GMC
24067 **Chevrolet Silverado & GMC Sierra** '07 thru '12
24070 **S-10 & S-15 Pick-ups** '82 thru '93, **Blazer & Jimmy** '83 thru '94,
24071 **S-10 & Sonoma Pick-ups** '94 thru '04, including **Blazer, Jimmy & Hombre**
24072 **Chevrolet TrailBlazer, GMC Envoy & Oldsmobile Bravada** '02 thru '09
24075 **Sprint** '85 thru '88 **& Geo Metro** '89 thru '01
24080 **Vans - Chevrolet & GMC** '68 thru '96
24081 **Chevrolet Express & GMC Savana** Full-size Vans '96 thru '10

## CHRYSLER

10310 **Chrysler Engine Overhaul Manual**
25015 **Chrysler Cirrus, Dodge Stratus, Plymouth Breeze** '95 thru '00
25020 **Full-size Front-Wheel Drive** '88 thru '93
**K-Cars** *- see DODGE Aries (30008)*
**Laser** *- see DODGE Daytona (30030)*
25025 **Chrysler LHS, Concorde, New Yorker, Dodge** Intrepid, **Eagle** Vision, '93 thru '97
25026 **Chrysler LHS, Concorde, 300M, Dodge** Intrepid, '98 thru '04
25027 **Chrysler 300, Dodge Charger & Magnum** '05 thru '09
25030 **Chrysler & Plymouth Mid-size** front wheel drive '82 thru '95
**Rear-wheel Drive** *- see Dodge (30050)*
25035 **PT Cruiser** all models '01 thru '10
25040 **Chrysler** Sebring '95 thru '06, **Dodge** Stratus '01 thru '06, **Dodge** Avenger '95 thru '00

## DATSUN

28005 **200SX** all models '80 thru '83
28007 **B-210** all models '73 thru '78
28009 **210** all models '79 thru '82
28012 **240Z, 260Z & 280Z** Coupe '70 thru '78
28014 **280ZX** Coupe & 2+2 '79 thru '83
**300ZX** *- see NISSAN (72010)*
28018 **510 & PL521 Pick-up** '68 thru '73
28020 **510** all models '78 thru '81
28022 **620 Series Pick-up** all models '73 thru '79
**720 Series Pick-up** *- see NISSAN (72030)*
28025 **810/Maxima** all gasoline models '77 thru '84

## DODGE

**400 & 600** *- see CHRYSLER (25030)*
30008 **Aries & Plymouth Reliant** '81 thru '89
30010 **Caravan & Plymouth Voyager** '84 thru '95
30011 **Caravan & Plymouth Voyager** '96 thru '02
30012 **Challenger/Plymouth Saporro** '78 thru '83
30013 **Caravan, Chrysler Voyager, Town & Country** '03 thru '07
30016 **Colt & Plymouth Champ** '78 thru '87
30020 **Dakota Pick-ups** all models '87 thru '96
30021 **Durango** '98 & '99, **Dakota** '97 thru '99
30022 **Durango** '00 thru '03 **Dakota** '00 thru '04
30023 **Durango** '04 thru '09, **Dakota** '05 thru '11
30025 **Dart, Demon, Plymouth Barracuda, Duster & Valiant** 6 cyl models '67 thru '76
30030 **Daytona & Chrysler Laser** '84 thru '89
**Intrepid** *- see CHRYSLER (25025, 25026)*
30034 **Neon** all models '95 thru '99
30035 **Omni & Plymouth Horizon** '78 thru '90
30036 **Dodge and Plymouth Neon** '00 thru '05
30040 **Pick-ups** all full-size models '74 thru '93
30041 **Pick-ups** all full-size models '94 thru '01
30042 **Pick-ups** full-size models '02 thru '08
30045 **Ram 50/D50 Pick-ups & Raider and Plymouth Arrow Pick-ups** '79 thru '93
30050 **Dodge/Plymouth/Chrysler** RWD '71 thru '89
30055 **Shadow & Plymouth Sundance** '87 thru '94
30060 **Spirit & Plymouth Acclaim** '89 thru '95
30065 **Vans - Dodge & Plymouth** '71 thru '03

## EAGLE

**Talon** *- see MITSUBISHI (68030, 68031)*
**Vision** *- see CHRYSLER (25025)*

## FIAT

34010 **124 Sport Coupe & Spider** '68 thru '78
34025 **X1/9** all models '74 thru '80

## FORD

10320 **Ford Engine Overhaul Manual**
10355 **Ford Automatic Transmission Overhaul**
11500 **Mustang '64-1/2 thru '70 Restoration Guide**
36004 **Aerostar Mini-vans** all models '86 thru '97
36006 **Contour & Mercury Mystique** '95 thru '00
36008 **Courier Pick-up** all models '72 thru '82
36012 **Crown Victoria & Mercury Grand Marquis** '88 thru '10
36016 **Escort/Mercury Lynx** all models '81 thru '90
36020 **Escort/Mercury Tracer** '91 thru '02
36022 **Escape & Mazda Tribute** '01 thru '11
36024 **Explorer & Mazda Navajo** '91 thru '01
36025 **Explorer/Mercury Mountaineer** '02 thru '10
36028 **Fairmont & Mercury Zephyr** '78 thru '83
36030 **Festiva & Aspire** '88 thru '97
36032 **Fiesta** all models '77 thru '80
36034 **Focus** all models '00 thru '11
36036 **Ford & Mercury Full-size** '75 thru '87
36044 **Ford & Mercury Mid-size** '75 thru '86
36045 **Fusion & Mercury Milan** '06 thru '10
36048 **Mustang V8** all models '64-1/2 thru '73
36049 **Mustang II** 4 cyl, V6 & V8 models '74 thru '78
36050 **Mustang & Mercury Capri** '79 thru '93
36051 **Mustang** all models '94 thru '04
36052 **Mustang** '05 thru '10
36054 **Pick-ups & Bronco** '73 thru '79
36058 **Pick-ups & Bronco** '80 thru '96
36059 **F-150 & Expedition** '97 thru '09, **F-250** '97 thru '99 **& Lincoln Navigator** '98 thru '09
36060 **Super Duty Pick-ups, Excursion** '99 thru '10
36061 **F-150** full-size '04 thru '10
36062 **Pinto & Mercury Bobcat** '75 thru '80
36066 **Probe** all models '89 thru '92
**Probe** '93 thru '97 *- see MAZDA 626 (61042)*
36070 **Ranger/Bronco II** gasoline models '83 thru '92
36071 **Ranger** '93 thru '10 **& Mazda Pick-ups** '94 thru '09
36074 **Taurus & Mercury Sable** '86 thru '95
36075 **Taurus & Mercury Sable** '96 thru '05
36078 **Tempo & Mercury Topaz** '84 thru '94
36082 **Thunderbird/Mercury Cougar** '83 thru '88
36086 **Thunderbird/Mercury Cougar** '89 thru '97
36090 **Vans** all V8 Econoline models '69 thru '91
36094 **Vans** full size '92 thru '10
36097 **Windstar Mini-van** '95 thru '07

## GENERAL MOTORS

10360 **GM Automatic Transmission Overhaul**
38005 **Buick Century, Chevrolet Celebrity, Oldsmobile Cutlass Ciera & Pontiac 6000** all models '82 thru '96
38010 **Buick Regal, Chevrolet Lumina, Oldsmobile Cutlass Supreme & Pontiac Grand Prix** (FWD) '88 thru '07
38015 **Buick Skyhawk, Cadillac Cimarron, Chevrolet Cavalier, Oldsmobile Firenza & Pontiac J-2000 & Sunbird** '82 thru '94
38016 **Chevrolet Cavalier & Pontiac Sunfire** '95 thru '05
38017 **Chevrolet Cobalt & Pontiac G5** '05 thru '11
38020 **Buick Skylark, Chevrolet Citation, Olds Omega, Pontiac Phoenix** '80 thru '85
38025 **Buick Skylark & Somerset, Oldsmobile Achieva & Calais and Pontiac Grand Am** all models '85 thru '98
38026 **Chevrolet Malibu, Olds Alero & Cutlass, Pontiac Grand Am** '97 thru '03
38027 **Chevrolet Malibu** '04 thru '10
38030 **Cadillac Eldorado, Seville, Oldsmobile Toronado, Buick Riviera** '71 thru '85
38031 **Cadillac Eldorado & Seville, DeVille, Fleetwood & Olds Toronado, Buick Riviera** '86 thru '93
38032 **Cadillac DeVille** '94 thru '05 & **Seville** '92 thru '04 **Cadillac DTS** '06 thru '10
38035 **Chevrolet Lumina APV, Olds Silhouette & Pontiac Trans Sport** all models '90 thru '96
38036 **Chevrolet Venture, Olds Silhouette, Pontiac Trans Sport & Montana** '97 thru '05
**General Motors Full-size Rear-wheel Drive** *- see BUICK (19025)*
38040 **Chevrolet Equinox** '05 thru '09 **Pontiac Torrent** '06 thru '09
38070 **Chevrolet HHR** '06 thru '11

## GEO

**Metro** *- see CHEVROLET Sprint (24075)*
**Prizm** *- '85 thru '92 see CHEVY (24060), '93 thru '02 see TOYOTA Corolla (92036)*
40030 **Storm** all models '90 thru '93
**Tracker** *- see SUZUKI Samurai (90010)*

## GMC

**Vans & Pick-ups** *- see CHEVROLET*

## HONDA

42010 **Accord CVCC** all models '76 thru '83
42011 **Accord** all models '84 thru '89
42012 **Accord** all models '90 thru '93
42013 **Accord** all models '94 thru '97
42014 **Accord** all models '98 thru '02
42015 **Accord** '03 thru '07
42020 **Civic 1200** all models '73 thru '79
42021 **Civic 1300 & 1500 CVCC** '80 thru '83
42022 **Civic 1500 CVCC** all models '75 thru '79

***(Continued on other side)***

**Haynes North America, Inc., 859 Lawrence Drive, Newbury Park, CA 91320-1514 • (805) 498-6703 • http://www.haynes.com**

# Haynes Automotive Manuals (continued)

NOTE: If you do not see a listing for your vehicle, consult your local Haynes dealer for the latest product information.

42023 Civic all models '84 thru '91
42024 Civic & del Sol '92 thru '95
42025 Civic '96 thru '00, CR-V '97 thru '01, Acura Integra '94 thru '00
42026 Civic '01 thru '10, CR-V '02 thru '09
42035 Odyssey all models '99 thru '10
Passport - see ISUZU Rodeo (47017)
42037 Honda Pilot '03 thru '07, Acura MDX '01 thru '07
42040 Prelude CVCC all models '79 thru '89

## HYUNDAI
43010 Elantra all models '96 thru '10
43015 Excel & Accent all models '86 thru '09
43050 Santa Fe all models '01 thru '06
43055 Sonata all models '99 thru '08

## INFINITI
G35 '03 thru '08 - see NISSAN 350Z (72011)

## ISUZU
Hombre - see CHEVROLET S-10 (24071)
47017 Rodeo, Amigo & Honda Passport '89 thru '02
47020 Trooper & Pick-up '81 thru '93

## JAGUAR
49010 XJ6 all 6 cyl models '68 thru '86
49011 XJ6 all models '88 thru '94
49015 XJ12 & XJS all 12 cyl models '72 thru '85

## JEEP
50010 Cherokee, Comanche & Wagoneer Limited all models '84 thru '01
50020 CJ all models '49 thru '86
50025 Grand Cherokee all models '93 thru '04
50026 Grand Cherokee '05 thru '09
50029 Grand Wagoneer & Pick-up '72 thru '91 Grand Wagoneer '84 thru '91, Cherokee & Wagoneer '72 thru '83, Pick-up '72 thru '88
50030 Wrangler all models '87 thru '11
50035 Liberty '02 thru '07

## KIA
54050 Optima '01 thru '10
54070 Sephia '94 thru '01, Spectra '00 thru '09, Sportage '05 thru '10

## LEXUS
ES 300/330 - see TOYOTA Camry (92007) (92008)
RX 330 - see TOYOTA Highlander (92095)

## LINCOLN
Navigator - see FORD Pick-up (36059)
59010 Rear-Wheel Drive all models '70 thru '10

## MAZDA
61010 GLC Hatchback (rear-wheel drive) '77 thru '83
61011 GLC (front-wheel drive) '81 thru '85
61012 Mazda3 '04 thru '11
61015 323 & Protogé '90 thru '03
61016 MX-5 Miata '90 thru '09
61020 MPV all models '89 thru '98
Navajo - see Ford Explorer (36024)
61030 Pick-ups '72 thru '93
Pick-ups '94 thru '00 - see Ford Ranger (36071)
61035 RX-7 all models '79 thru '85
61036 RX-7 all models '86 thru '91
61040 626 (rear-wheel drive) all models '79 thru '82
61041 626/MX-6 (front-wheel drive) '83 thru '92
61042 626, MX-6/Ford Probe '93 thru '02
61043 Mazda6 '03 thru '11

## MERCEDES-BENZ
63012 123 Series Diesel '76 thru '85
63015 190 Series four-cyl gas models, '84 thru '88
63020 230/250/280 6 cyl sohc models '68 thru '72
63025 280 123 Series gasoline models '77 thru '81
63030 350 & 450 all models '71 thru '80
63040 C-Class: C230/C240/C280/C320/C350 '01 thru '07

## MERCURY
64200 Villager & Nissan Quest '93 thru '01
All other titles, see FORD Listing.

## MG
66010 MGB Roadster & GT Coupe '62 thru '80
66015 MG Midget, Austin Healey Sprite '58 thru '80

## MINI
67020 Mini '02 thru '11

## MITSUBISHI
68020 Cordia, Tredia, Galant, Precis & Mirage '83 thru '93
68030 Eclipse, Eagle Talon & Ply. Laser '90 thru '94
68031 Eclipse '95 thru '05, Eagle Talon '95 thru '98
68035 Galant '94 thru '10
68040 Pick-up '83 thru '96 & Montero '83 thru '93

## NISSAN
72010 300ZX all models including Turbo '84 thru '89
72011 350Z & Infiniti G35 all models '03 thru '08
72015 Altima all models '93 thru '06
72016 Altima '07 thru '10
72020 Maxima all models '85 thru '92
72021 Maxima all models '93 thru '04
72025 Murano '03 thru '10
72030 Pick-ups '80 thru '97 Pathfinder '87 thru '95
72031 Frontier Pick-up, Xterra, Pathfinder '96 thru '04
72032 Frontier & Xterra '05 thru '11
72040 Pulsar all models '83 thru '86
Quest - see MERCURY Villager (64200)
72050 Sentra all models '82 thru '94
72051 Sentra & 200SX all models '95 thru '06
72060 Stanza all models '82 thru '90
72070 Titan pick-ups '04 thru '10 Armada '05 thru '10

## OLDSMOBILE
73015 Cutlass V6 & V8 gas models '74 thru '88
For other OLDSMOBILE titles, see BUICK, CHEVROLET or GENERAL MOTORS listing.

## PLYMOUTH
For PLYMOUTH titles, see DODGE listing.

## PONTIAC
79008 Fiero all models '84 thru '88
79018 Firebird V8 models except Turbo '70 thru '81
79019 Firebird all models '82 thru '92
79025 G6 all models '05 thru '09
79040 Mid-size Rear-wheel Drive '70 thru '87
Vibe '03 thru '11 - see TOYOTA Matrix (92060)
For other PONTIAC titles, see BUICK, CHEVROLET or GENERAL MOTORS listing.

## PORSCHE
80020 911 except Turbo & Carrera 4 '65 thru '89
80025 914 all 4 cyl models '69 thru '76
80030 924 all models including Turbo '76 thru '82
80035 944 all models including Turbo '83 thru '89

## RENAULT
Alliance & Encore - see AMC (14020)

## SAAB
84010 900 all models including Turbo '79 thru '88

## SATURN
87010 Saturn all S-series models '91 thru '02
87011 Saturn Ion '03 thru '07
87020 Saturn L-series models '00 thru '04
87040 Saturn VUE '02 thru '07

## SUBARU
89002 1100, 1300, 1400 & 1600 '71 thru '79
89003 1600 & 1800 2WD & 4WD '80 thru '94
89100 Legacy all models '90 thru '99
89101 Legacy & Forester '00 thru '06

## SUZUKI
90010 Samurai/Sidekick & Geo Tracker '86 thru '01

## TOYOTA
92005 Camry all models '83 thru '91
92006 Camry all models '92 thru '96
92007 Camry, Avalon, Solara, Lexus ES 300 '97 thru '01
92008 Toyota Camry, Avalon and Solara and Lexus ES 300/330 all models '02 thru '06
92009 Camry '07 thru '11
92015 Celica Rear Wheel Drive '71 thru '85
92020 Celica Front Wheel Drive '86 thru '99
92025 Celica Supra all models '79 thru '92
92030 Corolla all models '75 thru '79
92032 Corolla all rear wheel drive models '80 thru '87
92035 Corolla all front wheel drive models '84 thru '92
92036 Corolla & Geo Prizm '93 thru '02
92037 Corolla models '03 thru '11
92040 Corolla Tercel all models '80 thru '82
92045 Corona all models '74 thru '82
92050 Cressida all models '78 thru '82
92055 Land Cruiser FJ40, 43, 45, 55 '68 thru '82
92056 Land Cruiser FJ60, 62, 80, FZJ80 '80 thru '96
92060 Matrix & Pontiac Vibe '03 thru '11
92065 MR2 all models '85 thru '87
92070 Pick-up all models '69 thru '78
92075 Pick-up all models '79 thru '95
92076 Tacoma, 4Runner, & T100 '93 thru '04
92077 Tacoma all models '05 thru '09
92078 Tundra '00 thru '06 & Sequoia '01 thru '07
92079 4Runner all models '03 thru '09
92080 Previa all models '91 thru '95
92081 Prius all models '01 thru '08
92082 RAV4 all models '96 thru '10
92085 Tercel all models '87 thru '94
92090 Sienna all models '98 thru '09
92095 Highlander & Lexus RX-330 '99 thru '07

## TRIUMPH
94007 Spitfire all models '62 thru '81
94010 TR7 all models '75 thru '81

## VW
96008 Beetle & Karmann Ghia '54 thru '79
96009 New Beetle '98 thru '11
96016 Rabbit, Jetta, Scirocco & Pick-up gas models '75 thru '92 & Convertible '80 thru '92
96017 Golf, GTI & Jetta '93 thru '98, Cabrio '95 thru '02
96018 Golf, GTI, Jetta '99 thru '05
96019 Jetta, Rabbit, GTI & Golf '05 thru '11
96020 Rabbit, Jetta & Pick-up diesel '77 thru '84
96023 Passat '98 thru '05, Audi A4 '96 thru '01
96030 Transporter 1600 all models '68 thru '79
96035 Transporter 1700, 1800 & 2000 '72 thru '79
96040 Type 3 1500 & 1600 all models '63 thru '73
96045 Vanagon all air-cooled models '80 thru '83

## VOLVO
97010 120, 130 Series & 1800 Sports '61 thru '73
97015 140 Series all models '66 thru '74
97020 240 Series all models '76 thru '93
97040 740 & 760 Series all models '82 thru '88
97050 850 Series all models '93 thru '97

## TECHBOOK MANUALS
10205 Automotive Computer Codes
10206 OBD-II & Electronic Engine Management
10210 Automotive Emissions Control Manual
10215 Fuel Injection Manual '78 thru '85
10220 Fuel Injection Manual '86 thru '99
10225 Holley Carburetor Manual
10230 Rochester Carburetor Manual
10240 Weber/Zenith/Stromberg/SU Carburetors
10305 Chevrolet Engine Overhaul Manual
10310 Chrysler Engine Overhaul Manual
10320 Ford Engine Overhaul Manual
10330 GM and Ford Diesel Engine Repair Manual
10333 Engine Performance Manual
10340 Small Engine Repair Manual, 5 HP & Less
10341 Small Engine Repair Manual, 5.5 - 20 HP
10345 Suspension, Steering & Driveline Manual
10355 Ford Automatic Transmission Overhaul
10360 GM Automatic Transmission Overhaul
10405 Automotive Body Repair & Painting
10410 Automotive Brake Manual
10411 Automotive Anti-lock Brake (ABS) Systems
10415 Automotive Detailing Manual
10420 Automotive Electrical Manual
10425 Automotive Heating & Air Conditioning
10430 Automotive Reference Manual & Dictionary
10435 Automotive Tools Manual
10440 Used Car Buying Guide
10445 Welding Manual
10450 ATV Basics
10452 Scooters 50cc to 250cc

## SPANISH MANUALS
98903 Reparación de Carrocería & Pintura
98904 Manual de Carburador Modelos Holley & Rochester
98905 Códigos Automotrices de la Computadora
98906 OBD-II & Sistemas de Control Electrónico del Motor
98910 Frenos Automotriz
98913 Electricidad Automotriz
98915 Inyección de Combustible '86 al '99
99040 Chevrolet & GMC Camionetas '67 al '87
99041 Chevrolet & GMC Camionetas '88 al '98
99042 Chevrolet & GMC Camionetas Cerradas '68 al '95
99043 Chevrolet/GMC Camionetas '94 al '04
99048 Chevrolet/GMC Camionetas '94 al '06
99055 Dodge Caravan & Plymouth Voyager '84 al '95
99075 Ford Camionetas y Bronco '80 al '94
99076 Ford F-150 '97 al '09
99077 Ford Camionetas Cerradas '69 al '91
99088 Ford Modelos de Tamaño Mediano '75 al '86
99089 Ford Camionetas Ranger '93 al '10
99091 Ford Taurus & Mercury Sable '86 al '95
99095 GM Modelos de Tamaño Grande '70 al '90
99100 GM Modelos de Tamaño Mediano '70 al '88
99106 Jeep Cherokee, Wagoneer & Comanche '84 al '00
99110 Nissan Camioneta '80 al '96, Pathfinder '87 al '95
99118 Nissan Sentra '82 al '94
99125 Toyota Camionetas y 4Runner '79 al '95

Over 100 Haynes motorcycle manuals also available

7-12

Haynes North America, Inc., 859 Lawrence Drive, Newbury Park, CA 91320-1514 • (80_ _8-6703 • http://www.haynes.com